Monarchs of the Renaissance

ALSO BY PHILIP J. POTTER

*Gothic Kings of Britain: The Lives of 31
Medieval Rulers, 1016–1399* (McFarland, 2009)

Monarchs of the Renaissance

The Lives and Reigns of 42 European Kings and Queens

Philip J. Potter

McFarland & Company, Inc., Publishers
Jefferson, North Carolina, and London

LIBRARY OF CONGRESS CATALOGUING-IN-PUBLICATION DATA

Potter, Philip J., 1943–
Monarchs of the Renaissance : the lives and reigns of 42
European kings and queens / Philip J. Potter.

p.   cm.

Includes bibliographical references and index.

ISBN 0-7864-6806-5
softcover : acid free paper ∞

1. Europe — Kings and rulers — Biography.   2. Queens — Europe — Biography.
3. Renaissance — Biography.   4. Europe — History — 1492–1648.
5. Europe — Politics and government — 1492–1648.
6. Monarchy — Europe — History.   I. Title.

D226.7.P68   2012   940.2'10922 — dc23   2012002663

BRITISH LIBRARY CATALOGUING DATA ARE AVAILABLE

© 2012 Philip J. Potter. All rights reserved

*No part of this book may be reproduced or transmitted in any form
or by any means, electronic or mechanical, including photocopying
or recording, or by any information storage and retrieval system,
without permission in writing from the publisher.*

On the cover: George Gower, *Elizabeth I of England, the
Armada Portrait*, oil on panel, 52⁴⁄₁₀" × 41³⁄₁₀", circa 1588.

Manufactured in the United States of America

*McFarland & Company, Inc., Publishers
Box 611, Jefferson, North Carolina 28640
www.mcfarlandpub.com*

To Joyce

Table of Contents

Preface   1

PART I: RENAISSANCE MONARCHS OF ENGLAND   3
Genealogical Tables   4–5

Overview 6	Richard III 48
Henry IV 7	Henry VII 57
Henry V 15	Henry VIII 65
Henry VI 25	Edward VI 77
Edward IV 35	Mary I 85
Edward V 43	Elizabeth I 94

PART II: RENAISSANCE MONARCHS OF SCOTLAND   107
Genealogical Table   108

Overview 109	James IV 133
Robert III 110	James V 139
James I 116	Mary I 147
James II 122	James VI (I of England) .. 154
James III 127	

PART III: RENAISSANCE MONARCHS OF FRANCE   163
Genealogical Tables   164–165

Overview 166	Louis XI 180
Charles VI 167	Charles VIII 190
Charles VII 173	Louis XII 196

Francis I	206	Charles IX	224
Henry II	216	Henry III	230
Francis II	222		

PART IV: RENAISSANCE MONARCHS OF SPAIN 237

Genealogical Table 238

Overview	239	Joanna	264
John II	239	Charles I (V of Holy Roman Empire)	274
Henry IV	245		
Isabella	254	Philip II	280

PART V: RENAISSANCE EMPERORS OF THE HOLY ROMAN EMPIRE 295

Genealogical Tables 296

Overview	297	Charles V (I of Spain)	323
Sigismund	297	Ferdinand I	331
Albert II	305	Maximilian II	337
Frederick III	308	Rudolf II	344
Maximilian I	314		

Bibliography 349

Index 353

Preface

The European Renaissance was a dynamic period which dramatically advanced the supremacy of the monarchy as the dominant ruling institution through the empowerment of its kings and queens. It saw forceful monarchs who reduced the feudal authority of their nobles, waged war to expand their lands, defended the Catholic Church against the encroachments of the Protestant Reformation and sponsored the development of new art, architecture, literature and music. *Monarchs of the Renaissance* describes the reigns of the sovereigns between 1400 and 1600 in England, Scotland, France, Spain and the Holy Roman Empire during their struggle for power over Europe. It recaptures the lives and times of forty-two monarchs in the context of their era, evoking their personalities, accomplishments and failures.

The English Renaissance began with the usurpation of the monarchy by Henry IV by force of arms in 1399 and ended in 1603 after the death of Elizabeth I. The English kings and queens waged war against France, Scotland and Spain in defense of their sovereignty, fought a bloody and savage civil conflict in the Wars of the Roses and defied the power of the pope by establishing the independent Church of England. The two-hundred-year period is rich in celebrated monarchs, including Henry V, Henry VIII and Elizabeth I, while containing unjustly neglected rulers such as Henry VI and Richard III who had a significant influence on the history of England.

In the late fourteenth century, the Stewart dynasty inherited the reins of kingship in Scotland to rule through eight monarchs during the Renaissance. Throughout the era they fought recurring wars with England and battled internal rebellion by their nobility while creating an acknowledged European power. The Scottish throne reached its zenith during the reign of James IV, who established a golden age of culture and art while expanding his kingdom's influence in European politics.

France was ruled during the Renaissance by ten kings who finally drove the English out of their realm to end the Hundred Years' War, solidified their authority over the recalcitrant nobility, waged war against the Holy Roman Empire for supremacy in Europe and defended their church against the intrusions of the Huguenots during more than forty years of religious war. During the reigns of Louis XI and Francis I, the monarchy became recognized as the dominant European power, while during the rule of the last three Renaissance kings, the kingdom was torn apart by civil war.

The kingdom of Spain emerged during the Renaissance as the dominant Iberian power, bringing the independent fiefdoms into a united realm. The five Spanish sovereigns completed the reconquest of their lands from the occupation of the Moors of North Africa, began the exploration and conquest of the New World and created the preeminent European monarchy, which ruled half the known world. The kingdom began its ascent to dominance in the reign of Queen Isabella and reached the summit of its greatness during the monarchies of Charles I and Philip II.

The Holy Roman Empire began the Renaissance with the assumption of the imperial crown by the Habsburg dynasty, which governed more than three hundred years. The rule of the eight emperors reached its pinnacle in the reign of Charles V, who protected his lands against the of French and the Ottoman Turks and as the secular leader of the Catholic Church defended it against the advances of the Protestants. Under the disastrous regime of the last emperor, Rudolf II, the Holy Roman Empire was beset with internal dissent and the loss of imperial power and prestige, resulting in the eruption of the Thirty Years' War in Germany.

This book is arranged into parts for each of the five kingdoms. A chronological listing of each kingdom's rulers appears at the beginning of the part and is followed by a genealogical chart. An overview of the realm is presented, followed by a description of the reign of each sovereign. The biographies may be read individually and in any order. The dates given in the genealogical charts and with each ruler's entry correspond to the birth, beginning of rule and death of the monarch. In the case when a king or queen was forced to abdicate, four dates are given: birth, beginning of rule, date of abdication and death.

Monarchs of the Renaissance was written as a work of European history and as a reference for individuals, schools and libraries. Its goal is to describe the advancement of the Renaissance sovereigns as the central ruling powers and their clash for supremacy in Europe. With its many celebrated kings and queens, the era is of interest to all who enjoy studying and reading European history.

Part I

Renaissance Monarchs of England

House of Lancaster

Henry IV	1366–1399–1413
Henry V	1387–1413–1422
Henry VI	1421–1422–1471

House of York

Edward IV	1442–1471–1483
Edward V	1470–1483–1483
Richard III	1452–1483–1485

House of Tudor

Henry VII	1457–1485–1509
Henry VIII	1491–1509–1547
Edward VI	1537–1547–1553
Mary I	1516–1553–1558
Elizabeth I	1533–1558–1603

Genealogical Tables

House of Lancaster

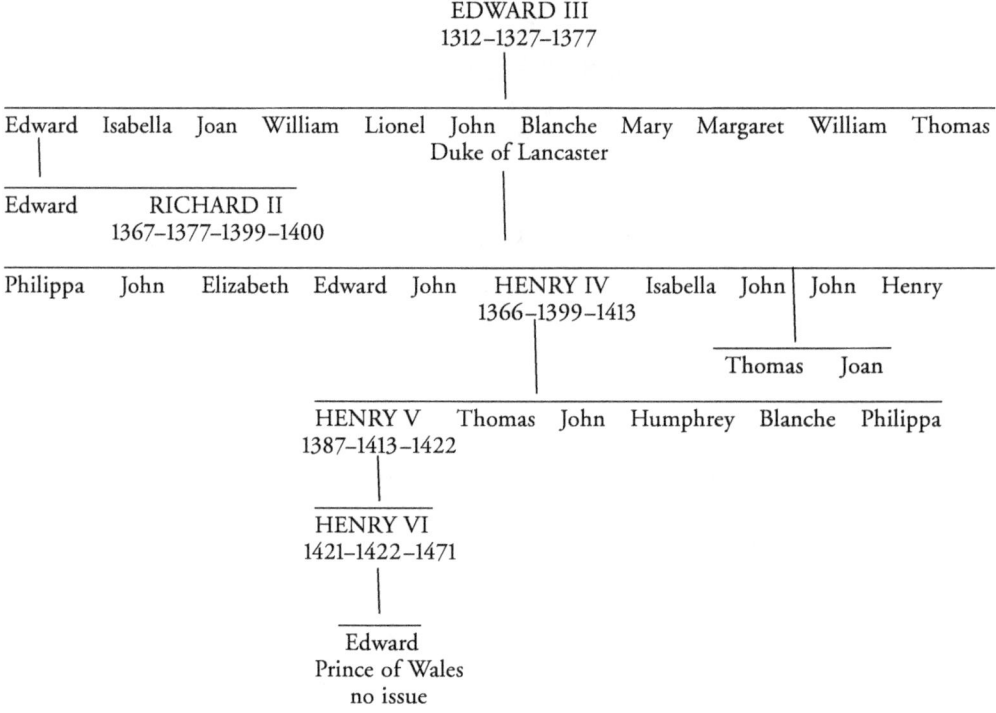

House of York

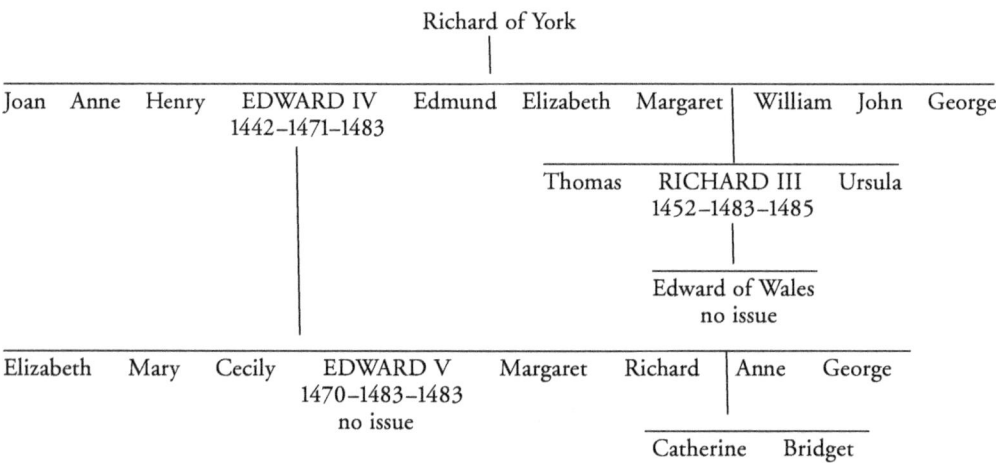

Kings and queens of England are in ALL CAPITALS

Genealogical Tables

HOUSE OF TUDOR

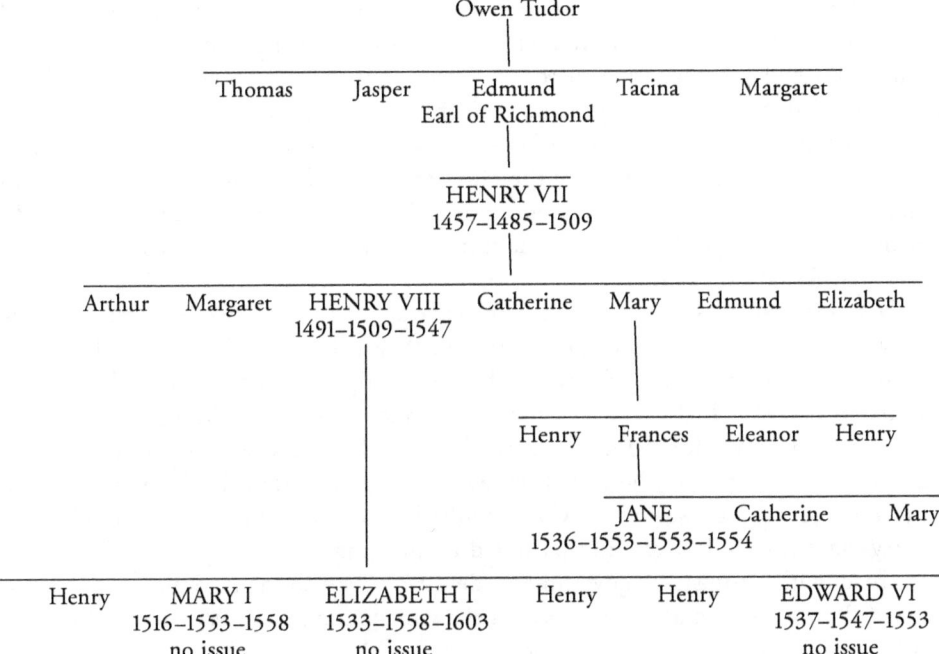

Overview

The seventeen year brutal and bloody civil war in England between the descendants of William the Conqueror was finally resolved with the succession to the throne of Henry Plantagenet, who established a dynasty that ruled for two hundred fifty years. His heirs fought in the crusades, defended their sovereignty rights against the encroachments of the barons, sanctioned the emergence of Parliament as a representative institution and invaded France in pursuit of hereditary blood claims to ignite the Hundred Years' War. Under the inept rule of the last Plantagenet, Richard II, England's conquests in France were lost and the conflict with the earls reemerged resulting in his dethronement in 1399 by Henry, Duke of Lancaster, who reigned as the first Renaissance king.

Henry IV's monarchy was directed at the consolidation of its newly won regime and suppression of revolt by the recalcitrant northern earls and Welsh. He bequeathed a loyal nobility and united English realm to his son, Henry V, whose kingship was dominated by the renewal of the Hundred Years' War. In 1415 he invaded France and won a magnificent victory at the battle of Agincourt against vastly superior forces. By his early death, the second Lancastrian king had been acknowledged as heir to the French crown and had conquered half of the kingdom. The third Renaissance monarch was Henry VI, who inherited the thrones of England and France, ruling for forty-eight turbulent years. Incapacitated by the king's frequent periods of insanity, his reign was beset with an unstable government, defeat on the continent resulting in the loss of the occupied French lands, and the eruption of the violent and savage Wars of the Roses.

Edward of York seized the Lancastrian monarchy in 1471 by decisively defeating the army of Henry VI at Tewkesbury during the Wars of the Roses to rule as the fourth monarch of the Renaissance epoch. He solidified his kingship by introducing reforms to his government designed to bring reconciliation with the nobles and expansion in the economy through increased trade with Europe and growth in agriculture production. At his death the stable and unified York regime was assumed by his minor son, Edward V, whose short reign was dominated by the power struggle for supremacy over the regency council between his uncle, Richard of Gloucester, and the political faction loyal to the dowager queen, Elizabeth Woodville. By seizing control of his nephew, Richard III outmaneuvered his opposition and usurped the kingdom, ordering the murder of Edward V in the Tower. However, his sovereignty was challenged by the last Lancastrian claimant to the crown, Henry Tudor, who invaded England in August 1485 and dethroned the king at the battle of Bosworth to end the Wars of the Roses.

With his victory at Bosworth Field, Henry VII claimed the English realm to rule as the seventh Renaissance monarch. After seizing control of the kingdom, he was forced to defend his sovereignty against the attempted usurpations of two pretender kings while initiating an energetic program of legal, political and financial reforms to his government. He bequeathed to his successor, Henry VIII, a peaceful, prosperous and unified England. Assuming the throne in 1509, Henry VIII's reign of thirty-seven years was defined by the quest for a legitimate male heir through his six marriages, dissolution of the Catholic Church in England and creation of a new Protestant religious institution under the dominion of the monarchy. The ninth English king of the Renaissance era was Edward VI, who continued his father's religious policies, expanding the assimilation of Protestantism while aggressively suppressing the Catholic faith. He was succeeded to the crown by his half-sister, Mary I, who initiated measures to reverse the rise of Protestantism and restore the supremacy of the Holy See of Rome. As resistance mounted against her regime, she authorized the persecution of the heretics and nearly three hundred anti–Papists were burned at the stake. When Mary I died childless in 1558, her half-sister, Elizabeth I, was recognized by Parliament as the eleventh and final Renaissance sovereign of England. Assuming power, she returned her realm to the Church of England, ending the authority of Rome. A dynamic and charismatic personality, the queen governed in an autocratic style, believing she was chosen by God to rule. As the result of her anti–Catholic policies, England became involved in war against Spain and in the summer of 1588 Elizabeth I reached the summit of her reign with the defeat of the Great Armada.

Henry IV, 1366–1399–1413

In the late summer of 1399 Richard II was deposed by his cousin, Henry of Lancaster, to begin the reign of the first English king of the Renaissance era. Henry was born at Bolingbroke Castle in April 1366 and was the only surviving male issue of Duke John of Gault and Blanche of Lancaster. The infant prince's father was the fourth son of Edward III and his mother was directly related to the Plantagenet lineage through Henry III. With his marriage to Blanche, the duke assumed control over her duchy of Lancaster and earldoms of Derby, Lincoln and Leicester. At his birth Henry was recognized as the heir to his father's extensive and rich lands. When Henry was three his mother died and with John of Gault frequently absent from the family estates at the court of Edward III, he was raised by Lancastrian appointed retainers. The duke took a special interest in his son's education, appointing renowned scholars for his instruction in reading, writing, religion, Latin and French, music and court etiquette. He received a well-rounded education, excelling in his studies. The Bolingbroke prince began his military training in 1374 in the battle skills of a knight, becoming accomplished in jousting and other field sports. When Henry was eleven, the Lancastrian duke ceded him the earldom of Derby. Bolingbroke was a devout follower of the doctrine of the Church of Rome, participating in the holy crusades in Lithuania against the pagan tribes and making a personal pilgrimage to Jerusalem in a visible display of his faith.

In 1377 King Edward III died and his grandson, Richard II, succeeded unchallenged to the English throne. While the Derby earl remained on the Lancaster lands continuing his academic and military education, his father assumed a dominant role in the regime of the new monarch. As the duke grew in prominence, his son began to increasingly appear at court and take part in the government. In 1383 he sailed to Calais with the Lancaster duke to negotiate a military agreement with the Flemish and in the following year acquired his first combat experiences during the war against Scotland. Henry actively participated in the many martial tournaments in England, gaining a reputation for his jousting successes, gallantry and chivalry. He traveled extensively throughout the Lancastrian properties, learning the skills necessary to manage the large family estates.

In July 1380 John of Gault arranged the marriage of his son to Mary Bohum, co-heiress to the earldom of Hereford. The marital agreement brought great wealth and rich estates to the Lancaster family. Henry and Mary had known each other since childhood and had become very close friends. The elaborate wedding ceremony took place in early February 1381 and the earl and Mary developed a loving and devoted relationship through their thirteen years of marriage. She actively supported the Derby earl in English politics, frequently traveling with him as he managed their lands and attended court and Parliament. They were both highly educated and cultured, sharing many common interests, including religion, collecting books and music. The earl and his wife played the harp, sang sacred music with their court choir and were patrons of renowned poets, including Geoffrey Chaucer. Their union resulted in the birth of four surviving sons and two daughters. However, in 1394 Mary died from complications giving birth to her second daughter, Philippa. Henry was greatly distressed by her death, repeatedly visiting her tomb.

In 1381 the weak regency government established by Parliament to rule during the minority years of Richard II was usurped by John of Gault and his Lancastrian allies. As the new regent asserted his power, a coalition in support of the independent reign of the boy king began to rally around Robert de Vere, earl of Oxford. The party in opposition initiated several plots in 1384 to overthrow the Lancaster regime, creating an atmosphere of mistrust and hostility at court. As the danger of civil war grew, the queen mother intervened to forge a fragile reconciliation. The uneasy peace was maintained until July 1385 when a combined Franco-Scottish army threatened to strike the northern English border counties. To thwart the anticipated invasion, John of Gault ordered a counter attack against the Scottish Lowlands. However, the royal troops, personally commanded by Richard II, and the private militias of the barons failed to achieve a decisive victory, when the two factions began to openly disagree over the conduct of the war. The political struggle intensified when the king's favorite, Robert de Vere, accused the Lancaster duke of conspiring to depose the monarchy.

While the threat of armed conflict escalated between Robert of Oxford and the governing regency of John of Gault, in 1385 the monarchy of Castile-Leon was embroiled with war against Portugal. The Lancaster duke possessed a blood claim to the kingdom through his second wife, Constance of Castile, and in the summer of the following year sailed to Spain to usurp the crown by force of arms and establish his independent reign. During his father's absence, Henry of Bolingbroke was appointed to oversee the numerous Lancaster estates. Without the dominant presence of John of Gault at court, the Plantagenet king overcame the opposition of the barons to impose his autonomous rule. While Henry remained occupied with the family lands, the leadership of the Lancaster party was seized by Richard II's uncle, Thomas of Woodstock, duke of Gloucester, who initiated a political campaign to depose his nephew and place himself on the throne. He forged a coalition known as the Lords Appellant with three high earls and Henry of Bolingbroke.

The Lords Appellant began to aggressively challenge the rule of Richard II, demanding the dismissal of his chief advisors. As their support from the barons escalated, the king was forced to agree to their ultimatum to thwart the threat of his dethronement. However, he delayed the removal of his favorites and allies from the government and began to raise an army to defend his royal prerogatives. The rebel magnates responded by accusing the sovereign's ruling council of corruption and treason.

As the political crisis grew, the Lords Appellant mustered their private militias and appointed Henry of Derby as commander. As the threat of armed insurrection escalated, de Vere advanced the royalists against the Derby earl at Radcot Bridge to force the acceptance of the Plantagenet crown's rule. In the ensuing encounter on December 20, 1387, the rogue troops led by Henry completely overwhelmed the king's army. Following the battle the victorious Appellants marched unopposed to London to besiege Richard II in the Tower. Without any prospects for rescue, he began negotiations with the earls to find a resolution to their ongoing revolt. Deserted by his allies, Richard II was compelled to agree to arrest his advisors but thwarted the attempt to usurp his throne by Duke Thomas of Woodstock. In February 1388 the Merciless Parliament met in London for the trial of the royal counselors, who were quickly declared guilty of treason. To replace the disgraced administration, the legislative assembly approved a new regime led by Thomas of Gloucester. Henry of Bolingbroke supported the trial and creation of the Gloucester government and was named to serve on the ruling council.

Acting under the authority of the Merciless Parliament, the Appellants began to govern the kingdom in the name of Richard II. However, they ruled as poorly as the prior administrations and their popularity and support steadily declined. They renewed the conflict against France but with disastrous results, while border unrest with Scotland flared up. The Gloucester regime's frequent requests for additional taxes to fund its wars caused a break in its once friendly relationship with Parliament, encouraging the king to assert his independent reign. On May 3, 1389, he announced his assumption of full power, replacing the Lords Appellant with a council of his choosing.

Following Richard II's overthrow of the Gloucester regime, Earl Henry of Derby continued to attend council meetings and court but increasingly under a hostile atmosphere. In November 1389 John of Gault returned from Spain and was welcomed back to the government, becoming a trusted friend and advisor to the king. Under his influence an uneasy reconciliation was forged between Richard II and the Lords Appellant but they exercised little prestige or power. As the king expanded his sovereignty and popularity, Henry became anxious to leave court and taking the advice of his father agreed to join the Teutonic Knights in their crusade against the pagan Lithuanians. The Teutonic Knights were a monastic military order created in 1190 during the siege against the Saracen occupied fortress of Acre to provide hospital care for German crusaders in the Holy Land and protection for pilgrims. In 1226 Emperor Frederick II gave the Teutonic Order the authority to establish an ecclesiastic fief in Prussia and by the end of the century the territory was under its control. With Prussia under their rule, the knights renewed their crusade into neighboring Lithuania, converting the heathen local tribes to Christianity and enlarging their demesne by force of arms.

In August 1390 Derby sailed from England into the Baltic Sea, landing in Prussia. After disembarking his small personal army, he traveled overland to join the crusader forces on the Lithuanian border. Marching into pagan territory the earl fought his first major engagement during the siege against Vilna, demonstrating his battle skills and bravery. However, despite repeated assaults against Vilna, the fortification garrison refused to surrender and the crusaders were compelled to withdraw to Konigsberg. With the onset of the harsh northern weather, the holy war was suspended and Henry remained in the city for the next four months. In the company of the German knights, he spent the winter jousting, hunting, participating in martial tournaments and attending banquets and religious festivals.

After spending over seven months in Prussia, in late March 1391 Henry of Bolingbroke sailed home to England. He returned to the royal court and joined his father's political faction, supporting the reign of Richard II. In the following year the king sent John of Gault and Earl Henry of Derby along with a large delegation to France to negotiate an end to the Hundred Years' War. However, the deliberations quickly became bogged down over the French demand for the return of the English occupied Calais enclave. As the talks dragged on, the earl decided to travel to Prussia to rejoin the Teutonic Knights' campaign against the pagans in Lithuania. He arrived at Konigsberg with his small private army in early September but was disappointed when no crusade was planned for the autumn. Thwarted in his quest to expand the Christian religion by force of arms into heathen lands, the earl became resolved to make a pilgrimage to Jerusalem in a visible display of his piety to the church. After sending part of his forces to England, the journey to the Holy City was begun by traveling to Prague and later Vienna, where he was lavishly entertained by the local rulers. Through the intervention of Duke Albert V of Austria, the earl was able to lease a Venetian vessel for his pilgrimage to Jerusalem.

Henry of Derby arrived in Venice in late November 1392 and was warmly received by the city's ruling council. He was given a grand reception in the doge's palace and remained for the next three weeks, preparing for his voyage to the Holy Land. While in Venice the earl was frequently entertained by Doge Antonio Venier. On December 23 the Bolingbroke lord sailed from Venice, landing in the Holy Land at the port of Jaffa after a brief stop in Rhodes for supplies. From the coast he traveled directly to Jerusalem; however, his stay was brief and was highlighted by visits to the Church of the Holy Sepulcher and Mount of Olives, where offerings and prayers were made. The return to England was made by sea to Venice and overland through Milan and France. On his long journey the earl met many of the powerful rulers of Europe, developing personal relationships, while enhancing his esteem and renown among their courts and the English nobility and church.

After his return from Jerusalem, Henry of Derby was welcomed back to court and Parliament as a part of his father's political faction. John of Gault remained a formidable supporter of the king and his son assumed prominent offices in the administration. When Richard II traveled to Ireland in 1394 to subjugate his recalcitrant English vassals and rebel Irish warlords, Henry was appointed to the governing regency council. As Derby continued his stay at court, the reign of Richard II became more popular following his successful military intervention in Ireland, the signing of a twenty-eight-year truce with France and growing domestic prosperity. With his throne secure he began to rule as a virtual dictator, ignoring his advisors and Parliament. The monarch had maintained his resentment and anger against the Lords Appellant for their usurpation of his crown and the death of his friends nine years earlier and now from a position of power ordered the seizure of three members of their alliance on charges of sedition. Henry of Bolingbroke was spared arrest for his recent faithful and loyal service to the Plantagenets. However, as the regime of Richard II grew more tyrannical, in December 1397 Henry was exiled for ten years for his alleged involvement in a new conspiracy to overthrow the government.

Following his banishment, Derby traveled to Paris and was warmly welcomed as a royal prince by the regime of Charles VI. In February 1398 Henry's father died and the Plantagenet king expanded his exile to life and seized all the Lancaster estates. After the forfeiture of his inheritance, the earl began to aggressively plot the overthrow of Richard II and usurpation of the English crown. Through his family's lineage to King Edward III, the Derby earl possessed a direct blood claim to the English monarchy and his quest for the throne was facilitated by the death in Ireland of the childless sovereign's designated heir, Roger Mortimer, Earl of March.

While Henry assembled his troops and allies in France for his revolt against the Plantagenet regime, in May 1399 Richard II launched a second campaign against the recalcitrant Irish magnates in retaliation for their continued rebellion and slaying of his favorite, Mortimer of March. Seizing on the absence of Richard II from England, in early July Henry of Derby and his small army of three hundred soldiers boarded three ships and sailed to Yorkshire. As he began his advance south his forces were joined by numerous Lancastrian supporters and the powerful Percy and Nevill families, as the size and strength of his army multiplied. Confronted with the overwhelming military might of the rebels, on July 27 the king's appointed regent, Edmund of Langley, first Duke of York, abandoned the Plantagenet crown to unite with Henry's uprising.

In early July Richard II received reports of Henry of Bolingbroke's attempted usurpation of his throne and quickly re-boarded his ships with his army, sailing to England. However, by the time he arrived in his kingdom, most of the great barons with their allies had joined the rebellion, pledging their allegiance to Henry's new regime. As the Plantagenet government was increasingly abandoned by its supporters, Richard II withdrew to the safety of Conway Castle. From the unassailable stronghold he remained defiant, refusing to surrender to his cousin. Nevertheless, with few friends to defend his monarchy, the king agreed to meet with the Derby earl and discuss the terms of reconciliation. However, when Richard II rode out of the Conway fortress, he was seized and taken to London by the retainers of Derby.

With control of the king and support from the great earls, church and cities, Henry of Derby laid claim to the English throne, quickly establishing his new government in London. To give added legitimacy to his usurpation, he personally met with his Plantagenet cousin in the Tower, forcing him to sign a letter of abdication. On September 30, 1399, Richard II formally renounced his monarchy in favor of Derby and thirteen days later Henry IV was anointed and crowned king of England in Westminster Abbey.

The deposed Richard II continued to be a threat to the legitimacy and survival of the new Lancastrian regime and in October 1399 he was moved from the Tower to the fortress of Pontefract for added security against escape. While most of his supporters had abandoned him, the Plantagenet king retained a hard core coalition of loyal friends. In December under the leadership of Sir John Holland of Huntingdon, Thomas Holland of Kent and the Earl of Salisbury, John Montacute, a faction was formed to restore Richard II to his kingdom with the planned murder of the Lancastrian monarch and his sons in the Epiphany Rising. John Montacute was the third earl of Salisbury and devoted friend of the Plantagenet king. He was an experienced soldier and veteran of the wars against France and the Teutonic Knights' crusade against the pagans in Lithuania. Salisbury was a favorite of Richard II and participated in the crown's campaigns in Ireland. Thomas Holland was the third Earl of Kent and nephew of Richard II. For his loyalty to the king, he was granted large estates and appointed Duke of Surrey. John Holland, Earl of Huntingdon, was the half-brother of Richard II and had remained a faithful ally of the Plantagenet throne. He fought in the Plantagenet wars against Scotland and served as constable of the army during John of Gault's expedition to Spain. For his fealty to the monarchy, Holland was appointed to numerous high offices in the government, including lord chamberlain and constable of the Western Marches on the Scottish border. In 1397 the Huntingdon earl along with Montacute and Thomas of Kent were sent by the Plantagenet council to arrest Duke Thomas of Gloucester and other members of the Lords Appellant. For their devotion to his reign, Richard II ceded them a share of the Appellants' honors and lands, later rescinded by the administration of Henry IV.

As the conspirators continued their plot to free Richard II and return him to the English throne, their revolt was revealed to the Lancaster council. Henry IV quickly assembled a large army in London, advancing to Windsor to confront the rebels. At the approach of the formidable loyalist forces, the rogues fled to the western counties and attempted to raise the banner of insurrection. However, their mutiny found little support and the coalition was easily defeated by the overwhelming military might of the king. The earls of Kent and Salisbury were seized and quickly executed for their treason. John Holland of Huntingdon managed to escape but was later captured and beheaded. The Epiphany Rising compelled Henry IV to authorize the assassination of the Plantagenet king to prevent a motive for future sedition. On February 14, 1400, the Lancastrian administration announced the death of Richard II.

The rebellion of the Epiphany Rising was quickly defeated and for several months Henry IV ruled his kingdom in peace. Early in his reign, he was widely supported by the English magnates, church and towns, despite the persistent rumors that Richard II was still alive and plotting his return to the crown. However, in September 1400 Wales rose up in a popular revolt in defense of Owain Glendower, who was disputing the seizure of his inherited lands by the English Lord Grey of Ruthyn. After failing to receive satisfaction to his claim from Henry IV, he declared himself prince of Wales and became leader of an increasingly widespread Welsh uprising. Glendower was directly related to the rulers of the princedom of Powys and was a wealthy nobleman with rich estates in the northeastern Welsh lordships. In 1383 he answered the Plantagenet regime's summons for military service, participating in campaigns in Scotland and France. Returning to Wales, Owain became the voice for local dissent against the overbearing English overlords.

As his rebellion gained strength, Owain Glendower attacked the lord of Ruthyn's castle at Rhuddlan in northern Wales, harrying the town and farm lands. The pillaging raid was expanded into the counties of Flint and Denbigh, which were looted and burned. In response to the uprising, Henry IV mustered a powerful army at Shrewsbury, advancing into Wales to confront Glendower. However, the Welsh prince withdrew to the mountains and engaged in only small scale skirmishes, ambushes and raids, while avoiding any decisive battle. The English retaliated by ravaging the Welsh towns and laying waste to the countryside. As the fighting dragged on, there were numerous atrocities by both armies as the conflict was marked by blood and plunder.

While the Lancasterian forces continued their Welsh offensive, Henry IV became increasingly hard pressed to find the money to finance his war, as Parliament resisted his request for additional taxes. His lieutenant for northern Wales, Henry Hotspur Percy of Northumberland, resigned his position in protest of the lack of financial support to pay his troops and purchase needed arms. Henry Hotspur was born on May 20, 1365, and was the son of the first earl of Northumberland, Henry Percy, and Margaret Nevill. He was heir to the earldom of Northumberland and leading member of the powerful northern English Percy family. He gained widespread renown at an early age for his military skills, bravery and quick temper in the wars against Scotland and France. In August 1388 he was captured by the Scots at the battle of Otterburn but later ransomed. Following his release Percy served the government of Richard II as governor for Bordeaux for two years. When Henry of Bolingbroke returned from exile in 1399, Henry Percy joined his rebellion against the Plantagenet regime and later was appointed as royal viceroy for northern Wales.

While the conflict continued in Wales, in February 1402 the lord of Ruthyn was captured and the English campaign suffered from the absence of his energy and leadership. Henry IV's offensive in Wales was dealt another serious setback on June 22 at the battle of Pilleth, when a formidable Lancaster army of over two thousand men under arms led by Edmund Mortimer was defeated by Glendower's troops and he was taken prisoner. The Mortimer family held strong blood rights to the English throne and the king strongly suspected that Sir Edmund had willingly deserted to the Welsh to gain their support in his quest for an autonomous crown. Henry IV refused to pay the ransom for Mortimer's release and seized his possessions.

In late 1402 the Scottish Earl of Douglas, Archibald, led a large pillaging force into northern England in pursuit of plunder and to support the Welsh war effort, ravaging and laying waste to the towns and farms. As he withdrew to Scotland, his army was intercepted by Henry, Earl of Northumberland, and his son, Hotspur Percy, at Homildon Hill. In the ensuing battle, the Scots were decisively defeated and Douglas and a large number of his lords taken prisoner. However, after their overwhelming triumph, relations between the king and the Percys deteriorated rapidly when the Lancastrian government failed to reward their success and prohibited Hotspur from ransoming his captives. The Percy family became increasingly dissatisfied and rebellious when the regime refused to reimburse them for their expenditures in defense of the throne in Wales and along the northern English border counties. In the autumn of 1402 Henry Hotspur traveled to London to press his demand for payment of his expenses but the talks ended in heated exchanges. After returning to Northumberland, Hotspur and his father abandoned their allegiance to the Lancastrian crown and joined the revolt of the Welsh.

While relations with the Percy family continued to deteriorate, in April 1402 Henry IV was married by proxy to Joan of Navarre. She was the daughter of the king of Navarre, Charles II, and widow of John IV, Duke of Brittany. In 1399 her first husband died and Joan became regent for her minor son. Henry and Joan had met several times in France beginning in 1396, developing a close friendship. The union was also a political agreement providing protection to Brittany against French aggrandizement and giving England an ally and friend against the hostile Valois regime. The official ceremony was held at Winchester Cathedral on February 7, 1403, and later in the month she was crowned queen at Westminster Abbey. The new Lancastrian queen was well educated and intelligent, quickly becoming a valued advisor and companion to her husband. She had previously ruled over Brittany and used her experiences and administrative skills to aid the king in governing the kingdom. Differing from many contemporary princes, Henry IV remained faithful to both Mary Bohum and Joan, never taking a mistress. Unlike his marriage to Mary, the second marital union resulted in no children.

In July 1403 Henry IV was informed of the Percy rebellion and their coalition with Owain Glendower, quickly ordering the mustering of his army to strike at the English rebels before they united with the Welsh. He marched to Shrewsbury intercepting the Northumbrians on July 21, as they advanced to join Glendower. After Henry IV's attempt to negotiate a reconciliation failed, the Lancaster and Percy forces formed into battle formation. The conflict began with a deadly volley of arrows from Hotspur's Cheshire bowmen. The royal right flank, personally led by the king, was attacked and steadily driven back under constant pressure from the rogue archers and men-at-arms. However, the left wing commanded by the monarch's heir, Henry of Monmouth, held his position and counterassaulted to ravage the rear of Percy's line. In the ensuing melee Hotspur was killed and his army overwhelmed, retreating in great haste. The three hour battle of Shrewsbury was bloody and savage with Henry IV actively engaged in the fighting, personally killing several Northumbrian knights. As the result of the Percy defeat, Glendower lost a powerful ally and the opportunity for Welsh independence.

Following the defeat of the Percy army, Henry, Earl of Northumberland, submitted to the Lancastrian crown and was compelled to forfeit several of his honors and castles for his involvement in his son's conspiracy. With the earl's reconciliation the northern lordships were again under Henry IV's rule. In January 1404 Parliament was called to London, where the king pressed for new taxes to fund his government and war against Wales. However, the assembly refused to grant additional revenue. Henry IV's offensive against Owain Glendower continued to suffer from insufficient money, soldiers, and arms, as the Welsh repeatedly thwarted the English campaigns. In 1404 Glendower seized control of the castles at Harlech and Aberystwyth, giving him sovereignty over central Wales. Several additional strongholds that were lightly garrisoned with troops due to the lack of funds also fell to the Welsh. As his power grew, Glendower summoned his Parliament to Machynlleth and was formally proclaimed prince of Wales in the presence of emissaries from France, Scotland and Ireland.

While Owain Glendower expanded his power and threatened the sovereignty of England, in February 1405 Earl Henry of Northumberland again defied his king by negotiating an agreement for the overthrow of the Lancaster regime and partition of the kingdom with the Welsh rebels. Under the Triple Convention, Earl Henry was promised northern England, the Mortimer family received the southern lordships, while all of Wales and the region west of the Severn River was given to Glendower. To justify their revolt and rally support to their cause, they issued a public proclamation, claiming Henry IV was an usurper, who illegally raised taxes and was responsible for the murder of Richard II. Many powerful warlords and prelates from the north, including Richard Scrope, archbishop of York, willing joined the growing insurgency. The archbishop was from a wealthy English family who rose rapidly through the church hierarchy. He was ordained into the priesthood in March 1377, first serving as cleric to the York ministry. Five years later he was named to the English delegation at the papal court and later participated in numerous diplomatic missions for Richard II. For his service to the Plantagenet regime, in 1398 Scrope was appointed as archbishop for the See of York. As the reign of Richard II grew more autocratic, the York prelate supported the usurpation of the kingdom by Henry of Bolingbroke and presided over his coronation as king. However, in 1404 when Henry IV threatened to tax the church lands to ease his financial burden, Archbishop Scrope joined the Percy rebellion.

In late May 1405 Henry IV learned of the new Percy revolt and began to muster his large army at Hereford. As he advanced toward Northumberland, his friend and ally, Ralph Nevill, Earl of Westmoreland, assembled his private militia in support of the Lancastrian crown to contend the York archbishop and his sympathizers. He intercepted the rebels at Shipton Moor, where the two opposing forces faced each other. To avoid the uncertainty of battle, Nevill offered to negotiate a reconciliation of the archbishop's grievances with the king. However, when Scrope agreed to meet with the earl, he and his lieutenants were arrested and charged with treason. They were taken to Henry IV and quickly placed on trial. The archbishop and his allies were declared guilty and in early June executed. The beheading of Richard Scrope of York caused widespread outcry against Henry IV, as his popularity continued to wane. He was threatened with papal excommunication and only avoided condemnation through the disunity in the church, resulting from the ongoing schism between Pope Innocent VIII in Rome and Benedict XIII in Avignon. Soon after the execution of Scrope, Henry IV became seriously ill, which the populous of Northumberland believed was God's justice for the killing of the archbishop. He eventually slowly recovered from his sickness but his health remained severely impaired.

Following the capture of Archbishop Scrope, the Percy rebellion quickly began to dissolve and Henry of Northumberland was forced to flee to Scotland to seek sanctuary. Under orders from Henry IV, the royal army advanced against the remaining rebel strongholds, capturing Prudhoe, Alnwick and Berwick. By July the uprising was suppressed and the north country once again under Lancastrian sovereignty.

While Henry IV was suppressing the Percy rebellion, in Wales the Lancastrian forces under the command of Prince Henry of Monmouth began to turn the tide against Owain Glendower and his rebels. In March 1404 the Welsh siege against Grosmont Castle was thwarted by the defiant resistance of the local garrison and two months later the English army gained another victory at Pwll Melyn. Glendower had earlier secured a military alliance with France and in July 1405 two thousand five hundred Valois infantry and men-at-arms began to arrive in Wales. In August their combined armies marched to the east to invade England in Worcestershire. At the approach of the allies, Henry IV assembled a large military force to defend his kingdom. However, no battle occurred after the English skillfully outmaneuvered and blocked the advance of the Franco-Welsh troops, compelling them to abandon their offensive and withdraw. After the retreat of Glendower, the power of the Lancastrians steadily improved as the strength of the uprising began to crumble. The 1406 Parliament at Westminster voted to appoint Prince Henry as permanent commander for the war against the Welsh. Under his skilled leadership, the English slowly began to recapture many of their seized castles and reassert the sovereignty of the king through force of arms.

Henry, Earl of Northumberland, had remained in exile for several years but when the

Scottish King David II ruling regency's relationship with England improved, he was forced to flee to the protection of the Welsh prince. However, finding little support from Glendower for a new attack from the north, the earl traveled to France to begin plotting the overthrow of Henry IV. In December 1407 he returned to Scotland and raised an army but his call to arms attracted only a small military force of Percy vassals and out of favor Englishmen. In February 1408 Earl Henry advanced into Northumberland with his poorly armed and trained troops and was met at Bramham Moor by the militia of Sir Thomas Rokeby, sheriff of Yorkshire. In the resulting battle, the rebels were decisively defeated and Henry of Northumberland killed. With his death the spirit of revolt in the north was broken and finally, after over eight years of internal strife, peace with the nobility was restored.

With the northern English counties firmly under royalist authority, during 1408 Henry IV directed his military initiatives against the destruction of the Welsh rebellion. He appointed his eldest son and heir, Prince Henry, as his deputy for all of Wales and sent him a powerful military force with capable lieutenants to conquer Glendower. After long sieges the great castles at Harlech and Aberystwyth were captured, which was a serious setback to the Welsh prince's autonomous rule. By 1409 Prince Henry had seized control of the major strongholds and towns, reasserting his father's kingship. Glendower was forced to escape to the Snowdonia Mountains, becoming a decreasing threat to the Lancastrians and by the end of the king's reign his revolt had ended. Owain Glendower was never captured and the last years of his life remained unknown.

As his son successfully pursued the offensive against Wales, Henry IV grew increasingly ill and was forced to temporarily appoint his friend and faithful ally, Archbishop Thomas Arundel, to rule during his periods of incapacitation. As the popularity and power of Henry of Monmouth increased, the king started to mistrust him, fearing his usurpation of the crown. A rival political faction was formed around the prince and in 1409 gained control over Parliament. His sympathizers began to plot the overthrow of the monarchy and succession of Henry of Monmouth to the throne. However, in the autumn of 1411 Henry IV partially recovered his health for a short time and reimposed his authority, removing the prince and his followers from the council. Nevertheless, later in the year, they were reconciled, when Prince Henry of Monmouth publicly denied he was raising an army to depose his father.

During much of 1412 Henry IV remained active in the governing of his kingdom and began to prepare for the succession of Prince Henry. The king was exhausted from the years of fighting in Wales and defending his usurpation of Richard II's crown, which caused him great mental anguish. His health was weakened from a severe skin disease and repeated strokes. Lacking the strength to ride a horse, he had to travel either by boat or litter. Henry IV died at age forty-six on March 20, 1413, at Westminster Abbey and was buried according to his wishes at Canterbury Cathedral after a reign of thirteen years.

Sources

Bevan. *Henry IV.*   Mortimer. *The Fears of Henry IV.*   Potter. *Gothic Kings of Britain.*

Henry V, 1387–1413–1422

In the aftermath of the death of Henry IV in March 1413 his English throne was assumed by his twenty-five-year-old son and heir, Henry V, who ruled as the second king of the Renaissance epoch. Henry was the eldest surviving issue of the Earl of Derby, Henry, and Mary of Bohum, Countess of Hereford, and was born on September 16, 1387, in southern Wales at Monmouth Castle. At birth he was recognized as successor to his father's extensive estates and titles. The young lord of Monmouth saw little of the Derby earl, who was actively involved in politics at court and Parliament. When Henry was seven years old, his mother died and with the earl frequently away from the family lands, he was raised along with his three brothers and two sisters by his maternal grandmother, Joan of Hereford. His uncle, Bishop Henry Beaufort, and other distinguished scholars were appointed as tutors for his education and he was instructed in reading, writing, religion, Latin and French, literature, music and court etiquette. Like his father and mother, Henry learned to play the harp and was always fond of music. At the age of ten Henry of Monmouth began his military training under the guidance of experienced knights, mastering the techniques of riding, jousting, fencing and hunting. He was a natural leader with a charismatic personality and later, under the martial tutelage of Henry Hotspur Percy, evolved into a skilled soldier. As Monmouth grew older, he began to attend court with the Earl of Derby, becoming a favorite of King Richard II.

While Henry of Monmouth resumed his education on the family estates, in December 1397 Henry of Derby was banished from England by the ruling Plantagenet council for his alleged plot to usurp the realm. However, the king continued to show favoritism to Lord Henry. In the following year Richard II mounted a second expedition to Ireland against the recalcitrant local rebels and took Monmouth with him as his ward. During the Irish campaign, Henry remained with the royal court, participating in the offensive against the rogues and was knighted for his loyalty and military service to the crown. Nevertheless, despite his friendly relationship with Richard II, when his father attempted to overthrow the regime by force of arms, he was arrested and imprisoned at Trim Castle. To defend his kingdom, the Plantagenet monarch quickly returned to England but was abandoned by his army and supporters, ensuring the seizure of the throne by Earl Henry of Derby.

Following his usurpation of the monarchy, the new king immediately ordered the return of Henry of Monmouth to court from his confinement in Ireland. On October 13, 1399, Henry IV was anointed and crowned at Westminster Abbey with his son assuming a dominant role as bearer of the sword of mercy in the grand and elaborate enthronement ceremony. After the coronation Lord Henry was invested with the titles of Prince of Wales, Duke of Cornwall and Earl of Chester. However, while the royal family celebrated their assumption of power, a plot to restore Richard II to the throne and murder Henry IV and his sons was organized by a faction of loyal Plantagenet sympathizers. As the rebels continued their preparations, the Epiphany Conspiracy was revealed to the Lancaster regime and the sovereign quickly mustered his army to crush their revolt. The attempted rebellion of the nobles served as Henry of Wales's introduction to court politics as a member of the ruling dynasty.

With his investiture as prince, Henry of Monmouth became overlord for most of northern Wales, while the English lords of the March governed the south and central counties. His power over the upper region was secured by control of the great castles at Caernarvon, Conway, Harlech and Rhuddlan. The English had gained sovereignty over the Welsh a century earlier, initiating a relentless and brutal policy of subjugation, which encouraged and kept alive a local spirit of nationalism and freedom. In late 1400 the Welsh quest for independence was given a charismatic and dynamic leader, when Owain Glendower rose up in revolt against English injustice over a land dispute with Lord Reginald Grey of Ruthyn.

As the rebellion of Owain Glendower gained momentum in northern Wales, Henry IV along with his son assembled a large army at Shrewsbury and in September advanced to impose the crown's sovereignty. As the English marched into Wales, Glendower withdrew into the Snowdonia Mountains, avoiding any major battle while engaging in only limited skirmishes and ambushes. After harrying the towns and countryside, the king returned to London, leaving Henry of Wales with an experienced council headed by Henry Hotspur Percy to restore order. Under the guidance of Percy, the Prince of Wales gained his first combat experiences and grew into a skilled commander. However, by the summer of 1401 the uprising had spread throughout the north and the English were hard pressed to contain the rebels as their ranks and strength grew by the day. Compounding the lack of success, the Lancaster initiative suffered from inadequate troop strength and shortages of money. In 1402 Hotspur resigned his office as royal lieutenant for northern Wales in protest of the insufficient aid from the throne. Despite the lack of support from Henry IV, his son's small army managed to retain control over the major Welsh castles. Without adequate forces, the English were compelled to fight a defensive campaign, launching pillaging raids against the Welsh from their base of operations in Chester.

While Prince Henry continued his limited campaign, the war became marred with atrocities by both armies, as the fighting was beset with increasing acts of brutality and barbarity. In June 1402 Owain Glendower fought his first major battle at Pilleth, defeating a large Lancastrian force led by the March lord, Edmund Mortimer. In the aftermath of his defeat, Sir Edmund was captured but soon abandoned his king to join the Welsh. The success at Pilleth and defection of Lord Mortimer gave Glendower a political triumph which enhanced his esteem and stature among the European courts as a legitimate ruler. Following the victory, the Welsh initiated a diplomatic offensive to win recognition from Scotland, France and Ireland as an independent realm.

While Prince Henry continued to attack the Welsh, the Percy family abandoned their allegiance to the crown and joined the rebellion of Owain Glendower. In the summer of 1403 the Percys mustered their private militia and allies, marching to unite with Glendower. When Henry IV received the reports of the uprising, the royal army was assembled and quickly sent to intercept the rebels before they could join the Welsh. As the monarch traveled north, Prince Henry advanced from the Welsh border region with his small army, meeting his father at Shrewsbury. On July 21 the opposing forces clashed with the king commanding the right wing and Henry of Wales leading the left. Occupying the high ground on a ridgeline, Hotspur's well positioned six thousand Cheshire and Welsh archers began the battle by firing a deadly storm of arrows, wounding the prince in the face. The impact of the volley and charge of Northumberland foot-soldiers forced Henry IV's royalists to fall back but his son rallied his infantry, charging into the flank and rear of the rogues. The bloody and savage melee lasted for over three hours; however, when Hotspur was killed his soldiers began to retreat. In his first major encounter Henry of Wales was recognized for his bravery and leadership skills by the crown.

Following his victory at Shrewsbury, Henry IV consolidated his military resources in a major initiative to suppress the Welsh rebellion but his campaign suffered from a lack of money and troop strength, allowing Owain Glendower to remain unchecked. While Prince Henry struggled to contain the rebels, the Welsh seized control over the central region and laid siege against several large royalists' castles. As their uprising gained momentum, Glendower secured wider European acknowledgement as prince after negotiating a treaty of alliance with the Valois regime. With fresh French reinforcements, he renewed his attack and conquered additional lands to hold power over most of the princedom. However, when Owain Glendower and his French allies were repulsed from Worcestershire, the impetus for Welsh independence began to wane. In 1406 the English Parliament recognized Prince Henry as lieutenant for

Wales and permanent commander for the suppression of the revolt. Under his strong and determined leadership, the English regained the upper hand, as many of the castles and towns previously lost were reconquered and the crown's authority reimposed.

Under Henry of Wales's relentless offensive, Glendower was forced on the defensive. In 1408 the great castles at Harlech and Aberystwyth were recaptured by the royalists after long sieges and by the next year most of the princedom was again under Lancastrian sovereignty. With the loss of his base of support, Prince Owain was compelled to seek safety in the mountains of Snowdonia. He continued to launch small attacks and ambushes against the prince's troops but his war of independence was shattered by the overwhelming military might of the English. The Prince of Wales emerged from over nine years of campaigning as a seasoned commander who repeatedly distinguished himself on the battlefield with his bravery and military skills. Constantly short of funds, he learned the necessity of possessing a rich treasury in order to wage a successful war.

While Prince Henry was winning the battle for Wales, he became increasingly popular with the English nobles and prelates. Henry IV was now frequently beset with debilitating strokes as a formidable political party began to form around his son, encouraging him to seize the crown. With the war in Wales well contained, the prince was able to meet on a regular basis with the king's council and assume a larger role in the administration of the government. When his father was incapacitated, he ruled as acting regent, as his authority and esteem escalated. Henry of Wales began to hold his own court and establish a network of influential allies.

In late 1409 Prince Henry's friends gained supremacy over Parliament and forced the dismissal of the ruling council. The assembly appointed nobles and prelates to govern the realm who were loyal to the prince. For most of the following year Henry of Wales held the reins of power, as his father suffered from reoccurring bouts of illness. However, in the autumn of 1411 the king partially recovered his health and assumed control of his regime, compelling Prince Henry and his supporters to resign their offices. After his withdrawal from court, relations between Henry and his father steadily deteriorated, as rumors spread that the prince was raising troops to usurp the throne. Despite the persistent talk of his impending revolt, in 1412 they were reconciled when the Prince of Wales appeared before the council to publicly deny any involvement in a plot to overthrow the crown. In December Henry IV suffered a serious stroke, as his health rapidly declined. On March 20, 1413, he died and Henry V succeeded to the monarchy unchallenged. At the time of his coronation, Henry V was physically described as unusually tall at over six feet, clean shaven with dark hair cut in a circle above the ears, ruddy complexion and lean face. His years of military campaigning in Wales had given him a robust health and a strong muscular body.

Assuming the reins of power, the new king quickly organized his government, replacing most of his father's advisors with his supporters and appointing his uncle and former tutor, Bishop Henry Beaufort, as chief counselor. On April 9, 1413, he was anointed in Westminster Abbey as King Henry V in an elaborate and solemn ceremony. To gain approval and support from the earls, who had been out of favor with Henry IV, he reinstated many of their honors and estates, which had been previously seized by the throne. To atone for his father's involvement in the murder of Richard II and dispel the persistent rumor that he was alive in Scotland, the king ordered the transfer of his body from the humble grave at Langley to a richly ornate tomb at Westminster Abbey. The restoration of lands and reburial served to fully solidify his father's forced usurpation of the Plantagenet crown and secured Henry V's supremacy over the realm.

Under the rule of his father, the danger of armed rebellion by the English high barons was eliminated during the wars against Northumberland, allowing Henry V to assume the monarchy with a loyal nobility. He gained the support of the prelates by initiating a policy of royal patronage, sponsoring the construction and refurbishing of churches, establishing new monastic orders and richly endowing monasteries and abbeys. However, despite winning the approval of the magnates and church, the king was forced to intervene to suppress the Lollards, who posed the threat of igniting religious conflict in his realm.

The Lollardy was a religious and political faction founded by John Wycliffe that aggressively pursued reforms in the church, fought against clerical abuses, opposed the sacraments, considered the pope as the antichrist and argued for more simplistic rituals. Wycliffe was a prominent theologian who was expelled from his teaching position at Oxford University in 1381 by Archbishop Arundel for his criticism of the church and demands for ecclesiastic changes. Henry V was deeply religious and a pious follower of the doctrines of Rome, pledging to uproot the Lollards' expanding crusade. He was forced to take action when his close friend, Lord John Oldcastle of Cobham, lay leader of the radical sect, refused to renounce his belief in the movement. Sir John Oldcastle earlier had served as a knight in the raids against southern Scotland and had fought with Prince Henry in Wales. He won favor with the prince for his bravery and military skills, assuming high command positions in the army. In 1411 he participated with distinction in the English campaign in France in support of Duke John II of Burgundy during the Armagnac-Burgundian civil war. After returning to England, Oldcastle became a prominent defender of the Lollards and was recognized as secular head of the heretic faith. Sir John was arrested on orders from the king and an ecclesiastic court found him guilty of heresy with a sentence of death. However, while Oldcastle remained in captivity in the Tower, his allies arranged his escape and he became the focus of open rebellion. Messengers were sent throughout England, announcing the mustering of their military forces at Fickett's Field near London on January 9, 1414. The goal of the Lollards was to seize the monarch, destroy the priesthood and establish a new church based on Wycliffe's teachings. The Lancastrian government soon learned of the conspiracy and Henry V raised a strong contingent of troops to protect his monarchy. When the unorganized and poorly led antipapists arrived in London, they were arrested and imprisoned virtually without a fight. Their uprising quickly dissolved and Henry V was acknowledged as protector of the church. As the result of his intervention in defense of the orthodox religion, Henry V exploited his new power and esteem to expand his control over the English church. While the revolt of the Lollards was easily defeated, their movement continued to stay active and was not fully suppressed until late in the king's reign.

By the spring of 1414 Henry V was securely in power with the full loyalty of the nobles, church and populace. With his kingdom at peace, he directed his policy toward France and the renewal of the Hundred Years' War. Through his great-great-grandmother, Isabella, sister of Philip IV and wife of Edward II, he had a blood right to the monarchy of France. Henry V had grown up hearing the tales of his ancestors' battlefield exploits against the French, fighting over lands each claimed. By the end of the fourteenth century, the English had been forced out of most of the territory and the new monarch was determined to assert his inheritance. In early 1415 he sent envoys to the Paris court, demanding the return of western France, payment of all unsettled financial claims and marriage with Princess Catherine, daughter of the Valois king, Charles VI. At the time of the negotiations, France was beset with civil war between the Armagnac faction of Count Bernard VII and John II of Burgundy for control of the insane Charles VI. The Armagnacs had recently seized the reins of power and rejected the English ultimatum. When the Lancaster king was informed of the failure of his emissaries, preparations for war were initiated.

During the early months of 1415 Henry V was energetically involved in the organization and preparation of his cross-channel offensive. His English fleet was made ready and additional ships and crews were leased from Flanders. The king found a ready source of experienced volunteers for his army from the marauding bands of unemployed former soldiers who were eager for plunder in the rich French lands. The nobility readily answered his call to arms with knights from the leading families pledging to join the campaign. The royalists began to assemble in April in southern England around the port of Southampton. The invasion force was made up of over eight thousand skilled archers, two thousand five hundred men-at-arms, a contingent of the latest artillery for siege warfare and numerous supporting troops, including fifteen minstrels. After assuming power, Henry V had adopted a conciliatory policy with Parliament, gaining the loyalty of the legislative body. He exploited his friendship with the assembly to secure generous grants of money for the French war. To supplement the treasury, loans were extorted from the nobles, church and towns as the monarch continued to plan for a well prepared and armed initiative. In early July there was a last minute attempt to reach a peaceful resolution with visiting French emissaries, but the negotiations ended at an impasse.

While Henry V finalized his preparations, Richard, Earl of Cambridge, began to intrigue against the Lancastrian government, drawing Sir Thomas Grey into his conspiracy to depose the king and place the young Edmund Mortimer, fifth Earl of March, on the throne. Edmund was born on November 6, 1391, and was the son of Roger Mortimer of March and Alice Fitzalan, daughter of the tenth Earl of Arundel, Richard. When the March earl was killed in Ireland, the six-year-old Edmund inherited his lands and titles. Mortimer was a direct descendant of Edward III through his father and rightful heir to the Plantagenet crown. After Henry IV's seizure of the English kingdom, Edmund was held captive at Windsor Castle and his estates and honors forfeited to the new regime. However, in 1413 he was freed and his titles and lands restored by Henry V. Edmund Mortimer remained loyal to the king, while Cambridge and his conspirators plotted the overthrow of the administration. After failing to gain support in the north for their revolt, the rebels traveled to Southampton and bribed Lord Henry of Scrope into joining their attempted usurpation. In July they revealed their scheme to Edmund of March but he soon exposed their plans to the Lancaster council. When the plotters were confronted with their sedition, they quickly confessed. All three were put on trial and condemned to death as traitors. Edmund Mortimer was cleared of any involvement in the mutiny and granted a full pardon. The Southampton Plot was the last threat of treason against the monarchy during Henry V's reign, as he was now master of England.

After appointing a regency council led by his brother, Duke John of Bedford, to govern England, on August 11, 1415, Henry V began his campaign to seize the French throne. After a two day journey across the channel, the fleet anchored in the estuary of the Seine River and the large army disembarked to besiege the port of Harfleur. The stronghold was well defended by a large, formidable moated wall and a determined garrison of archers and knights. After encircling the fortress, Henry V brought his siege guns forward to begin a daily bombardment of the defenses. Finally following six weeks of investment, with their food supplies exhausted and no relief forces arriving, the French were compelled to surrender. On September 22 Henry V entered the city in a triumphant procession and offered prayers at the Church of Saint Martin to thank God for his success. To establish a permanent presence in Harfleur, a new civil government was created and repair work begun on the battered fortifications. The residents who swore allegiance to the Lancastrian crown were permitted to stay, while the remainder were forced to leave their homes. While the king succeeded in capturing Harfleur, the victory was costly with over one-third of his army either killed or disabled by attacks from the French, desertion and disease. However, he was determined to continue the war but due to the large loss of troops and approach of winter, the scheduled offensive against Paris was abandoned. Henry V now planned to march straight to his enclave at Calais and lay waste to the countryside and villages enroute.

After leaving a large garrison under the command of his uncle, Thomas Beaufort, to guard his new colony, on October 8 Henry V began the long trek to Calais. After encountering only scattered resistance, he reached the Somme River but found the bridges and natural fords blocked by large contingents of French knights. The English were compelled to redirect their route up river to find an undefended crossing and by a series of rapid marches finally located an unguarded bridge. The journey toward Calais was continued but as the Lancastrian soldiers approached the village of Agincourt, their line of advance was barred by a large Valois army led by Count Charles d'Albret of Dreux. Confronted by an overwhelming military force, the Lancastrian king offered to abandon Harfleur and pay for the damages in exchange for passage to Calais. The Count of Dreux, sensing an easy victory, quickly refused and ordered his men-at-arms to make ready for battle in the morning.

Following the French refusal of his offer, Henry V was compelled to prepare his outnumbered soldiers for the coming encounter, choosing to defend a location that was lined on both sides by trees to protect his archers. The army was divided into three divisions with the king in his distinctive surcoat leading the center forces. The strength of the English was their archers, while Dreux depended on the shock effect of his heavy cavalry. On October 25 the two armies assembled into battle formation and in the late morning Henry V gave the order for his longbowmen to fire. In response the French mounted troops and foot-soldiers charged across the open wheat field into a deadly storm of arrows, which broke their initial assault. As the decimated knights struggled forward, the second wave launched its attack. When they finally reached Henry V's defensive line, a bloody and savage hand-to-hand combat ensued, as the king's men-at-arms now advanced into the melee. Henry V was actively engaged in the fighting, receiving several sword blows to his helmet, as he encouraged his forces forward. Due to the restricted battlefield, Dreux's offensive quickly lost the advantage of its cavalry as the English steadily gained command of the conflict. In less than an hour the engagement was over with two French divisions destroyed and the third in full retreat. The Lancastrian causalities were light, while French losses were close to eight thousand killed or captured.

In the aftermath of the Agincourt battle, Henry V's small, exhausted army became threatened by the large number of prisoners and the possibility of a new attack from the remaining French cavalry. To protect his vulnerable troops, he ordered the execution of all the captives with the exception of the high nobles, who could pay a large ransom. The slaughter was carried out by archers from his personal bodyguard. With the route to Calais now secure, in the following morning the English renewed their march north. When the army reached Calais, Henry V was given an elaborate welcome by the local governor, as preparations for the return to London were soon begun. On November 16, 1415, the monarch sailed to England, landing at Dover to a hero's welcome. On the road to London he was greeted by celebrations and large cheering crowds. In the capital the king attended a thanksgiving mass at Saint Paul's Cathedral to give praise to God for his victory. However, despite his magnificent triumph at Agincourt, he had gained only Harfleur and realized the larger task of imposing his sovereignty over all of France still remained.

Following its disastrous defeat at Agincourt, the French Armagnac regime of Count Bernard VII quickly recovered its footing, as preparations for the defense of the kingdom against further attacks were initiated. In England Henry V remained determined to assert his blood claim to the French crown by force of arms and plans for a second invasion began in the spring of 1416. With the king's widespread popularity, the Parliament voted increases in the taxes for the new war with little opposition.

The triumph at Agincourt resulted in dramatic increases in English prestige among the European courts. Exploiting his new widespread renown and esteem, Henry V initiated a diplomatic campaign to win approval from the continental powers for his right to the crown of France. However, while his envoys were pursuing acceptance of Lancastrian sovereignty, the king was compelled to intervene to safeguard his enclave at Harfleur against an attack by Bernard VII and the Armagnac army. In early 1416 a large French force laid siege against Harfleur, threatening to starve the garrison into submission. In August a relief army under the command of the sovereign's brother, duke John of Bedford, sailed to France. When the English fleet reached the mouth of the Seine River, the Bedford duke led an assault against the blockading ships of the Armagnac's Genoese ally. In the resulting naval battle, despite their larger and more powerful vessels, the Italians were defeated by the experienced and skilled English seamen and Harfleur relieved. The victory over the Armagnacs added to the escalating military prowess of the Lancaster regime.

While Henry V was preparing his military forces for the Harfleur relief campaign, in late April 1416 the Holy Roman emperor, Sigismund, was welcomed to England by the Lancastrian council. The emperor was touring the European capitals, attempting to gain international backing for an end to the long ongoing schism in the Church of Rome through the intervention of the Council of Constance. The king was anxious to secure the approval of Sigismund for his birthright to the French realm and negotiations were conducted during the summer to solidify his claim. To gain the imperial court's acceptance, Henry V offered to renounce his inheritance to the Valois throne in exchange for western France and Harfleur. English and imperial emissaries were sent to Paris to win Armagnac agreement but Bernard VII refused to surrender any of the kingdom's territory. With the deliberations reaching an impasse, Sigismund abandoned the talks in France and gave his full support to the English government. On August 15 the two rulers signed the Treaty of Canterbury, uniting their two regimes in a mutual military alliance. With the emperor as his ally, Henry V acquired the endorsement of the influential Holy Roman Empire for his succession to the French crown.

Following the agreement with Sigismund, the Lancastrians opened negotiation with Duke John II of Burgundy, attempting to gain his support for the usurpation of the Valois crown. The duke had personal aspirations for French land for his expanding fiefdom and refused to commit to an alliance. However, Henry V was encouraged with the talks and renewed his plans for the second French invasion.

During the winter of 1417, the king began to address the need for additional money to finance his French war. Parliament had already voted a large subsidy but more revenue was needed for the formidable invasion army. He used his royal regalia as collateral for loans and supplemental funds were exhorted from the church, nobles and towns. Recruitment for the army was initiated, while war supplies and weapons were purchased. To transport the large military force across the channel, the English navy was made ready, additional vessels purchased and ships hired from the Flemish. In March the troops started to muster in Hampshire and the fleet assembled. On July 31 the king sailed to France with over ten thousand well prepared and experienced soldiers to begin his conquest of a new kingdom.

After an uneventful channel crossing, Henry V landed in Normandy, quickly securing a bridgehead by capturing the fortified town of Bonneville. With a secure base of operations, on August 13 he advanced against Caen and after a three week siege the town was stormed and brutally ravaged. After garrisoning the fortress, the king continued his offensive to the south, easily occupying additional strongholds as the defenders surrendered without resistance, fearing the sacking of their towns. By December most of Lower Normandy was under control of the Lancastrians and to complete their subjugation of the region the royalists moved against the formidable castle at Falaise. The citadel was besieged and sorties mounted against the town militia. After a month's investment and no relief possible from the Armagnac regime, the French were forced to submit. By the spring of 1418 all of Lower Normandy was under Henry V's rule. The defeated towns were occupied with soldiers and a new civil government established under English officials.

While Henry V was gaining mastery over Lower Normandy, the ongoing truce between the Burgundians and Armagnac faction was broken and the civil war resumed. In May 1418 Duke John II of Burgundy formed an alliance with Charles VI's wife, Isabella, who declared herself regent for the incapacitated Valois king. With the military power of their combined forces, the new allies drove the Armagnacs out of Paris and established their ruling administration over northern France. During the encounter, Count Bernard VII was killed and the leadership of his party was assumed by the dauphin, Prince Charles, who retained authority over southern France.

As the result of the ongoing bloody civil war between the dauphin and John II, resistance against the onslaught of the English was seriously weakened and distracted. After the subjugation of Lower Normandy, Henry V marched steadily toward the ducal capital at Rouen, as town after town fell to his soldiers. By summer 1418 he had conquered the major castles in the duchy with the exception of Rouen and in late July siege operations were begun against the fortified city. Rouen was well protected by a high wall, deep moat and strong towers, presenting a formidable obstacle to the king. While the English were occupied in the south, the stronghold was reinforced with additional troops and food supplies and the garrison quickly refused Henry V's demand for surrender.

The strong defenses of the city could not be taken by storm and the English were compelled to starve the population into submission. The fortress walls were encircled, barring any relief from the French regime and siege operations initiated. Henry V remained with his troops, maintaining order and enforcing a strict discipline. After several of his soldiers deserted their post, they were publicly hung as a warning to the army. The king stayed close to the frontline to press the battle against Rouen and actively directed the counterattacks against the frequent sorties from the garrison, as the investment wore on into the winter months.

As the cold weather set in, food supplies in the fortification became exhausted and famine took an increasing toll on the population. To save food the garrison commander expelled thousands of sick residents from the stronghold. However, Henry V refused to allow them to pass through his lines and they were left in the moat to starve to death. As the new year began, the city had reached the limits of its resistance and negotiations for surrender were begun. After prolonged talks, a settlement was finally arranged on January 13, 1419. Under the terms of the agreement, the citizens who pledged fealty to the Lancastrian regime were permitted to stay in Rouen with their property, while all others were forced to leave. The survivors from the moat were readmitted to the city and properly cared for. On January 20 Henry V entered Rouen and attended a mass of thanksgiving in the cathedral. He stayed for two months in his Norman capital, establishing a new civil council under English officials, while his military lieutenants completed the conquest of the remaining French held Norman castles. By the summer of 1419 after two years of constant campaigning, the king claimed sovereignty over the entire duchy of Normandy and began preparations for the advance into the Ile de France region and Paris.

During the siege at Rouen, Henry V began negotiations for the settlement of his inheritance demands for France with both the Armagnacs and John II of Burgundy. The talks with the dauphin quickly reached an impasse but the discussions with the Burgundians were more successful. In May 1419 the rival envoys reached an agreement in principal with Henry V to receive sovereignty of Anjou, Maine, Touraine, Gascony and his recent Norman conquest. The treaty was to be sealed with the marriage of the warrior-king to Princess Catherine of Valois. A personal meeting between the two sovereigns was arranged at Meulan on May 30. At Meulan the deliberations lasted throughout the following month but ended in a stalemate over the size of the dowry.

After the meeting at Meulan ended in failure, Henry V renewed his offensive against Paris. His campaign in the Ile de France region encountered little opposition and the survival of the dauphin and Duke of Burgundy became increasingly threatened. To thwart the danger of English subjugation, the two bitter rivals began talks for reconciliation; however, when they met on the bridge at Montereau to finalize the settlement, John II was killed by a retainer of Prince Charles. The duke's son and heir, Philip III, assumed his Burgundian fiefs and exacted revenge for the assassination of his father against the Armagnacs by renewing the civil war and reopening negotiations with Henry V. A truce between England and the new duke was quickly arranged, while discussions for a treaty of alliance were initiated.

In May 1420 the Lancastrian monarch and Philip III met at Troyes to sign the final agreement. Under the terms of the Treaty of Troyes, Henry V was recognized as successor to Charles VI and appointed regent during the interim, while the dauphin, Charles, was disinherited. The accord was ratified on June 2 with the marriage of Henry V to Princess Catherine of Valois. During Catherine's childhood she was largely ignored by her father and mother and sent to be raised and educated by the nuns at the convent of Poissy, where she grew into a beautiful, cultured and poised princess. She was described by contemporaries as possessing elegance, charm and intelligence. Despite being an arranged marital union for political reasons, the king and Catherine quickly developed a loving and supportive relationship. During Henry V and Catherine's visit to London in February 1421, she was anointed and crowned queen at Westminster Abbey. In December the future succession of the Lancastrian monarchy was assured when she gave birth to the future Henry VI. Following the death of Henry V, she later married Owen Tudor and became the grandmother of the founder of the Tudor dynasty, Henry VII.

Following the wedding ceremony, on June 4 the new allies began to campaign together against Prince Charles. Riding side by side, Henry V and Duke Philip III marched their armies against the defenses of Paris. The surrounding fortified towns were attacked and occupied after brief sieges. Nevertheless, when the Anglo-Burgundians reached the great fortress of Melun, they were delayed for over four months by the heroic defense of the small garrison. Finally, with their food stocks depleted, the captain of the defenders was forced to submit. Despite their valiant resistance, many of the Melun captives were executed in an act of ruthlessness by the Lancastrian king. After the seizure of Melun, the road to Paris was clear and on December 1, 1420 Henry V and Charles VI entered the city in triumph to the welcome of the population. However, despite his astonishing achievement, the English monarch was recognized as ruler by only northern France, while the region south of the Loire River gave allegiance to Prince Charles. To win sovereignty over all of France, Henry V was compelled to continue his offensive against the dauphin.

The warrior-king had been absent from England for over three years and in late December 1420 preparations began for the return home. Before leaving Paris, Henry V met with the French Parliament to secure additional taxes for his war and initiated policies to promote economic growth. To impose his sovereignty, English nobles were appointed to rule the newly conquered towns, while the administration of the local governing institutions and church was left unchanged, albeit under the command of the king's men. With his government established, in late January 1421 Henry V and Catherine sailed for England to a hero's welcome.

The royal party landed in England on February 1, 1421, and traveled to a grand and lavish reception in London. Following the city's welcome, the king and Catherine spent the next two months touring the kingdom to renew the Lancastrian regime's bonds with the population. During the journey, Henry V pressed his need for additional money and troops for the French war with the local nobles, knights, church and towns, raising a considerable amount for his coffers. In May the monarch summoned Parliament to Westminster, where new subsidies were granted for the campaign and the Treaty of Troyes ratified. Henry V spent his remaining time in London occupied with English civil affairs and preparations for his return to France.

After four months in England, on June 10 Henry V sailed for Calais with reinforcements for the initiative in the Loire Valley against Prince Charles. Before leaving France in late January, he had appointed his brother, Duke Thomas of Clarence, as his surrogate commander. In March the duke renewed the war, advancing his cavalry and archers south toward Orleans. However, during the siege against Bauge Castle, he was killed and his forces routed in a surprise attack from a revived French army, which was augmented with fresh soldiers from its new Scottish ally.

In the aftermath of the Bauge defeat, the Earl of Salisbury, Thomas Montague, assumed leadership of the English army and continued the offensive into the Loire Valley but his campaign soon stalled. After arriving in Paris, Henry V took personal command of his troops, advancing against the formidable network of strongholds still loyal to the dauphin. The Lancastrian king marched his forces into the Loire and under his dynamic and energetic leadership captured castle after castle by siege. In October he besieged the great fortified town of Meaux. The defenses were skillfully led and offered a defiant resistance against the English assaults. The attack against Meaux lasted for over seven months but finally in early May the garrison submitted. Henry V remained with his soldiers, personally directing the cannon bombardments and sorties. However, during the long investment he began to show increasing signs of ill health.

After the surrender of Meaux, Henry V returned to Paris and reunion with Queen Catherine. However, his health continued to deteriorate and he grew increasingly weak from dysentery contracted during the siege at Meaux. In Paris he met with Duke Philip III and they agreed to combine their forces for a joint campaign into the Loire. However, before they could launch their offensive, Prince Charles attacked the castle of Cosne, threatening the safety of the Burgundian capital of Dijon. Henry V attempted to advance against the French but was too frail. He was taken by litter to Vincennes Castle, where the Lancaster king died on August 31, 1422, at age thirty-five and a reign of nine years.

Sources
Allman. *Henry V.*   Hutchison. *King Henry V.*   Neillands. *The Hundred Years' War.*   Seward. *The Hundred Years' War.*

Henry VI, 1421–1422–1471

While in pursuit of his birthright to the sovereignty of France, in August 1422 Henry V died from the effects of dysentery contracted during the siege at Meaux, bequeathing a legacy of heroic triumphs and conquests to his nine-month-old heir, Henry VI, who reigned as the third Renaissance king of England. Henry was the only child of Henry V and Catherine of Valois and was born on December 6, 1421, at Windsor Castle. By October of the following year with the death of his father and maternal grandfather, Charles VI, the infant-prince had inherited the kingdoms of England and France. In December 1422 the Lancaster Parliament recognized Henry V's brother, Duke John of Bedford, as regent for France, while appointing the new king's uncle, Humphrey of Gloucester, lord protector for England. After succeeding to the monarchy, Henry VI spent his early years under the protection of Sir Thomas Beaufort, whom Henry V had named as guardian for his son prior to his death, while the government of England was administered by Duke Humphrey and the conquest of France renewed by Duke John. Henry VI began his public life in November 1423, attending his first Parliament under the care of his mother. In 1428 he began his educational studies, when Richard Beauchamp, Earl of Warwick, assumed responsibilities for his academic and military training. The monarch was instructed in religion, reading, writing, languages, court etiquette, music and the battle skills of a knight. However, unlike his father, Henry VI was not a natural leader and had little interest in military affairs. He was raised in the Lancaster court with the children of prominent noble families under the guidance and influence of Queen Catherine and his tutors.

While Henry VI continued his preparations for kingship, in France Duke John of Bedford's campaign into the Loire was checked at the defensive walls of Orleans and the English war effort began to falter. In 1429 the French dauphin, Charles of Valois, was crowned king at Rheims Cathedral as the Lancastrian fortunes deteriorated further. To buttress the failing English resolve and fighting spirit, the Bedford duke urgently finally convinced the ruling government in London to make arrangements for the coronation of Henry VI in Paris as king of France. In early December 1431 he made his entrance into the French capital and was anointed ruler at Notre Dame Cathedral. The twice enthroned sovereign remained in his second kingdom for over a month before ending his first and only visit in February 1432. Returning to London he received a hero's welcome and was greeted with a lavish reception by the city council. A solemn mass of thanksgiving soon followed at Westminster Abbey. His formal succession to the monarchy of France generated an enormous sense of English patriotism and pride throughout the realm.

As John of Bedford defended his nephew's French lands, in England the policies of Duke Humphrey grew increasingly unpopular. The bishop of Winchester, Henry Beaufort, formed a party in opposition and began to openly confront the Gloucester regime. As the power struggle between the two factions intensified, the ruling administration was beset with indecision and stagnation. When Henry VI sailed to France in late 1431, Humphrey assumed the authority of regent and ruled without the advice of the council. With total control of the government, he initiated a political campaign to eliminate Bishop Beaufort, charging him with treason. As the crisis threatened to erupt into violence, acting under the influence and encouragement of Queen Catherine and his tutors, the young king intervened to personally force a reconciliation through the esteem and sovereignty of his crown. However, hostilities between the two rivals continued as England remained paralyzed.

By 1433 the conflict in France had reached an impasse and Duke John of Bedford returned to England to raise additional troops, money and support for his role as regent for France. However, the king's government under the regime of Duke Humphrey continued to be ineffective and weak and John was appointed by Parliament to rule in both England and France. He stayed in the kingdom until July 1434, endeavoring to reform the finances and secure a stable source of funds for the war in France. The duke succeeded in gaining new loans and guarantees for additional revenue from the royal lands before returning to Paris. After arriving in France with reinforcements, he assumed personal command of the army and began to buttress his defenses in Ile de France and Paris. Despite his attempts to revive the English war effort, the campaign against Charles VII remained at a deadlock and the Lancaster council agreed to open discussions at Arras for a settlement. The talks quickly ended in failure when Charles VII demanded total sovereignty for France. While the peace negotiations with the Lancastrian court were at an end, England's principal ally, Philip III, Duke of Burgundy, renewed his deliberations with the Valois envoys. In October 1435 he signed the Treaty of Arras, pledging to abandon Henry VI and join forces with Charles VII. The defection of the Burgundian army was a serious blow to English military might, which was exacerbated by the unexpected death of John of Bedford.

Without the resolve and skilled leadership of Duke John, the English campaign against the Valois king soon faltered. In April 1437 Charles VII entered Paris in triumph and was recognized as monarch by the southern half of the kingdom. While the French army pressed its attack into the Ile de France region, Henry VI began to increasingly assume personal power over his government. He regularly attended sessions of his council meetings, conferred with foreign emissaries and exercised royal prerogatives with the granting of honors, lands and money. By November 1437 the sixteen-year-old Henry VI was fully acknowledged as ruling sovereign. His tutors and advisors had every reason to expect that he would be an effective and energetic monarch. Henry VI was healthy, pious, intelligent, and scholarly but weak willed and disinterested in military affairs. He was easily influenced by his courtiers and his reign became beset with uncertain judgment and vacillation. The royal council was soon dominated by the Duke of Suffolk, William de la Pole, and Bishop Henry of Beaufort, who used their high offices to govern the realm. A faction in opposition was forged by Henry VI's uncle, Duke Humphrey, which aggressively confronted the policies of the regime, as the English administration remained stagnant, while lawlessness and social disorder became widespread.

When Henry VI assumed full power over England without opposition in 1437, the quest for his French inheritance still remained unresolved. After the conquest of Paris, Charles VII renewed his advance into the Ile de France region, driving the Lancaster army back toward Normandy. As his control over France deteriorated, the English regime agreed to begin peace discussions at Gravelines in June 1439 but the negotiations ended without a settlement over the continued demands for the French throne by Henry VI.

In the aftermath of the fruitless Gravelines negotiations, in July 1440 the Lancaster monarch reappointed Richard, Duke of York, as his lieutenant for Normandy and sent him a large army of reinforcements to renew the attack against Charles VII in Ile de France. Richard was born on September 21, 1411, and was the second son of the Earl of Cambridge, Richard, and Anne Mortimer. He was the largest landowner and most powerful magnate in England, second only to the king. As a direct descendant of the third son of Edward III, he had a better claim to the English crown than Henry VI, who was related to the fourth son. When he was four years old, his father, Richard, Earl of Cambridge, was executed for his involvement in the Southampton Plot and his son was denied his inheritance to the family's demesne. However, when his paternal uncle, Edward of York, died childless, Richard assumed his lands and later acquired the earldom of March after the death of his maternal uncle, Edmund Mortimer. In May 1436 he was appointed to replace Duke John of Bedford as military commander for the war against France and succeeded in regaining several towns and retaining control over Normandy. Nevertheless, in 1439 the duke resigned his office in protest at the lack of military and financial support from the Lancaster court.

After returning to Normandy, during the summer of 1441 York marched his forces into the Ile de France region, reoccupying towns and castles along the Seine and Oise rivers. However, his campaign soon began to suffer from the lack of money, troops and the king's wavering resolve, as his recent gains were soon reclaimed by the Valois soldiers of Constable Arthur de Richemont. In 1443 the Lancaster council diverted a large army to relieve French pressure against its southern duchy of Gascony, denying Richard of York of much needed reinforcements and supplies. Despite his shortages of manpower, York was able to defend the borders of Normandy against de Richemont's attacks, as both kingdoms became increasingly war weary and desirous of peace. In February 1444 Henry VI sent his chief advisor, William of Suffolk, to Tours to begin discussions for a settlement. The talks were initiated in April but no lasting reconciliation was possible with the Valois regime's continued insistence on full sovereignty for all of France. Nevertheless, a truce for two years and marital agreement between Henry VI and Princess Margaret of Anjou was signed as the means to advance a future permanent resolution.

Under the terms of the Truce of Tours, on April 22, 1445, Henry VI was married to Margaret of Anjou in England at the Titchfield Abbey. The marital agreement was strongly supported by the English regime as part of its peace initiative to solidify friendly relations with the court of France. Margaret was born on March 23, 1430, in the independent duchy of Lorraine and was the second daughter of Rene I of Anjou and Isabella, Duchess of Lorraine. Through her mother's lineage, the princess was closely related to the ruling Valois House of France. While her father was in Italy involved in a power struggle for the crown of Naples, she was raised by Isabella in Lorraine, receiving a well rounded education. Margaret was described by contemporaries as intelligent, beautiful and uncompromising. Possessing a dominating personality, she soon exerted a strong influence over her weak willed husband and played a major role in his policy decisions. After nearly eight years of childless marriage, the future of the Lancastrian dynasty seemed secured with the birth of Prince Edward on October 13, 1453.

Following their truce agreement at Tours, the two kingdoms remained in close contact in the quest for a permanent peace. Queen Margaret quickly gained influence over the highly impressionable Henry VI and aggressively supported the political initiatives of the French king, gaining her husband's approval for the return of the county of Maine to France and the personal meeting between the two rivals to further the cause for reconciliation. Despite several border incursions by both regimes, the truce was routinely extended, while the French repeatedly delayed any final negotiated settlement. As the Lancaster king pursued his peace policy, English defenses in occupied France were largely ignored and troop strength depleted. While Henry VI and William of Suffolk continued to exchange emissaries with the Valois court, Charles VII began an energetic campaign to reform and rebuild his military forces with the creation of a permanent professional army.

In numerous personal letters to Charles VII and meetings with French emissaries, the Lancastrian king had pledged to return the county of Maine to Valois control but the transfer date had been repeatedly extended. Finally, in March 1448 the French army advanced into Maine and laid siege against Le Mans to force the English to abandon the countship. After the loss of Le Mans, Henry VI's envoys negotiated the Treaty of Lavardin and agreed to withdraw from the disputed county. However, the expelled troops were garrisoned in strongholds and towns along the border region between Brittany and Normandy, which aroused the suspicions and concerns of the Breton duke, Francis I. The duke had earlier given his fealty to Charles VII and appealed to his overlord for protection. In defense of his ally, the French king ordered his local Valois forces to arrest the duke's brother, Gilles, who was a sympathizer of the English and involved in plots to seize Brittany. In April 1449 the Lancastrians retaliated on instructions from Henry VI's council by assaulting and seizing the Breton village of Fougeres in support of their ally. Charles VII considered the capture of Fougeres as a direct attack against his vassal, which breached the terms of the Tours agreement and was considered just cause for renewing the conflict. Despite attempts by the new Lancastrian lieutenant for Normandy, Edmund, second Duke of Somerset, to maintain the truce, the Valois army began to muster for the invasion of English occupied France. Edmund was born in 1406 and was the fourth son of John Beaufort, Earl of Somerset, and Margaret Holland. He was from one of the great English families with direct lineage to the royal house. After the deaths of his older brothers, Edmund inherited the duchy of Somerset. He was a veteran of the war against the French and in 1431 was appointed as commander of a Lancaster army. He later led a relief force to recapture the fortress at Harfleur and achieved additional victories against the Valois regime prior to his appointment as royal governor for the English held lands in France.

Following the declaration of war, the French king and Francis I of Brittany negotiated a mutual treaty of alliance. In the late summer of 1449 Charles VII invaded Normandy with the full power of the new Valois army while the Bretons advanced from the west. During the four years of truce, the local English forces and defenses had been largely ignored by Henry VI, leaving his lands and towns open to attack. Under the leadership of Constable Arthur de Richemont, the well prepared and armed French swept into Normandy quickly, overcoming the weak and scattered resistance to conquer the eastern region and in October the garrison commander of Rouen, John Talbot, earl of Shrewsbury, surrendered the city. After occupying Rouen, de Richemont continued his campaign in Normandy and by the end of the year the entire area south to Harfleur was once again under Valois control.

In April 1450 Henry VI managed to secure enough money to dispatch a small relief force commanded by Lord Thomas Kyriell to Cherbourg in an attempt to recover some of his lost lands. After the arrival of Kyriell in France, his army was augmented with a contingent of Norman soldiers sent by Duke Edmund of Somerset. With his military might strengthened, Lord Thomas advanced to recapture the Valois occupied town of Formigny. As he approached the town, his line of march was intercepted by the local French militia, which was quickly reinforced with the timely arrival of de Richemont and his infantry and knights. In the ensuing battle, Kyriell's troops were nearly annihilated by the superior French artillery and determined charge of the cavalry. With the destruction of the only English field army in France, the remaining isolated and demoralized Norman garrisons fell in rapid succession. After the seizure of Caen and Cherbourg, by August 1450 all of Normandy was once again under Valois sovereignty, while the English still retained control over the duchy of Gascony and the enclave at Calais.

While the Lancaster regime was losing power over Normandy, Henry VI's French peace policy grew increasingly unpopular in Parliament and among the English population. In the early summer of 1449 the legislative assembly met at Winchester and under the leadership of the House of Commons refused to grant the crown's request for war funds. As the losses in Normandy mounted, the Commons began to direct its opposition against Henry VI's chief advisor, William de la Pole, Duke of Suffolk. In February 1450 the duke was formally charged by Parliament with treason. He was accused of losing English control over Maine and Normandy and plotting the overthrow of the monarchy with the aid of a French invasion army. The Suffolk duke was arrested and imprisoned in the Tower to await trial by his peers. However, he retained the favor and backing of Henry VI and appealed directly to him for justice.

On March 17, 1450, the king personally intervened and sentenced de la Pole to banishment for five years. As he sailed into exile in Burgundy, the duke was seized by the sailors of his ship and beheaded in an act of justice in support of the Commons and popular condemnation of Henry VI's council.

After the death of Duke William of Suffolk, the shire of Kent rose in revolt in support of Parliament and in protest of unfair taxes and corrupt government. In June 1450 the peasants and craftsmen assembled and advanced to London to register their grievances. By the time they reached Blackheath, their ranks had grown to over three thousand dissenters. As the threat to his sovereignty escalated, Henry VI dispatched envoys to the rogues at Blackheath, demanding their withdrawal. The leader of the uprising, Jack Cade, refused the order, claiming his men were marching to London to protect the sovereign from his traitorous counselors and in defense of the House of Commons' attack against the royal council. To counter the defiance of Cade, the king mustered a large army and moved to directly confront the Kent protesters. At the approach of the formidable and well armed Lancaster military force, Jack Cade directed his followers to disband and return to Kent. As they retreated, the insurgents were attacked by the royalists and their lands ravaged. However, when Henry VI commanded his troops to pursue Cade's fleeing men, they mutinied and refused to fight. The Lancastrian soldiers soon deserted, leaving London open to attack by the Kent rebels. In early July the reassembled Kent dissidents marched against the capital, while Henry VI remained paralyzed with fear and inactivity at the great castle of Kenilworth guarded by a strong contingent of infantry and knights.

With London now virtually defenseless, the Kent rebels entered the city to make their demands known to the regime with a display of force. The Tower fortress was seized and the remaining royal counselors executed. Jack Cade and his peasant forces remained in the capital for three days, traveling over London Bridge at will from their base camp at Southwark to loot and pillage. However, on July 3 the city residents rallied around the remaining garrison troops and blocked Cade's entry into London at the bridge and fought his rogues to a standoff. After the battle the bishop of Winchester met with Cade and his men, offering a full pardon for their withdrawal. The Lancastrian government honored the amnesty and the insurgents returned to Kent in peace.

At the end of July 1450 Henry VI traveled to London and reassembled his scattered government to again take up the reins of power. In September he named his disgraced former lieutenant for France, Duke Edmund of Somerset, as the new constable and member of his council. Somerset was widely unpopular in England and his Norman policies were blamed for the loss of the duchy. His appointment added to the growing dissent against the Lancastrian government.

As the king struggled to enforce his rule, Richard of York sailed to England from his post as lord lieutenant for Ireland to renew his rebellion against the throne. Following his return from France, he had been sent to Ireland in July 1449 to restrict his influence and involvement in crown affairs. York was held in high esteem by the nobles, church and populace as a great lord who had a right to a prominent office in the administration. As his support and authority grew, he became the focal point of an increasingly disloyal faction in opposition, demanding reform to the government. At the November 1450 Parliament, the House of Commons petitioned the monarch to remove Somerset and his allies from the council with the full backing of York. In defiance of the assembly, Henry VI refused to dismiss his friends and favorites, as unrest escalated throughout the realm. However, he appeased the Commons with concessions and changes to his council, agreeing to annul all his prior grants of titles, honors and lands, while pledging to create a new commission of earls to approve all future subsidies. After the king mollified his detractors, Richard of York withdrew from court to his great castle at Ludlow on the Welsh border and became uninvolved in the conduct of the regime's policies.

Following the recovery of Normandy, Charles VII renewed his campaign of conquest for English occupied France by attacking the duchy of Gascony. In August 1450 Henry VI assembled a relief army to bolster the Gascon defenses but the expedition never sailed due to the lack of money. While English reinforcements remained stranded, the French advance encountered only light and scattered resistance as castle after castle fell before the might of the Valois army and with the capture of Bordeaux and Bayonne all of Gascony was under French rule.

From his sanctuary at Ludlow Castle, Richard of York remained absent from court and out of favor with the king. When Henry VI summoned him to answer charges of breaking the peace, the demand was ignored. As hostility between the two rivals escalated, in January 1452 the duke attempted to forge a peaceful reconciliation with the Lancaster council but his petition was disregarded. After his proclamation went unanswered, York began to muster an army to protect his rights and lands. As Richard sent requests to the nobles and towns for troops, Henry VI issued a decree, claiming York was preparing for rebellion against his crown and ordered his loyal supporters to assemble for war. In late February the formidable Lancastrian military force gathered near London and marched against Richard near Dartford. The sovereign's summons for the defense of his kingdom was answered by a large number of high magnates and knights and York was confronted by a powerful army. Opposed by the overwhelming military might of the royalists, the duke was compelled to submit, after presenting a list of complaints against the Duke of Somerset, charging him with the loss of France and plotting his downfall. Richard of York and his allies were soon granted a full pardon after pledging not to intrigue against the Lancaster throne.

After the suppression of York's revolt, Henry VI spent much of 1453 on a grand tour of his realm to reassert his sovereignty and justice through the force of his presence. Despite several brief uprisings in defense of York, England remained at peace and the rule of the king honored. While Henry VI actively imposed his authority, John Talbot, Earl of Shrewsbury, was given command of a new royal army and sent to reconquer the lost duchy of Gascony. The French had not regained the loyalty of the Gascons and with the arrival of Talbot and his troops, they rose in rebellion, overthrowing the occupation garrisons and supporting the English in the recapture of the duchy. After Shrewsbury's victories, the Reading Parliament voted Henry VI a large increase in his subsidy to defend the kingdom and continue the war in France. By the summer of 1453 he had fully enforced his power over the mutinous nobles and had become a respected and energetic monarch.

Henry VI had repeatedly made numerous grants of titles, offices and wealthy lands to his favorite, Edmund of Somerset. In July 1453 he personally intervened to enforce the transfer of the Welsh lordship of Glamorgan to Somerset from Richard Nevill, Earl of Warwick, who refused to relinquish control. Richard was born on November 22, 1428, and was the son of the earl of Salisbury, Richard, and Alice Montagu. He was the fourteenth Earl of Warwick and a powerful and wealthy nobleman. Through inheritances and marriage he had gained rich and extensive estates centered in the northern counties. The earl entered the government of Henry VI and was knighted for his services. He served in the king's army, participating in campaigns in the north and against Scotland. When Richard of York rebelled against Henry VI in 1452, the Warwick Earl remained loyal to the crown and was involved in the suppression of his conspiracy.

While Warwick continued to retain Glamorgan by force-of-arms, the monarch traveled toward the Welsh borderlands to personally assert his authority. In early August as the royal court advanced near Clarandon, Henry VI received the reports of John Talbot's death and his devastating defeat at the battle of Castillon. In the aftermath of Talbot's loss, the French expelled the English and subdued the rebellion, ending English sovereignty over Gascony. The shock of the disaster propelled the king into a severe state of depression, rendering him incapable of governing. With his absence as head of state, the council lacked the power to rule and the realm drifted into stagnation and indecision.

In October 1453 as the depression of Henry VI deepened into insanity, Queen Margaret gave birth to a son and heir, Edward of Lancaster. With a direct successor to the Lancasterian crown, Richard of York was no longer next in line to the throne and less of a threat to usurp the regime. He was now invited to rejoin the council as an equal of the great lords. However, soon after returning to the government, he reissued the charges against his enemy, Somerset, blaming him for the loss of English occupied France. Under the force of his personality and military might, he imposed his control over the ruling ministry and had Edmund of Somerset committed to the Tower. In March 1454 his supremacy over the monarchy was confirmed by Parliament and with the continued incapacity of the king, he was appointed protector and defender of the kingdom. With his authority honored by the high nobles and church, Richard replaced Somerset's supporters on the council with his allies and friends, establishing his own administration.

While Richard of York consolidated his office of protector, in Yorkshire Henry Holland, Duke of Exeter, formed an alliance with the Percy family in an attempt to seize northern England from the rule of York's regime and create a new realm under their authority. To defend the king's demesne, Richard quickly advanced north with a military force and issued a proclamation, charging Exeter and the Percys with treason. Under threat of attack by the protector and his northern ally, Richard Nevill, the rebels fled but were later captured and imprisoned. By exploiting the military power of his office in a show of force, by the summer of 1454 the York duke had regained full control over the kingdom.

As Richard of York continued to rule under the authority of Parliament, in early 1455 Henry VI began to recover his health. In February the king started to take back his government, ordering the release of the Percys and Exeter, while replacing York's appointees at court with his friends and supporters. In March he presided over his first council meeting and exonerated his favorite, Somerset, of the duke's charges, while reinstating him to his administration. The restoration of Edmund of Somerset, the Percy family and Holland to the favor of the monarchy was a direct threat to York and the Earl of Warwick, compelling them to flee from court for their safety and forge an alliance to protect their rights and lands. Under the influence of Edmund of Somerset, in April Henry VI commanded York and Nevill to attend his council at Leicester and disband their private militias. The duke ignored the demand and as the sovereign advanced to Leicester to impose his order, he was intercepted by the army of Richard at the town of Saint Albans on May 22. Confronted by the troops of York, the royalists took up defensive positions in the city, while negotiations for reconciliation were initiated. However, the discussions quickly broke down and the duke ordered his soldiers to attack. Possessing a superior military force, he quickly overwhelmed the loyalists and in the ensuing melee killed Somerset and many of the great earls, while capturing Henry VI to begin the thirty year Wars of the Roses.

In the aftermath of his defeat at Saint Albans, Henry VI was taken under Yorkish guard to London. He began to suffer a relapse of his insanity from the severe stress of his recent defeat and capture at Saint Albans rendering him unable to rule; allowing Richard to assume the lord protectorship. The king's council was dissolved and replaced with supporters of York. To consolidate his accession to power, the duke summoned Parliament to meet in early July

1455 at Westminster. The assembly was officially opened by Henry VI with Duke Richard close by his side. With control of the king, York utilized the authority of the monarchy to pressure the Parliament into approving a full pardon for the victors of Saint Albans and when the delegates reassembled in November Richard was again appointed as protector and defender to legitimize his seizure of the crown. However, his protectorship lasted only until February 1456, when Henry VI sufficiently regained his health to return to court. York was not immediately dismissed from the council but finally under the encouragement of Queen Margaret in August the monarch forced him and his friends from the government.

Following the birth of the Lancaster heir, Edward of Wales, the queen began to increasingly assert her influence over Henry VI. She was widely unpopular in the south and persuaded her husband to move the seat of his regime to her strongholds in the Midlands. The king had partially recovered his sanity but was only able to take part in the public duties of the monarchy, while the responsibilities of government rested with the great council, which was dominated by supporters of Margaret. During the periods when Henry VI was incapacitated, the administration of the kingdom became largely paralyzed by the inaction and indecision of the Lancastrian counselors. As the realm drifted without a leader, the monarch spent considerable periods of time isolated in the Midlands' abbeys and monasteries. Lacking the power of a functioning monarchy, Parliament was no longer summoned and the plight of the people ignored. Richard and his allies continued to attend council meetings but the political faction favoring Queen Margaret and her infant son began to aggressively oppose him, as the lords prepared for the renewal of the Wars of the Roses.

Queen Margaret had continued to retain her influence over the king as his bouts of insanity grew more frequent and severe. With control of her husband, she and her supporters gained full authority over the council to rule the realm. York and his friends were out of favor and withdrew to their estates, preparing for war. In May 1459 the Lancastrian government began to assemble its loyal nobles and their private armies around Leicester, while the Yorkish coalition mustered at Ludlow Castle on the Welsh border.

In late September Henry VI was at the head of an army marching west from Kenilworth Castle to subdue York and his allies at Ludlow. When the royalists approached the entrenched rebels at Ludford, many of the Yorkish soldiers defected to the crown after the promise of a full pardon. With his forces greatly depleted and now outnumbered, Richard and his remaining supporters abandoned the field and fled to safety abroad. York escaped to Ireland, while his son, Edward of March, and his chief advisors, Richard of Warwick and the Earl of Salisbury sailed to sanctuary in Calais. In the aftermath of the Lancastrian victory, Parliament was summoned to Coventry in November and under the influence of the queen's faction passed the Act of Accord, which outlawed the dissidents and seized their lands. In Ireland Richard assumed his former office of lord lieutenant and with the backing and protection of the local rebel Parliament was recognized as royal governor for Henry VI in defiance of the ruling council. From his haven he spent the first half of 1460 preparing with Warwick and Salisbury for their return to England and the armed rescue of the monarch from the control of his corrupt and incompetent counselors.

While the lord lieutenant remained in Ireland, Richard of Warwick, Salisbury and York's son, crossed the channel from Calais to England in late June 1460, arriving at Sandwich with an invasion force. After landing with their troops and war supplies, the earls were joined by many of their Kentish allies as they marched against London. Confronted by the large, powerful dissident army, the capital surrendered without opposition. Salisbury was placed in command of the city, while Warwick and Edward advanced against Henry VI and his royalists at

Northampton. The two armies clashed on July 10 with the rebels quickly defeating the Lancastrians and killing many of the throne's close advisors while capturing the king. With possession of the acknowledged legal power, the government was assumed by the friends of York and the crown's counselors replaced. In October 1460 Richard of York finally returned to London and before the assembled Parliament at Westminster claimed the English monarchy by right of blood and conquest. However, his attempted usurpation was strongly opposed by the earls and Commons, who had sworn allegiance to Henry VI. Facing the united resistance of his sympathizers, York was compelled to accept a compromise. Under the ensuing Act of Accord with Parliament, Henry VI remained as king until his death and York was recognized as successor presumptive with all the honors and rights of the heir. Despite the settlement, with the monarch's continued bouts of insanity, Richard of York immediately become ruler of the realm by the authority of the legislative assembly.

The compromise agreement was accepted by the king and Parliament but Queen Margaret and her allies refused to relinquish the inheritance rights of Prince Edward of Wales and renounced the reconciliation. In December the queen's supporters assembled their vassals and private militias in the north and advanced to reinstate the rule of the Lancaster monarchy. To counter the new threat, Richard of York and Salisbury quickly marched with their small contingent of available soldiers without waiting for reinforcements. The two rivals clashed at Wakefield and in the ensuing melee York was killed and his forces shattered. However, despite having no knowledge of the queen's rebellion, the king was widely blamed by the Lords and Commons for breaking the terms of his settlement with the Yorkists, and Margaret and her coalition were now considered rebels who had broken the peace by waging war against the acknowledged head of state. The duke's eldest surviving son, Edward, assumed his titles and lands and under authority from Parliament mustered the loyalists against the revolt. While Edward defeated a small Lancastrian army at Mortimer's Cross on the Welsh border, Margaret traveled south from Yorkshire with the northern lordships' militias to rescue her husband from control of the Yorkists. At the approach of the queen's forces, Richard of Warwick moved to block their advance at Saint Albans from a well fortified defensive position. However, during the second battle of Saint Albans, he was skillfully outmaneuvered with his left flank breached and his troops overwhelmed. During the ensuing melee, Henry VI was abandoned by Warwick and reunited with Margaret.

As the Lancastrians withdrew to the base of their support in the northern counties, in March 1461 Edward of York consolidated his authority over the south and entered London in triumph to be anointed king of England. With his power recognized by the southern lordships, he marched against the forces of Henry VI and Margaret and on March 29 the two armies collided in Yorkshire at Towton during a blizzard. The Lancastrians initiated the battle by abandoning their defensive positions and charging wildly into the Yorkist pikemen. The resulting melee was a bloody and savage close quarter encounter with heavy casualties on both sides. However, the tide of victory was turned in Edward's favor with the timely arrival of fresh reinforcements led by John Mowbray, third Duke of Norfolk. After their defeat at Towton, Margaret and Henry VI abandoned England with Prince Edward of Wales, taking refuge in Scotland at the court of James III.

In exile Margaret negotiated a treaty of alliance with the Scottish regime, giving up authority of Berwick Castle for military aid in the overthrow of the usurper. However, the surrogate troops of James III proved unreliable and their sorties against Yorkist controlled Carlisle were easily repulsed. Following the failed Scottish campaign, the queen sailed to France to seek support from her cousin, Louis XI. After meeting with the Valois king, the

French government agreed to provide a contingent of men-at-arms and in 1462 Margaret arrived in Northumberland with a small army commanded by Pierre de Breze. Breze won a few skirmishes against the Yorkists but lacking troops and money his attack soon failed. In the spring of 1463 Margaret abandoned her husband and returned to her father's estates in Anjou with Prince Edward. The insane Henry VI soon became a liability to James III's court and was expelled from the kingdom, taking up residence in the Lancaster city of Bamburgh. In the summer of 1464 he was compelled to flee the city, when the local garrison surrendered to the forces of Edward. The mad king spent most of the following year wandering through the countryside and villages, until he was finally captured near Clitheroe in July 1465. He was taken as a traitor to London and imprisoned in the Tower.

As Henry VI languished in prison, Edward began to exert his independent rule, resulting in conflict with his ambitious principal advisor, Richard, Earl of Warwick. As their relationship grew increasingly hostile, Warwick was compelled to seek sanctuary in France, where through the intervention of Louis XI his reconciliation with Queen Margaret was negotiated. In September 1470 he sailed to England to overthrow the usurper. With support from his northern allies and the sympathizers of the deposed Lancaster king, the duke of Warwick overwhelmed the Yorkists and forced Edward to abandon his crown and flee to Burgundy. Following the Lancasterian victory, Henry VI was restored to the throne to reign as the figurehead ruler under the control of Warwick.

While Henry VI assumed the reins of the monarchy under the guidance of Richard of Warwick, Edward began negotiations with the Burgundian court for support in reclaiming the English throne. He was the brother-in-law of the Burgundian duke, Charles, who agreed to provide him with a fleet and invasion army for an attack against the English regime. In April 1471 York returned to England with the professional troops of Charles, defeating and killing Warwick at the battle of Barnet. Shortly after Edward's victory, Queen Margaret and the eighteen-year-old Prince Edward of Wales crossed the channel from France and rallied the Lancastrian forces against the usurpers. Edward advanced to meet the new threat, completely overwhelming the queen's army and killing her son during the battle at Tewkesbury. In the aftermath of his victory, Edward returned to London and ordered the murder of Henry VI to prevent future rebellion in favor of the Lancastrians. The last Lancaster king died at age forty-nine and a disastrous reign of forty-eight years, resulting in the loss of two kingdoms.

Sources

Griffiths. *The Reign of King Henry VI.*   Seward. *The Hundred Years' War.*   Wolffe. *Henry VI.*

Edward IV, 1442–1471–1483

On May 4, 1471, Edward of York defeated the Lancastrian army of Henry VI at the battle of Tewkesbury to secure the crown of England for the Yorkish dynasty and reign as the fourth king of the Renaissance age. Edward was born in France at Rouen on April 28, 1442, and was the second son of Duke Richard of York and Cecily of Nevill. His father was directly related to the ruling Lancastrian monarchy and acknowledged as heir to the childless King Henry VI. Richard of York controlled extensive and rich estates centered at his great castle of Ludlow and was widely recognized as the greatest landowner and most powerful magnate in England. With the duke absent from his household for extensive periods, the young Edward was raised at Ludlow under the care and protection of a governor. Tutors were appointed for his education in reading, writing, Latin and French, religion, law, music and the social graces. The York prince took his studies seriously and received a well versed education. While continuing his academic instruction, he began his military training in the battle skills of a feudal lord, learning to hunt, ride, fence and joust under the guidance of experienced knights. As Edward grew older, contemporaries described him as having inherited the physical features of the Nevill family. He was over six feet tall, strikingly handsome with a muscular frame. The prince was a natural leader with a charismatic personality.

While Edward remained at Ludlow, continuing his education and military training, Duke Richard of York became the leader of the party in opposition to Henry VI. The king's rule had grown increasingly unpopular under the burdens of high taxes, escalating civil disorder and domination of the administration by his favorites and friends. After Henry VI was incapacitated by mental illness in August 1453, York was elected lord protector by Parliament and assumed control of the government with his son participating in his rule. However, early in 1456 the monarch recovered his health and the Yorkish faction was forced to flee from England. Edward had supported his father's regime and had taken part in several battles against the Lancastrians. He received the earldom of March in recognition of his bravery and loyalty. After the overthrow of the Yorkists, Edward was compelled to escape to Calais with the Earl of Warwick, Richard Nevill, while Duke Richard fled to Ireland.

The Earl of Warwick had earlier been appointed captain of Calais and had retained the loyalty of the local garrison's soldiers. From their secure base, Warwick and Edward began preparations for their return to England and seizure of the government by force of arms. In June 1460 they crossed the channel with as small army of supporters, landing at Sandwich and declaring their purpose was to replace the king's corrupt advisors and relieve the suffering of the people. As the earls advanced toward London, their ranks were joined by many thousands of armed sympathizers. Confronted by the large rebel force, the city quickly surrendered without opposition. After securing control of the capital, Edward and Richard Nevill moved north to confront Henry VI and his royalists. The two armies clashed on July 10, 1460, at Northampton with Edward in command of a large contingent of troops. In the ensuing encounter, the outnumbered Lancastrians were easily defeated and Henry VI captured. For his service during the battle, the March earl was recognized for his bravery and military skills.

With possession of the king, the Yorkists seized control of the government and ruled in his name. When Richard of York returned to London from Ireland, he was appointed as successor to Henry VI by Parliament and with the king's continued insanity seized control of the kingdom. While the agreement was accepted by legislative assembly and king, Queen Margaret and her sympathizers refused to relinquish the inheritance rights of her son, Prince Edward, to the throne. From her base of support in the north, she assembled her allies and marched toward London to confront the new regime by force of arms. Richard of York quickly mustered his available troops and without waiting for reinforcements advanced against the queen. As he traveled north additional soldiers were recruited but his military strength remained weak and when the two armies clashed near Wakefield, the Yorkists were greatly outnumbered. In the resulting battle they were completely routed by the Lancastrians and Richard of York killed.

Following Queen Margaret's victory at Wakefield, the road to the south was free of Yorkist defenders and her army turned toward the conquest of London. However, as the Lancastrians moved south, they began to sack and ravage the farm lands and towns. Fearing the pillaging attacks of the queen's troops, the southern earls and towns rallied to Edward of March, who was acknowledged as his father's successor and lord protector of England. After receiving reports that the Lancastrians were reassembling their forces, Edward of York advanced his vassals and supporters from the capital to defend his government. While Warwick protected London, the Yorkish duke marched his army against the Lancastrian forces of Jasper Tudor in the Welsh border region. The two rivals met at Mortimer's Cross, where Edward won his first victory as an independent commander.

While Edward of York was defeating the Lancastrians at Mortimer's Cross, Earl Richard of Warwick advanced his army from London to repel the threat of Queen Margaret. As he marched north, the two forces collided at Saint Albans on February 17, 1461. In the ensuing hard fought and bloody battle, Warwick's left flank was penetrated and his troops routed. During the melee Henry VI, who was held prisoner in Warwick's camp, was abandoned and later reunited with Margaret.

After gaining control of Henry VI, the recognized symbol of royal power, Queen Margaret and her allies abandoned their campaign against London and returned to the north. As the Lancastrians withdrew to the base of their support, Edward and Warwick joined their forces, returning to London but without possession of the king they lost their legal authority to rule. To regain lawful sovereignty, Edward petitioned the Yorkist dominated Parliament to issue a decree outlawing the Lancastrian king for violating the 1459 Act of Accord. At the death of his father, Edward had inherited his titles, lands and blood rights to the English kingdom. After the legislative assembly declared Henry VI a rebel, the Yorkish duke proclaimed the throne vacant and as the acknowledged heir on March 4, 1461, was anointed by the church as monarch at Westminster in the presence of the great southern earls. However, his supremacy was only accepted in the south and a formidable Lancastrian opposition faction still remained centered in Yorkshire.

To consolidate his rule over the entire kingdom, Edward of York hurriedly raised money and additional troops to contend the rebellion of Henry VI. On March 13, 1461, he left London with a large army, marching toward Yorkshire. As the Yorkists traveled north, Queen Margaret, who was acting as surrogate ruler for the insane Henry VI, and her allies mustered their forces to defend their claim to the throne. On March 19 the two formidable armies clashed at Towton in a long and brutal encounter. The battle was initiated with Edward's advance against the Lancastrians positioned on a ridgeline. His archers fired a devastating volley of arrows and in response Henry VI's infantry charged into the Yorkish ranks. A bitter and hard fought struggle followed with the battle finally won by Edward after the arrival of reinforcements from the Duke of Norfolk. The defeat was a crushing blow to the queen and her sympathizers, which broke their power in the north. However, Henry VI and Margaret managed to escape the melee, taking refuge in Scotland to remain the symbol of Lancastrian authority and continued threat to the sovereignty of Edward.

The victory at Towton had destroyed the Lancastrian army but many English lords and towns, especially in the north and west, still retained their loyalty to Henry VI. From Scotland the king and Margaret remained as the figureheads for the Lancastrian cause serving as a rallying point for resistance. To consolidate his sovereignty by force of arms, Edward appointed Richard Nevill as military commander with orders to crush the opposition. While the earl attacked the rebel castles in the north, Edward began a policy of reconciliation with the supporters of Henry VI.

While the Yorkish regime attempted to impose its rule, Henry VI and Margaret were welcomed by the court of the Scottish king, James III, and began to intrigue to regain their crown. Following a failed attack from Scotland against Carlisle, in April 1462 Queen Margaret crossed the North Sea to France and for her promise to return English held Calais to the French received military aid and money from her cousin, King Louis XI. After mustering her forces, she resumed hostilities by landing in Bamborough with French troops commanded by Pierre de Breze. When Edward received the reports of her return, he began to assemble an army to confront her invasion. His summons was answered by many of the great families, including lords from the north. However, Queen Margaret remained unpopular and her call to arms received little support. The army of de Breze was small and without reinforcements from the English magnates, she was compelled to abandon the campaign and sail to Scotland. With the threat of the queen eliminated, Edward utilized his large and formidable military force to capture many of the still defiant strongholds in Yorkshire to further solidify his power.

Richard Nevill of Warwick and his brothers, John and George, were the dominant earls in England and with their support the Yorkist regime was increasingly able to consolidate its power. The favor of the Nevill family was crucial to the continued rule of Edward and it was richly rewarded with grants of titles, lands and important offices on his council. While Warwick and the Nevills pressed their attacks against the remaining Lancaster castles, Edward began policies to ensure the loyalty of the nobles, church and population by improving the economy and ending ongoing lawlessness. He sent loyal lieutenants with royal troops to suppress the civil disorder and enforce his laws. Measures were introduced to expand foreign trade, agriculture and commercial activities. Reforms were made in the government to improve efficiency, while court expenditures were reduced and royal favoritism limited. The restructuring of his administration curbed cost and increased revenue, lowering the treasury deficit. Edward's initiatives resulted in a wider acceptance of his Yorkish authority and a more secure monarchy.

Edward's rule was now widely respected throughout the kingdom. However, in the spring of 1464 Henry Beaufort, Duke of Somerset, revolted against the Yorkish government and joined Henry VI's small court in the last rebel enclave at Bamburgh. After taking command of the few remaining Lancastrian sympathizers, he attempted to raise a rebellion in the north in the king's name. Nevertheless, his call to arms received little support and in April he was defeated at Hedgeley Moor by John Nevill, lord of Montagu. The battle at Hedgeley Moor was not a decisive defeat for the Lancastrians but on May 15 their army was routed at Hexham by the forces of Nevill. Somerset was captured during the encounter and quickly executed on orders from Sir John. The Yorkish initiative was continued under the leadership of Nevill and the castle at Bamburgh placed under siege. After bringing up heavy cannons and breaching the walls, the garrison was forced to surrender. During the attack Henry VI managed to escape but with the capture of the last Lancastrian stronghold his quest to regain the English monarchy was at an end.

Abandoned by his supporters Henry VI was forced to wander the English towns and countryside with only a single retainer, until he was finally captured in July 1465. He was taken to London and imprisoned in the Tower on orders from York. With the suppression of the Northumbrian uprising and the seizure of the king, Edward's control over the kingdom was secure but only as long as his government retained the loyalty of the powerful and influential Nevill family.

To increase his base of support, Edward extended his policy of patronage to additional noble families to reduce his reliance on the Nevills. Richard of Warwick was the most powerful magnate on the council and grew increasingly resentful at the loss of his prestige and influence in the government but still remained loyal to the regime.

England had a long history of friendship with Burgundy, which Edward supported. However, Warwick began independent talks for a treaty of alliance with the French court, which was the traditional Burgundian foe. The agreement was to be guaranteed by the marriage of Edward to a Valois princess. The earl strongly favored the accord with Louis XI, who promised him rich French estates and titles for the reconciliation. Nevertheless, in May 1464 Edward secretly married Elizabeth Woodville, which threatened to thwart Nevill's ongoing negotiations. The marriage was a formidable bargaining tool and when the union with Elizabeth was disclosed Warwick was outraged. Not only had Richard's planned coalition suffered a serious set back but the Woodville marital union advanced her family in status and wealth and weakened his position as the most powerful nobleman in the kingdom.

Elizabeth Woodville was the daughter of a minor English nobleman and a widow with two children. Her first husband had been killed fighting for Henry VI at the second battle of Saint Albans in 1461. Elizabeth was of humble origins and brought no political or monetary advantages to the Yorkish cause. However, Edward disregarded the shortcomings and out of love married her. She became devoted to her husband and despite his numerous mistresses, they developed a close and supportive relationship. He richly rewarded and advanced her family, which alienated many of the magnates and caused a reduction in his crown's base of support. Edward and the queen had ten children, including three sons, who secured the future succession of the Yorkish dynasty.

As Edward exerted his independent rule, relations with the Nevill family grew increasingly strained. Richard was still a powerful magnate with a large following and remained on the governing council as first minister. Edward was not yet strong enough to break away from the earl, who was allowed to renew his negotiations with Louis XI. However, Edward of York favored an alliance with Burgundy and in 1468 solidified relations with the duchy by arranging the marriage of his sister, Margaret, to Duke Charles. Thwarted in his attempt to form a French coalition, Warwick withdrew his support from the Yorkish regime and began to promote the quest for the English kingship by Edward's ambitious brother, George, Duke of Clarence. The Nevill family had a longstanding relationship with the lords in the northern counties and exploited their influence and prestige to raise a series of local revolts to weaken the power of the ruling administration.

While the pro–Nevill rebellions were contained by the loyalist government, Edward's popularity began to wane. His marriage to Elizabeth Woodville was highly unpopular and the recent uprisings resulted in the further loss of favor. As his support declined, the nobles and populace turned to Warwick, who issued a declaration demanding Edward reform his council and policies. With the backing of the high earls and towns, the Nevill alliance began to muster a large military force to depose Edward and place Clarence on the throne. In July 1469 the royalists advanced to defend their regime but they were defeated at Edgecott and Edward of York became surrounded near Coventry. Confronted by a formidable army, he was compelled to surrender to Richard of Warwick.

In the aftermath of his seizure of the monarchy, Warwick with George of Clarence's support attempted to establish a new government but they found little acceptance in Parliament for their assumption of the regime. Lacking the authority of an anointed ruler, their administration was ignored and civil disorder soon broke out in London and other regions, while a Lancastrian uprising erupted in the north. Without the power to quell the escalating violence, Richard and Clarence were forced to restore Edward to the throne. With military assistance from Warwick and his sympathizers, York sent his loyalists to suppress the lawlessness. In December 1469 the earl of Warrick and Duke George were publicly reunited with the crown. However, the reconciliation was only superficial and Warwick was soon in rebellion against the Yorkish council.

In March 1470 Richard and Clarence raised a large army in Lincolnshire and revolted in a new attempt to seize power. Edward quickly advanced against the rebels and surprised them with a powerful military force at Empingham. In the ensuing battle, the dissident troops were defeated and Warwick was forced to flee to France, seeking protection from Louis XI. To further his quest for the restoration of the pro–French Lancastrian alliance, the Valois king negotiated a reconciliation and coalition between the earl and Queen Margaret. Louis XI agreed to provide ships, soldiers and money for the English invasion, while Margaret pledged to appoint Richard regent for her son, Prince Edward of Wales.

In September 1470 Warwick and his French allies crossed the Channel, landing at Devon, while the Nevill family and its northern allies raised a rebellion in support of the invasion. In response to the uprising, Edward marched his troops north to contain the Nevills but with Warwick's attack in the south, his regime was ill prepared to fight a war on two fronts. His hold on the monarchy deteriorated further when John of Montagu defected with his army to the Lancastrian cause. Now greatly outnumbered, Edward was compelled to abandon England and flee to safety in the court of his brother-in-law, Duke Charles of Burgundy. After York deserted his regime, Warwick rode to London and seized control of the government. He released Henry VI from the Tower and placed him on the throne to rule as the figurehead king of the Nevills.

In early January 1471 Edward met with Duke Charles at Aire to secure Burgundian military support for his overthrow of Richard of Warwick. As rumors of the Yorkists' return to England escalated, Richard began to assemble his troops in the Midlands to defend his usurped regime. On March 11 Edward and his small army sailed to England, landing at Ravenspur and proceeding directly toward London. While he advanced south his forces were augmented by additional soldiers who declared their allegiance to the Yorkish cause. As his military might steadily grew, George of Clarence defected from the pro–Nevills, joining forces with his brother. When the large Yorkish army neared London, the city opened its gates without resistance, welcoming Edward as king.

As Edward took control of London, Warwick marched his army from the Midlands toward the capital. At the approach of the Nevill-Lancastrian allies, Edward ordered his troops to advance north and destroy the rebels before Queen Margaret arrived with reinforcements from France. On April 14, 1471, the two armies clashed in a dense fog at Barnet with Edward actively engaged in the fighting, leading his soldiers from the front. In the hard fought and bloody battle, the Yorkists outflanked the left of Warwick's line and broke his center. During the melee, Richard and his brother, John of Montagu, were killed, while their forces were routed.

While the Yorkists were crushing the Earl of Warwick at Barnet, his ally, Queen Margaret, landed in England and began to aggressively recruit troops in the southwest and Wales. When Edmund, Duke of Somerset, declared his fealty to the Lancastrian cause and joined the queen, their combined armies were marched toward Gloucestershire to unite with Jasper Tudor and his Welsh soldiers. Jasper Tudor was born in 1431 and was the son of Owen Tudor and the dowager English queen, Catherine of Valois. Through his mother, he was the half-brother of Henry VI and directly related to the Welsh high nobility by his father's lineage. In 1452 Henry VI appointed Jasper to the earldom of Pembroke. During the Wars of the Roses, he fought for the monarchy of Henry VI and maintained support for the Lancastrians in the Welsh border counties. In 1461 Jasper assumed custody for his brother's newly born son, Henry, Earl of Richmond, who later overthrew the Yorkish regime and established the Tudor dynasty.

Following Margaret's return from France, Edward began to assemble his army at Windsor and marched to contain the threat of the pro–Lancastrians. He traveled toward Gloucester pushing his troops hard to engage the rebels before they could link up with Jasper Tudor. Finally on May 4, 1471, they intercepted the queen and Somerset at Tewkesbury. Confronted by the loyalists, the Lancastrians commanded by Edmund of Somerset moved to a strong defensive position, which was protected by dense hedges and deep ditches. However, his attempt to outflank the Yorkish right wing commanded by Duke Richard of Gloucester was repulsed and his forces broke, fleeing the field. The battle now turned into a rout with hundreds of Lancastrians killed, including Margaret's only son, Prince Edward of Wales. The queen escaped the melee but was soon captured and remained the prisoner of the Yorkist government until finally ransomed to France in November 1475. With the defeat of her army and death of the Lancastrian heir, resistance against the Yorkish regime collapsed and Edward was recognized as king. On May 21 he reentered London and again assumed the reins of power. To remove the major Lancastrian symbol of opposition and rallying cause for future rebellion, he approved the murder of Henry VI in the Tower. With Richard of Warwick, his Nevill family and the last of the Lancastrians eliminated, Edward IV assumed the throne unchallenged to reign as king.

With uncontested control of the crown, Edward IV began to solidify his rule, ordering the execution of the remaining rebel leaders while pardoning their followers. However, Jasper Tudor was still not reconciled with the regime but his continued resistance was now pointless and he fled to Brittany, taking his nephew, Henry, with him. The fourteen-year-old Henry, Earl of Richmond, became the last surviving member of the Lancastrian dynasty and symbol of resistance. In Brittany the Earl of Pembroke became dedicated to the assumption of the English throne by Henry Tudor.

Jasper Tudor's flight from England eliminated the last organized resistance to the Yorkish regime and the king began to form his ruling council. With the skilled assistance of Lord John Howard and Thomas Stanley of Derby, the Yorkish government reintroduced its previous reforms designed to improve the economy and end the outbreaks of civil disorder. The measures resulted in a revival of economic growth, more efficient and responsive administration and end to the brigandage on the roads and in the countryside. To improve commerce, new roads and waterways were built and existing ones improved. New commercial activities with the continental powers were cultivated and the sovereign restored friendly relations with the Hanseatic League through the Treaty of Utrecht, as trading was once again resumed with Germany. Court costs were reduced and with tax revenues rising, the royal treasury's debt was abolished. Edward IV exerted an aggressive foreign policy by reestablishing historic relationships with the dukes of Brittany and Burgundy and Queen Isabella and King Ferdinand II of Spain. Negotiations were initiated with Scotland in an attempt to end raiding activities along the northern border. With England now at peace and returning to prosperity, the king's rule grew secure and more popular.

In 1475 Edward IV negotiated a military treaty of alliance with Duke Charles of Burgundy at the urging of Parliament and nobility who favored the resumption of the armed conflict with France with its prospects for the conquest of rich lands. Under their agreement, the English became committed to an invasion of western France in support of the Burgundians' ongoing war against Louis XI. Before leaving his kingdom to take command of the campaign, the king continued his deliberations with numerous bankers and merchants for loans to supplement his Parliament's war subsidy and appointed a council to rule in his absence. In July 1475 the Yorkish army of over fourteen thousand archers, infantry, men-at-arms and artillerymen landed in Calais, where the English monarch joined Duke Charles and his small contingent of soldiers. However, as the two forces advanced into France, the duke unexpectedly abandoned the offensive, returning to his main army, which was attacking the duchy of Lorraine. With their coalition against Louis XI dissolved, the Yorkish king agreed to independent talks with the French for a truce. He sent an embassy led by his brother-in-law, Sir Thomas Saint Leger, and John Howard to discuss the terms. Sir Thomas was a knight of the Order of the Bath and former ambassador to the court of Louis XI. He was married to the sister of Edward IV, Princess Anne of York, and was part of her brother's inner circle of close friends. His family had originated in Normandy and in 1066 had joined William I in his conquest of England. Several generations of Saint Legers had fought in the First and Third Crusades and had participated in the Barons' Wars against the Plantagenet monarchs, signing the Magna Carta in 1215. After two weeks of negotiations, a settlement was signed. Accompanied by Saint Leger, Lord Howard, his brother, George of Clarence, and other high earls, Edward IV met Louis XI on August 29 near Amiens to finalize the accord. Under the Treaty of Picquigny, the two sovereigns agreed to a seven year truce, the Valois regime pledged to pay an annual subsidy and the English were to depart France peacefully without any aggrandizement of territory. After ratifying the treaty Edward IV returned to Calais with his troops and on September 18 departed for England, receiving a hero's welcome.

Edward IV was a friend and patron of the arts during his reign. He assembled a large personal library and was fond of collecting illuminated manuscripts, mainly from Bruges. His regime became a sponsor of architects, jewelers, goldsmiths and sculptors and spent freely to maintain a lavish court. However, he directed his major patronage toward the refurbishment and enlargement of his royal palaces, disbursing large sums of money at Westminster, Eltham and Greenwich and in 1473 began construction of Saint George's Chapel at Windsor. During his exile in Burgundy in 1470, the Yorkish king was exposed to the recently invented printing press and became a patron of William Caxton, encouraging his efforts to print books in England.

Edward IV's ambitious brother, George, Duke of Clarence, had aspirations of acquiring a separate kingdom and had not favored the peace treaty with Louis XI, which ended his quest for French lordships. Despite receiving large grants of lands from the Yorkish crown, he remained hostile. As the second issue of Richard of York, he had been heir to the throne until the birth of Edward IV's son, Prince Edward, and began to spread rumors that his brother's marriage to Elizabeth Woodville was illegal and their children illegitimate. In 1477 Duke Charles of Burgundy was killed at Nancy and his strategic duchy inherited by his unmarried daughter, Mary. It was in the political interest of England that she marry into a powerful European family to prevent Burgundy's union with France. The wife of George of Clarence had recently died in childbirth and with the support of his sister, Margaret, dowager duchess of Burgundy, he actively promoted his marriage to Mary. However, George's prior activities had proven unreliable and disloyal and Edward IV refused to sanction the marital agreement. Rebuffed by his brother, Clarence began to plot the overthrow of the regime and his assumption of the English realm. His intrigues were soon discovered and the duke was arrested on charges of high treason. In January 1478 Parliament met to hear the indictment and after a two week trial he was declared guilty. The sentence of death was carried out in the Tower of London on February 18. The duke's vast estates were forfeited to the monarchy, which greatly enhanced the royal treasury's income. With possession of Clarence's demesne, Edward IV became the greatest land owner and richest lord in England, which strengthened his independent rule and weakened the power of Parliament and the nobility.

In the aftermath of George of Clarence's rebellion, Edward IV's rule was respected by the nobility and his kingdom both at home and internationally remained at peace. However, in early 1480 relations with Scotland became increasingly bellicose. Under French influence and increasing pressure from his Lowland warlords, who were seeking rich English plunder, in September the Stewart king, James III, launched a large raid into Northumberland, ravaging and burning Bamburgh and the neighboring farmlands. In response the English council ordered the monarch's brother, Richard of Gloucester, to counterattack. As the hostilities escalated, Edward IV began to prepare for war, raising money and recruiting troops for a large invasion of Scotland. However, despite several small forays, no major expedition was mounted and it was delayed until the following year due to the illness of the English king.

During his later years, the Yorkish king had become increasingly obese and lethargic, limiting his activities and interest in the government. In 1482 he suffered serious health problems and command of the planned Scottish invasion was given to Richard, Duke of Gloucester. As preparations for the attack continued, Alexander, Duke of Albany and brother of James III, rebelled against the Stewart regime and from his Paris exile began negotiations for an alliance with the English. In May Edward IV met with the Stewart duke to finalize their treaty. Under their ensuing accord, the English agreed to recognize Albany as the new Stewart king, while he pledged to give fealty to the Yorkish administration and end Scotland's friendship with Louis XI. In June 1482 Gloucester and Duke Albany invaded Scotland to overthrow James III. However, after advancing unopposed into the Lowlands, the fortress at Edinburgh defiantly refused to surrender and the attack was abandoned. While the encroachment failed to establish Albany on the throne, the Yorkish regime gained possession of the strategic city of Berwick.

Due to his declining health, the Yorkish king had not participated in the war against Scotland. In 1483 he became subjected to an increasing number of ailments and grew weaker. Early in the year Edward IV participated in Parliament and continued to rule his kingdom unchallenged but court factions were beginning to form to advance their positions, sensing his worsening condition. At the end of March he became ill with a fever, dying on April 9 at Westminster Palace. Edward IV reigned as undisputed king of England for eleven years and died at the age of forty.

Sources

Clive. *This Sun of York.*   Dockray. *Edward IV.*   Ross. *Edward IV.*

Edward V, 1470–1483–1483

After the death of Edward IV in April 1483, the English throne was assumed by his minor heir, Edward V, who was recognized as the fifth king of the Renaissance era. Edward was the first son of Edward of York and Elizabeth Woodville and was born on November 2, 1470, in London at Westminster Abbey. Prior to Prince Edward's birth, his father was forced to abandon his crown and flee to Burgundy after the seizure of the kingdom by Richard of Warwick, while Elizabeth sought sanctuary in Westminster Abbey. The infant prince spent his first five months in the abbey and was not united with his father until Warwick was overthrown in April 1471 by the Yorkish army. After the elimination of the Lancastrian threat to his monarchy, Edward IV was acknowledged as king without opposition. On June 11, 1472, he appointed his son Prince of Wales, Earl of Chester and later Duke of Cornwall in recognition of his hereditary rights to the English realm. To further guarantee his future succession, the monarch had the high secular and spiritual lords swear allegiance to Prince Edward and had his grants of honors and lands approved by Parliament. The young Edward made his first public appearance before the great lords and clerics in October to confirm the continuation of the Yorkish dynasty.

Prince Edward spent the majority of his first two years in London at the residences of his father, but in 1473 a personal household was established for him at Ludlow Castle near the Welsh border. A permanent council was chosen to administer his estates and court with the queen's brother, Anthony, Earl of Rivers, serving as governor. As the eldest son and successor to the monarchy, Edward was educated as the future ruler. Distinguished scholars were appointed for his instruction in reading, writing, religion, French and Latin and court etiquette. Under the guidance of his uncle, he received a well rounded education, excelling in his studies. In preparation for his role as captain general of the royal military forces, he was trained in the weapons of a feudal knight, learning the skills of riding, fencing, hunting, hawking and jousting. The sons of other prominent noble families were selected to reside at Ludlow and they shared the daily educational and recreational activities of the prince. While remaining at Ludlow Castle, Edward continued to participate in court functions with the royal family, performing his duties as heir.

In 1475 the four-year-old Edward was appointed to serve as the figurehead guardian of the realm, when his father sailed to France to wage war with the Burgundian duke, Charles, against King Louis XI. A ruling council of twenty nobles was established to administer the government and on May 12 the prince made his formal entry into London to assume nominal control of the regime. Before departing from England, Edward IV knighted his son in Westminster Palace before the assembled high lords and clergy. During the Yorkish monarch's absence, all acts of the regency were signed under the seal of Prince Edward. After three months in France, Edward IV returned to London to a hero's welcome and his son again assumed residence at Ludlow Castle under the protection and guidance of Lord Rivers.

At Ludlow Prince Edward continued his academic and military education under the guidance of his appointed tutors. However, he frequently traveled to the royal court to attend official functions, holidays and secular and religious festivals with the Yorkish family. While he remained on his Welsh estates, his uncle, George of Clarence, was executed on charges of high treason. The forfeiture of Clarence's vast lands to the crown greatly enlarged the future inheritance of the prince, making him the greatest landowner in England.

As the recognized successor, Prince Edward was the titular overlord for the principality of Wales, and his council was given responsibility for restoring and maintaining order in the region. Their authority was later expanded to include the prince's other possessions of Cornwall and Chester. As governor for Edward and head of his household, Anthony, Earl of Rivers, became the effective ruler for Wales and a powerful and respected lord. He was the son of Richard Woodville, first Earl of Rivers, and Jacquetta of Luxembourg and was born in 1440. As the brother of Queen Elizabeth, he was deeply loyal to the Woodville faction and promoted the enrichment of his family. The earl was highly educated and a patron of learning, personally sponsoring the printing of books in England by William Caxton. He was renowned for his military and diplomatic skills and many jousting feats. He had traveled extensively throughout Europe and as a devout follower of the Holy See of Rome had made several religious pilgrimages. Rivers had first served with the Lancastrian alliance against the Yorkish attempted usurpation of the English kingdom and had fought against them at the battle of Towton. He later changed his allegiance to Edward IV and was wounded at Barnet, leading his troops against

Richard of Warwick. Under the control of his uncle, Prince Edward was encouraged and influenced to become an advocate for the Woodville family and their advancement at court. The Rivers earl was devoted to Prince Edward, staying with him at Ludlow until the death of Edward IV in April 1483.

In May 1481 Edward IV finalized his ongoing negotiations for the marriage of his heir to Anne, the four-year-old daughter of Duke Francis I of Brittany. The successful talks followed prior failed attempts to arrange the marriage of Prince Edward to Isabella, heiress of Ferdinand II and Isabella of Spain, and later the daughter of the Duke of Milan. Under the terms of the treaty with Francis I, the eldest son of their union would inherit the English crown, while the second son would rule the independent French duchy. When Anne reached the age of twelve, she was to be sent to live in the Yorkish court in preparation for her future succession as queen and following the marital ceremony Prince Edward would assume the ducal throne. Brittany was the historic ally of the English and the agreement assured the Yorkish regime of its continued friendship and support.

By 1481 the health of the Yorkish king began to increasingly deteriorate. The planned punitive invasion against Scotland in retaliation for raiding activities in the north was delayed due to his continued illnesses. In the following year he still had not recovered his health and command of the Scottish campaign was given to his brother, Richard, Duke of Gloucester. However, the attack against Scotland ended in failure, bequeathing to the future reign of Prince Edward a hostile relationship with the Scottish regime and escalating unrest along the border region.

Edward IV continued to retain authority over his government, despite his steadily declining health. However, in March 1483 he became seriously ill with fever and died on April 9. Two days later Edward V was proclaimed king without opposition. At the time of his father's death, Edward V was twelve years old and still considered a minor, necessitating the creation of a ruling council. During his father's illness, Edward V had stayed at Ludlow Castle on the Welsh border under the custody of Earl Anthony of Rivers. With possession of the recognized monarch and symbol of sovereignty, the Woodville faction outmaneuvered their rivals led by Henry Stafford, second Duke of Buckingham, and Baron William of Hastings to seize power. Henry of Buckingham was born on September 4, 1455, and was the son of Humphrey, Earl of Stafford, and Margaret Beaufort. Through his mother's lineage, he had inherited a direct blood claim to the English throne. Both his father and paternal grandfather had been supporters of the Lancastrian monarchy and had been killed fighting against Edward IV's usurpation of the English crown. Following the Yorkish rise to power, he remained on his family estates uninvolved in court politics. However, when the Woodvilles attempted to seize the government, he quickly became allied with the party in opposition. His co-conspirator, William Hastings, was the first Baron of Hastings and faithful ally of the Yorkish dynasty. He had served with Edward IV at the battles of Mortimer's Cross and Towton against the Lancastrian king during the Wars of the Roses. After the establishment of the Yorkish regime in 1461, Hastings was appointed lord chamberlain and became a key figure in the new realm. When Edward IV was forced into exile in Burgundy, the Baron of Hastings was part of his small court. In the spring of 1471 he returned to England with the Yorkish invasion force, fighting at the decisive battles of Barnet and Tewkesbury. For his loyalty, service, military skills and administrative talent, Edward IV appointed the baron to the office of lord chamberlain and captain of the Calais enclave.

Following their seizure of the government, the queen and her allies sent instructions to Ludlow for the earl to bring Edward V to London for his coronation. As the anointed king, he would be legally considered to have reached his age of majority, and to thwart any challenge to their regime, the Woodvilles planned an immediate investiture. Edward V was still too young to personally assume the throne and without the appointment of a ruling council or lord protector by Parliament, the Woodvilles would continue to govern England unopposed.

While the Woodvilles had initially seized the government, the Hastings-Buckingham faction continued their quest for power by forging an alliance with Duke Richard of Gloucester, uncle of the new king. As Edward V and Anthony of Rivers traveled toward London, Gloucester assembled his personal militia and augmented with troops from Henry of Buckingham intercepted them at Stony Stratford. Taken by surprise by the overwhelming military might of the dukes, Rivers was arrested and the king placed into the custody of Gloucester and Buckingham. The dukes pledged to govern in the name of the king as loyal protectors. With the possession of the Yorkish monarch, the usurpers rode to London in slow stages to avoid arousing suspicion of rebellion.

When the news of Edward V's seizure reached London, Queen Elizabeth attempted to raise an army to rescue her son but her call to arms was widely ignored. Fearing hostile actions from Gloucester, she sought sanctuary in Westminster Abbey with her daughters and second son, Richard of York. With the king under his protection, Richard of Gloucester entered London on May 4 with only a small escort to dispel any threat of armed rebellion. He issued proclamations, declaring loyalty to his nephew and intent to remove the corrupt Woodville faction from power. Edward V was housed in the bishop of London's palace in a visible display of his continued rule. However, with control of the acknowledged head of state, Gloucester replaced the queen's supporters in the government with his allies. On May 8 the new council appointed Richard as lord protector for Edward V.

While the king remained in London secure in the bishop's palace, the Gloucester regime assumed full power, quickly announcing Edward V's coronation date for June 22 and summoning Parliament to meet two days later. The routine business of the government was continued with judges and sheriffs appointed and decrees issued for tax collection and subjugation of piracy. Following Edward IV's death, his truce with the French had collapsed and the Scots had remained hostile along the northern marchlands, forcing the Gloucester administration to initiate measures to defend the kingdom during the ongoing period of instability. All acts of the council were proclaimed in the name of Edward V as sovereign.

As the new regime steadily advanced its power, the lord protector ordered the king moved to the more protected Tower of London. Edward V was still treated as monarch with all the royal dignities and not denied visitors. To further consolidate his rule and purge the government of Woodville sympathizers, decrees were issued by Gloucester, appointing the Duke of Buckingham as constable, lord chamberlain and governor for Wales, while other faithful supporters received important high offices to displace lords of questionable loyalty. By mid–June the lord protector was firmly in control of the monarchy and began to prepare for his usurpation of the English crown. He sent secret letters to his friends in the northern lordships, ordering them to quickly muster their militias and march toward London, while security in the city was enhanced with his troops and additional forces from Buckingham. To secure his unfettered assumption of the throne, Gloucester had the king's brother, Richard of York, removed from Westminster Abbey on the pretense of preparing for his attendance at the forth coming coronation ceremony. With his authority uncontested, Richard announced the cancellation of Edward V's enthronement and the meeting of Parliament.

Baron William of Hastings had been a loyal supporter of Edward IV and had continued to strongly advocate the assumption of the crown by his son. As a powerful and influential nobleman, he became a threat to Gloucester's planned encroachment of power. On July 12 Hastings was called to the citadel in the Tower to attend a council meeting. However, he was soon accused of plotting the murder of the lord protector and usurpation of the government in support of Queen Elizabeth's faction. Hastings was given no opportunity to defend himself and was seized by troops led by the Duke of Buckingham. After last religious rites from a hastily summoned priest, Baron Hastings was taken outside the citadel and beheaded by Henry of Buckingham's men. The execution of Hastings served as a threat to other potential rebels and eliminated any remaining sympathy for the reign of Edward V out of fear of similar arrest.

By moving aggressively against possible dissent, the lord protector now had control of Edward V and the second-in-line to the crown, Richard of York, in the Tower, neutralizing the Woodville alliance and eliminating the opposition of the magnates. On June 16 Duke Richard ordered the removal of the king and York from the royal apartments to the inner rooms of the Tower and deprived them of their loyal retainers and servants. The two sons of Edward IV were frequently observed in the garden but as the days passed they were seen less and less.

With his seizure of the crown unchallenged by any organized resistance, on June 25 Gloucester assembled the ecclesiastic and secular lords at Westminster and issued a petition, claiming that Edward IV's marriage to Elizabeth Woodville had been illegal and their children illegitimate, which disqualified Edward V and his brother from inheriting the kingdom. The assembly, under fear of Richard's formidable military presence, voted their approval of the proclamation and his assumption of the monarchy as the legal heir of his brother.

Despite widespread support for Edward V's claim to the English throne, with his new regime authorized by the established governing institutions and defended by an overwhelming military force, Richard III succeeded in making himself king.

While preparations for the coronation of Richard III were being made in London, in the southern and western lordships support for the continued reign of Edward V grew. A broad coalition of alienated Yorkists, dissident Lancastrians and the Woodville faction led by the queen's brothers, Lionel, Richard and Edward, began to forge an alliance to restore Edward V to his rightful monarchy. However, he was too heavily guarded in the Tower's citadel to be rescued but a plot was formulated to free his sisters from Westminster Abbey. If Edward IV's daughters were able to flee to the continent, they could dispute their uncle's claim to the throne and act as a deterrent to the elimination of the deposed king and York. The Sanctuary Conspiracy was soon discovered by the many spies of Richard III and instructions were given to blockade all exits from the abbey to prevent escape. With Westminster closely protected, the plotters were forced to abandon their scheme and the usurper king's power remained unchallenged.

The Sanctuary Conspiracy and strength of dissent in the south finally convinced Richard III that the deposed king and his brother remained a serious threat to his rule while they remained alive. While he was absent from London on a tour of the western counties, orders were issued from Gloucestershire for the murder of his two nephews. Edward V was last seen in the Tower in July but the exact date and means of his death were never discovered. However, the most likely time for his execution was in August 1483. Edward V died at the age of twelve and a reign of less than four months.

Sources

Hicks. *Edward V.* Weir. *The Princes in the Tower.*

Richard III, 1452–1483–1485

In the summer of 1483 Richard III usurped the Yorkish throne of his twelve-year-old nephew, Edward V, to reign as the sixth English king of the Renaissance period. Richard was the fourth surviving and youngest son of Duke Richard of York and Cecily Nevill, daughter of the Earl of Westmoreland, and was born at Fotheringay Castle on October 2, 1452. Through his parents' bloodlines, he was directly related to the ruling English dynasty. Richard, Duke of York, was the first peer of the realm and heir apparent to the childless Lancastrian king Henry VI, while Cecily was from the wealthy and powerful northern Nevill family. Richard spent his early years at Fotheringay with his sister, Margaret, and brother, George, under the care and protection of the duchess's household, while the Duke of York became the leader of a hostile faction in opposition to the Lancastrian council. At Fotheringay distinguished tutors were appointed for Richard's education in reading, writing, religion, basic mathematics, law, French and court etiquette. He received routine military training as a feudal lord under the guidance of experienced men-at-arms, mastering the skills of fencing, riding, jousting and hunting. As a youth he suffered from poor health and was frequently ill.

In 1459 Richard of York was forced into exile in Ireland by the Lancastrian council, while Cecily and her children were captured by the loyalists and confined to the manor house of her sister, Anne Nevill. They remained under confinement until June 1460, when the Lancastrian regime was overthrown by supporters of the Yorkish duke. Following Richard's return to power, Cecily and her younger children were moved to London, residing at Baynards Castle. However, in December the royalists launched a new offensive against the Yorkish government and at the battle of Wakefield overwhelmed the army of the rebels and killed Richard of York.

Following the Yorkish disaster at Wakefield, Cecily was compelled to hastily escape with George and Richard to safety in the duchy of Burgundy. While they remained with a few trusted servants in Utrecht and later Bruges at the ducal court, in March Cecily's eldest son and heir to the family titles and lands, Duke Edward of York, destroyed the royalist army at Towton, forcing Henry VI to flee into exile in Scotland. With the collapse of the Lancastrian monarchy, Richard and George returned to England from Flanders and on June 28 played a prominent role in the lavish coronation ceremony of their older brother at Westminster Abbey. In November the nine-year-old Richard was created Duke of Gloucester and later admitted to the Order of the Garter. While the Yorkish regime assumed the crown, many English lords and towns, especially in the west and north, retained their allegiance to Henry VI, who remained the figurehead for the Lancastrian cause.

In the aftermath of Edward's succession of power, Richard along with Margaret and George were moved from London to the royal palace at Greenwich. As the brother of the Yorkish king, Richard was appointed admiral of England and commissioner for the northern counties. Early in 1464 when Henry Beaufort, Duke of Somerset, rebelled against the Yorkish regime and joined his private militia with the deposed Henry VI in Bamburgh, the eleven-year-old Duke of Gloucester, acting in his largely figurehead role as northern commissioner, recruited a contingent of troops and advanced against the rebels in defense of his brother's realm. However, the crown's ally, John Nevill of Montagu, decisively defeated Somerset at the battle of Hexham before the reinforcements arrived and Gloucester was denied his first combat experiences. As a member of the royal family, Richard was granted numerous honors and estates, including the Lancastrian forfeited lordships of Pembroke and Richmond, becoming a wealthy and powerful magnate, despite his young age.

As was the custom in English middle age society, in 1465 the Duke of Gloucester became a ward of his cousin, Richard Nevill, Earl of Warwick. He left Greenwich Palace and traveled north to Yorkshire, joining the earl's household at Middleham Castle. Under the guidance of Nevill, the duke's education and military training were renewed. The Earl of Warwick was the wealthiest and most powerful magnate in the north country and Middleham the center of political activities. As a member of the earl's court, Gloucester was exposed to the uniquely clannish culture and traditions of the local nobility, developing close friendships and relations that later formed the basis of his political faction.

Richard of Gloucester stayed at Middleham for three years before returning to the Yorkish court in London. While the duke was in the north, the once strong bond between the Yorkish king and his chief counselor, Richard of Warwick, began to unravel. The first break occurred when Edward IV secretly married Elizabeth Woodville, disrupting the earl's ongoing talks with Louis XI of France for a treaty of alliance, which was to be sealed with his marital union to a Valois princess. The final rupture took place in 1468 after the Yorkish monarch ignored Warwick's French peace initiative and signed an accord of friendship with the duchy of Burgundy. The agreement was sealed with the marriage of his sister, Margaret, to the ducal ruler, Charles. The Valois government was at war with the duchy and considered the treaty a breach of the peace. Soon after the wedding ceremony, England became allied with Burgundy actively backing its conflict against France. As the threat of an English invasion to aid the Burgundians escalated, Louis XI offered Warwick an independent Flemish fiefdom for his support against the Yorkish regime. Anxious to retain his influence and high offices in England and expand his estates into the Low Countries, Richard of Warwick accepted the proposal and attempted to lure Edward IV's brothers into his plot to seize the monarchy. While George, Duke of Clarence, was won to the earl's rebellion with the promise of his deposed brother's crown, Richard of Gloucester remained loyal to the government.

Early in 1468 at the encouragement of the Nevill family, rebellions erupted in the northern counties in opposition to Edward IV of York and his unpopular queen. As the level of violence grew, York mustered his soldiers, and with Richard of Gloucester at his side rode, north to impose his law. While the small army advanced slowly toward Norfolk, Warwick and Clarence sailed to Calais to recruit reinforcements, while the Nevill faction began to assemble its militia. On July 20 Warwick returned to England with fresh troops, marching against Edward and Richard, who had taken refuge in Nottingham Castle. Confronted with an overwhelming military force, the king was compelled to submit. With Edward IV his captive, the earl seized control of the government and attempted to assert his rule. However, lacking the acceptance of an anointed ruler his administration was largely ignored and lawlessness spread rapidly throughout the realm. While his brother remained imprisoned, Gloucester began to raise soldiers in the north with the royalist ally, William of Hastings, to force the release of Edward IV of York. However, by October Warwick had lost authority over the ruling council and was compelled to release Edward, who quickly reestablished his power. In December Warwick and Duke George were reconciled to the Yorkish regime but under an uneasy peace. For his continued loyalty to his brother, Richard of Gloucester was richly rewarded with many new honors and estates.

While Edward IV attempted to consolidate his rule, a small revolt broke out in western Wales. As the newly appointed administrator of justice for the principality, Richard advanced with his troops against the rogues and with an overwhelming military presence quickly crushed their uprising. However, while the Welsh were easily subdued, numerous new rebellions again erupted in the north country in support of the Earl of Warwick and Duke of Clarence. Edward

IV hastily raised a large army and marched north to suppress the rebels. Opposed by a formidable military force Warwick and George of Clarence refused to obey the royal summons to appear before the council and escaped to safety at the court of Louis XI. Under the influence of the French king, Warwick was united with the exiled Lancastrian faction and swore allegiance to Henry VI and Queen Margaret.

In September 1470 Warwick and Clarence returned to England and issued a proclamation, demanding the restoration of Henry VI to the throne. As they advanced toward London with a small army, many pro–Lancastrian lords with their private militias rallied to their cause. While the rebels were in France, Edward IV and Richard of Gloucester had remained in the north suppressing the local uprisings. Confronted by the earl's new attack against the capital and his formidable northern alliance, Edward lacked the military power to defend his kingdom and was compelled to abandon his crown, escaping to the continent. He rode to King's Lynn with his small band of supporters, including his brother and William Hastings, seizing control of a royal ship and several fishing boats and crossing the channel to sanctuary in Burgundy. Meanwhile, in London Warwick was welcomed by the city's mayor and population and quickly restored the insane Henry VI to the monarchy to rule as his puppet sovereign.

After landing on the coast of Holland, Edward IV and his allies came under the protection of Louis of Bruges and spent the autumn at his court in The Hague. The Burgundian duke, Charles, was currently at peace with France and anxious not to offend the pro–French Lancastrian regime in London by personally welcoming the exiles to his duchy. However, later in the year after Louis XI renewed the war with Burgundy, the duke agreed to talks with the Yorkish brothers for military aid. After meeting with Edward IV and his supporters at Aire, Charles pledged to supply ships, money and a contingent of troops for the overthrow of Warwick's government.

On March 11 the small mercenary army boarded ships and sailed from Flushing to England, landing at Ravenspur. While they advanced south toward London unchallenged, many of the local lords began to join their campaign. As their military might grew, Duke George of Clarence defected from the pro–Lancastrians after receiving Edward IV's promise of a full pardon, uniting his four thousand men under arms with the invading forces. The final negotiations for the reconciliation were conducted by the Duke of Gloucester, who convinced his brother to accept Clarence's submission. With his troop strength greatly enhanced, London opened its gates without opposition, welcoming Edward IV as sovereign.

With London securely under his control, Edward IV along with his brothers advanced north to challenge the forces of the Earl of Warwick. Late in the afternoon of April 13, 1471, the two rivals clashed at Barnet with Richard of Gloucester leading the royal vanguard and making the initial contact with the Nevill-Lancastrians. Early in the next morning the fighting was resumed with Gloucester commanding the royalists' right wing. In the bloody and hard fought battle with Edward IV and Richard personally engaged in the close combat, Warwick's left flank was shattered and his troops put to flight. During the savage melee, Richard of Warwick was killed and his army destroyed.

The supporters of the Lancastrian queen, Margaret, had been actively raising troops in anticipation of her return from France. On the same day that the Yorkish army destroyed her ally, Richard of Warwick, at Barnet, the queen landed in southern England. While she recruited local lords to her banner, Edmund, Duke of Somerset, joined his army with her forces and together they traveled toward Gloucestershire to unite with the militia of Jasper Tudor. In the aftermath of his Barnet victory, Edward IV returned to the south but when informed of Margaret's arrival quickly reassembled his cavalry and infantry. He moved rapidly to the west to intercept the Lancastrians' line of advance and by a series of rapid marches caught Margaret and Somerset at Tewkesbury before they could link up with Tudor. On May 4, 1471, Richard of Gloucester with command of the vanguard made the first contact with Somerset. The battle began with Duke Edmund's assault against the defensive line of Gloucester, which was repulsed by a contingent of well placed pikemen. With their charge rebuffed, Somerset's men began to panic and flee the field with Richard's troops in close pursuit. As the Yorkists pressed their attack, the encounter turned into a rout with many hundreds of Lancastrians killed, including Queen Margaret's only son, Prince Edward of Wales, who was cut down by Clarence's soldiers. Following Margaret's defeat, Lancastrian sympathy collapsed throughout the kingdom, but to eliminate the last symbol of resistance and rallying cause for future rebellion, Edward IV ordered the murder of Henry VI in the Tower. The victories at Barnet and Tewkesbury and the death of the insane king were the decisive blows for Edward IV, confirming his usurpation of the monarchy.

Richard of Gloucester had played a prominent role in his brother's triumph and was richly rewarded for his loyal support and battle skills with the grant of the majority of Warwick's forfeited estates and honors. With the assumption of the earl's lands, Gloucester replaced the Nevills as the most powerful magnate in the north. In the summer of 1471 he rode to Middleham Castle in Yorkshire, taking control of his new offices and demesne. He traveled extensively throughout the local lordships, asserting his authority and establishing political bonds with the noble families. As the chief military captain for the north, the duke directly interceded against the resurgence of Scottish raiding activities along the border, personally leading sorties against the Stewart warlords. However, his stay at Middleham was short and in September he was compelled to return to the London court to defend his estates and inheritance rights of his future wife, Anne Nevill, against the attacks of his brother, George of Clarence.

Anne was the second daughter of Richard of Warwick and co-heiress with her older sister, Isabel, to their mother's large and rich Beauchamp lands. Duke George was married to Isabel and schemed against Gloucester to deny Anne her share in the inheritance. As the hostilities between the two brothers grew, Edward IV intervened and ordered them to appear before his council to resolve their dispute. After meeting with the counselors, a compromise was reached with Richard agreeing to renounce his claim to the Beauchamp estates and part of Warwick's demesne for the right to marry Anne. Despite the public reconciliation, relations between the rivals remained bellicose and unsettled.

Under the settlement ordered by Edward IV, in late February 1472 Richard of Gloucester and Anne Nevill were married at Westminster. She had grown up at Middleham Castle and had been friends with Gloucester during his early years in the north. Through his marital union with the Nevill family, Richard solidified his support among the northern lords and towns, while inheriting a share of the Warwick lands. Although Anne and he were cousins, the marital ceremony was quickly held without a papal dispensation to avoid the interference of the Duke of Clarence. Following the wedding Richard returned to the governorship of the northern counties, residing with Anne in Middleham and Pontefract castles. Early in 1473 she gave birth to their only child, Edward of Middleham. When Richard became king, Anne frequently traveled with him on the royal tours, buttressing his assumption of the monarchy through her family's alliances and friends. Under the influence of his wife, the duke expanded his interest in music, attracting renowned singers, minstrels and musicians to his court. They were also patrons of the church and enthusiastic builders, funding new construction and renovation at Windsor, Westminster and Nottingham castles.

After his marriage to Anne, the Duke of Gloucester remained loyal to his brother, serving as royal governor for the north, while managing his large estates. He continued to travel throughout his lands, enforcing his rule and justice, while granting favors and privileges to gain the goodwill of the local lords and towns. With the encouragement of the nobility and Parliament, in 1475 the Yorkish council signed an agreement with Duke Charles of Burgundy committing to invade France in support of the Burgundians' war against Louis XI. As the second peer of the realm, Richard raised a contingent of archers and men-at-arms and in June sailed with the royal army to join forces with Duke Charles at Calais. However, the planned attack against France quickly dissolved when Charles unexpectedly withdrew from the campaign and returned to his main army fighting in Lorraine. With their offensive now shattered, the English opened negotiations with Louis XI for a truce and on August 29 the two kings met at Picquigny to ratify the accord. Under the treaty they agreed to honor a seven year truce, while the Yorkish regime promised to immediately leave France without any territorial aggrandizement and Louis XI pledged to pay a yearly subsidy. Richard of Gloucester was noticeably absent from the signing ceremony, signaling his disapproval of abandoning the war without any material gains of French lands.

Following a brief visit to the court of Louis XI at Amiens, on September 18, 1475, Richard of Gloucester sailed from Calais with the Yorkish army to England. He soon returned to Middleham Castle and resumed the governorship of the northern lordships. He remained in the border counties for most of the next two years, traveling throughout the region imposing justice and defending the frontier against Scottish forays. To better administer his demesne, he created the Council of the North to resolve disputes locally instead of referring them to London. The duke frequently visited York, Durham and Carlisle, preparing the cities' defenses against Scottish attacks. He also actively sought the favor of the northern churches and was a benefactor of the clergy, building new chapels and religious houses while repairing existing ones. Richard became highly popular in the north country, establishing a powerful base of support.

Richard of Gloucester became devoted to the northern lordships and spent little time at the London court. While the duke continued to defend the north as royal governor, in early 1480 James III of Scotland approved new cross-border raids by his Lowland warlords, who were seeking to plunder the rich English counties. In September the Scots mounted a large pillaging foray against Bamburgh, which was sacked and burned. In retaliation Gloucester, who had been appointed lieutenant general, raised an army and launched a punitive counterattack. As the hostilities escalated, Edward IV began to prepare for war and in March 1481 Richard traveled to London to plan the invasion against James III.

Meeting with the king and his council, Richard of Gloucester was given command of a combined land and sea initiative to impose English sovereignty over the Scottish border region. After traveling to the north, Gloucester raised troops from his local allies and advanced to besiege the Scottish held fortress of Berwick. The garrison led by the defiant Duke Archibald of Douglas refused to submit, forcing the English into a prolonged blockade. As the investment wore on into the next year, James III mounted several cross-frontier raids, burning and looting the towns before being driven off by the Gloucester duke. The lieutenant general remained active along the border defending his lands, while entrusting the naval campaign to Lord John Howard. Lord Howard assembled his ships and sailed up the Scottish coast, destroying James III's fleet at the Firth of Forth before returning to England to protect the shoreline against sea raiders. Howard was born in 1421 and was the son of Sir Robert Howard and Lady Margaret Mowbray of Norfolk. He was appointed captain of Norwick Castle and sheriff for the counties of Suffolk and Norfolk by Edward IV. He had a distinguished military career, first fighting in France against the Valois regime and later, after joining the Yorkish alliance, taking part in the battles of Saint Albans and Towton. He was rewarded for his administrative and military skills with appointments to high offices in the government and ennobled as a lord in the late 1460s. Following the overthrow of Edward IV in 1470, Lord Howard became a member of the party in exile in Burgundy. In the following year he recrossed the channel with the Yorkish invasion army and fought bravely with the king and Gloucester in the decisive battles of Barnet and Tewkesbury.

The campaign against Scotland was continued into 1482 with numerous skirmishes and raids by both belligerents, while the siege against Berwick remained ongoing. As preparations for the new English offensive were being made, Edward IV finalized his negotiations for a joint invasion of Scotland with Duke Alexander of Albany, exiled brother of James III. In May the duke arrived in England from France and signed the Treaty of Fotheringay. Under their agreement, the English pledged to provide an army for Albany's seizure of the Scottish crown and recognize him as King Alexander IV. In exchange for English support, he agreed to give homage for Scotland to the Yorkish regime.

In June the lieutenant general and Alexander IV mustered a large force of English troops and dissident Scots, marching across the border into the Lowlands, laying waste to the towns and farms as they moved toward Edinburgh. As they advanced unchallenged, the Scottish army rebelled and seized control of James III, retreating with him to the Edinburgh citadel. The defenseless city was occupied by the English but the stronghold refused to submit. Lacking siege guns and money for a long investment, Richard was compelled to withdraw to England, leaving Alexander IV to negotiate a reconciliation with his brother. However, the Gloucester duke gained some success for the English king by finally forcing the garrison at Berwick to surrender and his victory was greeted with celebrations all over the kingdom. The triumph over a foreign sovereignty propelled him into a national hero and greatly enhanced his military reputation as a skilled soldier. In late 1482 he traveled to London, receiving a hero's welcome. He was granted additional honors and lands in the north by his brother, expanding his martial and political power over the region, while becoming an increasing threat to the ambitions of the Woodville family and its supporters.

During the war against Scotland, Edward IV had remained in London, suffering from deteriorating health. In 1483 the seriousness of the ailments escalated as he grew increasingly weaker, dying on April 9 from a fever. His English throne was inherited by his twelve-year-old son, Edward V. The new king had not reached the age of majority, forcing the creation of an interim regime. Edward V had resided on the Welsh border at Ludlow Castle under the care of his Woodville uncle, Anthony of Rivers. With possession of the acknowledged monarch and symbol of authority, Queen Elizabeth and her Woodville allies outmaneuvered their rivals led by Henry Stafford, Duke of Buckingham, and Baron William of Hastings, seizing control over the council and appointing a regency under their dominance to rule. The queen sent instructions to her brother, Anthony, at Ludlow to immediately bring her son to London for his coronation. To thwart any opposition to their administration, the Woodvilles planned an early investiture to legalize the king's assumption of the crown. Under the precedent set after Henry VI's assumption of the monarchy, Edward V's minority would end with his anointment, giving the queen's faction unfettered power to govern.

Richard of Gloucester had remained in the north following Edward IV's death, keeping in touch with unfolding events in London through his spies. However, after receiving reports of the Woodville faction's usurpation of the monarchy and Edward V's planned investiture, he began to muster his northern coalition for the overthrow of the new regime. Reinforced with troops from Buckingham, the Gloucester duke intercepted the royalists at Stony Stratford as they traveled from Ludlow to London for the coronation, arresting Rivers and seizing custody of his nephew. As he advanced toward the capital with Edward V and a small escort, messengers were sent to the Woodville queen, pledging loyalty to her council to avoid the appearance of rebellion. Richard was highly popular with the lords and Commons, while Queen Elizabeth had little support. After arriving in London he assembled the magnates and with control of the recognized head of state was invested with full authority to rule. He was empowered as lord protector of the kingdom and established a new council with his loyalists' sympathizers. Duke Buckingham was rewarded for his unfettered loyalty with the governorship of Wales and the offices of constable and chamberlain, while Lord Howard was given other high positions in the government. Baron Hastings was retained in the administration but was not made a member of the protector's inner circle of advisors. To further solidify his hold on the realm, Richard ordered the execution of Rivers on charges of sedition and announced the cancellation of Edward V's anointment ceremony. He sent secret orders to his friends in the northern lordships, commanding them to march with all speed to London to protect his appropriation of power. Despite his accepted assumption of the Yorkish regime, his supremacy became threatened when his ally, Baron William Hastings, transferred his allegiance to Queen Elizabeth's party and advocated her son's immediate succession to the crown.

The Baron of Hastings had supported Gloucester's appointment as lord protector but had remained committed to the investiture of Edward V to the throne. He had held the high post of lord chamberlain under the government of Edward IV but lost the office to the Duke of Buckingham in the new regime and was scheming with the queen to regain his position. After the sovereign was moved from public view in the bishop of London's palace and placed in the secure confines of the Tower, he began to fear Richard's illegal seizure of the monarchy. His concerns were further heightened, when Edward V's brother, Richard of York, was taken from his mother and relocated to the Tower with the king. Gloucester was soon informed of the growing conspiracy and to protect his planned usurpation, on June 12 Hastings and his fellow rebels were summoned to attend a meeting of the council in the Tower of London. Soon after arriving in the Tower, the conspirators were accused of plotting the murder of the protector and arrested. Richard acted quickly to prevent any further dissension, ordering the immediate beheading of Hastings and his allies. Proclamations were issued by the government, announcing the revolt and execution of the insurgents, serving as a deterrent to future sedition.

With his rule now uncontested, on June 25 Richard summoned the lords to Westminster to legalize his usurpation of the throne by issuing a decree announcing Edward IV's marriage to Elizabeth Woodville had been illegal and their children illegitimate. The assembly approved the declaration, fearing the protector's powerful military presence and eager to avoid civil turmoil. With Edward V and York prohibited from inheriting the crown, Richard III was recognized as heir and proclaimed king by the assembled nobles and Commons. On the following day the formal proclamation was presented to him and the barons pledged their fealty. On July 6, 1483, Richard III was anointed at Westminster Abbey in a magnificent ceremony attended by the peerage of the kingdom with Buckingham, John Howard and Lord Thomas Stanley playing prominent roles.

While Richard III's succession to the monarchy had the acceptance of the high earls and prelates, support for Edward V's claim to the crown remained widespread. Rumors began to circulate in London of plots in the south and west organized by dissident Lancastrians and alienated Yorkists to rescue Edward V and Richard of York from the Tower. With his seizure of the throne and imprisonment of his nephews, Richard III had gone too far with his treasonous acts to ever permit them to rule. Without their elimination he risked losing all that had been gained over the past several months. The decision to murder the Yorkish princes was made after the discovery of the conspiracy to free their sisters from sanctuary in Westminster Abbey and establish them on the continent as a party in opposition. In July 1483 the king left London, traveling to the western counties and from Gloucestershire issued orders for the executions of Edward V and Richard of York.

From Gloucestershire the king resumed the western tour, enforcing his assumption of the throne and receiving the fealty of the local lords and towns. The journey was continued to the north, traveling to the base of his support in Yorkshire. When the members of his court entered the city of York, they received a magnificent reception with welcoming pageants and lavish displays. Richard III remained in York for three weeks of celebrations, banquets and tournaments, highlighted by the investiture of his son and heir, Edward of Middleham, as Prince of Wales. However, as he renewed his triumphant progress to Lincoln, news reached him that his close friend and ally, Henry, Duke of Buckingham, was in rebellion against his crown.

While Richard III toured the northern counties and celebrated his assumption of the crown with his Yorkshire friends, in London Queen Elizabeth began to plot his overthrow with Margaret Beaufort, mother of Henry Tudor. Twelve years earlier as the last Lancastrian claimant to the English throne, Henry had been forced into exile in Brittany but through the intervention of his mother an agreement for the usurpation of the monarchy was negotiated with the Woodville faction. The union of the two houses was to be sealed with the marriage of the dowager-queen's eldest daughter, Elizabeth, to Henry. As the news of the insurgency movement spread across the western and southern lordships, many powerful and influential nobles joined the Tudor alliance. Many of the lords in revolt were former members of Edward IV's household and supporters of the inheritance rights of his sons. The leaders of the conspiracy began to meet secretly with Henry, Duke of Buckingham, convincing him of the weakness and vulnerability of Richard III's reign and political necessity of uniting with their opposition party. As the first peer of the kingdom and chief advisor to the king, his defection brought military might and prestige to the rebels' cause.

By the end of September the preparations for the rebellion were finalized with Buckingham playing the dominant role in the campaign. Under the agreed plan he was to lead an uprising from Wales into the Yorkish western counties, while Henry Tudor landed with an invasion army from Brittany. However, the king was soon informed of the conspiracy and assembled his forces at Leicester, while the newly appointed Duke of Norfolk, John Howard, reinforced the defenses in the region surrounding London against the expected attack of the Kentish insurgents. On October 18 Buckingham launched his offensive into Herefordshire but his incursion quickly lost momentum under the constant harassing sorties of the loyalists and unremitting rainstorms, which restricted his line of march. With the initiative in shambles, the demoralized troops deserted the rebel army and the duke was later arrested. After the elimination of Buckingham's threat, Richard III concentrated his soldiers in the west against the remaining dissidents of the Woodvilles and the queen's brother-in-law, Sir Thomas Saint Leger. After receiving reports of Buckingham's destruction and with the royalists rapidly approaching, many of the west country conspirators abandoned the war against the Yorkish regime. Many of the leaders of the revolt fled to France, while Buckingham, Saint Leger and other prominent supporters of Edward V were executed.

While his rebel allies were being overwhelmed by the Yorkists, Henry Tudor finally sailed from Brittany in late October with fifteen ships and five thousand Breton mercenaries. However, as he approached the coast of southwestern England his fleet was struck by a storm, which dispersed his vessels. When the two remaining ships entered the port of Plymouth, the Lancastrian pretender was informed of the defeat of Buckingham's rebellion and now with his attempted usurpation of the Yorkish throne in shambles, the invasion was abandoned. After returning to Brittany, Henry Tudor of Richmond was united with many of the exiled pro–Lancastrians and supporters of Edward V in the ducal capital of Rennes, forming an alliance for the overthrow of Richard III.

In the aftermath of the failed uprising, Richard III traveled to London and celebrated Christmas and his triumph in the west with lavish banquets and festivals. In January he rode to Kent, imposing his sovereignty and justice against the rebellious local lords and towns. By the end of the month he had returned to the capital to attend his first Parliament as king. To solidify his rule the assembly declared Edward IV and Elizabeth Woodville's marriage illegal and approved Richard III's inheritance of the throne, while acknowledging Prince Edward of Middleham as heir apparent. To gain the approval of the population, he pressed the Lords and Commons to pass a series of legal reforms to ensure the rule of law was carried out without prejudice. He granted large estates and titles to Duke John Howard of Norfolk, Thomas and William Stanley, John de la Pole of Lincoln and other prominent nobles to bind them to his monarchy. The offices of sheriff, judge and castle captain were filled with faithful Yorkish supporters who were richly rewarded for their loyalty.

In March 1484 Richard III renewed his political campaign to enhance his popularity and strengthen his hold on the throne, traveling to central England and holding court in Cambridge and Nottingham Castle, enforcing his rule through the power of his presence. In Nottingham he received the news that his only son, Edward of Wales, had died at Middleham Castle. The death of his son had serious ramifications for the king, leaving him without a direct heir to ensure the continuance of the Yorkish dynasty and weakening his authority and support among the nobles. The death of the Prince of Wales also gave added encouragement to Henry Tudor, who continued to plot the overthrow of the king from Brittany. To guarantee the uninterrupted rule of his family, Richard III appointed his nephew, John de la Pole, Earl of Lincoln, as his successor apparent.

The death of his son and Henry Tudor's continued threat of invasion jeopardized and weakened Richard III's power to govern. The maintenance of peace with Scotland was now essential to buttressing his defenses against an internal revolt and the return of the pretender. In July the English launched a large land and sea punitive raid against the Scottish king, James III, threatening his control over the Lowlands and compelling him to negotiate a settlement. In September the English monarch and his council met with the Scottish envoys and after ten days of talks, a three year truce and treaty of friendship was signed. The agreement freed Richard III to concentrate all his military might against Henry Tudor and an uprising of the English earls without the distraction of fighting along the northern border region. After securing peace with Scotland, he returned to London and renewed his preparations for war. He spent the winter months raising money to defend his reign, sending his agents to secure loans from the towns and lords, while ensuring the readiness of his army. In June 1485 the king moved his court to Nottingham Castle in central England in anticipation of the Tudor invasion. He deployed his loyal and capable lieutenants to protect the vulnerable locations on the coastline and dispatched orders for the troops to be prepared to march.

While Richard III waited for the expected usurper's invasion at Nottingham Castle, on

August 7, 1485, Henry Tudor and his small army of only five hundred dissident Englishmen and two thousand French troops arrived in southwestern Wales at Milford Haven. The Tudors marched slowly to the east through Pembrokeshire, recruiting additional reinforcements as they advanced. When the reports of Tudor's landing reached the king on August 11, messages were sent for the royalists to mobilize at Leicester.

As Henry Tudor approached the area of Market Bosworth, the English king assembled his forces on Ambion Hill and prepared for battle. On August 22, 1485, the two forces clashed in a bloody and savage encounter. As the struggle wore on with the royalists slowly gaining the advantage, from the ridgeline of Ambion Hill Richard III identified Henry by his red dragon banner and to end the battle with a single blow charged down the hill with his household cavalry to engage his enemy. However, in the resulting melee, he was unhorsed and killed by the rebel pikemen. Richard III had ruled England for two years and was thirty-two at his death.

Sources

Cheetham. *The Life and Times of Richard III.*   Ross. *Richard III.*   Seward. *Richard III England's Black Legend.*

Henry VII, 1457–1485–1509

In August 1485 Richard III was killed at the battle of Bosworth defending his crown against the Lancastrian claimant to the monarchy, Henry VII, who by right of birth and conquest established the Tudor dynasty to rule as the seventh Renaissance king of England. Henry Tudor was born on January 28, 1457, in Wales at Pembroke Castle and was the only son of Edmund, Earl of Richmond, and Lady Margaret Beaufort. Edmund had been a supporter of the reigning Lancastrian regime against the House of York during the Wars of the Roses, defending its presence along the Welsh border region. However, he was captured by Sir William Herbert and died in prison on November 1, 1456, forcing Lady Margaret to seek protection with her brother-in-law, Jasper Tudor. At his birth Henry was recognized as successor to his father's lands and title of earl of Richmond. He was directly related to the ruling Lancastrian family through his father, who was a half-brother of Henry VI, and by Lady Margaret, who was the great-great-granddaughter of Edward III. Through his paternal grandfather, Owen Tudor, the Richmond earl was a direct descendant of the princes of Wales.

Henry of Richmond's first years were spent at Pembroke Castle under the guardianship of his uncle, Jasper Tudor, Earl of Pembroke, who supported the Lancastrian cause during the Wars of the Roses and was appointed as captain for several strategic strongholds along the Welsh border. However, in March 1461 the royal army was defeated by Edward of York at the battle of Towton and Jasper was forced to flee from England. Pembroke Castle was seized by Sir William Herbert, who was named as Yorkish lieutenant for South Wales. The three-year-old Henry Tudor was placed under the protection and care of Herbert and moved to the center of his power at Raglan Castle. At the stronghold in Wales, Richmond was raised in Sir William's household with his other children. Tutors were appointed for his education and under the guidance of his protector; Henry received a well rounded education. He was a gifted and serious student, excelling in his studies of reading, writing, French, mathematics and religion. His military training was assumed by a local knight, Sir Hugh Johns, and the earl was taught the skills of a feudal warrior, learning to fence, ride, joust and hunt. In 1470 during the brief revival of the Lancastrian monarchy, Henry of Richmond was taken to London by

Jasper Tudor and presented to Henry VI. The journey to London was the first time he had left Wales and served as his introduction to life at court.

Henry Tudor's first fourteen years were spent in relative obscurity in Wales. However, in early 1471 Edward of York returned from banishment in Burgundy and after defeating the Lancastrian army at Tewkesbury again seized the English crown. In the aftermath of the death of the Lancastrian heir to the crown at the battle of Tewkesbury and the murder of his father, King Henry VI, in the Tower, Henry of Richmond became the last claimant of the dynasty to the English kingdom. With his hereditary rights to the throne, he was a threat to the legitimacy of the Yorkish monarchy and forced to escape for safety to the continent. Henry was secretly taken to a friend of Lady Herbert and reunited with his uncle, Jasper. From their haven, they traveled with several trusted retainers to the Pembrokeshire coast, where a ship took them to exile in Brittany.

Jasper Tudor and his fourteen-year-old nephew landed in Brittany at Brest on June 2, 1471, and were welcomed by Duke Francis II, who pledged to protect them from Yorkish England. Henry of Richmond spent the next fourteen years in the duchy, becoming a pawn in the diplomatic intrigues of the Breton duke. He was not free to travel in the duchy and was detained in several castles under close confinement and supervision. With possession of the claimant to the Lancastrian throne, Francis II attempted to play England against France to his best political advantage. Nevertheless, despite the duke's continuing schemes, the earl remained in Brittany during the reigns of Edward IV and his son, Edward V. However, the usurpation of the crown by Richard III in 1483 opened the way for Henry Tudor to seize the English monarchy.

As the reign of Richard III grew increasingly unpopular with the English secular and ecclesiastic lords, Lady Margaret Beaufort began to cautiously negotiate his overthrow with Queen Elizabeth Woodville, mother of the murdered Edward V. To give legality to their usurpation, their two royal houses where to be united with the marriage of Henry Tudor to the dowager queen's eldest daughter, Elizabeth of York. After the queen agreed to the plot, Lady Margaret's agents began to secretly recruit large numbers of conspirators to their cause, including the crown's closest advisor, Duke Henry of Buckingham. As the first peer of the realm and an experienced soldier, he was chosen to command the rebellion. While the rebel leaders prepared for the uprising, messengers were sent by Buckingham to Henry of Richmond, asking him to sail to England and free the kingdom from Yorkish tyranny. Large sums of money were dispatched to the earl with instructions to raise a mercenary army and land in Wales in October to support Buckingham's revolt.

While the Duke of Buckingham finalized his preparations for the uprising, Henry Tudor negotiated the Breton duke's approval to recruit a local mercenary army and fleet in his duchy for the English invasion. On October 19, 1483, he sailed toward the Welsh coast with five thousand soldiers in fifteen vessels. While Tudor crossed the channel, Henry of Buckingham launched his offensive against the Yorkish regime but his rebellion quickly faltered under the constant attacks of the royalists. The attempted usurpation of the English monarchy suffered a further setback when Henry Tudor's flotilla was dispersed by a violent storm and many of ships were forced back to Brittany. Richmond finally struggled into the port of Plymouth with only one other vessel, soon learning of the defeat of Buckingham's campaign. With the revolt against Richard III now a disaster, the earl abandoned the invasion and returned to Brittany. In the aftermath of the failed seizure of the English crown, many rebel lords were compelled to flee England, joining Henry's exile court in Brittany. On Christmas Day 1483 in the Rennes Cathedral, the earl pledged before his assembled supporters to conquer Richard III by force of arms, while they offered fealty to him as the rightful king of England.

From his haven in Brittany, Henry Tudor remained a threat to the rule of Richard III. To protect his monarchy, the Yorkish king established a network of spies in Brittany and sent envoys to the ducal court to urge the surrender of Henry. After the English pledged to provide a large contingent of archers and infantry to the duchy, in June 1484 Francis II agreed to relinquish control of the Richmond earl. However, Henry was soon informed of the conspiracy and secretly escaped to France. He was welcomed by the Valois regime of Charles VIII and granted sanctuary and financial aid. In Paris Richmond was joined by his supporters from Brittany, while new English exiles were steadily added to his anti–Yorkish coalition. He kept in close contact with his sympathizers in England and Wales and continued to proclaim his blood right to the throne.

During the summer of 1485 Henry Tudor secured a large loan from Charles VIII and began to recruit a local mercenary army for his second invasion of England. With additional financial support and troops from the Valois crown, on August 1 he sailed from Harfleur with a force of five hundred English and two thousand French soldiers. The fleet crossed the channel, landing on the Welsh coast at Milford Haven in Pembrokeshire. As the earl advanced inland to the east, his army was joined by many Welsh and anti–Yorkish recruits, as his military might steadily grew. In the middle of the month he entered England and marched his troops toward the assembled loyalists of Richard III in the rural district of Market Bosworth.

On August 22 Henry Tudor's vanguard clashed with the royalists. Henry had little combat experience and gave command of his troops to John de Vere, thirteenth Earl of Oxford, who ordered an attack against the king's forces on the ridgeline of Ambion Hill. To confront the Oxford earl's attack, Richard III commanded his vanguard of archers and pikemen, led by Duke John Howard of Norfolk, to charge downhill into the ranks of the Tudor army. Initially Oxford held off the Yorkish infantry but his outnumbered forces slowly began to give way as the loyalists pressed their assault. Confronted by the powerful military might of Richard III, the success of Henry's invasion now depended on convincing Sir William Stanley to desert the Yorkists and join his soldiers with the usurper's army. Sir William had been a faithful supporter of the Yorkish king but had refused the order to unite his militia with the royalists, remaining away from the battle on a nearby hilltop. Henry Tudor, protected by with a small escort of men-at-arms, rode toward Stanley's position to personally seek his intervention. From Ambion Hill Richard III identified Henry by his distinctive red dragon banner and to end the battle with a single strike charged down the hill with his household cavalry to challenge his adversary. After personally killing several rebel knights, Richard III reached Richmond and engaged him in close combat, trading blows with their weapons. With the earl's life in danger, William ordered his men to support the Tudors. In the ensuing onslaught, the Yorkists were overwhelmed by the attack of Sir Stanley's reinforcements and the king was unhorsed and killed. With the battle lost the royalists began to flee the field, while the Tudor army shouted, "*God save King Henry.*"

Following his victory at Bosworth, Henry rode to London, entering the city on August 26, 1485, to a grand reception. He established his residence in the bishop of London's palace and formed his new government by appointing his loyal supporters to high offices in his administration. He richly rewarded his friends and allies, naming his uncle, Jasper, Duke of Bedford and granting titles and estates to the Earl of Oxford and William Stanley. On October 30, Henry VII was anointed king in Westminster Abbey by the archbishop of Canterbury in a lavish and magnificent coronation. To confirm his assumption of power, on November 7 Parliament assembled at Westminster to declare Henry VII as sovereign of England and petition him to marry Princess Elizabeth of York. The marriage to the daughter of Edward IV was a political agreement to secure the new Tudor regime's rule. The wedding ceremony was held on January 18, 1486, and united the Houses of Lancaster and York to end the Wars of the Roses.

Under the terms of the agreement between the dowager queen, Elizabeth, and Margaret Beaufort, in January 1486 Henry VII was married to Elizabeth of York. In spite of being a politically arranged union, the king and Elizabeth developed a supportive and loving relationship. The Tudor queen was described by contemporaries as possessing beauty, charm, piety and graceful features. She had been well educated in the Yorkish household and was highly popular with the English people. Elizabeth took little role in the administration of the regime but was fully involved in the social life of the court.

Despite Henry VII's acceptance as king by Parliament and the high secular and spiritual lords, support for the Yorkish cause continued to be widespread, especially in the northern counties. To assert his sovereignty by the force of his presence, during the spring of 1486 he planned a prolonged tour of the shires of Lincoln and York, where strong sympathy still remained for the Yorkists. However, while traveling through the northern towns, he was informed of the growing rebellion in Yorkshire. Henry VII responded quickly to the danger of the rebels by ordering Jasper of Bedford to recruit an army and issuing a decree promising a pardon to all dissidents who willingly submitted. His proclamation and the threat of attack from the formidable Tudor forces led to the mass desertion of the rogue troops and seizure of their leaders by the loyalists. With the threat of open revolt ended, the city of York welcomed the Tudor king and pledged its loyalty. In August he returned to London with his rule now respected in the north. During the following month, Queen Elizabeth gave birth to a son and heir, Prince Arthur, which united the Yorkish and Lancastrian families, assuring the succession and continuance of the Tudor dynasty.

The rapid suppression of the northern rebellion and birth of a heir seemed to secure the Tudor monarchy. However, in November 1486 rumors began to circulate of a new plot to place a Yorkish usurper on the throne. The Yorkish pretender was reputed to be Edward of Warwick, son of Duke George of Clarence, who allegedly escaped captivity from the Tower and was claiming the crown as the rightful successor. However, the role of claimant had been assumed by the ten-year-old Lambert Simnel, son of an Oxford tradesman, who had been coached by a local priest, Roger Simon, to impersonate the Warwick earl. Under the tutelage of Simon, he had received a well rounded education and had been instructed in proper court etiquette. As the conspiracy spread, Simnel was taken to Ireland by the plotters and presented to the local lords and prelates as Edward of Warwick. The Yorkish family had a large following among the Irish and Lambert was widely acknowledged as the rightful heir to the English kingdom. As the news of the pretender circulated through the European courts, the sister of Edward IV and dowager duchess of Burgundy, Margaret, rallied to his cause, providing financial aid and raising an army of local mercenaries for the overthrow of the Tudor king. In late April 1487 the rebel force of over one thousand seven hundred seasoned soldiers under the command of Martin Schwartz sailed to Ireland, where they were welcomed by the supporters of Simnel. As the reports of Schwartz's arrival spread, his troops were soon augmented with contingents of pro–Yorkish Irish militiamen. With the strength of the rebellion growing rapidly, in May Lambert was anointed in the cathedral of Dublin as King Edward VI.

As the danger of the pretender's invasion from Ireland escalated, Henry VII assembled his troops and marched to the Midlands to defend his newly won crown. On June 4, 1487, Edward VI and Schwartz's rebel forces landed on the Lancashire coast and moved inland toward Nottinghamshire, gathering only a few local recruits as they advanced. On June 16 the two armies clashed at Stoke with John de Vere of Oxford leading the Tudor king's vanguard. The battle began with Schwartz's attack against Oxford's vanguard troops, which was held in check with great difficulty. However, after reinforcements arrived from Henry VII, the earl steadily overwhelmed the Irish and Burgundian soldiers. During the melee Schwartz was killed and the pretender's army put to flight. Lambert Simnel was captured but serving only as the figurehead for the rebellion was pardoned and given a position in the royal household.

On November 4, 1487, Henry VII returned triumphantly to London, receiving a hero's welcome. Five days later Parliament assembled and enacted decrees of attainder against the leaders of the pretender's uprising. However, the king acted with restraint, pardoning most of the rebel lords after receiving their pledges of loyalty and initiated a policy of reconciliation to bring peace to England after years of civil war.

England had been ravaged by the Wars of the Roses for over thirty years and Henry VII needed an extended period of order and prosperity to consolidate his reign. To ensure peace with the European courts, he initiated an aggressive and energetic campaign of diplomacy to win their support and friendship. He received papal recognition for the legitimacy of his crown with Pope Innocent III threatening to excommunicate anyone who challenged his right to rule. In July 1488 the English council negotiated a treaty of trade and security with Brittany. However, France had territorial ambitions in the duchy and sent an army of conquest to overthrow Duke Francis II. Under the military might of Charles VIII's forces, by the following year most of the duchy had been occupied and the duke compelled to acknowledge France as his overlord under the Treaty of La Verger. The English had provided financial aid to the Bretons but had sent only a small contingent of reinforcements under Edward Woodville to bolster the duchy's defenses. Under the agreement of La Verger, Woodville and his troops were forced to return home with the English losing their historic influence and presence in Brittany. However, Francis II died a few days after signing the settlement and Charles VIII demanded custody of his minor heir, Duchess Anne. To retain their local autonomy, the Breton lords united to resist the Valois guardianship of Anne and rebelled against Charles VIII's occupation.

England, Spain and the Holy Roman Empire each held territorial and commercial interests in preserving Breton independence and with the duchy again at war the allies agreed to send troops and financial aid to support their resistance. However, they were late in responding to French aggression, allowing Charles VIII to seize control and compel Anne to marry him. Due to the difficulty of securing financial grants from Parliament for his campaign, Henry VII was only able to raise a large military force in late September 1492. He sailed to Calais with twenty-five thousand men-under-arms and on October 18 besieged the well fortified and garrisoned stronghold of Boulogne. As the English established their siege lines, Charles VIII dispatched emissaries to seek peace terms and the withdrawal of the Tudor soldiers. With only a small war coffer and confronting a formidable enemy, Henry VII willingly agreed to negotiate. Under the ensuing Treaty of Etaples, the English pledged to peaceably abandon their French invasion for the payment of an annual cash subsidy. The treaty was widely unpopular in England but the king was satisfied with strengthening his friendship with France and reducing his dependency on Parliament for money.

While policies were initiated by Henry VII to retain English influence and presence in Brittany, envoys were sent to Spain to renew historic ties with the monarchy of Queen Isabella and King Ferdinand II. In March 1489 the Tudor king signed the Treaty of Medina with Spain, restoring their former alliance and establishing favorable customs duties for English merchants. The new agreement was ratified by the marriage of Prince Arthur to Catherine of

Aragon, daughter of the Spanish monarchs. The English government continued its foreign diplomacy by reinstating the treaty of friendship and trade with Portugal and issued a charter confirming the commercial Treaty of Utrecht with the Hanseatic League, previously negotiated by Edward IV. The Tudor regime also pursued favorable trade policies with the Baltic and Italian states. Through the energetic initiatives of the crown, the English economy improved as the amount of commerce with Europe expanded and the reign of the Tudor monarchy became more popular.

Henry VII's forceful suppression of Lambert Simnel's attempted usurpation of the crown and his foreign peace and trade policies had produced a more stable and accepted monarchy with the secular and ecclesiastic lords and towns acknowledging his rule. However, in 1491 he was again confronted with the threat of another pretender to his throne, Perkin Warbeck. Perkin was born in 1475 and was the son of a Flemish boatman. In 1491 he was hired by a Breton silk merchant, who took him to Cork, Ireland, to display his rich clothes. Dressed in the fine garments of his employer, the city residents claimed he was Richard of York, second son of King Edward IV. Despite his initial denials, the Irish continued to press their assertion and Warbeck finally agreed to impersonate York. While his quest for the usurpation of the English monarchy received strong support from the population of Cork, the Irish nobles refused to offer financial or military aid and his planned overthrow of the English kingdom faltered. However, as the reports of the new pretender spread to the European courts, Charles VIII invited him to his realm. In the summer of 1492 Warbeck was received by the French king as a royal prince. Despite his friendly reception by the Valois regime, in November Charles VIII negotiated the Treaty of Etaples with the English to end their invasion of Brittany and under its terms the government agreed to expel the pretender from France.

In the aftermath of his expulsion from France, Perkin Warbeck found refuge in Burgundy under the protection of the dowager duchess, Margaret of York, who acknowledged him as her nephew. Many of the Yorkists, who had been forced into exile by the Tudors, had settled in Margaret's court and quickly rallied to the pretender's cause. With support and financial aid from the duchess, the conspirators began a diplomatic campaign to gain acceptance of Warbeck as the rightful heir to the English crown from the European monarchies. As a member of Margaret's small court of outcasts, Perkin became friends with Duke Philip of Burgundy and during the summer of 1493 was recognized by him as the rightful claimant to the throne. In August the pretender traveled to Vienna with Philip, meeting his father, Archduke Maximilian, and attending the funeral of Emperor Frederick III. In Austria Warbeck was acclaimed as Richard IV by the new Holy Roman emperor, Maximilian I. As the danger of rebellion from the pretender's followers grew, Henry VII sent envoys to Burgundy, demanding the surrender of Perkin Warbeck but Philip refused to abandon him.

While Perkin Warbeck continued to gain wider recognition from the European courts as the claimant to the crown, in England Lord William Stanley and other pro–York loyalists began to conspire with him and his supporters in Flanders. Henry VII was soon informed of their sedition by his network of secret agents and in early 1495 ordered their arrest. In January Stanley and his allies were tried for treason by Parliament at Westminster and convicted of the charges. The swift execution of the plotters served as a deterrent to future rebels.

In early July 1495 Warbeck recruited an invasion army of English volunteers and mercenaries with funds proved by Margaret of York and Emperor Maximilian I, crossing the channel from Burgundy to the Kent coast and landing near Deal. As Richard IV marched inland, the men of Kent remained loyal to Henry VII and refused to rally to his banner, as his planned uprising failed to develop. When the local militiamen attacked their forces,

Warbeck and his rebels abandoned the English usurpation attempt and sailed to Ireland to raise additional troops. They landed near Waterford and laid siege against the English controlled fortress. However, the Tudor king had reinforced the local garrison and buttressed its defenses and the insurgents' assaults against Waterford were repelled by the royalists, despite receiving military support from the Earl of Desmond, Maurice Fitz Gerald.

Following his failed attack at Waterford, Warbeck was granted sanctuary by James IV of Scotland and welcomed to his court at Stirling Castle, where he was acknowledged as King Richard IV. The appearance of Warbeck and his pro–Yorkist sympathizers threatened the ongoing truce between England and Scotland, which Henry VII was determined to enforce. As hostilities along the border escalated, the English king began to prepare for the anticipated Scottish invasion by reinforcing his defenses in the region, while sending emissaries to the Stewart council to discuss peace terms and a marital treaty between James IV and his daughter, Margaret. However, the talks dragged on without any reconciliation and in September 1496 the Scottish army, augmented by Warbeck's contingent of Yorkists and mercenaries, launched an attack into England. The pillaging foray was largely unopposed, as James IV's troops ravaged the Northumberland towns and farm lands. As they advanced deeper into the northern counties, the usurpation cause of Richard IV received little support from the local population and with the approach of a large force of English militiamen; the Scottish king withdrew his soldiers across the border.

In the aftermath of James IV's raid into the north country, the English Parliament granted Henry VII a substantial tax increase to fund a retaliatory attack against the Scots. In early 1497 the Tudor king began to recruit troops and purchase war supplies in anticipation of a large land and sea invasion of Scotland. However, the heavy levy imposed by Parliament was highly unpopular throughout the kingdom but especially in impoverished Cornwall, where civil unrest soon erupted, forcing the delay of the Scottish incursion. In May a rebel army of over five thousand protesters mustered at Saint Keverne and marched toward London to demand the dismissal of the king's corrupt council and end to the excessive taxes. As the dissidents advanced through the west country, their ranks steadily grew with new recruits. When they entered the city of Wells, command of their military force was given to a local lord, Sir James Touchet of Audley, a devoted supporter of the Yorkish regime and an experienced soldier.

With his crown now in peril, Henry VII initiated energetic measures to defend London from the approaching fifteen thousand Cornish protesters. He ordered all the bridges to the capital fortified and mustered reinforcements, while recalling Lord Giles Daubeney and his eight thousand man Scottish invasion army. On June 17, 1497, at Blackheath, Audley's troops attempted to seize the bridge at Deptford Strand but Daubeney led a decisive charge with his spearmen, destroying the Cornish rebels and thwarting their threat to the Tudor government. Lord Touchet and the leaders of the revolt were captured and later executed for treason, while the remaining conspirators were pardoned after paying fines. Following his triumph at Blackheath, Henry VII entered the city over the London Bridge to a hero's welcome and attended a mass of thanksgiving at Saint Paul's Cathedral.

After receiving the reports of the Cornish rebellion, James IV organized a double pronged attack against England, sending Perkin Warbeck with a small army of Yorkist volunteers and mercenaries to Cornwall to rally the local rebels to his banner, while the Scots launched an incursion across the border. After leaving Scotland, Warbeck first sailed to Ireland to muster reinforcements, which delayed his arrival in the west country until after the destruction of the insurgent forces at Blackheath. Landing on the Cornish coast near Land's End, the pretender proclaimed himself Richard IV and advanced toward Exeter, recruiting additional soldiers to his cause. He laid siege against Exeter but after eleven days of assaulting the fortress, the investment was abandoned with over three hundred of the seditionists killed. His call to arms had received little support from the Cornish men after their devastating defeat at Blackheath and with his campaign now in shambles, the pretender became disillusioned and surrendered to the king on October 5. After making a full confession of his impersonation as Richard of York before the Tudor council, Perkin Warbeck was treated with clemency and confined to the royal court under only minimal restraint. In June 1498 he attempted to flee but was quickly recaptured and imprisoned in the Tower. While in the stronghold, in August 1499 he began to plot his escape with Edward, Earl of Warwick, and other Yorkist prisoners but their conspiracy was soon discovered. The dissidents were tried for attempting to escape by bribing their guards and executed for treason.

While Warbeck was advancing through the western counties, in July James IV assembled a large army and personally commanded an attack against the English fortress at Norham. He besieged the stronghold and pounded the defensive walls with his heavy artillery. Despite his energetic assaults, the well fortified castle garrison refused to surrender and with the earl of Surrey approaching with the local militia, the Stewart king was forced to return to Edinburgh after harrying the border towns and farm lands.

In the aftermath of the failed Scottish incursion against Norham Castle, Henry VII again sent his emissaries to the court of James IV to discuss terms for a lasting peace. With both rivals favoring negotiations, an agreement for a seven year truce was soon signed, while talks for a permanent reconciliation continued. Finally after prolonged deliberations, in January 1502 the Treaty of Perpetual Peace was ratified. The accord provided for the marriage of James IV to the English king's daughter, Margaret, and the automatic renewal of the peace settlement following the succession of each new monarchy. The treaty was formally recognized by the papacy, which became committed to the excommunication of any king who failed to honor the resolution.

The March 1489 Treaty of Median had committed both the Tudor government and Spain to the marriage of the English heir, Prince Arthur, to Catherine of Aragon, daughter of Isabella and Ferdinand II. Negotiations to settle the final terms of the marital agreement had continued but no settlement had been signed. The Spanish regime held reservations about the security of Henry VII's usurpation of the throne, which were reinforced by the appearance of the pretenders, Lambert Simnel and Perkin Warbeck. However, with the defeat of the imposters and peace restored with Scotland, the Spanish court finally became assured of the king's hold on his realm and agreed to the union. In the summer of 1499 a proxy wedding was held in London and two years later Catherine arrived in England to widespread rejoicing. The formal ceremony was held on November 14, 1501, uniting the two kingdoms in friendship. The marriage to a princess from the powerful Spanish dynasty signaled the acceptance of Henry VII's rule and propelled him to equal status with the monarchies of Europe. Following a month of lavish celebrations with numerous banquets, jousting tournaments and pageants, Prince Arthur and Catherine traveled to their new residence at Ludlow Castle on the Welsh border. However, five months later the Prince of Wales died and the death of his beloved son was a devastating blow to the Tudor king.

During the second half of his reign Henry VII maintained a splendid court, sparing no expense to impress the monarchies of Europe and gain their acknowledgement as the legitimate English king. He dressed in rich robes of gold and silver cloth and spent freely on jewels, furs and silks for his household. A strict palace etiquette was established with formal receptions, banquets and processions. He was a patron of learning and arts, attracting renowned musicians, poets and historians to his regime. The king funded a permanent body of court musicians and chapel choir to provide music for state and private occasions. As his kingship grew more secure, he initiated an ambitious building program. Westminster Palace was expanded, while the London residence of Baynards Castle was rebuilt into a lavish town house. The monarch continued the construction begun by Edward IV on Saint George's Chapel at Windsor and when the royal residence at Sheen was destroyed by fire, it was replaced with the magnificent Gothic style Richmond Palace. Within two years the new building was ready for occupancy and was richly decorated with turrets, gardens and a great tower. To emphasize his Lancastrian heritage, he glorified the sovereignty of Henry VI by constructing a new chapel in Westminster Abbey as a shrine to his martyrdom. In the style of the French court, Henry VII created the elite Yeomen of the Guard with their distinctive red uniforms and black hats as a personal bodyguard.

In the aftermath of his triumph at the battle of Stoke in 1487 against the pretender, Lambert Simnel, the Tudor king began an energetic domestic program of financial and legal reforms based on the autocratic regime of Edward IV. He appointed experienced and skilled nobles and clerics to his council, many of whom had served during the reigns of the Yorkish sovereigns, and created new specialized committees to administer the princedom of Wales, judicial system, treasury function and foreign policy. The Tudor monarch actively participated in his government and regularly attended council meetings. He took a special interest in the collection of royal revenue and personally audited the account books. Modifications were made in the procurement of rents and taxes, eliminating waste and corruption, while increasing receipts to put the Tudor treasury on a sound footing. To expand the economy, he reformed the realm's industrial and agrarian sectors while putting the coinage on a firm financial basis. Commercial agreements were negotiated with Burgundy and other trading partners, securing special privileges for English merchants. The king initiated policies to ensure peace with the European powers and in 1496 England joined Pope Alexander VI's Holy League to restrain Charles VIII's aggrandizement into Italy. Following Christopher Columbus's discovery of new lands in the west, Henry VII sponsored voyages of exploration to the New World. In 1496 he authorized the expeditions of John Cabot under the English flag. Cabot's first voyage in the following year discovered Newfoundland, which resulted in a highly profitable English fishing trade. Other ventures followed, which explored the coastline of North America, giving Henry VII a claim to the territories.

During the final years of his reign, the reform measures were continued by the royal council but Henry VII became increasingly isolated from his court. The king's rule became more autocratic after his regime reestablished its power over the nobles and created a strong centralized government. In February 1508 he became seriously ill, worn out from the stresses of civil war and imposing his sovereignty. By the following year he was nearing death, suffering from gout and consumption. Henry VII died at Richmond Palace on April 21, 1509, at age fifty-two after a reign of twenty-four years.

Sources

Bevan. *Henry VII.*   Chrimes. *Henry VII.*   Lockyer. *Henry VII.*   Williams. *The Life and Times of Henry VII.*

Henry VIII, 1491–1509–1547

At his death in April 1509 Henry VII bequeathed a wealthy and united kingdom to his heir, Henry VIII, who reigned for thirty-seven years as the eighth Renaissance king of England.

Prince Henry was born on June 28, 1491, at Greenwich Palace and was the third child of Henry VII and Queen Elizabeth of York. He spent his first years at Eltham Palace in Kent under the care and protection of his mother. In October 1494 he was given the title of Duke of York and later received additional honors, including Earl Marshal of England, Warden of the Scottish Marches and Lord Lieutenant for Ireland. As the second son, Henry was destined for a career in the church at an early age and initially received ecclesiastic training. However, under the influence of Queen Elizabeth, the focus of his education became more secular and distinguished scholars were appointed for his academic training. He was a gifted and dedicated student, excelling in his studies of reading, writing, literature, Latin, French, Spanish, astronomy, religion, mathematics and court etiquette. While acquiring a well rounded humanist education, he was exposed to the arts and became devoted to music, playing the harp, lute and organ. Prince Henry studied musical theory and composed instrumental and vocal songs. While at Eltham he began military training under the tutelage of experienced knights, mastering the skills of riding, archery, hawking, hunting and jousting. The prince was a natural leader with a charismatic personality and evolved into a skilled politician and soldier.

In November 1501 the king's heir, Prince Arthur, was married to the Spanish princess, Catherine of Aragon, and sent to the Welsh border at Ludlow Castle to prepare for his kingship. However, four months later he died and the ten-year-old Henry became the successor designate. He immediately assumed Arthur's title of Duke of Cornwall and ten months later was created Prince of Wales and succeeded to the earldom of Chester. The duke was moved from Eltham to Richmond Palace and provided his own household albeit under the close supervision of Henry VII. Unlike his older brother, Henry was not associated with his father's government and received little preparation for his future assumption of the Tudor throne. He was not permitted to attend meetings of the ruling council or be present during audiences with nobles and foreign emissaries.

In the aftermath of Prince Arthur's death, the Spanish regime sent its envoys to negotiate the marriage of Prince Henry to the newly widowed Catherine of Aragon. In spite of the political advantages to the English, the deliberations soon became stalled over the payment of the remaining dowry and were not resolved until the spring of 1503 when the Spanish king, Ferdinand II, reduced his financial demands. On June 3 the marital alliance between Spain and England was signed in London. Under the terms of the settlement, the wedding was to take place after the receipt of the final installment of the dowry, the Prince of Wales reaching the age of fifteen and the delivery of a papal dispensation for the prior union between Arthur and Catherine. Nevertheless, Ferdinand II continued to delay paying the agreed amount and Henry VII initiated new talks for a marriage treaty with the duchy of Burgundy, France and Emperor Maximilian I. Before the ongoing negotiations were finalized, Henry VII died at Richmond Palace and his heir inherited the Tudor crown as King Henry VIII. Following his accession to power, Henry VIII ended the marital discussions with the European courts and notified the Spanish ambassador of his decision to marry Catherine. The ceremony was held in the Franciscan church at Greenwich on June 11, 1509. Eighteen days later he was anointed before the great secular and ecclesiastic lords of the realm by the archbishop of Canterbury in Westminster Abbey in a lavish and opulent coronation service. The investiture ritual was followed by many days of banqueting, festivals and jousting tournaments.

After his assumption of the reins of power, Henry VIII consolidated his new realm, making few changes to his father's administration. With his kingdom united and prosperous, he took little interest in domestic issues and left the routine decisions of state to his council under the leadership of Thomas Wolsey and Bishop Richard Fox. Wolsey was the son of a wealthy cloth merchant and was born in 1475 at Ipwich. He studied theology at Oxford College and was ordained a priest in 1498. After excelling in numerous ecclesiastic positions, in 1507 he entered the service of Henry VII as royal chaplain. Thomas Wolsey was a gifted administrator and with his exceptional organizational skills and energy rose quickly to high offices. At the beginning of the reign of the new Tudor regime, he was named to the ruling council, becoming a close friend and confidant of Henry VIII. For his later diplomatic successes in Europe, Wolsey's services were richly rewarded with appointments as lord chancellor, archbishop of York and in 1515 cardinal.

While largely ignoring internal issues, the king began to plan the renewal of the war against England's historic foe, France. In his youth he had heard the stories of his ancestors' heroic exploits during the Hundred Years' War and was determined to seek personal glory on the battlefield by attacking the Valois regime of King Louis XII. In May 1510 the Tudor king negotiated an alliance with Ferdinand II of Spain for a joint invasion of southern France. While the Anglo-Spanish allies planned their offensive, the Holy See of Rome under the guidance of the warrior pope, Julius II, formed a Holy League to reclaim Valois occupied northern Italy. To gain the approval of the pope for their initiative, in November 1511 England joined the coalition, pledging with Ferdinand II to conquer the French Aquitaine in the name of the papacy. During the winter months of 1512 English troops were recruited, ships assembled and war supplies purchased for the monarch's first military campaign. In June the fleet carrying the Tudor army sailed for Spain to unite with the forces of Ferdinand II. However, soon after landing at San Sebastian, the Spanish soldiers were diverted to conquer the small kingdom of Navarre and without an ally the English were compelled to abandon the attack against France.

While his first attempt at waging war was a fiasco, Henry VIII remained resolved to invade France. As his foremost advisor, Thomas Wolsey, planned and organized the new English offensive, the king used his political skills to reconcile his monarchy to the nobility, towns and Parliament to raise additional tax revenue to fund the campaign. In April he signed a treaty of alliance with the imperial emperor, Maximilian I, for a combined initiative against Louis XII. In June the largest invasion army since the reign of Henry V sailed from England landing at Calais. After three weeks of final preparations, the nearly thirty thousand Tudor troops marched against the fortress town of Therouanne. While the English established their siege lines, they were joined by the small Habsburg army of the emperor. Henry VIII was actively engaged in the attack, encouraging his men by his presence, personally adjusting cannon fire against the citadel and commanding sorties to confront the harassing assaults of the French men-at-arms. To defend his kingdom as the investment wore on, Louis XII sent a large cavalry force to break the siege. As they approached Therouanne, Maximilian I led a counterattack, defeating the French at the battle of Guinegate. After the allies' victory, with no relief now possible and food supplies exhausted, the garrison soon surrendered. On August 24 Henry VIII and the emperor entered the city in triumph, attending a religious service of thanksgiving at the local church. Three days later the strategic stronghold was destroyed to eliminate a barrier to future English campaigns against the Ile de France region and Paris.

After razing Therouanne the allies advanced unchallenged to attack the bishopric of Tournai, which was captured after a short siege of only eight days. Unlike Therouanne the bishopric remained under Henry VIII's control and was garrisoned with his troops and administered by his civil officials to serve as a base for new offensive operations against the Valois crown. After the seizure of the two towns, the Tudor king traveled to Lille, meeting with the envoys from Madrid and the Holy Roman Empire to negotiate the renewal of their military alliance. Under the ensuing treaty, the allies agreed to continue the war in the spring of 1514 with the English and imperialists attacking Picardy and Ferdinand II striking against southern France. The accord was to be sealed with the marriage of Henry VIII's younger sister, Mary, to Archduke Charles of Burgundy, grandson of the emperor.

While the English were attacking the Valois king, Scotland declared war against Henry VIII in support of its traditional French ally. In August 1513 James IV crossed the Tweed River with a large army, seizing several English border strongholds. While the Scots pillaged and burned the local towns and countryside, the Tudor regime's northern lieutenant, Sir Thomas Howard of Surrey, mustered the local militia and advanced to confront the Stewart king. The two armies clashed at Flodden Hill on September 9 with Howard outmaneuvering and destroying the Scottish forces. At the end of the year, Henry VIII's personal victories in France along with the Earl of Surrey's overwhelming triumph at Flodden Hill had greatly enhanced the reputation of English military might and had won recognition and respect for the Tudor crown as a powerful ally from Maximilian I and Spain.

Following his return from France, Henry VIII energetically prepared for the renewal of his war against the Valois regime. While he made arrangements for a large invasion army, in January 1514 Ferdinand II and the emperor began secret negotiations with Louis XII to end their ongoing conflict. After receiving the French king's pledge for the marriage of his daughter, Renee, to a Habsburg prince with the dowry of Milan and Genoa both Spain and the imperialists were won to the treaty. In spite of the desertion of his allies, Henry VIII refused to abandon the spring campaign and mustered his troops and ships for the coming attack. However, Pope Julius II had died in February 1513 and his successor, Leo X, had little interest in continuing the French war, launching a diplomatic initiative to bring peace to Europe. He sent his legates to London to persuade the Tudor government to begin talks for a reconciliation with France. After the loss of his comrades in arms and under heavy papal pressure, Henry VIII finally agreed to open discussions with the Valois court. In August he signed a peace treaty, pledging to honor the status quo in France, while Louis XII committed to pay a war indemnity and recognize the recent English conquests. The settlement was secured by the marriage of the Tudor king's sister, Mary, to Louis XII.

In October 1514 Princess Mary was formally married to Louis XII and crowned queen at Saint Denis Basilica. However, the union between London and Paris was short lived when the fifty-two-year-old French king died in early January 1515 and was succeeded by his cousin, Francis I. The new Valois ruler was young, ambitious and like Henry VIII eager for personal glory on the battlefield. Soon after consolidating his rule, he began preparations to continue his predecessor's quest for aggrandizement in northern Italy. In August 1515 the French army under the personal command of Francis I crossed the Alps into Lombardy, defeating the Milanese mercenaries at the battle of Marignano and entering Milan in triumph. In the aftermath of the victory, with the status quo in Europe now threatened Henry VIII began discussions for a military league with the major European powers to force the Valois occupation troops out of northern Italy. Despite repeated attempts by the English crown's first minister, Cardinal Wolsey, no treaty of alliance resulted and the French remained firmly in control of the duchy of Milan.

Following the failure of his diplomatic initiatives to drive the French out of Italy by force of arms, Henry VIII began secret discussions with Francis I for a universal European peace. While the Anglo-French deliberations continued, Cardinal Wolsey sent his agents to the European courts, seeking their approval of the non-aggression pact. In October 1518 the Tudor and Paris regimes agreed to participate in the new détente, which bound all realms to perpetual peace. Under the accord if any kingdom suffered foreign aggression, the remaining signatories were collectively committed to expel the offender. After ratification of the agreement by Henry VIII and Francis I, the emissaries of the major European powers and lesser fiefdoms signed the non-aggression covenant in London. To celebrate the Treaty of London the king, ambassadors and English secular and ecclesiastic lords gathered at Saint Paul's for a service of thanksgiving led by Wolsey. The London rapprochement was followed by a separate treaty between the Tudor and Valois councils, which bound the two kingdoms in friendship with the marriage of Henry VIII's two-year-old daughter, Princess Mary, to the dauphin, Francis, and arranged the personal summit between the two kings.

After several prolonged delays, in early 1520 Cardinal Thomas Wolsey began preparations for the meeting between his king and Francis I under the terms of their separate London Treaty. In March the English delivered large quantities of tents, pavilions, building supplies and food to France for the more than five thousand expected courtiers, while temporary banqueting halls, chapels and palaces were constructed. In late May Henry VIII and Queen Catherine sailed to Calais with a massive flotilla in a visual display of English naval power. On June 7 the two kings met near Calais at Balinghem for the first time, embracing each other in friendship. The event lasted for two weeks with Henry VIII and Francis I participating together in the daily jousting tournaments, archery competitions and military games, while attending banquets and parties filled with music and dancing. The conference ended with a mass conducted in an open air chapel by Cardinal Wolsey. The meeting became known as the Field of the Cloth of Gold because of the rich, elaborate arrangements and the use of great amounts of gold thread. Despite the enormous expense, the summit failed to result in any lasting agreements.

In the aftermath of the Treaty of London, Henry VIII initiated a policy of preserving the peace in Europe. Despite his energetic diplomatic efforts, in the spring of 1521 hostilities between the new Habsburg emperor, Charles V, and France continued to escalate. War erupted between the two belligerents when Francis I sent his surrogate, Lord Robert III of Marck, to invade Habsburg lands in Flanders, forcing the emperor to counterattack. In May the English regime with papal approval and acting under the London Treaty ordered Cardinal Wolsey to Calais to mediate the dispute. However, the meetings with the Valois and Habsburg envoys did not produce any resolution and Henry VIII began to increasingly favor direct negotiations with Charles V for a military league against France. In August Wolsey renewed the Calais peace conference but no agreement resulted. With little prospects for peaceably resolving the ongoing conflict, the cardinal traveled to Bruges to discuss terms for an alliance with the emperor. Under their resulting treaty, despite imperial demands for an immediate declaration of war, London agreed to invade France only in May 1523 to give Wolsey additional time to find a reconciliation. During the ensuing months numerous attempts to bring the French and Habsburgs to the peace table were initiated but all failed. While returning to Spain from Flanders, in late May 1522 Charles V made a brief visit to England to finalize the plans for a joint campaign in the next year. On June 16 the Treaty of Windsor was signed, which formally committed the two realms to war against the Valois government of Francis I.

While the Tudor council was negotiating the terms of the Treaty of Windsor, the regent of Scotland, John Stewart of Albany, increased hostilities along the English border, ravaging and destroying the towns and countryside. As the likelihood of war against their northern neighbor escalated, the English became increasingly reluctant to commit a large armed force to France. In the summer of 1522 Henry VIII authorized a pillaging incursion from Calais against the Picardy region by Thomas Howard, newly appointed Duke of Norfolk, to quell imperial demands for military assistance. The small foray accomplished little but temporarily mollified Charles V. During the winter of 1523 the English regime agreed to send an army to confront Francis I and in August over ten thousand troops under the leadership of Charles Brandon, Duke of Suffolk, sailed to France. The duke was the son of Sir William Brandon and Lady Elizabeth Bruyn and was born in 1484. Following the death of his father at the battle of Bosworth, Charles was raised and educated in the royal household, becoming a close friend and favorite of the future king. He served in the Tudor army, quickly rising to positions of high command and was recognized for his bravery and military skills during the sieges at Therouanne and Tournai. Brandon won widespread distinction for his many jousting triumphs and acts of chivalry. After taking charge of the royal army, he landed at Calais and advanced toward Paris, razing the towns and threatening the environs of the capital. However, after over three months of campaigning and with the onset of wintry weather, the Tudor offensive lost momentum compelling Brandon to withdraw to Calais.

Following Brandon's failed campaign in the Ile de France region, Henry VIII became disillusioned with the French war and with his coffers depleted and confronting a hostile Parliament showed little enthusiasm to send a new army against Francis I in the coming year. While maintaining discussions with the Habsburg court for a new offensive, he began secret peace talks with the Valois regime at Calais. During the spring months of 1524 no arrangements for an incursion against France were made but when the imperial ally, Duke Charles III of Bourbon, invaded and advanced unchallenged into Provence, the English hurriedly prepared to muster their military forces in support of the emperor. However, when the duke's initiative stalled during the siege against Marseille, Henry VIII abandoned the planned attack. Despite the lack of Tudor success against France, in February 1525 the European balance of power dramatically shifted in the Habsburgs' favor when Francis I was defeated and taken prisoner during hostilities at Pavia in Lombardy.

In the aftermath of Francis I's disaster at Pavia, his kingdom was defenseless and without an anointed sovereign. From his prison in Spain he was forced to sign the Treaty of Madrid, agreeing to all of Charles V's demands to secure his freedom. With the rise of imperial power and the weakening of France, the security of the English regime became threatened and the focus of London's foreign policy shifted to a more pro–Valois policy. The Tudor kingdom began talks with the French and Henry VIII's government became more closely allied with Francis I against the Habsburgs. When the Valois court attempted to forge the League of Cognac to limit the emperor's aggrandizement in Italy, the Tudor administration aggressively encouraged Pope Clement VII, Florence and Venice to actively participate. The English king's main objective now was to limit imperial expansion without going to war. In August London and Paris pledged to not reach a separate agreement with the Habsburg emperor and in the following year they signed a treaty of eternal peace at Amiens. The accord was to be ratified with the marriage of Princess Mary to the Duke of Orleans, Charles. The Amiens Treaty ushered in a decade of Anglo-French détente.

Following a series of miscarriages, stillbirths and early infant deaths, in February 1516 Queen Catherine delivered a healthy girl, Princess Mary. After the many prior disappointments, the king was encouraged his next child would be a healthy son. However, several more miscarriages followed and by 1525 he lost hope of having a male heir with the queen. Henry VIII became increasingly concerned that England would be plunged into civil war at his death without a recognized successor. To provide a male heir, he promoted the hereditary rights of his illegitimate son, Henry Fitzroy. To gain validity for his future accession to the Tudor crown, in 1527 Fitzroy was created Duke of Richmond, appointed lord high admiral and later sent to govern the north country. However, as an illegitimate issue his inheritance would likely be challenged causing the monarch to consider a divorce from Catherine. In May 1527 he asserted that his marital union with the queen was illegal and his failure to produce a legitimate successor was divine punishment for the sin of marrying his deceased brother's wife.

In July 1527 the Tudor king sent a delegation to Rome to secure his separation from Queen Catherine on the grounds that the papal dispensation granted by Pope Julius II for his marriage was invalid. He now had an added incentive for obtaining the divorce after falling passionately in love with Anne Boleyn. His agents in Rome were instructed to seek Clement VII's approval for a papal inquiry in England to examine the validity of his claim. After great reluctance, in June 1528 the pope empowered a commission led by Wolsey and his personal legate, Cardinal Lorenzo Campeggio, to try the case and issue judgment. However, Charles V was the nephew of the English queen and was determined to prevent the annulment. With virtual control over Italy, he openly threatened the papacy if a ruling was found in favor of Henry VIII. Accordingly, secret instructions were given to Campeggio, ordering him not to pronounce a sentence. On May 31, 1529, at Black Friars, the court finally assembled with both the king and queen testifying. After hearing numerous petitions and arguments from the lawyers, in compliance with Clement VII's directive in late July the papal legate refused to render a decision and adjourned the hearings, referring the lawsuit to Rome. Henry VIII was bitterly disappointed at the outcome and directed his anger against Cardinal Wolsey.

While the papal inquiry in London dragged on, in January 1528 as the ally of Francis I England became ensnared in war against Charles V. The prospect of a costly conflict with an interruption of trade with Europe was widely unpopular among the English merchant class, causing riots in opposition to soon break out. Confronted with overwhelming dissent and a hostile Parliament, Henry VIII refused to support the Valois war and sent his envoys to negotiate peace with the emperor. In June the English signed a truce with the Habsburg regime, which was followed in the following year by the Peace of the Two Ladies between the French and the emperor. The separate Franco-imperial peace treaty had serious ramifications for Henry VIII when the Valois government pledged to repudiate its claim to Lombardy, leaving Charles V as the virtual master of Italy. Pope Clement VII was now forced to seek friendlier relations with the emperor and ratified an agreement, pledging to suppress the Tudor king's petition for divorce.

The repudiation of the English king's divorce appeal served as the catalyst for the downfall of Cardinal Wolsey. In addition to his failure to secure the annulment of the marriage, the lord chancellor's policies had proven disastrous for England, resulting in higher taxes and the loss of esteem in European politics. The blood and treasury of the kingdom were squandered for no gain and Henry VIII's rule was now widely unpopular. In October 1529 the king ordered the cardinal's arrest on the serious charge of attempting to introduce papal law into England. After his indictment by Parliament, Wolsey pleaded guilty and was deprived of most of his offices and lands but Henry VIII permitted him to retain the archbishopric of York. In the spring of 1530 the cardinal established his residence in York and assumed his ecclesiastic duties. However, he soon began to intrigue with the European powers to raise a rebellion to recover his forfeited properties and offices and in November was accused of treason by the English high court. Shortly after his arrest, exhausted by his years at court in the service of the throne, Cardinal Wolsey died at Leicester Abbey en route to face trial in London.

Henry VIII had maintained his ongoing love relationship with Anne Boleyn and in January 1533 she became pregnant. His divorce petition continued unanswered in Rome but now it was critical for the first marriage to be quickly dissolved for Anne's issue to be recognized as legitimate. However, while Pope Clement VII remained under Habsburg control no annulment was expected. The Tudor king was compelled to pursue a different remedy, turning to the English church and the archbishop of Canterbury as the highest ecclesiastic authority in his realm. The archbishopric had been vacant since the death of Archbishop William Warham in August 1532 and under the influence of the Boleyn family, the king appointed Thomas Cranmer as his successor. Cranmer was born in Nottinghamshire in 1489 and as the second son was placed on an early path to a clerical career. After receiving a humanist education at Jesus College, Cambridge, he was ordained into the priesthood. He stayed at Cambridge serving as a resident scholar until his appointment to the English embassy in Spain. In 1527 he returned to court and assisted Cardinal Wolsey with the papal divorce initiative. In January 1532 Cranmer was named as resident envoy to the court of Charles V, becoming exposed to the Protestant reform movement in Germany.

During the divorce proceedings Henry VIII had maintained cordial relations with the Holy See and his petition for Thomas Cranmer's appointment as Canterbury's archbishop was quickly approved in February 1533 without opposition. With Cranmer's assumption of the archbishopric, the king had a friendly prelate who willingly supported his marriage nullification. To further pursue his annulment from Queen Catherine, the king sent the Act of Appeals to Parliament for ratification and after days of debate on April 3, 1533, it was passed with only small dissent. The act empowered the archbishop of Canterbury to settle all marital issues in England without appeal to Rome, while proclaiming that marriages like Henry VIII's to Catherine were impeded by divine law and therefore null and void. The Appeals Act, later confirmed by the Act of Supremacy, invested Henry VIII with the authority to decide all matters both secular and ecclesiastic without interference from any foreign power and gave total control of the church to him as its supreme head. On May 10 the archbishop opened his ecclesiastic court at Dunstable to resolve the king's divorce case. Queen Catherine refused to appear or recognize the legality of the hearings. After four days of testimony, on May 23 Cranmer ruled that Henry VIII and Catherine had never been married, their daughter, Mary, was illegitimate and the pope was powerless to approve such unions. Five days later he declared the Tudor monarch's secret marriage in January to Anne was lawful and their children legitimate heirs to the crown. On May 31 Anne was anointed by the Canterbury archbishop at Westminster Abbey as queen of England. Despite a lavish and magnificent coronation ceremony, the new queen remained unpopular with the people of London, who retained their loyalty and support for Catherine.

The legalization of Henry VIII's marriage to Anne was a direct challenge to the ecclesiastic authority of Rome, and Clement VII responded by threatening to issue a bull of excommunication. In support of the Holy See, the Habsburg court initiated plans to invade England, but when confronted with the loss of the highly profitable Flemish cloth trade and rebellion in the Low Countries, Charles V became resolved to allow the pope to defend his own rights through diplomacy. Francis I remained neutral, not willing to break the ongoing status quo with England. While the European powers were adopting a policy of nonintervention, in England opposition to the monarch's divorce from Catherine was widespread, especially in Kent. A local nun, Elizabeth Barton, had earlier publicly threatened the king if his separation from the queen was pursued. After the annulment was announced, Elizabeth became the focal point of popular dissent in Canterbury, when she predicted the death of Henry VIII for his act of heresy. As the danger of rebellion grew, the nun and her band of followers were arrested and in April 1535 hanged for treason.

In the aftermath of the Kent unrest, the Tudor king moved decisively to eliminate Bishop John Fisher and Sir Thomas More, who were the focus of major support from the opposition factions in England and on the continent. Bishop Fisher had been a member of both Henry VII's and his son's councils but had refused to abandon Queen Catherine, while More had been a prominent attorney and had held the high office of lord chancellor for Henry VIII but would not acknowledge him as the supreme head of the church. After over a year spent languishing in the Tower, in the summer of 1535 they were beheaded for treason. The executions of the two eminent statesmen served as a warning to the English that the powers of the king would be enforced and any dissent not tolerated. In Europe the new pope, Paul III, responded to the death of Fisher and More by attempting to raise a crusade to dethrone Henry VIII by force of arms, but his appeals were largely ignored. Now confronted with little resistance the king aggressively renewed his offensive to fully impose his royal supremacy. The English religious houses were powerful and rich and at the center of pro-papacy challenges to change from Henry VIII. Under the leadership of the lord chancellor, Thomas Cromwell, a program was initiated to confiscate the great wealth of the church. Royal agents were sent to the churches, monasteries, nunneries and abbeys to find legal grounds for their appropriation. A detailed listing of each religious house was compiled during the visitations with charges, largely of lax morality, justifying their seizure. The dissolution of the ecclesiastic property was a great financial windfall for the regime; however, large grants of land were given to the nobles to ensure their loyalty and guarantee their acceptance of Henry VIII's new prerogatives. The suppression of nearly six hundred monasteries doubled the crown's annual income and greatly extended its property holdings.

To Henry VIII's great disappointment in September 1533 Anne gave birth to a daughter, Elizabeth. Two stillborns and a miscarriage followed, giving the king little hope of producing a male heir with his queen. As his relationship with Anne grew increasingly strained, he sought the company of new favorites, taking several mistresses and paying special attention to Jane Seymour, who was a lady-in-waiting to the queen. In early 1536 Anne suffered another miscarriage and, convinced that she could not provide him a son, Henry VIII became resolved to take a new wife. A royal commission led by Cromwell and the Duke of Norfolk, Thomas Howard, was created to find evidence of treason against Anne. Within days they drew up a list of her adulterous affairs with five men, including her brother, George Boleyn. After a short trial Queen Anne was found guilty and sentenced to death. On May 19 she was beheaded by a French swordsman in the courtyard of the Tower. Shortly after the death of his second wife, Henry VIII married Jane Seymour in the great hope of finally securing a legitimate successor to the Tudor dynasty.

The Tudor king's dissolution of the monasteries and profound changes to the structure of the English Church created widespread dissent throughout his kingdom. In the south there was local talk of resisting the new religion but in the north country a series of rebellions known as the Pilgrimages of Grace erupted in support of the Church of Rome and against the region's stagnant economic conditions. In October 1536 a riot broke out in Lincolnshire that spread rapidly to Yorkshire. The Yorkshire revolt was led by Robert Aske, who issued a proclamation to the government demanding the legitimization of Lady Mary and restoration of the church's powers. Henry VIII lacked the military might to forcibly subdue the pilgrims' uprising and ordered Thomas Howard to negotiate a settlement. The duke pledged a pardon to the rebels who peaceably returned home and the summoning of the Parliament to resolve their grievances. While the majority of the pilgrims accepted the offer, in February 1537 new civil disorder flared up in Cumberland and the king sent the local militia under the command of Howard to arrest the conspirators. Fewer than two hundred peasants were seized and hanged but the rebellion was crushed. In the aftermath of the Pilgrimages of Grace, Henry VIII created a permanent Council of the North to firmly enforce his sovereignty over the frequently recalcitrant northern counties and his royal authority was now fully respected.

While the subjugation of the north country was unfolding, during the spring of 1537 Henry VIII received the happy news of Jane Seymour's pregnancy. He became the doting and devoted husband, caring to her every need. With the outbreak of plague in London, the queen spent the summer months at Windsor Castle. In September she was moved to her apartments at Hampton Court and after three days of labor delivered the long awaited healthy son, Edward. To celebrate the birth of his heir, the king ordered services of thanksgiving in every church and a plethora of lavish feasts and magnificent pageants through the realm. However, his joy was soon muted when Queen Jane became seriously ill with a fever and died on October 24. He showed genuine and sincere grief at the loss of his queen, arranging a funeral of great pomp and grandeur in Saint George's Chapel at Windsor.

After years of conflict, in 1538 Francis I and Emperor Charles V personally met in southern France near Nice to sign a treaty of truce and agreed to further pursue a permanent peace settlement. The Franco-imperial treaty altered the ongoing European balance of power, leaving England without an ally. To protect his kingdom against foreign invasion, Henry VIII began an aggressive construction program, buttressing his coastal defenses by reinforcing existing harbor fortifications and building new ones, while doubling the size of the royal navy by adding new and larger warships, including the *Great Harry* and *Mary Rose*. In need of a continental partner, England initiated negotiations with the German Protestant Schmalkaldic League, but the talks ended in failure over religious differences. The king remained resolved to strengthen his ties with Europe, using his marriage to secure an ally. Overtures were made to the French and imperial courts but no agreement resulted. In January 1539 discussions were begun with Duke William of Cleves for the marriage of Henry VIII to his sister, Anne. The duchy was strategically located in the Rhineland, bordering Habsburg Netherlands and was closely associated with the Schmalkaldic League. Thomas Cromwell greatly favored the marital union as a means of driving a wedge between France and the Habsburgs. Under the influence of his lord chancellor and after viewing a portrait of Anne painted by Hans Holbein, the king was finally won over. However, when he first saw her at Rochester, Henry VIII was greatly disappointed at her appearance and physical features, rejecting the marriage. Nevertheless, for reasons of state he was forced to marry Anne of Cleves in January 1540.

Despite the English king's great displeasure with the marriage to Anne, the union with Cleves had the desired political effect of making Charles V more insecure in western Europe. In the spring of 1540 the emperor traveled from Spain to the Netherlands to personally enforce his rule and renew the friendship with Francis I. While France and the Habsburgs remained on cordial terms, Henry VIII was compelled to maintain the marriage to Anne. However, within six months the Franco-imperial détente deteriorated and the king was able to pursue his divorce. He ordered Cromwell to find legal grounds to dissolve the union and a review of the marital documents revealed that Anne's previous contract to marry the son of the Duke of Lorraine was still a binding agreement and not just a promise to wed. In July 1540 his marriage to Anne of Cleves was revoked without being consummated and Henry VIII was free to marry Catherine Howard, the new love of his life.

In the wake of the failed Cleves marriage, Henry VIII moved decisively and quickly to remove Thomas Cromwell from his government. The lord chancellor had been the architect of the Cleves alliance and had grown widely unpopular with the high nobles and Parliament for his radical religious beliefs and harsh suppression of the monasteries. Cromwell was from a humble birth as the son of a blacksmith and was born at Putney in 1485. He spent much of his early adulthood on the continent, serving as a soldier with the French army in Italy and working for a cloth merchant in Antwerp. He returned to England to study law and was elected to Parliament. Thomas later became a member of Cardinal Wolsey's staff and soon gained the favor of the king. Cromwell was appointed to the royal council and after the downfall of Wolsey replaced him as lord chancellor. In June 1540 Henry VIII ordered his arrest on charges of heresy and treason and after his conviction by Parliament Thomas Cromwell was executed.

Even before the divorce from Anne was finalized the king had fallen under the spell of Catherine Howard. She was the beautiful niece of the powerful and influential Duke of Norfolk, who aggressively promoted her relationship with Henry VIII to advance his family's position at court. Catherine had had many prior sexual encounters before coming to court and had continued her promiscuous affairs as a lady-in-waiting to the queen. Henry VIII now spent more and more of his time with his new love, favoring her with lavish gifts of jewels and gold. Shortly after Parliament ratified his separation from his fourth wife, on July 28, 1540 he was married to Catherine Howard.

With his young bride by his side, Henry VIII spent the summer months participating in magnificent parties, jousting tournaments and hunts, leaving the affairs of state to the inner council led by Thomas Howard of Norfolk. The 1540 Christmas season was observed with lavish celebrations with Catherine rejoicing in her new role as queen. The sovereign granted her rich estates, castles and jewelry, becoming devoted to her happiness. However, Catherine had continued her adulterous affairs with many of the courtiers, secretly meeting them nightly in her bed chambers.

In the summer of 1541 the Tudor king made his first progress through the recalcitrant north country, taking his court of over five hundred with him. At each stop the queen met secretly with Thomas Culpepper to renew their love affair. When Henry VIII was first informed of her indiscretions, he refused to believe the charges and only after Archbishop Cranmer confirmed them was an investigation ordered to collect evidence. Interrogations were held by the royal council and the queen and Culpepper were found guilty of treason. The judgment was confirmed by Parliament under the Act of Attainder and in early January the queen along with Thomas Culpepper and her other lovers were executed.

During his kingship, Henry VIII was a patron of the Renaissance era, creating a monarchy dedicated to architecture, learning, art and music. Throughout his reign he remained actively involved in architecture and became a builder-king. After assuming the crown, he spent heavily on repairs and extensions to his existing estates, including Windsor, Richmond and Bridewell. After Cardinal Wolsey's fall from power in 1529, the king seized and enlarged his magnificent palaces at Hampton Court and York Place for use as royal residences. Between 1532 and 1540 he built a lavish new dwelling in London at Saint James. The Tudor king began construction of his most ambitious building project in 1538 at Caddington a few miles southeast of Hampton Court. Over two thousand acres were acquired for Nonsuch Palace, which was to rival Francis I's great Loire chateau at Chambord in size and grandeur and celebrate the power and magnificence of the Tudor dynasty. While his main interest was architecture, Henry VIII was a patron of music, employing renowned vocalists and musicians, including lutenists and keyboard players from Italy and the Netherlands, while sponsoring the works of composers, including William Cornysh and William Crane. Music played a major role in the Tudor royal household with performances given for ceremonies, entertainment and church services. Henry VIII was an amateur composer and performer, personally writing many compositions and frequently accompanying his singers at court. To embellish the interiors of his palaces, he collected tapestries, objects of art and paintings, while inviting the artist Hans Holbein to his court.

In the summer of 1542 hostilities again erupted between Francis I and Emperor Charles V and the English regime opened negotiations with the Habsburgs for a treaty of alliance. While the talks continued, Henry VIII sent the Duke of Norfolk to ravage and plunder the southern Scottish Lowlands to eliminate the threat of attack from France's ally. The Scottish army attempted to retaliate but was soundly destroyed at the battle of Solway Moss, leaving the kingdom open to invasion. However, the king's main objective remained the conquest of lands in northern France and acquisition of the lost realm of his ancestors. On July 1, 1543, England signed a treaty of peace with Scotland to be sealed with the marriage of the sovereign's son, Edward, and the infant Queen Mary I.

In February 1543 the emperor and Henry VIII ratified a treaty for the joint invasion of France with each promising to field an army of forty-five thousand. While the large military force was being recruited, during the summer the English sent a small contingent of troops commanded by Edward Seymour to harry the Artois region from Calais in support of the imperial war effort, but his foray accomplished little. However, as the Tudor preparations continued, Scotland broke its pledge of peace and renewed its alliance with France. To eliminate the threat of a Scottish attack in the north, Henry VIII dispatched Edward Seymour to plunder and burn Edinburgh and Saint Andrews. With his northern border at least temporarily safe, in July 1544 the king personally led his massive army to France, albeit from a litter due to his deteriorating health. Remaining in Calais, Henry VIII ordered his troops under the command of Charles Brandon and Duke Thomas Howard to besiege the stronghold of Boulogne. On September 18 the garrison surrendered and the English now held control over much of the Picardy region. In spite of Henry VIII's conquest, the Habsburg initiative into eastern France failed to achieve any meaningful gains and Charles V separately negotiated a reconciliation with Francis I, leaving the English again isolated without an ally. The Tudor throne's envoys attempted to reach a settlement with France but the talks reached an impasse over the return of Boulogne.

While England was in the midst of the war with France, on July 12, 1543, Henry VIII married Catherine Parr in the private chapel at Hampton Court. She was the daughter of a Northamptonshire nobleman and was born in 1512 in the northwestern county of Westmoreland. Following the death of her second husband, Catherine joined the household of Lady Mary, where Henry VIII first met her. She had a lively and pleasing appearance and her intellectual interests were similar to the king's. Henry VIII and his sixth queen developed a close and supportive relationship and he came to rely on her advice and steady presence. When he sailed to France with his invasion army in 1544, Queen Catherine was appointed as regent and governed in his name for three months. During his final years Henry VIII grew increasingly obese and immobile, depending on Catherine as a loyal companion and caregiver.

In retaliation for the seizure of Boulogne and to force the English back to the peace talks, during the summer of 1545 Francis I launched a large seaborne attack against southern England. Confined to a litter Henry VIII personally assumed command of the coastal defenses and sent his navy to engage the Valois galleys. On July 19 the two fleets met in an inconclusive engagement but the English suffered the loss of the battleship *Mary Rose*. When the French attempted to land their thirty thousand invasion troops, the Tudor ships blocked their advance, forcing them to retreat. Later in the year the war became stalemated and with the coffers of both realms depleted negotiations were resumed. In July 1546 the Treaty of Ardes was signed with peace restored between both kingdoms and the English pledging to abandon Boulogne following the payment of a large indemnity.

With peace reestablished in Europe, Henry VIII spent his final months largely isolated from his government under the care of Catherine Parr. His health had been steadily declining in recent years and now he suffered from bleeding leg ulcers and increasingly frequent fevers. He was unable to walk and forced to be carried by litter. In late January the king became seriously ill with a high fever, growing weaker by the day. Early in the morning of January 28, 1547, he died in London at Whitehall Palace at age fifty-five and a reign of over thirty-seven years. Henry VIII was buried according to his wishes in Saint George's Chapel at Windsor Castle alongside Queen Jane Seymour.

Sources

Erickson. *Great Harry.* Lacey. *The Life and Times of Henry VIII.* Pollard. *Henry VIII.* Robinson. *The Dukes of Norfolk.* Scarisbrick. *Henry VIII.* Simpson. *Henry VIII.*

Edward VI, 1537–1547–1553

In January 1547 Henry VIII died and his son, Edward VI, inherited a legacy of royal supremacy over the state and church to rule with absolute power as the ninth English king of the Renaissance era. Edward was the only surviving son of Henry VIII's six marriages and was born on October 12, 1537, at Hampton Court Palace. Shortly after his birth his mother, Jane Seymour, died and the heir designate was placed under the care and protection of a court appointed governess. As the acknowledged successor, he was proclaimed Duke of Cornwall and later Prince of Wales. In March 1538 a separate household was created for him and much of the Prince's infancy was spent at Richmond Palace and smaller manor houses on the outskirts of London. During the summer of 1544 the six-year-old Prince Edward was moved to Hampton Court, where a court was established for him and tutors named for his humanist education. He was a gifted and dedicated student, excelling in his studies of reading, writing, Latin, French, religion, geography and mathematics. Like his father, Edward was fond of music and kept an ensemble of musicians and singers in his household. He also received instruction in music and played the lute and violin. While at Hampton Court, he began his military training, learning the skills of fencing, equestrianship, jousting and hunting. He was raised with the children of high noble families, developing many close friendships. Edward spent little time with his father but the king was devoted to his son's health and education, providing him with the best doctors and scholars. By the time the Tudor prince reached the age of nine, he had acquired an excellent basic education and was prepared to master the art of kingship that would soon be thrust upon him.

By late 1546 Henry VIII's health had seriously deteriorated and he was dangerously close to death. To gain supremacy over the government of the minor heir, two court factions began to contend for dominance. The conservatives were led by the powerful and pro–Catholic Howard family, while the liberal Protestant party was controlled by Edward Seymour. By December the radicals had gained the favor of Henry VIII and the Howards were arrested on charges of plotting to usurp the Tudor crown. On January 13, 1547, Henry Howard was convicted of treason and six days later beheaded in the Tower. His father, Duke Thomas Howard, was later declared guilty but escaped execution when the monarch died on January 28.

Before his death Henry VIII had rewritten his will and testament, giving control of the minor Prince Edward to the Protestant faction. A regency council of sixteen high nobles and prelates was created to reign in the name of the new king. As the leader of the political party,

Edward Seymour assumed the titles of lord protector of England and first Duke of Somerset, ruling with few restrictions. The appointment was later confirmed by a letter of commission signed by Edward VI, giving the duke power to govern until the young monarch reached the age of eighteen. Seymour was born in 1506 and was the son of Sir John Seymour, a prominent courtier of Henry VIII, and Margery Wentworth, who was a descendent of King Edward III. In 1536 his sister, Jane Seymour, became the third wife of Henry VIII and through her influence Edward was named Earl of Hertford and Warden of the Scottish Marches. Through his close association to the Tudor court, he gained the favor of the king and was richly rewarded for his administrative and military skills. The earl served the Tudor crown as commander of campaigns against France and Scotland, winning widespread repute for his martial triumphs. He was responsible for the brutal sacking of Edinburgh in 1544 and later the energetic defense of Boulogne against the attacks of the French. He was an advocate of the Protestant Reformation and supported an independent church in England.

In the aftermath of Henry VIII's death, on January 31, 1547, Edward VI was brought to London from Enfield and housed in the royal apartments at the Tower to prepare for his coronation. Following the burial of his father at Windsor, on Saturday, February 19, the monarch rode to Westminster Abbey in an elaborate procession dressed in a gown of gold cloth over a vibrant white jacket trimmed with silver and decorated with diamonds and pearls. His horse was richly adorned with a red satin cover embroidered with pearls and gold. On the progress to the abbey, the streets were lined with magnificent plays, pageants, decorations and displays, celebrating Edward VI's succession and depicting the power and grandeur of his monarchy. After spending the night at Westminster, on the following day he was anointed by Archbishop Thomas Cranmer as the absolute ruler, who was answerable for his actions to only God and not the people as in past enthronement ceremonies. In the lavish ritual the king was invested with three separate crowns by Seymour and Cranmer. The service was followed by a large banquet at Westminster Hall and two days of jousting, military tournaments, plays and feasting.

Following Edward VI's coronation ceremony, Edward Seymour moved decisively to solidify his personal rule. Soon after his appointment as lord protector, he ordered the arrest of the lord chancellor, Thomas Wriothesley of Southampton, who was aggressively opposing his assumption of power and obstructing his policy initiatives. To further consolidate his primacy, in early March 1547 the sixteen member regency was replaced with a Privy Council of seven nobles and clerics, who were chosen by the protector. The new council soon acted to expand the supremacy of Edward Seymour by granting him authority to govern as near absolute ruler. From his position of dominance, he gained jurisdiction over Edward VI, appointing loyal supporters to his household and totally controlling his access and activities. The king was now tutored by zealous Protestants, who energetically advanced the doctrine of the new religion.

With his reign unquestioned, Edward Somerset directed his domestic policy toward the advancement of the anti-papist movement. There had been earlier local attacks against the traditional Catholic rituals, which had been approved by Somerset's government. However, in the summer of 1547 the protector ordered a royal visitation to every church to promote Bible readings and services in English instead of Latin and the outlawing of iconic worship. The use of the rosary and candles was prohibited and veneration of all images, including stained glass and statues of saints, was banned.

While Edward Seymour continued to enforce the doctrines of the reformist movement to advance England as a fully Protestant kingdom, during the summer of 1547 preparations for a massive land and sea invasion of Scotland were hastily made. In Scotland the widow of James V, Mary of Guise, had regained supremacy over the regency government of her daughter, Queen Mary I, and had negotiated a treaty of alliance with the Valois court, which threatened English interest in the north and in France. As a result of Seymour's earlier campaign in 1544 much of the Scottish Lowlands remained under English subjugation and the Tudor regime was determined to expand its control over the entire realm by force of arms. The Somerset duke assumed command of the army and in late August reached Berwick, while the fleet sailed up the coast toward Edinburgh. To avoid war, he offered peace if the Stewart council accepted a marriage agreement between Edward VI and Queen Mary I. When the proposal was ignored, the English marched toward Edinburgh, where on September 10 they encountered the waiting Stewart troops led by James Hamilton, Earl of Arran, at Pinkie Cleugh. The battle began when the undisciplined and poorly commanded Scots abandoned their strong defensive position to charge wildly into the strength of Somerset's forces. The well placed Tudor artillery decimated Hamilton's ranks as his soldiers panicked and deserted the melee. As the Scots fled the field, the English cavalry attacked to completely destroy the Stewart army. In the aftermath of the Pinkie Cleugh victory, the duke occupied southern Scotland and garrisoned the strategic strongholds with his troops.

Shortly after securing control over the southern Scottish lordships, Somerset returned to London to confront the growing insurrection of his brother, Thomas Seymour. Despite his earlier appointment as lord high admiral and grants of rich estates, Thomas demanded the governorship of his nephew and a larger role in the government. Following the death of Henry VIII, Thomas Seymour had defied the protector by marrying the dowager queen, Catherine Parr, to create an early environment of hostility between the two brothers. The belligerence was further increased after Catherine's death in childbirth, when Seymour attempted to expand his power by arranging his marriage to the king's half-sister, Elizabeth. While the Somerset duke was in Scotland, Thomas formed a party in opposition with several members of the Privy Council and tried to discredit his brother. He attempted to gain favor and influence over Edward VI by winning his friendship with gifts and money. The lord high admiral encouraged his nephew to dissolve the protectorship and assume personal rule but his advances were rejected by the monarch, who remained loyal to the duke and his council.

Thwarted by his failed intrigues to gain power, Seymour forged a military league with numerous high nobles and began to recruit troops and acquire weapons for armed revolt. To provide financial funding for his planned insurrection, he gained the support of Sir William Sharington, who was treasurer of the Bristol Mint. Through his father-in-law, John Bourchier, chancellor of the exchequer, Sharington had earlier met and befriended Thomas Seymour. When Thomas's sister, Jane, became the third wife of Henry VIII, Sir William used his influence with the Seymour family to acquire positions in the royal household, quickly rising to high offices. Sharington later became a large land holder in Wilshire and member of Parliament for Heytesburg and Bramber. In 1546 he was appointed as master of the newly reestablished mint at Bristol, which was the only facility besides London authorized to produce gold coins. At the coronation ceremony of Edward VI, he was knighted and served in Parliament as a nobleman from his shire.

The admiral had earlier used his influence to protect Sir William from prosecution on charges of forgery and now in need of money, he induced him to counterfeit coins for his conspiracy. Sharington agreed to forge enough money to keep ten thousand soldiers in the field for a month. With the cash from the Bristol Mint, Thomas Seymour fortified his stronghold at Holt and prepared to kidnap Edward VI, who was to be imprisoned at his castle. On

January 16, 1549, he broke into the royal apartments and attempted to seize his nephew. However, his plot ended in failure and the lord high admiral was arrested. He was tried before the Privy Council with Elizabeth and Edward VI testifying against him. A bill of attainder was introduced in Parliament by Somerset and on March 5, 1549, Thomas Seymour was declared guilty of high treason. Two weeks later he was executed at Tower Hill. The insurrection of his brother resulted in serious repercussions for Edward Seymour, weakening his hold on the kingdom and threatening to undermine his supremacy as absolute ruler.

Under the leadership of Edward Seymour, the government of Edward VI had begun to enforce extensive Parliamentary reforms into the realm to alter the theology, institutions and practices of the English church along more Protestant lines. The changes were widely unpopular in the southwest, which remained loyal to the Catholic Church of Rome. After religious processions and pilgrimages were barred, the king's regime ordered its royal agents to remove all symbols of the old faith. In April William Boyd was sent to destroy the Catholic images in Cornwall but his presence sparked a local rebellion, ending with his murder at Holston. Seven of the rioters were later arrested and executed for their treason, but the region remained hostile to any revisions to their church rituals. In the following year Parliament passed the Act of Uniformity, which made it illegal to use the Latin Prayer Book. In June the new Edwardian Common Prayer Book, written by Archbishop Cranmer, was introduced into practice in the county of Devon at the village of Sampford Courtenay but the congregation refused to allow its usage, forcing the priest to perform mass in Latin. The revolt quickly spread through northern Devon and into Cornwall. The rebels demanded the restoration of traditional religious images, ceremonies, holy water and bread and the elimination of the new prayer book. As the strength of the uprising grew, the Cornishmen joined their forces with the Devon insurgents to defy the king and attack his city of Exeter.

With the southwest in revolt, Edward VI and his counselors sent Lord John Russell, first Earl of Bedford, to relieve the siege at Exeter. Russell had served with distinction as a diplomat and soldier during the reigns of Henry VII and his son. During the English invasion of France in 1513, he took part in the captures of Therouanne and Tournai and later was knighted for his military skills during the attack at Morlaix in Brittany. Russell was made a privy counselor in 1536 and helped to suppress the Pilgrimages of Grace uprising in Yorkshire. He developed a close friendship with Henry VIII and was appointed lord of the Council of the West, lord admiral and high steward for Cornwall. In the campaign against Boulogne in 1545, Lord Russell was named to command the army's vanguard and participated in the seizure of the French fortress. After the death of Henry VIII, he became a member of the new regency council for Edward VI's government and in January 1549 was created Earl of Bedford.

As the Bedford earl approached Exeter, the rebel commander, Sir Humphrey Arundel, blocked his advance at Fenny Bridge, and in the ensuing battle the loyalists were compelled to retreat. However, when the earl was reinforced with the one thousand German mercenaries of Lord William Gray, the attack was resumed. After two bloody and hard fought victories with thousands of Catholic supporters killed, Russell's army of over eight thousand men-under-arms destroyed the remnants of the rogues at Sampford Courtenay to restore the king's rule. Arundel escaped the onslaught but was soon captured and taken to London, where he was executed for treason in the Tower.

While Lord John Russell was suppressing the rebels in Devon, in the east central county of Norfolk a new revolt erupted over agrarian grievances. The dissidents were protesting the corrupt government, high rent and mismanagement of the land by the local nobles and were led by a Norwick tanner, Robert Kett. The rebellion had been sparked on July 6, 1549, after a riot broke out at Wymondham during an illegal celebration honoring the sainthood of Thomas Becket. The civil disorder quickly spread to other towns and on July 12 the rioters marched against Norwick to enforce their demands. As they approached the city, the mayor closed the gates, compelling Kett to establish an armed camp at nearby Mousehold Heath. His ranks soon swelled to over fifteen thousand as Norfolk artisans and peasants joined his uprising. After ten days the insurgents' food supplies became depleted, forcing Kett to lead an attack against Norwick. After a hard fought battle, he overcame the resistance of the royalists to gain control of the city.

As the insurrection spread into the central eastern counties, Edward VI ordered William Parr, marquess of Northampton, to restore order. On July 31 he advanced against the rebels at Norwick but his ill planned and poorly led attack quickly failed. With the dissidents still in defiance of the Tudor crown, the Earl of Warwick, John Dudley, was sent north by the king with a large army, including German and Spanish mercenaries, to crush the rebellion. John Dudley was born in 1504 and was the eldest son of Edmund Dudley and Elizabeth Grey. After his father was executed for treason against the government of Henry VIII, he was raised and educated in the household of Sir Edward Guildford. John was a distinguished Tudor diplomat, admiral and soldier, serving during the reigns of Henry VIII and Edward VI. Dudley was a court favorite, excelling in jousting, archery and combat tournaments and gained widespread recognition for his martial successes. He participated in Charles Brandon's 1523 campaign in France, winning a knighthood for his bravery and military skills. Sir John was a member of the royal household, rising to high offices and serving as an envoy to France and Spain. He later was appointed lord high admiral and became a member of the Privy Council. During Edward Seymour's 1544 Scottish invasion, Sir Dudley commanded the English navy, taking part in the sacking of Edinburgh. In the following year he successfully directed fleet operations against the French sea attacks in southern England. John Dudley was a close friend and confidant of Henry VIII and supported his initiatives to reform the English church. After the death of Henry VIII, he was elected to the regency council and promoted the assumption of power by Edward Seymour. In 1547 Sir John was rewarded for his many triumphs and loyalty to the Tudor throne by his appointment to the earldom of Warwick.

After arriving in Norfolk Sir John Dudley offered a pardon to the rebels if they agreed to peaceably disperse. When his overture was rejected, the earl stormed Norwick with an elite contingent of German mercenaries and compelled Kett to flee the city with the remnants of his troops. Two days later after reorganizing his army, Kett counterattacked the royalists at Dussindale but possessing an overwhelming military might Dudley destroyed the insurgent forces. Robert Kett escaped from the onslaught but was later captured and taken to London for trial on charges of treason. He was declared guilty and hanged at Norwich Castle to discourage further local sedition.

By late 1549 Edward Seymour's continued rule as lord protector became increasingly threatened by the relentless attacks of the Privy Council against him. His invasion and occupation of Scotland had resulted in an unsustainable drain on the royal coffers and his slow and ineffective responses to the recent rebellions had given cause to the king's advisors to plot his downfall, drawing John Dudley of Warwick into their insurrection. When Somerset received the reports of the growing conspiracy, he withdrew to Hampton Court and under the signature of Edward VI began to raise troops, while ordering Lord John Russell to come to his aid. However, Russell ignored his call to arms and joined the insurgency of John Dudley. By October 11 with the military might of the Earl of Bedford backing him, Dudley gained control of the council and ordered the arrest of the lord protector. Seymour was taken to the

Tower and charged with negligence, personal enrichment and governing without the consent of the council. Under interrogation he confessed to the list of charges and was imprisoned in the Tower of London.

In the aftermath of his rise to power, John Dudley was elected lord president of the Privy Council and to solidify his rule appointed new loyal allies to his regime. However, unlike the Somerset duke, he was not empowered with unrestricted authority and was compelled to govern with the consent of the counselors. To better control Edward VI's activities and access, the earl reorganized the royal household, replacing Seymour's sympathizers with his trustworthy friends. In 1549 the Tudor king began to attend meetings with his counselors and play a larger role in his government. Warwick chose new tutors for Edward VI to further his education in preparation for his assumption of the kingship. Dudley developed a close and friendly relationship with the king and greatly influenced his political training.

As the king's uncle, the Duke of Somerset still retained a large base of popular support and during the spring of 1550 the Warwick earl was forced to arrange his release from confinement and return to the Privy Council. Despite their apparent reconciliation, relations between the two rivals quickly grew increasingly hostile, as Edward Seymour began to plot his restoration to power. He soon attracted political sympathizers to his conspiracy and attempted to obstruct and defeat the earl's policies. As the rumors of his intrigues grew, in October 1551 to retain the loyalty of the nobles, Dudley created numerous new peerages, raising his ally, Lord Henry Grey, to the duchy of Suffolk and creating the Northumberland duchy for himself. Nevertheless, Somerset continued to attack him, and after he ordered the murder of the lord president his arrest was authorized by the council. After a trial by his peers at Westminster Hall, Edward Seymour was declared guilty of plotting rebellion and executed on January 22, 1552. With the elimination of his closest contender, Northumberland now ruled with near absolute supremacy.

The Franco-Scottish initiatives of Edward Seymour had resulted in an unsustainable drain on the royal treasury, forcing the lord president to decrease costs. After Henry II of France declared war on England in August 1549 and launched an attack against the Tudor held enclave at Boulogne, Dudley agreed to open talks for a permanent settlement to the hostilities between the two kingdoms to reduce court expenditures. In March 1550 the Treaty of Boulogne was signed with the English pledging to abandon the French stronghold for the payment of an annual indemnity. The accord was to be sealed with the marriage of Edward VI to the Valois princess, Elizabeth. To further lower royal expenditures and end the threat of war with Scotland, Dudley withdrew the English troops from the occupied Lowlands and negotiated a treaty of peace with the regency government of Queen Mary I. However, the Tudor crown retained its large presence in Calais, despite the high cost. A new policy of neutrality was initiated with France and Emperor Charles V, which was designed to keep England at peace with the continental powers.

While Northumberland's foreign initiatives had lowered crown expenditures, the English economy was still beset with slow growth, escalating inflation and debased coinage. To bring financial stability to Edward VI's kingdom and reduce the risk of popular rebellion, Dudley reorganized the treasury function by appointing loyal and competent officials to restore confidence in the monetary system and expand agriculture and business growth. The coinage was established at a set metal standard to end the practice of debasement. To decrease corruption and enhance the acquisition of taxes, the king's government centralized the revenue collection procedures. In 1552 there were finally good harvests after years of poor crops and with inflation diminishing, the economic expansion resumed. The cost reduction measures were energetically continued and with tax payments rising, the deficit in the royal treasury began to fall.

To expand international business, the Tudor regime encouraged trading with the west coast of Africa, sending ships to establish commercial ties. Utilizing the earlier discoveries of John Cabot, the English council began to sponsor explorations to the New World, funding voyages to the northern coastline of the new continent. In 1552 Edward VI chartered the Company of Merchant Adventurers in London to discover a Northeast Passage to China. In the following year Sir Hugh Willoughby and Richard Chancellor sailed with a small fleet to search for the passage. During the voyage into the North Sea, Chancellor in the *Edward Bonaventure* was separated from the other two vessels during a storm but continued eastward to discover the entrance to the White Sea. After anchoring in the port of Archangel, he was taken to the court of Czar Ivan IV in Moscow. The czar was anxious to open sea trading routes with the west and issued letters of commerce, inviting English merchants to his realm. While Richard Chancellor was establishing contacts with Russia, Willoughby became entrapped in the winter ice on the Lapland coast and died with the crews of his ships. As the policies of Dudley produced a growing prosperity, increased foreign commerce and smaller price rises, the reign of Edward VI became more popular and secure.

Edward VI was raised as a Protestant and became fully devoted to the teachings of the new religion. In 1552 the Common Prayer Book was revised to include the demands of the reformist for more liberalization and the king supported its implementation. Unlike the introduction of the earlier 1549 Prayer Book, the reaction to the second edition was largely muted with little dissent resulting from the nobles and populace. Following the acceptance of the revised book, Edward VI empowered his council to make a new inventory of the remaining church plate, wealth and land endowments. In 1553 after the visitations were completed, the Tudor king ordered the confiscation of the property to supplement his treasury. As a devout Protestant, he encouraged the greater use of liberal religious doctrines and suppression of the Catholic rituals. However, while he approved the dissolution of the office of bishop, Archbishop Thomas Cranmer intervened to block his government's initiative. Nevertheless, Edward VI remained firmly committed to the advancement of the anti-papist dogma.

As the appropriation of church property resumed, relations between Edward VI and his half-sister, Lady Mary, rapidly deteriorated over religious differences. Mary was as zealous about her Catholic faith as the king was committed to Protestantism, which created an atmosphere of hostility. In defiance of the crown, she continued to observe mass in Latin with the traditional prayer book, while her half-brother demanded her obedience to his laws. She refused to comply and threatened to invoke the protection of her cousin, Emperor Charles V, if religious freedom was not granted to her. Confronted with the risk of war with the formidable Habsburg Empire and local Catholic insurrection, the monarchy was forced to permit her the use of the religious ceremony according to the old rituals. However, Mary was restricted to mass in her private chapel with only a few close courtiers and friends.

In February 1553 Edward VI became ill with a prolonged fever, which persisted for several months, rendering him increasingly weak and frail. As his condition deteriorated, he developed a chronic lung infection and seemed incapable of recovery. Under his father's will and the Parliamentary Act of Succession, at his death without issue the Tudor throne passed to Mary. As a devout Protestant, the succession of his Catholic half-sister was unacceptable to the king and measures were taken to change the order of inheritance. Edward VI personally wrote *My Devise for the Succession,* which excluded both Mary and Elizabeth as illegitimate daughters of Henry VIII and transferred the crown to his cousin Lady Jane Grey and her male heirs. Lady Jane was born in Leicestershire in October 1537 and was the eldest of the three daughters of Duke Henry Grey of Suffolk and Frances Brandon. Through her mother's lineage, she was directly related to the reigning Tudor dynasty. She received a broad based scholarly education and excelled in her studies. Her father actively encouraged the English Reformation movement and through him Jane became committed to Protestantism. In 1546 Lady Jane Grey was sent to live as a ward of Queen Catherine Parr and in her royal household she met and became friends with her cousin, Prince Edward Tudor. To advance the position of her family at court, on May 21, 1553, she was married to the fourth son of the lord president, Lord Guildford Dudley.

To give legality to the altered will of Henry VIII and the Act of Succession, letters patent were written authorizing Edward VI to exercise his rights to appoint Lady Jane Grey as his heir apparent. The document was signed by the Privy Council and other prominent members of the government, including Archbishop Cranmer and Duke John Dudley. The Northumberland duke, as a committed Protestant and head of the Tudor administration, had the most to lose if Lady Mary ascended to the crown and to enhance Jane's stature he aggressively encouraged the acceptance of the patent by the lords, church and Parliament. On June 19 writs were issued, summoning a new Parliament to meet in September to give added legitimacy to the succession of Lady Jane by approving the revised inheritance. Dudley attempted to buttress his position as lord president by granting new estates and titles to gain the support of the prominent noble families. To prevent rebellion in defense of Mary's claim to the throne, he ordered the recruitment of troops and reinforcement of the strategic strongholds.

As the legal arrangements for the assumption of power by Jane Grey were finalized, the king remained confined to his apartments at Greenwich Palace. On June 27, 1553, he appeared briefly in public for the last time from the window of the palace, as his health steadily deteriorated. On July 6 Edward VI died at age fifteen and after a reign of six years. His death was kept secret for four days to prepare for the proclamation of Lady Jane Grey's accession to the Tudor throne. Edward VI was later buried at Westminster Abbey on August 8 in a magnificent funeral ceremony.

In the immediate aftermath of the death of her cousin, on July 10, 1553, Lady Jane Grey was taken by boat from Syon House in a grand procession to the royal apartments in the Tower of London and proclaimed queen of England. However, few lords or towns rallied to her assumption of the throne as support for Mary steadily grew. John Dudley with three thousand troops attempted to enforce Jane's acceptance as sovereign but most nobles and towns remained loyal to Mary. While the Duke of Northumberland was in Cambridge, London abandoned Jane and accepted Lady Mary as the lawful heir of Edward VI. She now had sufficient political and military backing to ride into London in a triumphant procession, taking control of the kingdom and ordering the arrest of Dudley. With the attempted usurpation of Dudley's faction crushed, Parliament was summoned to formally recognize Mary Tudor as the rightful successor, while revoking Jane's claim to the monarchy. Lady Jane Grey ruled for only nine days and remained imprisoned in the Tower until her execution for treason on February 12, 1554. Mary I officially succeeded her half-brother, Edward VI, on October 1, 1553, in Westminster Abbey, when she was anointed and crowned as queen of England.

Sources

Loach. *Edward VI*. Skidmore. *Edward VI*.

Mary I, 1516–1553–1558

In July 1553 the Protestant king, Edward VI, died childless and was succeeded by his Catholic half-sister, Mary I, who reigned during a period of great political and religious turmoil as the tenth English sovereign of the Renaissance epoch. Princess Mary was born on Monday, February 18, 1516, at Greenwich Palace in Kent and was the daughter of Henry VIII and Queen Catherine of Aragon. She was the only surviving issue of the king's first marriage, which was beset with numerous miscarriages, stillbirths and early infant deaths. On February 21 the Tudor princess was christened in the friar's church near the palace with prominent noblemen and ladies serving as godparents and sponsors. As the only legitimate child of the monarch, Mary was acknowledged as successor apparent and later invested with the title of Princess of Wales. Soon after her birth, she was separated from her father and mother but often visited them and spent the religious holidays at their royal court. Henry VIII created a separate household for his daughter with a small personal and administrative staff, including a chamberlain, treasurer and priest. While the Tudor monarch saw little of his heir, he was devoted to her health and care, personally appointing her tutors. Renowned scholars were chosen for her humanist education and as a gifted student Mary excelled in her studies of reading, writing, religion, French, Italian, philosophy and the social graces of music, dancing and court etiquette. She was encouraged to take outside exercises, learning to hunt and ride horses. Like her father, the princess was fond of music and learned to skillfully play the lute and virginal. In 1525 at the age of nine, she was sent to live at Ludlow Castle near the Welsh border with a large body of retainers and experienced counselors to govern the marchlands as Princess of Wales. However, in the following year she was again at court to meet the French ambassador, Admiral William Gouffier of Bonnivet, who was in England to discuss her marriage to Francis I. Similar to two prior marital negotiations, the treaty was never ratified due to the rapidly changing political environment in Europe.

While Princess Mary's birth had been preceded by many failed attempts to produce a male heir, Henry VIII was encouraged that the next child would be a healthy son. However, several additional miscarriages followed and by 1525 he began to consider a divorce, convinced that Queen Catherine could not give him a male successor. In 1527 he asserted that his marriage to the queen was illegal by church law and the failure to acquire a legitimate heir was God's punishment for the sin of marrying his deceased brother's wife. His quest for an annulment was given an added incentive after he fell in love with Anne Boleyn. With Anne now in residence at court and Catherine banished, the relationship between Henry VIII and his first queen increasingly deteriorated with Mary seeing them less frequently. The princess with her household was sent to live at Richmond Palace and later New Hall in Essex. Remaining isolated from the royal court, she had little contact with her mother but was occasionally visited by the king.

To protect her daughter's succession rights to England, the queen defied Henry VIII's demands for a divorce and refused to admit their marriage was unlawful, appealing directly to the papacy for support. With the annulment decision delayed in Rome, under the influence of his lord chancellor, Thomas Cromwell, the king dissolved the Catholic Church and had himself appointed supreme head of the English church under the Parliamentary Act of Appeals. In May 1533, acting under the act, the archbishop of Canterbury declared the sovereign's union with Catherine void and his recent marriage to Anne Boleyn legal. Anne was anointed and crowned queen in June, while Catherine was virtually imprisoned in the castle at Kimbolton with a small personal staff, and her daughter remained isolated in Essex away from court. Catherine stayed secluded in a small room and saw only her maids of honor, Spanish retainers, priest and physician. The castle grounds were guarded and access to her restricted on orders from Henry VIII. By late 1535 she had become seriously ill from the prolonged mental stress of the divorce, loneliness and melancholia, dying on January 7.

Under the Act of Succession passed by Parliament in 1534, the children of Henry VIII and his second wife were made heirs to the Tudor throne and Mary declared illegitimate. When Anne Boleyn gave birth to Elizabeth, the king's eldest daughter was compelled under duress to renounce her title as royal princess and become recognized as Lady Mary. However, she refused to publicly accept the Acts of Appeal and Succession and regarded her father's second marriage as illegal. Henry VIII grew increasingly angered by her continued defiance and first reacted by reducing her personal staff before forcing her to live at Hatfield House in the household of Elizabeth. Mary was disliked by Queen Anne and had a hostile and antagonist relationship with her stepmother. Under the influence of the queen, Henry VIII deprived his eldest daughter of her personal staff and made her serve as a lady-in-waiting to Princess Elizabeth. At Hatfield House Mary remained in a menial position and was frequently ill from the stresses of her isolation and harsh treatment. When Queen Catherine died, the king denied Mary permission to attend the funeral and refused to permit her the few objects of value bequeathed from her mother. As her confinement grew worse, she initiated plans to escape to the continent with the encouragement and help of the Habsburg ambassador of her cousin, Charles V, but the scheme became too dangerous and was abandoned.

While Mary languished alone at Hatfield, Anne suffered two stillbirths and a miscarriage, giving Henry VIII little hope of producing a male successor with her. When she miscarried again in 1536, he became determined to dissolve their union and take a third wife, turning his attention to Jane Seymour. After establishing a royal commission to find evidence of treason, Anne was arrested and charged with adultery and incest. She was declared guilty after a short trial and beheaded on May 19, 1536. Shortly after the execution, the monarch was married to Jane Seymour in the expectation of finally having a son.

Unlike Anne Boleyn, the new queen was not threatened by the presence of Lady Mary and encouraged Henry VIII to reunite with her. He finally agreed to accept letters from her but rejected any reconciliation until she fully complied with his terms. She again refused to admit her illegitimacy, despite increasing intimidation. However, after her life became endangered by the threats of the crown, she signed a new proclamation from the royal council, acknowledging that her mother's marriage was illegal and accepted Henry VIII as supreme head of the English Church. In spite of consenting to the decree, she soon asked the imperial ambassador to obtain a secret papal dispensation for ratifying the papers under duress. In July Mary's father and Queen Jane visited her at Hunsdon House but their meeting did not result in a return to full favor. Nevertheless, she received an increase in her living allowance and the household staff was enlarged. Lady Mary was permitted greater freedom to travel and receive frequent guests. In the absence of a male heir, on August 30 she was proclaimed successor apparent to the throne.

While relations with her father had dramatically improved, they soon became more polarized when rebellion erupted in Yorkshire, demanding the legitimization of Lady Mary and restoration of the Catholic rituals. The monarch increasingly feared that Mary would become the center of a popular uprising, threatening his continued reign. He ordered a close surveillance on his daughter and restricted her travels. However, his concerns were alleviated when Queen Jane delivered a healthy son, Edward, on October 12, 1537. With a successor whose legitimacy was not questioned, Mary was relegated to second-in-line to the throne. She now regained more favor with the king and played a prominent role in the funeral of the queen, who died shortly after the birth of her son. Nevertheless, the Tudor lady was still restricted largely to her own residences and spent her time practicing her musical instruments, reading and playing cards with her courtiers.

In July 1538 Francis I and Emperor Charles V personally met in southern France to sign a truce to end years of war. With the two former foes now at peace, England began to search in Europe for a new ally, exploiting the marriages of Henry VIII and Lady Mary to secure a coalition. Talks were initiated with the Duke of Cleves for the union of his sister, Anne, to the English king, while separate negotiations were held with the duchy of Bavaria for a marital treaty between Mary and the Protestant Duke Philip. In December 1539 Philip arrived in England and visited the Tudor lady at Enfield, presenting her with a cross of diamonds and pearls as a symbol of his esteem. She preferred not to wed a Protestant but indicated to the royal council her father's wishes would be obeyed. While the deliberations with Bavaria continued, in January 1540 Henry VIII was married to Anne of Cleves with both his daughters participating in the wedding ceremony. The king was greatly disappointed with the appearance and physical features of Anne and initially rejected their union but for reasons of state was compelled to finally agree. However, after six months he had the marriage dissolved, following the breakup of détente between France and Charles V and after finding just legal grounds.

Even before his separation from Anne of Cleves was finalized, Henry VIII had fallen under the spell of the young and beautiful Catherine Howard. After Parliament ratified the annulment of his fourth marriage, on July 28, 1540, he was wed to Catherine. Unlike her relationship with her father's third wife, Mary disliked the new queen and remained away from court confined to her personal residences. However, the new queen had continued her promiscuous affairs with many of the courtiers and in the summer of 1541 Henry VIII was informed of her infidelities. He ordered her arrest and after a brief trial she was executed on charges of treason.

Following the execution of Queen Catherine, relations between Lady Mary and her father again improved and she was invited back to court. The king and his daughter grew closer after his sixth marriage to Catherine Parr. The new queen and her step-daughter became close friends and shared a common interest and bond in education and religion. Catherine showed her great kindness and influenced her husband to increase Mary's living allowance. With a secure environment and without the daily stresses of loneliness and melancholia, the Tudor lady's health steadily improved and she finally found a period of happiness. By late 1546 Henry VIII had grown increasingly ill and summoned Mary to his deathbed, asking her to take care of his only son. On January 28, 1547, he died and under his will and earlier Parliamentary Act of Succession, Edward Tudor and his heirs were recognized as successors to the Tudor crown followed by Mary and Elizabeth. With her formal acknowledgement as heir apparent, Mary gained widespread support and acceptance among the nobles and populace.

On February 20, 1547, the nine-year-old Edward VI was crowned king of England at Westminster Abbey. A sixteen member regency council was created under Henry VIII's will to rule for his minor son, but Edward Seymour quickly formed a political faction of supporters and seized power to govern in the name of the king as lord protector. From his position as near absolute ruler, he gained jurisdiction over the monarch and controlled his access and activities. Seymour was dedicated to the suppression of the Church of Rome in England and appointed tutors of the radical religion to educate Edward VI. Under their strong influence, he became committed to the advancement of the new theology in his kingdom. Lady Mary remained a devout Catholic and her half-brother's anti-papist beliefs created a growing division between them. As the atmosphere at the royal court became increasingly hostile, she continued to live at her personal residences, only visiting Edward VI occasionally. For the next two years the Tudor lady stayed isolated with her private household of Spanish retainers and friends. She again began to suffer from mental anguish, loneliness and despair, as her health declined.

While Lady Mary remained away from court, the government of Edward VI aggressively implemented new reforms to the English church, making it illegal to hear mass or use prayer books not approved by the royal council. Under the leadership of the lord protector, Parliament passed the Statute of Uniformity, which increased the penalties for disobedience to the king's laws. As a devout Catholic, Lady Mary was threatened by the new decrees and carefully avoided offering any public support for the old religion, while expressing her loyalty to her half-brother. To safeguard her freedom to worship, she sought the protection of her cousin, Charles V, who pledged to intervene if religious freedom was denied to her. Throughout the Catholic suppression campaign, she was faithful to her beliefs, hearing mass in her private apartments. However, while not practicing her faith in public, she continued to defiantly guard her Catholic rights and directly challenged the regime by adhering to the church laws of her father.

In October 1549 Edward Seymour was overthrown as lord protector by a political coalition of privy counselors led by John Dudley, Earl of Warwick, who was elected lord president. With the government under his control, he rigorously renewed the restructuring of the English Church, demanding that the king's laws be obeyed without exception. Lady Mary received letters signed by her half-brother, asking her to abide by his statutes by abandoning her Catholic beliefs. As the danger escalated, she again considered escaping to the imperial court and appealed to Charles V to make the arrangements. However, Warwick was soon informed of the plot and initiated measures to prevent her rescue, forcing Mary to remain in England.

Following the failed escape attempt, Dudley pressed Mary to fully submit to Edward VI's wishes. In March 1551 the Tudor lady was summoned to the Privy Council and ordered to obey the king's laws but she refused to change her faith. She appealed to the imperial court for protection and Charles V threatened to declare war if his cousin was denied her religious freedom. In August the English regime ignored the emperor's warning and sent members of the Privy Council to compel Mary's obedience with the statutes. After she again declined, the king's advisors demanded her compliance but indicated no force would be used to make her adopt the new religion, if her worship was restricted to her private chapel with only a few courtiers.

In the aftermath of her encounter with the Privy Council, Mary remained in her household with her friends and ladies. She was permitted the freedom to travel and frequently entertained guests. While she stayed isolated with her small court, the health of Edward VI steadily declined from the prolonged effects of fever and chronic lung infection. In February 1553 she visited her half-brother at Westminster Palace and was well received by him and his counselors. During the following months the monarch grew increasingly weak and frail and seemed incapable of recovering. Under the will of Henry VIII and the Parliamentary Act of Succession, the English crown passed to Lady Mary and her heirs should Edward VI died without issue. The accession of a Catholic queen was unacceptable to the Protestant king and Privy Council and initiatives were taken to alter the order of inheritance. Under the influence of the lord president, John Dudley, the king was persuaded to write *My Devise for the Succession*, which excluded both Mary and Elizabeth as illegitimate and assigned the Tudor throne to his cousin Lady Jane Grey and her male heirs.

On July 6, 1553, Edward VI died and four days later Lady Jane Grey was taken to the

Tower of London to prepare for her coronation as queen of England. When Lady Mary was informed of the king's death, she immediately departed from Hunsdon and traveled to Kenninghall in Norfolk to raise troops in defense of her inheritance. From Kenninghall she wrote to the Privy Council, asserting her birthrights and proclaiming her succession to the throne. As the reports of her arrival in Norfolk spread, many of the local nobles with their private militias began to rally to her cause, while her support among the populace steadily grew. As her military might escalated, John Dudley mustered an army in London in the name of Queen Jane Grey to capture Mary and crush the growing rebellion. While he made his final campaign preparations, Lady Mary assembled her forces at Framlingham Castle in Suffolk, which by late July had swelled to over twenty thousand knights and peasant soldiers. Remaining in Suffolk, sympathy for the Tudor lady's assumption of the crown spread from town to town, as they recognized her as queen. When Jane Grey's Protestant troops advanced to Cambridge, Mary rode into her armed camp to give encouragement and confidence to her army for the expected battle with Dudley.

In Suffolk Mary's army grew larger and stronger every day while the lord president was confronted by an expanding mutiny among his troops, who joined the ranks of the rebels. In London the Privy Council withdrew its support for Dudley and ordered his arrest. On July 19 the counselors abandoned Lady Jane Grey and proclaimed Mary queen of England. Following the rapid collapse of Jane Grey's regime, on August 3, 1553, Mary rode triumphantly into London preceded by nearly a thousand armed knights. She was dressed in a purple gown richly decorated with precious stones, gold and pearls and was enthusiastically greeted with shouts of "Long Live Our Queen." After receiving the symbols of office from the city's lord mayor, she went to the state apartments in the Tower to prepare for the establishment of her new government and the funeral of her half-brother.

Following the Protestant funeral service on August 8, 1553, for Edward VI, Queen Mary I traveled to Richmond Palace to begin the task of asserting her power and assembling a new regime. The queen had little personal experience in government and depended on her council for support. Her advisors were drawn from her faithful household officers, previously disgraced officials from the prior monarchies and selected members of Edward VI's reign. She relied on her lord chancellor, Bishop Stephen Gardiner of Winchester, and Lord William Paget, who assumed dominant roles in her early administration. As a devout Catholic, one of her first decrees was to restore the mass to religious services, but the reintroduction of the ritual caused widespread dissent, especially in largely Protestant London and the southern lordships, compelling her to limit any future initiatives. While relying heavily on her council, she sought the advice of Charles V, who cautioned against any sudden radical changes. While the queen remained at Richmond, John Dudley was captured and brought to London for trial. The hearings were held at Westminster, where Dudley made a full confession and begged for mercy. He was quickly found guilty and sentenced to the traitor's death of drawing, hanging and quartering. The queen later commuted the verdict to death by beheading.

In late September 1553 Mary I moved to London from Richmond to prepare for her coronation. On September 30 she left the Tower for Whitehall Palace preceded by over five hundred nobles and court officials. The queen was carried in a lavishly adorned litter drawn by six horses through streets richly decorated with displays, exhibitions and pageants, glorifying her succession to the throne. She was dressed in a long white robe trimmed in fur and gold and embellished with precious stones. After spending the night at Whitehall Palace, early the next morning she traveled the short distance to Westminster Abbey for the Catholic enthronement ceremony. Mary I was anointed with holy oil and invested with three separate crowns by the bishop of Winchester, Stephen Gardiner, as queen of England. The inauguration service was followed by a holy mass and later a magnificent banquet at Westminster Hall.

The coronation ceremony was followed four days later by the new queen's first Parliament. She had never approved the religious policies of her father or Edward VI and wanted to quickly restore the authority of Rome to her kingdom. Under the reigns of her two predecessors, Protestantism had firmly taken hold in many regions, compelling Mary I to accept only limited modifications to the statutes. The legislative assembly agreed to pass an act repealing Henry VIII's divorce from Queen Catherine of Aragon, which restored Mary I's legitimacy. The Houses of Commons and Lords also rescinded most of the religious laws of her half-brother, while the Edwardian Prayer Book was replaced by the Catholic service and clergy were again forbidden to marry. The statute increasing the penalties for disobedience to the royal laws was revoked. While the changes were modest by the queen's desires, they provoked strong dissent among the Protestants and Charles V continued to caution her to move slowly.

During the reigns of Henry VIII and Edward VI, numerous initiatives were made to negotiate the marriage of Mary I to European prince but all attempts ended in failure. With her assumption of the English crown, it was now necessary for her to quickly marry and produce a successor for reasons of religion and state. Her Privy Council proposed various English lords, while her Habsburg cousin advocated his son, Prince Philip of Spain. As Mary I continued to vacillate on making a decision, the imperial ambassador bribed and flattered Lord William Paget into supporting the cause of the Spanish prince. Influenced by the advice of Paget, the queen was finally convinced to choose Philip. Despite the initial opposition of her council and Parliament to a foreigner, they agreed to accept the Habsburg prince. In January 1554 a large Spanish delegation arrived in London to finalize the marriage treaty.

While the terms of the marital agreement were being resolved by the London and Brussels courts, the English people grew increasingly hostile to the queen's marriage to a foreign prince, resulting in the eruption of armed revolt. The opposition was led by four prominent Protestant noblemen, Sir Thomas Wyatt of Kent, Sir James Croft from Herefordshire, Sir Peter Crew from Devon and Duke Henry Grey of Suffolk, father of the deposed Queen Jane Grey. Under their planned insurrection, each of the lords was to raise a popular uprising in his region and unite to march on London to place Lady Jane Grey on the throne. However, the rebellions in the Midlands and west country failed and only Wyatt succeeded in mustering a large military force of over four thousand men.

As the rebels advanced from Kent, the queen's council sent Duke Thomas Howard of Norfolk with a small contingent of Londoners to suppress Wyatt but when five hundred of his troops deserted to the enemy, the remnants of the royal army were compelled to retreat. The road to the capital was now clear of defenders and Wyatt marched into the outskirts unopposed. At the approach of the dissidents, Mary I went to the Guildhall to encourage and rally her forces in defense of her monarchy. She ordered the bridges over the Thames River destroyed and the fortifications reinforced. Despite her initiatives, Wyatt repaired the bridge at Kingston and on February 7, 1544, launched his attack into the city. They encountered the waiting loyalists near Hyde Park but were outmaneuvered and destroyed. Wyatt and many of his soldiers were captured and imprisoned in the Tower. In spite of the risk to her life, the queen had remained in her capital, emboldening and supporting her royalists. In the aftermath of the failed Wyatt's Rebellion, Lady Jane Grey was implicated in her father's aborted uprising and Mary I signed her death warrant on February 8 to eliminate a symbol for future Protestant resistance. Wyatt and over fifty of his captains were convicted of treason and executed, while his remaining forces were pardoned after pledging allegiance to the queen.

In early March 1544 the imperial envoys returned to London to sign the final terms of the marriage treaty. After the agreement was ratified, Mary I was formally betrothed at Whitehall Palace on March 6 with the Flemish Count of Egmont acting as proxy for Philip. The Habsburg prince had never favored the Tudor union and continued to delay his departure from Spain. However, under the repeated exhortations of his father, he finally sailed from Corunna with a fleet of over two hundred ships and a large company of Spanish troops for protection against French sea raiders and as a display of his power and prestige. He arrived off the coast of Southampton in his flagship, *The Holy Ghost,* on July 19 and was greeted by Bishop Stephen Gardiner and a contingent of Catholic nobles. While he remained in the city, Mary I traveled to Winchester to prepare for the wedding ceremony. On July 23 the Habsburg prince left Southampton, riding through a heavy rain storm to Winchester, where he was first introduced to Mary I. Two days later Philip and the Tudor queen were married in Winchester Cathedral in a Catholic ritual of great magnificence with a rich mixture of secular pomp and spirituality. The wedding was followed by a great banquet with Philip and Mary I enthusiastically participating in the dancing and enjoying the musical performances. After spending a few days in the city, the royal party made a slow journey to London, staying at several palaces en route. On August 19 they entered the capital to be greeted with cheering crowds and lavish decorations.

Despite the concerns of Charles V, his son began to win the support and recognition of the English nobles with his charm and generous use of bribes. He quickly developed a close relationship with Mary I and they seemed to be happy together, despite their dissimilar cultural and age difference of eleven years. They were both deeply religious and devoted to the protection of the Church of Rome, while sharing a common interest in art, music and sculpture. As her consort, he was unable to assume power but was limited to only providing advice to the queen. Mary I pressed her council and Parliament to allow her husband to be crowned and govern as co-ruler. However, the Houses of Commons and Lords strongly opposed the assumption of the monarchy by a foreign prince, compelling Philip to serve as only an advisor.

After her succession to power, the queen's Catholic dominated Privy Council, led by Bishop Gardiner of Winchester, began measures to reverse the rise of Protestantism and restore the supremacy of the Catholic Church. At the encouragement of Mary I, in late 1554 Pope Julius III sent his personal legate, Cardinal Reginald Pole, to reestablish the Roman church in her realm. The cardinal was born in March 1500 at Stourton Castle in Staffordshire and was the son of Sir Richard Pole and Lady Margaret. Through his mother's lineage, he was directly related to the House of York and was a member of the royal dynasty. At an early age Pole exhibited an exceptional talent for learning, receiving his initial education at the Sheen Charterhouse before attending schools at Oxford and in Italy at the expense of Henry VIII. After his return to England, he entered the service of the Tudor regime, becoming a favorite of the court and was rewarded for his administrative skills with the grants of many wealthy church lands. When Henry VIII began his quest for a divorce from Queen Catherine of Aragon, Reginald Pole was sent to France to search for evidence to buttress the royal appeal to Rome. Following Pole's return to England, the king offered him the archbishopric of York for his support in the creation of a new independent English church. As a devout Catholic he disapproved of the break with Rome and chose exile to preserve his faith. Pole sailed to the continent, joining the Holy See of Rome, quickly rising to high offices and in 1536 was received into the clerical order and appointed a cardinal by Pope Paul III. The new cardinal continued to serve the papacy in various diplomatic and ministerial positions, working to rally the European Catholic powers against the Tudor kingdom.

With her assumption of the government accepted by the English people, in late 1554 Mary I summoned Cardinal Pole to England to reinstate the supremacy of the Catholic Church. On November 28 he appeared before Parliament to explain his mission of reuniting the Tudor kingdom with the Roman church in a spirit of benevolence and friendship. The Houses of Lords and Commons soon passed the Petition for Reconciliation with Rome, which repealed all the decrees limiting the authority of the papacy. The approval of the statute was followed by the cardinal's absolution for the realm's schismatic sins of the past two reigns. The return to the Catholic religion was greeted with calm as the majority of the population initially accepted the law of their queen. However, the Parliament also revived the heresy laws, giving the bishops the power to order the arrest and trial in the church courts of anyone suspected of anti–Catholic beliefs, which soon resulted in the eruption of new rebellions in support of the Protestant faith.

As the reports of the new anti–Protestant statutes spread through the realm, there were unorganized acts of violence against Catholics and their churches. A wave of new rumors circulated, inflaming the resistance to the queen. In response to the rising unrest, Mary I authorized the persecution of the heretics to restore her authority. In late January 1555 John Rogers of Saint Paul's Cathedral, Bishop John Hooper of Gloucester and several other prominent Protestant leaders were arrested on charges of breaking the religious laws and tried before the ecclesiastic court of Bishop Gardiner. They became the first of nearly three hundred reformers to be burned at the stake as punishment for their crimes against God. Many leading Protestants fled the kingdom and sought sanctuary in Germany and Switzerland. From the continent they unleashed a broad based propaganda campaign of books, poems, lampoons and pamphlets against the Tudor regime. The most influential of the publications was John Foxe's *Acts and Monuments of These Latter and Perilous Days,* which recorded the lives of the executed martyrs and their deaths in vivid detail. During the rest of the year Gardiner's court continued to try the accused Protestant radicals with the flames consuming Archbishop Thomas Cranmer in March 1556. As the number of executions grew, the Habsburg emperor, fearing a violent rebellion by the anti-papists, pressed his cousin for restraint, but Mary I ignored his advice.

While her regime aggressively suppressed the Protestant heretics, in late 1554 Mary I announced her pregnancy to the court and in April moved her personal household to Hampton Court to await the delivery of her child. However, as the expected birth date passed without signs of labor, doubts began to grow about her pregnancy. With a swollen abdomen the queen refused to believe that she would not give birth to the heir so desired by her and Philip. After several months passed beyond the due date, she was finally compelled to accept the diagnosis of her doctors. The queen's personal grief was made worse by the pending departure of Philip to join his father in Brussels. In September he left England, leaving his wife to mourn the loss of the expected child and her husband.

Before his departure from Greenwich Palace, Philip used his influence in the government to reorganize the ruling council and appoint Cardinal Reginald Pole as his wife's principal advisor. Pole was a zealous Catholic and was completely trusted by the queen. Without the guidance of her husband, she depended increasingly on Pole for support. In October she returned to London and opened the newly elected Parliament with the assistance of Pole and Bishop Gardiner. Her council had been reduced to only nine members but the queen continued to distrust their advice and relied only on Gardiner and Pole. However, in late November the bishop died and Cardinal Pole became Mary's sole loyal and devoted counselor.

As the church courts continued to send convicted Protestant activists to their deaths in the heresy fires, in early 1556 a plot to overthrow the queen was revealed to Cardinal Pole.

The conspirators planned to steal funds from the royal treasury for the payment of French mercenaries and English exiles, who were to launch an attack against the southern coast of England. While the invasion force led by Sir Henry Dudley landed on the Isle of Wight, the local rebels were to rise up in revolt and unite with the foreign soldiers to march on London. With the early betrayal of the rebellion, the dissident leaders were quickly arrested, thwarting the danger to the crown. While the uprising never materialized, it became evident that its support was widespread and reached deep into the queen's government and court. The effects of Dudley's Rebellion left Mary I feeling isolated and threatened and her anxiety was increased after Cardinal Pole left Greenwich Palace to assume the archbishopric of Canterbury. She again began to suffer from severe mental anguish and despair from the stresses of ruling virtually alone and pressed Philip to return from Flanders. As her health continued to deteriorate, she recalled Pole from Canterbury and placed the administration of her kingdom under his authority.

In the autumn of 1556 Philip II, who had been granted the Netherlands and the thrones of Spain and Naples by his father, was drawn into war against France and Pope Paul IV. England attempted to remain neutral but the Spanish king was in need of money, troops and arms and pressed Mary I for assistance. In March 1557 he returned to London to personally use his influence with the council and Parliament to acquire the necessary military aid. Initially he found little support for his foreign conflict and secured only small loans. While Philip II remained at the Tudor court, in France the English dissident exile Sir Thomas Stafford, with a subsidy and encouragement from King Henry II, mustered a small force of refugees and sailed from Dieppe to raise a rebellion in northern England. Landing in Yorkshire, the small contingent of rebels quickly captured Scarborough Castle, but their call to arms received little enthusiasm. Stafford and his men were soon captured and imprisoned by the sixth Earl of Westmoreland, Charles Nevill. In the aftermath of Stafford's failed attack, the French involvement in his revolt and the earlier Dudley Rebellion aroused a wave of public sympathy for the Franco-Papal War. In May the queen recalled her Paris ambassador and declared war on Henry II on June 7.

Following the Tudor alliance with Spain, in June 1557 Philip II returned to Flanders to command the war against the French. In support of the Habsburg war effort, the queen ordered the defenses at the English enclave of Calais reinforced and buttressed with additional troops while a Tudor army was recruited and sent to Flanders. In August the captain general of the allied forces, Emmanuel Philibert of Savoy, invaded France and laid siege against the fortress of Saint Quentin with the English soldiers participating in the attack. When Henry II attempted to raise the investment, his army was virtually destroyed by the Habsburg-Anglo forces.

The victory at Saint Quentin was greeted with wild rejoicing and services of thanksgiving in London and throughout the kingdom. However, the English joy was short lived when the French led by Francis II, Duke of Guise, attacked Calais in December, driving the defenders from the outer defenses and besieging the stronghold. The English and their Spanish allies were unable to send any relief and on January 7, 1558, the garrison surrendered. In England the loss of the prized French possession, which had been captured by Edward III in 1346, was met with widespread despair and anger against the queen. After the loss of the important foothold in France, the English population and Parliament turned against the alliance with Spain and Mary I had difficulty recruiting additional troops and raising money for the war effort. She continued to distrust her Privy Council and was again forced to rule virtually alone when Cardinal Pole became seriously ill. As Mary I struggled to find the resources to continue the fight against the Valois regime, she grew more distressed and tormented, as her health deteriorated under the constant stress. By late 1558 it was obvious to her court that the queen was dying and under pressure from the council she agreed to the succession of her half-sister, Elizabeth. In the morning of November 17, Mary I died in London at Saint James Palace at the age of forty-two and a reign of five years. She was buried in Westminster Abbey in a service of Catholic rituals performed by the bishop of Winchester, John White.

Sources

Erickson. *Bloody Mary.*   Prescott. *Mary Tudor.*   Roll. *Mary I.*   Tittler. *The Reign of Mary I.*

Elizabeth I, 1533–1558–1603

The eleventh and final sovereign of the English Renaissance era was Elizabeth I, who inherited the Tudor crown from her half-sister, Mary I, and ruled for nearly a half century during a period of internal turmoil and foreign war. In January 1533 Henry VIII secretly married Anne Boleyn while negotiations for his divorce from Queen Catherine of Aragon were pursued with the English Parliament. Under the resulting Parliamentary Act of Appeal, the Catholic Church in England was dissolved and on May 23 Archbishop Thomas Cranmer voided the king's first marriage and legalized his union with Anne Boleyn. Princess Elizabeth was born at Greenwich Palace in the afternoon of September 7, 1533, and was the only surviving issue of Henry VIII and his second wife, Queen Anne. At her birth she was recognized as heir presumptive to the English throne, usurping the inheritance rights of her half-sister, Mary. Three days later she was christened Elizabeth, Princess of England, in an elaborate ceremony attended by the high secular and religious lords in the nearby friary church. Henry VIII was greatly disappointed Anne had delivered a daughter but was encouraged that the next child would be a healthy son. When the Tudor princess was three months old, a separate household was created for her at Hatfield House in Herefordshire with her own administrative and personal staff. Although she remained at Hatfield away from court, Henry VIII and the queen frequently visited her and personally managed her household.

While Princess Elizabeth stayed isolated at Hatfield and several nearby royal palaces, in early 1536 her mother suffered another miscarriage after two previous stillborns and the king was now convinced she could not give him a male successor, becoming resolved to take a new wife. To find just cause for an annulment, he ordered his lord chancellor, Thomas Cromwell, to establish a royal commission to find evidence of her treason. While Elizabeth was at Greenwich Palace, her mother was arrested on May 2 and after a quick trial declared guilty of adultery and plotting the death of the sovereign. The execution was carried out seventeen days later on the Tower Green and was followed by the Tudor king's marriage to his new court favorite, Jane Seymour. Henry VIII's third marriage had serious repercussions for Elizabeth, when Parliament passed a second Act of Succession, which recognized the children of Queen Jane as the only lawful heirs to the throne and declared the daughter of Anne illegitimate. She was deprived of her royal title as Princess of England and acknowledged as only Lady Elizabeth. In October the queen gave birth to a healthy son, Prince Edward, while Elizabeth was returned to live at Hatfield with a reduced living allowance and staff.

At Hatfield House a governess was appointed for the care and protection of the young Elizabeth and with the approval of the king, tutors were chosen for her classical education.

Like her father, she was a gifted student, excelling in her studies of reading, writing, history, French, Latin, and the new Protestant religion. She also received instruction in the social graces of dancing, music and court etiquette, while mastering the skills of archery, hunting and riding. Elizabeth saw her father only rarely, however, frequent progress reports were sent to him.

While Elizabeth remained away from court, Jane Seymour died shortly after the birth of Prince Edward. The death of the king's third wife was followed by his unsuccessful marriages to Anne of Cleves and Catherine Howard. The Tudor lady saw little of her father during this turbulent period, but when he married Catherine Parr the royal children were returned to court. Under the influence of the sixth queen, Elizabeth's education was expanded and she was given access to the scholars and libraries of her half-brother. The royal tutors instructed her in the new studies of Greek, Italian and classical literature while continuing her lessons in French, Latin and religion. Queen Catherine provided a stable and secure environment for Elizabeth and her life became more orderly and peaceful. While the Tudor lady stayed in the royal household, her father grew increasingly ill and weak, suffering from high fevers and bleeding leg ulcers. In late 1546 with his death imminent, the three royal children were sent to separate residences and were not permitted to visit their father during his last days.

Following the death of her father on January 28, 1547, Lady Elizabeth resided with the dowager queen, Catherine, at her Chelsea Palace. Under Henry VIII's will and the Parliamentary Act of Succession, the Tudor throne was inherited by his only son, Edward, while a sixteen member regency council was created to rule in the name of the minor king. However, the new king's uncle, Edward Seymour, forged an alliance of royal counselors and seized the government, assuming the title of lord protector. With virtual dictatorial authority, he appointed his brother, Thomas, as lord high admiral but denied him any real power. Ambitious and jealous of his older brother's high offices, Lord Thomas began to conspire against the lord protector and to gain political influence and esteem married the dowager queen, Catherine. At Chelsea Palace he became friends with Lady Elizabeth lavishing her with so much attention and affection that in May 1548 the dowager queen arranged for her to move back to Hatfield House to protect her reputation as the king's half-sister.

After the death of Catherine Parr in early September 1548 following the birth of a daughter, Thomas Seymour renewed his relationship with Elizabeth as part of a plot to marry her and seize the English crown. In January 1549 he broke into the royal apartments and attempted to kidnap Edward VI. His attack was thwarted and he was arrested on charges of high treason. Lady Elizabeth was implicated in the conspiracy because of her close association with the lord high admiral and subjected to interrogations by the Privy Council but not enough evidence was found to incriminate her.

In the aftermath of her involvement with Thomas Seymour's conspiracy, Elizabeth remained at Hatfield House continuing her studies, spending time on her lands hunting and riding, practicing her musical instruments and playing cards and games with her ladies-in-waiting. She visited her half-brother at court occasionally and was graciously received. With her striking physical features, intelligence and charismatic personality she became a favorite of the nobles.

In early 1552 the lord protector was overthrown and the reins of power seized by John Dudley, Duke of Northumberland. As a committed Protestant, he intensified the ongoing royal policy of Catholic suppression and expansion of liberal religious doctrines. In the summer the Protestant King Edward VI became seriously ill with a fever and chronic lung infection. If he died without a direct heir, the Tudor crown passed to his zealous Catholic half-sister,

Mary, which threatened the future of the new reformist faith. To change the order of accession to the monarchy, the king with the assistance of Dudley issued *My Devise for the Succession*, appointing his Protestant cousin Lady Jane Grey as his heir and excluding both Mary and Elizabeth as illegitimate. While Lady Elizabeth remained at Hatfield House continuing her education and keeping informed with events at court, on July 6, 1553, Edward VI died and Northumberland proclaimed Jane Grey as queen. However, Lady Mary had a widespread base of support among both papists and Protestants for her inheritance rights and marched against London with her large army, deposing the new queen and usurping the throne.

Elizabeth was at Hatfield as events in London unfolded. After learning of Mary I's succession to the monarchy, she traveled to the capital to proclaim her allegiance to her half-sister. As a Protestant and now heir apparent, she was in a dangerous position and had to be careful not to pose a threat as a rival claimant. When the queen approached the city, Lady Elizabeth rode out to greet her, kneeling to pledge her loyalty. The Tudor lady was accepted into the royal court and treated with respect as the successor designate. As the queen's government restored the Catholic faith to England, Elizabeth stayed away from mass and other papist religious rituals, continuing with her Protestantism. However, Mary I demanded she convert and attend mass, sending members of her Privy Council to intimidate her with imprisonment in the Tower. Under duress Elizabeth was forced to outwardly conform and acknowledge the Church of Rome. While the Tudor lady remained at court, her relationship with the queen grew strained, as she greatly resented being subservient to her half-sister.

Mary I was betrothed to Prince Philip of Spain in late 1553, despite the disapproval of her council and Parliament. As the negotiations for the marital treaty were finalized, opposition to the foreign prince spread throughout the realm and rebellion erupted in Kent under the leadership of Sir Thomas Wyatt. He assembled an army of over four thousand soldiers to march against the queen while Elizabeth was away from London at Ashridge House. As the rebels approached the capital, Mary I rallied her troops and the city's population to crush Wyatt's forces. Before initiating his uprising, Sir Thomas had made personal contact with Lady Elizabeth, informing her of his impending revolt and encouraging her to participate as the claimant to the throne. After Wyatt's defeat she was implicated in the failed conspiracy and summoned to court. Fearing her arrest she stayed at Ashridge, claiming illness. However, Elizabeth was compelled to return to London, when the queen sent two doctors to escort her to the royal court. After arriving in the city she was taken to the Tower and given apartments with her small household staff in the Bell Tower. Her future now depended on the decision of the Privy Council but they could not reach a decision and lacking any real evidence, the queen ordered her release. On May 4 the Tudor lady was removed from the prison by the Tower constable, Sir Henry Bedingfield, and taken to Woodstock Palace in Oxfordshire. At Woodstock she was kept under close house arrest with Bedingfield acting as the queen's local representative and guardian.

In late 1554 Mary I announced to her court that she was pregnant and in April traveled with her personal household to Hampton Court to await the arrival of the child. Under the influence of Prince Philip, who actively encouraged a reconciliation between the two half-sisters to enhance Spanish prestige and influence in the government, the queen agreed to permit Elizabeth's return to court. After over ten months at Woodstock she was brought to Hampton Court, but initially Mary I refused to see her. When finally granted an audience, she pleaded her innocence in Wyatt's rebellion and proclaimed her loyalty to the crown. Following their meeting, the Tudor lady was given greater freedom and allowed to reside at Hatfield. Elizabeth's standing as heir apparent was threatened by the impending birth of the queen's child but her pregnancy proved to be false. With the income from her estates at Hatfield, she established a small household and renewed her previous peaceful life of reading, playing the virginal, entertaining guests, playing cards and games, while engaging in hunting, falconry and riding. There were several attempts by Mary I and her council to arrange a marriage for Elizabeth with a foreign prince, suggesting Duke Emmanuel Philibert of Savoy and Charles of Spain, but she refused to leave England. When Philip sailed for Flanders in June 1557 to pursue the Anglo-Habsburg war against France, Elizabeth visited her half-sister more frequently and they developed a closer relationship. As the conflict in France grew more unpopular and the persecutions of the heretic Protestants intensified, opposition to Mary I's reign increased, while support for Lady Elizabeth spread throughout the kingdom. The Tudor queen had suffered from declining health for many years and in 1558 became seriously ill. With death approaching, under pressure from her Privy Council she acknowledged the succession rights of Elizabeth to the English monarchy. On November 7 Mary I died and Elizabeth I ascended to the Tudor throne at the age of twenty-five.

Elizabeth I received the news of Mary I's death and her succession to the English throne at Hatfield House and immediately established her new ruling council, appointing her friend and supporter, Lord William Cecil, as her royal secretary. Cecil was born in September 1521 in Lincolnshire at Bourne and was the only son of Richard Cecil, who was a minor official in the court of Henry VIII, and Jane Heckington. William began his education in Stamford before attending Cambridge College. In 1547 he participated in Edward Seymour's military campaign in Scotland and later in the year was elected to Parliament from Stamford. He later joined the government of Edward Seymour of Somerset, serving as his personal secretary. When Somerset was overthrown in October 1549, William Cecil was briefly detained in the Tower. After his release he entered the new regime of John Dudley and was recognized for his administrative skills with his appointment as state secretary. Cecil survived the downfall of Dudley and was named to a minor office during the reign of Mary I.

The Tudor queen first met with her Privy Council on November 18, 1558. She increased the number of her advisors to nineteen, appointing both Catholic and Protestant members, while retaining thirteen counselors from Mary I's regime. Elizabeth I rewarded her faithful supporters with high offices in her new administration and included many of her friends and relatives from her household staff. With her government established, on November 23 she traveled in a grand procession from Hatfield to London to prepare for the coronation. While arrangements for the investiture continued, she held meetings with the Privy Council and met with a steady flow of ambassadors, courtiers and visitors in the royal apartments at Whitehall Palace. From the beginning of her reign, Elizabeth I governed in an imperial style, believing she was chosen by God to rule.

The enthronement was held on January 15, 1559, with the queen riding to Westminster Palace dressed in a gold robe in a splendid procession of soldiers, noblemen, ladies and courtiers through streets lavishly decorated with tapestries, displays and pageants, glorifying her assumption of the English throne. The following morning the ceremony was held at Westminster Abbey with the bishop of Carlisle, anointing and crowning Elizabeth I as queen of England. The service was followed with a magnificent banquet with the queen enjoying the entertainment, music and dancing. Ten days of feasting, parties and jousting tournaments were held after the investiture.

On January 25, 1559, the queen opened her first Parliament at Westminster Hall, which was dominated by religious issues. Elizabeth I was determined to rule with the same English church and powers as her father and under the ensuing Parliamentary Act of Uniformity, a moderate religious settlement was approved, which was Protestant in doctrine and Catholic in appearance. The authority of Rome was abolished and the Church of England restored with the queen recognized as supreme governor. She resisted attempts by the extremist Protestants to eliminate her supremacy as head of the Church but permitted the adoption of the more progressive 1552 Prayer Book of Edward VI. The Catholic archbishop of Canterbury, Reginald Pole, died in late 1558 and Elizabeth I appointed Matthew Parker as his successor. The new primate was a centrist Protestant, who opposed the radical beliefs of both religions and was trusted by the queen to implement her policies.

Queen Elizabeth I was the only surviving member of Henry VIII's immediate family and to ensure the security of the kingdom and avoid the question of a future successor, the council and Parliament encouraged her to quickly marry. Soon after her accession, the Spanish ambassador was sent to court with a marriage proposal from Philip II. The offer was politely declined due to the differences in their religion and her unwillingness to convert to the Catholic faith. The Spanish overture was followed by advances from the Austrian Habsburg Archduke Charles and the heir to Sweden, Prince Eric, but the queen informed their envoys of her desire not to marry in the near future. Despite rejecting the foreign princes, she was attracted to two English lords, Robert Dudley and Sir William Pickering, but their relationship remained only platonic. When Dudley became Elizabeth I's favorite, their impending marriage was widely rumored by the courtiers but she would not make a commitment. Lord Robert was born on June 24, 1532, and was the fifth son of John Dudley, Earl of Warwick, and Lady Jane Guildford. He received a broad based humanist education and excelled in his studies. His father held high posts in the government of Edward VI and Robert accompanied him to court, mastering the skills of a courtier. In the summer of 1549 he served with the royal army suppressing the Kett Rebellion in Norfolk. After the death of the childless Edward VI, he supported his father's attempt in 1553 to place Lady Jane Grey on the throne and was sent with a force of three hundred troops to capture Mary Tudor in Norfolk. When the plot failed, Robert was arrested for treason and imprisoned in the Tower. He was finally released in October of the following year but remained under suspicion of treason by Mary I. To promote his return to court, Lord Robert joined the Anglo-Spanish army and fought at the great battle of Saint Quentin in France. Following the death of the Catholic queen, Dudley regained favor and was recalled to court, quickly becoming a favorite of Elizabeth I.

After the queen became seriously ill with smallpox and was in danger of dying in October 1562, her Privy Council pressed her to acknowledge a successor. Despite the pleas of her advisors, she would not choose a husband or appoint a designated heir. Queen Elizabeth I's repeated refusals to recognize a successor created an inheritance crisis during her illness, threatening the security of the realm with internal rebellion and foreign invasion. There were four contenders for the throne but the Catholic queen of Scotland, Mary I, held the strongest blood claim as first cousin to Elizabeth I. In August 1561 Mary I returned to rule in Scotland following the death of her husband, King Francis II of France. She began to correspond with the English council, advancing her birthright to the crown. She sent her counselor, William Maitland, to London to persuade her cousin to publicly acknowledge her as heir. The English queen diplomatically declined to make any commitment but continued to communicate with the Stewart government. When the Scottish administration initiated negotiations for a marriage agreement for Mary I with the Habsburg Emperor and Spain, the cordial relationship between the two regimes grew increasingly strained.

While the English court continued to negotiate with Scotland, Lord William Cecil increasingly exhorted the queen to marry. He favored an alliance with the Holy Roman Empire and advocated Elizabeth I's union with Archduke Charles. As the deliberations were begun with the imperial council, the queen chose a new favorite, Thomas Butler of Ormonde, ignoring the ongoing discussions with the emperor. When the Parliament met in October 1566, the Commons refused to approve the crown's request for additional taxes until Elizabeth I settled the succession issue. She angrily responded that her marriage was not the business of the assembly. The impasse with Parliament was finally resolved after she reduced her petition for funds and agreed to consider the marriage overture with the Habsburgs. Elizabeth I now took an active role in the talks with the imperial court but no agreement was possible due to their religious differences. The failure of the marital proposal satisfied the monarch, who continued to disregard the pleas of her privy advisors and Parliament to wed.

As part of the ongoing talks with Edinburgh for the acknowledgement of the blood claim of Queen Mary I, the Stewart council pardoned the previously exiled Scottish Earl of Lennox and his son, Henry Stewart, Lord of Darnley, in a show of good faith. The English reciprocated by permitting Lennox and Lord Henry to return to Scotland. In Edinburgh Darnley quickly became a favorite at court. With his handsome looks and charismatic personality, he developed a close relationship with Mary I. By early 1565 she had fallen in love with him and was considering marriage. Elizabeth I strongly opposed her cousin's union with Darnley and offered to favorably consider her inheritance rights as designated heir if she married an English peer. The Scottish queen disregarded the Tudor government and in July was wed to Lord Henry in a Catholic ceremony at Holyrood Abbey. However, their marriage was a disaster for the reigning queen when Lord Darnley attempted to usurp her throne. His revolt was easily suppressed, and Darnley murdered by Mary I's loyal allies. However, Darnley's plot divided and weakened support for Mary I and the Protestant lords rebelled to overthrow her in 1568. Following her defeat at the battle of Langside, she was compelled to flee to England and seek sanctuary with her Tudor cousin. The Stewart crown was assumed by her young son, James VI, who ruled under a regency regime led by his uncle, James Stewart of Moray.

In the aftermath of the Stewart queen's dethronement, Elizabeth I sent an envoy to the new Scottish government threatening to invade and reinstate Mary I to the throne by force of arms. Before the military campaign was organized, Mary I escaped to England and was held at Carlisle Castle. It was English foreign policy to gain political influence in Scotland by thwarting any Stewart alliance with France and suppressing the local restoration of the Catholic faith. To advance the crown's quest for power in Scotland, the Tudor queen ordered the appointment of a commission led by the Duke of Norfolk, Thomas Howard, to determine Mary I's involvement in the death of her husband. Thomas Howard was born in the early morning of March 10, 1538, at his family's principal seat of Kenninghall Castle and was the first son of Henry Howard and Lady Francis Vere, daughter of the fifteenth Earl of Oxford. When his father was executed for treason by Henry VIII, the eight-year-old Thomas was raised by his aunt, Mary Fitzroy, Duchess of Richmond. After the accession of Mary I, Lord Thomas Howard was recognized as Earl of Surrey and created a knight of Bath. When Prince Philip of Spain came to England, the Surrey earl served in a high office in his household. He succeeded his grandfather on August 25, 1554 as the fourth duke of Norfolk, becoming the largest landowner in the realm. After Elizabeth I assumed the monarchy, the duke was named to the Privy Council in 1562 and acknowledged as the first peer of the royal blood and cousin of the queen. He was a prominent member of the royal council and actively contended with Lord Robert Dudley and William Cecil for power and influence.

The Scottish queen was accused of arranging the murder of Lord Darnley by the Duke of Norfolk's commission. If she was declared blameless, Mary I was to be returned to Scotland

and restored with Tudor military assistance to reign as the English figurehead ruler. However, no supporting evidence of her guilt or innocence was produced and on January 10, 1569, Lord Cecil issued the official report, which reached no conclusion. Mary I continued to be imprisoned and was moved to Wingfield Castle for greater security. While at Wingfield, she became involved in a plot with Thomas Howard agreeing to marry him and jointly rule England. The Earl of Northumberland, Sir Thomas Percy and Charles Nevill, Earl of Westmoreland, were drawn into the insurrection along with other discontented Catholic nobles. The queen's spies soon informed her of the growing revolt and Howard was summoned to court. Appearing before the council, the duke was charged with treason and sent to the Tower. Elizabeth I ordered the remaining rebels to London but they refused to leave their northern stronghold. On November 10, 1569, they marched their militias to seize Durham, igniting the Northern Rebellion. The earls issued a call to arms to the northern warlords to free Mary I from her captivity and restore the Catholic religion. In an act of defiance Northumberland and Nevill entered Durham Cathedral with their supporters, destroying the Protestant Communion table, burning the heretic Bibles and prayer books and hearing mass with the old rituals.

In early December the rebel army of over five thousand soldiers marched south to rescue Mary I. With possession of the queen and holding control over the north country, the earls would pose a formidable threat to the Tudor regime. Queen Elizabeth I was without a standing army but ordered the Viscount of Hereford, Walter Devereux, to muster a large local military force to suppress the conspiracy. While he assembled his soldiers, the insurgents captured the castle of Barnard, but as they continued south their rebellion found little popular support. As Devereux advanced from York with over seven thousand men-under-arms, the earls were compelled to retreat north, dispersing their troops and fleeing to Scotland. Many of the dissidents were captured and imprisoned at York Castle, where over seven hundred suffered the traitor's death at the command of Elizabeth I. Both Percy and Nevill escaped death but their estates were seized by the crown and given to the queen's loyal allies. In support of the Northern Rebellion, in early 1570 Pope Pius V issued a papal bull excommunicating Elizabeth I and declaring her deposed, while authorizing her assassination. She responded by ending her policy of religious toleration and began the persecution of her Catholic enemies.

Duke Thomas Howard had been imprisoned in the Tower since the Northern Rebellion but after nine months was released when no evidence of his treason was found. However, in 1571 he was involved in a new plot to free Mary I and assassinate the Tudor queen. The conspiracy was instigated by the ardent Catholic Florentine banker, Roberto Ridolfi. Under the plan presented to Howard, the Habsburg governor of the Netherlands, Fernando Alvarez, third Duke of Alba, was to invade England with a large Spanish force while the duke raised a rebellion in the north. The two armies were to later unite and march on London. The insurrection was quickly discovered by the crown's spies and Norfolk arrested. He was tried before the peers at Westminster Hall and declared guilty of treason. On June 2, 1572, he was beheaded at Tower Hill. In the aftermath of the Northern Rebellion and the attempted Ridolfi Plot, the queen was exhorted by Parliament to prosecute Mary I for her sedition, but she refused to prosecute a close blood relative and co-monarch. For greater security the Scottish queen was moved to Tutbury Castle, where she spent the remaining years of her captivity.

The risk of Spanish involvement in the Ridolfi Plot made England even more dependent on a continental ally and negotiations were initiated with the French regency government of Catherine de Medici for a treaty of alliance and marriage of the Tudor queen to a Valois prince. In April 1571 the French queen sent a proposal to the English council for the marital union between her third son, Duke Henry of Anjou, and Elizabeth I. The offer was rejected when the Valois regime demanded the anointment of Duke Henry as king and his continued open worship as a Catholic. While the marriage deliberations failed, discussions were renewed for a coalition between the two realms and in April 1572 the Treaty of Blois was signed, which bound each signatory to defend the other if attacked.

As the marriage negotiations with France remained at an impasse, the Dutch rebelled against Spanish suppression, threatening the European status quo. To protect Tudor trade with Flanders, Elizabeth I offered to mediate a settlement between the warring parties but her proposal was ignored by Philip II. In the Netherlands the new Spanish governor, John of Austria, issued the Perpetual Edict, pledging to evacuate his foreign troops if the Dutch laid down their arms. However, when he began preparations to invade England with the withdrawn occupation army and replace the Tudor queen with Mary I of Scotland, the English council granted large loans to the rebels to encourage their continued resistance. To further buttress the Dutch rebellion, the Tudor government funded the German Protestant forces of Count John Casimir, who mounted a campaign against the Spanish. With the Low Country in turmoil, the heir to the French throne, Duke Francis of Valois, forged an alliance with the Dutch dissidents and launched an attack against John. The new danger to peace in Europe revived Elizabeth I's stalled marriage discussions with Queen Catherine of France.

To solidify the Treaty of Blois, Catherine de Medici advanced the marriage of her youngest son, Francis of Anjou, and the English queen. As the deliberations with the French dragged on with little success, Queen Elizabeth I met with her Parliament and Privy Council to address the routine business of state, while attending court with her friends and courtiers. The queen continued her close association with Lord Robert Dudley and had numerous favorites but the relationships only served as an amusement. However, in April 1578 Francis arrived in England to meet the queen and personally pursue the marital negotiations. Despite their age differences, with his quick wit, charm and charismatic personality he made a favorable impression on Elizabeth I. When he sailed to Paris two weeks later, she sent a proposed marriage agreement to the French regime.

While the talks with Anjou continued, Tudor relations with Spain grew increasingly strained with the escalation of English plundering raids in the New World. Francis Drake led attacks against Spanish ports and shipping bringing rich treasures back to the Tudor government. In 1580 he returned to England after navigating around the globe in the *Golden Hind* in a three year voyage of discovery and privateering. Drake was born in March 1540 in the southwestern county of Devon and was the eldest son of a local Protestant minister, Edmund Drake, and Mary Mylwaye. He became an apprentice seaman at the age of twelve, sailing on vessels trading with cross-channel ports in Flanders and France. In 1560 he assumed command of his first ship and three years later began pillaging Spanish treasure fleets and settlements in the New World. Drake continued to sail for the Tudor monarchy and captured a large cargo of gold and silver on the Panama Isthmus in 1573.

To retain the possibility of an Anglo-French military coalition as a deterrent to Spanish aggression, Elizabeth I continued her ongoing relationship with Francis, exchanging flattering letters, jewelry and elaborate gifts. The duke made two additional visits to Elizabeth I's court; however, by the summer of 1581 she had tired of him and with the constant opposition of Lord Cecil to the French marriage the discussions were ended. She had no intention of ever marrying and had used Francis as a diplomatic tool to keep the Spanish threat neutralized with the potential union between her kingdom and France.

Queen Mary I of Scotland continued to remain under captivity at Tutbury Castle and was the center of numerous plots to place her on the English throne. There were rumors of the planned murder of Elizabeth I by zealous English Catholics and impending papal invasions of the realm by foreign troops. As the risk of conspiracies against the crown increased, the queen of the Scots was kept under stricter confinement and denied contacts with her friends and foreign courts. Despite the enhanced security, in 1583 Elizabeth I's spies thwarted the scheme to use a Spanish army from the Netherlands to restore the papist religion to England with Mary I as queen. Three years later the Stewart queen began to secretly correspond with Philip II in Madrid. Her messages were intercepted by the government's agents, which revealed a new plan to assassinate the queen and occupy the kingdom with a large Spanish military force. The Catholic conspirators in England were led by Sir Anthony Babington of Derbyshire, who was recruited by Mary I's secret envoys to organize and raise a revolt against the Protestant Tudor regime. However, with the incriminating information from the seized letters, the plotters were arrested and their insurrection foiled.

As the English council began preparations to formally indict Mary I on charges of conspiracy against the throne, the commander of the Dutch opposition movement, William of Orange, was assassinated and his demoralized troops defeated by the Spanish governor, Alexander Farnese, prince of Parma. Without a recognized resistance leader, the Spanish soon regained supremacy over many of the large cities and much of the countryside, compelling the rebels to turn to Elizabeth I for military intervention. In August 1585 she signed the Treaty of Nonsuch Palace, promising to send an army to the Dutch to help them recover their independence. The declaration of war was popular with her subjects and served to unite England in a common cause. The expeditionary force was commanded by the queen's favorite, Lord Robert Dudley, but after landing in the Netherlands the Tudor council opened peace talks with Philip II, undermining Dudley's Dutch campaign. The English initiative was further limited by Elizabeth I's refusal to provide the army with needed money and supplies. Without the full support of the Tudor regime and confronting a seasoned professional military force, Dudley's offensive floundered. In late 1587 the queen ordered him to begin peace discussions with Parma to resolve the conflict.

Under continuing pressure from Lord William Cecil, the Tudor queen finally but reluctantly agreed to the indictment of Mary I and on August 11, 1586, the council charged her with acts of treason against the crown. In September she was moved to Fotheringhay Castle in Northamptonshire, while a commission was appointed to determine her involvement in the Babington Conspiracy. After a two day trial, she was declared guilty of plotting the murder of the queen and usurpation of the throne. On February 1, 1587, Elizabeth I signed the death warrant and seven days later the queen of the Scots was publicly executed in the great Hall of Fotheringhay in front of three hundred witnesses.

Like her father, Elizabeth I's monarchy evolved into a center for Renaissance culture, music, and literature. She was highly fond of music and subsidized renowned singers, musicians and composers with her royal patronage. William Byrd was appointed master of music and became a favorite of the queen. During her reign, there was a blossoming of literary works from new poets and novelists, including Christopher Marlowe, Edmund Spenser and John Lyly. The queen was a sponsor of the English theater and established her own company of actors. She and her courtiers actively supported the leading dramatists, including William Shakespeare and Ben Johnson, with many of their plays performed at court before the queen. She traveled frequently between her many different palaces but preferred to reside at Richmond, Hampton Court and Windsor. During the summer progresses, the queen rode through the kingdom, asserting her rule with the power and grandeur of her presence.

To promote and encourage the growth of English foreign commerce, she maintained

Edward VI's earlier diplomatic contacts with the imperial court of Russia and created a commercial relationship with the Barbary Coast of Africa. Trading ties were established with Morocco and English goods were exchanged for sugar, spices and other local products. The Tudor regime chartered the Levant Company to trade with the Ottoman Empire and exchanged envoys with the sultan's government. Late in her reign Elizabeth I authorized the creation of a new colony in the New World, extending her patronage to Sir Walter Raleigh to establish the first English settlement in Virginia at Roanoke.

Following England's intervention in the Dutch war and the execution of Mary I of Scotland, relations with Spain rapidly deteriorated. In 1587 Philip II began preparations to conquer England and usurp the crown for himself. The Great Armada of nearly two hundred warships was mustered, which was to ferry the duke of Parma's army from the Netherlands across the channel to invade the heretic realm. On July 22, 1588, the Armada sailed to England with Alonso de Guzman, Duke of Medina Sidonia, commanding the Spanish fleet. After entering the English Channel, he maneuvered his vessels into an impregnable crescent shape formation, thwarting the attacks of the Tudors. However, when the Spanish anchored off Calais to await the arrival of Parma, the English sent eight fireships to drift into Guzman's moored flotilla. At the approach of the burning ships, the Spanish cut their anchor lines, escaping into the channel. The fire attack broke the duke's defensive formation and near Gravelines the Tudor sea captains led by Sir Francis Drake destroyed part of the armada. The remnants of the Spanish fled toward Scotland and abandoned the invasion of England. Elizabeth I's great triumph was greeted with celebrations and church services of thanksgiving throughout the kingdom.

While the defeat of the Spanish Armada was a decisive victory for England, the conflict with Philip II continued unabated. To weaken the Habsburg king's war effort, in 1589 Sir Francis Drake led a naval force against Lisbon to aid the Portuguese rebels, who were resisting the usurpation of their kingdom by the Spanish crown but his intervention achieved little success. In a further attempt to contain Philip II's expansionist and anti–Protestant policies in Europe, Elizabeth I agreed to send military and financial assistance to bolster the inheritance rights of the new Protestant king of France, Henry IV, who was at war with the Spanish sponsored Catholic League. Baron Fulke Greville of Willoughby was given command of a small contingent of English soldiers and served with the French king during operations in Normandy. However, with persistent shortages of manpower and money his campaign was ineffective. A second expedition was mounted two years later but when the English were defeated by the league at the battle of Craon in northwestern France, the shattered remnants of the army were withdrawn. After the failure of the two armies, in July 1591 Elizabeth I sent her new court favorite, Robert Devereux, Earl of Essex, to buttress Henry IV's siege against Rouen. Despite Essex's martial skills and personal bravery during the investment of Rouen, his attacks were unsuccessful and his troops returned to England in January 1592. Robert was the son of Walter Devereux, first Earl of Essex, and Lady Lettice Knollys and was born on November 19, 1566, at Netherwood in Herefordshire. His maternal great-grandmother was Mary Boleyn and through her lineage he was directly related to Queen Elizabeth I. He was raised on his father's estates in southwestern Wales and Staffordshire at Chartley Castle and was educated at Trinity College, Cambridge. At the death of his father in 1576, Robert inherited his Essex lands and title of earl. When Lady Lettice remarried two years later, the earl became the stepson of Lord Robert Dudley. In 1586 he joined the English expeditionary army of Dudley to aid the Dutch in their war against Spain and participated in the siege against the fortress of Zutphen, gaining recognition during the battle for his energy and courage.

During the final years of Elizabeth I's reign, the war with Spain dragged on, while the tax burden grew and the economy suffered from the loss of trade with Europe and poor harvests. In 1598 Lord William Cecil died and the queen was without her most skilled and experienced counselor. The new Privy Council was dominated by his son, Robert, but lacking his father's power and influence internal strife soon erupted in the government. A bitter rivalry resulted between Cecil and the Earl of Essex for control of the regime, as the queen's personal rule grew unpopular. While the population suffered with the economic slowdown, Elizabeth I expanded her policy of subjugation against the English Catholics to prevent the threat of rebellion.

The queen's martial expeditions against the Spanish in Europe accomplished little in restraining the power of Philip II and with the outbreak of insurrection in Ireland, the English were compelled to redirect their military operations away from France and toward the enforcement of their rule against the rebelling clans. The English had claimed overlordship in Ireland for over four hundred years but still only held firm control over Dublin and the enclave in the southeastern region. In 1591 the Tudor council approved a campaign to expand its dominance over the entire island. After suppressing the Irish clans in the lordships of Monogham and Longford, the English viceroy advanced north to gain supremacy over Ulster. The local ruler, Hugh O'Neill, earl of Tyrone, attempted to negotiate a settlement but when his talks failed, revolt soon erupted. To quell Tyrone's rebellion, the English government in Dublin sent an army to subjugate the earl by force of arms. However, its attacks were repeatedly defeated by Tyrone's well armed and disciplined troops. His victories encouraged the remaining Irish clans to join his insurrection and the rebels gained authority over most of the island with the exception of the large fortified cities.

With the Tudor sovereignty challenged, the queen appointed the Earl of Essex, Robert Devereux, as her lord lieutenant for Ireland and sent him with seventeen thousand soldiers to crush Tyrone's rebellion. After reasserting the throne's control over the south, he garrisoned the castles and fortified towns and advanced to confront O'Neill in Ulster. As the lord lieutenant marched north, his forces were repeatedly harassed by Tyrone's troops as his military strength and supplies steadily declined. When the Tudor army finally entered Ulster, its forces were weakened by disease and battle causalities and were unable to actively combat the Irish. With his campaign in shambles, Essex began negotiations with Tyrone and without consulting with London agreed to a truce. Disillusioned with the Tudor war effort, Devereux abandoned his army and returned to London with the northern lordships still under Irish authority. For his disobedience in deserting his command, the queen placed him under house arrest and deprived him of all of his offices and court patronage.

After remaining under close confinement for nearly a year, Robert Devereux was released by the queen in late 1600. To regain his lost dominance over the ruling council, he assembled a small coalition of three hundred sympathizers and began to plot the seizure of the government and overthrow of Robert Cecil. The Privy Council soon learned of his conspiracy and summoned him to appear at Westminster. Essex ignored the order and attempted to raise a rebellion in London, charging Cecil's administration was in league with Spain and the Infanta Isabella would be appointed the queen's successor. The city's population refused to support his uprising and on February 8, 1601, he was arrested at Essex House on charges of sedition. He was tried before his peers and found guilty of treason. After some reluctance, Elizabeth I signed the death warrant and on February 25 Earl Robert Devereux of Essex was executed. After the fall of Essex, Robert Cecil's power over the Privy Council was uncontested and his influence with the queen unchallenged.

Elizabeth I had refused to recognize a successor, in spite of the persistent exhortations of her Parliament and Cecil. She was now approaching the age of seventy and still in good health, despite an earlier serious illness with smallpox, which left her with facial scars and permanent hair loss. She continued to stay actively engaged in her government until early 1603, when rumors of a new conspiracy to usurp her crown caused her to suffer from severe despair and alienation, prompting her to withdraw to her private apartments at Richmond Palace. Elizabeth I remained isolated, refusing to eat or sleep, as her health steadily declined. On March 22 the Privy Council gathered in her chambers, pressing the queen to name the next ruler but their pleas were again ignored. In the early morning two days later, Elizabeth I died after a reign of forty-five years while Cecil sent messengers to Scotland to announce the succession to the English throne by James I from the House of Stewart. On April 28 Queen Elizabeth I was buried in Westminster Abbey with the Privy Council members, high peers and clerics attending the funeral ceremony.

Sources

Chidsey. *Elizabeth I.* Erickson. *The First Elizabeth.* Marshall. *Elizabeth I.* Robinson. *The Dukes of Norfolk.* Williams. *The Life and Times of Elizabeth I.*

General Sources for England

Ashley. *British Kings & Queens.* Ault. *Europe in the Middle Ages.* Blum; Cameron; Barnes. *The Emergence of the European World.* Cannon; Margreaves. *The Kings and Queens of Britain.* Frazer. *The Lives of the Kings and Queens of England.* Pickering. *Lancastrians To Tudors.* Read. *The Tudors.* Wernham. *Before the Armada: The Emergency of the English Nation.*

PART II

Renaissance Monarchs of Scotland

HOUSE OF STEWART

Robert III	1337–1390–1406
James I	1394–1406–1437
James II	1430–1437–1460
James III	1452–1460–1488
James IV	1473–1488–1513
James V	1512–1513–1542
Mary I	1542–1542–1567–1587*
James VI (I of England)	1566–1567–1625

Four dates indicate birth, succession, abdication and death.

Genealogical Table

HOUSE OF STEWART

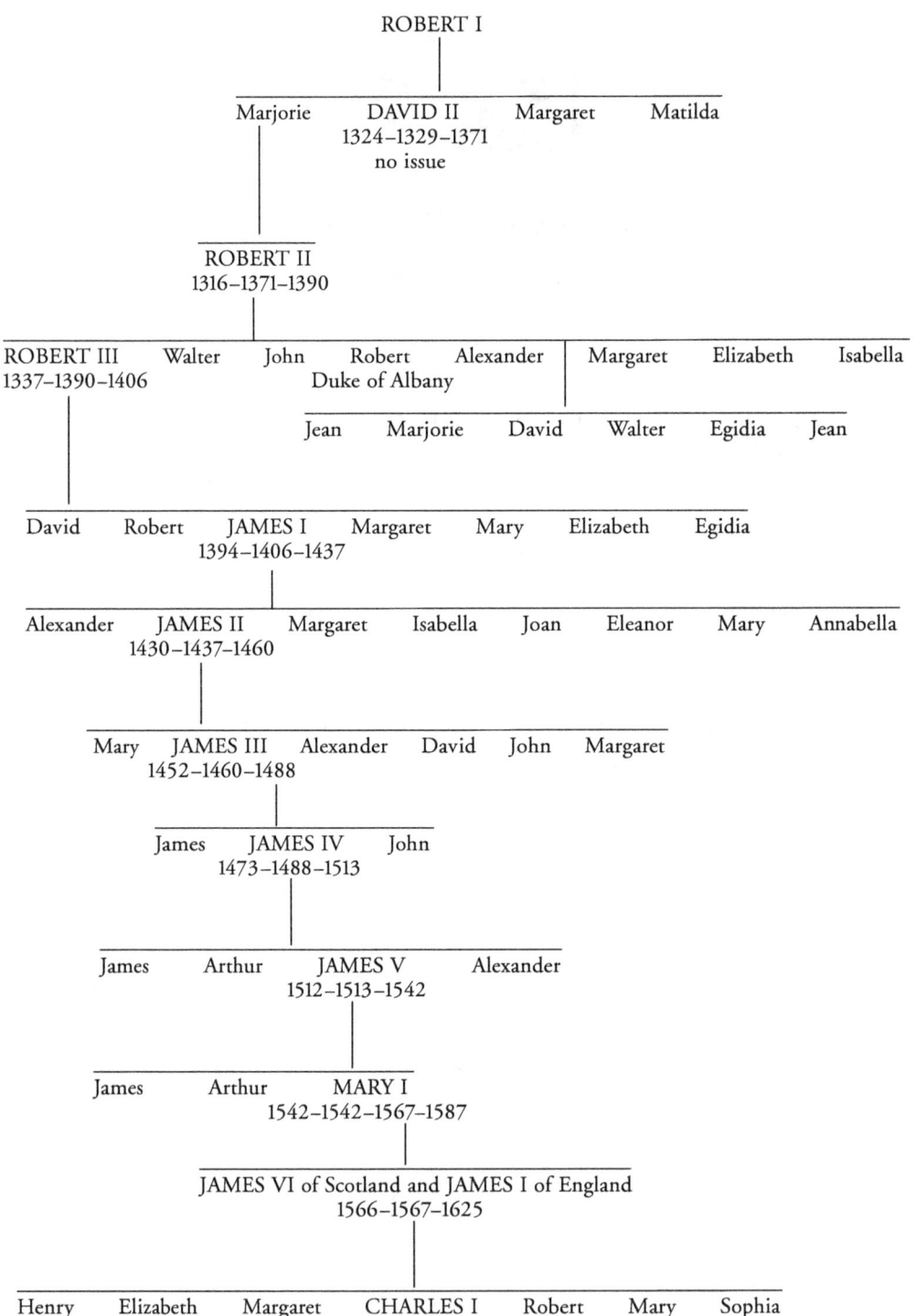

Kings and queen of Scotland are in ALL CAPITALS

Overview

The kingdom of Scotland was united by the Canmore dynasty in 1058 through force of arms, ruling for over two hundred years until the death without a direct successor of its last monarch, Queen Margaret I. After the dissolution of the Canmore monarchy, the realm was propelled into years of bloody civil war and subjugation by the Plantagenet throne of England. As Scotland struggled under foreign occupation, in 1304 Robert Bruce, through force of personality and military might, began the long reconquest of independence and establishment of the Stewart regime, which reigned during the Renaissance era. The Stewart family ruled through eight monarchs, who battled against internal rebellion, defended their borders against English encroachments and created a recognized European power.

The reign of the first Renaissance king, Robert III, was dominated by the rebellion of his son, David, and an ongoing struggle to contain the aggression of the Plantagenet monarchy. While he continued to confront the attacks of England, his brother, Robert of Albany, attempted to seize his realm and establish a new Stewart dynasty. The second monarch of the Renaissance epoch was James I, who assumed the kingship in 1406, while a prisoner of the English government. After eighteen years of imprisonment, he claimed the crown from his usurper cousin, Murdac of Albany, and initiated a relentless campaign of suppression against his recalcitrant nobles to restore Stewart sovereignty over Scotland. Through the power of his administration, he expanded his kingdom's international presence and repute while increasingly participating in European state affairs.

James I was followed to the throne by his son, James II, in 1437 at age six. After years of misrule and rebellion during the ensuing regency administration, in 1450 he assumed the monarchy, asserting control over the warring magnates through martial might to end the threat of internal conflict. With unimpeded authority, he initiated reforms to expand Scotland's economy and restore its judicial system, resulting in a period of prosperity and peace. The fourth Stewart king was James III, who inherited the reins of kingship in the aftermath of a series of inept regency governments. As he attempted to impose his supremacy, his relentless and brutal suppression policies directed against the recalcitrant nobles resulted in civil war and his death in battle at Sauchieburn in defense of his sovereignty. He was succeeded to the crown by James IV, whose reign was dominated by a golden age and advancement of Renaissance art, architecture and science. Under his rule Scotland became a recognized international power, actively engaging in European politics. He continued Scotland's historic friendship and military alliance with France, participating in the Holy League War against the papacy and England. In 1513 James IV commanded a large pillaging raid in support of his French ally into the northern English counties, resulting in his death at the battle of Flodden Hill.

After a turbulent regency administration, in 1528 James V assumed the monarchy to reign as the sixth Stewart king. Under his reign the sporadic war against England and subjugation campaign to impose the regime's power over the nobility were continued. The rule of his heir, Mary I, was dominated by her forced abdication and subsequent involvement and execution in the plots to enforce her hereditary rights to the English crown through the attempted assassination of Elizabeth I. The last king of the Renaissance era was James VI, who fully asserted his sovereignty by military might over the rebellious Scottish magnates and church to govern unchallenged. He initiated policies to bring détente with the court of Elizabeth I and in 1603 after her death inherited the English kingdom as the acknowledged successor by blood birthright.

Robert III, 1337–1390–1406

In the aftermath of the death of Robert II in April 1390, John Stewart, Earl of Carrick, formally succeeded to the monarchy of Scotland as Robert III to rule as the first Renaissance king for the next sixteen years. After assuming the throne, he chose the name of his father and great-grandfather to more closely associate his reign with the prior Stewart dynasty. John was the first of the four sons of Robert of Stewart, high steward of Scotland, and his first wife, Elizabeth Mure, and was born in August 1337 in the Priory at Scone. At an early age he was granted the lordship of Kyle in southwestern Scotland by the steward and spent the majority of his first years on his father's extensive estates. Tutors from the church provided his education and he was taught the basics of reading and writing along with religious dogma. While receiving only a limited academic education, renowned masters of arms were appointed for John's military training in weapons and battle tactics in preparation for his future assumption of power as high steward of Scotland and head of the Stewart family. The Kyle lord and his brothers and sisters were initially considered illegitimate by the Scottish church due to the close consanguineous relationship between Robert of Stewart and his wife. However, in 1347 his father received a papal dispensation from Pope Clement VI, which officially ended any uncertainty about the legality of the marriage.

In October 1346 after the Scottish king David II was defeated and captured by the English at the battle of Neville's Cross, the high steward was appointed by Parliament to lead a regency government and drive the invaders out of their newly seized lands. John of Kyle began his public career by serving as commander for a contingent of soldiers, attacking the English forces in the western lordships. In support of his father's rule, he was actively engaged in reasserting the sovereign's authority over the earldom of Carrick from English occupation. By the time of David II's release from captivity in 1357 and his assumption of the Scottish crown, John's aggressive campaign had eliminated the foreign troops from the Carrick region. As a prominent magnate and heir to the Stewart demesne, the Kyle lord was later compelled to serve as one of twenty hostages to England, guaranteeing the ransom of the Bruce king.

Following his release as a hostage in England and return to his lands, in March 1363 John energetically defended his father's participation in the brief War of the Three Earls against the Scottish crown. As the leader of a western fief, the lord of Kyle served in several attacks by the rebel forces against the Bruce regime's troops and vassals. However, the Stewart family's involvement in the revolt was short and by April along with the high steward, John had submitted to David II. Despite the formal reconciliation with the royal court, relations between the Bruce king and Stewart alliance remained distant and hostile. When the government launched a political offensive to replace the Steward as heir apparent, the Stewarts enthusiastically challenged the throne's initiatives. Robert of Stewart rallied the majority of the magnates, prelates and burghs to his defense, thwarting the attempted usurpation of his inheritance rights. As the eldest of his sons, John would assume the title of successor designate if the king died childless, and he actively supported his father's campaign to preserve his standing in the line of succession.

As the king continued to rule without a direct heir, John's popularity and prestige among the Scots escalated, compelling David II to increasingly rely on him for support. To more closely bind John to his kingship, in 1367 the monarch arranged the marriage of the western lord to his wife's niece, Annabella Drummond. Soon after the wedding, John was granted the earldom of Atholl by the steward. As further recognition of his standing in the royal succession, in the following year David II named the Atholl prince as overlord for the traditional Bruce earldom of Carrick. However, later in the year the Stewart family's seemingly secure inheritance rights to the crown became threatened when David II suddenly announced plans to divorce Queen Margaret Drummond and marry again in the quest for a direct heir.

The Drummonds had risen to positions of importance and power in the Scottish regime through the marriage of Margaret to David II. The politically arranged marital union between John of Carrick and Annabella Drummond brought the Stewart family increased presence at court and prestige among the Scottish warlords. After Robert III assumed the monarchy in 1390, Annabella took an active interest and role in crown affairs, serving as a trusted advisor to her husband. At the direction of the king, she served as an envoy to England, promoting peace by negotiating directly with the council of Henry IV. The union resulted in the birth of seven children, including the future King James I in 1394.

The second marriage of David II to Margaret Drummond was childless and politically disruptive. While he campaigned to gain papal approval for a divorce from the queen, relations with the Stewart family steadily deteriorated as John of Carrick energetically attempted to thwart the king's legal separation to protect his bloodrights to the Scottish crown. As the initiatives of the Steward and his son grew more aggressive and hostile, in 1369 David II ordered their arrest, while their lands were occupied by royal troops. The period of captivity was short as the powerful Stewart faction rallied to their support, quickly compelling David II to arrange their release.

During the next two years John largely remained isolated from the Bruce court, residing on his western lands. However, in February 1371 the Scottish political environment changed dramatically in the Stewart family's favor with the death of David II without direct issue. As the acknowledged rightful successor by birthright, Robert Stewart was proclaimed king by Parliament and in March anointed as Robert II at Scone Abbey. Later in the year the Scottish Parliament confirmed John's place in the order of succession by naming him heir apparent. John was already recognized as the dominant magnate in the western region and his formal acceptance as successor designate brought him increased power and prestige among the bishops, burghs and nobles. Using his dominance as a formidable magnate in the regime, the Carrick earl began to expand his authority and influence into the Lowland fiefs, forging an alliance with William, first Earl of Douglas, and the Lindsey family to secure his hold over the southern region.

While the Stewarts were firmly establishing their sovereignty over Scotland, in England the boy-king, Richard II, succeeded his grandfather, Edward III, to the monarchy in June 1377. With the Plantagenet government occupied with an internal power struggle, the southern Scottish warlords under the energetic leadership of John of Carrick began a military campaign to reconquer their seized estates from English occupation. As the result of his attacks, the local lords increasingly recognized the earl as the defender of their liberties and lands. In the border region the regime's law and justice were enforced by John as he became the crown's ruling authority and power. The court formally confirmed his position in 1381 by appointing him royal lieutenant for the Lowland earldoms. In this capacity he also became the throne's envoy for the resolution of frontier disputes with the English, which further enhanced his supremacy among the area's prelates and lords.

By late 1384 John Stewart had acquired a reputation as an energetic and skilled military leader and guardian of Scottish rights and lands. He exploited his standing among the nobles and churchmen to forge a formidable power base which was used to seize the government from his father. Robert II's rule had grown increasingly unpopular in recent years, due to the repeated lawlessness in the northern fiefdoms and his regime's lack of interest and energy in supporting an escalation in the punitive raids against England. When the Parliament met at Holyrood in November, the Carrick earl was appointed lieutenant for Scotland, usurping the monarchy of his father.

To consolidate his government after assuming the guardianship for Scotland, John of Carrick directed his first policy initiative against his rebellious brother, Alexander, Earl of Buchan and Ross. The younger Stewart had secured control of the northern Scottish princedoms through a relentless program of suppression and brutality, which had incurred the alarm and disfavor of the southern lords and the church. Robert II had been unable to impose his authority over his son, weakening the Stewart regime's prestige and stature among the earldoms. To win the support of the Lowland burghs, clerics and lords, the Carrick earl launched a political and military offensive to subdue Alexander. However, the campaign was abandoned when the Stewart regency became increasingly distracted by the threat of war against England on the southern border.

As cross-border plundering encroachments and tensions between Scotland and the Plantagenet regime intensified, the Stewart court negotiated a treaty of alliance with the French crown in 1385 and with the promise of troops and money preparations began for a large raid into England. In July after the arrival of the pledged aid, the Scottish-Franco forces launched their punitive offensive. The lieutenant of the realm's attack initially encountered little resistance as the English border towns and farms were brutally pillaged and burned. However, as the allies advanced farther south, the campaign was abandoned with the approach of a formidable English army. The political prestige of John Stewart was seriously damaged with the magnates and prelates when the soldiers of Richard II were permitted to continue their initiative unchallenged into southern Scotland. The heir's lack of intervention in confronting the English caused a serious erosion in his ability to govern the kingdom. During the following three years, he retained his office with the support of the Lowland warlords and clergy. However, after the death of his chief allies, James, second Earl of Douglas, and James Lindsay, at the battle of Otterburn and the growing power of his ambitious brother, Robert, Earl of Fife, in December 1388 the Edinburgh Parliament overthrew the lieutenancy of John Stewart. In the aftermath of John's ouster, the legislative assembly appointed the Fife earl to succeed his brother as lieutenant. Robert of Fife was the third son of King Robert II and Elizabeth Mure of Rowallan and was born in 1340 at Dundonald, Ayrshire. As the third son he was not educated for the kingship but through the force of his charismatic personality assumed a leading role in his father's government. Through his marriage to Margaret Graham, he inherited the earldoms of Fife and Mentieth. The earl was appointed high chamberlain by his father in 1382 and commanded numerous successful pillaging raids into England in defense of Scottish territorial rights, building a reputation as an energetic and skilled military commander.

With the loss of his guardianship, John returned to his western estates while Robert Stewart assumed the government of Scotland. However, in April 1390 King Robert II died and as his acknowledged heir, John launched an energetic campaign to succeed to the monarchy with unrestricted authority. His quest for Parliament's approval was aided by the continued brutal attacks of Alexander of Buchan into the Moray earldom in defiance of the Earl of Fife's regime, which weakened his prestige and popularity among the prelates and magnates. The political initiatives of the Carrick earl combined with Robert's inability to protect the north resulted in John Stewart's recognition as successor to his father. On August 14, 1390, at the Scone Abbey, he was anointed and crowned as Robert III. However, his assumption of the monarchy was impeded when his brother was reaffirmed as guardian for the realm, severely limiting the new king's ability to rule independently. The power to govern the kingdom and establish policy remained under the control of Robert, Earl of Fife, as regent for Scotland, compelling the Stewart king to form an opposition faction to regain full sovereignty and safeguard the inheritance rights of his son, David.

Soon after the investiture, Robert III began a political offensive to end the guardianship of his brother. Using the authority and prestige of the crown and his strong relationship with the southern warlords, he began to establish a counter-faction centered on his heir, David Stewart. Through the liberal use of royal pensions and privileges, the king and his son were able to draw numerous magnates and prelates to their cause. To further enhance his esteem, David was appointed earl of Carrick and his court was soon dominated by churchmen and lords from the southern fiefs. David Stewart and his allies became the focal point of the throne's initiative to regain unrestricted control of the monarchy. As the Carrick earl's popularity increased, the Stewart government's power base grew, undermining Robert of Fife's position as guardian. Under the mounting influence of Robert III's alliance, in February 1393 the Scottish Parliament withdrew the regency of the Earl of Fife and restored the king to total sovereignty.

After the end of the lieutenancy of Robert of Fife, the fifty-six-year-old king increasingly withdrew from the ruling council and David assumed authority to rule in the name of his father. Through his initiatives, the royal supremacy was further advanced into the southwest by a series of political alliances with the local warlords. The king's new allies were rewarded with offices in the government and granted honors and titles, securing the realm's control over the area. The Earl of Carrick also mounted sporadic attacks into the Highland earldoms against his recalcitrant uncle, which enhanced his stature and power as the defender of the crown's rights. As part of his campaign to pacify the northern region and enforce the regime's law, in September 1396 the earl arranged to settle the ongoing dispute between two warring families by judicial trial by combat. The Battle of the Clans was fought to the death between two contingents of warriors, armed with swords, shields and crossbows. The trial was personally attended by the monarch and his court as evidence of his ability to impose the royal will over the rebellious Highlanders. Robert III and his son departed from the north with their prestige and authority enhanced as the protectors of Scottish law and justice.

Through the use of royal patronage and partisan alliances, by 1398 David Stewart became the leader of crown policy, overthrowing his father's rule. As the heir assumed supremacy over the government, Robert III's personal authority and sovereignty were largely ignored. The Earl of Carrick had been made a permanent member of the royal council and had assumed the mantle of defender of Scottish independence. In April 1398 David was named Duke of Rothesay by Parliament in recognition of his new political power and influential status at court, as Robert III became increasingly viewed with dissatisfaction and scorn. As his control over Scotland rapidly deteriorated, in the summer he attempted to regain his popular support by personally commanding siege operations against the rebellious lord of the strategic castle of Dumbarton. However, after three months the investment was abandoned after his treasury was depleted and many of his troops deserted, severely weakening the power and acceptance of Robert III. In January 1399 the leading magnates and bishops assembled at Perth, removing the king from the monarchy and replacing him with a regency government led by the Duke of Rothesay and aided by an advisory committee, dominated by nobles loyal to the newly created Duke of Albany, Robert Stewart of Fife.

Following the Scottish victory at the battle of Otterburn in 1388, a truce had been signed with the English crown which had resulted in peace in the border counties. However, in September 1399 Richard II of England was overthrown by Henry Bolingbroke, Duke of Lancaster, who assumed the monarchy as Henry IV. His usurpation resulted in a period of internal conflict and uncertainty which was exploited by the Lowland Scots to launch a series of raids against the rich lands in northern England in search of plunder. As the border incursions grew in strength and frequency and all attempts by the English to negotiate a peaceful resolution failed, in June 1400 Henry IV assembled a formidable army at York to force his will on the Scots. As the Lancastrians launched their attack, the king remained on his western estates, relegating the defenses of the realm to his son and regency administration. However, as the invading forces marched north from York, the Scottish troops under the command of the regent refused to confront the powerful army, withdrawing to the protection of Edinburgh Castle. As the English began siege operations, the Scottish garrison, commanded by the Rothesay duke and the fourth Earl of Black Douglas, Archibald, resisted all attempts to seize the stronghold. As the siege at Edinburgh wore on, after two weeks of fruitless talks and lacking money and arms to continue his attack, Henry IV was compelled to abandon the campaign with few tangible gains. Archibald was the eldest son of Archibald of Douglas and Joanne of Bothwell and was born in 1372 at Threave Castle in western Scotland. In 1390 his father ceded him the right to rule the regions of Ettrick Forest and Lauderdale. Through his marriage to Margaret of Carrick, daughter of Robert III, he gained a close association to the royal court and government. As a trusted and loyal member of the royal family, Archibald was appointed captain of the strategic castle of Edinburgh by his father-in-law. At the death of his father, he was acknowledged as the successor to the vast Douglas lordships and created earl. The Black Douglas was the most powerful and wealthy magnate in Scotland, commanding a large alliance of Lowland warlords. In recognition of his prominence in the south, he was appointed warden of the Marches by Robert III. In early 1400 in defense of his lands, Archibald defeated a large marauding force led by Sir Henry Percy, gaining renown for his military skills and energy.

While David Stewart and the Duke of Albany had largely cooperated during the English invasion, in the following year dissent erupted between them. The discord developed soon after the death of the queen and chief prelate, who had exercised a strong measure of restraint on the ambitious David. Without the constraining influence of his mother and the church, the Rothesay duke began to appropriate royal funds for his personal use, ignoring the office of treasurer held by his uncle. By late 1401 his actions became more open and aggressive as he defiantly disregarded the Duke of Albany and regency council to rule as an independent monarch. However, when he schemed to seize control of the rich Saint Andrews Bishopric, a coalition of high magnates was formed in opposition by Robert of Albany. With the support of his formidable allies, he ordered the arrest of Rothesay, imprisoning him at his Falkland Castle. Robert aggressively moved to neutralize the duke's sympathizers and by intimidation and bribery secured their approval for the confinement of his nephew. David's powerful ally, Archibald of Douglas, was bribed with lands from the earldom of March to approve the seizure of the government. The continued imprisonment of the heir and usurpation of the king's government were implemented without any opposition from Robert III, who remained isolated and ignored.

As Robert of Albany consolidated his usurpation, David remained in captivity at Falkland Castle. However, even from his imprisonment the duke retained a large following of supporters, who posed a potential danger to the rule of Albany and his allies. To secure his seizure of the kingdom and end the threat of his nephew, Robert ordered the murder of the Rothesay duke by starvation. David Stewart died in March 1402 as a result of his uncle's quest for power. After the death of the duke, in May the Parliament was summoned to Edinburgh to officially recognize Robert's appointment as the lieutenant of the kingdom and his assumption of unrestricted authority.

After the elimination of the threat from David of Rothesay, the realm's lieutenant solidified his rule further by appointing the powerful Lowland warlord, Archibald of Black Douglas, as his chief advisor. Archibald still retained his hereditary rights to many English occupied Lowland fiefs and under his influence the lieutenant approved an attack against Henry IV. As relations with England quickly deteriorated and truce negotiations collapsed, in September 1402 Archibald, Earl of Douglas, personally commanded a large pillaging army into England. However, when the Scots marched south toward Newcastle, the northern English barons led by the Earl of Northumberland and his son, Henry Hotspur Percy, countered the incursion by advancing their militia to meet Sir Archibald at Homildon Hill. In the resulting battle, the invading forces were routed by the well commanded and disciplined troops of the Percys. The English victory at Homildon Hill resulted in disastrous repercussions for Robert of Albany, as the political unity forged with the Black Douglas in the south was shattered.

At the battle of Homildon Hill, the majority of the Scottish army had been recruited from the border counties. In the aftermath of the defeat, the Earl of Douglas and many of the regent's most powerful allies had been either killed or captured. The loss created a large power vacuum among the southern princedoms, leaving the region open to further English counterattacks. In early 1403 Henry IV became resolved to press his Homildon Hill victory by forcibly annexing the unprotected south of Scotland. His campaign of conquest was begun by granting the estates of Archibald of Douglas to the Earl of Northumberland and empowering him to mobilize his army to enforce the Lancaster crown's will. In the spring of 1403 Henry Percy's militia moved against the castle at Cocklaws to begin the subjugation of southern Scotland. However, when the Percy family became directly involved in the plot to overthrow Henry IV, they withdrew their troops from the war, leaving Scotland free of English forces.

While Sir Henry Percy was besieging the Scottish castle at Cocklaws, the guardian was unable to raise sufficient troops to relieve the investment. However, with the Percys' participation in the rebellion against Henry IV, the border lordships were largely void of English forces and Robert assembled his vassals to mount a counterattack against the lightly garrisoned strongholds. The campaign met with little opposition and the recently seized fiefdoms were quickly reoccupied. While the kingdom suffered no loss of land, the early success of the English offensive resulted in a severe deterioration of Robert of Albany's prestige and repute, as the defender of Scottish freedom and territorial rights.

As support for the Duke of Albany's continued rule declined, in 1404 the Scottish king ended his self-imposed exile and launched a political campaign for his restoration to power. He personally attended the Parliament at Linlithgow to announce his resumption of the monarchy and the purge of his brother's allies from the royal council. As he increasingly enforced his will, Robert III began to closely associate his young son and heir, James, with his new regime. The king had previously established a long standing relationship with the southern lordships and with his return to the government forged a new alliance with his former sympathizers. By the end of the year, through the aggressive and energetic interventions of the crown, Robert III once again became the center of court power and influence. In the following year he traveled extensively through the southern fiefs, attempting to reassert his authority by the generous use of royal patronage. However by 1406, his continued granting of political favors directed at only a small close circle of friends and advisors created hostility and resentment from the coalition loyal to Robert of Albany. As the belligerent threat from his brother grew in strength, in March 1406 Robert III began preparations to send his only surviving son, James, to safety in France.

As James Stewart began his journey to France, his escort party was intercepted by allies of the Duke of Albany. In the ensuing melee, James managed to escape, finally finding passage across the North Sea on March 22. However, English pirates captured his ship and he was taken to London as the prisoner of Henry IV. While James was attempting his escape to France, the health of Robert III declined rapidly and after hearing the reports of his son's captivity, he died on April 6, 1406, at age sixty-nine and a reign of sixteen years.

Sources

Boardman. *The Early Stewart Kings.*   Oram. *The Kings & Queens of Scotland.*   Penman. *David II.*

James I, 1394–1406–1437

In April 1406 Robert III died and the Scottish Parliament recognized his son, James I, as his successor to reign as the second Renaissance king. James Stewart was born late on December 10, 1394, at Dunfermline Priory and was the third son of Robert III and Queen Annabella Drummond. The royal prince's early childhood was spent in the secure environment of his mother's household. She arranged for his education by appointing the bishop of Saint Andrews to employ scholar monks and he was instructed in the basics of reading, writing, religion and languages. As James approached the age of seven, the king provided renowned knights for his son's initial military training as a knight.

As James remained on his father's western estates, in 1402 his uncle, Robert of Albany, attempted to overthrow the monarchy of the ruling Stewart family by arranging the murder of the heir designate, David, Duke of Rothesay. However, after the death of the duke, his eight-year-old brother, James, was recognized as successor by the Scottish Parliament, thwarting the assumption of sovereign power by the cadet Albany Stewart line. Despite the initial setback, Duke Robert continued his campaign to seize his brother's crown and by early 1406 had usurped the throne, while consolidating his authority over Scotland as the acknowledged guardian. With control of the regime, his attacks against Robert III's household grew increasingly hostile. In March the king began to fear for the safety of his son, making preparations to send him to the protection of the French court. However, as James began his voyage to France, his ship was captured by sea-raiders loyal to Henry IV of England.

Following his seizure, James was taken to the Tower of London as the prisoner of the Lancastrian crown. While remaining in the Tower, in April 1406 his father died and James I was recognized as successor to the monarchy in the following month by the Scottish Parliament. However, with the king's continued confinement in England, the high nobles and prelates reappointment Robert of Albany as guardian for the realm. With his election Robert was king in all but name as he firmly seized control of the government in the absence of the royal family. The regent showed little interest in arranging talks with the English to negotiate terms for the release of his nephew as he schemed to establish a new Albany dynasty in Scotland.

With the prospects for an early settlement shattered, James I was taken to the security of Pevensey Castle, where Henry IV provided for his care and education. Sir John Pelham, lord of Sussex, was appointed as governor and tutors were employed for his instruction in the liberal arts and sciences. The Stewart king had a natural aptitude for learning, exhibiting an energetic and inquisitive intellect. He was a serious student, excelling in his studies of reading, writing, literature, religion and the languages of Latin and French. He developed a special interest in English poetry, becoming devoted to the works of Chaucer. The Stewart king wrote several renowned pieces of prose in the Chaucerian style. He was exposed to the social graces, mastering various forms of music, particularly the singing of ballads. However, the focus of his education was directed at his training in the military skills of a knight. James I was instructed in the use of the lance, sword and poleax and mastered the techniques of jousting while becoming an accomplished equestrian. He was physically described as medium in height with broad shoulders and muscular in frame with a natural athleticism and charismatic personality.

While the king remained in captivity, he was provided a largely Scottish household. Through the small royal court, James I maintained contacts with his kingdom as numerous attempts were made to enforce his sovereignty rights and influence crown affairs. The communications with Scotland served to remind the magnates and prelates of their allegiance to the Stewart monarchy and James I. There were frequent visitors from Scotland who kept the monarch informed on local matters and the governorship of Robert of Albany. As his imprisonment wore on, Archibald of Douglas led several attempts by loyal Stewart allies to negotiate his ruler's ransom but his initiatives ended in failure.

The Scottish king had been held under limited confinement during the reign of Henry IV and had been a frequent visitor and guest to his household. However, after the succession of the second Lancastrian king, Henry V, in 1413 the imprisonment became more stringent with James I's removal to the Tower of London. With the northern English border counties at peace, the Scottish prisoner had little political negotiating value and it was not until the status quo changed during the ongoing Hundred Years' War in France, that James I was once again able to play a role in crown politics.

In 1417 Henry V invaded the duchy of Normandy and began to drive the French into the Ile de France region. As the English relentlessly pursued their attack, in late 1420 the Valois army was compelled to abandon Paris. After Henry V occupied Paris and advanced his campaign into the Loire Valley, the French regency government of the dauphin, Charles, began negotiations with Scotland for an alliance. The Stewart regime under the regency government of the aging Robert of Albany and his aggressive and ambitious son, Murdac, pledged to send a strong force of knights and infantry to augment the hard pressed French war effort. After the arrival of fresh troops and experienced military commanders, the dauphin's forces were able to inflict several stinging defeats on the English to limit their offensive.

As the Lancaster attack stalled, the government offered James I command of a contingent of English troops in France. His active participation in the war rendered the Franco-Scottish alliance illegal and in opposition to the will of their acknowledged ruler. In 1420 James I crossed the English Channel, joining the Lancaster campaign south of Paris to confront the French during the summer. In the following year he returned to France to play a more significant role in the ongoing conflict as commander of the siege at Dreux and was later knighted by Henry V for his military skills and leadership. The Scottish king became an active member of the Lancaster regime and was involved with local politics, steadily building a reputation as a friend and ally of the English court.

To enhance his relationship with the Lancastrian regime after his return from France, in 1421 James I befriended the powerful Beaufort family. Thomas and Henry Beaufort were uncles of Henry V and trusted advisors to his council. Through his relationship with the Beauforts, the Stewart king first met their niece, Joan. Over the next three years Joan and he developed a devotion and love for each other and were married in February 1424. She later became the subject of one of his most famous poems. After the Stewart monarch assumed power in Scotland, his queen became a close and trusted advisor, exerting a strong influence over crown affairs. She maintained contacts with the English court and James I used her family's standing and friends in the Lancaster household to influence negotiations with Henry VI. James I and Joan had six daughters and twin sons born in 1430 but the first son, Alexander, died soon after birth, leaving Prince James to secure the monarchy for the Stewart dynasty.

In August 1422 the charismatic and triumphant military captain Henry V suddenly died in France and was succeeded by his infant son, Henry VI. A regency council was established to rule in England under Humphrey, duke of Gloucester, and James I continued his friendship with the new administration. As the regency regime of Robert of Albany and Murdac Stewart expanded its military presence in France in defiance of the king's policy, the English attempted to ransom their Stewart prisoner to end the Scots' involvement in the ongoing war. James I's efforts to obtain his release were further aided by his relationship and marriage into the prominent Beaufort family, who utilized its standing at court to promote his cause. By 1423 he had pressed the Lancastrian council into renewing negotiations with the Scottish government of his cousin, Murdac Stewart, who had succeeded his father, Robert of Albany, as guardian for the realm three years earlier. However, Murdac initially exhibited little interest in seeking James I's freedom, only agreeing to talks after strong political opposition from the pro–Stewart faction under the leadership of the powerful and influential earl of Black Douglas, Archibald, and the king's uncle, Walter Stewart of Atholl. After prolonged deliberations, the Treaty of London was signed, which granted the freedom of the Scottish king in exchange for the payment of an indemnity and promise to end all aid to the French war effort. In April 1424 James I finally crossed the border into Scotland to begin his personal kingship after eighteen years of imprisonment.

While James I was imprisoned in London, his kingdom suffered years of misrule by his uncle, Robert of Albany, and later the incompetent and self-aggrandizing administration of his cousin, Murdac. Murdac Stewart was the only son of Robert of Albany and Margaret of Menteith and was born in 1362 at Dundonald. Through his father's lineage, he was a member of the ruling Stewart family and nephew of King Robert III. In defense of Scottish territorial rights, he commanded several raids against England and was captured in battle. After his release from confinement, he served in his father's regime, assuming high positions in the ruling council. When his father died in 1420, he inherited the duchy of Albany and earldoms of Fife and Menteith and was appointed as successor to the regency government by Parliament. Under the two Albany guardianships, the power and stature of the monarchy were greatly eroded with the loss of crownlands and tax revenues, while the realm was plunged into a costly war in France, resulting in the death of many nobles, including the Black Douglas who was killed at the battle of Verneuil in August 1424. By the time of the monarch's return, the authority and prestige of the Stewart sovereignty had been reduced to the level of a regional magnate. Many warlords had taken the period of lax government as an opportunity to establish their own autonomous princedoms in open defiance of the regents.

When James I finally assumed control of his monarchy, he directed his policies against the powerful Albany family to end the threat of rebellion from his cousins. In May 1424 the king ordered the arrest of Walter Stewart, eldest son of Murdac, on charges of treason. Walter had earlier created an independent fiefdom in Lennox and after the return of James I had continually defied his laws. In the following year, the king renewed his offensive against the rebellious Albany Stewarts, ordering the imprisonment of Murdac, his son Alexander and over twenty nobles from their alliance on charges of sedition against the kingdom. Late in 1425 after revolt erupted in Lennox, in support of the Albany Stewarts, he summoned the Parliament to Stirling Castle, securing authorization for the execution of his cousins and annexation of their estates to eliminate the major opposition to the imposition of his full sovereignty.

After the elimination of the Albany threat, the king directed his subjugation offensive against numerous rogue magnates in the northern earldoms and by the use of royal patronage and direct intimidation received their oaths of fealty. After reasserting his authority over the Highlands, the royal court advanced its initiative to the south, where the suppression of the earls and minor warlords was greatly facilitated by the crown's historic alliance with the Douglas faction. During James I's imprisonment, the Lowland fiefs had largely been consolidated under the leadership of Sir Archibald. His family had a long history of mutual friendship with the Stewart monarchy and through their support the king reclaimed sovereignty over the lower Scottish lands. By the end of 1425 he had eliminated the Albany danger and dramatically altered the balance of power between the monarchy and nobles in his favor. In the aftermath of the defeat of the recalcitrant lords, James I was free to reign without fear of revolt.

During his years of captivity in the Lancaster court, the Stewart king had been exposed to English institutions, customs and laws. After asserting his kingship, he introduced a new series of measures based on the English government to reform the structure of the Scottish administration and tax system. The procedures for the collection of royal revenues were made more efficient with all payments now made directly to the crown. To further weaken the wealth and power of the magnates, many of their long standing pensions and grants of royal patronage were eliminated, while influential regime offices were given to the lesser nobles and clergy, who had loyalty to only the Stewarts. The royal council was reorganized with the legal and treasury functions separated into independent offices. To pay the English ransom payments, attempts were made to impose new taxes, which proved to be widely unpopular and were later modified or withdrawn. Changes were made to the judicial system, unifying and strengthening the criminal and civil laws to apply equally throughout the kingdom, while the legal courts were revised and expanded. There were efforts to improve agriculture output and the amount of foreign trade with continental Europe. James I continued the monarchy's sponsorship of the Scottish church by actively supporting new religious orders, construction of monasteries and initiating programs to strengthen the doctrines of the clergy.

James I's suppression of the Albany Stewarts in the Highland earldoms had been aided by his alliance with Alexander, Lord of the Isles, who controlled a large and powerful fiefdom in the northwest. The magnate had shared a common hostility against Murdac and his sons but following the destruction of the dissident faction, he increasingly defied royal policy and law. In 1428 Alexander began to plot to annex the earldom of Ross to his already extensive lands. While the Lord of the Isles continued to act as an independent prince, James I began military preparations to reassert his supremacy over the northwestern region. As the royalists advanced against the Isles' warlords, in August 1428 envoys were sent to Alexander and his allies to negotiate a settlement. However, when the talks began at the royal castle at Inverness, the rogues were arrested by the king and under threat of imprisonment and forfeiture of their estates; they rendered their pledge of loyalty to the Stewart crown. Nevertheless, soon after gaining his freedom and returning to his demesne, Alexander broke his oath by leading a large punitive raid against Inverness and in defiance of the Stewart monarchy supported the claim of James Mor, son of Duke Murdac, to the throne. To confront the new challenge to his authority, James I initiated a second military campaign, marching the regime's army against the rebels in late June. As he moved into the lordship of Badenoch, the Stewart troops attacked the ill prepared forces of Alexander at Lochaber, completely overwhelming him, as many of his allies quickly deserted to the king.

Following the victory at Lochaber, the king spent the summer months relentlessly pursuing Alexander and occupying his estates and castles. As the Stewart army remained in the north, the Lord of the Isles was finally compelled to surrender and fully submit to the crown. Alexander was taken to Perth where after a brief trial the Parliament ordered his imprisonment and forfeiture of lands. After the elimination of the threat, James I appointed the Earl of Mar, Alexander, as his northern lieutenant to renew the campaign to enforce his rule in the northwest against the continued rebellion of the allies of the Lord of the Isles.

As James I imposed his authority over the Scottish magnates and burghs to secure his rule, his power and prestige escalated in the realm and among the European courts, posing an increasing threat to the security of England. In 1427 the yearly ransom payment due for his release from Lancaster captivity was ignored, as relations with Henry VI grew increasingly strained. In the following year, to strengthen Scottish independence from the danger of English domination, the Stewart regime negotiated a military alliance with France, which included a provision for the marriage of the king's infant daughter, Margaret, to the heir of Charles VII. The treaty brought increased esteem and stature among the European kingdoms, raising the Stewart monarchy to new levels of international respect. To further his quest for greater autonomy, the king reformed and modernized his military and began the practice of maintaining a permanent standing household army. Under James I's sovereignty, there was an increased emphasis on the use of artillery and new cannons were purchased from continental manufacturers.

With Scotland's new international recognition, James I began to assume a more aggressive diplomatic role in European politics. He actively pursued reforms in his local church and discouraged papal interference in Scottish ecclesiastical affairs. The Scots had long defended the anti-popes of Avignon during the Great Schism and had only reluctantly acknowledged an unified Holy See after the election of Pope Martin V in 1417. As the new pontiff attempted to reimpose his autocratic rule, James I openly backed the rebel clergymen at the Council of Basel, who met to restrict the authority of the papacy. The defeat of Martin V would preserve the benefices and legal powers to enforce church law, which the monarchy had earlier seized during the schism. James I became allied with the French court as both kingdoms opposed the Holy See in its quest for greater religious independence. The anti-papacy alliance with France also served to distance Scotland from the Lancastrian regime, which supported the restoration of the pontiff in Rome with full primacy.

As the prestige of the Stewart regime grew, the king began to spend lavishly to enhance the image of a powerful and wealthy realm. The royal residence at Linlithgow was rebuilt in the opulent style of a Renaissance pleasure palace. Enhancements were made to other crown properties designed to emulate the European courts and openly display the new prosperity and stature of the Scottish kingdom. The royal apartments were richly decorated in the latest fashion and new luxury items were imported from Europe. However, James I's extravagant lifestyle distanced his monarchy from the population, while increasing his growing unpopularity under the weight of heavy taxes.

While James I was aggressively reasserting his kingship and enhancing Scotland's international presence, the need for additional taxes to support his numerous political and military initiatives was greatly expanded. As the crown's financial demands grew, there was escalating resistance from the Parliament for more levies, compelling the king to find new sources of funds. The Stewart court borrowed heavily from the religious orders and forced the nobles and burghs to grant large loans, which it was slow to repay. In 1431 James I attempted to introduce a direct tax, which was met with a storm of protest and quickly withdrawn, as relations between the royal regime and the magnates, clergy and towns grew increasingly hostile. The inability to generate additional money served to seriously check the ambitions of the throne.

After appointing Alexander, Earl of Mar, to administer his policies and justice in the northern fiefs, James I renewed his campaign of suppression against the high magnates in the Lowlands. In 1431 he ordered the arrest of the region's principal leaders, Archibald, fifth Earl of Black Douglas, and Sir John Kennedy. The warlords were later reconciled with the crown, but their base of power and support among the Lowland lords was reduced as the regime enhanced its control and repute over the southern earls. James I continued to maintain a policy of hostility toward his nobles, taking every opportunity to reduce their prestige and authority but at the cost of distancing his monarchy from its primary sources of support and revenue.

In July 1435 the stability and peace in the northern lordships was shattered with the death of Alexander of Mar. He died without a direct heir and two prominent families began to maneuver to gain his vacant titles and lands. To secure control over the Mar earldom, Robert Erskine forged a political coalition among the local magnates, while Elizabeth of Mar, widowed daughter-in-law of Alexander, became the focus of a faction in opposition. As the two rivals schemed to gain dominance over the earldom, the Stewart king intervened to ensure his continued rule over the rich demesne. To gain sovereignty over Mar, James I became allied with Elizabeth and arranged her marriage to William Sinclair, who was a close friend and trusted advisor to his council and court. With the loyalty of the earldom guaranteed by the presence of Sinclair, in late 1435 Mar was granted to Elizabeth by the Stewart throne. After the rejection of his claims, Robert Erskine began to form a series of alliances with the regional warlords to confront the Stewart crown.

While the Stewart regime was dealing with the growing prospects of revolt in the Highland lordships, James I was compelled to confront the escalating breaches in the border truce with Henry VI. In the summer of 1435 the Lowlands Earl of March, Patrick Dunbar, rebelled against the Scottish throne and began independent talks with the English court for military aid. The Stewart king responded to his sedition by declaring his lands forfeited, forcing him to flee to London, where he negotiated an alliance with the Lancaster government. In September an English army and dissident Scots attacked southeastern Scotland in support of the deposed Earl of March. The raiders were intercepted and easily defeated by the crown's local lieutenant but the incursion signaled serious future problems for the Stewarts continued control over the Lowland lordships.

In February 1436 James I renewed his military alliance with Charles VII of France and finalized the marriage of his daughter, Margaret, to the dauphin, Louis. In the following month when she sailed to the Valois court, the king sent a Scottish army to directly aid the Valois war against Henry VI. As part of the new treaty, James I also pledged to open a second front against the Lancastrian regime by attacking the English border counties. Before launching his offensive, the king spent several months attempting to buttress his support and loyalty among the southern lords. After receiving their pledges of fealty, during July the royal army was assembled for the encroachment against England. In early August the Stewart troops crossed the frontier and were soon assaulting the Lancastrian stronghold at Roxburgh. The English garrison was well prepared and skillfully commanded, rejecting all offers of surrender. Confronted with the defiance of the castle's defenders, the Scots were compelled to establish siege operations. However, the Stewart crown's intervention quickly turned disastrous when internal dissent and mutual mistrust erupted among the warlords and all discipline and military order disappeared. As the magnates withdrew their soldiers from the investment and with the approach of a large English relief force, the campaign was abandoned. The failure to capture Roxburgh created serious political repercussions for James I, resulting in the deterioration of his prestige and loyalty among the nobles, prelates and towns, weakening his power to rule.

James I continued to sanction border raids against the English and began plans for another large invasion in the following year. In February 1437 James I summoned his Parliament to meet at Perth, where additional taxes to pursue the English war were requested. Under the leadership of his uncle, Walter Stewart, the legislative assembly rejected the demand with widespread hostility. Walter Stewart was born in 1358 and was the second son of King Robert II and his second wife, Euphemia of Ross. In 1390 he acquired the earldom of Caithness and later was ceded the Atholl earldom by the regency government of Robert of Albany. Walter energetically negotiated with the English regime to secure the release of James I from his London imprisonment. He was a member of the Parliamentary jury, trying Murdac Stewart and his two sons on charges of treason, authorizing their execution. The earl had once been a close advisor to James I and had been the recipient of royal patronage. However, by 1436 as the crown's requirements for money grew, many of Walter's rich grants were repealed. As the dissension intensified, during the winter months of 1437, the Atholl earl began to conspire to assassinate his nephew. Open rebellion occurred when the throne appointed James Kennedy to the vacant bishopric of Dunkeld in Walter's earldom of Perthshire. The new bishop was James I's nephew and the earl considered his succession to the bishopric as the Stewart council's first initiative toward the royal annexation of his Perthshire lands.

In February 1437 the Earl of Atholl began to forge an alliance for the assassination of James I with Robert Graham and other magnates, who were former sympathizers of the deposed Albany Stewarts and had suffered the loss of their estates and authority, as the result of the regime's subjugation of the nobility and expansion of its rule. The conspirators planned to murder James I in Perth during his stay at the Dominican Abbey and seize control of the realm's government by placing Walter Stewart in power as guardian for the king's young son. Early on the morning of February 21, the assassins led by Robert Graham entered the royal apartments at the Dominican Priory, attacking and killing James I. However, the plotters' attempted coup quickly ended in failure when the nobles and prelates led by Queen Joan rallied to the monarch's son, James II. The second Stewart king died at age forty-two after a reign of twenty-one years.

Sources

Brown. *James I.*   Donaldson. *Scottish Kings.*   Oram. *The Kings & Queens of Scotland.*

James II, 1430–1437–1460

In February 1437 James I was assassinated at the Dominican Abbey in Perth and was succeeded to the Stewart crown by his young son, James II, who ruled as the third Scottish king of the Renaissance era. James Stewart was born at Holyrood Abbey on October 16, 1430, and was the sole surviving son of James I and Queen Joan Beaufort. His early childhood was spent in the household of his mother with his six older sisters. At the age of one, he was named Duke of Rothesay in recognition of his status as heir apparent. After remaining in the queen's court during his infant years, the duke was placed in the custody of John Spens, who was a trusted counselor of the king and captain of Edinburgh Castle. For his safety he was taken to Edinburgh Castle, where Spens provided for his care, education and initial military training.

In late 1436 a conspiracy began to develop in opposition to the repressive policies of James I. The Stewart regime's initiatives, directed at the suppression of the nobles, increased taxes to support its foreign policy and lavish lifestyle paired with the recent failed military campaign against England had created a tide of rising unpopularity and resentment among the nobility. The plotters had suffered the seizure of their wealth and estates by the royal court and began to conspire to murder the king and seize control of the realm. In the ensuing power struggle, on the early morning of February 21, 1437, James I was assassinated in his chambers at Perth, but the attempt to kidnap his six-year-old heir failed. After the death of the king, loyal friends of the royal household quickly took the Duke of Rothesay to the safety of the queen. Under her protection James II was formally crowned king of Scotland one month later at Holyrood Abbey.

In March the Scottish Parliament was assembled in Edinburgh to officially recognize Queen Joan as guardian for her son and regent for the kingdom. Archibald, fifth Earl of Black Douglas, who controlled a large and powerful league of Lowland warlords, was appointed as her principal advisor and co-regent. As the new regime enforced its power, Walter Stewart and his co-conspirators in the murder of James I were captured and executed, as the guardians quickly eliminated an immediate danger against the new regency government. During the following two years, the king remained with his mother's court, as she attempted to impose her authority over the nobles and prelates. However, from the beginning of the regency a mutual distrust developed between the queen and Douglas which undermined the policy initiatives and legitimacy of the crown. Without a strong and unified central administration to defend the throne's laws and justice, civil unrest and open rebellion soon erupted, as the warlords began to assert their independence. The political stability and autocratic rule that had been crafted by the suppression offensive of James I was quickly destroyed.

As the queen attempted to enforce her regency administration, in 1439 Archibald Douglas died from the plague, leaving a large power vacuum in the Scottish government. To give her regime a strong base of support, Joan struggled to replace the earl with an equally dominant warlord but the suppression policies of James I had eliminated many of the high magnates, while other noble houses had disappeared after failing to produce heirs. Without a strong central government, the minor lords began to contend for supremacy and authority against Queen Joan.

While the regent struggled to establish a stable government, two families from the lower nobility began to aggressively challenge for hegemony over the kingdom. The Livingstons led by Lord Alexander of Callendar had been an influential member of James I's council, acquiring wealth, estates and high offices, including guardianship of Stirling Castle. They were opposed by the alliance of Sir William, first Lord of Crichton, who had been appointed master of the king's household and keeper of Edinburgh Castle, along with other prominent positions in the Stewart court. The fight for supremacy between these two rival factions and later the Black Douglas family dominated the minority years of James II's rule.

The appointment of Sir William of Crichton as captain of the Edinburgh stronghold gave him immediate possession of James II and as guardian for the young sovereign, he overthrew the queen's administration and usurped the Scottish kingdom. To challenge the loss of her regency, Joan negotiated a counteralliance with Alexander Livingston and his faction. With the military might of the Livingstons backing her, in the summer of 1439 she regained custody of her son, taking him to the security of Stirling Castle. With the support of her allies and control of the king, she reasserted her authority over Scotland. After regaining acceptance as regent, the queen attempted to establish her independent rule by marrying James Stewart of Lorne and forging a new coalition with his family. However, to prevent the seizure of their government, Lord Alexander and his Livingston sympathizers ordered the arrest of Joan and her new husband, seizing personal control over the royal court. The queen was forced to sign the Appointment to gain her release, agreeing to retire to her private household and take no part in future crown affairs. With the elimination of the queen and jurisdiction over James II, the Livingstons secured their dominance over the Scottish regime. Nevertheless, Sir William, Lord of Crichton, quickly thwarted the assumption of the realm by his rival by forcibly kidnapping James II and forming a party in opposition. As the Crichton and Livingston houses vied for supremacy, Scotland became ravaged by lawlessness and the private wars of local warlords, as neither family commanded the power to enforce its rule.

While the realm slipped into anarchy, William, sixth Earl of Douglas, forged a formidable league with the Lowland lords, becoming an influential counter force in Scottish politics. As the power and prestige of the Douglas earl grew, the Livingston and Crichton factions put aside their differences and united to eliminate their new rival. They negotiated an alliance with William's great-uncle and heir designate to the Douglas House, James, to secure the loyalty and participation of a southern faction of warlords. On November 24, 1440, Sir William was arrested while at dinner with James II and quickly executed in what became known as the Black Dinner. After the death of William, the extensive Douglas properties were assumed by James as the seventh earl, making him the single most important powerful magnate in Scotland. The Livingston, Crichton and Douglas triumvirate now ruled the kingdom, as each intrigued independently for supremacy, leaving Scotland with a weak and fragmented government.

As Scotland continued to suffer from the lack of a united government, in 1443 Alexander of Callendar and William Crichton again assumed control of the ruling council after the death of the Black Douglas. While the Livingstons and Crichtons struggled to enforce their rule, the Douglas lands were inherited by the earl's charismatic and ambitious son, William. William was born in 1425 and was the eldest son and heir of James, seventh Earl of Douglas, and Beatrice Sinclair. After the death of his father, William asserted his overlordship over his Lowland vassals and towns and restored the power and wealth of the Douglas family by reacquiring the lands of Galloway, Bothwell and Wigtoun, which were previously seized after the murder of the sixth earl at the Black Dinner. As the Lowlands' most formidable warlord, when war erupted with England in 1447, he commanded a large Scottish raid into the border counties, gaining widespread repute for his ravaging of Alnwick and Warkworth. As the kingdom's richest and most powerful nobleman, William became a part of the royal court, developing a close friendship with James II. Two years later the eighth Earl of Douglas used his relationship with the king and his stature and influence with the nobility and church to negotiate a separate political union with Lord Alexander of Callendar. Together they forced the Crichton House out of the administration with the Livingstons becoming the dominant member of the new regime. While the Lord of Callendar gained control of the major court and government offices, Earl William forged a series of alliances with formidable northern and western warlords to consolidate their new regency.

In October 1444 the Scottish Parliament officially ended the minority of James II but the Livingston-Douglas coalition refused to recognize his assumption of power, remaining in control of the monarchy. As the virtual prisoner of the regents, the Stewart king was isolated from the administration of his kingdom and had little preparation or support for his accession of the throne. With only limited participation in his government and lacking a large following, he was forced to rule through the existing regime of the Livingston-Douglas faction. It was not until his marriage in July 1449 to Mary of Guelders, niece of the powerful and wealthy Duke of Burgundy, Philip III, that James II was finally able to begin actively asserting his personal kingship. The marital union with one of the premier royal houses of Europe brought prestige to the Stewart regime and opened the vastly rich Flemish markets to Scotland, which greatly enhanced the king's stature among his high nobles and bishops, enabling him to begin the formation of his own political party.

The Scottish royal council began negotiations in 1448 with Arnold, Duke of Guelders, for the marriage of his daughter, Mary, to the Stewart king. The marital agreement was ratified in April of the following year and Mary sailed to her new kingdom in late June. The royal wedding was held on July 3 in Holyrood Abbey in a grand and elaborate celebration. Philip III was a formidable and wealthy ally of France and exerted a strong influence over continental affairs. His court was a center of political activism and Mary experienced the ducal statecraft as the duke held audiences with foreign ambassadors, court officials and vassal lords. She was raised and educated in the household of her uncle and exposed to the latest in the arts and letters of the Renaissance. The queen had an active and inquisitive intellect and with her exposure to the Burgundian government became a trusted and valuable ally to her husband. Under the influence of the queen, the art, architecture and music of the Renaissance were brought to Scotland. James II and Mary had six children, including the future James III born in 1452.

Soon after the marriage to Mary, the king began a political campaign to assert his personal rule over Scotland by first eliminating the Livingston faction from his government. He summoned the Parliament and ordered the trial of Lord Alexander and members of the Livingston family on charges of embezzlement. When the legislative assembly met in January 1450, the Livingstons and their allies were declared guilty of financial fraud and their titles and offices seized by the crown, giving James II control over all future appointments to his government. After the dismissal of the Livingstons, he established his first council and began to solidify his personal reign.

With the elimination of the Livingstons, the royal council moved to restrain the dominance of the Black Douglas faction. In early 1451, while Earl William was on a pilgrimage to Rome to celebrate the papal jubilee, James II seized his fief of Wigtoun. The crown's forced annexation of the region was widely unsupported and unpopular among the magnates, who feared a revival of the suppressive policies of James I. To avoid a future cause for rebellion, when the Black Douglas returned to his estates, the king negotiated a settlement and agreed to restore Wigtoun for his public submission to the throne's sovereignty. However, as hostilities continued between the two rivals, James II launched a political campaign to weaken the earl's southern faction through the liberal use of royal patronage. By granting titles, royal honors and with the threat of coercion, many of the warlords broke their allegiances to their overlord to join the Stewart regime and William of Douglas's authority over the Lowland magnates was now only marginally acknowledged.

To counter the loss of his support and military might, William formed an alliance with the Lord of the Isles, John Macdonald, and Alexander Lindsay, fourth Earl of Crawford, to protect his lands and wealth. With his sovereignty threatened, in February 1452 James II ordered William of Douglas to attend a meeting of the royal council and negotiate a resolution to the escalating danger of rebellion. The Black Douglas was issued a safe conduct and met with the king and his advisors at Stirling Castle on February 21. During the audience, James

II demanded the earl dissolve his coalition with Macdonald and Lindsay and submit to him. After two days of fervid and unsuccessful deliberations, James II became enraged at the continued insolence and defiance of William, drawing his knife and stabbing him to death. The Stewart king later successfully defended his assault before the general Parliament, as a justifiable act in defense of his kingdom.

After the death of William, the earldom of Douglas and leadership of his Lowland alliance were assumed by his brother, James. The ninth earl openly challenged the royal court by renouncing his family's oaths of fealty to the throne and sacking the towns surrounding Stirling Castle. Following the withdrawal of his allegiance to the Stewart crown, James Douglas sent envoys to Henry VI, offering to give homage to England in exchange for military aid. The Stewart king countered the acts of treason by launching a series of punitive raids into the southern earldoms, as the kingdom moved closer to civil war. While the regime pursued its armed campaign of suppression, James II continued to use royal patronage to win the loyalty of the Douglas allies. With his base of support weakening, in late August the earl was compelled to agree to peace terms and an uneasy stalemate resulted between the two rivals.

Following the settlement with the ninth Black Douglas, the Stewart council aggressively renewed its campaign to destroy his political party. Over the next three years the patronage policy of favoring the Lowland nobles with grants of royal offices, titles and lands was continued, resulting in the desertion of many of the earl's vassals and friends. With the Douglas power base further eroded, in March 1455 James II mobilized a formidable army and augmented with new artillery launched his offensive against the remaining allies of James Douglas. The rebel coalition was quickly defeated, as the regime directed its attack against the heartland of the Douglas family. The earl's castle at Abercorn was stormed after a month's siege and James was forced to flee to England for sanctuary. Despite the flight of their overlord, the surviving Lowland faction continued to resist the king but after the crown's decisive victory at the battle of Arkenholm in May and capture of Threave Castle, the Black Douglas rebellion was finally destroyed. The Earl of Douglas was later tried by the Scottish Parliament for treasonable acts against the kingdom and his extensive lands forfeited to the throne.

The successful campaign launched in March 1455 eliminated the threat of civil war and secured the independent rule of James II. With his monarchy unchallenged, the Stewart king energetically initiated a series of programs to enhance the economy. The continental relationships and prestige of his wife's family were utilized to expand the kingdom's commerce with the merchants of Flanders and France. New measures to improve agriculture output and wool trade production were introduced. James II reformed the judicial system by appointing new sheriffs and court officials and the law was aggressively enforced throughout the realm. Parliaments were summoned on a regular basis and relations between the monarch and the legislative assembly remained cordial. Under the influence of his well educated and pious queen, James II became a dedicated patron of the Scottish church and arts. The Stewart court maintained a close association with the high prelates and clergy to strengthen their bonds of mutual support. He sponsored new religious orders, monasteries and churches, while efforts were made to aid the poor and sick. The Renaissance style was beginning to take hold in Europe and Queen Mary imported artists and craftsmen to refurbish the royal castles in the latest fashions. The practice of royal patronage was expanded with the creation of new earldoms and the title of Lord of Parliament was established for the minor magnates. A new nobility class was originated, which owed its loyalty solely to the Stewart regime. James II's initiatives proved largely successful and enhanced the authority and popularity of the Stewart reign.

The suppression of the Scottish nobility enabled James II to initiate a more aggressive foreign policy. In 1455 the royal court traveled extensively throughout the western fiefdoms to strengthen the crown's authority and enforce the will of the king over the frequently recalcitrant warlords. To enhance his power over the region, James II opened negotiations with the Danish king, Christian I, to free Scotland from the existing feudal obligations for the Western Isles. The talks remained ongoing and were later expanded in 1459 to include a marriage alliance between the Duke of Rothesay and the daughter of Christian I. Overlordship for the Scandinavian controlled isles of Orkney and Shetlands was transferred to Scotland as security for the dowry.

In the border counties between Scotland and England, the local lords had maintained peace during the early reign of James II, despite sporadic raids by both kingdoms. However, freed from the threat of civil unrest and with a united kingdom, in 1455 the Stewart king began a more hostile policy toward his southern neighbor. In England a civil war had erupted for control of the monarchy between the Houses of Lancaster and York. In the ensuing Wars of the Roses, as internal conflict and strife erupted, James II exploited the opportunity to capture the two remaining Scottish enclaves still under English control at Berwick and Roxburgh. Under the crown's direction, the Scots mounted several punitive raids into Northumberland, while sorties were made against the castle at Berwick in preparation for a large attack. The war was renewed in the following year when a Scottish invasion force was launched against the English held Isle of Man, but the army of Henry VI was well prepared and drove back the king's troops.

Over the following three years there were sporadic raids into the northern counties but no large encroachment was initiated. However, in July 1460 the political stability in England was once again shattered, when the Yorkish army of the Duke of Warwick won a decisive victory over the Lancastrians, capturing Henry VI at Northampton and the English throne was claimed by the Duke of York, Edward. The Yorkish faction had earlier supported the Black Douglas in his rebellion against the Scottish crown and was hostile toward the kingship of James II. In the ensuing internal uncertainty and confusion in England following Edward IV's usurpation of the crown, the Stewart court was determined to seize the occupied enclaves at Berwick and Roxburgh. By the end of the month a formidable military force, augmented with a large contingent of the latest artillery, was mobilized and the campaign initiated with an attack against the castle at Roxburgh. The royal regime had utilized the assistance of Philip III of Burgundy to acquire the most advanced and largest cannons available. James II took a special interest in the artillery and was familiar with its operations. As the Scots besieged the Roxburgh Castle, on August 3, 1460, the king was participating in the firing of the heavy guns, when one exploded, killing him. At his death the third Stewart king was twenty-nine years old and ruler of Scotland for twenty-three years. He was succeeded to the monarchy by the eight-year-old Duke of Rothesay, as James III.

Sources

Barrell. *Medieval Scotland.*   Mackie. *Kings & Queens of Scotland.*   Oram. *The Kings & Queens of Scotland.*

James III, 1452–1460–1488

In early August 1460 James II was killed during his army's siege against the English occupied Roxburgh Castle and was succeeded to the Scottish throne by his son, James III, who reigned as the fourth Renaissance king. James Stewart was born in May 1452 at Saint Andrews Castle and was the eldest son of James II and Queen Mary of Guelders. Soon after his birth, he was named Duke of Rothesay to acknowledge his position as heir designate. The duke's childhood was spent in his mother's household with his three sisters and two brothers. His father appointed prominent scholars and theologians as tutors for his education and James was instructed in languages, reading, writing, religion and law. Under the influence of the queen, the duke developed an interest in the arts and architecture of the newly evolving Renaissance movement, which were actively pursued during his kingship. The captain of the strategic castle of Edinburgh was assigned as his military instructor and at the age of seven he began training in the weapons and skills of a medieval warlord.

In 1455 the uneasy truce between James II and the Lancaster regime was broken by a series of sporadic Scottish raids into the northern English border counties. As the war intensified, in the summer of 1460 the Stewart army launched a large campaign to capture the English held stronghold at Roxburgh. During the siege operations, on August 3 James II was killed by an exploding cannon. The eight-year-old Duke of Rothesay was readily acknowledged as the successor to the Scottish throne and one week later anointed and crowned in Kelso Abbey as King James III.

After the death of his father, James III remained under the custody of Queen Mary, as she assumed the monarchy in the name of the newly consecrated sovereign. In February 1461 the Scottish Parliament was summoned to Edinburgh to formally elect Mary of Guelders as her son's guardian and regent for the realm. A seven member administrative council led by the bishop of Saint Andrews, James Kennedy, was created by the legislative assembly to advise the queen. James Kennedy was the third son of Sir James Kennedy of Ayrshire and Princess Mary Stewart and was born in 1408. After completing his basic studies, he was sent to the continent to complete his education in theology and canon law. Following his return to Scotland, he first served as canon at Dunkeld before his election as prelate to the bishopric in June 1437. Assuming his ecclesiastic duties, Bishop Kennedy introduced new reform measures to end abuses in the church and attended the council of Florence to obtain Pope Eugene IV's support for his initiative. In the aftermath of the death of the bishop of Saint Andrews, while in Florence Kennedy was appointed as his successor. After his investiture of the prestigious bishopric, he renewed his religious reforms and worked to end the schism in the Holy See of Rome.

After her appointment as regent, Mary of Guelders quickly established her dominance over her counselors by the force of her strong willed personality, intelligence and energy. The dowager queen had been a trusted and skilled advisor to her husband and after taking power retained his governmental programs. James II had earlier supported the Lancastrian faction during the English Wars of the Roses and after his death the regent renewed his policy. However, in February 1461 Henry VI's army was defeated at the second battle of Saint Albans and Mary of Guelders offered him and his wife sanctuary from the Yorkish regime in exchange for the ceding of the Lancaster held enclave at Berwick. While Scotland regained the stronghold, her initiative resulted in a breach with Bishop Kennedy, who backed the new Yorkish king, Edward IV. Two rival political alliances were soon formed around the New Lords led by the queen and Old Lords centered on the leadership of James Kennedy. Despite the ongoing power struggle between the two rival factions, the central government remained stable and no unrest developed as Mary continued to maintain her supremacy.

While the Stewart court favored the Lancastrian cause, the Yorkish claimant to the English throne, Edward IV, forged an alliance with the dissident and exiled Scottish Earl of Douglas and the Lord of the Isles. Reinforced with a strong contingent of English troops, in 1462 James Douglas attacked the Scottish border fiefdoms in an attempt to raise rebellion. As the rogue army advanced into Scotland, the local warlords remained loyal to James III and the earl was soon forced to withdraw after his encroachment failed to gain support. In the summer of 1463 the Scots retaliated against Douglas's foray by mounting a punitive raid against Norham Castle. The stronghold was well defended by the Yorkish garrison and the campaign failed to gain any English concessions. However, the unsuccessful siege and continued deterioration of Scottish backing for the Lancaster faction among the high nobles and prelates resulted in a policy change in the queen's government. Under the new Stewart initiative, the deposed Henry VI was abandoned and negotiations for a truce were initiated with the envoys of Edward IV.

In December 1463 Queen Mary died and the Scottish Parliament elected Bishop James Kennedy of Saint Andrews as custodian for James III and regent of the kingdom. The bishop had earlier supported the Yorkish party, developing close contacts and friends with the English lords and church and after the overthrow of the Lancastrian regime better relations resulted between the two realms. The guardian found the Yorkish court more receptive to negotiating a settlement to their ongoing border disputes. Deliberations were undertaken and soon produced an agreement for a fifteen-year truce and English abandonment of James Douglas's cause. With his southern borders protected, the regent was free to direct his policy initiatives against the still recalcitrant Lord of the Isles and his Highlands allies. During the summer of 1464, James III and his army were sent north to reassert the crown's authority and justice. With a strong royal presence and show of force, the Upland lords were compelled to reaffirm their allegiances by pledging fealty to the king. The bishop's campaign of suppression in the north produced a peaceful and united kingdom for James III's monarchy.

Following the death of James II, the political stability of the Scottish government had been maintained by the partnership between Queen Mary and James Kennedy. After the queen's death, the bishop retained the power base necessary to establish his independent regency administration through the support of the party of Old Lords. However, in 1465 the guardian died, resulting in a power struggle for supremacy over the ruling council. Two rival factions began to contend for leadership of the realm and wardship of the king. The Kennedy alliance was under the control of the bishop's brother, Gilbert, while Robert, Lord of Kilmarnock, led the Boyd family. The nobles and clerics of both coalitions had been granted high court offices and custody of strategic castles. In the summer of 1466 Robert Boyd seized James III, taking him to the security of Edinburgh Castle, which was under the authority of his brother, Alexander. With possession of the symbol of royal primacy, the Boyds were in a formidable position to assert their dominance over the regime. In October Robert negotiated an agreement with the Scottish Parliament, usurping the Kennedys' rule. Under the ensuing settlement, guardianship for James III was granted to Robert Boyd, along with the office of chamberlain and keepership of the crown's strongholds. With the royal power of James III backing him, Lord Boyd had his son, Thomas, appointed Earl of Arran and added large and wealthy estates to his extensive demesne. However, his policy of self-aggrandizement created widespread resentment among the magnates and particularly James III, who was forced to sanction the seizure of royal titles and lands by Robert and the marriage of his sister, Princess Mary, to Thomas Boyd.

In 1468 James III began to assert his personal kingship in defiance of the Boyd government. With the support of the high magnates and bishops, in November 1469 he summoned Parliament to meet and brought charges of treason against the Boyd family, forcing Robert to flee to England, while his brother, Alexander, was captured and executed. Their lands were declared forfeited and annexed directly to the crown. The downfall of the Boyd political faction signaled the full ascension to the monarchy by James III at age sixteen.

In 1459 the government of James II had begun ongoing negotiations for the marriage of the heir to Princess Margaret, daughter of the king of Denmark-Norway, Christian I. The marital agreement was ratified ten years later and the wedding ceremony between James III and Margaret held at Holyrood Abbey on July 13, 1469. She was physically described as a royal princess of great beauty and refinement, who earlier had been exposed to the arts and letters of the Renaissance at the Danish court. Margaret was deeply pious and became a devoted patron of the Scottish church. James III and Margaret had three sons, including the future James IV born in 1473. To secure the terms of the marriage settlement, the Norwegian controlled Orkney and Shetland Islands had been pledged as the dowry to the Scottish throne as security. However, Christian I was unable to fulfill the financial terms of the treaty and in 1470 James III formally annexed the territories to Scotland.

While James III was consolidating his personal rule, in 1471 Edward IV of York had eliminated the Lancastrian challenge to usurp the monarchy of England. The Stewart king actively cultivated friendly relations with the York regime and maintenance of peace on his southern borders. Following the birth of the Scottish heir in 1473, the Stewart court initiated negotiations with the English for a marriage agreement between the daughter of Edward IV, Cecilia, and James, Duke of Rothesay, to ensure a closer alliance. However, his policy of pursuing friendship with Scotland's traditional enemy was received with little enthusiasm by the magnates, especially the Lowland warlords, who still remained hostile to the English.

As the result of his father's marriage to a princess from the powerful and wealthy House of Burgundy and his union to the daughter of the king of Denmark-Norway, the court of James III achieved a level of European prestige and stature unknown to prior Scottish regimes. The new influence led directly to an ambitious policy of intervention in continental affairs by the Scottish government. The Stewart king began initiatives to expand his territorial holdings across the North Sea into Flanders and Brittany. From his mother, daughter of the Duke of Guelders, James III inherited a claim for the Flemish duchy and began preparations to invade and annex the region directly to Scotland. He also planned to mobilize an army of Scottish and mercenary troops to conquer the independent duchy of Brittany. The adventurous schemes for Stewart self-aggrandizement along with his ongoing policy of promoting English friendship were strongly opposed by the prelates and magnates, resulting in further erosion to the crown's popularity.

After the assumption of his autonomous reign in 1468, James III established the seat of his government in Edinburgh. He quickly abandoned the practice followed by his predecessors of traveling extensively throughout the realm to personally enforce his will and laws. The kingdom's administration became centralized in the capital and as a result pockets of disorder developed among local feuding warlords. The lack of personal contact with the nobles, clergy and burghs caused further losses of prestige and favor for the Stewart crown. The king also pursued the unpopular financial policy of pardoning serious crimes for the payment of a fine, while increasing numerous taxes. To raise new revenue, the coinage was frequently debased, producing periods of rising inflation. The royal initiatives received the growing disapproval of Parliament, causing several clashes between the regime and the assembly which served to undermine the authority of the throne.

James III's mother and Queen Margaret had been raised and educated in prominent European households with a tradition of patronage to the Renaissance movement, which they both imported to Scotland. Through his relationship with the dowager-queen and his wife, the monarch became a dedicated sponsor of scholarship and the arts. Like his father, James III took an interest in the promotion of literature and many noted poets received his royal favor. Through the continental family and friends of the queen, many accomplished musicians and artists were encouraged to reside at the Stewart court. James III employed eminent architects and craftsmen and encouraged new construction in the latest Renaissance style. Under his direction, there was a revival in the construction of new royal and burgh buildings, churches and abbeys. The king had a broad range of interest, bringing distinguished scholars and artisans to his kingdom and establishing a reputation of culture and learning for his court among the European regimes.

While the Stewart king was an energetic sponsor of the letters and arts, he was also a pious and devoted patron of the Scottish church. He took an active interest in the establishment and embellishment of numerous churches and contributed from the royal treasury to their building projects and decorations. The Stewart crown defended the independence of the Scottish bishoprics and challenged the authority of the papacy to interfere in local ecclesiastical issues. After the Holy See raised the Saint Andrews diocese to an archbishopric with full control over the Scottish Church, the Stewart court with support from Parliament defended its rights to appoint local bishops and tax the bishoprics against the usurpation of the Church of Rome.

James III's practice of governing from Edinburgh and attempting to rule through local royal officials gave cause to growing civil unrest among the warlords, especially in the frequently rebellious northwestern lordships. In 1475 John Macdonald, Lord of Ross and the Isles, ignored royal sovereignty by establishing his autonomous overlordship and negotiated a secret treaty with Edward IV to support him in the conquest of Scotland. To reassert his kingship over the recalcitrant warlord, James III formally summoned him to Parliament to answer charges of treason. When the Lord of Ross refused to appear, the king declared his lands forfeited to the crown and a royal lieutenant was appointed to occupy the region. After the loss of his estates, in July 1476 Macdonald finally appeared at Parliament, where he publicly submitted to the throne's authority. After pledging his fealty to the regime, he was granted the lordship of the Isles as a vassal of the court. James III's aggressive initiative resulted in the annexation of the earldom of Ross to the monarchy and ensured a period of peace and stability in his northern fiefs.

While the Stewart king had successfully suppressed the revolt of the Macdonald family, by 1479 his ruling council's policies had generated a deepening wave of dissatisfaction and resentment against the crown. James III had continually ignored the base of his power among the earls and prelates by surrounding himself with an inner council of lowborn favorites who dominated the royal government and court. The nobles' loss of presence and influence in the regime paired with the policy of promoting a closer détente with England and aggressive taxation caused the magnates and clerics to turn to the king's two brothers, Alexander, Duke of Albany, and John, Earl of Mar, for support against the throne. A formidable counterpolitical faction began to be centered on the younger Stewart brothers, which increasingly became a threat to the reign of James III. When the Albany duke and Mar earl began to openly confront the royal administration, the sovereign ordered their immediate imprisonment. John died under suspicious circumstances, while still a prisoner while Alexander managed to escape from Edinburgh Castle, taking refuge in France. Alexander was born in 1454 and was the second son of King James II and Mary of Guelders. In recognition of his status in the royal family, he was appointed Duke of Albany and Earl of March. He became a member of his brother's government and served as the Stewart crown's warden for the Marches. As warden, Alexander defended the southern Scottish border against English encroachments and energetically commanded pillaging raids in retaliation, gaining a reputation for his military skills and energy.

As the discontent among the earls intensified, in 1480 the border warlords began to openly defy crown policy by mounting numerous marauding raids into northern England in pursuit of plunder. Edward IV grew increasingly hostile as the encroachments continued, sending a battle fleet to sack the Scottish east coast and preparing for war. In response to the Yorkish aggression, the militant Lowland magnates forced James III to counter the attack by launching a punitive foray into Northumberland. As the peace between the Stewart regime and England deteriorated, in 1482 Alexander of Albany began negotiations from France with the Yorkish court for an alliance against his brother. In May he traveled to England to formally ratify the Treaty of Fotheringhay. Under the terms of the accord, Edward IV agreed to provide an army for the conquest of Scotland, while the duke pledged to cede large sections of the Lowlands to the English realm and become the vassal of the Yorkish monarchy.

In June 1482 the English king appointed his brother, Richard of Gloucester, to command the campaign against Scotland and a formidable invasion force was mobilized, marching into the Lowlands unchallenged. In defense of his kingdom, James III assembled the royal army near Edinburgh and advanced south to thwart the offensive. However, as his troops maneuvered for battle, the nobles mutinied with their militias, refusing to fight unless the crown's inner council of favorites was dismissed and replaced with earls and bishops. James III rejected the demands and was promptly arrested, while several members of his court were hanged. After their rebellion, the Scots abandoned the war, returning to Edinburgh with the king as their prisoner.

James III was imprisoned in Edinburgh Castle, as the duke of Albany and Gloucester's soldiers advanced unopposed against the stronghold. The Scottish garrison refused all demands of surrender, forcing the English into the prospects of a prolonged siege. The Yorkish army lacked adequate money, war supplies and cannons for a long investment and was compelled to abandon the campaign while the Albany duke began independent negotiations with James III and the dissident faction. Under the terms of their ensuing agreement, the duke and recalcitrant Scottish earls were reconciled to the crown and the king's brother was appointed lieutenant general of the realm. Despite the settlement, Alexander was soon again allied with the rebellious Scottish lords and intriguing with the York court for the usurpation of the kingdom. However, the plot was discovered and the Duke of Albany was forced to flee to safety in England. In the following year he raised a small army of Scottish malcontents and English troops and unsuccessfully mounted an attack into the Lowlands. After the failed foray, Alexander of Albany returned to France, where he was killed in 1484, participating in a jousting tournament.

After the defeat of Alexander's rebellion, James III reestablished his sovereignty over the lords and clerics. His inner council of close friends was recalled, while supporters of the magnates were dismissed from their court offices and the king returned to his autocratic rule. Excluded from the government, the warlords renewed their alliance against the crown, drawing the king's eldest son and heir, James of Rothesay, into their cause. The rebelling nobles led by Alexander, Lord of Hume, and Sir Patrick Hepburn proclaimed the fifteen-year-old duke as governor of Scotland, as he became the figurehead of the revolt against his father. In June 1488 James III mobilized his remaining loyal allies and soldiers to counter the growing insurgency. The royal army marched west from Edinburgh, defeating Prince James and his small band of renegades in an indecisive battle near the town of Blackness. The Rothesay duke withdrew from the initial encounter, escaping to join the larger force of rebels assembling along the border. James III continued to advance toward Stirling Castle where the two armies clashed on June 11, 1488, at Sauchieburn. The battle soon developed into a series of small sporadic charges, ending with the complete rout of the royal troops. James III was actively engaged in the melee and during the fighting was killed. He had reigned for twenty-eight years and was thirty-six at the time of his death. James III was buried at the Cambuskenneth Abbey alongside Queen Margaret and was succeeded to the Stewart throne by his son, James IV.

Sources

Barrell. *Medieval Scotland.* Donaldson. *Scottish Kings.* Oram. *The Kings & Queens of Scotland.*

James IV, 1473–1488–1513

In the summer of 1488 Prince James of Rothesay, heir to the Scottish monarchy, became the figurehead leader of the insurgency of Lowland warlords directed against the suppressive regime of James III. In the resulting rebellion, his father was killed at the battle of Sauchieburn and the Duke of Rothesay claimed the crown as James IV to rule as the fifth Scottish king of the Renaissance epoch. James Stewart was born on March 17, 1473, at Stirling Castle and was the eldest son of James III and Margaret of Denmark. His early childhood years were spent in the queen's household at Stirling with his two brothers. Soon after his birth James was appointed Lord of Cunningham and later Duke of Rothesay to acknowledge his inheritance right as successor to the throne. The queen assumed responsibility for his initial education, employing eminent scholars as his tutors. James was a serious and gifted student, exhibiting an interest in a broad range of subjects. He received an exceptional education, excelling in his studies of reading, writing, languages to include French and Latin, religion, history and the sciences. He was also instructed in the social graces of dancing, court etiquette and music. Under the influence of his mother, who had been raised in the highly cultured Danish court, Prince James became attracted to the arts and letters of the Renaissance movement, which were enthusiastically pursued during his kingship. As the heir approached the age of seven, he began military training in the weapons of a warrior to include the lance, battle-axe, archery and sword. He became highly proficient in jousting, developing a reputation for his martial skills and chivalry. Away from his formal studies, James was an active hunter and energetically participated in field sports. Physically the Rothesay duke was described as medium in height with a muscular frame and possessing a noble bearing and handsome appearance.

By 1488 the political policies of James III had grown widely unpopular among the Scottish lords, clerics and burghs, giving cause to open rebellion. While the insurgency movement gained momentum, the Duke of Rothesay remained isolated at Stirling Castle away from the royal court and ruling council. During the escalating crisis, the king increasingly ignored the heir, favoring his second son, James of Ross, with special patronage and esteem. Abandoned by the throne and threatened with the loss of his birthright, the prince joined the growing revolt of the southern warlords. In June 1488 warfare erupted between the two rival factions as the rebels led by the Rothesay duke, Lord Alexander of Hume and Sir Patrick Hepburn, Lord of Hailes, advanced to resolve their grievances by force of arms. After an indecisive initial encounter at Blackness, the two armies met at Sauchieburn, where the royalists were routed and James III killed during the battle. James of Rothesay was recognized as the successor to the crown and on June 24 anointed as king at Scone Abbey.

James IV assumed the monarchy at age fifteen with only a small party of sympathizers and limited personal experience in the administration of the royal government. Lacking a formidable power base to impose his authority, the victorious warlords at Sauchieburn led by Alexander of Hume and Patrick Hepburn united to form a political coalition to usurp the crown and establish a regency to rule in the name of the minor king. Sir Alexander had earlier joined the alliance of Earl William of Douglas in opposition to the reign of James II. He continued his close association with the earl, traveling with him to the papal jubilee in Rome. In 1473 he was appointed Lord of Parliament and later renewed his resistance to the oppressive policies of the Stewart monarchy, becoming allied with the Hepburn faction. Patrick was the son of Adam Hepburn, Lord of Hailes, and inherited his family's properties in 1482. He became a member of the royal court and served as a diplomat for James III, negotiating a truce with the English in 1484. However, he soon revolted against the increasingly suppressive policies of the king, allying with the rebel lords. After taking the reins of power in the name of James IV, Lord Alexander was appointed Earl of Mar and chamberlain, while Patrick of Hailes acquired the earldom of Bothwell and leadership of the royal household. Members of both families were named to high offices at court as the new regime consolidated its control and dominated the minority years of the monarch.

The Hepburn-Hume alliance had been the leading force behind the overthrow of James III in June 1488 and with custody of the king, the two families moved to quickly consolidate their assumption of power against the remaining friends and allies of the deposed monarchy. Support for the dethroned James III had been strong in the northeastern lordships and to ensure control over the recalcitrant nobles, royal summons were issued to them to answer charges of treason. When the lords appeared before Parliament, they pledged their fealty to the crown, becoming reconciled with the new regime. Acting in the name of the Stewart government, by the end of 1488 Patrick Hepburn and Alexander Hume had restored the peace and solidified the government of James IV.

After the overthrow of James III, the Hume and Hepburn factions united to seize total and independent control of the Scottish realm, barring other powerful nobles from their administration. The Earl of Lennox, John Stewart, and Lord Robert of Lyle had been prominent supporters of the recent rebellion but had been excluded from the new regime. To confront the Hume-Hepburn alliance's usurpation of the kingdom, in the spring of 1489 the two southwestern warlords with their vassals and allies revolted against the crown. To confront the new uprising, Parliament was summoned to Edinburgh, where in June the rebels were declared guilty of treason and their lands forfeited to the king. The royal army was mobilized to seize the earldoms and in July James IV personally commanded siege operations against Lord Robert at Duchal Castle. The stronghold was quickly overwhelmed, as large cannons reduced the defensive walls. While the Duchal stronghold was easily subdued, the rogues' principal fortress at Dumbarton defiantly repelled the Stewart assaults.

Emboldened by the strong resistance of the Dumbarton Castle's garrison, new uprisings soon erupted among the warlords in the northeastern lordships. The Lord of Huntley, Alexander Gordon, broke his pledge of loyalty by assembling his allies and retainers, marching to support the Earl of Lennox's cause. With his army reinforced with the arrival of Gordon, in early October John Stewart of Lennox led his formidable forces against Stirling Castle to capture the king and seize the government. To thwart the threat of the Lennox earl, James IV mustered his soldiers, advancing to meet the approaching renegades. On October 11 the two armies clashed at the Field of Moss, where the royalists repulsed the repeated charges of the insurgents. However, their victory was not decisive and Lennox and his coalition escaped with their army to still pose a danger to the throne.

At the battle of the Field of Moss, the Stewart regime lacked the military might and resources to fully enforce its will, compelling the Hepburn-Hume coalition to adopt a more conciliatory policy toward the rebel faction. In February 1490 Parliament was summoned to Edinburgh, where under petitions from James IV's council, the previous forfeitures against the lords of Lennox and Lyle were withdrawn and all grants of royal patronage to the regime's allies made since the coronation voided. A program of reconciliation, inclusion and toleration was adopted, giving greater access to the crown's ruling council and court. The composition of the royal administration was expanded to include nobles from the earldoms, giving them broader involvement in the Stewart government. The accommodation initiative succeeded in ending the cause for rebellion and brought peace, despite occasional flare-ups in the upper northwestern lordship of the Isles.

In 1488 James IV had backed the rebellion against his father, actively participating in the battle at Sauchieburn. However, he had not been closely associated with James III's administration and had not developed an autonomous political power base. Without a party of supporters, he was forced to accept the rule of the Hepburn-Hume alliance. Nevertheless, by 1493 through the force of his personality, James IV began to assume a more independent role in the government. The regime of Alexander Hume and Patrick Hepburn had imposed the crown's control over most of the kingdom with the exception of the frequently recalcitrant Lord of the Isles, John Macdonald, and his allies. John Macdonald was born in 1434 and was the son and heir of Alexander, Earl of Ross, and Elizabeth Seton, daughter of Alexander Seton, Lord of Gordon. At the death of his father in 1449, he inherited the titles and lands. Three years later he revolted against James II, forming an alliance with Duke William of Douglas. When William was murdered by the king, John continued to resist the authority of the Stewart crown with impunity. The Lord of the Isles later became involved in a territorial dispute with James III and in defense of his claims seized the royal castles of Inverness and Ruthven. He pressed his independence rights by negotiating the Treaty of Westminster with Edward IV, agreeing to support the English conquest of Scotland in exchange for the region north of the Forth River.

As James IV increasingly asserted his power, in May 1493 the lands of Macdonald and his faction were declared forfeited to the crown, for their continued rebellion, but the rebel coalition continued to defy the Stewart throne. To counter the revolt of Macdonald, in the spring of 1495 the king began preparations for a major campaign to subdue the northwestern lordships. A small fleet was constructed and in May the Stewart army assembled at Dumbarton Castle. In the early summer the troops boarded the ships, sailing against Macdonald and his supporters to enforce the kingship of James IV. Through his personal presence and military might of his army, the local warlords were compelled to pledge their fealty. The Stewart court's authority was further enhanced in the following year when James IV returned to the lordship of the Isles to fortify his strongholds and increase the strength of his garrisons. However, John Macdonald refused to submit and continued to resist the Stewart regime. The Earl of Argyll, Archibald Campbell, was named royal lieutenant for the region and additional sheriffs were appointed to ensure obedience to the Scottish laws and justice. Despite these measures, there were periodic uprisings, which did not end until the capture of the Lord of the Isles.

In 1485 Henry Tudor overthrew the Yorkish monarchy of Richard III, seizing the throne of England as Henry VII. After the death of the last Yorkish king at the battle of Bosworth

Field, the Scottish crown recognized the pretender, Perkin Warbeck, as successor to the English kingdom. Warbeck claimed to be the second son of Edward IV and rightful heir to England. Despite an ongoing truce, relations between the Stewart and Tudor regimes grew hostile, as cross border raids by both rivals increased and Henry VII's fleet seized several Scottish ships without just cause. As the belligerence escalated, in 1496 the Pretender was welcomed to the Stewart court and James IV threatened to break the armistice by invading England. By September the Scottish kingdom was finally resolved to war and began to mobilize the royal army for a punitive raid. On September 20 the king, augmented with Warbeck's contingent of supporters and mercenaries, crossed the Tweed River into Northumberland. Their advance was largely unopposed, as the Scottish troops pillaged and ravaged the local towns and countryside. As the raiders marched deeper into England, the usurpation cause of the pretender found little favor among the population and Warbeck quickly withdrew from the conflict, leaving James IV to continue his plundering attacks. However by September 25, the English barons had mustered their military forces at Newcastle and were moving to counter the Scots' marauding. At the approach of the Tudors, James IV ordered his army to abandon the incursion and return to Scotland, having achieved the objectives of his campaign to harry Northumberland. The brief encroachment was widely popular among the Scots, establishing the monarch as an aggressive and successful military commander and defender of the realm's territories and rights.

Following the pillaging encroachment of the Stewart regime, Henry VII revoked the ongoing truce and began plans for a combined land and sea retaliatory campaign. As the Tudor forces prepared for their offensive, during the winter months James IV toured his border fortifications and ordered garrison reinforcements and defensive improvements to the strongholds in anticipation of the English invasion. When Henry VII was compelled to delay his Scottish incursion due to rebellion in his duchy of Cornwall, in July a large Stewart army with the latest artillery pieces was mustered for an attack against Norham Castle in Northumberland to counter the mounting threat. In early August the fortress was besieged and the large cannons pounded the defensive walls. However, the English garrison refused to surrender and James IV lacked the money and supplies to continue with a prolonged siege. After plundering the borderlands, the foray was abandoned and James IV returned to Edinburgh.

While Henry VII was preparing for his land and sea invasion of Scotland, in his duchy of Cornwall the local barons led a revolt against the regime's excessive taxes to finance the Scottish war effort. The Tudor government was forced to divert large resources away from its planned punitive incursion to restore peace in Cornwall. With the loss of the opportunity to counter the Scottish raids, the English court began to make overtures for a truce accord. An armistice for seven years was quickly signed, while deliberations for a permanent reconciliation were continued with Patrick Hepburn leading the Stewart envoys. After prolonged negotiations the Treaty of Perpetual Peace was ratified in January 1502. The settlement provided for the marriage of James IV to Margaret, daughter of Henry VII, and the automatic renewal of the agreement at the succession of each new monarchy. The Perpetual Peace was formally sanctioned by Pope Alexander VI, who committed the Holy See to the immediate excommunication of any king who failed to honor or renew the treaty.

Under the marriage terms of the Perpetual Peace Treaty, in early August 1503 Margaret Tudor crossed the border into Scotland and was met by James IV, who personally escorted her to Edinburgh. The wedding ceremony was held on August 8 at Holyrood Abbey and was followed by a celebration of great pomp and spectacle. There were five days of festivals, pageants, feasts and dancing in the newly renovated abbey. A grand jousting and martial skills tournament was held, which attracted knights from all over Europe, including the Scottish king. At the time of her marriage, Margaret was only thirteen years old and had little in common with her older husband. James IV and the queen maintained separate households and he continued his relationships with numerous mistresses, having several children with them. The politically arranged union resulted in the birth of six children, however, only one son, James, survived into adulthood. The marriage between the Houses of Stewart and Tudor resulted in the consolidation of England and Scotland under a single monarchy one hundred years later.

James IV had been instructed by an exceptional group of learned scholars and theologians, receiving an enlightened humanist education. He was highly intelligent with an enthusiastic interest in a wide array of disciplines, which were actively pursued during his monarchy. Under his personal direction, the Stewart court became a center for the Renaissance movement, energetically sponsoring its ideals to create a golden age in Scotland. James IV's regime was at the vanguard of promoting the arts, letters, sciences, architecture and music among the European courts. The king was a patron of literature, encouraging noted poets to reside in Scotland. Under his crown's sponsorship, the first printing press was imported into the realm, producing a wide variety of religious and literary publications. He took an active interest in science and medicine and was personally attracted to surgery and dentistry. Under his orders, the Royal College of Surgeons was established in Edinburgh for the advancement of medicine. The royal treasury supported and financed the study of alchemy in the quest to turn lead into gold. The Stewart administration promoted Scottish education by requiring all nobles to send their eldest son to school to acquire basic instruction. The availability of higher learning was expanded with the founding of Scotland's third university at Aberdeen in 1495. There was a revival in building activity with extensive renovations at Holyrood with the construction of a French style tower and new projects at the Falkland and Linlithgow palaces. The castle at Stirling underwent major additions with a Renaissance inspired royal chapel and great hall. The composition of new music played a vital role in the Stewart household and noted composer Robert Carver was backed and encouraged by the throne. James IV spent lavishly on his cosmopolitan court, military, building projects and government and was regarded as a prince of the Renaissance.

At the beginning of James IV's reign, Scotland was without a permanent navy, leaving the merchant fleet highly vulnerable to attacks from pirates and English raiders. To protect his expanding foreign commercial interest and give the kingdom an offensive weapon against potential Tudor aggression, in 1502 the Stewart crown began the foundation for a new royal navy. An aggressive naval procurement initiative was mounted to acquire vessels by purchase and construction. In 1505 the *Treasurer* and *Colomb* were purchased from French merchants, forming the nucleus of the fleet. The king's first battleship, *Margaret,* was launched in 1506 and fitted with five cannons. As the size of the Scottish naval forces expanded, an arms race developed between the Stewart and Tudor regimes, when the English countered James IV's acquisition program by building the *Mary Rose* and later *Great Harry.* In 1512 the Stewart court launched its most formidable and expensive battleship, *Great Michael,* which was armed with twenty-seven cannons and manned with a crew of three hundred sailors, making it the largest armed vessel of the day. A smaller third capital ship, *James,* was later added to the fleet and the realm augmented its growing flotilla by hiring numerous privateers. The building of a powerful sea force of over thirty-eight armed vessels gave a feeling of pride to Scotland and strengthened the prestige of the throne among the European courts.

As James IV continued with his many building and patronage initiatives, measures were begun to reform the judicial system by adding new royal sheriffs to enforce the law and increasing the number of courts to administer justice. He traveled extensively to personally attend regional courts, issuing judgments in the name of the crown and imposing his authority. Fewer Parliaments were summoned during James IV's reign, as the royal council came into greater use and a strong central administration dominated the government. Under the Stewart monarchy peace and order were restored and the king's sovereignty was readily accepted and obeyed.

The maintenance of a lavish court, many building projects and creation of a navy required huge sums of money. The primary source of income was the revenues generated by the extensive royal estates. However, as the Stewart king expanded his spending his personal lands proved inadequate and new sources of funding were sought. After assuming power, James IV augmented his financial needs by increasing the tax base with Parliamentary approval but over time this became insufficient and by 1501 was received with growing resistance. To meet his ever escalating money requirements, James IV began to increase the rents on his crown properties by charging an annual fee and demanding a periodic renewal payment. To raise additional income, the wealth of the church was exploited by the seizure of vacant benefices and imposition of direct levies against the clergy. These two measures were highly successful in enhancing the royal coffers, allowing the monarchy to continue with its numerous spending programs.

The mother of James IV was the sister of the king of Denmark, Hans I, and in 1492 a treaty of friendship and mutual defense was signed between the two kingdoms. In 1501 the Danish king's Swedish and Norwegian vassals revolted and a request for military assistance was made to the Stewart court. Under the terms of the treaty, James IV sent Sir James Hamilton of Arran with a fleet of four privateers, augmented with the crown ship, *Christopher,* and an army of two thousand soldiers under the command of his chamberlain, Alexander of Hume, to buttress the Danes' attack. The Scottish forces crossed the North Sea in 1502 and served in Hans I's campaigns against Norway and Sweden. The Stewart throne later dispatched a relief naval force to Lubeck to aid the Danes against the rebelling city and threatened to intervene in Flanders in support of the sovereign's cousin, Charles, Duke of Guelders. The Danish and Lubeck expeditions accomplished little militarily for Scotland but enhanced the Stewarts' continental presence and stature as an European power and served as an impetus to the establishment of a permanent royal navy.

Under the terms of the Treaty of Perpetual Peace signed by the Stewart regime and England in 1502, raids along the border fiefdoms were to end. However, there continued to be clashes on both sides of the marchlands, which increased in 1509 after the succession of the new English monarch, Henry VIII. Hostilities between the two realms escalated when the Stewart navy expanded its presence in seas once dominated by the Tudor fleet. There were unprovoked attacks against Stewart ships and when James IV's vessels, *Lion* and *Jenny Pirwin,* were seized in open water, the Scottish court accused the Tudor government of breaking the terms of the Perpetual Peace.

As relations between Scotland and England steadily deteriorated, in Europe the fragile status quo was shattered in 1509 with the invasion and conquest of the duchy of Milan by the French Valois king, Louis XII. The warrior-pope, Julius II, countered the occupation of Lombardy by negotiating a Holy League with the Republic of Venice, Ferdinand II of Spain and Henry VIII to protect the Ecclesiastic States and drive the French out of northern Italy. Scotland had been the historic ally of France and Louis XII forged a mutual defense alliance with James IV and Denmark. In June 1513 Henry VIII honored his commitment to Pope Julius II by mounting a large encroachment into western France from his enclave at Calais. With an attack against Scotland's traditional friend and ally paired with just provocations from the English border raids and seizure of his ships, James IV formally declared war and in May sent his fleet, including the *Great Michael,* to molest Tudor shipping interests.

While the naval expedition was sailing to engage the English in support of the Valois war effort, the Scottish king summoned his allies and vassals for a large raiding foray into Northumberland to divert Henry VIII's forces away from France. By late August 1513 an army of twenty-five thousand well-armed soldiers, including the flower of Scottish nobility, was mobilized outside Edinburgh. Under the personal command of James IV, the Scots crossed the Tweed River, seizing the strongholds at Norham, Ford and Etal. Before departing for France, the English king had appointed Sir Thomas Howard, Earl of Surrey, as his lieutenant in the north to guard against a Scottish invasion. The earl was an experienced and highly skilled military commander who defended Northumberland with a militia of twenty thousand troops. On September 4 Howard gathered his forces at Alnwick and began his march to the north to contend the pillaging Scots. At the approach of the English, James IV moved his knights and infantry to a strong fortified position atop Flodden Hill. It had been raining for several days, which made the slopes of the hill even more unassailable. While the Stewarts remained protected on Flodden Hill, the English maneuvered around the Scots to approach from the north. Attempting to engage Howard on September 9, James IV abandoned the defensive high ground and shifted his army to Branxton Hill to better confront the earl's advancing formations. In the late afternoon the battle was initiated by a strong cannonade from the Scots but the artillery largely fell harmless when the gunners could not adequately aim their cannons down the hill. Sir Thomas's guns answered with devastating effect, decimating rows of spearmen in the schiltrons. With their ranks depleted, James IV personally led a charge of his remaining pikemen down the slippery slopes into the waiting English. In the ensuing close quarter melee, the long Scottish pikes proved ineffective against the much shorter halberds and the Stewart troops were completely overwhelmed. In excess of five thousand Scots were killed, including over forty nobles, six prelates and the Stewart king. The battle of Flodden was a decisive defeat for Scotland that put the kingdom's continued existence as an independent and separate kingdom in jeopardy. James IV was forty years old at the time of his death and ruler for twenty-five years. His badly mutilated body was taken as a war prize to London, where he was later buried at Sheen Abbey. James, Duke of Rothesay, the seventeen-month-old and only surviving son of James IV, was readily recognized as successor and Scotland again faced the uncertainty and weak government of a long regency period.

Sources

Blackie; Donaldson; McKenzie. *James IV: A Renaissance King.* Donaldson. *Scottish Kings.* Macdougall. *James IV.* Oram. *The Scottish Kings & Queens of Scotland.*

James V, 1512–1513–1542

In September 1513 James IV was killed in the battle of Flodden Hill during a pillaging raid into England and was succeeded by his infant son, James V, who ruled as the sixth Renaissance king of Scotland. The Stewart Prince was the third son of James IV and Margaret Tudor of England and was born at Linlithgow Castle on April 10, 1512. With the earlier deaths of his two older brothers in infancy, the young James became the acknowledged heir, and when his father was killed at Flodden on September 9, 1513, he inherited the throne. In the aftermath of the king's death, Queen Margaret was quickly recognized as acting regent and guardian for her son. However, her assumption to power was opposed by many nobles and prelates, who resented the rule of the English born queen, favoring an administration led by James V's first cousin, John Stewart, duke of Albany. John of Albany was the son of Alexander Stewart, brother of James III, who earlier had been forced to seek sanctuary in the French Valois court in 1484 after his failed rebellion against the Scottish monarchy. John Stewart was born in France and raised on his father's extensive estates. Following the death of Duke Alexander, his son assumed his Scottish and French titles and lands. Through his service to the Valois court as a diplomat and soldier, John received additional honors and properties. After James IV's death at Flodden Hill, John Stewart became the widely recognized Scottish heir presumptive. As support for the regency of the Albany duke increased, to solidify her government Margaret hastily had James V crowned as monarch in Scone Abbey on September 21. After the ceremony he was taken to Stirling Castle, remaining for the next two years as two political factions contended for control of the kingdom, while Scotland was plunged into political disorder.

As the queen's popularity steadily declined, a powerful alliance of high nobles and prelates united to actively promote the creation of an Albany regime. The party in opposition to the regency was under the leadership of the archbishop of Glasgow, James Beaton, Lord Alexander Hume and James Hamilton, first Earl of Arran. Hamilton was born in 1475 and was the only son of Lord James Hamilton and Mary Stewart, sister of King James III. When his father died in 1475, he inherited the titles and lands. The young lord was appointed as the sheriff of Lanark and royal counselor by his cousin, James IV. The Arran earl was a prominent member of the king's inner council, serving as a soldier and diplomat. He negotiated the king's marriage to Margaret Tudor and later was appointed as envoy to the Valois court of Louis XII. In 1502 Hamilton commanded the royal fleet sent to aid King Hans I of Denmark in his war against Norway and Sweden and later during the Cambria War supported Scotland's ally, France, by leading the navy to attack English shipping and ports in Ireland.

With the majority of the leading magnates and clerics rejecting her guardianship, Margaret was compelled to seek support from the sixth Earl of Angus, Archibald Douglas. The earl was the head of a formidable Scottish noble house and the regent appointed him to prominent positions in her administration. However, he used his offices at court to appoint members of his family to high posts in the queen's government, incurring the hostility of the pro–Albany faction. As the dissent between the two rivals grew, to assure his dominance over the kingdom Douglas skillfully used his influence with the queen to convince her of the political necessity of their marriage to consolidate their control. Under pressure from the Douglas alliance, the queen agreed to the marriage to Sir Archibald and the ceremony was held in August 1514. However, Margaret was unaware that James IV had bequeathed the wardship for their son to her for only as long as she remained a widow. After her marriage to Douglas, she was forced to renounce her regency and accept John of Albany as regent.

In May 1515 John Stewart arrived in Scotland and on July 10 was formally installed as regent at Edinburgh Castle. The advisors of the queen were soon dismissed from their offices and to solidify his new government the Duke of Albany demanded custody of James V. Margaret defiantly refused to give up possession of her son, forcing the regent to threaten a siege against her at Stirling Castle, while Sir Archibald and his allies rose in revolt in her support. When the crown's army approached the Stirling stronghold, Margaret reluctantly agreed to surrender the king's guardianship. With control of the symbol of royal authority and power, the Albany duke consolidated his regime but his rule was beset with frequent periods of internal disorder and conspiracy.

After the overthrow of Queen Margaret's government, John of Albany solidified his rule and was acknowledged as regent for James V. However, his assumption of the government was strongly opposed by many formidable Lowland lords who had grown disillusioned at their lack of influence at court and loss of power. In late 1516 the Earl of Arran, James Hamilton, formed an alliance with the Hume family, revolting against the new regency administration. To counter the growing dissent against his regime, John Stewart assembled the royal army and advanced against the rebellion, imposing his authority over the southern fiefdoms by force-of-arms. In November the Scottish Parliament officially recognized Albany's supremacy by appointing him as heir apparent.

With his power in Scotland secure, in 1517 the Albany duke's administration began talks with the Valois government to renew their treaty of friendship and military assistance. As the deliberations continued, in June he made plans for travel to France to personally negotiate the agreement. Before his departure to the French court, he appointed a regency council to govern in his name and moved the five-year-old James V to Edinburgh Castle. A household was established for his education and care and the young king spent his early years in a nurturing and secure environment. In France John Stewart met with the Valois regime, finalizing the Treaty of Rouen. Under the provisions of the Rouen accord, the two kingdoms agreed to a mutual defense alliance and the marriage of James V to a daughter of the French king.

As John of Albany remained in France, the regency council appointed to govern Scotland in his absence became beset with an internal power struggle. Two factions soon emerged from the political upheaval to contend for supremacy. Archibald Douglas commanded the Angus family, while the Arran alliance was centered on James Hamilton. However, neither coalition was strong enough to assert its will and usurp the kingdom, as social disorder and lawlessness erupted. While John Stewart stayed in France, Henry VIII and Francis I negotiated a truce to their ongoing war. Before agreeing to the settlement, the English king had demanded a secret clause preventing the duke from returning to Scotland to ensure unrest in the realm. Without the presence of the Albany duke, the turmoil and violence continued unabated until November 1521, when he was finally permitted to travel to Scotland. With the support of the Scottish Parliament, the regent asserted his rule to end the political chaos. To break the power of the parties in opposition, John Stewart advanced his army against Archibald Douglas, forcing him and many of his allies to flee to England for safety while the Hamiltons were brought into his new government.

While John of Albany was reestablishing his administration, the peace agreement between Henry VIII and Francis I was broken and both realms were once again at war. Fearing an encroachment from Scotland in support of the Rouen Treaty, the English threatened not to renew their ongoing truce with the Stewarts unless the pro–French regent was exiled. The Parliament defiantly rejected the demand and the Tudor regime responded by launching a pillaging raid against southern Scotland to force acceptance of its demand. As hostilities escalated, in September John of Albany retaliated against Henry VIII's attack by leading his army against the Tudor enclave at Carlisle. However, as his forces approached the fortress, the Scottish warlords refused to fight outside their borders and the campaign was abruptly abandoned. The Stewart government of Albany was compelled to quickly negotiate a truce with the English to temporarily end the conflict.

With his offensive against the Tudors thwarted, to secure new military aid for a second invasion of England, in late 1522 John Stewart again formed a regency council to govern the kingdom and returned to France. In September 1523 he landed in Scotland with a large contingent of French troops, money and war supplies as preparations were immediately begun for a new campaign against the Tudors. In the following month, the Franco-Scottish forces were mustered and advanced south to attack the castle at Wark. The stronghold was besieged, but even after repeated assaults the garrison refused to surrender. As the investment dragged on, the harsh winter began to deplete the army's strength and when a large English relief force approached, the Albany duke was compelled to retreat to Scotland. Early in the next year he sailed to France to negotiate additional financial and military assistance. However, the duke soon joined the French in their war against Emperor Charles V, later leading their army against the Spanish in Naples. With his prolonged absence from Scotland, in July the Parliament revoked his regency.

With John of Albany out of power, Queen Margaret began to plot to regain control of her son and the government. She negotiated an alliance with James Hamilton, Earl of Arran, and with the military might of his faction supporting her cause, reclaimed possession of the king and seized authority over the kingdom. To consolidate her usurpation, the minority of James V was declared ended and on July 26, 1524, at age twelve he was formally invested with the symbols of sovereignty.

While James V was in the custody of John of Albany and following his nominal assumption of the kingship, tutors from the Scottish church were appointed for his academic education. Like his father, the Stewart king was a gifted and serious student, excelling in his studies of reading, writing, languages to include Latin and French, religion and history. James V also received instruction in the social graces, developing into an accomplished musician, mastering the playing of the lute. At an early age he began training in weapons and equestrianship on a routine basis, becoming skilled in jousting. Away from his studies, James V enjoyed hunting and hawking and enthusiastically participated in field sports and military tournaments.

With the elimination of John Stewart's regime and assumption of power by the queen's faction, the Douglas family was free to end their forced exile in England. Archibald Douglas, Earl of Angus and husband of Queen Margaret, quickly returned to Scotland and was reconciled with his wife through the intervention of her brother, Henry VIII. While Margaret reluctantly agreed to include Sir Archibald in her government, she secretly pursued a legal separation. With the aid of her friend and ally, James Hamilton, the Holy See of Rome granted Margaret a divorce in 1525.

As the leader of the formidable Douglas House and through the force of his personality, the Earl of Angus soon gained dominance over the queen's council, despite the loss of her support. With the military might of his alliance backing him and control of the government, he forced the Parliament to approve the removal of James V from his mother's custody, effectively ending her regency. However, the earl lacked the necessary power and base of support to usurp the regime and could only rule through possession of the king. To gain Parliament's approval for his guardianship of James V, he was compelled to create a rotating custodianship with the four leading high magnates. Archibald secured the first regency and with control of James V seized the realm, refusing to relinquish his custody. The queen's allies and sympathizers were dismissed from their court offices and replaced with Douglas family and friends. James V remained under the direct protection of the guardian as a virtual prisoner with access to only the Angus faction. However, many of the nobles and prelates refused to accept the Douglas usurpation of the kingdom, forming an opposition coalition under the leadership of John Stewart, third earl of Lennox.

As the dissent against Archibald Douglas intensified, John Stewart seized control of Stirling Castle and issued a summons for the high Scottish lords to rally to his cause to rescue the king and overthrow the Angus regime. Many great warlords joined his revolt and in September 1526 the rebels advanced against Edinburgh. As the rogue troops approached the city, the Douglas army maneuvered to give battle and in the ensuing encounter the uprising was crushed and John Stewart killed. Despite the defeat of Lennox's rebellion, James V remained defiant of the Angus faction and determined to secure his escape and assumption of independent sovereignty.

Over the next two years, the Stewart king remained in the possession of the Douglas family, where his education was neglected and he was encouraged to indulge in licentious pursuits. However, James V was resolved to enforce his birthright and in late May 1528 gained his freedom, escaping to the safety of Stirling Castle. From the security of the stronghold, he declared his minority at an end and his intentions to rule with full and independent power. After the issuance of his royal decree, the nobles, bishops and towns rallied to James V, pledging their total support. Nevertheless, the Douglas alliance still remained a powerful and defiant force, which continually ignored the crown's demands to appear before Parliament to answer charges of sedition. To impose the authority of the Stewart regime, in the autumn the royal army advanced against the Douglas' castle at Tantalton but was unable to storm the formidable defensive walls. After the abortive attack, James Hamilton assumed command of the campaign against the rebels and through his relentless assaults against their lordships, finally broke their resistance, forcing Archibald Douglas and his sympathizers into exile at the Tudor court. Following the suppression of the Angus faction, their estates were declared forfeited to the Stewart throne, while James V rewarded his loyal magnates with grants of castles, honors and lands. A new government was formed with skilled and loyal allies and friends, while the king asserted his personal reign without restrictions.

During the regency government of the Douglas family, private wars and lawlessness had gone unchecked in the Highlands and among the southern border lords. To reimpose the crown's authority and justice against the recalcitrant northern warlords, a formidable campaign was mounted in early 1529, resulting in their suppression by the royal army and pledges of obedience to the king's laws. In the following year, the powerful and rebellious Lowlands magnate, John Armstrong, was captured and executed for his continued acts of defiance as James V made clear his intentions of ruling unopposed. The throne's decisive interventions in the frontier earldoms produced peace and obedience to the king's will. After the subjugation of the southern lords, in 1530 the royal council advanced to reduce the might and defiance of the Campbell family in the Western Isles. A loyal and skilled lieutenant, Alexander Macdonald, was appointed the regime's lieutenant for the region and through his energetic offensive; the dissent of the local nobles was eliminated. Throughout his reign James V moved aggressively to check the power of the high magnates. However, his relentless and energetic policy caused the loss of support and favor among the earls, resulting in future disastrous revolts that threatened to topple his monarchy.

After his forced exile to England in 1528, Archibald Douglas had become a ward of Henry VIII. He was granted lands in the northern English counties and continued to conspire against the Stewart regime. He used his influence at the Tudor court and charismatic personality to promote unrest along the borderlands and encourage revolt among the southern Scottish lords. As a result of his intrigues, cross-frontier raids were increased by both rivals as the two kingdoms moved closer to open warfare. In January 1533 James V's lieutenant for the Lowland lordships began to mobilize his Scottish troops to thwart new Tudor raids. After he was reinforced with a contingent of Highland levies, measures were taken to fortify the marchlands against further attacks and threaten northern England with a punitive incursion.

As the prospects for war grew, James V intensified his diplomatic efforts to secure a military alliance with the Holy Roman Empire and France. As the talks continued and the outlook for an agreement increased, Henry VIII became less bellicose and more receptive to negotiations. In May 1533 the Tudor court agreed to open discussions at Newcastle to find reconciliation. In the following year after prolonged deliberations, a treaty was ratified in London, which committed the two kingdoms to keep the peace on their borders and end all raiding activities.

While Scotland was involved with the escalating conflict on its southern border, envoys were dispatched to the European kingdoms to negotiate a marriage treaty for the king. Attempts were made to enforce the provisions of the Treaty of Rouen with Francis I for the marriage of James V to his daughter, Madeleine. However, France was at peace with England and had no desire to give the appearance of a new alliance with Scotland. Following the failed talks with the Valois regime, discussions were held with the imperial court for the marital union to a Habsburg princess, while emissaries were sent to Pope Clement VII to secure an agreement for the marriage of the Stewart king to his ward, Catherine de Medici. While both initiatives were rejected, the papal deliberations offered the prospects of acquiring a much needed source of funding for the Stewart crown from the local church's coffers.

In England Henry VIII had recently broken with the Holy See over its denial of his petition for a divorce from Catherine of Aragon, resulting in the creation of a separate and independent Tudor church. With the Protestant Reformation spreading across Europe and recent rejection of the Catholic faith in England, it was in the best interest of Pope Clement VII to retain the goodwill of James V. The favorable political climate permitted the throne's envoys to negotiate an agreement with Rome for a special tax on the Scottish church to be paid over a four-year term. The ecclesiastic subsidy greatly relieved the ongoing financial crisis that James V had assumed at the beginning of his independent rule. The exploitation of church properties was continued by the crown's granting of rich abbeys and bishoprics to numerous members of the king's immediate family with papal approval.

Under the agreement negotiated by his envoys, the Scottish church of James V remained committed to the doctrines of Rome. In 1532 the Parliament passed a resolution confirming the crown's support for the Holy See and active suppression of the Protestant movement. The new religion was slow in coming to Scotland and during the reign of James V there were only limited persecutions and a small number of executions for heresy. However, the Stewart king's muted policy of subjugation against the Protestant religion and his continued rejection of Henry VIII's proposals for an independent Scottish church mollified the papacy's concerns and the Stewart regime retained its cordial relationship with Rome.

While the initial negotiations for a marital agreement binding Scotland to a European power had failed, James V remained committed to a Valois wife. Discussions were reopened with France, however, Francis I refused to approve the marriage contract for his favorite daughter, Madeleine, proposing Mary of Bourbon, daughter of the Duke of Vendome, as a suitable substitute. With his succession still unsecured and little progress in obtaining an imperial princess, the Stewart king reluctantly accepted the offer and the treaty was soon ratified. After appointing a regency council to govern in his absence, in September 1536 James V sailed to France for an unofficial meeting with his prospective wife, Mary. He spent several days with the Vendome household at Saint-Quentin but James V quickly became unhappy with Mary and renewed talks with Francis I for his marriage to Madeleine.

Remaining in France, the Stewart monarch traveled to the Valois court at Chapelle to personally press his initiative for a Valois wife and negotiated the contract for his marriage to

Madeleine. The agreement was signed in November with the official ceremony taking place on January 1, 1537, in Paris at the cathedral of Notre Dame. The wedding to the French princess was celebrated with an elaborate and grand display of banquets, military tournaments and balls, lasting over several weeks. Following the many festivals, James V stayed in France until May, becoming exposed to the magnificence and grandeur of his father-in-law's court with its emphasis on the Italian Renaissance style of art, music and architecture. The Stewart king was greatly impressed by the Valois castles and furnishings, which were later brought to his kingdom.

In May the Stewart court finally returned to Scotland with the new queen. The union with one of the most powerful and wealthy royal houses of Europe brought stature and prestige to James V; however, the marriage lasted only an additional two months. Madeleine was described as intelligent and ambitious, possessing beauty, charm and grace but burdened with a frail health. Despite her attempts to actively participate in court affairs, shortly after her arrival the queen grew increasingly ill and weak, dying on July 7 in Edinburgh.

The early death of Madeleine left James V still without a legitimate successor, while his foreign policy remained committed to a French marriage to underpin Scotland's friendship and military alliance with the Valois regime. Accordingly, the archbishop of Saint Andrews was sent to negotiate a new marital agreement. With war threatening with Charles V and England, Francis I was anxious to permanently bind together the two kingdoms through marriage, offering Mary of Guise, daughter of the powerful and influential Guise duke, Claude, as a second wife. After a suitable period of mourning, the wedding ceremony was held by proxy in Paris on May 18, 1538. The new queen arrived in Scotland in June and was welcomed by the high lords and bishops of the realm in a grand procession. Mary was described as a princess of beauty, tall with reddish hair, well educated and possessing a strong, pious belief in the doctrines of Rome. With an assertive personality, she exerted a forceful influence on James V, especially concerning ecclesiastic affairs and the new dogma of the Reformation. The Stewart king and Mary had two sons both of whom died in infancy and one daughter, Mary, who was acknowledged as heir.

James V's aggressive and relentless policy of subjugation against the nobility and especially the Douglas alliance succeeded in asserting his sovereignty over the Lowland fiefs. However, pockets of resistance still remained and in 1536 John, Lord of Forbes, who was married to a sister of Archibald of Angus, was accused of plotting to assassinate the king. The evidence presented against him was mostly anecdotal and he was widely believed to have been executed because of his support for the Douglas family. The persecution against the Angus faction was renewed the following year when Lady Janet of Glamis, sister of Earl Archibald, was burned at the stake for planning the overthrow of James V. The executions aroused extensive public sympathy, serving to further distance the crown from the magnates. However, the monarch continued his personal campaign to eliminate the threat of the allies of Archibald by launching new attacks to purge the last remnants of the Douglas party from his kingdom.

While the crown maintained its constant pressure on the southern nobles, in 1539 the Western Isles rose in revolt against royal authority. In response to the uprising, in the following year James V mounted a naval expedition to end the lawlessness and reimpose his sovereignty. The initiative was both a campaign of suppression and royal tour, permitting the king to defend his monarchy by military might and the power of his presence and personality. The fleet of twelve vessels sailed north to the Orkney and Shetland islands to assert the throne's control before entering the Hebrides Sea and the Western Isles. The navy made stops at the rebellious burghs, where the Stewart troops enforced James V's kingship and secured his rule over the local lordships.

James V's relentless subjugation of the magnates had increasingly alienated him from the major base of his power. To further impose crown authority, shortly after his return from the Western Isles, charges of treason were brought against Sir James Hamilton of Finnart, who had once been a friend and favorite of the Stewart government. Despite his relationship with the regime and lack of supporting evidence, Hamilton was soon put on trial and executed with his lands forfeited. The death of a close associate of the Stewarts caused further deterioration in the support of the nobles, who believed no one was safe from persecution. Increasingly, the Scottish lords withdrew from court, fearing for their safety.

In 1541 Emperor Charles V and Francis I were once again at war with Henry VIII allied to the imperial regime, while Scotland supported the Valois realm. As an ally of France, the Stewart crown began to fear an English invasion and envoys were sent to the Valois kingdom to secure financial and military aid in preparation for the coming conflict. Through the year tensions escalated between England and Scotland, as both rivals prepared for war. In the marchland fiefs, cross border raiding activities intensified and in August a small Tudor army attacked southern Scotland. The incursion was met by the well prepared Scots at Haddon Rig, where the English were easily repulsed; however, the encounter signaled the beginning of hostilities.

After his defeat at Haddon Rig, Henry VIII assembled a formidable army at York under the command of the Duke of Norfolk, John Howard. James V was forced to thwart the threat posed by Howard by summoning an unreliable nobility that had been repeatedly persecuted and suppressed by his government. In November the English invaded the borderlands with a large pillaging raid, as the Stewart king marched south to defend his demesne. The Norfolk duke soon ended his marauding assault, withdrawing across the frontier after laying waste to the eastern Scottish counties. As James V approached the border in pursuit of the Tudors, his troops mutinied and refused to advance into England, forcing the campaign to be abandoned.

Following its failed initiative, the Stewart court remained determined to confront Henry VIII and planned a two pronged offensive into northern England. James V appointed Sir Oliver Sinclair of Pitcairns to command one wing of the campaign, while he led the second attack. However, the king suddenly became seriously ill and was compelled to abort his encroachment. As Sinclair marched into Cumberland, on November 25 his troops encountered a small force of local militia under Sir Thomas Wharton near Solway Moss. As the Scots began to maneuver into combat formations, many of the nobles rebelled against the leadership of the king's favorite, withdrawing from the battle. In the ensuing engagement, many of the lords willingly surrendered to the English, resulting in the total rout of Sinclair's army.

James V was shattered with the reports of the mutiny of his nobles and the crushing destruction of the army. His court spent the next several days traveling aimlessly from castle to castle before establishing his government at Falkland. With his borders open to English invasion and already suffering a serious illness, he was taken over by melancholia and despair, growing increasingly weak, dying on December 14, 1542. James V ruled Scotland for twenty-nine years and died at age thirty. The sixth Stewart king was succeeded by his newly born daughter, Mary I.

Sources

Bingham. *James V: King of Scots.*   Cameron. *James V.*   Donaldson. *Scotland: James V—James VII.*

Mary I, 1542–1542–1567–1587

In the aftermath of the sudden death of James V, the monarchy of Scotland was assumed by his infant daughter, Mary I, who reigned as the seventh ruler of the Renaissance. Mary Stewart was born at Linlithgow Castle on December 8, 1542, and was the only surviving issue of James V and Mary of Guise. Six days after the Stewart princess's birth, her father died and as heir apparent she inherited his crown. After the premature death of James V, the Scottish kingdom was forced to once again confront the political uncertainty and insecurity of a long regency government. Two factions began to contend for custody of the queen and control of the regime. The Protestant and pro–English James Hamilton, second Earl of Arran, advanced his claim to power as the successor designate, attracting a large following of nobles. Hamilton was born in 1520 and was the eldest son of the first Earl of Arran, James Hamilton, and Janet Bethune. Through his father's lineage, he was directly related to the ruling Stewart dynasty. In 1529 the first Earl of Arran died and the nine-year-old James inherited his estates and titles and was raised and educated by his half-brother, James Hamilton of Finnart. Following the death in France of the childless heir to the Scottish throne, John Stewart of Albany, Hamilton was recognized as his successor to the Stewart monarchy.

While the Hamiltons struggled to gain control, they were opposed by David Beaton, archbishop of Saint Andrews, whose challenge for power was based on his alleged bequeathal of the guardianship for Mary I by her father. The archbishop favored a pro–French Catholic policy, which would bind Scotland to the Holy See and away from Protestant England, while the Hamiltons promoted the cause of the Tudor court and spread of the new religion. Intervening to secure peaceful relations and goodwill with Scotland, in January 1543 Henry VIII supported the assumption of the regime by James Hamilton and ordered the release of the captured Solway Moss prisoners, on condition they rally to the earl's banner. A new coalition of repatriated captives, led by the former exile, Archibald Douglas, was formed, joining with the Hamiltons to overthrow Beaton. In March the Scottish Parliament formally appointed the Arran earl as regent for Scotland and guardian for Queen Mary I.

Assuming power the Hamiltons quickly dismissed the allies and friends of Beaton from office, creating a pro–English administration. With the new ruling council favoring a closer détente with the Tudor court, negotiations were soon opened to more closely bind the two kingdoms through the marriage of Mary I to Prince Edward, the five-year-old son of the English king. Henry VIII approved the marital agreement provided the queen was raised in his household and the strategic castles at Stirling, Dumbarton and Edinburgh were surrendered to Tudor control. The Scottish regime strongly objected to the loss of local independence and foreign occupation, refusing to accept the terms. After the initial rejection of his conditions, the talks were renewed and the English finally agreed to withdraw the restrictive provisions. The formal treaty was ratified on July 1, 1543, at Greenwich, providing for the marriage of Mary I at the age of ten to Edward and guarantees for an autonomous Scotland. However, Henry VIII's demeaning demands had damaged support for the pro–English faction, as many magnates and prelates began to fear domination by their powerful and aggressive southern neighbor.

The growing dissent against the Tudor alliance was further energized with the return from France of the regent's pro–Valois half-brother, John Hamilton, who was next in line to the crown following his older brother. The deposed archbishop of Saint Andrews, David Beaton, quickly brought the popular and influential former exile into his party, rallying the nobility and church around his pro–French coalition. The rejuvenated Beaton faction soon regained control over Parliament, forcing the regent to relinquish his power and repudiate the Treaty of Greenwich. With the assumption of the regime by the anti–English government, tensions between Henry VIII and Scotland mounted and in July Queen Mary I was taken from Linlithgow under armed guard to the secure castle at Stirling as fears of her kidnapping intensified.

With his influence and favor in Scotland shattered by the new Beaton government, Henry VIII began to muster his military forces for a two pronged campaign of conquest. In May 1544 Edward Seymour, Earl of Hereford, commanded a sea-borne invasion army of over thirty thousand men-under-arms, landing at Newhaven and first laying waste to the seaport before moving inland to attack Edinburgh. Much of the city was ravaged and burned but the castle escaped capture. While Seymour pillaged the countryside and burghs around Edinburgh, a second, larger force advanced north overland, sacking the southeastern borderlands. However, unlike the marauding encroachments of the past, the English troops were not withdrawn and remained in the southern earldoms as an army of subjugation and occupation to continue their devastation of the local population.

The unimpeded destruction and occupation of the southern counties resulted in the discrediting of the Beaton regency, while James Hamilton and many of the leading earls rallied to Mary of Guise as guardian for the queen. As the Tudor pillaging attacks against the Lowland lordships continued, the Scottish warlords allied with the dowager queen overthrew the Beaton regime and launched a counteroffensive against the troops of Henry VIII. However, their sorties were only sporadic and limited, as the Scots lacked the military might, finances and resources to openly challenge the formidable English army.

While Scotland struggled under Tudor oppression, the queen remained sheltered under the protection of her mother at Stirling Castle, spending her early years in a loving and supportive court. On September 9, 1543, Mary I was formally invested as sovereign, as the high magnates and bishops pledged their fealty. The Stewart queen stayed at Stirling until September 1547, when security concerns in southern Scotland forced her removal to the more remote and secure Inchmahome Priory and later Dumbarton Castle. The living conditions were more difficult for the five-year-old Mary I, as most of her friends and mother's household were abandoned. However, Mary of Guise continued to personally provide for her care and security, as the child-queen grew healthy and robust.

For over three years the southern Scottish earldoms remained under English subjugation, as the local towns and population suffered terribly from the oppressive attacks of the occupation troops. However, in 1547 the balance of power began to shift away from the Tudor court. In late January Henry VIII died and was succeeded by the boy-king, Edward VI, under a regency council headed by his uncle, Edward Seymour. The political upheaval in England was followed in March by the death of the French king, Francis I, and the succession of his son, Henry II. The Seymour government continued to support the Scottish suppressive policies of Henry VIII, while the new French administration, dominated by the powerful and influential Guise family of the dowager queen, favored a close détente with Scotland.

While the Stewart court pursued friendly relations with France, Edward Seymour, assuming the office of lord protector, launched a formidable invasion into the Scottish southeastern borderlands to fully subdue and occupy the region. Once the Lowland lordships were under his control, he planned to gain full overlordship of Scotland by forcing the marriage of Edward VI to Mary I under the terms of the Treaty of Greenwich. As the lord protector's army marched north and the Tudor fleet commanded by Sir John Dudley sailed toward Edinburgh, the Scots under the Earl of Arran assembled their troops from the southern nobles and Highlands, maneuvering to meet the English at Pinkie Cleugh. The battle was initiated on September 10, when the undisciplined Stewart forces abandoned their well-fortified positions, charging into the strength of Seymour's artillery. As the Scottish ranks were decimated by the well placed cannons, the English cavalry attacked the flanks to complete the rout. With the overwhelming defeat, the south of Scotland was completely occupied and strategic strongholds garrisoned with Tudor soldiers.

With the English in control of the Lowlands and lacking Scottish military forces to confront their occupation troops, in November 1547 the pro–French government of James Hamilton sent emissaries to the court of King Henry II to seek the intervention of his soldiers and to negotiate the marriage of Mary I to the dauphin. After meeting with the Valois regime, the deliberations resulted in the Treaty of Haddington and in June 1548 under the terms of the agreement, a French army began to land near Edinburgh to begin the slow reconquest of the kingdom. By the following year, the combined attacks of the Franco-Scottish armies and the failure of Seymour's interventionist policy to subdue the local Stewart resistance created a loss of favor for the lord protector in Parliament and his overthrow. As the fighting continued unabated, the English legislative assembly grew tired of the high cost of the unsuccessful war and in September 1549 the campaign was abandoned and peace talks initiated with the Hamilton regency.

As the result of the Haddington Treaty, on August 7, 1548, the Stewart queen sailed to France and a new life in the Valois court. In October Mary I met her four-year-old future husband, Francis, in Paris and they soon became close friends, as she assumed the role of the dominant and overprotective older sister. A large French household was provided for her every need and tutors appointed for the continuance of her education. She quickly learned to speak French and it remained her language of choice. Mary I's academic studies included reading, writing, Latin and Italian and the social graces of dancing, art and music, where she excelled in playing the lute. Mary was not trained as a governing monarch but as the future dauphine of France.

In March 1558 the Scottish Parliament sent envoys to France to finalize the treaty for the marriage of Mary I to Prince Francis. Under the ensuing agreement, the two kingdoms were to be united under the French king but with Scotland acknowledged as a separate realm. If there was a surviving male heir from the marriage, he would inherit both thrones; however, if there was no legitimate successor, the House of Arran would be invested with the monarchy of Scotland. Despite the settlement's provisions protecting the independent sovereignty of her throne, shortly before the wedding Mary I secretly signed a separate covenant, effectively ceding Scotland to France if she died without a direct heir. The formal ceremony was held in Paris at the Notre Dame Cathedral on April 24, 1558, amid a grand and elaborate series of celebrations.

In July of the following year, Mary I's position at the Valois court changed dramatically when Henry II died as the result of an injury suffered in a jousting tournament and the sickly Francis II and his wife inherited the throne. However, their reign lasted only seventeen months, ending with the death of the king on December 5, 1560. Francis II was succeeded by his ten-year-old brother, Charles IX, but his mother, Catherine de Medici, quickly seized power, ruling in the name of her son. As the dowager queen, Mary I, was out of favor with the increasingly hostile Valois regime and in August 1561 returned to Scotland to assume the monarchy as queen at age eighteen.

During Mary I's absence from Scotland, James Hamilton of Arran was appointed by Parliament as regent to rule in the name of the queen. However, in 1554 the Arran earl was forced from the government under pressure from the Guise family of the dowager queen. As the French court's political power increased in Scotland, Mary of Guise was elected to replace Hamilton as regent for her daughter. While she consolidated her rule, the advisors of Arran were replaced by her loyal supporters, as foreign officials now increasingly dominated the new regency and a large French army was garrisoned in the towns and castles to enforce her authority. Resentment against the alien occupation quickly grew among the nobility and church but it was the growth of the Protestant Reformation that finally propelled the kingdom into open civil war.

The new religion had first appeared on Scotland's east coast during the 1520s and had slowly begun to spread through the nobility and burghs. There were periodic outbreaks of violence as the Calvinists pressed for additional religious concessions from the government. The response from the Hamilton and Guise councils was weak and slow in suppressing the reformers, permitting the Protestant church to become firmly established. However, in 1558 the Catholic queen of England, Mary I Tudor, died and was succeeded by her Protestant half-sister, Elizabeth I. The pro–French Guise party began to fear an English intervention in support of the Scottish reformers. The religious climate was inflamed further the following year, when the French regime began the hostile subjugation of its heretic faction, which encouraged Mary of Guise to become more militant in Scotland. When she summoned the Calvinist leaders to her court to answer charges of disobedience, revolt soon broke out. John Knox was the recognized head of the Protestants and openly encouraged attacks against Catholic priests and institutions. He received his education from Saint Andrews University and after completing his studies entered the Catholic priesthood. However, Knox soon came under the influence of the growing church reform movement, joining the Presbyterian Church as chaplain for Saint Andrews Castle. When the rebel fortress was seized in 1546 by the French troops of Mary of Guise, he was captured and forced to serve nearly two years as a galley slave before his ransom by English Protestants. After his release, Knox joined the Church of England, rising to royal chaplain for King Edward VI. When Mary I Tudor reestablished Catholicism Knox fled to Geneva and became associated with John Calvin. Following his return to Scotland, Knox assumed the leadership of the local Protestant Reformation.

Under the exhortations of Knox, in May 1558 the Calvinists attacked and occupied Edinburgh as the religious conflict grew increasingly hostile. To advance their cause and give legitimacy to their rebellion, the reformer party established a new governing administration with James Hamilton as the nominal head of state. With the heretic offensive steadily gaining momentum, Mary of Guise aggressively responded by sending her French troops to recapture Edinburgh, suppressing the uprising by force of arms. As the fighting escalated, in January 1560 Elizabeth I intervened to defend the Protestants by sending her army into Scotland. As the English advanced across the border a stalemate soon developed and with the death of Mary of Guise in June both factions agreed to a settlement. Under the ensuing Treaty of Edinburgh, the Tudor council and French pledged to withdraw their soldiers and allow the Scots to resolve their religious conflict.

To settle the ongoing Protestant rebellion, in August 1560 the Scottish Parliament met to establish a governing council and determine ecclesiastic policy for the realm. The legislative assembly was quickly dominated by the Protestant faction, which created a new pro-reformer government and passed laws to abolish the Catholic mass and authority of Rome. However, with the Scottish monarchy still vacant, the Parliament failed to decide on a new ruling royal house, leaving the issue unresolved until late 1560 when the French king died, permitting negotiations to begin for the return to Scotland of Mary I Stewart. In April 1561 the regency council sent envoys to the Valois court to offer the kingdom to Queen Mary I and after reaching an agreement with the French regime, in August she arrived in Edinburgh to begin her personal reign.

During her years in France, Mary I had grown into a strikingly beautiful eighteen-year-old, standing just over six feet tall with large greenish eyes, reddish hair and possessing a graceful, elegant royal bearing. Assuming control of the ruling Stewart administration, she began her monarchy with energy, toleration and a spirit of reconciliation with the reformists. Through the Scottish Parliament, she granted freedom of worship to all who wished to practice the Calvinist belief. During her first year, the Stewart queen traveled extensively through the Highlands and the southern counties where her court was welcomed with great enthusiasm and acclaim. William Maitland of Lethington and Mary I's half-brother, James Stewart, who were both Protestant and highly skilled and competent advisors, were appointed to the royal council and they quickly dominated her regime. James Stewart was born in 1531 and was the illegitimate son of King James V and his favorite mistress, Lady Margaret Erskine, daughter of the Lord of Erskine, John. James was an early convert to Protestantism, joining the anti–Catholic warlords to oppose the administration of Mary of Guise and her campaign to suppress the new religion. He became a member of James Hamilton's regency government, negotiating the return of Queen Mary I from France in 1561. Under the leadership of James Stewart and Maitland, crown policy showed no favoritism to any faith, becoming the protector of both churches and prosecuting the law without bias. While Mary I initially succeeded in ending the religious strife, the ultra anti-papist faction led by John Knox remained defiant in their opposition to the Catholic dogma.

Soon after assuming the reins of power, Mary I mustered the Scottish army and advanced to crush the remaining pockets of resistance to her government. Her first attack was launched against the defiance of the Protestant Hamilton family. Under the military might of her forces, the Earl of Arran was defeated and imprisoned, while his political league was shattered. Following the subjugation of the Hamiltons, the Stewart regime mounted a campaign to suppress the formidable Catholic Huntly alliance in the north led by Lord George Gordon. In the summer of 1562 Mary I mobilized a small army, marching into the Highlands to reimpose her authority by force of arms. At the approach of the royalists, Gordon of Huntly attempted to negotiate a reconciliation, but the queen defiantly refused, forcing the earl to assemble his soldiers to defend his demesne. Under the skilled command of James Stewart, newly appointed Earl of Moray, the Stewarts routed the Huntly forces, killing Lord Gordon. The crown seized his estates and castles with the Moray earl granted the majority of his lands. Mary I's quick and decisive actions eliminated two powerful opposition factions, securing her hold on the monarchy and permitting the unimpeded implementation of her policies.

With the return of Mary I to Scotland, the Stewart regime once again became the center of learning and culture in Scotland. In the Valois household of Henry II, the young Mary I had been exposed to the Renaissance style of arts and letters, music and architecture, which were brought to her kingdom. She actively encouraged noted scholars and artisans to reside in her court. Under her reign there were frequent hunting parties during the day and at night plays, dancing and parties. Like her grandfather, James IV, the queen was an accomplished musician, skillfully playing the lute. She took an interest in reading, acquiring a large personal library on many subjects, while developing a fondness for poetry and the classics.

As the granddaughter of Queen Margaret Tudor, Mary I was the successor to the English crown by birthright should Elizabeth I die without issue. The queen's chief counselors, Moray and Lethington, favored a political union with England to protect the independence of Protestant Scotland in a largely Catholic Europe. To preserve the kingdom's future, the two advisors began negotiations with the Tudor court to encourage Elizabeth I to officially recognize Mary I as heir, offering the English the choice of a husband for her to secure their approval. However, the initiatives were ignored by the Tudor regime.

As part of the negotiations with England for the recognition of Queen Mary I as heir to the Tudor crown, in a show of good faith the Stewart regime pardoned the exiled Earl of Lennox and his handsome and charismatic son, Henry Stewart, Lord of Darnley. Henry Stewart was the son of Matthew Stewart and Margaret Douglas and was born in Leeds, England, in 1545. He was the second cousin of the queen and next in succession to the Scottish throne. He had been raised and educated at the English court and had many close friends and contacts in the Tudor government. In the winter of 1565 Lord Darnley met his cousin and quickly became a regular member of her household. He possessed good looks, an easy manner with abundant charm and Mary I was soon deeply in love with him, becoming determined to marry Henry. On July 29, 1565, in a Catholic ceremony at Holyrood Chapel, Mary I was married to Henry Stewart.

Following the queen's marriage, James Stewart of Moray withdrew from the government with his office of chief council advisor threatened and his ambition to acquire the monarchy for himself thwarted by the presence of Lord Darnley. He formed an alliance with the discredited Earl of Arran and Hastings family. The allies hastily raised an army in an attempt to seize the crown but Mary I countered their rebellion by summoning her vassals and supporters and personally marching against them. No battle resulted, as the Moray earl soon realized his cause was lost and abandoned his uprising, seeking asylum in England.

While the revolt of her half-brother had been easily subdued, the queen was soon confronted with the deviant and eccentric behavior of her husband. Darnley showed himself to be shallow, unstable and utterly without loyalty. He formed his own counter court packed with scheming low nobles and became a threat to usurp the crown by forging an alliance with the treasonous magnates, headed by James Douglas, fourth earl of Morton. Douglas was born in 1525 and was the second son of Sir George Douglas of Pittendriech and Elizabeth Drummond. He inherited the earldom of Morton in 1553 after the death of his father-in-law and became a prominent member of the Stewart council, serving as lord chancellor. Under the leadership of Darnley and Lord Morton, the rebels directed their uprising against the queen's personal secretary, David Rizzio, whom they claimed had gained too much royal favor and patronage and was a secret agent of the Holy See. On March 9, 1566, Rizzio was murdered at Holyrood Palace by Lord Darnley's supporters led by James Douglas. After the death of the secretary, Mary I's husband panicked and abandoned the insurgency, begging for reconciliation with his wife. As the rogues advanced against him in retaliation, the queen began to fear for her life and was quickly reunited with Henry of Darnley. On March 11 they escaped from the palace, traveling to safety at Dunbar Castle, where James Hepburn, Earl of Bothwell, with his small army joined the queen's faction. With the military might of Bothwell backing her, Mary I marched to Edinburgh again taking command of her government. Hepburn was the son of Patrick Hepburn, third Earl of Bothwell, and Agnes of Sinclair and was born in 1534. He was popular in the Lowland fiefs and succeeded to the earldom of Bothwell in 1556 after the death of his father. He inherited the title of lord high admiral of Scotland and become an experienced naval captain, sailing throughout the North and Baltic Sea regions. He met Mary I and Francis II in Paris several times and when the French king died in 1560 made the arrangements for her return to Scotland. After Mary I's assumption of the throne, he became a member of her court but was soon charged with treason and imprisoned for a short period at Edinburgh Castle.

Soon after her triumphant return, Mary I gave birth to her only surviving child, James, on June 19, 1566, at Edinburgh Castle. He was appointed Duke of Rothesay and acknowledged as heir to the Scottish throne in recognition of his blood rights. After the birth of their son, the reconciliation between Mary I and Darnley quickly ended, when he began to plot to seize control of Prince James and depose his wife. During the late autumn of 1566, Mary I was increasingly pressed by her supporters to petition Pope Pius V for a divorce. As hostilities with Henry Stewart escalated, she finally agreed to pursue the dissolution of the marriage. However, not willing to wait on papal approval, a coalition of the queen's allies began to plan the murder of Darnley. On February 9, 1567, the plotters placed kegs of gunpowder under his residence and early in the morning the building was demolished. Darnley's body was found in the garden unmarked by the explosion and the cause of death was never determined. No one was ever convicted of the crime, although Bothwell was charged but released after a mock trial.

Mary I's authority and prestige with the leading nobles and prelates was seriously damaged by the suspicion that she was involved in the murder of her husband. As the opposition to her reign intensified, she increasingly turned to James Hepburn of Bothwell, as her defender and protector. While Hepburn led a formidable faction of southern warlords, he was unpopular with the high magnates and welcomed the opportunity to advance his favor with the throne. As his esteem and power grew at court, he began to conspire to usurp the Scottish crown through his marriage to the queen. His initial proposal was rejected by Mary I; however, after Hepburn kidnapped her, she agreed to the marriage under duress. On May 15, 1567, the Protestant ceremony was held at Holyrood Palace with few members of the nobility and church present, as the queen became further distanced from her base of support.

Over the past two years of her rule, Mary I had grown increasingly unpopular with her high lords, bishops and burghs with her favoritism of Darnley and later James Hepburn. On May 1 the magnates rose in revolt, agreeing to restore Mary I to the throne only if she abandoned Bothwell. The rebels marched to Dunbar Castle to openly confront the queen but no battle resulted when Hepburn's troops refused to fight and Mary I and her new husband were compelled to accept the terms dictated by the insurgents. Bothwell was forced into exile, while the queen was taken to Edinburgh under heavy armed guard as the virtual prisoner of the rogue nobles. On July 24 the leaders of the insurrection league demanded the abdication of Mary I from the Stewart crown in favor of her thirteen-month-old son, James. Suffering from shock and depression from the recent miscarriage of twins and with no visible friends or allies, she signed the agreement, ending her reign.

After the overthrow of the queen, her half-brother, James Stewart, earl of Moran, returned to Scotland from his English exile and was appointed regent for a new government by the rebel lords. However, Mary I still retained many supporters as the legitimate ruler among the nobility and George Douglas, brother of the keeper of Lochleven Castle, formed an alliance with her friends to restore her to the throne. Through the intervention of the Douglas faction, on May 2, 1568, the queen escaped from Lochleven, traveling toward the protection of Dumbarton Castle. As she passed through the countryside, many nobles with their troops joined her cause and Mary I was determined to seize her crown by force of arms. Upon learning of his half-sister's flight, the newly elected regent and his chief advisor, James Douglas of Morton, marched from Glasgow to defend the regime. In the ensuing encounter at Langside, the well commanded soldiers of James Stewart held the high ground and out maneuvered Mary I's forces, completely overwhelming her army. She was compelled to flee the battlefield and with a small band of followers escaped to England, resolved to regain the kingdom with the aid of her cousin, Elizabeth I.

When Mary I arrived in England, she was received in friendship by Elizabeth I's government, however, the deposed queen was quickly confined at Carlisle Castle and later moved for greater security south to Bolton Castle. To advance England's ongoing quest for supremacy over Scotland, Elizabeth I soon became involved in local politics by appointing a commission headed by Thomas Howard, Duke of Norfolk, to determine her cousin's involvement in the murder of Darnley. However, when the council issued its final report in January 1569, no conclusion for the cause of Darnley's death was given. With the lack of a definitive decision, the English were compelled to abandon their initiative to return Mary I to her Scottish throne as their figurehead ruler and she continued to remain the prisoner of her cousin.

During the following year, Mary I was frequently moved from castle to castle out of security concerns. While at Wingfield Castle, she became part of a plot engineered by Thomas Howard to overthrow Elizabeth I and place Mary I on a restored Catholic throne of England. The conspiracy was discovered by double agents and resulted in more severe confinement for the deposed queen with little possibility of rescue.

As Mary I remained in captivity, Scotland was thrust into civil war following the murder of the regent, Moray. Two alliances were soon formed to contend for control of a new government; the King's Party favored the monarchy of James VI, while the Queen's Men supported the restoration of Mary I. The bloody conflict dragged on unresolved until April 1573, when the Tudor court sent troops to intervene in support of the King's Party and their combined armies destroyed the last remnants of the Queen's Men coalition, finally bringing peace.

After the failed escape attempt from Wingfield, the deposed Stewart queen was moved to the bleak castle of Tutbury, where she spent the greater part of her captivity. Throughout the remainder of her life Mary I never stopped involving herself in numerous schemes to secure her freedom and the English crown. In 1583 a conspiracy was discovered by spies of Elizabeth I, which centered on a Spanish invasion of England and restoration of the Catholic faith with Mary I as queen. This was followed by a plan to assassinate the Tudor queen, which again entangled Mary I in a web of treasonous activities. Finally, in early 1586 a Catholic priest named John Ballard and his co-insurrectionist, Anthony Babington, formed a plot to kill the English queen and place her cousin on the throne with the aid of a Papal-Spanish army. However, the secret agents of Elizabeth I infiltrated the conspirators and captured incriminating letters from Mary I, which resulted in her arrest on August 11 on charges of treason. In September she was taken under heavy armed guard to Fotheringhay Castle, where her two-day trial was held the following month. On October 25 the judges found Mary I guilty of intriguing to murder Elizabeth I with a sentence of death. The execution warrant was signed on February 1, 1587, and seven days later the queen of Scots was beheaded in the Great Hall of Fotheringhay. She was initially buried in Peterborough Cathedral and later reinterred in Westminster Abbey alongside Elizabeth I. The seventh Stewart monarch died at the age of forty-four and reigned in Scotland for twenty-five years.

Sources

Donaldson. *Scottish Kings.*   Fraser. *Mary Queen of Scots.*   Morrison. *Mary—Queen of Scots.*

James VI, 1566–1567–1625

Following the forced abdication of Queen Mary I in 1567, the thirteen-month-old James VI was recognized as the eighth Scottish king of the Renaissance era. James Stewart was born on June 19, 1566, at Edinburgh Castle during a period of internal disorder and rebellion among the nobility. The Stewart prince was the only surviving son of Queen Mary I and Henry Stewart, Lord of Darnley. In acknowledgement of his inheritance right of succession to the Scottish kingdom, James was named Duke of Rothesay. After his birth he was placed in the care of the Erskine family and raised and educated at Stirling Castle. In accordance with the wishes of his mother, he was baptized as a Catholic, which caused a storm of protest from the majority Protestant nobles. In 1567 Mary I's alleged implication in the murder of her second husband, Lord Darnley, and remarriage to the unpopular and ambitious Earl of Bothwell, James Hepburn, gave cause to revolt among the high magnates. After a failed attempt to defend her rule by force of arms, the queen was seized at Dunbar Castle and forced to abdicate the Stewart throne in favor of her son, James. On July 29 in a Protestant coronation ceremony at Stirling Castle, the two-year-old James VI was formally invested with the crown of Scotland.

While the infant-king remained at Stirling under the custody of John Erskine, the Scottish Parliament appointed the Earl of Moray, James Stewart, as regent to govern the kingdom in his name. Moray had the support and favor of many of the powerful noble families and through his skilled rule brought peace and a stable administration to the realm. However, in January 1570 he was assassinated, resulting in a series of weak governments. To confront the unstable Protestant regime, the Queen Men's alliance was formed by Sir William Maitland of Lethington with the leading Catholic warlords to promote the restoration of the deposed Queen Mary I, propelling the crown into civil war with the defenders of James VI. The bloody struggle dragged on until 1573, when the King's Men faction of James VI recognized James Douglas, fourth Earl of Morton, as regent. In February he negotiated a reconciliation with a breakaway party of Catholics, who had grown war weary, and with the aid of English troops provided by Elizabeth I finally destroyed the queen's remaining allies by storming Edinburgh Castle and executing the Lethington lord.

The early years of James VI's childhood were spent at Stirling Castle away from the ongoing brutal civil war. The Erskine family provided for his protection and care in a stern and strict court, where he was denied personal affection and love. At the age of four his academic education was begun with tutors appointed by the regency. He was a gifted and dedicated student, excelling in his studies of reading, writing, history, mathematics, science, Calvinist doctrine and languages to include Latin, French, Greek and Italian,. A large library was available for his use, containing a wide variety of books on many subjects. He received an exceptional humanist education from his distinguished private instructors, developing into a scholar. Members of the Erskine family provided his military training in weapons but he took little interest in the instruction. The king enjoyed field sports, especially golf and archery. James VI became an accomplished equestrian with a fondness for hunting, which was pursued passionately throughout his life.

The defeat of the Queen's Men in 1573 secured the regency of James Douglas of Morton, permitting him to govern Scotland in the name of James VI. Douglas restored the king's authority and laws over the realm by brutally thwarting all challenges to his power by the rebel factions, while maintaining stability on the southern border by actively promoting peace with England. The regent reigned as an independent overlord, including few noble families or Presbyterian churchmen into his administration, which served to separate him from important bases of support. By 1578 the earl was growing increasingly unpopular and with their power and prestige at court weakened by their denial of royal offices, militant alliances of magnates began to form in opposition, resulting in his brief overthrow in March. Despite the failure to assert their control, the rogue lords remained resolved and defiant, continuing to plot the downfall of the regent. As resistance against his rule mounted, James Douglas continued to exclude the monarch from his regime and under influence from the Erskine family, James VI was drawn into the escalating revolt, joining the dissident movement as figurehead leader. With custody and support from the young king, a formidable insurgent party was formed by alienated Presbyterians and high magnates, forcing James Douglas to resign from the government.

In the summer of 1579 the king's cousin, Esme Stewart, arrived in Scotland from his family estates in France and began to exert a steadily expanding dominance over James VI. Esme was the son of John Stewart, fifth Lord of Aubigny, and was born in 1542 in France. In 1567 his father died and Esme inherited his titles and lordship of Aubigny. He became a prominent member of the Valois court and was sent to Scotland by the Guise faction to improve French influence with the Stewarts. The two cousins soon developed a close friendship and through his relationship with the sovereign, Esme was appointed to the council. He was showered with gifts, honors and in 1580 named to the vacant earldom of Lennox. Using his association with the king, the Lennox earl seized control of the crown to rule the kingdom. However, as a foreigner and Catholic, he had few friends or defenders in the nobility and lacked a political base of support, as opposition forces quickly rallied against his regime. After Esme's assumption of power, James VI began to attend council meetings and actively participate in the government, while the high warlords were largely ignored and excluded from the administration. As the earl grew increasingly unpopular, his implication in the Spanish conspiracy to rescue the deposed Mary I from her imprisonment in England and restore her to the Scottish throne gave cause to revolt by the magnates. With Esme's reign discredited and fearing the forced restoration of the Catholic queen, in August 1582, a coalition of rebels led by William Ruthven, first Earl of Gowrie, plotted to overthrow the monarchy and take custody of James VI. The earl was from a prominent Presbyterian family with estates in Perthshire and earlier was a member of the conspiracy to murder Queen Mary I's personal secretary, David Rizzio. On August 22, 1582 William Ruthven led an alliance of Presbyterian lords and kidnapped the monarch at Ruthven Castle, forcing him to exile Esme. The Gowrie earl quickly usurped the realm and with the backing of the Protestant church and wardship of James VI consolidated his authority.

Following his seizure by the dissident coalition, James VI was imprisoned at Ruthven Castle and defiantly began to plot with his supporters to regain his freedom. While he remained under confinement, the new Ruthven regency attempted to exert its rule, however, despite financial support from Elizabeth I's regime, the Gowrie earl's government grew increasingly unpopular and ineffective. As his administration's power continued to wane, the king exhorted his loyal magnates to unite and secure his release. Finally in June 1583, an escape plan was arranged and as James VI traveled to Saint Andrews his guards were overwhelmed by the conspirators and he was freed after being held prisoner for ten months. The rebel lords were arrested but later pardoned to prevent a cause for future revolt.

In the aftermath of the overthrow of the Ruthven council, the anti–English Earl of Arran, James Stewart, was appointed by Parliament to rule in the name of the king. While the Arran regime asserted its power, the seventeen-year-old James VI began to increasingly participate in the government and take personal control of his kingdom. The fall of the Ruthven administration had resulted in the loss of English influence in Scotland and the Tudor court attempted to regain its lost favor by encouraging the rebels to renew their revolt with promises of military and financial aid. In April 1584 William Ruthven and his supporters launched their coup, attacking and seizing Stirling Castle. In defense of his monarchy, James VI and the Arran alliance assembled a large army, forcing the conspirators to surrender. William Ruthven and the leaders of his insurgency were captured and later executed for their acts of treason.

After the elimination of the Ruthven conspiracy and the king's continued suppression of the rebellious lords, by 1584 the Stewart throne had gained unrestricted power over the nobility. However, the Presbyterian Church still remained defiant of the Stewart council's authority and James VI launched a political campaign to limit its independence. He issued a decree reaffirming his authority as head of the church's governing body, the Kirk, forcing the Presbyterians to acknowledge his sovereignty. While the Kirk continued to function as a separate entity, its ruling members accepted the supremacy of the king. By its aggressive and determined initiatives against the nobles and church, the Stewart crown reasserted its power and recognition to an extent not known since the reign of James IV.

With a secure monarchy James VI began to direct his foreign policy away from his realm's historic ally and friend, France, and toward conciliation with Elizabeth I. The Tudor court was initially antagonistic toward any agreement with Scotland, however, in late 1584 as war with Spain increasingly threatened, Elizabeth I became less bellicose. The Stewart regime sent Patrick Gray to London in October to arrange a settlement. In need of a secure northern border to direct all its resources against Spain, the English were willing to negotiate in good faith and in the following year a treaty was signed. The formal agreement was ratified in July 1585, providing for the two former rivals to actively enforce peace on their borders and form a military coalition. For abandoning the traditional French alliance, James VI was to be paid an annual annuity. In February 1586 the first challenge to the new détente occurred with the trial and execution of the king's mother, the deposed Queen Mary I. The Scottish council issued a strong public protest but privately gave assurances of its desire not to disrupt the recent resolution. Both kingdoms found it disadvantageous to renew hostilities and no serious border incidents occurred. James VI exploited England's increased tension with Spain to press for his formal recognition as Elizabeth I's successor but his petitions were ignored.

During 1587 Philip II of Spain began to assemble his Great Armada for the long expected invasion and conquest of England. As the threat of war grew, Elizabeth I sent envoys to the Stewart government to ensure her alliance with Scotland would be honored. The prospects of receiving formal recognition of James VI as the queen's heir designate was skillfully exploited by the Tudors to hold any anti–English initiatives by the Scots in check. Nevertheless, as the probability of a Spanish victory grew, James VI began to seek the goodwill of his non–Calvinist nobles to protect his regime against revolt in support of Philip II and to remain on friendly terms with papist Europe. The Catholic Earl George Gordon became a favorite of the monarch and part of his royal regime. Gordon was the fifth Earl of Huntly and educated as a member of the Church of Rome in France. After his return to Scotland, he joined the faction in opposition to the rule of James Douglas of Morton and participated in his overthrow. In June 1583 he was part of the plot that resulted in the escape of James VI from his Ruthven captors.

It was Stewart policy to outwardly promote rapport with both the Catholic and Protestant courts of Europe to thwart the expected Spanish triumph against England. In July 1588 as Philip II's navy approached England, Elizabeth I's ambassadors offered James VI many of his demands to receive his pledge of support. He accepted the proposal and promised Scotland's full military cooperation. However, after the Great Armada was largely destroyed by the attacks of Sir Francis Drake and summer gales, James VI received little from their negotiated agreement. The continued reluctance of Elizabeth I to honor her commitments finally convinced the Scots that she would never publicly acknowledge the Stewart king as her rightful successor. Without the assurance of the English crown, James VI directed his initiatives toward gaining the friendship of both the Scottish and European Catholics to maintain peace within his predominately Protestant realm.

Despite James VI's efforts to retain the goodwill of his non–Protestant nobles, by early 1589 a faction headed by the Earl of Huntly conspired with Philip II, offering its support for a second Spanish invasion of England. To honor its pledge to the Tudor court, the Stewart throne dismissed Gordon from the council and court, exiling him to his estates. To regain his lost offices and honors, the earl assembled his Catholic allies and vassals and advanced against the king at Edinburgh. To counter the challenge to his sovereignty, James VI summoned a large army and marched to oppose Gordon's revolt. At the approach of the formidable royal army, the rebel forces of Gordon quickly surrendered. Huntly was arrested but later pardoned for his rebellion, as the crown remained committed to promoting the favor of the Catholics to maintain peace and avoid isolating Scotland from pro-papist Europe.

The Scottish king had received an excellent education from his tutors, developing a special interest in the arts and poetry. His regime attracted the leading scholars, artists, poets, dramatists and musicians, sponsoring and encouraging their many works. The Stewart king enthusiastically participated in the reading of poems and dramas at his court, contributing many of his personal writings. Many fine examples of his prose still exist. James VI also published several books dealing with issues of theology and justification of kingship through divine right. He wrote *Basilikon Doron* for the education of his heir, Henry, and *The True Law of Free Monarchies* to explain his theories of religion and government, in addition to numerous political essays.

James VI had no immediate successor and after peace was imposed in Scotland his council increasingly pressed him to marry to secure the Stewart dynasty. Envoys were sent to the European courts in search of a wife and by 1589 the choice of a royal princess was reduced to two, Catherine of Navarre and Anne, daughter of the king of Denmark. The Danish realm offered the advantages of a large dowry and an alliance with a wealthy Baltic power. Negotiations were begun with the Danes and a marital treaty was quickly finalized. The ceremony was held by proxy on August 20 with the new queen soon sailing for Scotland. However, bad storms forced the escort fleet to seek shelter in Norway. As Anne remained stranded, James VI grew impatient to meet his new wife, leaving his kingdom to join her in Oslo. From Norway the queen and king returned to Denmark, spending the winter with her father and not departing for Scotland until May 1590. During the first years of their marriage, James VI and Anne developed a loving and supportive relationship, but in the later years they drifted apart with each pursuing separate interests. She became an energetic patron of the arts and letters and did much to promote and encourage their growth in Scotland and later England. The succession to the throne was secured with the birth of Prince Henry in February 1594 and was followed by six additional children, including the future King Charles I in 1600.

Following his return to Scotland, James VI was confronted by rumors that the Baltic storms that disrupted Anne's voyage were arranged through witchcraft to prevent the marriage. In sixteenth century Europe, the practice of demon worship was widely accepted and feared. As the unrest spread, the Stewart government ordered an investigation, resulting in the North Berwick Trials and the execution of numerous alleged witches. While the crown's initiative against the exercise of sorcery continued, in April 1591 Francis Stewart, Earl of Bothwell, was accused of involvement with the Berwick witches and plotting the death of the king through wizardry. Bothwell was arrested and imprisoned but soon escaped, avoiding all attempts at recapture and for the next three years unleashed a campaign of personal terrorism directed against the Stewart court. In the summer of 1594 Francis of Bothwell withdrew to the north, seeking sanctuary with his cousin, George Gordon of Huntly. The royal army under the command of James VI advanced against the two rogue earls, quickly subduing their rebellion. However, Bothwell again escaped going into exile. Huntly submitted to the throne and was banished but permitted to return in 1596 after pledging fealty to the Stewart regime.

Through the subjugation policy of James Douglas of Morton, the rule of James VI was not seriously challenged by his nobility after his assumption of the crown. However, the governing body of the Presbyterian Church, the Kirk, attempted to act independent of royal authority under the leadership of Andrew Melville. Melville was educated as a scholar, excelling in his studies of classical languages, civil law and theology at the universities of Saint Andrews and Paris. He later became dean of the school at Saint Andrews, greatly expanding the quality and size of the course curriculum. In 1583 Melville was appointed to lead the Presbyterian Church and participated in the organization of the Kirk, defiantly supporting the rights of his religion against the encroachments of the Stewart court. Two years later he fled to England to avoid charges of treason for his energetic defense of freedom of worship, remaining in exile for over one year.

The king remained a devoted Calvinist but was widely accepted by the other Protestant churches with the exception of the Melville extremists. James VI considered the Kirk subordinated to his authority, while under Melville's dogma his church was responsible only to God. To promote friendship with the Presbyterians, early in 1592 the Stewart regime ratified the Golden Act, granting the Kirk the right to create its own functioning bureaucracy, while the throne still retained limited powers. However, after religious riots erupted in Edinburgh in support of religious freedom, to enforce his control over the militant churchmen, James VI decreed that his government must approve all future appointments of ministers. In 1597 the Presbyterian General Assembly responded by appointing a council to advise the monarch in his choices of clergymen, which the Stewart administration skillfully used to dominate the church and outmaneuver the ultra–Melville faction to reassert its full sovereignty over the Protestants.

While Elizabeth I refused to publicly acknowledge the king of the Scots as her immediate heir, the European courts and English Parliament considered him as the successor designate. James VI held the superior claim by birthright and union with England would end countless years of war between the two kingdoms. As the Tudor queen entered the last years of her reign, in February 1601 James VI dispatched secret envoys to London to open private discussions with the English first minister, Robert Cecil. They were assured of the Stewart king's succession by Cecil and advised to take no actions to harm the status quo. Following their return to the Stewart regime, a long correspondence was begun between the Scottish crown and Lord Cecil, which served to inform and instruct James VI on the art of kingship in England.

As the Stewart administration impatiently awaited the death of the English queen, James VI used the power of his monarchy to impose order and justice in his realm and mount an energetic international diplomatic campaign to gain the favor of the Catholic courts of Europe in his quest for the English regime. In Scotland the Stewart council enhanced the rule of law by increasing the number of crown sheriffs and reforming the local court system by expanding the royal appointed judiciaries. James VI skillfully exploited the queen's recent conversion from Lutheranism to the Catholic Church, by sending emissaries to the European papist governments, seeking their support for his kingship of England. The initiative received generally favorable responses and with Pope Clement VIII's approval, there were no major continental obstacles to James VI's succession to the English throne.

By early 1603 Elizabeth I was beginning to show clear signs that the end of her reign was nearing. She died early in the morning of March 24 and a few hours later a royal courier was sent north to bring the news to Scotland. After a three day ride to Edinburgh, James VI was informed of his inheritance of the throne of England, as King James I. The official proclamation from Parliament reached him five days later, as preparations for a grand procession south through England were well underway. On April 5 he left Edinburgh accompanied by many English and Scottish nobles, arriving in his new realm to the cheers of the local population. The king and queen were officially invested with the crown of England at Westminster Abbey on July 25, 1603.

James I had initiated private contacts with the English regime's first minister, Robert Cecil, prior to the death of Elizabeth I and following his investiture the king continued to rely on him for advice and recommendations in establishing his government. With the earl's support, the Stewart council began the difficult task of confronting Parliament and limiting the growing power of the Puritans. Soon after his arrival in England, James I clashed with the religious extremists over their demand for changes to the Anglican Church's doctrine. An ecclesiastic assembly was summoned to Hampton Court to resolve the escalating dissension, where James I made clear his intentions to make no modifications to the established dogmas. While the Hampton Court Conference failed to resolve the religious differences, it did authorize a commission of church scholars to write a new English version of the Bible. After four years the final work was published in 1611, as the King James Version. However, it was the English Catholics in their quest for greater freedom of worship and not the Puritans that created the first crisis of the new reign.

Under Queen Elizabeth I's government, the English Catholics had been subjected to severe persecutions and restrictions and looked to the new monarch for greater tolerance and the repeal of the anti-papist laws. Despite the Stewart regime's repeated initiatives to promote religious tolerance, Parliament refused to approve all attempts to weaken the legislation and the Catholics became disillusioned with James I. In May 1604 a militant faction of extremist Catholics, dissatisfied at the lack of religious freedom, began to plot the overthrow of the government and assassination of the king by blowing up the House of Lords. In October 1605 thirty kegs of gunpowder were placed under Parliament House and made ready for the opening of the legislative session on November 3. However, the conspiracy was discovered and the plotters arrested. The Gunpowder Plot resulted in further restrictions on the Catholics and they were required to swear an oath, acknowledging James I as king and repudiating the papacy's right to depose Protestant rulers.

From the beginning of James I's rule in England, relations with Parliament were hostile. The delegates clashed with him over taxes and his belief in kingship by divine right. The Parliament demanded additional rights regarding taxation and complained about the crown's selling of monopolies and charging duty on imported goods. To resolve the ongoing conflict over revenues, the monarch offered the legislative body the Great Contract, proposing to restrict the use of royal prerogatives in exchange for a large cash infusion to payoff the royal debt from the reign of Elizabeth I. When the royal legislative assembly responded by offering a smaller settlement, James I refused any further compromise, dissolving Parliament.

In 1614 a new Parliament was summoned to London but like the previous legislative sessions the members soon became bogged down over the crown's demand for new taxes and the right of royal prerogative. The king's skilled first minister, Robert Cecil, had died in 1612 and his new counselors lacked the experience and repute to control the royal legislature. As a consequence, no legislation was enacted and in frustration James I again dismissed the delegates, not calling a new assembly for seven years.

While the Stewart monarchy continued to struggle with the English Parliament, in Scotland James I established a separate government, which was well administered by his chosen counselors. Instructions were sent north on a regular basis with the council fully executing the king's demands. There were frequent Scottish visitors to the London court, who kept the regime fully informed on local affairs. While the northern and Lowland lords remained under the authority of the monarchy, in 1608 the Hebrides Islands rose in revolt in the pursuit of greater autonomy. Operating under orders from London, the Scottish administration empowered the Earl of Argyll to restore royal sovereignty. The earl advanced the Stewart troops into the rebellious lordship to quickly impose James I's supremacy. Following the suppression of the Hebrides uprising, the Macdonald faction rebelled in 1614, attempting to recreate the usurped Kingdom of the Isles. The crown's military forces were again mustered and marched north to crush the Macdonald renegades. So effective was the functioning Scottish council that James I did not return to his homeland until March 1617, staying for only three months.

Under the reign of the Tudor monarchies, England had shown little interest or desire in establishing an overseas empire in the New World. After assuming the throne, James I became an enthusiastic supporter of American exploration and in 1607 sanctioned the Virginia Company to begin a permanent settlement at Jamestown. The successful Virginia colony was followed by additional enclaves in Bermuda, India and in 1620 at Plymouth, Massachusetts. The Stewart king took a special interest in the development of his colonies, issuing charters to many of his favorites. However, the majority of the ventures were ill conceived, ending in failure, financial loss and scandal for the crown.

The promotion of peace had been at the center of James I's foreign policy in Scotland and following his inheritance of the English crown, the initiative was zealously pursued. In 1604 a resolution to the ongoing twenty years of conflict with the Spanish court was finally negotiated under James I's personal direction. To thwart the opposition of Catholic Europe against the rise of Protestantism, the Stewart government sponsored a grand alliance of pro-reformer princes, which was consolidated with the marriage of the king's daughter, Elizabeth, to the Count of Palatine, Frederick V. However, instead of ensuring peace for England in European affairs, the political union with Protestant Palatine involved James I in the Thirty Years' War.

In 1619 Frederick V was elected to the throne of Bohemia after the overthrow of the Catholic Habsburg emperor, Ferdinand II. James I's détente with Philip III of Spain was seriously threatened when the Madrid government became an ally of Habsburg Austria in the war against Bohemia. In 1620 with aid from Philip III, the Catholic army defeated the Protestants at the battle of White Mountain, deposing Frederick V in Bohemia and the Palatinate. To reinstate the count to his lands, the Stewart king was compelled to send English troops to support his son-in-law. However, the royal treasury lacked the necessary funds to provide adequate military forces and arms and when the Stewart regime summoned Parliament in January 1621, the delegates revolted, refusing to approve the petition for additional money. The result was a stalemate and no new taxes were voted for the conflict in the Palatinate.

Following Parliament's failure to grant new war taxes, the English king began a political campaign to reclaim Frederick V's usurped lordship through negotiations with Spain. Relations between the two kingdoms had become hostile during the reign of Philip II and in 1623 to restore friendship the Stewart heir, Prince Charles, was sent to Madrid. He met with the Spanish king, Philip IV, and his advisors but failed to establish a new détente. In the aftermath of the unsuccessful Spanish talks, James I was compelled to summon Parliament to approve the necessary subsidies to support England's involvement in the Thirty Years' War. However, the legislative assembly never met, as the regime's relations with the delegates continued to deteriorate, forcing James I to contest the Catholic threat in Europe with only limited funds. A naval expedition against Cadiz was thwarted and attempts to reinforce the French Protestants at the port of La Rochelle were repulsed, while the Catholic powers retained supremacy over the Palatinate. The English intervention in the Thirty Years' War in defense of the Protestant cause remained in shambles.

In the final years of his monarchy, James I's health steadily declined and he increasingly withdrew from the daily functions of his government, becoming a weak and despondent ruler. His heir and numerous court favorites assumed a larger role in administering the crown's policies, frequently with disastrous results. On March 5, 1625, James I suffered a stroke while hunting and died twenty-two days later at Theobalds Park at age fifty-eight and a reign of fifty-seven years.

Sources

Bingham. *James VI of Scotland.*   Donaldson. *Scotland: James V—James VII.*   Fraser. *King James VI of Scotland.*

General Sources for Scotland

Lynch. *Scotland: A New History.*   Magnusson. *Scotland*

Part III

Renaissance Monarchs of France

House of Valois

Charles VI	1368–1380–1422
Charles VII	1403–1422–1461
Louis XI	1423–1461–1483
Charles VIII	1470–1483–1498

(Valois-Orleans Branch)

Louis XII	1462–1498–1515

(Valois-Angouleme Branch)

Francis I	1494–1515–1547
Henry II	1519–1547–1559
Francis II	1544–1559–1560
Charles IX	1550–1560–1574
Henry III	1551–1574–1589

Genealogical Tables

House of Valois

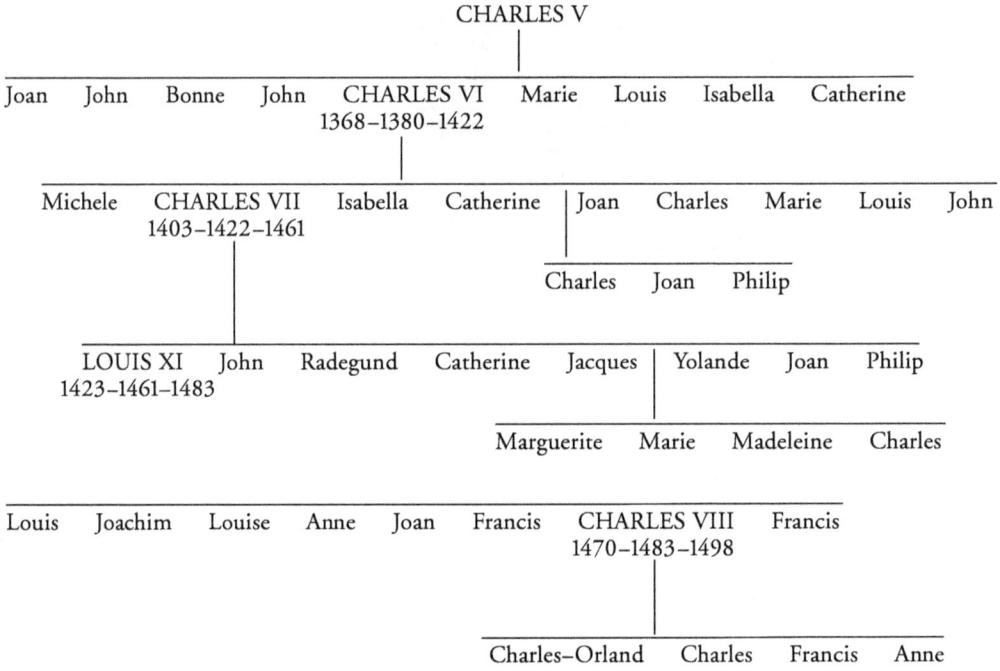

Valois–Orleans Branch

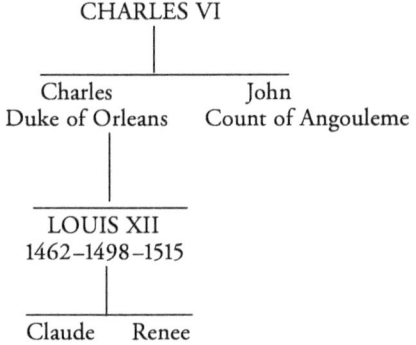

Kings of France are in ALL CAPITALS

Valois–Angouleme Branch

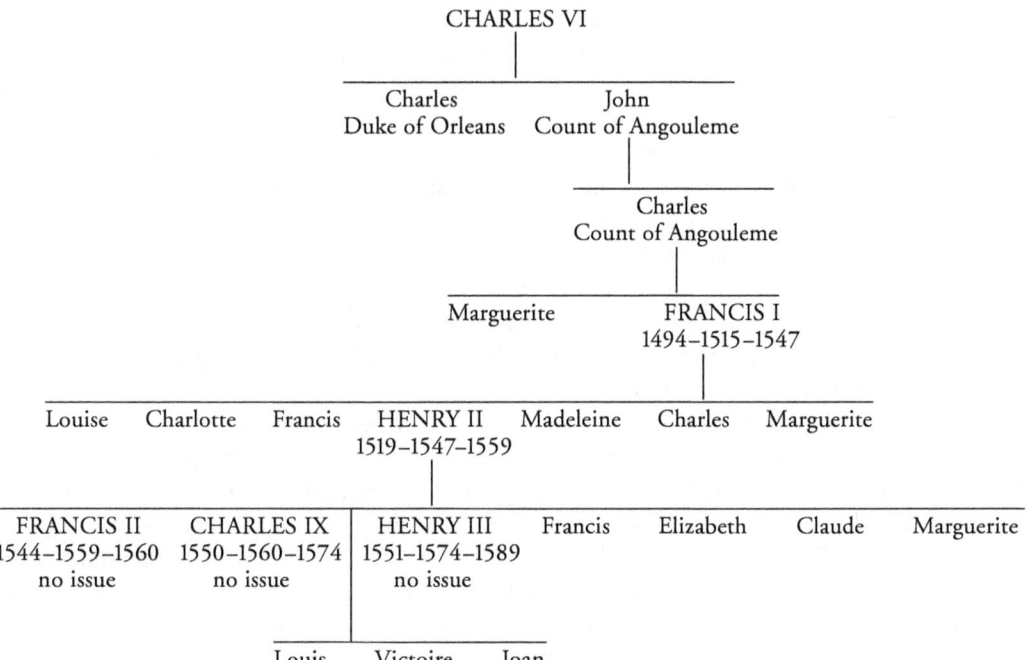

Overview

The kingdom of France was usurped in 987 by the House of Capet, who united the fragmented realm to rule for nearly three hundred years. The Capetian kings reestablished their royal authority over the autonomous nobles, defeated the Angevin Empire to regain control of western France, participated in the Crusades and created a medieval European power. In the aftermath of the death of the last Capetian king in 1328, the French monarchy was inherited by the Valois family, who reigned during the near destruction of France during the Hundred Years' War, internal struggles of the Protestant Reformation and wars in Italy with their introduction of the Renaissance spirit into France.

During the Renaissance epoch, France was ruled by ten monarchs beginning in 1380 with the regime of Charles VI, whose kingship was dominated by his increasingly frequent and severe periods of insanity and renewal of the Hundred Years' War with the devastating English invasion and conquest of Henry V.

The second Renaissance king was Charles VII, who assumed a divided crown in 1422 and through the force of his personality united the kingdom to drive the English from France. He was succeeded by his son, Louis XI, who aggressively asserted the authority of his throne to permanently break the feudal powers of the nobles by military might, negotiations, bribery and intimidation. The sovereignty of his heir, Charles VIII, was directed at the annexation of the duchy of Brittany and beginning of the quest for Italian aggrandizement by force of arms. The fifth Renaissance king was Louis XII, whose reign was occupied with war against the Habsburg Empire for dominance over the duchy of Milan. In 1500 he sent his armies into Lombardy to seize the region, ruling for twelve years as duke before his government was overthrown.

Louis XII was followed to the throne by his cousin, Francis I, who resumed the quest for Lombardy by involving France in a series of conflicts with England and the Holy Roman Empire. While energetically pursuing the conquest of Milan, he became a great patron of Renaissance painters, musicians, architects, poets and sculptors, accumulating a massive collection of art objects, which formed the foundation for the Louvre Museum. At his death in 1547, he was succeeded by his son, Henry II, whose reign finally ended the ongoing Franco-Habsburg wars and began the active resistance of the Valois crown against the escalating threat of the Protestant Reformation. The eighth Renaissance monarch was Francis II, who inherited the French domain in 1559 after the death of his father in a jousting tournament. During his short seventeen month monarchy, hostilities against the Huguenots intensified as the kingdom became increasingly divided by religious civil strife. Francis II died childless in 1560 and the regime was claimed by his brother, Charles IX. After he came under the influence of the ultra-Catholic Guise family, the French royalists aggressively renewed the religious struggle by force of arms against the heretics. The last Renaissance king was Henry III, whose sovereignty was beset with the continued attacks of the anti-papists led by his cousin, King Henry of Navarre, and rebellion of the militant Guise faction in opposition to his more tolerant religious policies toward the Huguenots. To resolve the war, Henry III abandoned the ultra-Catholics and negotiated an alliance with the Protestants. However, as they were besieging Paris, Henry III was assassinated by a fanatic Dominican priest. Before his death he named Henry of Navarre as his successor to end the rule of the French Renaissance kings.

Charles VI, 1368–1380–1422

The first French king of the Renaissance epoch was Charles VI, who was born near Paris on December 3, 1368, and was the third son of Charles V and Queen Jeanne of Bourbon. After the earlier death of his two older brothers, he was acknowledged as the successor to the Valois crown at his birth. The heir spent his early years in the loving and secure environment of the royal court, where his father took special interest in his education. Distinguished scholars and theologians were appointed for his academic instruction; however, Charles was not a gifted or serious student. He developed an interest in military and weapons training, becoming skilled in equestrianship and archery. During his childhood there were several incidents of mental instability, which foreshadowed his later psychological illness. As Charles grew into adolescence, he was described as tall and muscular with a fondness for physical activities and field sports.

As the health of Charles V began to seriously deteriorate, in 1380 preparations were begun for the succession of his eleven-year-old son to the monarchy. Four of the dauphin's uncles were appointed to a regency government to rule in his name during his minority years. Louis of Anjou was named as head of the new administration, but after the death of Charles V in September a power struggle soon developed between him and Philip II of Burgundy for supremacy over the governing council. Philip II was the fourth son of King John II of France and Bonne of Luxembourg and was born at Pontoise on January 17, 1342. During the Hundred Years' War against England, Philip served in his father's army and was recognized by the Valois crown for his bravery and military skills at the battle of Poitiers. Following the death of the last Capetian Duke of Burgundy in November 1361, he was appointed lieutenant general for the duchy and later invested with the ducal throne by John II. Through his marriage to Margaret of Dampierre, the duke gained control over Flanders, Brabant and Artois and an increased presence in the Low Countries. As the recognized first peer of the kingdom and Burgundian Duke, he assumed a position of authority and preeminence in France and became the founder of the Burgundian cadet branch of the Valois House. Holding great wealth and power, he was a patron of the Renaissance and sponsored many artists, sculptors, goldsmiths and musicians at his elaborate court. Following the coronation of Charles VI at Rheims Cathedral in November, the Burgundian Duke formed an alliance with the two uncommitted regents, Louis of Bourbon and John of Berry to further his usurpation cause against the Anjou Duke. With the support of his allies, Philip II began to challenge the policies of the Duke of Anjou, resulting in a weak and disunited regime.

Soon after assuming control of the regime, the regents replaced the capable and experienced officials of Charles V with their family and favorites. Louis of Anjou and Duke Philip II both had territorial ambitions and used the power of the throne to advance their individual causes. After the ruling council came under the dominance of the Duke of Burgundy, the kingdom's government was increasingly misruled for his self aggrandizement and the royal coffers were soon empty. As the financial crisis deepened, the regents were compelled to summon the Estates-General to grant new taxes. However, their demands for funds were met with widespread resistance as violence broke out in Paris and numerous provisional towns, forcing the petition to be withdrawn.

In January 1382 new attempts were made to raise money through the reimposition of an indirect tax. In opposition to the levy, the city of Ghent erupted in new uprisings and the local ruling Flemish count, Louis II, issued an appeal to the Valois crown for military support. To restore order in Flanders, the French army was assembled and under the nominal command of Charles VI advanced north to suppress the rebellion. As the royalists approached Ghent, the Flemish militia under the command of Philip van Artevelde prepared to defend its city by force of arms. In the ensuing battle at Roosebeke on November 27, 1382, the loyalists outmaneuvered the rebels with the skillful use of cavalry, killing over twenty-five thousand to restore peace to the region.

While the Valois forces were victorious at Roosebeke, open rebellion still raged in large parts of France. To impose the king's rule, the royal army marched from Flanders against Paris and with a show of military might compelled the rogues to surrender. As the news of the city's subjugation spread, the throne's authority was quickly reestablished over the remaining insurgent areas. With their power restored, the regents summoned the national Parliament to authorize new taxes and under threat of attack the money was approved with little opposition.

After the withdrawal of the French troops from Flanders, the rebellion was soon resumed in the Ghent province. To augment their defenses, the Flemish towns negotiated an alliance with the English court of Richard II for military aid. In May 1383 Henry Despenser, bishop of Norwich, crossed the channel in support of the Flemish revolt, capturing Dunkirk and Graveline from the French. Despite his triumphs, when a large Valois army advanced into the region, the bishop was forced to abandon his conquest and return to England with the Flemish fiefdom once again under French control.

With peace restored in France and Flanders under occupation, the Valois regency council began preparations for a two-pronged invasion of England in an attempt to force an end to the ongoing Hundred Years' War. However, the attack against London was delayed by the renewal of the Flemish revolt and the second encroachment into northern England from France's ally, Scotland, achieved little. Following two additional aborted campaigns, peace negotiations were begun with the regime of Richard II resulting in a three-year truce.

In 1385 Philip II of Burgundy negotiated an agreement for the marriage of Charles VI to Isabella of Bavaria-Ingolstadt. The union with the formidable Wittelsbach dynasty brought France power and presence in the southwestern Low Countries, where the family controlled a large demesne. Isabella was intelligent, ambitious and assertive and quickly began to form her own political faction to influence regime policies. She had been raised in the wealthy Wittelsbach household and reintroduced an ostentatious court, which was unpopular with many of the nobles and church. Charles VI and the queen's personalities were ill-suited to each other, resulting in a stormy relationship. Her many adulterous affairs brought further dissension to their marital union. Despite their turbulent marriage, the king and Isabella had twelve children, securing the Valois succession in 1402 with the birth of the future Charles VII.

After the expiration of the truce with England in 1386, the agreement was again extended, freeing the Valois regents to intervene against the resurgence of French armed rebellion against their administration. Despite the resolution of the earlier uprisings, new dissension continued to grow throughout the kingdom in dissatisfaction to the rule of Philip II of Burgundy's council. William, Duke of Guelders, openly defied the regime in September 1387, threatening to seize the neighboring province of Brabant. To enforce the crown's authority, the royal army was mustered under the nominal command of Charles VI and advanced against the rebellious lord. After a brief campaign William was forced to submit and offer fealty to the king. To thwart the danger of future revolts from the throne's vassals in opposition to the unpopular reign of Philip II, the eighteen-year-old Charles VI was encouraged by his high nobles and churchmen to declare an end to the regency and take personal charge of the government.

Following the suppression of revolt in Guelders, the king returned to Paris and dismissed the regency council to assume independent power. To establish a stable and effective government, the capable prior ministers of Charles V were reinstated to the administration, the former policies restored and skilled bureaucrats were appointed to the offices of state. Reforms were enacted to expand economic growth by reducing taxes, curtailing military and court expenditures and restructuring the regional Parliaments. The measures produced a growing prosperity and peace, resulting in a more popular and accepted monarchy. However, in the summer of 1392 Charles VI suffered his first serious attack of mental instability and his continued incapacity to govern resulted in the return of the disastrous rule of his uncles.

In June 1392 the monarch's constable and close friend, Oliver Clisson, barely escaped an assassination and in defiance of the crown Duke John IV of Brittany offered the assailant protection. Clisson was an experienced and renowned Breton soldier who had been raised in England and after his return to Brittany had become allied with Duke John IV to fight against the French. However, in 1370 he abandoned his alliance with the duke and joined the Valois regime, serving with distinction in the campaigns against the English in Normandy and siege at Brest. He commanded the throne's troops against the Ghent uprisings, defeating their militia at Roosebeke in November 1382 and later led the army in Poitou and Flanders. Following the assault against his constable, Charles VI pledged to arrest the assassin and in August 1392 led a contingent of knights into Brittany to enforce his law. As the summer afternoon heat grew more intense, he was confronted by a leper, who warned him of treasonous acts in the future. Shortly after the meeting with the leper, the loud clash of a fallen lance on the helmet of a page frightened and confused the Valois king, who drew his sword charging wildly into a group of his attendants, killing four of them before he was subdued. It was several weeks before he regained his sanity. With the inability of Charles VI to rule, the government was again assumed by Philip II of Burgundy as regent. The encounter in Brittany was the first of many periodic bouts of insanity, which were to plague the king for the rest of his life.

Philip II was a powerful and ambitious lord, who ruled extensive and strategic fiefs in western Europe centered on Burgundy and Flanders. After the duke's seizure of the regency, the king's younger brother, Louis of Orleans, began to openly oppose his uncle's assumption of power. Louis held large estates in central France and was intelligent, energetic and bold, mounting a political campaign to seriously challenge the authority of Philip II of Burgundy. However, the Duke of Burgundy skillfully outmaneuvered his nephew by forming an alliance with many of the high magnates to thwart his attempted usurpation of the council. Philip II replaced Charles VI's administrative officials with his allies and friends to solidify his supremacy over the kingdom.

The Hundred Years' War between France and England had begun in 1337 and had remained unresolved despite repeated attempts to arrange a permanent peace. With his regency unchallenged, in 1394 Philip II of Burgundy opened talks with the Plantagenet regime of Richard II to find a lasting settlement. After prolonged deliberations, the negotiations were at an impasse over the French claim for Calais and English demands for reparations. However, the discussions were continued and in March 1396 the two rival kingdoms agreed to a twenty-eight-year truce and marriage of Richard II to the young daughter of the French monarch. The treaty was formally ratified on October 30 at Ardres in a splendidly staged meeting between the two courts. At Ardres the Valois king and Richard II further pledged to send envoys to Avignon and Rome to negotiate an end to the schism in the church and lead a crusade against the Muslims' advance in the east.

While Charles VI continued to suffer from reoccurring bouts of insanity, France remained firmly under the control of Duke Philip II of Burgundy's regency until his death in 1404. In the ensuing power vacuum, the king's brother, Louis of Orleans, forged a formidable political coalition and with the support of Queen Isabella seized the regime. While Louis ruled unopposed, in January 1406 the successor to the duchy of Burgundy, Duke John II, was appointed to the council and dissension soon erupted between him and Louis. The duke was born at Dijon on May 28, 1371, and was the son of Philip II and Margaret of Dampierre. As the acknowledged heir to his father's titles and lands, he was named count of Charolais. When Pope Boniface IX summoned the knights of Europe to assemble for the holy crusade against the Muslims in the Balkans, in the summer of 1396 John led a large contingent of French to Hungary. He united his men-at-arms with Emperor Sigismund's forces in Buda and participated in the siege against the Turkish castle at Nicopolis. The count gained widespread glory and fame throughout the European courts for his heroic cavalry charge against the Ottoman defenders. After becoming a member of the regency administration, hostilities between the cousins mounted over the next two years, as the Burgundian duke increasingly challenged for supremacy of the government. Finally, in late November 1407 he ordered the assassination of Louis to gain unimpeded authority. However, after the death of Louis his attempted usurpation failed, when he was forced to admit his involvement in the murder. The duke was denounced by the king and forced to withdraw to his estates.

While in exile John II's allies interceded with the government in his defense, winning the support of many of the high nobles and prelates. In February 1408 the duke returned to Paris and issued a proclamation claiming he had acted only to protect the king from the treason of Louis. He was quickly pardoned by Charles VI and restored to the council. During the following year, John II purged the regime of his enemies and in late December 1409 was appointed as guardian for the dauphin, Louis, to gain full control of the realm. However, many magnates opposed his rule and a counter coalition began to form under Count Bernard VII of Armagnac, father-in-law of the murdered Louis of Orleans. The count was an experienced and skilled soldier, who had earlier fought with his brother, John, against the Spanish in Catalonia for possession of the fief of Roussillon. He gained influence and presence at the French court through the marriage of his daughter, Bonne, to Duke Charles of Orleans. While France moved closer to civil war, Charles VI continued to struggle with increasing attacks of insanity.

In the summer of 1411 as the kingdom moved closer to civil war, Bernard VII forged the Gien League with the dukes of Orleans, Berry and Brittany and the towns south of Paris, while John II's base of support remained in the northern French lordships. Hostilies between the two factions soon erupted as Bernard VII advanced against Paris. To counter the threat to his government, the Burgundian duke marched his troops to meet the Armagnacs near the town of Montdidier but no battle resulted when he suddenly withdrew to his Flemish lands, when confronted by superior forces. From his Flemish town of Arras he negotiated an alliance with the Lancastrian regime of Henry IV to reinforce his military might and in November augmented with English soldiers, attacked and drove the Armagnac army from Paris. With control of the king and his capital, the duke once again assumed power and issued a decree in the name of Charles VI outlawing Bernard VII and his allies. However, the Armagnacs still retained authority over the south and with both rivals' treasuries depleted a truce was arranged.

During 1413 John II of Burgundy attempted to raise additional funds by summoning the Estates-General but no taxes were approved when the Paris citizens revolted in protest. As the duke's rule grew increasingly unpopular, Charles VI regained his sanity and with encouragement from the dauphin denounced the Burgundian regent and joined forces with the

Armagnacs. With the loss of the throne's support, John II was accused of treason against the regime and fled to Flanders for safety. A new government was appointed by the king with Bernard VII and Charles of Orleans acting as regents.

While the Armagnac party ruled France, the English warrior-king, Henry V, succeeded his father in 1413 to the Lancastrian crown. Over the next two years he imposed his authority over the kingdom and with his power secure began to plan for the renewal of the Lancastrian inheritance claim to the French monarchy. After the failed attempt to negotiate a peaceful resolution, Henry V prepared for an invasion of France and revival of the Hundred Years' War.

In August 1415 the English army landed in Normandy and after a six-week siege captured the port of Harfleur. However, the victory was costly to the Lancastrian throne with over one-third of its troops killed or injured. Due to the heavy losses, the attack against Paris was abandoned and Henry V decided to march to his Calais enclave and pillage the countryside enroute. As the English advanced north, they encountered the assembled French at Agincourt. In the morning of October 25 the opposing forces were mustered into combat formation and through his brilliant battle plan Henry V's outnumbered troops won a magnificent triumph over Charles VI's army.

Despite the English victory at Agincourt, the French quickly recovered their footing and the government of Charles VI led by the Armagnac party remained unchallenged and prepared to defend the kingdom against further attacks. While the triumph at Agincourt had failed to advance the English quest for the Valois crown, Henry V remained resolved to claim his birthright. In 1416 he opened negotiations with the exiled John II of Burgundy, attempting to forge a military alliance. The Burgundian duke was noncommittal but Henry V was encouraged by the talks and began plans for a second French invasion.

Following the defeat at Agincourt, Count Bernard VII's council remained in control but in 1417 Duke John II regained his influence and power over northern France through the force of his charismatic personality and military might. He renewed his initiative against the Armagnacs, resuming the civil war. To further his campaign to take the French throne, the duke forged an alliance with Queen Isabella, who issued a proclamation recognizing his regency. As the northern coalition continued to gain more power, John II established an opposition regime at Troyes and his new government began to rule in the name of the king. The duke's attempted usurpation of the crown was buttressed by the death of the dauphin, who had favored the Armagnac faction. Without the prestige and authority of the Valois prince backing the count, hostilities between the two rival parties soon resumed with the Armagnacs steadily losing supremacy over Paris. In an attempt to seize the kingdom, in May 1418 with the aid of the queen and her allies, John II advanced his army against Paris to confront the Armagnac regency. At the approach of the duke, Bernard VII assembled his troops to defend the city but in the ensuing battle was killed and his forces defeated. The followers of the Armagnac coalition were compelled to flee to their southern strongholds. The duke of Burgundy now reigned over the northern half of France, while the king's new heir, Charles, with the support of the Armagnacs formed a counter administration in the city of Bourges.

In early August 1417 Henry V returned to France in pursuit of his blood claim to the monarchy. He landed in Normandy with a formidable army and after establishing a secure coastal enclave to protect his lines of communications with England advanced to capture Caen. The walled city was placed under siege and after a month of relentless attacks, the defenders were forced to surrender. After garrisoning the citadel with troops, the offensive was renewed into lower Normandy, which was soon under Henry V's control. With half of the duchy occupied, the English marched against the regional capital at Rouen. The Valois regime had earlier reinforced the garrison and its defenses, enabling the French to withstand the Lancastrian assaults and cannon bombardments until January 1419. With the seizure of Rouen, the English king had gained full authority over Normandy. After leaving a strong contingent of soldiers to maintain order in the duchy, Henry V advanced his campaign to the east into the Ile de France region and Paris.

While Henry V advanced against little organized opposition toward Paris, the civil war between the Burgundians and Armagnacs continued with neither faction able to enforce its will. In September 1418 John II of Burgundy was assassinated on the bridge at Montereau by allies of the dauphin and was succeeded to ducal throne by his son, Philip III. The Lancastrian king began negotiations with the Burgundian party and found the new duke more willing to compromise than his father. On May 20, 1420, Charles VI, who was under the control of Philip III, and the English signed the Treaty of Troyes. Under the terms of the agreement, Henry V was to assume the monarchy at the death of the French king, while the dauphin, Charles of Valois, was disinherited. The accord was sealed with the marriage of the Valois princess, Catherine, to the Lancastrian monarch. Duke Philip III received guarantees for his lands and appointment as English regent for France. Following the ratification of the Troyes Treaty, Henry V renewed his offensive toward Paris and late in the year the city's population declared its loyalty to him. On December 1, 1420, with Charles VI riding at his side, he entered the capital in triumph. The English occupied the area of France north of the Loire Valley, while the divested heir claimed the south, establishing his capital at Bourges.

With control of the upper half of France, Henry V remained determined to continue his campaign of conquest against the dauphin and his coalition. In 1421 the attack was advanced south of Paris but the towns in defense of Charles of Valois's rule refused to surrender, forcing the English into prolonged sieges. Despite the delays, the offensive moved steadily south, expanding the territory under the Lancaster king's authority. With his army's unremitting progress, Henry V returned to England to raise additional troops, appointing his brother, Thomas, Duke of Clarence, as the local commander. With his lands and power increasingly deteriorating under the relentless Lancastrian assaults, during the winter of 1421 the French heir began talks with the Scottish regency government of Robert of Albany and his son, Murdac, for their military aid. The negotiations resulted in a treaty of alliance and in the spring Scottish forces under the command of John Stewart, Earl of Buchan, began to arrive to revive the failing Armagnac war effort.

In March 1421 Thomas of Clarence renewed the campaign of conquest, marching his English army south toward Orleans. After pillaging the local towns and farms, he turned west to besiege Bauge Castle. While the English attacked the stronghold, John Stewart led a force of six thousand French and Scottish soldiers to relieve the investment. As the dauphin's army approached Bauge Castle, Thomas of Clarence advanced to engage them. In the ensuing bloody and hard-fought battle, the Lancastrian duke was killed and his troops overwhelmed. For his victory Stewart was appointed as constable of France by the dauphin. The English defeat and death of Duke Thomas caused their offensive to stall and Henry V was compelled to return in June with reinforcements.

Assuming command of the English campaign, the Lancaster king renewed the initiative into the Loire Valley and continued to push-back the forces of Charles, while occupying additional territories and towns. However, the English war effort suffered a serious set back when Henry V unexpectedly died of dysentery at the castle of Vincennes east of Paris. He was succeeded to the Lancastrian throne by his nine-month-old son, Henry VI.

While his kingdom was being ravaged by civil war and the English pursuit of the Valois crown, Charles VI remained isolated in Paris under the control of Queen Isabella. As he grew older, the periods of insanity became more intense and frequent. After 1392 the king was largely incapable of ruling and took little part in the governing of his realm. Charles VI died on October 22, 1422, in Paris at age fifty-two and a reign of forty-two years. At his death, the infant heir of Henry V was acknowledged as monarch by the lordships north of the Loire Valley, while Charles VI's only surviving son, Charles, claimed the southern half of France.

Sources

Denieul-Cormier. *Wise and Foolish Kings—The First House of Valois.* Knecht. *The Valois: Kings of France 1328–1589.* Neillands. *The Hundred Years' War.* Vaughan. *Philip the Bold.*

Charles VII, 1403–1422–1461

After the death of Charles VI in October 1422, the Valois crown was inherited by his only living son, Charles VII. However, with the English regime of Henry VI occupying the region north of Paris, the second Renaissance king of France was only acknowledged by the southern lordships. Charles of Valois was the eleventh child of Charles VI and Isabella of Bavaria-Ingolstadt and was born in Paris on February 22, 1403. As the third surviving male issue, he was not expected to rule the realm and received little training or preparation for kingship. With his mother's numerous adulterous affairs, the legitimacy of his birth was frequently questioned; however, he was always treated as the rightful son of the monarch. The Valois prince occupied his childhood in the royal household with his six surviving siblings where his education was begun by private tutors. He received instruction in reading, writing, history, religion, geography and languages, including Latin. However, Charles's education was limited, as his parents took little interest in the raising of their children. He spent his early years in an unstable and insecure environment where court life was dominated by the intrigues and plots of the queen and his father's insanity.

In 1413 the Valois regime negotiated the marriage of the ten-year-old Charles to Mary of Anjou. The House of Anjou centered in central France at Angers possessed a blood claim to the kingdoms of Naples and Aragon and the union with the powerful family enhanced the Valois's presence and prestige in the region. To unite the two houses in friendship, the French prince was removed from the insecure surroundings of the royal court and sent to reside in the Anjou household. In Angers he quickly developed a close personal bond with Mary's father, Duke Louis II of Naples, and mother, Yolande of Aragon, who exerted a strong influence and provided a stable and supportive environment. After assuming the reins of power, Charles repeatedly turned to the House of Anjou for many skilled and trusted counselors and friends. In 1422 he was formally married to Mary and their union resulted in the birth of four surviving children, including his successor, Louis XI. The marriage was generally happy until 1443, when Charles VII became involved in an adulterous affair with Agnes Sorel. She was as intelligent and ambitious as she was beautiful and under the force of her personality the king abandoned the queen, becoming totally devoted to his mistress. Agnes served as a trusted advisor to Charles VII and actively participated in the governing of the realm. Their relationship lasted for four years, ending with the death of Agnes under suspicious circumstances.

Charles spent more than three years at the Anjou court where Yolande acted as surrogate mother, arranging for his care and education. While he remained in Angers, the civil war for supremacy over France between John II of Burgundy and the Armagnac faction of Bernard VII again erupted into hostilities. In early 1417 Count Bernard VII regained control over Paris and under the influence of the Anjou family, the Valois prince became allied with him and his coalition. On April 15, 1417, the dauphin, John, died and Charles was readily acknowledged as the heir and successor to the throne. In September he established his residence in the Paris royal palace and began to increasingly participate in the Armagnac regency government. Charles continued to have the support and encouragement of Yolande, who provided distinguished tutors for his education and advisors for his private council. Under the guidance of Bernard VII, the dauphin began to learn and master the skills of kingship required to rule his realm.

In August 1417 the English army of King Henry V returned to France to resume its quest for the Valois crown by force of arms. While the Lancastrian king was advancing in Normandy virtually unchallenged, John II of Burgundy formed an alliance with Queen Isabella and in May 1418 their combined forces drove the dauphin and the Armagnac government out of Paris. The Burgundians now ruled the northern lordships, while Charles claimed power over the Loire Valley region. However, as all resistance against the Lancastrian offensive collapsed, Duke John II and the Armagnacs increasingly realized the danger of English subjugation and agreed to negotiate a resolution to their ongoing hostilities. On September 10, 1418, Prince Charles and the duke met on the Montereau Bridge northeast of Paris but their talks ended in disaster when a retainer of the dauphin killed John II. The duke's son, Philip III, assumed his fiefdoms and titles and believing the assassination was a plot initiated by the dauphin, quickly resumed the civil war. Philip was born on July 31, 1396, at Dijon and was the son of Duke John II and Margaret of Bavaria. In early 1404 he was appointed Count of Charolais in recognition of his hereditary rights to the Burgundian duchy. Under the long forty-eight-year reign of Philip III, his demesne was greatly enlarged through his skillful use of diplomacy and military might. Through the force of the duke's personality, Burgundy reached its zenith of prosperity and stature, while under his patronage the court became a center for the art and letters of the Renaissance.

With the renewal of fighting between Burgundy and the dauphin, the remaining French garrisons in Normandy received little support from the government to confront the advance of Henry V. By early 1419 after the capture of Rouen, the whole of western France was under English rule. With his fiefs threatened by the English regime's onslaught, Philip III began negotiations with the Lancastrians to protect the autonomy of his demesne against their occupation. In the resulting Treaty of Troyes, the dauphin was disinherited and the Lancaster king recognized as successor to Charles VI, while the duke agreed to an alliance with England and received guarantees for his continued sovereignty over his lands. During the summer the English resumed their march against Paris and on December 1, 1420, Henry V with Charles VI at his side entered the city in triumph.

While the English occupied northern France, Prince Charles was acknowledged as successor to the crown by the southern lordships. As Henry V renewed his campaign south of Paris, the dauphin energetically defended his lands in the Loire Valley against his advance. To thwart the Lancastrian offensive, he negotiated a military alliance with Scotland and in the spring of 1421 under the leadership of John Stewart, Earl of Buchan, the new troops began to enter the war. Nevertheless, the combined Lancastrian-Burgundian military might relentlessly pushed the dauphin's forces back, occupying the towns and enforcing the rule of the Henry V's regime. However, in July 1422 the English king unexpectedly died from dysentery and was succeeded to the throne by his infant son, Henry VI. Two months later Charles VI died and under the terms of the Treaty of Troyes, Henry VI was recognized as the king by the northern half of France under the regency government of his uncle, Duke John of Bedford.

Under the experienced and skilled command of the Lancastrian regent, the united English-Burgundians steadily advanced against the inadequate and poorly led forces of the dauphin. As the allies pressed their offensive into the Loire Valley, Charles's troops were decisively defeated at the battle of Cravant. In the following year he reinforced his depleted army with the arrival of six thousand fresh Scottish men-at-arms and archers led by Sir Archibald, Earl of Douglas, who was appointed lieutenant general of the realm. Archibald was the fourth Earl of Douglas and the wealthiest and most powerful nobleman in Scotland. He was an experienced and renowned soldier, fighting against the English in numerous battles and cross border raids. The earl was active in Scottish politics and led the failed negotiations for the release of King James I from captivity in London. Under the influence of his son, Archibald of Wigtoun, he agreed to support the dauphin's war effort. The French further augmented their military might by hiring two thousand heavily armored mercenary knights from Lombardy.

With his army reinforced, in the summer of 1424 Charles ordered his generals to aggressively pursue the war effort. Under the leadership of John VIII, viscount of Aumale, and Archibald of Douglas, the dauphin's force of over fifteen thousand knights and infantry marched from Bourges against Duke John of Bedford. The united French and Scottish forces advanced to the west attempting to drive the English from their Norman border fortifications. After the Valois troops seized the fortified town of Verneuil, Duke John responded by leading his soldiers to confront the allies. On August 17 the two armies deployed into battle formations near the village of Verneuil. In the ensuing encounter, after the devastating charge of the heavy Italian cavalry, John quickly reorganized his shattered forces and counterattacked, completely overwhelming the dauphin's foot soldiers and men-at-arms. Over half of the allies were either killed or captured, including Earl Archibald and John Stewart, who both lay dead on the battlefield.

After their decisive victory at Verneuil, the English advanced virtually unopposed into the heart of the Loire region, occupying town after town. With the loss of his best commanders and troops and the treasury depleted, Charles possessed little means to assert his birthright to the crown. By the beginning of 1429 it appeared that his southern kingdom would be overrun by the relentless offensive of the Lancaster-Burgundian army. However, the impending defeat was turned to triumph with the arrival at the Valois court in Chinon of Joan of Arc.

Joan was a young peasant from the small northeastern village of Domremy. At age fourteen she claimed to have been visited by heavenly visions and angels, carrying messages from God. She later said the saints told her to break the ongoing English siege at Orleans and drive the invaders away from Rheims to allow the coronation of Charles as king. In early 1429 Joan traveled to the royal court at Chinon, where after persistent requests Charles reluctantly agreed to meet her. Following their talks, the dauphin refused to believe in her mission and dismissed her. However, she would not abandon her quest and under continued pressure, the Valois heir sent her to his counselors and clerics for interrogation. While remaining at Chinon, she found a supporter and sponsor in Yolande of Aragon, who pressed her cause with Charles. When the royal council could not dispute her claims and under the influence of Yolande, the dauphin finally became convinced in the truth of her visions. Joan was given command of the Valois army and sent to Tours to prepare for the attack against the English at Orleans.

By the end of April Joan had assembled the relief force and had begun the march north to confront the Lancastrian investment against Orleans. With the city's resistance steadily weakening under the persistent English-Burgundian assaults, she rode ahead of the slow moving army with a contingent of cavalry to buttress the defenders and prevent the citadel's surrender. As the vanguard approached the fortress, she skillfully evaded the besiegers and entered Orleans on April 29. Joan was readily recognized as commander by the garrison with her presence bolstering the fighting spirit of the French. On May 7 the king's soldiers finally arrived at Orleans and advanced to attack the allies as Joan led a spirited sortie from the stronghold. The English were trapped between both Valois armies, as a fierce struggle ensued lasting until dark with the Lancaster troops driven from the battlefield. On the following day the English abandoned their siege lines and retreated north.

As the allies withdrew, Joan renewed her offensive advancing toward Rheims and on May 12 captured the city of Jargeau. As the French relentlessly pursued the Lancastrian forces, their campaign gained momentum, occupying numerous towns and castles on the road to Rheims. On June 18 they encountered the retreating English at the village of Patay and in the ensuing battle the charge of Joan's knights broke the defenses of the Lancastrian troops, killing or capturing over two thousand. Following the victory at Patay, the attack was aggressively pressed, while the Duke of Bedford's army continued to fall back toward Paris. By the end of June the region around Rheims was cleared of the English, while Charles began the journey to be formally anointed sovereign. On July 16 Rheims opened its gates and declared its loyalty to the new regime. On the next day Charles VII entered the city and at the historic Rheims Cathedral was crowned king of France according to the ceremony of great pomp and spirituality followed since the days of Clovis I.

The fighting spirit of the French troops and resolve of Charles VII against the threat of English usurpation were reenergized by the presence and triumphs of Joan. Under her leadership, the army rediscovered its confidence, energy and determination to inflict a series of stinging but not decisive defeats on the allies, as they retreated toward Paris. While the French approached the capital, John of Bedford took command of the war effort and blocked Joan's attempts to besiege the city. Late in 1429 she was compelled to suspend the attack and withdraw into winter quarters.

In the spring of 1430 Joan resumed the offensive against Paris but her initiative soon lost momentum, as the allies counterattacked, driving the royalists from the environs of the city. The campaign against the capital was abandoned under the relentless attacks of John of Bedford. While her troops were retreating, Joan returned to Charles VII's court at Chinon and was confronted by the hostility of the council. Under the influence of his advisors, the king soon lost confidence and trust in Joan, removing her from command of the Paris army and sending her to relieve the Burgundian siege at Compiegne, which was under the personal leadership of Duke Philip III. Assuming control of the city's defenders, Joan led a spirited sally against the forces of Philip III, however, during the battle she was captured. The Burgundians later ransomed her to the English and Joan was taken to Rouen in Normandy. Imprisoned by the Lancastrian government, she was charged with heresy and witchcraft. After a trial lasting over three months, Joan was declared a witch and burned at the stake on May 30, 1431.

After the duke of Bedford thwarted the Valois seizure of Paris, his advance against the retreating French soon stalled and the war became stalemated. In 1432 largely through the intervention of Yolande of Aragon, the French regime became reconciled with its former constable, Arthur de Richemont. Arthur was born in Brittany on August 24, 1393, and was a younger son of Duke John V and Joanna of Navarre. He fought bravely at Agincourt and was wounded and captured during the battle. Following his ransom from the English, Arthur became a supporter of Joan of Arc and joined her forces at Patay, participating in the march against Rheims. After his return to the royal court and through the support of Yolande, he became a counselor to Charles VII. Arthur was instrumental in the removal of several corrupt advisors from the ruling council and under his influence a restructuring of the government and army was initiated.

With the hostilities against the Valois regime remaining at an impasse and the English war effort suffering from the shortage of money, troops and lack of support from London, Philip III of Burgundy began talks with the government of Charles VII for a separate reconciliation to preserve the autonomy of his duchy from a revival of French military might. After meetings between the duke's envoys and de Richemont, a two-year truce was signed. Following the loss of his ally and as the French continued to carry out small indecisive attacks against his Paris defenses, John of Bedford agreed to begin peace negotiations, consenting to an international congress.

During the summer of 1435 the conference assembled at Arras with representatives from Burgundy, the Holy Roman Empire, Pope Eugene IV, Valois government, and the Lancastrian regime led by the cardinal of Beaufort. The English offered to cede the lands already conquered by the French but claimed sovereignty over the entire kingdom. The Valois envoys countered by demanding the Lancaster court renounce its rights to the French crown and withdraw from the occupied territories. On September 1 the cardinal rejected the proposal and retired from the Parliament. However, Philip III continued the negotiations with the French, agreeing to a separate peace in October. Under the Treaty of Arras's terms, the duke pledged to abandon the Lancastrian war effort and was permitted to retain his demesne as an autonomous duchy.

In September 1435 Duke John of Bedford died in Rouen, and without his support and energy, the English resolve to retain their conquest in western France began to wane. The young king, Henry VI, had little enthusiasm for foreign conflicts and was more interested in scholarly pursuits and religion. The Lancastrian war effort suffered from the lack of leadership and money as their military presence and determination in the Ile de France region was increasingly reduced. As the English continued to withdraw troops from Paris, in February 1436 Constable de Richemont marched against the capital's weakened defenses and began siege operations. The garrison put up only a token resistance for several weeks before agreeing to surrender. On April 13 Charles VII returned triumphantly to Paris, establishing the official seat of his government in the city and proclaiming sovereignty over all of France.

After gaining control over Paris, Charles VII's rule as king was acknowledged by the southern half of the kingdom and in parts of the Ile de France. To consolidate his authority and power, he initiated a series of measures to reform the government, economy and army. To expand and encourage economic growth, the financial system was restructured and the currency put on a sound monetary basis. The Estates-General approved a permanent tax, eliminating the uncertainty and need for legislative approval to provide a stable source of income for the king. The regime made changes to its council and administrative organizations, improving overall efficiency. Under the guidance of de Richemont, the military was remodeled with the creation of the first permanent army and independent contingents of artillery. The reforms increased the acceptance and independence of the monarchy over the nobles and church to solidify the supremacy of Charles VII.

While the reform programs were continued, Charles VII intervened to thwart attempts by Pope Eugene IV to broaden his power into French ecclesiastic affairs. In defense of its religious prerogatives, the regime issued the Pragmatic Sanctions, which limited the Holy See's control over the local church by restricting the appointment of bishops and abbots, while limiting papal rights to interfere in judicial concerns. The sanctions expanded the king's supremacy over the French church and its revenues and bound the institution more closely to the will of the Valois crown. During his reign, Charles VII made many sweeping changes to his government, military, economy and church that remained in effect until the French Revolution.

As the Valois regime continued to energetically enforce its authority and enact reforms to the military, the independent power and prestige of the nobility steadily declined. To expand the supremacy of the monarchy further, the government demanded the dissolution of all private armies. Confronted with the loss of their military might, in 1439 the magnates rose in revolt in defense of their feudal privileges. The Praguerie Rebellion was led by Charles I, Duke of Bourbon, who formed a coalition with Philip III of Burgundy, John VI of Brittany, Prince Louis of Valois, and other dissident warlords. The rebel lords began to plot the replacement of de Richemont and overthrow of the king. As the conspiracy spread, the formidable and influential John II, Duke of Alencon, soon joined the growing alliance. He had a long history of service against the English and had participated in the battle of Verneuil, fought with Joan in the Loire River Valley and had commanded soldiers in the Norman offensive. Charles VII responded quickly and forcefully to the threat of insurrection, sending his constable at the head of a large army to attack and seize the lands of the rogues. Under the skilled leadership of de Richemont, the royal troops marched into Poitou using the new artillery to batter the castle walls of the rebels. By 1440 the uprising had been suppressed and Duke Charles I, John II of Alencon and their allies compelled to seek terms.

While the French were distracted with the subjugation of the Praguerie Rebellion, the English government of Henry VI became determined to regain its lost lands in France and began to reinforce its forces and defenses in Normandy in preparation for the new offensive. With his troop strength augmented, a new campaign commanded by Richard, Duke of York, was mounted into Ile de France. The advancing Lancastrians encountered only sparse resistance from the weakened French garrisons and numerous towns and castles were soon occupied by the Duke of York. However, after the resolution of the Praguerie Rebellion, Charles VII sent Arthur de Richemont to the area west of Paris to contest the recent gains of the English army. By the end of 1441 the constable had driven the soldiers of Henry VI back to their strongholds in Normandy and secured the rule of the Valois regime over the region.

With Ile de France again under Valois authority, de Richemont advanced into Normandy but his offensive soon encountered the well entrenched English and little progress was made. The war quickly developed into a stalemate, as both rival realms became increasingly war weary. With the regimes anxious for a settlement, negotiations for a truce were begun in Tours in April 1444. The talks soon produced the Truce of Tours with both kingdoms agreeing to honor the status quo for two years. The English were left in control of Normandy, Maine and Gascony with Charles VII holding the remainder of France.

The Truce of Tours was extended several times over the next five years despite numerous border incidents by both regimes. With peace restored to his kingdom, Charles VII energetically renewed his campaign to reform and rebuild his army. Under de Richemont's skilled command, major improvements were made in the training, discipline and armament of the troops and by 1449 the French were strong enough to resume the war in Normandy. The Lancastrian government provided just cause for breaking the ongoing peace by attacking the Breton town of Fougeres. The region was in the demesne of Duke Francis I of Brittany, who was allied with the French. The seizure of Fougeres was considered an assault against the Valois kingdom and Charles VII responded by declaring war in defense of his lands.

With the outbreak of new hostilities, Charles VII ordered Arthur de Richemont to invade and conquer Normandy. His offensive was aided by the uprising of the local population, who had grown tired of the harsh repressive policies of the English occupiers. As the constable continued his advance, Francis I of Brittany sent his forces into western Normandy in support of the French. Under the combined attacks of the allies, the eastern region of the duchy quickly fell and in October 1449 Charles VII was with his troops before the defensive walls of Rouen. The Lancastrian garrison was under the command of the experienced and capable John Talbot, Earl of Shrewsbury, who defiantly refused to surrender. John of Shrewsbury had a long history of distinguished military service to the English crown, participating in the siege at Orleans and campaigns in Maine and Normandy. However, following a short siege the city's residents revolted against the English and after several days of fighting, the Earl of Shrewsbury was compelled to seek terms. Following the occupation of Rouen, the initiative was resumed into the Seine River Valley and in December the port of Harfleur was recaptured by the French constable.

Following the collapse of English rule in Rouen, in 1450 the Valois army moved south of the city encountering light resistance as numerous castles and towns were quickly seized. As the French continued their advance, the Lancaster council sent reinforcements to Cherbourg to regain their lost lands. With their military might strengthened, the English force of over four thousand men-under-arms, under the command of Thomas Kyriell, marched against the city of Formigny. As the English approached Formigny, Kyriell was intercepted by a small French army. In the ensuing encounter, as Charles VII's cavalry charged the advancing Lancastrians, de Richemont arrived with his Breton soldiers and artillery to support its attack. He positioned his cannons to fire directly on the English archers driving them from the protection of their palisades. They were forced into an open field, where they were nearly annihilated by the assaults of the French knights. The victory at Formigny destroyed the only Lancastrian field army in Normandy, allowing the constable to advance unimpeded against the remaining strongholds. By August through the use of bribery, diplomacy, intimidation and force of arms, all of Normandy was under the control of Charles VII after the capture of Cherbourg.

With Normandy cleared of foreign occupation, Charles VII ordered his military to march against the English in the southwestern duchy of Gascony. The French forces, augmented with Norman and Gascon troops, encountered only scattered resistance and by August 1451 had seized the last stronghold at Bayonne. However, in the following year Henry VI launched an invasion to reclaim his hereditary Gascon duchy, sending a new army of three thousand men-at-arms and archers under John Talbot of Shrewsbury to Bordeaux. The Gascons had been under English rule for over three hundred years and fearing the destruction of their profitable wine trade with the Lancastrian regime, the population rose in revolt. With the support of the Bordeaux rebels, Talbot recaptured the city, as most of the duchy rebelled and was soon lost to the French. The Valois king responded energetically to the new threat, returning his army under John Bureau to the region. Bureau had participated in the campaign in Normandy and had been appointed as the crown's master of artillery. As the French approached Bordeaux, the earl of Shrewsbury advanced to attack at Castillon. John Bureau deployed into a strong fortified position, placing his artillery on the parapets and awaiting the assault of the English men-at-arms. In the ensuing battle, Sir John's cavalry charge against the French defenses was destroyed by the well placed cannons fire and Talbot killed. The Valois soldiers continued their offensive, laying siege against Bordeaux. After a three month investment, the garrison was compelled to surrender and Charles VII made a triumphant entrance on October

9, 1454. After the occupation of the city, all resistance ended and the duchy was fully brought back under authority of the French king, who sent trusted and skilled administrators to enforce the loyalty of the Gascons. The Valois victory at Castillon marked the end of the Hundred Years' War with the only remaining English enclave at Calais.

With the English defeat at Bordeaux, peace returned to the French kingdom after over one hundred years of intermittent war. The numerous reform measures initiated earlier by the regime began to produce an expanding economy with prosperity returning to the towns and countryside. Trade and business activities recovered and many areas experienced a dramatic increase in commercial and agricultural growth. While the economy revived, the influence of the merchant class grew as they increased their presence in the administration, forming a strong bond with the monarchy. The king appointed experienced and capable advisors, who continued his restructuring programs of financial and governmental reforms.

By 1461 the king's health had grown steadily worse under the stresses of several illnesses and exhaustion from many years of war against England and internal strife. Charles VII died on July 22, 1461, near the Loire town of Bourges at age fifty-eight and a reign of over thirty-eight years. He was succeeded to the crown by his heir, Louis XI.

Sources

Denieul-Cormier. *Wise and Foolish King—The First House of Valois.* Knecht. *The Valois: Kings of France 1328–1589.* Vale. *Charles VII.*

Louis XI, 1423–1461–1483

When Charles VII died in July 1461, Louis XI succeeded to the throne as the recognized heir presumptive, ruling as the third French king of the Renaissance era. Prince Louis was the first son of Charles VII and Queen Mary of Anjou and was born on July 3, 1423, at Bourges. At the time of his birth, the Valois regime was actively resisting the attempted usurpation of the kingdom by Henry VI and as his English army threatened Bourges, the heir was sent to Loches Castle for protection against pillaging raids. Local nobles were appointed for his security and care and he spent the next eight years at Loches largely separated from the royal family. In 1429 Louis was provided tutors by the Valois court for his academic education. He was a gifted and serious student with a natural aptitude and desire for learning, excelling in his studies of reading, writing, religion, history mathematics and languages, while developing a special interest in economics and business. At Loches skilled masters of arms were appointed for his military training and the prince received routine instruction in the warfare and weapons of a feudal knight.

By 1433 the northern Loire region had been reconquered from the Lancastrian regime and Louis was moved to the chateau of Amboise, where he was reunited with the royal family. His literary education was renewed and he began to receive political training in kingship in preparation for his future assumption of power. At the age of eleven, Louis was sent to Tours to begin his public life and gain experience in the management of the local government. During his two years in the city, he participated in the meetings of the ruling council and was tutored in the administration of the lordship. His education was resumed in Tours, which provided better access to scholars and libraries for the advancement of his studies.

While Louis remained in Tours, in 1436 Charles VII negotiated the marriage of his son to Margaret of Scotland, daughter of King James I. The political treaty formally united France to its historic ally and ensured military aid and troops for the ongoing war with England. Louis displayed little enthusiasm for the marriage and only reluctantly agreed to the wedding. After the ceremony he was granted a separate household and court with his own experienced and skilled advisors. In the following year the Valois prince gained his first combat experiences by campaigning with his father in the attack against the English garrison protecting Paris. He personally commanded a contingent of soldiers during the siege and led several assaults against the fortifications. After the English surrender, he entered the city in triumph with Charles VII.

Following the capture of Paris, Louis remained with the Valois court becoming closely associated with his father's regime. In 1439 he was given his first independent command and sent to the south central fiefdom of Languedoc as lieutenant general to end the growing civil unrest. The local population was continually ravaged by bands of brigands and the economy was in shambles with the government unable to enforce the king's authority. With the threat of rebellion mounting against Charles VII's sovereignty, Louis established his administration in Toulouse and formed an energetic and forceful council of experienced and loyal advisors who initiated policies to end the pillaging raids and restore order. He traveled extensively through Languedoc, receiving the fealty of the warlords and towns, while asserting the will of the Valois crown. Under his rule the reform measures produced an expanding economy and suppression of the marauders' attacks, enhancing his reputation and support among the Languedoc populace. The dauphin stayed in Toulouse until he was recalled by the Valois throne to participate in the subjugation of the Praguerie Rebellion.

In late 1439 Charles I of Bourbon and Duke John II of Alencon rebelled against the Valois kingdom's military reforms and outlawing of the nobles' private armies. Seeking to restore their historic feudal rights, many warlords soon joined the growing uprising. As part of the regime's campaign against the recalcitrant magnates, Louis was named lieutenant general and dispatched to the countship of Poitou to impose the sovereign's will. He established his governing council in Poitiers and initiated reforms similar to those in Languedoc. While Charles VII continued to struggle against the English in the Ile de France region and the ongoing threat from the Praguerie Rebellion, Louis increasingly considered his father a weak and ineffective king, who was too easily controlled and manipulated by his counselors. As his restructuring measures started to succeed and his power and popularity in Poitou grew, the dauphin began to ignore the Valois court and assert his self-rule. To secure his independence from the crown, he opened negotiations with Charles I and his allies, agreeing to join the Praguerie Rebellion. As the danger of the nobles' insurrection escalated, Charles VII sent a formidable army under the command of his experienced and skilled constable, Arthur de Richemont, to Poitou to enforce his authority. Marching into the countship, he quickly suppressed the revolt and the dauphin was compelled to seek reconciliation with his father. With his support in Poitou deteriorating, Louis was forced to accept the throne's terms, receiving a full pardon for his pledge of loyalty.

Following the failure of the Praguerie Rebellion, Louis returned to his father's court, participating in the government of the realm and campaigning against the English in Ile de France. In September 1441 he advanced with the French army into the region west of Paris to confront the Lancaster regime. During siege operations at Pontoise, the dauphin personally led the final assault against the defenses, gaining recognition for his battle skills and bravery. He remained with the king for the next two years, energetically engaged in asserting his father's fealty over the nobles and towns, administering the crown's justice and forcing the English out of Ile de France.

In the summer of 1443 Louis was rewarded for his administrative and military skills and loyalty to the throne with the appointment to command the relief forces against the ongoing English blockade against Dieppe. The seaport had been nearly surrounded and its surrender imminent. The dauphin assembled the royal army near Paris and quickly advanced to the west to relieve the defenders at Dieppe. On August 11 he arrived at the siege and began preparations for an attack against the English defenses. Louis personally commanded the assault forces in a well planned sortie, compelling the Lancaster troops to abandon their campaign and retreat. Following the Dieppe victory, Louis returned to his father's court at Tours and was recognized for his battle success while continuing to gain the favor of his father. However, despite his outward appearance of loyalty, the dauphin renewed his secret negotiations with factions of dissident magnates, plotting for his assumption of the crown.

In the following year the Holy Roman Emperor, Frederick III, appealed to the Valois kingdom for military aid in his ongoing war against the Swiss Cantons. The French had historic claims to lands in the western Cantons and the government agreed to launch an invasion to enforce its rights and support the emperor's initiative. Louis was given command of the campaign and ordered to raise a new army of mercenaries. With the Hundred Years' War at a stalemate, the dauphin found a ready source of experienced and skilled soldiers, hiring the unemployed English and Burgundians. A military force of over ten thousand was mustered and Louis began his offensive by marching against the city of Basel.

The Valois army advanced into the Cantons, encountering only light scattered opposition and began siege operations against the Basel stronghold, while opening talks for its surrender. As the blockade wore on, the Swiss Confederation countered the invasion against its territory by ordering its military to relieve the investment and drive the French back across the border. As the Swiss approached Basel, on September 24 the Valois prince formed his troops into battle formation and maneuvered to attack. In the ensuing encounter at Saint Jacob, the numerically superior French completely overwhelmed the Swiss pikemen but suffered large losses from their determined and stubborn resistance. Following his victory at Saint Jacob, Louis renewed his negotiations with Basel, demanding the city abandon its alliance with the Swiss regime and place the canton under his protection. While the deliberations continued, Louis captured several towns and castles to further consolidate his rule. However, during the assault against the fortress at Dambach, he was wounded in the leg by an arrow and forced to withdraw from the war. Charles VII ordered his son to return to France, ending his involvement in the campaign.

The dauphin's victories at Dieppe and Basel established his reputation as a skilled and energetic commander, while earning the favor and trust of his father. His participation in the Praguerie Rebellion was forgiven and he began to serve on the ruling council and act as emissary for the regime. However, Louis had not abandoned his rebellious allies and continued to plot against the crown for his assumption of power. In September 1446 Charles VII learned of his son's insurrection, removing him from court and sending him to personally govern the Dauphine lordship in southeastern France.

As the heir presumptive, Louis had earlier been invested with the Dauphine fief as his birthright. In January 1447 he arrived in his capital at Grenoble and began to enforce his rule. He traveled extensively through the region, receiving the fealty of the magnates and towns. The prince established his government in Grenoble, appointing local nobles and churchmen as his principal advisors and court officials. To solidify his authority, Louis initiated a series of reform measures to weaken the power of the lordship's warlords, forcing them to obey his laws. The Dauphine judicial system was restructured and a Parliament created, while the tax structure was reorganized to promote growth in the economy. Under Louis's regime, the ruling administration became more efficient and responsive, while agriculture and commercial activities revived. While remaining in Dauphine, he continued to maintain his contacts and spies at his father's court, retaining his faction in opposition to the policies of the king.

Following the dauphin's return from the campaign in Basel, his wife, Margaret of Scotland, suddenly died in July 1445. He had never favored the marriage and had spent little time with the dauphine. While Louis continued to govern the Dauphine, he began to secretly negotiate his marriage to Charlotte, daughter of Louis, duke of Savoy. The marital agreement would provide a rich dowry and secure a loyal ally on his southern border, while allowing direct access into Italy where Louis had aspirations of establishing an independent kingdom. When the Valois council was informed of the talks, Charles VII refused to approve the marital treaty. Nevertheless, the dauphin disregarded his father and on March 9, 1451, was married to Charlotte of Savoy. However, he had little interest in his new wife and their relationship remained distant and strained. The union resulted in eight children, including the heir, Charles, who was born in 1470.

Charles VII did not approve of his son's marriage and responded by withdrawing his pension and demesne. As the prince's relationship with the king grew more hostile, in the summer of 1452 the Valois regime threatened to invade Savoy, compelling Duke Louis to abandon the dauphin and acknowledge French protection. Following the elimination of the heir's ally, the crown began preparations to attack the Dauphine and force Louis's subjugation. However, the campaign was cancelled, when the English returned to Gascony to reclaim their lands by force of arms.

With the Valois regime distracted with the renewal of the Hundred Years' War, in the spring of 1453 Louis began talks with his uncle, Rene I of Anjou, to command the duke's army during his invasion of Italy. Rene was born at Angers on January 9, 1409, and was the second son of King Louis II of Naples and Yolande of Aragon. At the age of thirteen, he was married to Isabella of Lorraine and was raised and educated in her father's court. Rene became sympathetic to Prince Charles's cause in the war against Henry VI, joining the army of Joan of Arc. He participated in the offensive against the English in the Loire Valley and Normandy and served as one of Joan's captains during the siege against Paris. When his elder brother, Louis III, died in 1434 Rene I inherited the kingdom of Naples. However, his assumption of the Italian crown was opposed by Alfonso V of Aragon and after four years of war Rene I was defeated and forced to flee to France. However, he retained his hereditary claims to the Naples kingdom and began to plan a new campaign to enforce his rights to an independent Italian realm. The Anjou duke formed a coalition with Cosimo de Medici of Florence and Duke Francesco I of Milan, pledging to provide them military aid in their ongoing war against Venice for their support of his quest for a new princedom. With the French still occupied in Gascony, Charles VII had little opposition to his son's involvement in the expedition and Louis was named to lead Rene I's troops. He advanced the invading forces over the Alps to the allies' assembly point at Villanova. However, after arriving in Italy the dauphin plotted to abandon the attack against Venice and redirect the initiative against the poorly defended city of Genoa in pursuit of a separate kingdom for himself. All of northern Italy began to fear Louis's self-aggrandizement and demanded Rene I return him to France. To protect his interest in Lombardy, the duke was compelled to order his nephew back to Dauphine.

After his failed attempt to create an autonomous princedom in Italy, Louis returned to his court in Grenoble with his rebellion against his father still unresolved. Negotiations for reconciliation were renewed, but after prolonged unsuccessful talks, the king became determined to compel his son's obedience by force of arms, sending his army to Grenoble to arrest him. As the royal troops approached Dauphine, Louis fled his demesne, seeking refuge in Burgundy in the duchy of his uncle, Duke Philip III.

On October 5, 1456, Louis arrived in Brussels at the court of Philip III and was warmly welcomed and granted protection against the French regime. The dauphin was provided a pension and household in the Genappe Castle. He soon became active in the Burgundian government and in the spring of 1457 spent several months with the duke, touring the duchy's prosperous Flemish towns. The Valois prince renewed his interest in commerce and economics, questioning the wealthy merchants and burghers about their trading activities. In the summer Charlotte of Savoy joined him and they established their formal court in the castle at Genappe. Louis and his wife routinely entertained the Burgundian nobles and clerics with festivals, banquets and hunting parties. From Brussels he remained in contact with his friends and secret agents in the Valois kingdom, keeping well informed on affairs of state. In March 1461 Duke Philip III sent his nephew to England with a contingent of Burgundian troops to support his ally, Edward of York, in the war against the Lancastrian monarchy. After arriving in London, Louis joined the Yorkish campaign, advancing north to participate in the decisive battle at Towton during the Wars of the Roses.

After his return to Burgundy, in July 1461 the dauphin began to receive reports of the growing deterioration in his father's health and initiated preparations for his return to Paris. He sent his envoys to the Valois court to negotiate with the high nobles and churchmen to ensure their loyalty against an attempted usurpation of the crown by his brother, Duke Charles of Berry. On July 22, 1464, Charles VII died, while his son was rapidly traveling to Paris to impose his blood birthright. As Louis crossed the border into France, he was met by Philip III and a large contingent of Burgundian troops to guarantee his uncontested assumption of the monarchy. On August 15, 1461, he was anointed king in the Rheims Cathedral in an elaborate ceremony of great pomp and spirituality. Following the coronation, Louis XI rode to Paris and began to form his government. Many of his father's advisors and officials were dismissed and replaced with friends and allies of the new king. He traveled throughout the kingdom receiving the fealty of the nobles and towns, while asserting his authority. With his administration established, measures were introduced by the regime to encourage agriculture and business growth by granting the towns special trading privileges, revenue exemptions and tax free fairs. To further promote an economic revival, new roads and waterways were constructed while existing ones were improved and repaired. The reforms won the favor of the towns and merchants and they became a source of support to the Valois throne.

As Louis XI was imposing his rule over the nobles and towns, his government initiated reforms to broaden its control over the French church by increasing its power to appoint new clerics and expanding the ability to tax its possessions. As relations with Rome deteriorated, the Pragmatic Sanctions enacted by Charles VII were voided to gain the favor of the papacy. However, when Pope Pius II attempted to increase his local authority over the French church, Louis XI reinstated the sanctions and introduced new measures to tax the clergy. Contacts with the Holy See of Rome remained strained as the crown aggressively pursued the independence of its church.

While Louis XI continued to aggressively assert his supremacy, the nobility and church became increasingly threatened by the loss of their traditional feudal autonomy under the relentless subjugation of the Valois crown. As they began to conspire against the regime's policies of centralization, the revolt against the French king by Duke Francis II of Brittany led to his direct confrontation with the royal government and involvement of the disgruntled French lords. Brittany had pledged only nominal fealty to Louis XI and had largely remained independent. In 1465 as the Breton throne enforced its local rule, Francis II demanded the bishop of Nantes offer homage to him instead of the Valois kingdom. The prelate refused and was compelled to flee from his bishopric and seek protection from Louis XI. As Francis II increasingly ignored his feudal obligations and usurped the rights of the French administration, Louis XI summoned the high magnates to his court to launch a punitive campaign against Brittany. However, seeking to regain their lost historic rights, the nobles refused to commit their armies, uniting in defiance of the crown. To challenge the ruling Valois council, they formed the League of the Public Weal and declared the king's brother, Duke Charles of Berry, as regent of France. The league appointed Duke John II of Bourbon as captain general for the military and began preparations for war by raising troops and money.

As the threat of open revolt escalated, in March 1465 to preserve the peace Louis XI offered a pardon to the nobles if they deserted the league. Many of the minor lords quickly agreed but the peers of France remained committed to the cause of the Public Weal League, continuing their war preparations. As the rebel army began to assemble, Count Charles of Charolais became the recognized leader of the Public Weal. Charles was born on November 10, 1433, at Dijon and was the son of Duke Philip III of Burgundy and Isabella of Portugal. He was raised in his father's splendid Renaissance court, becoming exposed to the latest in art, literature and science. He received a broad based humanist education, excelling in his studies. Charles was appointed Count of Charolais and made a knight of the Golden Fleece by the Burgundian duke in recognition of his birthright as heir. Under the guidance of his father, Charles became a skilled and ambitious warrior and in 1462 began to assume control of the duke's large demesne.

As the rebellion against the Valois crown gained momentum, Louis XI defended his monarchy by attacking the lands in central France of the Public Weal's ally, John II of Bourbon. When the king advanced south from Paris, Charles of Charolais mustered an army of over twenty-five thousand knights and infantry and began to march against the defenses of Paris. When the French king learned of the danger to his capital, the campaign against John II was abandoned and his forces rushed north to confront Count Charles of Charolais. When the French approached the town of Montlhery, on July 16 Louis XI encountered the vanguard of the league led by the Count of Saint-Pol, Louis of Luxembourg. The count had been a close friend of the king, fighting with him against the English in Flanders and Normandy but had recently rebelled to join the Public Weal. The battle at Montlhery was begun with the cavalry charge of Count Louis, who was quickly reinforced by the troops of Charles. The bloody encounter lasted until nightfall with the royalists finally compelled to withdraw in defeat.

After the rebuff at Montlhery, Louis XI reassembled his battered troops and marched to the north, while the league, supported by the forces of Charles of Burgundy, renewed their siege against the capital. The two armies met near Paris, facing off against each other on opposite banks of the Seine River. With his forces in a fortified position, the Valois king traveled to Normandy to rally additional soldiers to his cause. With his army reinforced he offered to negotiate a settlement with Charles and the nobles of the Public Weal. As the talks dragged on and the unity of the league began to weaken, the Charolais count was compelled to agree to terms. Under the ensuing Treaty of Conflans, the Valois regime pledged to cede Normandy to the king's brother, Duke Charles of Berry, restore Burgundian rule to the Picardy towns along the Somme River and countships of Boulogne and Guines, while the league committed to recognize and honor the sovereignty of Louis XI.

Following his investiture of Normandy under the terms of the Conflans Treaty, Duke

Charles of Berry traveled to the new demesne to assert his power and receive the homage of the nobles and towns. While Charles rode through the duchy, he was joined by his ally and friend, Francis II of Brittany. As Francis II remained in Normandy, the local magnates began to fear the usurpation of their lands by the Bretons. To defend their rights, they arrested the king's brother and held him captive. When Louis XI was informed of the rebellion and seizure of Charles, he sent his army to reimpose the Valois crown's rule. At the approach of the royalists, the Normans quickly surrendered and accepted the authority of Louis XI. Duke Charles was forced to renounce his Norman duchy to the Valois throne and was later granted the countship of Champagne as compensation. The monarch's energetic and decisive intervention reestablished his sovereignty over Normandy and overturned part of the unfavorable terms of the Conflans Treaty.

While Louis XI was contesting the League of the Public Weal, his regime began to intrigue to gain possession of lands in northern Spain. The Valois court had earlier supported the Castilian king, Henry IV, during his civil war against John II of Aragon, negotiating a settlement between the two rivals. With a political and military presence established and with John II again distracted with the renewal of the conflict with Castile, in 1463 the Valois king ordered his army to invade the Aragonese counties of Roussillon and Cerdagne, which were quickly conquered and annexed to the crown. Ten years later the monarch of Aragon attempted to reclaim his fiefdom by mounting an attack against the French troops in Roussillon, but the Aragonese were defeated by the occupation forces and the Valois sovereignty remained secure over northern Spain.

In June 1467 Duke Philip III of Burgundy died and was succeeded to the ducal throne by his son, Charles. The new duke had participated in his father's diplomatic and military initiative to expand Burgundian lands and was determined to unite his scattered demesne into a single princedom drawn from French and German territories. To confront the Valois regime, he negotiated an alliance with Edward IV of England, Francis II of Brittany and numerous rebel French warlords, while building a professional Burgundian army of heavily armored cavalry, well-armed foot soldiers, Italian mercenaries and English archers. With the support of his military and allies, Charles mounted a political campaign of intimidation to gain the fealty of the southern Flemish lordships. However, the nobles remained loyal to Louis XI, compelling the duke to intervene with force of arms. The Burgundians advanced into Flanders, sacking the towns to enforce the rule of Duke Charles.

While Charles was asserting his supremacy over southern Flanders with military might, Duke Francis II rebelled against the French regime, launching an invasion into southern Normandy in support of his Burgundian ally. With Francis II in defiance of his rule, Louis XI was compelled to delay his counterattack against Burgundy to enforce his feudal rights over Brittany. He sent a formidable army against the Bretons, which quickly overwhelmed the duke's troops, forcing his withdrawal from Normandy and pledging of fealty.

With peace restored to Brittany, Louis XI dispatched envoys to the Burgundian regime to open talks to resolve their ongoing border conflict. Duke Charles invited the king under safe conduct to meet with him in the Somme River town of Peronne. However, before leaving his court Louis XI sent secret emissaries to the Flemish bishopric of Liege to encourage its revolt against the Burgundian duke's figurehead bishop, Louis of Bourbon. In October 1468 the Valois king traveled to Peronne to begin his negotiations with Charles. Soon after the discussions started, Liege rebelled against Burgundy's harsh rule, expelling the bishop and declaring its allegiance to France. When the duke was informed of the uprising and Louis XI's involvement, he ordered his arrest and imprisonment. Fearing for his life, the king was forced to negotiate with Charles and accept his severe terms. Under the resulting Treaty of Peronne, a one-year truce was declared and numerous concessions surrendered to Burgundy. Louis XI further agreed to assist in the duke's punitive assault against Liege, which was savagely sacked and burned with many thousands killed. In late October he was finally freed and returned to the Valois realm to prepare for the renewal of the war against Charles.

Following his failed attempt to secure peace with Charles at Peronne, the Valois king mounted a diplomatic campaign to isolate Burgundy from its allies. He opened talks with his brother, Duke Charles, receiving his pledge of loyalty and military aid in exchange for the duchy of Guyenne. While the French government continued to strengthen its attack through political intrigues with the Burgundian duke's sympathizers, Louis XI began preparations to resume the conflict, raising new troops and money. In 1471 he summoned Charles to his court to answer charges of treason. When he refused to appear, the Valois regime declared war and sent its soldiers into Picardy, while a second force attacked Burgundy from Dauphine. As the royalists marched into the Somme River region, numerous towns and castles were captured, while Amiens willingly submitted its homage. As the French renewed their advance, Charles mustered his army and launched a counteroffensive of brutality and pillage against the Picardy towns and countryside. When he reached Amiens, it was besieged with his large cannons relentlessly battering the defenses. However, despite his furious and energetic assaults, the garrison refused to surrender. After three weeks the Burgundians abandoned the investment and negotiated a truce with Louis XI.

During the armistice with France, Charles reorganized his army and recruited additional troops and in June resumed his attacks against the Somme River towns but was rebuffed by the determined resistance of the Beauvais garrison. The Burgundians abandoned their siege against the castle and marched south to ravage the Pays de Caux region of Normandy. By late autumn after a campaign of savage pillage and destruction, the initiative began to lose momentum and with his coffers nearly empty the duke retreated to Flanders. In November he began negotiations with the French and both rivals quickly agreed to a truce, while pledging to honor the existing status quo during the following year.

As the French regime defended its crownlands against the Burgundian encroachments, Louis XI continued the campaign to break the feudal power of his nobles and eliminate the allies of Duke Charles. In May 1471 the king's brother died and his Guyenne duchy was reclaimed by the throne. Royal sovereignty was increased in Brittany when Louis XI's army forced Francis II to abandon his coalition with Burgundy and pledge loyalty to him. As the French pursued their overlordship against Brittany, Count John V of Armagnac disregarded his oath of fealty to the monarchy and joined the Burgundian alliance. To reassert its authority, the Valois government sent its soldiers into the countship to suppress the revolt. Confronted with the power of the French forces, the recalcitrant count was compelled to surrender and render his homage. He was pardoned for his treason but soon rebelled, rejoining the war against the Valois kingdom. Louis XI ordered his troops to brutally sack the rogue's towns and during the assault against his stronghold at Lectoure John V was killed. His demesne was declared forfeited and annexed directly into the royal domain. By 1474 through bribery, intimidation, negotiation and military might, the sovereign had enforced his supremacy over his vassals and laid the foundation for the absolute rule that followed in subsequent monarchies.

While the Valois crown was asserting its authority over the recalcitrant lords, Duke Charles of Burgundy directed his policies toward unifying his scattered fiefs into a single united Burgundian kingdom. He purchased the Upper Alsace from Duke Sigismund of Austria and later seized the duchy of Guelders by force of arms to further solidify his lands. To further advance his aggrandizement initiative, in 1473 the duke met with the Holy Roman emperor, Frederick III, in Trier to negotiate his appointment as king of the Romans. However, the talks ended in failure and on unfriendly terms with the emperor departing in haste. After his rebuff at Trier, Charles intervened in support of Rupprecht of the Palatinate, archbishop of Cologne, establishing a vassal principality. However, while Duke Charles was extending his territories, a large coalition under Louis XI was uniting against him.

To counter the escalating threat of Burgundy, the French king sent envoys to negotiate a military alliance with the Swiss Confederation, imperial free cites along the Rhine River and Rene II of Lorraine. In early 1474 the league of Constance was formed in opposition to the aggression of Charles of Burgundy. In preparation for war, the Valois crown fortified its border towns, reorganized the military and raised revenue to finance the campaign. After the Burgundians began siege operations against Neuss, the League declared war. As Charles continued his investment at Neuss, his initiative became bogged down and after six months of fruitless assaults the Burgundians were forced to abandon the attempt to seize the city. With the duke distracted with his attacks against Neuss, the formidable Swiss army quickly captured Upper Burgundy and much of Franche-Comte, while French troops invaded Picardy and Luxembourg.

While Burgundy was expanding its territories along the Rhine River, Duke Charles began negotiations with Edward IV of England to enlarge his war against Louis XI with a new initiative directed at the seizure of western France. In 1474 a treaty was signed, which committed the English to an invasion of France in support of the duke. To further buttress the campaign, Francis II of Brittany was promised Lancaster military aid for his participation, while Count Louis of Saint-Pol pledged to join the league and permit unfettered access to his strategic lands, which lay between France and Burgundy. In July 1475 Edward IV landed in Calais, joining his forces with Charles of Burgundy. However, the English king was disappointed at the lack of troop support provided by the duke, who had earlier sent the bulk of his army to invade the duchy of Lorraine. Nevertheless, the two rulers agreed to advance along the Somme River through the friendly demesne of Count Louis and lay siege against Rheims. However, as the Lancastrian army marched to Saint-Quentin, the Saint-Pol count abandoned the coalition and launched an attack against the English, while Duke Charles suddenly announced his return to the conflict along the Rhine River. After the alliance against Louis XI quickly dissolved, Edward IV lost all faith in the duke and opened talks with the French for a truce. On August 29 the two monarchs met at Picquigny near Amiens, where a peace accord was finalized. Under the terms of the Picquigny Treaty, the English pledged to depart from France peacefully, the Lancastrian regime was to receive an annual subsidy payment and a seven-year armistice was to be honored. With the Burgundian strategy for the conquest of France shattered, Charles agreed to a separate nine-year truce with Louis XI in September.

After the return of the Lancastrian army to England and elimination of the threat to western France, Louis XI continued to financially aid and encourage the league of Constance in its war against Burgundy. In March 1476 the Burgundians suffered a devastating defeat at Grandson in western Switzerland, where their forces were nearly annihilated and Charles barely escaped capture. The duke managed to raise a new army and advanced against Bern, where his troops were again overwhelmed by the Leaguers. Despite the reverses, he refused to abandon his quest for a kingdom and in December besieged Nancy in Lorraine. However, the Burgundians were taken by surprise by the combined forces of Rene II of Lorraine and the Swiss on January 5, 1477, and Duke Charles killed during the battle. Louis XI was overjoyed at the death of his greatest enemy and immediately began preparations to seize his ducal territories.

Following the collapse of Charles's regime, in March 1477 Louis XI ordered his army to occupy the towns along the Somme River and the counties of Artois and Flanders. The Picardy region offered little resistance and pledged its allegiance to the Valois court. However, several towns defied the French king and declared their loyalty to the duke's heir, Mary of Burgundy. To suppress their opposition, Arras was brutally sacked and quickly captured. The city was heavily garrisoned with French troops and compelled to pay a large fine. After the severe subjugation of Arras, the remaining rebellious fiefs quickly surrendered and offered fealty to the French crown.

After the occupation of Picardy, the French resumed their offensive, advancing into Flanders. However, the resistance of the towns against Valois rule was strengthened in August 1477 when Mary of Burgundy married Archduke Maximilian of Habsburg. He assumed command of the local army and in the following year in defense of his wife's inheritance launched an attack to recover the recently seized lands. The city of Cambrai was recaptured and when the French attempted to send reinforcements to Flanders, Maximilian defeated their relief forces at Guinegate. Following the rebuff, Louis XI agreed to a papal sponsored truce, which remained in effect until the following year.

While the Valois king was personally involved in the conquest of Flanders, his administration sent two former allies of Duke Charles to negotiate his sovereignty over the southern Burgundian lordships. To assert his rule peacefully, the local nobles were granted pensions and government offices, while the towns were given special privileges and tax exemptions. After the offers of liberal royal patronage, the duchy of Burgundy declared its loyalty to the crown but the Franche-Comte region rebelled, pledging its fealty to Mary. To suppress the growing Franche-Comte uprisings, the ruling council in Dijon was replaced by Louis XI and an army dispatched to enforce the throne's will by force of arms. By late July 1477 the rebels were subdued and on July 31 the king made a triumphant entrance into Dijon.

Following the expiration of the truce between France and Archduke Maximilian, in 1478 hostilities were again resumed. However, after four years of inconclusive fighting, negotiations for a permanent resolution were finally begun following the sudden death of Mary of Burgundy in a riding accident. Maximilian of Habsburg had ruled Flanders in the name of his wife and after her death the local towns refused to accept a foreign prince. Led by the burghers of Ghent, the cities rebelled and initiated independent peace talks with the Valois court. In the ensuing Treaty of Arras, Louis XI gained sovereignty over Franche-Comte, Artois, Picardy and the Burgundian lordships, while the Habsburgs retained Flanders. The settlement was to be guaranteed by the future marriage of the archduke's daughter, Margaret, to the dauphin, Charles.

With peace restored to his borders, Louis XI continued his policies directed at the suppression of his magnates and strengthening of his sovereignty by usurping additional fiefdoms for the royal domain. In 1480 Rene I of Anjou died and the Valois crown annexed his lordship of Bar. When Rene I's successor, Charles IV, died without a direct heir his counties of Maine, Provence and Anjou were bequeathed to the regime. As the king ruled the kingdom with a stern hand, he began to suffer from periodic strokes, which increased in severity and duration. The seizures left him unable to walk or speak and increasingly his advisors governed the realm. Following his attacks, he withdrew from all public appearances and saw only a few counselors in private. After a period of rest, the effects gradually subsided and he temporarily regained his health but still remained frail. In early 1483 he began to plan for the succession of his thirteen-year-old heir, Charles, appointing his daughter, Anne, as regent for his minor son. On August 30, 1483, Louis XI died at age sixty and a reign of twenty-two years. Under his kingship the feudal powers of the nobility had been permanently broken, the boundaries of the royal demesne greatly expanded and France was at peace with the economy steadily moving to prosperity.

Sources

Champion. *Louis XI.*   Cleugh. *Chant Royal: The Life of Louis XI.*   Kendall. *Louis XI.*   Putman. *Charles the Bold.*

Charles VIII, 1470–1483–1498

Charles VIII inherited the Valois monarchy in late August 1483 to rule for nearly fifteen years as the fourth Renaissance king of France. He was born on June 30, 1470, in the royal castle at Amboise and was the only surviving son of Louis XI and his second wife, Charlotte of Savoy. The dauphin spent his childhood at Amboise and was raised in the protected and loving household of his mother. Louis XI provided distinguished scholars for his son's education, however, unlike his father the Valois prince was not a gifted student, displaying little desire or aptitude for learning. He was taught the basics of reading, writing, mathematics and religion and was instructed in the social graces of dancing, court etiquette and music. Charles later developed an interest in French history and dreamed of participating in foreign adventures and crusades to Jerusalem. During his early years, he was frequently ill and isolated from the royal regime. As a result of his illnesses, he was not closely associated with the ruling council and received little preparation or training for his future succession of kingship. On August 30, 1483, his father died and Charles VIII was recognized as king at age thirteen. Before his death Louis XI had established a governing regency for his minor son under the direction of his daughter, Anne. Charles VIII readily accepted his sister's assumption of power, preferring to remain uninvolved in court policies and politics. Anne of France was born at the chateau of Genappe in the lordship of Brabant on April 13, 1461, and was the eldest child of Louis XI and his second wife, Charlotte of Savoy. At the age of twelve, she was married to Peter II, lord of Beaujeu.

Anne was the older sister of the monarch and with her husband claimed the regency by blood right. However, when she attempted to consolidate her rule, the Valois princess was challenged by her cousin and acknowledged heir designate to the French throne, Duke Louis of Orleans. As the hostilities between the two rival factions escalated, the Estates-General was summoned to Tours to resolve the disputed succession. Anne had inherited her father's intelligence and energy and when the assembly met in early February 1484 she mounted an aggressive political campaign to win the approval of the Estates. With custody of the king, who was the recognized symbol of royal authority, she outmaneuvered Louis and with Peter II was appointed co-regent of France. The duke refused to honor the vote and began to conspire to usurp the kingdom by kidnapping Charles VIII and forcing his prisoner to name him regent. His plot was quickly discovered by Anne, who removed her brother to the safety of the fortified town of Montargis. With his demands for control of the monarchy thwarted, Louis of Orleans was forced to abandon his quest for power and withdraw to his estates.

With their reign unchallenged, Anne and Peter II consolidated their administration and began to govern the realm in the name of the king. However, in 1485 Duke Louis resumed his intrigues against the Valois throne with Francis II of Brittany and numerous dissident

French warlords, beginning a series of sporadic conflicts known as the Mad Wars. He appealed to Charles VIII to dismiss his sister and her husband from court and return to Paris to assume his personal rule. Under the influence of Anne, the young monarch refused and sent the royal army to enforce his power over the recalcitrant Orleans duke. As the Valois troops advanced against him, Louis quickly surrendered and pledged his fealty. Nevertheless, later in the year he again rebelled, forming an alliance with Count Charles of Angouleme and Viscount John of Foix in defiance of the crown, igniting the Second Mad War. Before their uprising could gain momentum, the regents mounted an attack against the Loire lands of Louis, forcing him to submit to terms. Under the Peace of Bourges signed in November 1485, he was compelled to accept his removal from the ruling council and the garrisoning of Valois soldiers in his towns.

In June 1486 Archduke Maximilian of Habsburg launched an attack against France to enforce his claims to disputed border towns and with the Valois regime distracted in Flanders, Louis of Orleans revolted, joining Francis II in Brittany. Many of the Breton warlords refused to participate in the uprising of their duke and appealed to Charles VIII for protection. To gain their support and allegiance, he negotiated the Treaty of Chateaubriant with them and in May 1487 sent his army with a contingent of Bretons to invade the duchy, beginning the Third Mad War. By the following year, the French had seized many strategic strongholds in the south and had captured Louis of Orleans during the battle of Saint-Aubin. After the rebels' defeat, the resolve of the duchy was broken and with their alliance shattered by the seizure of the Duke of Orleans, the Bretons were compelled to seek peace terms. Under the ensuing Treaty of Le Verger signed on August 20, Francis II agreed to expel his foreign troops and seek French approval before negotiating the marriages of his two minor daughters, Anne and Isabella.

Two days after the end of the Third Mad War, Francis II died, leaving the appointment of guardians for his heir and successor, Anne, in dispute. The Bretons favored the naming of a local high magnate as regent, while Charles VIII with the backing of his sister and Peter II asserted his custody by blood right. As the duchy resisted Valois guardianship for Anne and Isabella, in December 1488 French troops again invaded Brittany to impose their claims by force of arms and after a short campaign overran most of the fiefdom. However, other neighboring kingdoms had vital security and trading interests in preserving Brittany's autonomy, uniting to counterattack Charles VIII. The duchy's allies, Henry VII of England, Isabella and Ferdinand II of Spain and Maximilian of Austria, sent soldiers and money to buttress the resistance of the Bretons. Reinforced by the foreign armies, the supporters of Duchess Anne forced the French out of lower Brittany. At the end of the campaigning season, in October 1490 a six-month truce was arranged with Charles VIII retaining control over many fortified towns in the northern region of the duchy.

During the winter of 1491 the Breton nobles finalized their quest for a permanent protector for the duchy by negotiating the marriage of Duchess Anne to Archduke Maximilian. However, he was occupied in eastern Europe settling dynastic disputes in Lower Austria and Hungary while the truce in Brittany expired and hostilities resumed in May. The French army, reinforced with numerous rebel Breton lords and their vassals, marched into the duchy virtually unopposed with only Rennes resisting their onslaught. While Charles VIII's forces were occupying most of Brittany, Isabella and Ferdinand II were distracted with the conquest of Granada and Maximilian remained in Hungary, while the English were slow to respond due to the lack of support from Parliament. Deserted by her allies and many of her magnates, Duchess Anne was compelled to begin talks with the French for a settlement. With Princess Anne and Lord

Peter II leading the French negotiations, after prolonged deliberations an agreement was finally ratified in November. Under the treaty, peace was to be guaranteed by Anne of Brittany's marriage to Charles VIII with the provision that should he die without a successor Brittany reverted back to her. The formal ceremony was held on December 6, 1491, at the chateau of Langeais. The political marriage effectively ended the independence of Brittany and brought peace to France. The signing of the accord signaled the king's full assumption of the monarchy and end of his sister's regency.

Despite being a marital agreement negotiated for political gain, Charles VIII and Anne were well suited to each other and their marriage was generally happy. She was described physically as possessing attractive features with a small body and walking with a slight limp. The queen was intelligent and inquisitive, becoming a close and valued advisor to her husband. During the war in Naples, she was appointed as co-regent with Lord Peter II and with her prior exposure and association with the Breton government the Valois kingdom was skillfully ruled under her administration. Anne continued to remain dedicated to the independence of Brittany, intervening against the French council to defend the duchy's rights. The king and Anne had two children, including the dauphin, Charles Orland; however, both died in infancy leaving Charles VIII without a direct successor.

During the Breton wars, England had supported the independence of Francis II and his successor, Anne, with troops and money. However, following the truce of October 1490 Henry VII withdrew his forces from the duchy. The English had a long history of influence and trade in Brittany and after the marriage of Charles VIII to Anne the Tudor regime countered the loss of its power and presence by landing a large army at Calais to enforce their rights by force of arms. Henry VII marched against Boulogne in October 1492 and besieged the stronghold. In response to the Tudor threat, the French king sent his emissaries seeking peace terms and withdrawal of the English soldiers from his domain. The Tudor king was more willing to negotiate than wage war and a final settlement quickly resulted. Under the Treaty of Etaples, Henry VII pledged to abandon his campaign and honor peace between the two realms for an annual subsidy payment.

After the signing of the Etaples Treaty, Charles VIII began negotiations with Spain to resolve the ongoing disputes along his southern border. In November 1492 the Valois government agreed to return the usurped Spanish counties of Roussillon and Cerdagne to Queen Isabella and Ferdinand II. The formal treaty was signed on January 19, 1493, creating an alliance between the two kingdoms with both regimes pledging to respect the newly established frontier boundaries and remain at peace.

The two peace treaties negotiated by Charles VIII's government had destroyed the anti–French coalition that had been forged to restrict the aggression and expansion of the Valois regime. Without the military support of his allies, Archduke Maximilian's quest to reacquire his Valois seized Burgundian lands in Flanders and eastern France was weakened. The Treaty of Arras signed in 1483 had been guaranteed by the future marriage of the archduke's daughter, Margaret, to Charles VIII with the dowry of Franche-Comte and Artois. The French king's marriage to Anne of Brittany adjured the agreement and the Habsburg prince demanded the return of the two lordships. When the Valois court ignored his claim, he invaded France-Comte quickly capturing much of the region. While the Habsburgs continued their offensive, the French ruling council agreed to hold peace talks and in May 1493 the Peace of Senlis was ratified. Under the treaty's terms, Maximilian regained the eastern French countships, Artois and several small Flemish cities, while the remainder of the Burgundian demesne was retained by the Valois crown.

In 1494 France was at peace, united and returning to prosperity. With his reign secure Charles VIII began to direct his policy initiatives toward Italy and his claim to the throne of Naples through his inheritance from his great-uncle, Rene I of Anjou. The peninsular of Italy was a patchwork of large and small princedoms dominated by Florence, Milan, Venice, Naples and the papacy. In 1494 King Ferdinand I of Naples died and Charles VIII was pressed by Duke Ludovico Sforza of Milan, Florentine banking families, Pope Alexander VI and many Neapolitan nobles to usurp his crown. The seizure of southern Italy would also provide a strategic and safe assembly point for a new crusade to regain Jerusalem from Saracen control, which the French king and the Holy See highly favored. While he received widespread support and encouragement from the Italian princes, the French nobility and towns disapproved of the foreign expedition. They preferred political and military campaigns against the vulnerable lands of Emperor Maximilian I along the border lordships, where they had opportunities for personal gains. However, the Valois king remained determined to secure the conquest of Naples and assert his birthrights. When the French crossed the Alps into Lombardy in August, it was the beginning of a series of sporadic Franco-Italian wars that lasted over the next sixty years.

Early in 1494 military preparations were begun for the Italian initiative. The Valois king established a ruling council to govern in his absence, appointing Queen Anne and Peter II of Beaujeu as co-regents. Money for the campaign was exhorted from the nobles, church and towns, while additional funds were raised by an increase to the unpopular hearth tax. In the summer Charles VIII began to muster his forces around Tours. The royal army of over twenty thousand was composed of cavalry, Swiss pikemen, French infantry, archers and a large contingent of artillery. In August the French crossed the Alps into northern Italy, receiving triumphant receptions from the towns as they marched south. On September 9 the king made a grand entrance into Turin and was welcomed by the ducal regent of Savoy, Blanche of Montferrat. From Savoy the Valois troops advanced to Milan, where they were greeted by Duke Ludovico. During his stay in the city, Charles VIII negotiated a treaty of alliance with the duke, who pledged to support the attack against the new Neapolitan ruler, Alfonso II.

From Milan the invading army moved toward Rome but as the French approached Tuscany, Charles VIII was met by envoys from the ruler of Florence, Piero de Medici, who denied access through his demesne. Piero was born in Florence on February 15, 1472, and was the eldest son of Lorenzo de Medici and Clarice Orsini. He was educated to succeed his father as head of the Medici family and governor of the Florentine Republic. The Valois king needed the support of Florence to secure his lines of communications with Milan and began preparations to invade the fief. Piero had inherited control of the governing council at the death of his father in 1492 amid the mounting tide of religious opposition against the secular Medici regime. As he attempted to raise money and troops to defend the city, his exhortations received little backing from the Florentines. With Florence defenseless against the massive French forces, Piero entered Charles VIII's camp and willingly agreed to all his demands, conceding all the Republic's important fortresses. However, the ruling council refused to accept the treaty and Piero was overthrown and compelled to flee the city. The Valois king was forced to negotiate a new settlement with Piero de Gino Capponi, who had assumed command of the government. After agreeing to concessions, on November 17 Charles VIII entered the city and received the homage of the population. He remained for the next eight days, touring the Renaissance style churches and palaces, while viewing the art and sculptures. When the French soldiers resumed their march south to Rome, they were greeted with open gates and pledges of fealty from every town as the campaign became a grand triumphant procession.

On December 31 Charles VIII entered Rome and from the residence of a French cardinal began negotiations with the papacy for its support in the conquest of Naples. As the French approached the Holy City, Pope Alexander VI became increasingly alarmed at the presence of a large and powerful foreign controlled kingdom on his southern border, which would be independent of his authority and a threat to his Papal States. However, after two weeks of deliberations, the king and pontiff finally met and resolved their differences. Alexander VI was born Rodrigo Borgia on January 1, 1431, in the Spanish kingdom of Aragon. When his maternal uncle was elected to the Holy See as Pope Calixtus III, Rodrigo was made a cardinal and assumed important offices in his uncle's papacy. He later served in the Roman Curia, acquiring wealth, influence and administrative skills. He was chosen pope on August 11, 1492, taking the name of Alexander VI. Soon after his election to the papacy, Alexander VI pursued an aggressive policy of nepotism for his four children, granting them papal fiefdoms and archbishoprics and later scheming to use the French presence in Italy to gain new lands and titles for his family. On January 20, 1495, he celebrated mass with Charles VIII in Saint Peter's Cathedral and the following week the Valois army continued its march toward Naples with his blessings.

While the invading Valois army was advancing toward Naples, Ferdinand II of Spain sent reinforcements to buttress the resistance of his nephew, King Alfonso II. In early February the French crossed the border into the Naples kingdom and marched to besiege the great fortress of Monte San Giovanni. When the newly arrived Spanish garrison refused the demand to surrender, the Valois artillery began to bombard the defenses. After a large breach in the walls was opened, Charles VIII launched a brutal infantry assault, which quickly overpowered the Spanish with many thousands killed by the savage onslaught.

Following the fall of Monte San Giovanni, the French advanced south into the kingdom, meeting only scattered resistance from the Neapolitan-Spanish defenders. When the forces of Charles VIII approached the city of Naples, the local population revolted against Alfonso II, who abdicated his crown in favor of his son, Ferdinand II, and retired to a Sicilian monastery. The new Neapolitan king attempted to rally his troops but when his strongholds at Capua and Gaeta fell, he was compelled to retreat to Messina. On February 22 Charles VIII entered Naples with only the castle at Ovo offering any opposition. The Spanish garrison at Ovo refused to surrender and the Valois artillery began to bombard the fortress with heavy cannons, forcing Ferdinand II's soldiers to seek terms. With the city under French control, the offensive was renewed into the southern provinces. The towns offered only token opposition and by the end of March the entire realm of Naples was under the authority of the Valois throne.

Charles VIII established the seat of his government in Naples and began to solidify his rule. His friends and Italian allies were rewarded with offices and lands, while a French dominated council of state was formed. The regime confirmed the privileges and exceptions previously granted by the old administration to gain the favor of the Neapolitans. The local nobles were given titles, honors and high positions at court to win their support. The sovereign traveled extensively throughout his new kingdom from town to town asserting his authority and receiving the homage of the population. On May 12 Charles VIII was crowned king of Naples.

While Charles VIII was occupied with the subjugation of Naples, the major European powers became increasingly alarmed at his aggrandizement of new lands and wealth and the dissolution of the Italian political status quo. Under the leadership of Pope Alexander VI, on March 31, 1495, a Holy League was formed with Mantua, Doge Agostino Barbarigo of Venice, Milan, Isabella and Ferdinand II of Spain and Emperor Maximilian I to force the French out of Italy. The league elected Francesco II Gonzaga of Mantua to lead its military campaign. Francesco was born in Mantua on August 10, 1466, and was the eldest son of Marquess Federico I Gonzaga, who had served as a successful mercenary captain for Milan. When his father died in 1484, Francesco II inherited his lands and titles. In 1490 he married Isabella d'Este and under her influence his court became a center for Renaissance art and culture. Francesco II was an experienced and skilled soldier, who had served as captain general of the Venetian army. After assuming command of the league's forces, in May Francesco II began to attack the scattered Valois garrisons guarding Charles VIII's lines of communications. With his overland routes for reinforcements, resupply and retreat threatened, the French king was compelled to return to his realm and personally raise additional money and troops and negotiate new alliances.

On May 20 Charles VIII left Naples with half of his forces and began the march north. Gilbert d'Montpensier was appointed to command the remaining Neapolitan troops and ordered to maintain control over the scattered strongholds. By the end of the month the retreating French had advanced through Rome and continued into central Italy, avoiding contact with the Leaguers. As they traveled toward the Apennines Mountain region, their route was blocked by the waiting soldiers of Mantua and Venice at the town of Fornovo. On July 6 Francesco II formed his army into battle lines and launched his light cavalry against the French front. Their charge was repulsed but the Leaguers renewed their attack, slowly pushing the French from the field. However, when the Italians began to plunder the rich baggage train, the Valois troops reorganized and withdrew to a fortified hilltop. The battle turned into a stalemate and the next day Charles VIII was able to break contact and resume his advance to the north reaching the Italian border in November. As he approached France, the Valois king's ally, Lord John II Grimaldi of Monaco, protected his retreat along the Riviera region. John II was later rewarded by the Valois throne for his support with the appointment of the captain-generalship for the Riviera and his lordship was confirmed as a protectorate of France.

As the Valois king was advancing north, his Naples occupation forces under the command of d'Montpensier were attacked by the Venetians in the east, while from Sicily King Ferdinand II began to confront the French in the southern province of Calabria. During his exile in Sicily, the deposed Neapolitan king forged an alliance with his cousin, Ferdinand II of Spain, who promised to provide military aid for the war against the French. In May 1495 a small Spanish army arrived in Messina under the command of Gonzalo de Cordoba. He had fought with distinction with the Spanish soldiers in Portugal and later in Granada against the Moors. For his bravery and martial skills, he had won the favor of Queen Isabella and was appointed to command her escort troops.

Reinforced by his cousin's soldiers, Ferdinand II advanced against the French held fortresses in Calabria and quickly captured several lightly defended strongholds while occupying the town of Seminara. To counter the allies' offensive, the local Valois governor, Bernard Stewart, Lord of Aubigny and captain of the King's Scottish Archers, consolidated his scattered garrison troops and marched to meet the invaders. Bernard Stewart had earlier served with the French forces in the English army of Henry Tudor during the usurpation of the Yorkish regime and had fought bravely at the battle of Bosworth Field. At the appearance of Stewart's soldiers, on June 28 Ferdinand II moved out of Seminara and formed into battle formation. In the ensuing encounter, the inexperienced and poorly trained Calabrian militiamen panicked at the approach of the seasoned Lord of Aubigny's Swiss pikemen and fled the field. The Valois army seized the initiative and drove the allies from the battlefield with the Neapolitan king barely avoiding capture.

However, despite suffering a decisive defeat, the Neapolitan-Spanish renewed their attacks and with the support of the local populace Ferdinand II recaptured Naples on July 7, when the city rose in revolt against the French. As the Neapolitans entered the capital, de Cordoba resumed the campaign against the French forces and by a series of small and limited engagements seized control of Calabria. The French attempted to consolidate their remaining troops but were trapped at Atella and compelled to surrender. With the defeat of the Valois government's local commander, Gilbert d'Montpensier, the occupation of the Naples kingdom was abandoned, but Charles VIII never relinquished his title of Neapolitan king or the quest for an Italian realm and began plans in 1498 for a second invasion.

The campaign to seize the kingdom of Naples was a financial and military disaster for France. It seriously weakened the regime's power and prestige in European affairs and left a severe debt burden. However, the experiences in Italy resulted in exposure to the Renaissance movement, which was imported to France by the king and nobles. As the invading forces traveled to Florence, Milan, Pisa and other prosperous towns they came into contact with the architecture, culture and art of the Renaissance. Paintings, books, tapestries, sculptures and all manner of artworks were collected by the crown's agents and sent to France. Architects and craftsmen from Italy were employed and the new Renaissance style of buildings and gardens began to appear in the Valois realm.

After his return to France from Italy, the king assumed control of his government and soon began a political initiative to reform his realm. The administration of justice was revised with the addition of new courts and regional Parliaments. The financial sector was restructured, resulting in greater efficiency and tax revenues. With his kingdom at peace and prospering, in 1498 Charles VIII began to make preparations for a second invasion of Naples. The papacy's Holy League had recently dissolved with the defection of Milan and the Valois ruling council opened negotiations with Francesco II of Mantua for an alliance against Naples. However, on April 7, 1498, while at his favorite chateau of Amboise, Charles VIII accidentally struck his head on a low door beam falling unconscious. He died several hours later at age twenty-eight and a reign of fifteen years.

Sources

Bernardy. *Princes of Monaco.* Butler. *Twice Queen of France.* Denieul-Cormier. *Wise and Foolish Kings— The First House of Valois.*

Louis XII, 1462–1498–1515

In April 1498 Charles VIII died without a direct heir and his cousin, Louis of Orleans, succeeded to the crown of France, reigning as the fifth king of the Renaissance. He was born on June 27, 1462, in Blois and was the only son of Duke Charles of Orleans and his second wife, Mary of Cleves. The House of Orleans was a cadet branch of the ruling Valois dynasty, and the young prince was not in the direct line of succession. In 1465 Charles of Orleans died and Louis inherited his ducal lands and titles. Following the death of his father, Louis remained in Blois with his two sisters under the care and protection of Mary of Cleves. Louis XI took special interest in his education, appointing his principal tutors. However, the duke showed little interest in his studies of reading, writing, history, Latin and mathematics, preferring to participate in field games and hunting. He became a skilled equestrian and energetically pursued the popular sport of jousting. The Orleans duke was frequently engaged in military tournaments throughout France, gaining widespread renown for his martial triumphs. As a young knight, he was physically described as tall with a muscular and athletic body, while possessing handsome features and a regal bearing.

Several days after Prince Louis's birth, his father signed an agreement with Louis XI binding his son to marriage with the Valois Princess Jeanne. However, she suffered from numerous physical deformities which made her unattractive and incapable of producing children. As she grew older the disfigurements became more apparent and the king demanded the marital contract be renewed. Initially Louis refused to obey the order, only reluctantly complying after threats of royal intervention against his demesne. The official wedding was held three years later but following the ceremony the duke abandoned Jeanne, traveling alone to Blois. He was later forced to reconcile and return to his new wife. Louis remained with Jeanne at his Linieras Chateau for the next seven years having little contract with her. He occupied his time away from Linieras in the pursuit of parties, hunting and participating in jousting tournaments, while engaging in many adulterous affairs.

In 1483 Louis XI died and was succeeded by his thirteen-year-old son, Charles VIII. The young king was the only surviving male issue of the direct Valois dynasty and as his closest relative Louis of Orleans was acknowledged as the new dauphin. Before his death Louis XI had established a regency council for his minor son led by his daughter, Anne, and her husband, Lord Peter II of Beaujeu. As the recognized heir, Louis aggressively challenged the right of the regents to rule. He began to form a faction in opposition, joining with Francis II of Brittany and other powerful French magnates to confront Anne and Peter II's government. As the threat of open rebellion grew, the Estates-General was summoned to Tours in February 1484 to resolve the succession dispute.

When the assembly met in Tours, Anne mounted an aggressive political offensive to gain the favor of the Estates. As the acknowledged guardian for the king, she used his royal prestige and authority to outmaneuver Louis and secure her election as co-regent with her husband. After failing to gain control of the regime, the Orleans duke initiated negotiations to form an alliance with rebel French lords to usurp the monarchy by force of arms. With his allies he began to plot to seize Charles VIII and compel him to dissolve the government of his sister. A new ruling council was later to be established with Louis appointed as regent for his cousin. However, Anne soon discovered the conspiracy and removed her brother to the safety of Montargis Castle. With his insurrection in shambles, the duke was forced to withdraw from court and return to his estates.

Following the failure of Louis of Orleans's attempted revolt, Anne and Peter II ruled the kingdom unchallenged during the following year. However, in 1485 the duke renewed his conspiracy against the regime, traveling to Brittany to forge an alliance with Francis II and numerous dissident French warlords, beginning the First Mad War. In response to the danger of rebellion, the Valois government sent the royal army to assert the king's authority quickly forcing Louis to submit and swear his homage. Despite his promises of fealty, the Duke of Orleans remained determined to gain control of the monarchy and rebelled with Count Charles of Angouleme, Lord John of Foix and other recalcitrant French magnates. Anne soon discovered the new insurgency and summoned Louis to court to answer charges of treason. He refused to appear before the council and fled to Brittany. To counter his continued defiance, Princess Anne's regency advanced its soldiers against the rogues, forcing their surrender before their uprising gained momentum. The Orleans duke was compelled to sign the Peace of Bourges, pledging his loyalty and agreeing to the garrisoning of Valois troops in his towns, ending the Second Mad War.

Despite his two unsuccessful attempts to overthrow the regency of Anne, in 1486 with her Valois regime distracted in Flanders against a punitive encroachment by Archduke Maximilian of Austria, Louis renewed his coalition in opposition to the throne with Francis II, igniting the Third Mad War. However, many Breton nobles rose in revolt against their duke's alliance and agreed to unite with the French in the suppression of the rebels. In the summer of 1487 the army of Charles VIII invaded Brittany and with support from its local allies conquered most of the southern region of the duchy before the end of the campaigning season. In the following year the attack was renewed and in June the troops of Louis of Orleans were defeated at the battle of Saint-Aubin near the ducal capital of Rennes. During the encounter, the duke was captured and imprisoned for the next three years at Bourges.

During Louis's period of captivity, Jeanne relentlessly petitioned her brother, King Charles VIII, and sister, Anne, for his freedom. She frequently visited her husband at Bourges, attending to his care and needs, however, he refused to acknowledge her and continued his hostile relationship. While Jeanne campaigned for his pardon, many of the duke's friends and allies also advanced his cause with the regime. After the end of the Third Mad War, the monarch had dismissed the regency administration of Anne, assuming full independent power. Without the influence of his sister, in June 1491 he granted the release of Louis for his pledge of fealty. His offices at court were restored and he was appointed as royal viceroy for the duchy of Normandy. Assuming control of the Norman government, Louis abandoned his pursuit for the kingship, becoming a loyal and close advisor to Charles VIII.

While Louis of Orleans continued to serve on the regime's council and govern his personal lands and Normandy, Charles VIII began preparations for the conquest of the kingdom of Naples to impose his blood claim inherited from his great uncle, Rene I, the deposed Neapolitan king. In the summer of 1494 the Valois army was assembled at Tours and Louis appointed to lead a large contingent of cavalry. He had hereditary rights to the county of Asti through his grandmother, Valentine Visconti, and in August as the French crossed the Alps into Italy, the duke asserted his title to the lordship. Through the Visconti family he also had a claim against the neighboring duchy of Milan, which had been usurped by Ludovico Sforza. Ludovico had earlier seized the ducal crown from his minor nephew, Gian Galeazzo, holding him in harsh confinement. After his death under suspicious circumstances, Ludovico assumed the Milanese government, ruling as duke. However, without his formal investiture of the ducal title he was regarded as a usurper and was alarmed at the presence of a new potential challenger in nearby Asti. To secure his throne, the duke offered possession of Genoa to the French, if Louis was named as governor. To retain the loyalty and friendship of his ally, the king agreed and sent Louis to take command of Genoa.

In August 1494 Duke Louis traveled to Genoa, assuming control of the local government. While he consolidated his ruling administration and reinforced the city's defenses, King Alfonso II of Naples sent his fleet north to invade Genoa. When the king's ships approached the seaport, the Neapolitan naval commander landed his troops on the coast to seize the city. To counter the threat to his governorship, Louis ordered his infantry to attack the Neapolitans and thwart their advance, while he personally led his warships against Alfonso II's fleet. However, the Italian admiral refused to engage the French and sailed away, leaving his land forces stranded. Without the support of their vessels, the Neapolitan army was quickly overwhelmed and compelled to surrender. Following his victory, the Orleans duke returned to Asti to meet with Charles VIII, who was preparing to resume his campaign into southern Italy. During their discussions, the king appointed Louis as his governor for Lombardy and ordered him to guard his lines of communications with France and retain control over Genoa during his absence in Naples.

As the Orleans duke protected the Valois interest in northern Italy, in early 1495 Charles VIII advanced into Naples and by May had seized control of the kingdom. As he consolidated his government, Pope Alexander VI began to increasingly fear the presence of a formidable foreign power in Italy and formed the Holy League with Mantua, Venice, Spain and Milan in opposition to the French. The Valois regime's former ally, Duke Ludovico Sforza, now became a threat to the small army of Louis in Asti. To defend his lands against an attack from the Milanese, the Orleans duke sent an urgent appeal to France for additional troops and began to reinforce his strongholds.

While Louis continued to buttress his defenses, the neighboring fief of Novara rebelled against the overlordship of Ludovico Sforza, seeking protection from the French. Louis quickly agreed to intervene, sending his troops to occupy the region. In response to the loss of his demesne, Sforza sent his Milanese soldiers and Swiss pikemen against the city of Novara, placing the citadel under siege. As the blockade wore on and Louis's garrison came under increasing attacks, Charles VIII was defeated and compelled to abandon Naples, ordering a retreat north from Italy. When the French arrived in Asti, the king ordered relief forces dispatched to Novara to break the investment. At the approach of the large Valois army, Ludovico opened negotiations for a settlement, not willing to engage his undependable Swiss mercenaries in battle. In the ensuing treaty the Orleans duke was forced to withdraw from Novara and the French regime pledged not to support his quest for Milan, while Sforza agreed to respect the boundaries of Asti and accept Louis's local rule.

After the signing of the treaty with Milan, the Duke of Orleans rejoined the Valois army as it resumed the march north and at the end of October crossed the Alps into France. He renewed his close association with Charles VIII and participated in the regime's council while assuming the governorship of Normandy. As he ruled his private lands, in December 1495 the dauphin, Charles Orland, died and the Orleans duke once again became the acknowledged heir to the crown. Two years later, Queen Anne gave birth to another son, which threatened Louis's inheritance right. However, when the new dauphin died a month later Louis was recognized as the monarch's successor. As he continued to faithfully serve the Valois court, in April 1498 at the Amboise Chateau Charles VIII accidentally hit his head on a low beam, falling into a coma. When he died several hours later Louis was proclaimed king. On May 27, 1498, he was anointed at Rheims Cathedral at age thirty-eight in a grand ceremony of secular and spiritual splendor and pomp.

The king consolidated his government without opposition while confirming many of the appointments of Charles VIII and naming his friends and allies to offices in his court. To rule the kingdom, he created a new high council of his close and trusted advisors which initiated sweeping reforms to the financial and judicial systems, reviving the economy and ending costly corruption. To provide a more responsive and efficient administration, the number of regional Parliaments was increased and the tax burden reduced. The measures were widely popular throughout the realm, resulting in an expansion in the economy and a growing prosperity.

Several months after his coronation at Rheims, Louis XII began negotiations with the dowager queen, Anne, for their marriage. Under the terms of her marital contract, if Charles VIII died without a male heir she committed to marry his successor. On August 18, 1498, Anne pledged to honor the terms of the treaty, agreeing to the union with Louis XII. Following her acceptance, the king immediately sent envoys to the Holy See, seeking an annulment of his marriage with Jeanne. Pope Alexander VI, who wanted to gain the goodwill of the new regime, approved the establishment of a papal council to hear the petition. In October the Papal Court met in Tours, where Louis XII claimed a too close blood relationship and non-consummation of his marriage with the queen as justification for the divorce. The hearings lasted for over two months before the papal inquisition voted in the monarch's favor. Jeanne yielded to the ruling without protest and was appointed royal governor for the duchy of Berry. Two years later she withdrew from public life and founded the religious Order of the Annonciades, which was devoted to aiding the poor and sick. Her death in 1505 was soon followed by reports of numerous miracles and healings, which were attributed to those who prayed at her tomb. In 1950 Pope Pius XII granted Jeanne sainthood.

Following his legal separation from Queen Jeanne, in February 1499 Louis XII and Anne of Brittany were married in the cathedral at Nantes. After the wedding the king abandoned his debauchery and became devoted to his new wife. She became an influential and trusted advisor and they established a loving and supportive relationship. The queen continued to defend the rights of Brittany and frequently intervened against her husband's policy in support of her duchy. Louis XII and Anne had two daughters, Claude and Renee, but no surviving male issue.

The first two years of Louis XII's kingship were devoted to asserting the authority of his rule and initiating financial and judicial reforms. To expand the economy, further measures were introduced to improve commerce and agriculture. With France at peace and steadily returning to prosperity, the kingdom became the most powerful and wealthy in Europe. With his reign secure the Valois king began to direct his policy toward the conquest of the duchy of Milan to enforce his hereditary right from his grandmother, Valentina Visconti. To protect his frontiers against foreign invasion during his absence in Lombardy, he pursued a diplomatic campaign to negotiate non-aggression treaties with his neighboring realms. An agreement was signed with Duke Philip of Burgundy, ensuring peace in northern France. The Treaty of Etaples negotiated by Charles VIII with England was renewed, guaranteeing security in the western fiefdoms. To guard the southern region, a treaty of friendship was ratified with Ferdinand II and Isabella of Spain, while the Holy Roman emperor, Maximilian I, pledged to respect the eastern border.

With France's borders protected from the threat of foreign attack, Louis XII's diplomatic initiative was directed at securing Italian allies for his invasion. After prolonged negotiations a treaty was signed with Doge Agostino Barbarigo of Venice, who pledged to supply an army for an attack against eastern Milan. An agreement for military support was made with Pope Alexander VI, who promised papal troops for the war in return for a fiefdom for his son, Cesare Borgia. To facilitate the advance through Italy the king's cousin, Duke Philibert II of Savoy, granted him unimpeded access through his duchy for the payment of an annual pension.

After securing allies for the Milan campaign, Louis XII began military preparations by first collecting a large treasury to finance the war. Funds were borrowed from the nobles and church while a general tax increase generated additional revenues. In early August 1499 the Valois army of over twenty-five thousand began the advance into Italy, using the king's county of Asti as an assembly point. Under the direct command of Marshal Gian Trivulaio, the French marched into western Milan encountering little opposition and quickly occupying many towns and castles. As the marshal continued his offensive, the Venetians attacked the eastern region of the duchy to reinforce the initiative of Louis XII. Opposed by two formidable military forces, the Milanese duke abandoned his capital, fleeing to the protection of Emperor Maximilian I. Deserted by their ruler, the council of Milan began negotiations for the submission of the city and on September 17 signed the surrender agreement. The monarch made his triumphant entrance into Milan on October 6, receiving the homage of the population. To protect his conquest, he garrisoned the duchy's strategic towns and fortresses with his troops and returned the Sforza family's usurped privileges and properties to gain the support and favor of the local residents. The Valois king remained for the next six weeks, establishing his regime and creating a new government while appointing his allies and friends to high offices in the ruling council.

With his regime in Milan secured, in late November 1499 Louis XII returned to France, dismissing the regency council and taking personal control of the kingdom. However, soon after his departure from Lombardy, the French government initiated a reign of suppression and brutality, giving cause for revolt by the Milanese residents. As the dissent spread, Ludovico began to raise an army of Swiss mercenaries with financial support from Maximilian I to reassert his ducal authority. In January 1500 he advanced his troops into the duchy unopposed. As his Swiss forces approached the capital, on January 25 the local population rose in rebellion, forcing the Valois council and garrison to flee from Milan, allowing Duke Ludovico Sforza to again assume the ducal throne.

Despite the retreat from Italy, Louis XII remained determined to enforce his blood rights to Milan and by March had reinforced his Italian army with additional cavalry and a contingent of mercenary pikemen from the Swiss Cantons. As his troops marched into the Milanese fiefdom of Novara, Sforza advanced with his Swiss forces to defend his demesne. However, when the Valois soldiers approached the assembled army of Sforza, his Canton mercenaries refused to fight their fellow Swiss and deserted the battlefield. Ludovico attempted to escape to Germany but was captured and later imprisoned in France at the chateau of Loches where he died in 1508. With the dissolution of the duke's militia, the French again secured control of the duchy. A new government was established with a separate military and civil governor appointed to rule, while a Parliament was created with both French and Italian representatives to advise the regency administration. The viceroys acted aggressively to curb the violence and abuses of the occupation troops while securing the crown's authority. Under the reign of the co-governors, commercial and agriculture activities revived and slowly the economy returned to prosperity. A large army was stationed in Milan to maintain peace as the population accepted the new Valois sovereignty.

After the reconquest of Milan, Louis XII began to prepare for further expansion in Italy with the seizure of Naples. The treaties with the papacy and Venice were renewed, assuring their loyalty, additional troops and money for the campaign. Negotiations were initiated with Ferdinand II of Spain, who was supporting his cousin, King Frederick IV of Naples, with soldiers and a sizeable subsidy. Confronted with the overwhelming military might of the Valois alliance and eager to expand his presence in Italy, the Spanish king abandoned his cousin and signed the Treaty of Grenada. Under the accord, the two sovereigns agreed to jointly capture Naples and partition it between their two crowns with Louis XII gaining control of the northern half, including the capital and title of king. Under the command of Lord Bernard Stewart of Aubigny, in May 1501 the French force of over fifteen thousand, with a strong contingent of Swiss mercenaries, began the advance from France down the Italian peninsula to Naples. In July he invaded the Neapolitan kingdom, meeting only scattered opposition and entered the capital in the following month. While Stewart secured Valois power in the north, Gonzalo de Cordoba, who had earlier driven the occupation forces of Charles VIII from Naples, returned from Spain with an army to take supremacy over the southern fiefs.

Following the conquest of the Naples kingdom, Louis XII established his local government by appointing Duke Louis d'Armagnac of Nemours as viceroy. However, he was an inept and corrupt ruler whose administration soon alienated the Neapolitan population. Under his governorship, relations with Gonzalo rapidly deteriorated as they argued over their respective zones of occupation. To enforce their rights to Capitanata, the Spanish attacked the French garrisons, driving them from the fiefdom. As the border dispute escalated into war, in the summer of 1502 Louis XII returned to Italy with reinforcements and personally defeated Cordoba to reestablish his power over the kingdom.

With his authority over Naples secured, Louis XII reappointed the Duke of Nemours as governor and returned to France, leaving the Spanish in control of a small enclave on the east coast. While the French attempted to consolidate the king's power over the Neapolitan realm, Ferdinand II sent reinforcements to Gonzalo de Cordoba with orders to renew the war. Advancing from his enclave, in April 1503 he launched a counteroffensive against the Valois occupation forces, overpowering them at the second battle of Seminara and on April 21 at Cerignola. During the encounter at Cerignola, Cordoba's army of eight thousand, supported with a strong contingent of arquebusiers, occupied the high ground in a well fortified position and was opposed by a much larger French force under Louis d'Armagnac. The battle began with the charges of the Valois cavalry, which were repulsed by heavy cannon fire. During the assault, d'Armagnac was killed by the arquebusiers and his soldiers soon began to retreat in disarray as the Spanish infantry counterattacked to totally overwhelm the French. Following the defeat, the Spanish quickly seized the Valois occupied towns and strongholds, forcing the remnants of the French military to withdraw to the northern fortress of Gaeta to await a relief army.

Following de Cordoba's defeat of the French, Louis XII quickly organized a new army for the reconquest of Naples under Marshal Louis II la Tremoille. In July the marshal traveled over the Alps into Italy. After his arrival in Rome, he was compelled to delay his march to Naples to defend Pope Alexander VI from the danger of a local rebellion by dissident Roman residents. After a prolonged stay in Rome, la Tremoille advanced south toward the Garigliano River but was blocked by the Spanish. In December he was outmaneuvered in a surprise night attack and compelled to retreat, abandoning the defenders at Gaeta. With the threat of a relief army thwarted, de Cordoba laid siege against Gaeta. Without any hope of rescue, the garrison commander soon asked for terms and under the ensuing accord agreed to withdraw from Naples. In September 1504 Louis XII ratified the Treaty of Blois with Ferdinand II, giving up all French claims to Naples for an indemnity. The failed attempt to conquer the southern Italian kingdom resulted in a loss of French prestige and dominance in European affairs, while also weakening the realm's military might and wealth.

Louis XII's marriage to Anne resulted in the birth of two daughters but no surviving male heir. After the queen gave birth to a stillborn son in 1502 there was little probability that the sovereign would have a direct successor. To secure the continued rule of the Valois dynasty, negotiations were pursued for the accession to the crown of the king's cousin, Francis of Angouleme. In 1505 a secret marital agreement was signed, binding his eldest daughter, Claude, to the heir presumptive. Francis was taken under the care and protection of the royal court and provided a household at the chateau of Clos-Luce in Amboise. To prepare him for his assumption of power, he was closely associated with the governing council and later commanded the army.

While Louis XII had lost sovereignty over the kingdom of Naples after reigning for three years, the French retained control over the Italian fiefs of Milan, Genoa and Asti. However, in 1506 the Genoese revolted, overthrowing the Valois administration and murdering the local garrison troops. A new Genoese government was established with a doge elected to rule. To reassert his authority by force of arms, in the following year the French king personally mustered his army of cavalry and Swiss pikemen in Asti and advanced against the rebels. As he approached Genoa, the doge fled and the rogue council quickly began peace negotiations.

Louis XII entered the city, receiving the pledges of fealty from the population and reestablishing his local regime, appointing Raoul de Lannoy as viceroy. Genoa was annexed directly to France and the residents compelled to pay an indemnity for their rebellion. After the subjugation of the uprising, the monarch traveled to Milan to renew his bond of friendship and loyalty with the duchy.

In September 1506 the balance of power in Europe shifted to France's favor with the death of Duke Philip of Burgundy and the succession of his six-year-old son, Charles. A regency council was created by his grandfather, Maximilian I, to govern the Burgundian demesne and his daughter, Margaret of Austria, was appointed as guardian for Charles. Margaret was a skilled politician and as governor pursued a policy of peace between Louis XII and the Habsburgs, acting as intermediary between her father and the French court.

Under the rule of the new regent in the Low Countries, relations between France and the imperial empire steadily improved. The two realms soon discovered a mutual threat in the Republic of Venice, whose western expansion into Lombardy had usurped lands where the Habsburg and Valois regimes had territorial claims and ambitions. With the support and encouragement of Margaret, in December 1508 negotiations between France, Ferdinand II of Spain and the emperor resulted in the Treaty of Cambrai directed at halting the aggression of Venice. Pope Julius II later joined the league to advance the Holy See's rights against the Republic of Saint Mark. Julius II was born Giuliano della Rovere on December 5, 1443, near the Italian town of Savona and was the son of Rafaelo della Rovere and Theodora Manerola. He followed his uncle, Pope Sixtus IV, into the priesthood and was educated by the Franciscan Order. Through the influence of his uncle, Giuliano was appointed a cardinal and served as captain general of the papal army. He later was named papal legate to France and the Netherlands. Through his military, administrative and diplomatic skills, the cardinal acquired great wealth, prestige and power. Julius II was elected to the papacy in 1503, following the death of Pius III. He was a shrewd self-serving politician and skilled military captain who was resolved to the aggrandizement of new fiefs. Following his assumption of the throne, he reasserted the Church of Rome's supremacy over the ecclesiastic princedoms previously seized by the Borgia family of Alexander VI and was determined to regain control over Bologna and Romagna. While Julius II aggressively pursued a policy of expansion, he was a patron of Renaissance art, music and literature. He began construction of the new Saint Peter's Basilica and sponsored many works by Raphael and Michangelo while commissioning the painting of the ceiling in the Sistine Chapel.

In early 1509 Louis XII began preparations for war against Venice, amassing an army of over twenty thousand and in April crossing the Alps to Milan. While he made final plans for the offensive into the Venetian occupied region of eastern Lombardy, Pope Julius II demanded the withdrawal of Doge Leonardo Loredan's soldiers from the Papal States. The Saint Mark Republic ignored the ultimatum, giving just cause to the declaration of war. In May Louis XII personally led the French against the Venetians to ignite the War of the Cambrai League. As he advanced into the republic's mainland territory, his troops encountered only scattered resistance. However, after the French captured the fief of Perugie, the doge sent his mercenaries to defend his demesne and on May 14 the two rivals clashed at Agnadello. In the ensuing battle, Louis XII isolated a large force of Venetians commanded by Bartolomeo d'Alviano, destroying much of his army. Following the decisive victory, the fortified towns of Cremona, Crema and Brescia were quickly seized. With the defeat of Doge Loredan's mercenaries, the Valois king occupied eastern Lombardy and in September returned to France with his enhanced power and prestige recognized by the European courts.

While the League of Cambrai succeeded in forcing the Venetians from their mainland possessions, the unifying bond for the alliance was now shattered and soon dissolved. Fearing the domination of French power in northern Italy, in February 1510 Julius II signed a separate peace with Doge Loredan and rescinded the papal interdict against Venice. To further isolate France from its allies, he negotiated a treaty with the Swiss Confederation, denying the use of their mercenaries to Louis XII and offered the investiture of Naples to Ferdinand II to detach him from the league.

After the dissolution of the Cambrai League, in the summer of 1510 Pope Julius II invaded the duchy of Ferrara in pursuit of his territorial ambitions. With his demesne threatened, Duke Alfonso I appealed to the Valois ruling council for military support. Alfonso was born on July 21, 1476, at Subiaco and was the eldest son and heir of Ercole I d'Este and Leonora of Naples. After the death of his father in 1505, Alfonso I succeeded to the ducal throne. He joined the Cambrai League and remained a loyal ally of the French regime. Alfonso I was a great patron of the Renaissance movement and sponsored the works of Giovanni Bellini and Titian while amassing a large collection of paintings. The duke also encouraged renowned musicians and composers to come to his court, creating a distinguished musical center known throughout Europe. After the pope seized the Ferraran city of Bologna, Louis XII sent troops to buttress the duke's war effort. On May 23, 1511, the combined Franco-Ferraran army under the command of Alfonso I counterattacked the Holy See's occupation forces, compelling Julius II to retreat from the city. However, despite the triumph at Bologna, neither rival possessed the military might to force a decisive victory as the war entered a stalemate.

With his offensive against Ferrara stalled, in 1511 Pope Julius II formed a new Holy League with Ferdinand II of Spain and Venice to force the French out of Lombardy. In February 1512 the combined papal–Spanish army of Ramon of Cardona, viceroy of Naples, advanced against Bologna, besieging the stronghold. With the strategic city under threat of seizure, the newly appointed French general, Gaston of Foix, Duke of Nemours, marched his forces, augmented with a contingent of Ferraran troops led by Alfonso I, to relieve the investment. Gaston was the nephew of Louis XII and after assuming command of the army energized the Valois's war effort through the force of his charismatic personality and military skills. By traveling rapidly to Bologna, Foix outmaneuvered the allies and broke their siege. Following his victory, he attacked the city of Brescia, storming the citadel and overwhelming the Venetian defenders.

The two quick defeats of the league compelled Julius II to abandon his conquests in Ferrara and Lombardy and retreat to the safety of the Papal States, giving the Nemours duke control over much of northern Italy. To force a decisive encounter with the league, the French advanced against the papal city of Ravenna on the Adriatic coast. At the approach of Foix, the papal–Spanish commander, Ramon of Cardona, established a strong defensive position behind a barrier of entrenchments and obstacles. In the ensuing battle on April 11, Gaston skillfully placed his artillery in the rear of the allies, forcing Cardona to abandon the field with large casualties. However, the Valois regime suffered a significant loss when Gaston Foix was killed leading his cavalry in an attack against the retreating Spanish rearguard. With his death Louis XII lost his most talented and energetic commander, seriously weakening his war effort.

Following Louis XII's victory at Ravenna, Emperor Maximilian I and the Swiss Cantons agreed to unite with the papacy's alliance, fearing the presence of French military might in northern Italy. In early May 1512 a large force of Swiss infantry commanded by Cardinal Matthaus Schiner joined the Venetians near Verona and together they marched against the French in Milan. Schiner was the bishop of Novara and papal legate for Italy and Germany.

He was a skilled diplomat and as the personal envoy of Julius II was instrumental in the Swiss uniting with the Holy League.

After the death of Foix, the Valois king named Lord Jacques of la Palice to command his troops in Italy. However, when the papacy's allies advanced with overwhelming military strength, Jacques was compelled to withdraw from eastern Lombardy. Pope Julius II gave command of his Papal forces to his nephew, Duke Francesco Maria della Rovere of Urbino, who quickly restored Bologna and Ravenna to his uncle's rule. Driven out of the Papal States, la Palice was compelled to retreat toward Milan, but Cardinal Schiner with his Swiss troops outmaneuvered him and killed or captured much of his army. After the league's triumph, the remnants of the French troops were forced to abandon Italy and return to France. Following the withdrawal of la Palice, the cities of Milan and Genoa rebelled against their Valois garrisons, overthrowing Louis XII's sovereignty. In December 1512 after the defeat of the French, Cardinal Schiner placed Massimiliano Sforza, son of Ludovico, on the ducal throne of Milan to end Louis XII's rule over Lombardy.

In the aftermath of his expulsion from Italy and the election of the pro–French Pope Leo X to the papacy, the Valois king renewed his quest for Milan by force of arms. He recruited a new army with Marshal Louis II la Tremoille appointed as captain general and in May the invasion was launched. After crossing the Alps and entering the duchy of Milan, the French encountered only light and scattered resistance. As the marshal advanced against the ducal capital, the local population rebelled against the harsh policies and excessive taxes of the Sforza regime. The duke's Swiss mercenaries were unable to contain the rebels and withdrew from the city, marching to the protection of Novara Castle. La Tremoille reoccupied Milan unopposed and after garrisoning the stronghold pursued the Leaguers to Novara. The citadel was besieged by the French and an intense cannon bombardment begun. While the Valois soldiers were occupied with the investment, the Swiss Cantons sent a large relief force to Novara to break the ongoing attack. At the approach of the powerful Leaguer's army, la Tremoille was compelled to abandon his siege against Novara. However, as he retreated the Swiss mounted a surprise night assault, catching him unprepared and destroying the majority of his infantry. The defeat at Novara resulted in the loss of all the recent conquests and Louis XII was once again vanquished from Lombardy.

Encouraged by the defeat of the Valois regime in Milan, in April 1513 Henry VIII signed an alliance treaty with Spain and Emperor Maximilian I for a joint invasion of France. In May the Tudor monarchy began its initiative against Louis XII by sending a formidable army to Calais under the command of Henry VIII. Mustering their troops the English advanced into Artois, besieging the fortress at Therouanne, which protected the entrances to Ile de France and Paris. While the English king continued to enforce the investment, Louis XII sent a large force of cavalry to support the garrison but it was intercepted and destroyed by Maximilian I at Guinegate. After a two-month blockade, with their food stocks exhausted and no relief possible from the Valois realm, the defenders were compelled to surrender. The loss of the stronghold was followed by the capture of the bishopric of Tournai after only token resistance. By the end of the campaigning season, the English had seized two strategic castles and consolidated their hold on Artois.

As the English attacked northern France, in September 1513 the Swiss Cantons launched an invasion from the east, besieging the Burgundian capital of Dijon. Lacking adequate troop strength to resist the Swiss onslaught and with the king unable to send a relief army, the crown's governor was compelled to open negotiations for terms. In the resulting Treaty of Dijon, the city government agreed to renounce all claims to Lombardy and pay a large indemnity, while the Cantons pledged to abandon the recent conquest and peacefully retreat.

Following his defeat in Lombardy, Louis XII remained determined to assert his sovereignty rights to Milan and renounced the terms of the Treaty of Dijon. However, the English still maintained a large army in Artois, threatening Ile de France and Paris. In the summer of 1514 the Valois king began negotiations with London for the settlement of their ongoing war. Under the ensuing treaty, Louis XII agreed to pay a large indemnity and recognize the recent English conquests, while Henry VIII pledged to withdraw his troops and honor the status quo. Their accord was secured by the marriage of the sister of the Tudor king, Mary Rose, to Louis XII. The ceremony took place by proxy in August and the new queen finally arrived at the French court in October.

With his borders protected, the French king began preparations for a new invasion of Milan. However, he was growing increasingly weak and ill from the stresses of war and state and the effects of gout. Louis XII died on January 1, 1515, in Paris at age fifty-two and a reign of sixteen years. At his death he had no male successor and was succeeded to the French crown by his cousin, Francis of Angouleme, as Francis I.

Sources

Baumgartner. *Louis XII.*   Knecht. *The Valois Kings of France 1328–1589.*

Francis I, 1494–1515–1547

In January 1515 Louis XII died without a direct heir and the Valois throne was assumed by his cousin, Francis of Angouleme, who reigned for thirty-two years as the sixth Renaissance king of France. Francis was born on September 12, 1494, at the castle of Cognac and was the only son of Count Charles of Angouleme and Louise, daughter of the duke of Savoy. The Angouleme House was a minor branch of the ruling Valois dynasty and the young lord was not in the direct line of succession. In January 1496 Count Charles died and his son inherited his lands and titles under the guardianship of his mother. While Francis remained in Cognac under the care and custody of Louise, in 1498 Charles VIII died and was succeeded by Louis of Orleans. The new monarch was without a male heir and as his closest relative, Francis, was recognized as dauphin. He was taken under the direct protection of Louis XII and provided a household at the chateau of Clos-Luce in Amboise. Under the tutelage of Louise of Savoy, distinguished scholars were employed as tutors for her two children and they received a well-rounded humanist education. Francis and his older sister, Marguerite, were both gifted and dedicated students, excelling in their studies of reading, writing, geography, religion, history, science and languages to include Latin, Spanish and Italian. At Amboise they were exposed to the social graces of music, dancing and court etiquette. Marguerite later became a valued advisor to her brother and acted as an intermediary with foreign powers. She was a generous patron of Renaissance writers and artists, while gaining widespread acclaim for her personal poetry and plays. Marguerite supported reforms to the Catholic Church and used her influence with Francis I to protect heretics during the growing Protestant Reformation movement. While continuing his academic education, the dauphin received military training from renowned masters of arms in the weapons of a knight, becoming skilled in archery, fencing and equestrianship. He developed a special interest in field games, hunting and the sport of jousting. As Francis grew into adulthood, he was physically described as unusually tall at over six feet with a firm muscular frame and imposing regal bearing.

Louis XII's marriage to Queen Anne had resulted in the birth of two daughters but no surviving male successor. As the acknowledged heir, in 1505 preparations were begun for Francis's future assumption of power. To provide a direct and uncontested line to the monarchy, a marital agreement was signed binding the Angouleme count to the king's eldest daughter, Claude. He became more closely associated with the governing council and later assumed command of the military. By 1514 through the force of his energetic and charismatic personality, he was widely accepted as the dauphin and played an increasingly important role in the regime as the health of Louis XII began to fail. In 1514 Francis was married to Claude of France, solidifying his bond to the ruling Valois family and the kingship. In December the sovereign grew weaker from the stresses of war and state and the effects of gout, dying on New Year's Day 1515. Francis I was readily recognized as king and on January 25, 1515, rode to the Rheims Cathedral for his enthronement and anointment by Archbishop Robert Lenoncourt. Francis I entered the cathedral dressed in a long tunic of white damask edged in ermine. After taking the oath of office, he replaced his jacket with the coronation robe of blue decorated with gold fleur-de-les and was anointed with holy oil by Archbishop Lenoncourt. The French king then received the sword of Charlemagne and the archbishop placed the gold crown covered with large sapphires, emeralds and rubies on his head. Following the ceremony, the French ladies, lords and dignitaries shouted, "Long life to the King."

After his coronation ceremony, Francis I asserted his authority over the kingdom and established his ruling government without opposition. In 1515 France was at peace with the European courts and steadily returning to prosperity through the economic reforms of Louis XII. With his reign secure the king directed his policy toward the renewal of Valois expansionism in Italy. At the time of his succession, all the former French possessions in Lombardy had been lost with the duchy of Milan under the rule of Duke Massimiliano Sforza and in Genoa an independent republic had been created. While a youth in Amboise, Francis I had been exposed to stories of military glory and the magnificence and grandeur of Renaissance Italy from army veterans, travelers and clerics becoming determined to personally expand French power into the region by force of arms. Through his great grandmother, Valentina Visconti, he had a blood claim to the duchy of Milan and after solidifying his kingship began preparations for the conquest of the Lombardy fief to enforce his hereditary rights and reimpose Valois supremacy.

To protect his borders from foreign attack during his absence in Italy, the king renewed the prior non-aggression accords of Louis XII with the European powers and under the Treaty of Paris received the pledge of neutrality from the new Duke of Burgundy, Charles of Habsburg. To secure an ally for the conquest of Milan, a military alliance was negotiated with Doge Leonardo Loredan of Venice, who agreed to launch an offensive campaign in support of the French war effort. A regency government was formed to rule the realm with Louise of Savoy appointed as regent. In August 1515 a formidable invasion force of forty thousand troops, augmented with a large contingent of German landsknechts, mustered in southern France, crossing the Alps into Lombardy to expel Duke Massimiliano Sforza from power. Francis I advanced into the Milanese duchy, defeating the papal cavalry commanded by Prospero Colonna at Villafranca and compelling the allies of Duke Sforza to retreat to the capital. Colonna was a veteran of the Franco-Italian wars and earlier had fought against the Valois armies of both Charles VIII and Louis XII in Naples. As reward for his faithful service to the papacy, he was granted numerous fiefs, becoming a great feudal lord in southern Italy.

Following the victory at Villafranca, Francis I continued his advance to the east, reaching the environs of Milan near the small village of Marignano in early September unopposed. As the French established their fortified camp, on September 13 the Swiss under the command of Cardinal Matthaus Schiner marched from the city to defend the regime of Massimiliano Sforza. As Schiner approached Marignano, the French deployed into battle formation to thwart the advance of the mercenaries. The ensuing battle began in the afternoon with the inconclusive bloody fighting lasting until late in the night. In the morning Cardinal Schiner reorganized his infantry and charged the French lines, quickly breaking the left flank. As the king's position became seriously threatened, a relief force of mercenary cavalry under the employ of Doge Loredan arrived and counterattacked to drive the Swiss pikemen from the field. Schiner and the shattered remnants of his army retreated to Sforza Castle, where Massimiliano was forced to submit, going into exile in France. On September 16 Francis I entered the city in triumph to reimpose Valois supremacy over the duchy of Milan.

Francis I established a new government in Milan, appointing the duke of Bourbon, Charles III, to rule as viceroy. Charles III was born at Montpensier on February 17, 1490 and was the second son of Gilbert, count of Montpensier, and Clara Gonzaga of Mantua. When his elder brother, Louis II, died in 1501 he inherited the family lands and title of count. Four years later Charles married Suzanne of Bourbon and through her assumed control of her duchy of Bourbon. He was a veteran of the Italian wars, gaining widespread renown and acclaim for his distinguished service to the Valois crown. The Bourbon Duke was the commander of the vanguard during the battle of Marignano, winning recognition for his military skills and bravery from Francis I, who rewarded him with the governorship of Milan. However, as the administration attempted to assert its power, Pope Leo X, the Swiss and Emperor Maximilian I still posed a danger to French sovereignty. To protect his victory at Marignano, the Valois king negotiated a treaty with eight of the Swiss Cantons, gaining their withdrawal from Italy and neutralizing their threat. Peace talks were begun with the papacy and Leo X agreed to meet in December with Francis I at Bologna to find a settlement. Under the ensuing Concordat of Bologna, the French pledged to void the Pragmatic Sanctions, which had been previously issued by Charles VII to restrict the Holy See's control over the French church, while the king was granted the right to name local clergy. Both regimes promised to respect the peace and Francis I's recent conquests were acknowledged by Rome.

With his gains in Italy solidified and Charles III's government established, in January 1516 Francis I returned to France spending much of the year touring the kingdom as he slowly made his way to Paris. While the royal court traveled to the capital, in March Emperor Maximilian I invaded Lombardy, advancing against Milan. However, as his army began siege operations against the city, he unexpectedly abandoned his largely Swiss mercenary troops, leaving Italy. Without the presence of the emperor, the attack against Milan failed and the Swiss Cantons negotiated a separate peace with the Valois regime, pledging to evacuate Lombardy for the payment of an annual subsidy and not take up arms against the French. After the defeat of his offensive, the emperor agreed to open peace talks with Francis I and in March 1517 the Treaty of Cambrai was signed, which further guaranteed the Valois conquest of Milan. With France at peace, a period of economic growth and prosperity followed with significant expansions in commerce and agriculture.

In January 1519 Maximilian I died, creating a threat to the security of France and its possessions in Italy. Charles of Burgundy was the Habsburg heir of the emperor and already ruled Spain, the Low Countries and Naples. With his election as Holy Roman emperor, the Valois kingdom would be surrounded on its borders by a powerful and unified hostile rival. To protect his monarchy and gain the prestige associated with the Holy Roman crown, Francis I mounted a political campaign to secure his appointment. The formal election procedure had been established in 1356 by Emperor Charles IV with the issuance of his Golden Bull, which named seven German princes to choose the new emperor. However, the selection process became subjected to widespread abuse and corruption with the electors demanding bribes and favors for their votes. The French king sent numerous envoys under the leadership of Lord William of Bonnivet into Germany armed with chests of gold to influence the decision. Nevertheless, when the election was held in June, Charles V was chosen as imperial emperor. After his succession to the throne of the Holy Roman Empire, a lifelong rivalry began between Francis I and the emperor.

As the danger of hostilities between Francis I and the empire escalated, France and England were politically drawn closer together. The Valois regime needed an ally against the formidable Habsburgs and aggressively pursued improvements in relations with the Tudor council. Negotiations were begun with Henry VIII's chief envoy, Cardinal Thomas Wolsey, resulting in a treaty that committed both governments to honor the peace and defend the other if attacked. The accord was ratified by the personal meeting of Francis I and Henry VIII on June 7, 1520, at the Field of the Cloth of Gold at Balinghem near the English enclave of Calais. It was a gala event lasting over two weeks with huge feasts, music, jousting tournaments, military games and archery displays. Elaborate arrangements were made for the tents of the two kings and their nobles with so much gold and silk thread used that the meeting was named after the expensive cloth. Francis I ordered a magnificent tent of gold topped with a golden statue of Saint Michael killing the dragon. However, the summit did not produce any meaningful agreements but only served as an opportunity for both courts to display their wealth and power.

Following his election to the crown of the Holy Roman Empire, Charles V still lacked his formal investiture by the papacy. As he initiated preparations to meet with Pope Leo X for his coronation, in October 1520 the Valois king began to increasingly fear his presence in Italy with the imperial army and the opportunity to expel the French from Milan. To keep the emperor occupied in the Low Countries, Francis I encouraged and supported Lord Robert III of Marck to invade the Habsburg demesne. Robert III had fought with the army of Louis XII in the wars in Italy and later had participated in the Milan campaign of Francis I, winning special recognition for his bravery and skills at the battle of Marignano. When the lord of Marck led his campaign into Flanders, Charles V was forced to delay his imperial anointment in Rome to mount a counterattack to reimpose his rule. As the prospects for war between France and the empire escalated, in June 1521 Cardinal Wolsey, acting as papal legate, convened a peace conference in Calais. However, the meeting ended in failure and in August the Habsburg troops launched an incursion into northeastern France, besieging Mezieres. In defense of his territory, Francis I assembled a large relief force advancing to break the investment. The conflict dragged on inconclusively into November when the imperialists withdrew to winter quarters as the weather deteriorated.

While the war in the north remained at a stalemate, in Milan Charles III of Bourbon was replaced as Valois governor by Odet of Foix, viscount of Lautrec. However, the new administration abandoned the peace and reconciliation policies of Bourbon and began an initiative of repression and brutality against the local population. As the threat of revolt grew, Charles V sent a Swiss army to seize the duchy. When his mercenary troops approached the capital, the residents rose up in rebellion, expelling the French garrison and compelling Lautrec to desert the region. In the following spring, Francis I attempted to regain control of the

Milanese duchy, dispatching additional soldiers to buttress Viscount Lautrec's campaign. With his army strengthened, Foix assembled his forces and marched to reassert French power by attacking the citadel at Milan. However, his sorties against the heavily fortified castle walls were repulsed by the garrison led by Prospero Colonna. After their unsuccessful assaults, the French abandoned their offensive against Milan and traveled south to besiege the weaker protected city of Pavia. Following the withdrawal of Lautrec, papal troops were rushed to the aid of Prospero Colonna. With his army reinforced Colonna advanced against the French at Pavia, forcing Odet of Foix to lift his siege. As Lautrec retreated toward Monza, on April 27 he mounted an attack against the well defended position of Colonna at La Bicocca. In the ensuing battle, the Valois king's forces were routed and compelled to evacuate Italy.

Despite the failure of Lautrec's campaign, Francis I remained defiant in his pursuit of the conquest of Milan and in the summer of 1523 assembled his forces for a third invasion. In August he appointed his mother as regent and traveled to Lyon to assume command of the offensive. However, he was compelled to return north to central France and personally intervene against the threatened rebellion of Duke Charles III of Bourbon. Two years earlier the duke's wife had died and in a property dispute with the Valois regime her lands had been seized by the crown. In response to the loss of his inheritance, Charles III secretly negotiated an agreement with Emperor Charles V, pledging to lead an attack against southern France with his private troops and German mercenaries.

While the defection of the Bourbon duke caused Francis I to remain in France to guard against a possible internal revolt, the royal army under the command of Admiral William Gouffier, lord of Bonnivet, traveled across the Alps into northern Italy. Lord Gouffier was a childhood friend of the king and favorite of the Valois court. He had first won widespread renown during the War of the Holy League for his military skills and bravery during the siege at Genoa in 1507 and later at the battle of Guinegate in northern France. In 1515 Bonnivet was appointed admiral of France by Francis I and served during the Italian campaigns. He was sent on several diplomatic missions for the regime to England and the Imperial Diet at Frankfurt. After advancing into Lombardy and crossing the Ticino River, the admiral forced the papal-imperial troops of Colonna to retreat to the protection of Milan. Marching to the capital the French besieged the formidable fortress but the defenses were too strong to be taken by storm. The lord of Bonnivet was compelled to spend the harsh winter in his investment lines, where his forces suffered from exposure, disease and constant harassing sorties from Colonna's garrison. As the initiative wore on, in April 1524 Charles V dispatched a powerful Spanish relief army from Naples to break the ongoing blockade. With his military strength greatly depleted by the prolonged attack against Milan and with the approach the Spanish, the admiral was compelled to abandon his campaign and withdraw from Italy. .

As the Bonnivet lord was besieging Milan, a powerful English army under the command of Charles Brandon, duke of Suffolk, attacked Picardy from Calais in support of Emperor Charles V's war effort. The duke advanced east into the Ile de France region, threatening the environs of Paris and laying waste to the countryside and towns. However, his initiative soon lost momentum, and with the approach of winter Brandon retreated to Calais. After the disappointment of Suffolk's campaign, in May 1524 the emperor and his ally, Henry VIII, entered into an agreement with Duke Charles III of Bourbon for a simultaneous three pronged invasion against France. In the early summer the duke began to assemble his forces around Genoa. To facilitate his advance into Provence, he negotiated a treaty with Lord Augustin Grimaldi of Monaco to use his lordship as a supply base for the incursion. Under their accord Monaco became a protectorate of the emperor and Grimaldi agreed to abandon his French alliance.

In July the Bourbon duke launched his offensive from Italy, initially meeting only limited opposition. However, both Charles V and the Tudor king failed to mount their attacks and without the backing of his allies and delayed by the prolonged siege against Marseille, Charles III's encroachment bogged down. As his supplies became exhausted and his troop strength grew increasingly depleted by disease, desertion and summer heat, he was compelled to abandon the invasion and withdraw to Italy.

Following the defeat of Charles III in Provence and with the imperial alliance of the emperor in shambles, the Valois king again renewed his quest for the ducal throne of Milan. In October 1524 the royal troops began to muster in southern France and after appointing Louise of Savoy as the head of his regency council, Francis I assumed personal command of the campaign. Crossing the Alps he advanced into Lombardy largely unchallenged. As his forces approached Milan, the imperial and papal garrison withdrew to join the army of the duke of Terranova at the fortress at Pavia, allowing the French to enter the city uncontested. While Francis I gained possession of Milan, the Spanish and imperial troops of Antonio of Leyva, duke of Terranova, in the city of Pavia still posed a threat to his control of Lombardy. Leyva was an experienced military commander, serving in the Spanish conquest of Grenada and later in the Italian wars. He participated in the battle of Ravenna, where he was wounded and in 1524 fought with Charles III of Bourbon in the unsuccessful invasion of Provence.

After garrisoning Milan, the monarch advanced against the allies and began investment operations against Pavia. The fortress was well protected on three sides by formidable walls and the Ticino River to the south, forcing the French to spend the winter in their siege lines where they were exposed to disease, harsh weather and skirmishing sorties from the allies. As the blockade continued, in February with his food supplies nearly exhausted Leyva launched a massed attack in desperation. He began his assault at dawn, catching the French by surprise. The Valois infantry was unable to muster into battle formation, despite a heroic cavalry charge led by Francis I. The king's foot soldiers struggled to mount a counterattack but were decimated by the firepower of the Spanish arquebusiers. The bloody battle lasted until noon, ending with the decisive defeat of the Valois army and the seizure of Francis I. French casualties were high with over eight thousand killed or captured, including Admiral Bonnivet along with many peers and nobles of the realm.

With Francis I held prisoner at the Italian castle of Cremona, Louise of Savoy began negotiations for his release with the imperial court. Charles V initially demanded the return of all French seized Burgundian lands, restoration of Charles III of Bourbon to his estates and renunciation of all Valois claims to Italy. On orders from her son, the terms were quickly rejected by Louise as too harsh. After three months at Cremona, in June 1525 the king was sent to Spain to better facilitate the fruitless discussions. He was given a small household in the Madrid Alcazar where the talks resumed. In the late autumn his sister, Marguerite, arrived in Spain to personally press for a resolution. However, Charles V remained defiant and in January the regent was forced to accept his conditions. Under the ensuing Treaty of Madrid, to secure the freedom of Francis I, his regime pledged to surrender Burgundy to the emperor, reinstate Charles III to his demesne, forfeit all rights to Italy and the king agreed to marry Charles V's sister, Eleanor of Austria. The treaty was guaranteed by the exchange of Francis I for his two sons as hostages. On March 17 the dauphin, Francis, and Henry, Duke of Orleans, were surrendered and the Valois king released after being held captive for over a year.

While Francis I was held prisoner in Madrid, in June 1524 Queen Claude died at age twenty-four. Despite being an arranged marriage for political and dynastic reasons, the king and Claude developed a close and caring relationship, in spite of his many amorous affairs.

As the daughter of Queen Anne of Brittany, she inherited her lands and after Claude's death the duchy was later annexed to France. The marriage resulted in seven children, including the dauphin, Francis, born in 1518.

After his return to France, Francis I assumed personal power from his mother's regency and quickly reasserted his royal authority. A new ruling council and court were appointed, replacing the many high nobles killed or captured at Pavia. Following the creation of the government, the regime launched an aggressive diplomatic campaign to repudiate the Treaty of Madrid. Francis I challenged the legality of the agreement, claiming the terms were imposed under duress and coercion. He offered a settlement in gold for the release of his two sons but Charles V refused to renegotiate any of the conditions of the accord. To force the emperor to free the dauphin and his brother for the payment of a ransom, the king formed the League of Cognac with Doge Andrea Gritti of Venice, Ippolito of Florence and Pope Clement VII. In response to the league's opposition to his rule, in late 1526 Charles V sent the imperial army under Charles III of Bourbon into Italy to force the pope from the league by invading the Papal States. However, the mostly Protestant German troops had not been paid for many months and in May 1527 they mutinied to pillage Rome. With the imperialists occupied with the prolonged sacking of Rome, in September Francis I again attacked Lombardy in pursuit of Milan. While the French occupied most of the duchy, they failed to capture the capital city. The war soon reached a stalemate and Francis I began to search for a peaceful resolution. Charles V was eager to reach a settlement with his eastern borders threatened by attacks from the Ottoman Empire and mounting hostilities in Germany from the Protestant Reformation. Finally in July 1529 the king's mother, Louise of Savoy, and the emperor's aunt, Margaret of Austria, personally intervened to negotiate a reconciliation. Under the ensuing Treaty of the Two Ladies, peace was restored between both realms, while Charles V abandoned his claim to Burgundy but received full recognition of his sovereignty over the Low Countries. Francis I pledged to repudiate his hereditary rights to Italy and pay a large payment in gold for the release of his two sons.

With the end of hostilities against the Holy Roman Empire, the French economy quickly revived and with the return of prosperity the Valois regime rebuilt its depleted coffers and military forces. The king's reign grew increasingly popular and his authority was readily accepted. While the kingdom was experiencing economic growth and political stability, in Germany the escalating Protestant movement increasingly endangered the security of Charles V's rule. In France the government largely ignored the local growing Huguenot religious reformers. However, in 1528 they became more belligerent against the doctrines and rituals of the Catholic Church. The monarch's sister, Marguerite, who exerted a strong influence over her brother, had taken an interest in the Protestants and persuaded him not to intervene. For the next five years he held the reactionary papist factions in check until the Day of the Placards. During the evening of October 17, 1534, radical Huguenots posted numerous placards throughout Paris and other large cities denouncing the papacy, the Catholic Church and its institutions. Many of the posters threatened violence against the Catholics and destruction of their churches. The followers of the Holy See became alarmed and began to attack known Protestants, resulting in rioting in Paris and the death of thousands of Huguenots. Francis I was compelled to abandon his policy of toleration, issuing decrees to suppress the heretics. Persecutions against the Protestants soon followed with many burned at the stake as heretics.

Under the terms of the Peace of the Two Ladies, in 1530 Francis I married the emperor's sister, Eleanor of Austria. She was the widow of Manuel I of Portugal and was sent to the Lisbon court in 1518 to facilitate friendship between the two realms. Eleanor was the eldest and favorite sister of Charles V and the French regime utilized her contacts and prestige with the imperial household to promote better relations. However, Francis I and the queen were ill suited to each other and their marriage was unhappy. The king continued his numerous adulterous affairs, developing a special relationship with Anne of Pisseleu, Duchess of Etampes. The duchess exerted a strong influence over Francis I, serving as his unofficial advisor and establishing her own political faction of nobles and clerics to direct Valois policy.

Following the signing of the Treaty of Madrid, Francis I remained determined to aggrandize Milan and directed his government's policy toward decreasing Charles V's power in Europe. In Germany the Lutheran princes became increasingly hostile to Habsburg intervention, forming the Schmalkaldic League in 1531 to defend their religious freedom and lands. Francis I encouraged and supported the league against the initiatives of the emperor, forging an alliance with the militant warlords. While interceding in Germany, the French formed a relationship with the Ottoman figurehead king of Hungary, John Zapolya, sponsoring his opposition against Charles V. Contacts were also established with the Ottoman Empire, exhorting Sultan Suleiman I to attack the imperialists on their eastern border. To improve relations with the Tudor court, the Valois king openly backed Henry VIII's divorce from the emperor's aunt, Catharine of Spain, and attempted to use his influence with Pope Clement VII to win his approval. Francis I's political campaigns succeeded in keeping Charles V distracted in Germany and against Ottoman expansion in the Balkans, while weakening him financially and militarily.

As relations between Francis I and Charles V grew increasingly belligerent, in 1535 Duke Francesco II Sforza of Milan died without leaving a direct heir, creating a succession dispute. Through his mother, Francis I held a hereditary right to the duchy of Savoy and invaded the northern Italian region to gain a base of operations to further his quest for the vacant crown of Milan. In May Emperor Charles V countered the threat to his Italian controlled territories by sending his imperial soldiers to force the French out of Savoy. After restoring Charles III to his ducal throne, in July 1536 the emperor declared war against France and launched an attack against Provence with a formidable military force. As the imperialists began to advance into southern France, Duke Anne Montmorency was appointed by Francis I to defend his realm. Anne was born on March 15, 1493, at the chateau of Chantilly and was the son of Guillaume Montmorency and Anne Pot. The Montmorency family was closely associated with the French crown through generations of faithful service, gaining wealth, lands and influence. Anne was a close childhood friend of the king and veteran of the Italian wars, fighting at Ravenna and winning repute at Marignano and Pavia for his battle skills and bravery. He was an influential member of the Valois court, serving as diplomat and statesman and in 1522 was named marshal of France. When the imperialists marched into France, the duke assumed command of the army and withdrew to Avignon, adopting a scorched earth strategy as he retreated. The imperialists were drawn away from their supply bases into a barren land, finding little shelter or food. As the summer wore on, the combined effects of heat, food shortages and disease depleted the emperor's troop strength. By September Charles V was compelled to abandon his campaign, returning to Italy with his army in shambles.

The Franco-Habsburg War was renewed in 1537, when Francis I sent his troops under the command of Duke Montmorency to invade Artois. The duke captured several cities that had been previously ceded to Charles V under the Peace of the Two Ladies. However, the imperialists launched a counteroffensive to reclaim much of the lost territory. The war dragged on with neither army able to force a decisive battle. A stalemate soon resulted as both realms became war weary with greatly depleted coffers. Under the sponsorship of Pope Paul III a truce was readily accepted in June 1538 by Charles V and the Valois king.

After the signing of the truce with the imperial emperor, the Valois regime began talks with the papacy and Charles V to find a permanent peace. The king's diplomatic initiative was directed by Montmorency, who pressed Paul III to personally intervene. At the encouragement of the French, the pope arranged the direct meeting between the two rivals at Aigues-Mortes near Nice in July. At their summit Francis I and Charles V expressed their mutual friendship and agreed to a ten year truce, while pledging to continue their deliberations for a lasting resolution. After the ratification of the Truce of Nice, relations between the French and imperial court remained cordial with frequent exchanges between envoys, as peace discussions were resumed. In late 1539 a tax rebellion erupted in Ghent and Charles V utilized his friendly relationship with the Valois court to negotiate his overland passage from Spain through France to the Flemish city. He was met at the border and personally escorted through the kingdom by Francis I. As they traveled north toward Flanders, the towns provided elaborate welcoming ceremonies and lavish entertainment of festivals, tournaments and banquets. The journey was planned by the Valois government to display the grandeur and magnificence of French Renaissance art, music and architecture. During the emperor's visit both monarchs renewed their promise of cooperation and determination to find a permanent settlement.

Several months after his arrival in Flanders, in March 1540 Charles V sent a peace agreement to Paris to resolve their ongoing dispute. He proposed the marriage of his daughter, Mary, to the king's son, Charles, with both jointly ruling Burgundy and Flanders, while the French regime renounced its claim to Milan. Francis I quickly rejected the offer in early April and suggested an alternative settlement, which gave him sovereignty over Milan. His treaty was ignored by the imperialists, while additional negotiations were continued until June. However, no resolution for the succession to Milan was found and in October when the emperor ceded the duchy to his son, Philip of Spain, the Valois council began preparations to renew the war with the Habsburgs.

Following the signing of the Nice Truce, the Valois kingdom utilized the resulting peace to rebuild its depleted treasury, military stores and army. As the threat of hostilities against the empire escalated, new diplomatic initiatives were launched to secure allies in Lutheran Germany and with Sultan Suleiman I. After the murder of two French envoys in Milan, Francis I accused the emperor of breaking the Truce of Nice and in March 1542 declared war. To force concessions from the Habsburgs, the French army advanced into Flanders but they encountered stiff resistance from the well prepared local troops, while a second attack against Perpignan in northern Spain under the command of the dauphin, Henry, failed to breach the fortress's defenses. The campaigning season of 1542 ended in disappointment for Francis I with only small gains achieved against the imperialists.

To buttress his war against Francis I, in February 1543 Charles V ratified an agreement with the Tudor king for a joint invasion of France. However, before the allies launched their offensive, the French renewed their attack against Flanders, seizing several large cities and ravaging the countryside. The emperor was forced to delay his campaign in support of Henry VIII to mount a counter initiative in the Netherlands, which recovered much of the lost territory. While the imperialists were driving the French back in Flanders, Henry VIII began a large pillaging raid into Artois, burning and destroying farms and towns to reinforce the war effort against Francis I. By the end of the campaigning season, the conflict had become stalemated as both rivals withdrew to winter quarters with only limited gains.

After two years of fruitless war, in late December 1543 Henry VIII and the emperor pledged to resume their joint invasion against France with the imperialists advancing from Germany and the English attacking from Calais into Picardy. In July Charles V launched his offensive, quickly overrunning Luxembourg and continuing into eastern France. The English army encountered little opposition, capturing much of Picardy and beginning investment operations against Boulogne. However, as the imperial forces marched deeper into the kingdom, they became bogged down by the unexpected defiant resistance of the garrison at Saint Dizier. Delayed by the long siege against the stronghold, the emperor's initiative lost momentum and with his finances and troop strength depleted he was compelled to order a retreat to Germany.

With the imperialists and English campaign shattered, Francis I began peace talks with the emperor and Tudor regime. With both France and the Habsburgs war weary and their coffers depleted, the Treaty of Crespy was soon signed in September. Under the terms of the reconciliation, peace was reestablished between France and the empire and the agreement was to be secured by Duke Charles of Orleans's marriage to either Charles V's daughter, Mary, with a dowry of Flanders, or his niece, Anna, with the endowment of Milan. Francis I agreed to renounce his inheritance rights to Savoy and aid the emperor against the Lutheran Germans and Ottomans. The negotiations with the English continued but no resolution resulted with the return of Boulogne blocking any settlement.

Following the failure of deliberations with Henry VIII, the Valois king sent an army under the command of Dauphin Henry to force the English from Boulogne. The Tudor regime had earlier strengthened the defensive walls and towers and had garrisoned the stronghold with a large contingent of soldiers. Henry attempted to storm the citadel but his attacks were repulsed, compelling him to begin siege operations. While the investment at Boulogne continued, Francis I launched a sea raid against the south coast of England to force Henry VIII back to the peace talks. A large navy of over two hundred forty ships and thirty thousand invasion troops was assembled at Le Havre, sailing in July to the Isle of Wight. After an inconclusive naval engagement, where the great English warship *Mary Rose* sank, the French attempted to land their army but were driven off by Henry VIII's fleet. Late in the year, the war turned into a stalemate and negotiations were finally resumed. After prolonged discussions, the Treaty of Ardes was ratified on July 7, 1546. Under the agreement, peace between the two kingdoms was reestablished and the English king pledged to abandon Boulogne for the payment of two million in gold coins.

Francis I's invasions into Lombardy had exposed him to the beauty and grandeur of the Renaissance. He became a friend and patron of the arts and letters, personally sponsoring many artists, architects, musicians and writers and encouraging them to reside at his court. The king was a dedicated art collector, sending his agents to Italy to purchase the latest paintings, sculptures and decorative treasures. Many valuable works were given to him as gifts by the papacy and other Italian princes. As the result of his first campaign against Milan, the Valois king met Leonardo da Vinci, convincing him to resettle in France. A chateau was provided in Amboise close to the royal residence and he spent his remaining years in the employment of the French court. Through its relationship with da Vinci, the regime acquired many of his paintings, including the *Mona Lisa*. Francis I's private art collection became the foundation for the Louvre Museum.

While exhorting the latest in art to his realm, Francis I supported the building of new chateaux in the Renaissance style, especially in the Loire River Valley. He erected a massive palace of over four hundred rooms at Chambord with the advice of da Vinci. Under his direction, the castle at Fontainbleau was rebuilt, while the new hunting chateau of Madrid was constructed near Paris. The king extended his patronage to music, which played an important role in his palace life. He encouraged the most talented composers, singers and musicians to join his court and they provided music for the royal church, ceremonies and entertainment. He also sponsored many authors and poets and personally wrote many verses of poetry.

Francis I took an active interest in supporting the exploration of the New World and the search for new trade routes to the East. France gained territorial rights in the Western Hemisphere through his personal financial backing of many voyages of discovery. The regime's treasury funded the expeditions of Giovanni de Verrazano to the New World. He navigated and mapped the coastline between present day North Carolina and Massachusetts, looking for a northwest passage. The Valois court financed the three voyages of Jacques Cartier to explore the region beyond Newfoundland in the quest for a shorter route to the East. The king gave Cartier his flagship, *Grande Hermine,* which was used on his second and third expeditions. Cartier traveled the coast of Canada, discovering and exploring the Saint Laurence River. The explorations of de Verrazano and Cartier gave the Valois kingdom a claim to lands that were later colonized as New France in the following century.

By 1542 the health of Francis I began to decline rapidly. He suffered from infections, high fever and the prolonged effects of syphilis. Despite his deteriorating condition, he continued to maintain firm personal control over the government. However, in early 1547 his illnesses grew worse and the king began to prepare for the succession of his sole surviving son and heir, Henry. The dauphin became more closely associated with the ruling council and assumed more power. On March 31, 1547, Francis I died at age fifty-two and after a reign of thirty-two years at the chateau of Rambouillet on the southern outskirts of Paris. On May 22 he was buried at the traditional interment site of the French monarchy at the Saint Denis Basilica.

Sources

Knecht. *Renaissance Warrior and Patron.*   Hackett. *Francis the First.*   Seward. *Prince of the Renaissance: The Life of Francis.*   Wilkinson. *Francis in All His Glory.*

Henry II, 1519–1547–1559

Following the death of Francis I in March 1547, Henry II assumed the Valois throne as the recognized heir to reign as the seventh Renaissance king of France. Henry was the second son of Francis I and Queen Claude and was born at the chateau of Saint Germain on March 31, 1519. Shortly after his birth he was appointed duke of Orleans. The prince spent his early childhood in the royal household with his five surviving brothers and sisters and the children from the high nobles. Under the terms of the Treaty of Madrid, in March 1526 the Orleans duke and his older brother, Francis, were exchanged as hostages for their father to secure his freedom from Habsburg captivity. In Madrid they were held in a prison fortress under harsh and unhealthy conditions and not released for over three years. After Henry's return to France, his formal education was resumed and distinguished tutors were provided for his instruction in reading, writing, history, science, religion and languages. However, unlike his father, he was not a gifted or serious student, preferring to pursue field sports, hunting and jousting. Growing up in the French court, Henry was exposed to the arts, music and letters of the Renaissance, developing an interest in the study of architecture. As the second of three sons, the Orleans duke was not acknowledged as heir to the Valois crown and not closely associated with the regime's government, receiving little training or preparation for his future assumption of power.

While Henry continued his education, in 1533 to enhance his quest for the duchy of Milan and bind his kingdom to the papacy in friendship, Francis I negotiated a military alliance with Rome and his son's marriage to Catherine de Medici, niece of Pope Clement VII. She was the daughter of Duke Lorenzo II of Urbino and Countess Madeleine of Boulogne and was born in Florence in April 1519. Shortly after her birth both her parents died and Catherine was raised by her aunt, Clarissa Strazzi. Under the tutelage of her aunt, renowned scholars were appointed as tutors and she received a broad based humanist education. She possessed an energetic and inquisitive intellect, excelling in her studies. In October 1533 the Orleans duke and Catherine were married, and despite being a political union they developed a close and supportive relationship, in spite of his many mistresses. After ten years of marriage, in 1544 she gave birth to the dauphin, Francis. Henry and Catherine had ten children with seven surviving beyond childhood, including three sons, who became kings of France. Following Henry II's assumption of the monarchy, the new queen exerted little influence at court but during the reigns of her three ruling sons became the power behind the throne.

In 1536 the dauphin, Francis, died and Henry became the acknowledged successor designate. However, the king refused to associate him with the government and the new heir was ill prepared for his future assumption of the kingship. Isolated from the regime, he formed a political faction with out of favor nobles and clerics in opposition to the policies of his father. While Henry continued to openly challenge the initiatives of the royal court, in early 1547 the health of Francis I began to rapidly decline and the Orleans duke finally took a greater role in the ruling council. In late March the monarch died and Henry II ascended the throne of France unopposed.

After his coronation at Rheims Cathedral on July 26, 1547, Henry II quickly reformed the administration, replacing most of his father's advisors with his friends and sympathizers. However, with only limited exposure to the government he lacked the necessary experience and confidence to rule independently and relied heavily on the counsel of his favorites. The previously disgraced Duke Anne Montmorency was appointed as his chief minister and constable of France, but the king continued to seek the advice of his mistress, Diane of Poitiers. She had been a lady-in-waiting to both queens, Claude and Eleanor of Habsburg, and increasingly had become a favorite at the royal court. Diane was Henry II's most trusted ally and possessed an astute political intellect exercising great influence over his regime's policies.

Henry II spent the first months of his reign establishing and consolidating his government. By 1548 he had asserted his authority and began to direct his policy toward reclaiming the seized fortress of Boulogne, which had remained under Tudor occupation. To distract England away from its interest in France, the Valois king opened negotiations with the Stewart court of Queen Mary I for an alliance against the new Tudor regency regime of Edward VI. The Scottish Lowlands had been recently conquered by the English armies and the Stewart ruling council needed financial and military support to recover its demesne. Under the terms of the ensuing Treaty of Haddington, the French pledged to provide money and troops for the war, while the Scots committed to the marriage of Mary I to the dauphin, Francis. In June 1548 a Valois army landed near Edinburgh and with the soldiers of Mary I slowly drove the forces of Edward VI back toward the border. With the Tudors occupied in Scotland, Henry II personally led the attack against Boulogne. After the stronghold's garrison refused to surrender, several attempts were made to storm the walls but the sorties were repulsed and siege operations initiated. While the investment continued, peace talks began between the two rivals. Finally in March 1550, the English agreed to abandon the city for a cash indemnity. After satisfying the payment conditions, in May Henry II entered the enclave in triumph, reuniting the region to his realm.

The Valois family held hereditary claims against the duchy of Milan and had been at war with the Habsburgs for over fifty years for control of the region. The French were forced out of northern Italy in 1525 and Henry II began negotiations with Pope Paul III for an agreement to recover the lost duchy. Relations between the Holy See and Emperor Charles V had steadily deteriorated over the possession of the duchies of Parma and Piacenza and the pope was favorable to a French alliance. With papal financial and military support, in the spring of 1548 Henry II assembled his army in southern France and advanced across the Alps into Lombardy. However, before the French launched their attack against Milan, the king was forced to abandon the campaign and return to his kingdom when rebellion erupted in western France over the imposition of a new salt tax. Despite the delay in the offensive, Henry II remained committed to the recapture of Milan.

While Henry II was pursuing the war against the Habsburgs, his regime was forced to intervene against several internal revolts. The most serious uprising occurred in western France, when the salt tax was increased to raise additional revenue to fund the war against Charles V. With the region in rebellion, the king was compelled to abandon his ongoing offensive against Milan and return to France with his army. As the insurrection spread, the Valois council appointed Duke Anne of Montmorency to restore royal supremacy. In the summer of 1548 he advanced against the mutinous lordships, quickly enforcing the crown's authority. The local officials were replaced with loyal royalists, while the Valois troops aggressively pursued the insurgent leaders, who were arrested and executed. Large fines were imposed on the rebel towns and Henry II's sovereignty was fully reasserted by the force of Montmorency's presence.

With his regime's campaign to reclaim Milan postponed, Henry II directed his policies toward confronting Charles V in Germany and began negotiations with the Lutheran princes for an alliance. The Protestant fiefs had continued to resist all attempts by the emperor to end their religious freedom and to buttress their rights they agreed to the Treaty of Chambord with the Valois court. Under the settlement's terms, the French pledged to provide substantial financial aid and launch an attack into Germany in support of the Protestants in exchange for the bishoprics of Metz, Verdun and Toul. In February 1552 Henry II declared war against the Habsburg emperor and prepared his army for the invasion into western Germany.

In April 1552 the Valois government mustered its forces and began its advance into Germany, where Henry II was welcomed as a liberator and protector by the local population. A contingent of his troops under the command of Duke Montmorency quickly occupied Metz, while Toul and Verdun were captured by Henry II. The cities were heavily garrisoned with French soldiers and with the seizure of the three ecclesiastic fiefs, Valois power was extended to the Rhine River. However, after reaching a separate peace agreement with the German princes, in November, Charles V attempted to regain French occupied Metz, laying siege against the stronghold. The garrison's defenders, led by Francis II, Duke of Guise, refused to surrender and defiantly resisted the attacks of the imperialists. Francis II was born in the duchy of Lorraine on February 17, 1519, and was the eldest son of Duke Claude and Antoinette of Bourbon. He was raised and educated in the royal household with his Valois cousins and was a favorite of the court. He served in the armies of King Francis I and was wounded during the siege against Boulogne in 1545. For his services as a soldier and diplomat, in 1551 the regime named him as grand chamberlain of France. As the imperial investment at Metz wore on through the winter months, the emperor's army suffered from exposure, disease and harassing sorties from Duke Francis II. Finally with his military might and finances depleted, Charles V was compelled to order a retreat early in 1553 to secure French control over the bishopric.

Following the loss of the three German ecclesiastic fiefdoms, in 1553 Charles V renewed the Franco-Habsburg War, invading Picardy and capturing the strategic stronghold of Therouanne. To counter the emperor's offensive, the French regime mounted a counterattack against southern Flanders under the personal command of the Valois king, who occupied parts of the region by force of arms and compelled the imperialists to abandon Therouanne. In the following year Henry II resumed his campaign, seizing several strategic fortresses and driving Charles V's army from the lower Flemish lordships.

While Henry II was occupied with the campaign in Flanders, the war against the Habsburgs was renewed in Italy. When the city of Siena rebelled against imperial occupation and established an independent republic, the Valois king provided financial and military support to the new regime, sending troops to buttress the city's defenses against an imperial counteroffensive. Through his intervention in Tuscany, Henry II gained a foothold in central Italy for future initiatives against Milan. To further his war effort against Charles V, the sovereign signed an alliance agreement with the Ottoman Empire, resulting in the joint naval attack and conquest of the imperial occupied island of Corsica.

With the French presence remaining in Tuscany, the emperor formed a coalition with Duke Cosimo I of Florence for a combined offensive against Siena to reimpose his imperial influence and authority. Cosimo I was born in Florence on June 12, 1519, and was the son of the renowned mercenary captain Giovanni della Bande Nere and Maria Salviati. He spent his youth in the northern Italian village of Mugello and received only a limited education. Cosimo I was from a minor blood branch of the Medici family and assumed the ducal throne in 1537 after the assassination of his distant cousin, Alessandro. Through the force of his charismatic personality, he was recognized as the head of the Florentine regime. However, his assumption of power was not opposed and in July the duke led his troops to enforce his supremacy, defeating the rebels at the battle of Montemurls. With his reign secured, he began to expand his lands and negotiated an agreement with Charles V for imperial support to reinforce his quest for the conquest of Tuscany. In 1553 Cosimo I mustered his army and augmented with Spanish troops advanced against the French in Siena. The city was besieged but the defenders defiantly thwarted all attempts to storm the walls, forcing the duke's soldiers to remain in their investment lines for over a year before the garrison finally submitted. Following the occupation of the city, the fief was annexed to the growing Tuscan domains of Cosimo I. Despite the loss of Siena, Henry II refused to abandon his quest for Italian aggrandizement and in the next year dispatched an army to buttress the campaign of Pope Paul IV against the imperialists. The French seized several strategic fortresses on the main invasion route to Milan in preparation for a future attack against the duchy.

In October 1555 Emperor Charles V abdicated the imperial throne, appointing his son, Philip II, to rule Spain, the Netherlands and large parts of Italy, while the Habsburg Austrian lands and Holy Roman crown were assumed by his younger brother, Ferdinand I. In the following year, Charles V retired to a monastery in Spain, where he died on September 21, 1558. Philip II had recently married Queen Mary I of England and was anxious to consolidate his inheritance and establish his authority over his new empire. Soon after the abdication of his father, the Spanish king began peace negotiations with the Valois court. The French had grown increasingly war weary from years of constant conflict and with their coffers depleted were agreeable to terms. The Truce of Vaucelles was quickly signed with both kingdoms pledging to respect the peace and status quo.

While Philip II and the French government honored the truce, in Italy Pope Paul IV began to intrigue against the presence of the Spanish Habsburgs in Naples. He was determined to expand papal power into the south and began talks with Henry II for his support. Under the influence of Duke Francis II of Guise, an agreement was signed with the French promising military and financial aid in exchange for the Holy See's investiture of Milan and Naples to the two sons of Henry II. In the spring of 1556 the papal army attacked several Spanish occupied towns, provoking a counteroffensive from Philip II. When the Habsburg troops under the command of Fernando Alvarez of Toledo, Duke of Alba, invaded the Papal States, Henry II exploited the threat against Rome as a pretext to break the truce and dispatch a relief force to southern Italy. The Duke of Alba was an experienced and skilled military commander and veteran of many imperial campaigns, serving with Charles V during the battles at Tunis, Muhlberg and Metz. He was later appointed commander of all imperial forces in Italy and viceroy of Naples. While the Alba duke advanced into the ecclesiastic lands, the Valois army was led south by Duke Francis II, who marched unopposed to Rome. With the papal defenses reinforced with the arrival of the French, Alba withdrew his Spanish soldiers to Naples. However, the duke of Guise was unable to continue his initiative against Naples when Pope Paul IV unexpectedly abandoned his alliance with Henry II and signed a separate peace treaty with Philip II.

As Francis II was in Italy supporting the papacy against the Spanish Habsburgs, Philip II resumed the war in Flanders, sending a formidable imperial-Spanish army under the command of Emmanuel Philibert to invade northern France. Emmanuel Philibert was born on July 8, 1528, at Chambery, Savoy, and was the only surviving son of Duke Charles III and Beatrice of Portugal. When the duchy of Savoy was overrun by France, he was forced to flee to the imperial court for protection. In 1545 Emmanuel Philibert joined the army of Charles V and was recognized for his military skills and bravery during campaigns in France, Germany and the Netherlands. When his father died in 1553, Emmanuel Philibert succeeded to his usurped ducal throne. He continued in the service of the Habsburgs, winning repute for his capture of Hesdin from the French. He was later appointed governor for the Netherlands by his cousin, Philip II of Spain.

Assuming command of Philip II's imperial-Spanish-Anglo army, Emmanuel Philibert advanced into Valois territory, laying siege against the fortress at Saint Quentin. To counter the Habsburg threat to his stronghold, the French king sent troops under Constable Anne Montmorency to break the investment. However, as his forces approached the town, he was unexpectedly attacked by Emmanuel Philibert and in the ensuing battle suffered a decisive defeat with over half of his soldiers either killed or captured. After the destruction of the Valois relief force, Emmanuel Philibert attempted to march on Paris, but Philip II refused to grant permission, satisfied with the victory and weakening of the French war effort.

Following the Holy See's withdrawal from the league against Naples, Francis II had returned to France with his army. After Montmorency's capture and defeat at Saint Quentin, the Guise duke assumed the dominant role in the Valois council. Under the duke's influence, Henry II agreed to send him with the French army to attack the Habsburgs' ally, England, at Calais. In December 1557 he advanced against the Tudor enclave, driving the defenders from their outer fortifications by the end of the month. As the English troops retreated to the citadel, Francis II began siege operations. With Calais blockaded and Queen Mary I and the Spanish unable to send relief forces, on January 7, 1558, the garrison commander surrendered and the Valois king soon entered the city in triumph.

By 1558 the French and Spanish regimes had become exhausted from years of war and in October were agreeable to begin negotiations for a permanent resolution. After prolonged deliberations, the Treaty of Cateau-Cambresis was signed on April 4, 1559. Under the terms of the settlement, peace was restored between the rivals, Henry II pledged to renounce all claims to Italy and abandon his occupation of Savoy, which was returned to Emmanuel Philibert. The Valois crown received the right to retain Calais and the three ecclesiastic bishoprics, while acknowledging Naples and Milan as fiefs of Spain. The treaty was sealed with the marriage of Henry II's daughter, Elizabeth of Valois, to Philip II, whose second wife had recently died. The accord ended sixty-five years of near constant warfare between the Valois and Habsburg courts, which had dominated the reigns of four French kings and three imperial emperors.

The growing Protestant Reformation had been largely ignored during the reign of Francis I. However, the French Huguenot movement continued to spread, creating a threat to the sovereignty of Henry II. The Valois regime reacted aggressively against the reformers, increasing persecutions and creating special heresy courts. The authority of the regional Parliaments was increased and they were empowered to issue judgments without the right of appeal. Nevertheless, the initiatives failed to curtail the anti-papists' expansion and harsher measures were begun. Under the influence of Diane Poitiers, in July 1551 the king issued the edict of Chateaubriant, which imposed sweeping repressive reforms. The Edict strengthened the crown's courts, granting them more power to intervene against suspected Huguenots. Anti-Catholic censorship was enforced and local officials were encouraged to actively pursue and arrest religious radicals. Adherence to the Catholic religion and its doctrines and rituals was made mandatory and the judicial system was periodically searched for Protestants. The harsh suppressive laws caused many nobles and commoners to abandon France and seek safety and religious freedom in the Calvinist haven of Geneva.

Despite the adoption of the harsh repressive policies against the Huguenots, they continued to expand their presence, as missionaries from Calvinist Geneva were sent to France to spread the reformist doctrines. Under the influence of the Swiss radicals, many nobles abandoned the Catholic Church to join the Protestants, while numerous towns, especially in the southern and western lordships, openly supported the new religion. As the danger of the heretics grew, the Valois council issued the Edict of Compiegne, which strengthened the existing penalties against the anti–Catholics. However, the increased restrictive measures failed to subdue the Huguenots and Henry II began preparations for the use of military might to destroy the Protestant movement in his kingdom.

While France remained at war against the Habsburgs and Philip II, the Valois regime was unable to exploit the strength of its army to impose its authority over the Huguenots. However, following the signing of the Treaty of Cateau-Cambresis, Henry II began preparations for a military offensive against the enclaves of the heretics, while his initiative to eliminate the reformers from the government and regional Parliaments was intensified. In June 1559 he issued the Edict of Ecouen, which authorized the ruthless persecution of the anti–Catholic faction.

Through the court of his father, Henry II was exposed to the Renaissance and his regime continued to patronize the arts and letters. The construction of the great chateau at Chambord was resumed, along with the rebuilding of the Louvre and additions to Fontainebleau. He also encouraged his advisors and friends to build palaces in the Renaissance style of architecture. Renowned sculptors, woodcrafters and artists were employed to lavishly decorate the new structures. The king engaged artists to embellish the ceilings and walls of the rooms with large murals, while the sponsorship of portrait artists was renewed. While Henry II was primarily interested in the visual arts, his reign also supported many writers and poets and under the influence of Queen Catherine the royal theater began to develop.

As Henry II was preparing for religious war against the Huguenots, on June 22, 1559, at the cathedral of Notre Dame in Paris his daughter, Elizabeth, was married by proxy to Philip II of Spain under the provisions of the Cateau-Cambresis Treaty. To celebrate the wedding, the king ordered a large succession of grandiose banquets, parties and festivals to be followed by a magnificent military tournament, where he planned to compete. After the ceremony, on June 30 he took an active role in the jousting event, but during the third bout was struck in his helmet visor by the lance of the captain of his Scottish Guard, Gabriel, Count of Montgomery and Lord of Lorges. The force of the blow caused several splinters from Montgomery's shattered lance to become lodged in Henry II's upper forehead. He was rushed from the field unconscious to the Tournelles Palace, where he seemed to recover over the following days. However, on July 9, 1559, the king fell into a coma, dying the next day at age forty and a reign of twelve years.

Sources

Knecht. *French Renaissance Monarchy: Francis I and Henry II.*   Knecht. *The Valois: Kings of France, 1328–1589.*

Francis II, 1544–1559–1560

In July 1559 Henry II died from injuries suffered during a jousting tournament and was succeeded to the Valois monarchy by his fifteen-year-old son, Francis II, who reigned as the eighth Renaissance king of France for only seventeen months. Francis was the first son of Henry II and Queen Catherine de Medici and was born on January 19, 1544, at the chateau of Fontainbleau. As the eldest son of the king, he was acknowledged as dauphin and heir to the French throne at birth. Under the guidance of his mother, distinguished scholars were appointed as tutors for his education but the royal prince had little aptitude or interest in his studies. He preferred to pursue hunting and in particular the sport of hawking. Growing up in the French court of Francis I and Henry II, the dauphin was exposed to the music, arts, literature and poetry of the Renaissance movement. Francis was physically described by contemporaries as possessing handsome features with a regal bearing. However, he suffered from poor health and was frequently seriously ill. In April 1558 he was married to Mary I of Scotland under the terms of the treaty of alliance between the Valois regime and Stewart court. Shortly before the wedding, the two kingdoms were further united in friendship when Mary I signed a secret agreement ceding the Scottish crown to France should she die without a direct heir. The marriage ceremony was held at Notre Dame Cathedral in Paris and was followed by a series of grand and elaborate celebrations, festivals and banquets. The Scottish queen had come to France at an early age and was raised in the royal household with Francis. They developed a close bond with Mary I asserting her strong personality over the prince. She was two years older than Francis II and was described as exerting great charm, culture, beauty and intelligence.

In July 1559 Henry II unexpectedly was killed during a jousting tournament and as the recognized successor, Francis II, assumed the monarchy of France without opposition. However, he had not been closely associated with his father's ruling council and lacked any training or experience in the administration of the regime. He depended heavily on the advice of Catherine de Medici and his wife and they exploited their influence to reorganize the court with their favorites. The royal advisors of Henry II were replaced by the Guise family and its loyal friends and allies. Under the leadership of Duke Francis II and his brother, Cardinal Charles of Lorraine, the Guise faction quickly asserted its dominance over the policies of Francis II's government.

Catherine de Medici had received a humanist education in her native Florence and had been greatly influenced by the rich Renaissance regime of Francis I. At the French court she was exposed to the leading painters, poets, sculptors and artisans of Europe. Following her rise to power during the reigns of her three sons, she became a patron of the arts and letters, encouraging the most renowned artists and writers to reside at her court. The dowager queen was an ambitious collector of paintings, tapestries, maps, sculptures and objects of art. Under her sponsorship a royal theater was begun and productions of music, ballet and drama were presented. Catherine initiated an aggressive construction program in the Renaissance style, building new palaces at the Tuileries in Paris and Hotel of the Reine, while resuming her husband's projects at Chenonceau and Saint-Maur-des-Fosses.

After assuming control of the Valois government, the Guise family initiated a series of reforms to curtail court expenditures, while generously rewarding their friends and allies with rich grants of land, money, honors, titles and high positions in the regime. To further decrease spending, the size of the army was cut back and pensions reduced or suspended. The measures were highly unpopular among the magnates and towns, who lost many of their privileges and tax exceptions. However, Francis II supported the cost reduction policies after his mother intervened to encourage his approval.

While the Huguenots continued to expand their religious presence and power in France, they were opposed by Duke Francis II of Guise and his brother, who were ardent champions of the Church of Rome. The Guise government made the destruction of the heretic movement their primary domestic goal. While Duke Francis II strengthened and intensified his prosecution of the anti–Huguenot laws and forced the Protestant nobles from court, the dissidents recruited an army and raised money in defense of their lands and religious rights. As the acknowledged head of the Protestants, Louis I, prince of Conde, organized a conspiracy to kidnap the king at his chateau of Amboise and compel him to dismiss the Guise faction from the council. The prince was the younger brother of the king of Navarre, Antoine of Bourbon, and founder of the House of Conde. He was a veteran of the wars against Emperor Charles V, fighting at Metz and Saint Quentin. However, the royal regime was soon informed of the insurrection and on March 16, 1560, when the rebels attacked the castle, they were ambushed by the crown's troops and easily defeated. The surviving conspirators were soon captured and executed with their mutilated bodies left to hang from the chateau's walls as a warning against future revolt. The prince of Conde was implicated in the insurgency and forced to flee to his brother's kingdom of Navarre for protection.

After the failure to seize Francis II, an attempt at reconciliation was made with the Huguenots under the increasing influence at court of Catherine de Medici. In late March 1560 the Valois government issued the first Edict of Amboise, which granted a general amnesty to all heretics and initiated a policy of restraint and toleration. However, the Protestants considered the concessions as a sign of retreat and weakness and increased their belligerence against the regime with personal attacks against the Guise family and holding illegal religious demonstrations. To reduce the escalating violence, the royal council summoned the Huguenots and high Catholic nobles to meet at Fontainbleau at an Assembly of Notables.

When the assembly gathered in August 1560, Catherine pressed the Catholic and Protestant nobles to adopt measures to bring reconciliation to her son's realm and end the suffering of the population. Under the leadership of Gaspard of Chatillon, lord of Coligny and admiral of France, the Huguenots petitioned the king for freedom to worship and an end to all religious persecutions. Gaspard was a Gascon nobleman and veteran of the French wars in Flanders and Italy, where he was recognized for his bravery and military skills. In 1552 he was promoted to admiral and later commanded the garrison at Saint Quentin during the imperial siege of Emmanuel Philibert. The Coligny lord converted to Protestantism in 1558 and became closely allied with Louis I of Conde. After contentious negotiations between Gaspard of Chatillon and the Guise family, the Assembly of Notables issued an agreement pledging to reform the French church, encourage the heretics to return to the Catholic faith and summon the Estates-General to meet. However, the Parliament failed to reassure the anxieties of the Protestants, who began to collect arms and money to defend their religious rights, while hostilities broke out between supporters of Duke Francis II and Gaspard of Chatillon.

While the danger of religious war intensified, Prince Louis I of Conde began to raise a Protestant army to force the Guise faction from the government. The Guise family was still the dominant political power in the regime and Duke Francis II used his influence over the king to have him order the Conde prince to appear at the royal court to answer charges of treason. While traveling to Paris to defend his actions, the prince was seized at Orleans by troops under the employment of the Guise alliance. The Huguenots responded to the arrest of their leader by threatening armed rebellion. In an attempt to restore the fragile reconciliation, the queen mother intervened with her son to arrange the release of the prince of Conde. The peace was again honored but tensions remained high.

As religious war continued to threaten, in November 1560 Francis II, who had been a frail child and subjected to reoccurring health problems, developed an inner ear infection. By early in the following month, the inflammation spread to the brain and on December 5 in the city of Orleans the king died at age sixteen after a reign of seventeen months. He was buried in the traditional site of interment at the Basilica of Saint Denis north of Paris and was succeeded to the French throne by his ten-year-old brother, Charles IX.

Sources

Knecht. *The Valois: Kings of France, 1328–1589.*

Charles IX, 1550–1560–1574

When Francis II died without a direct heir at the beginning of the French Religious Wars, his brother, Charles IX, succeeded to the throne to rule as the ninth Valois king of the Renaissance epoch. Charles was born at the chateau of Saint Germain on June 27, 1550, and was the third son of Henry II and Catherine de Medici. Shortly after his birth he was named as the Count of Provence. He spent his early childhood in the royal household with his brothers, sisters and children from the high noble families. His mother employed renowned scholars as tutors for the education of the royal prince, but he had little interest or ability in his studies of reading, writing, religion, history and languages. With his older brother, Francis, he preferred to pursue field sports and hunting activities. However, his weak and frail health limited his active participation. As Charles grew older, he was physically described as unusually tall, while possessing handsome features and a gracious manner. As the third son of the monarch, he was not expected to assume power and was not associated with the governing council, receiving little training or preparation for his future assumption of power. Growing up in the Valois court, the Provence count became exposed to the arts, music, theater and literature of the Renaissance under the influence of the queen.

On December 5, 1560, Francis II died without a direct heir and as the next in line to the Valois crown Charles IX was readily acknowledged as the successor at age ten. The new king had not reached the age of majority and under existing law the Estates-General appointed his mother to rule as regent. Catherine de Medici quickly asserted her dominance over the royal council to govern in the name of her son. To restore peace with the increasingly militant Huguenot faction, she initiated a policy directed at religious toleration and reconciliation. To gain the support of the Protestants, the Guise party was dismissed from court, while nonpartisan and moderate nobles assumed their high positions in the regime. All heretics imprisoned by the Guise government were released and prior convictions pardoned. New laws were issued to reform the judiciary and administrative systems, ending the widespread corruption and improving efficiency.

As Catherine attempted to bring peace to her son's realm, the Huguenots pressed for more religious freedoms by initiating a more defiant and aggressive opposition against the royal government. They began to openly hold prayer meetings and attack Catholic churches, priests and rituals. Under the more tolerant policies of the queen mother, many new converts joined the Protestants as the Valois crown's authority began to decline further. The Catholics responded to the rising reformer belligerence with counter acts of violence, and frequent armed clashes soon resulted. As the danger of anarchy escalated, the more militant papist nobles and clerics abandoned Charles IX's court and formed an alliance with the duke of Guise to force Catherine's regency administration to reinstate the repressive anti–Huguenot laws. As the turmoil spread and intensified, the queen mother issued a summons for the Catholic and Huguenot magnates to meet at Poissy in a national council to resolve their growing religious differences.

In late July 1561 the colloquy of Poissy assembled with Charles IX issuing a personal appeal for compromise from both rival factions. Over the next two months the Catholics and Protestants met to discuss their doctrinal differences and proposals for reconciliation but no settlement was found and in October the Colloquy ended without any agreement. Following the failed Poissy council, the Huguenots and pro-papists became more hostile and prepared for war. In January 1562 Catherine made another attempt to restore peace by decreeing the Edict of January, which granted additional religious freedoms to the heretics. They were permitted to hold open prayer meetings outside the town walls but only during the day, while the previous religious concessions were confirmed. However, her edict had little effect as Charles IX's kingdom moved closer to civil conflict.

Despite numerous small skirmishes, no serious attacks had occurred between the Huguenots and Catholics. However, on March 1, 1562, Duke Francis II of Guise led a bloody and savage assault against a large group of reformers who were assembled for a prayer meeting. The Protestant faction responded to the deadly atrocity by issuing a call for money and arms in defense of their religious rights. As the level of dissent grew, the Huguenots rose up in revolt, brutally pillaging Catholic churches and murdering many papist followers. The anti–Protestants countered with acts of violence, as the realm moved closer to civil war. As the military forces of the heretics began to assemble, Duke Francis II persuaded Catherine and her royalist supporters to join his militant league to protect the throne of Charles IX. When the Huguenots were expelled from court, Louis I of Conde united his troops with Admiral Gaspard of Chatillon and together they seized control of Orleans and other towns in the south and west. Louis I circulated a proclamation, announcing his intent to rescue the king from the Guise alliance and ensure freedom of religion for all. At the encouragement of Duke Francis II, the queen mother ordered the royal army to retake the lost towns and restore her son's authority, resulting in the beginning of the First Religious War.

As the Valois army under the command of Constable Anne Montmorency and Duke Francis II marched south to impose the king's rule, on December 19, 1562, they intercepted the Protestant forces of Louis I of Conde at Dreux. In the ensuing engagement, the Catholics deployed into a strong defensive position and with their superior infantry repeatedly repulsed the charges of Conde's cavalry. The heretics were unable to break the constable's line of pikemen and arquebusiers and were compelled to withdraw from the battlefield. The causalities were heavy on both sides with many nobles killed or captured, including Conde and the seventy-year-old Montmorency, who were both held as prisoners. After the success at Dreux, the Catholic troops of the duke of Guise continued their campaign against the rebels, recapturing many of their towns in the south and west. Under Francis II's aggressive and brutal leadership, the royalists began to overwhelm the Huguenots and reestablish Charles IX's usurped authority. However, most of the victories were followed by savage acts of pillage, looting, rape and murder, which aroused the wrath of the anti-papists and encouraged new recruits to join the Protestant army.

After his victories in the south, Duke Francis II advanced against the rebel stronghold at Orleans. However, while besieging the city, he was assassinated by a radical Protestant, leaving an uncertain power vacuum in the leadership of the royalist war effort. With the loss of the popular and charismatic duke, Catherine once again imposed her dominance over the ruling council of Charles IX. She was anxious to find a religious compromise and using Conde and Montmorency as negotiators, the Treaty of Amboise was soon signed on March 19, 1563. The agreement restored peace between the two rival religious factions and allowed the Huguenots freedom to worship in one town in each judicial district where they were currently holding services. However, the treaty limited the heretics to the towns they already controlled and was widely unpopular with the Huguenots.

Following the murder of Duke Francis II, Catherine ruled the kingdom independent of the reactionary Guise faction. In August 1563 Charles IX was recognized as reaching the age of majority and formally assumed the monarchy, ending the regency of his mother. On August 17 he appeared before the princes of the blood, high nobles and clerics at the Parliament of Rouen to announce his succession to the throne of France. However, Catherine continued to hold the powers of government, establishing royal policy for her thirteen-year-old son.

The peace established by the Treaty of Amboise was only partially successful in ending the acts of religious violence. To enforce the truce, the king created a new commission of royal envoys who traveled across France to resolve local disputes and impose his authority. They succeeded in settling many disagreements, bringing greater stability and unity to the reign of Charles IX. To expand the success of the initiative, in 1564 Catherine planned an extended tour of the realm by her son to promote the acceptance of the Amboise Treaty and allow the towns to personally receive his justice. The grand progression was organized by Constable Montmorency, who made the travel arrangements for the large court and ensured the safety of Charles IX and Catherine. In each town the dowager queen and her son pressed the Huguenots and Catholics to honor and respect the compromise agreement and end their hostility. When the royal court reached Aix-en-Provence, the local council defied the king and refused to register the Amboise Edict. The Valois crown quickly dismissed the officials and appointed loyal royalists who acknowledged the treaty. Traveling through southern France, in Bayonne Charles IX met the personal emissary of his brother-in-law, Philip II of Spain, who encouraged him to repeal his policies of toleration and renew the persecution of the heretics. After the talks between the two Catholic regimes, the French Protestants began to fear an increasingly hostile Spanish influence in Charles IX's administration, but he quickly renewed his calls for compliance to the Amboise accord. The tour lasted from March 1564 until May 1566 and covered most of the kingdom, ending with the Valois government believing peace was restored.

The spread of the Protestant Reformation from Germany had not been limited to only France but had also made significant gains into the neighboring Spanish Netherlands. In 1567 Philip II sent an army under the command of Fernando Alvarez, Duke of Alba, to Brussels to assert his authority over the Dutch heretics. With the presence of a large and powerful Habsburg force across the border, the Huguenots became alarmed that the kingdoms of France and Spain would unite in a grand Catholic League directed against them. The threat escalated further when the king hired six thousand Swiss mercenaries and authorized the return to court of the cardinal of Lorraine, who the Protestants believed would influence the regime to reinstate the religious persecutions and anti–Huguenot laws.

Fearing the loss of their religious freedom, the Protestants organized a plot to seize the monarch and force him to replace the Guise faction in his government with a pro-reformer council. The revolt was launched in September 1567 as troops from the rebel towns marched against the king at Meaux. However, as the anti-papist cavalry attacked, the royal infantry repulsed their charge, allowing Charles IX to escape to safety in Paris. The attempted kidnapping resulted in an escalation of hostilities between the two religious parties, forcing the Valois regime to abandon its toleration doctrine and adopt the militant policy of the Guise alliance. Preparations for war began as new soldiers were mustered and money raised. Royal envoys were sent to Pope Pius V and Philip II seeking their support and financial aid for the renewal of the conflict. Under the leadership of Louis I of Conde, the Protestants responded by mobilizing their armies and mounting sorties against Catholic held strongholds to begin the Second Religious War.

After the resumption of the religious conflict, the Protestant faction captured several large cities in the south, including Orleans. As his campaign gained momentum, Louis I of Conde marched against Paris to force the Guise family from the government. The Huguenots laid siege against the capital and after nearly a month as food supplies became exhausted, Constable Anne Montmorency was ordered by the king to attack the rebels and break their investment. On November 10 he advanced the royalists against the army of Louis I, driving the heretics from the battlefield with a spirited cavalry charge. However, the Catholic victory was won at the loss of Montmorency, who was killed leading the sortie. His death resulted in the absence of a strong voice of restraint and moderation in the royal council, which was replaced by the militant Cardinal Charles of Lorraine.

Following the defeat of his forces at Paris, Prince Louis I withdrew to the south, besieging the city of Chartres. However, the stronghold was too well protected and with the approach of the royal army under the command of the king's brother, Henry of Anjou, the Protestants retreated to the base of their support in the southern and western lordships. As the inconclusive conflict continued to drain the financial and military resources of the Valois regime and Huguenot alliance, both rivals readily agreed to open truce negotiations. The Peace of Longiumeau soon followed and was signed on March 28, 1568, reconfirming the terms of the Edict of Amboise, while the Huguenots pledged to disarm and abandon their seized towns.

Despite the approval of the Longiumeau Treaty, there continued to be widespread breaches of peace by both religious factions. The papist sympathizers and Huguenots began to raise money and recruit new troops in preparation for the resumption of hostilities. Under the influence of Cardinal Charles of Lorraine, on September 25, 1568, Charles IX issued an edict denouncing the Reformation movement and repealing his policy of toleration and restraint, signaling the beginning of the Third Religious War. The royalists, under the command of Duke Henry of Anjou and Gaspard of Saulx, Lord of Tavannes, were sent to the southwest to subdue the Huguenot forces of Louis I of Conde. Lord Gaspard of Tavannes was a veteran of the Italian and Habsburg wars, winning renown for his bravery and battle skills at Pavia and the campaign in Provence. In 1552 with Duke Anne Montmorency he captured Metz and six years later participated in the conquest of Calais from the English. As the king's forces advanced into Protestant controlled territory, on March 13, 1569 the two armies clashed at Jarnac where the Tavannes lord's cavalry outmaneuvered the Huguenots, driving them from the battlefield. Louis I of Conde was captured and later murdered by the Anjou duke's personal bodyguard, inflaming the resolve of the Protestants. To fill the vacuum left by the death of the Conde prince, Admiral Gaspard Coligny of Chatillon assumed sole command of the heretic army.

The Huguenot army had been bloodied at Jarnac but still remained largely intact. As Admiral Coligny withdrew to reorganize his troops and raise new recruits, Henry of Anjou resumed his attacks against the Protestants, reimposing his brother's rule over many of the realm's towns. In early July the admiral's forces were reinforced with the arrival of fourteen thousand German mercenaries under the command of Duke Wolfgang of Zweibrucken, whose campaign in support of the Huguenots was financed by Queen Elizabeth I of England. The Protestant duke was an experienced soldier, fighting in the German religious wars against the encroachments of Charles V and later in opposition to the Ottoman Empire's invasion of the Balkans.

Reinforced with Zweibrucken's German soldiers, Admiral Gaspard Coligny's army under the nominal command of Louis I of Conde's young nephew, Henry of Bourbon, renewed the war against the Anjou duke. Henry was heir to the Protestant kingdom of Navarre and after the death of his uncle became the acknowledged leader of the Huguenot faction. He was a cousin of Charles IX and recognized as the next in line to the throne after the ruling Valois dynasty. As the heretics launched their offensive, numerous Catholic enclaves and towns in the south were attacked and captured as the new Protestant campaign slowly regained momentum. While the anti-papists renewed their initiative, Henry of Anjou received additional troops and financial aid from Pope Pius V and Philip II of Spain. With his forces reinforced, the Anjou duke advanced toward Poitiers to confront the reformers. On October 3, 1569, the two armies clashed at Moncontour, where Lord Gaspard of Saulx led a spirited royalist cavalry charge against the forces of Admiral Coligny, driving the Protestants from the battlefield in disarray with many thousands of causalities. However, Duke Henry failed to aggressively pursue the fleeing Huguenots, permitting the admiral to withdraw to the south to raise new recruits, arms and money.

In the spring of 1570 Prince Henry of Navarre's army was reinforced with additional troops and arms and a new aggressive campaign launched against the royalists. Attacks were made against numerous Catholic strongholds and towns as Henry advanced closer to Paris. However, by the summer both rivals had grown war weary and with their treasuries depleted negotiations were initiated for a truce. On August 8, 1570, the Peace of Saint Germain was signed. Under the terms of the agreement, the Protestants were granted the occupation of four fortified towns, freedom of religion in the areas where it previously existed and the nobles were recalled to the Valois court.

With peace established in the Valois kingdom, Catherine de Medici initiated negotiations with Emperor Maximilian II for the marriage of his daughter, Archduchess Elizabeth, to Charles IX to improve relations with the Holy Roman Empire. After prolonged talks an agreement was ratified and the wedding of great pomp and extravagance was held on November 26, 1570, in Paris. Despite being a politically arranged union to bind France closer to the imperial regime and protect the eastern border, the king and Queen Elizabeth were well suited to each other, developing a caring and supportive relationship. She was described as one of the most beautiful princesses in the European courts with great charm and intelligence. Elizabeth had been raised in the pious Catholic household of her Spanish mother and was devoted to the Church of Rome and its doctrines. The marriage resulted in one child, Marie-Elizabeth, who was born in 1572.

In the aftermath of the wedding between the French king and Elizabeth of Austria, the Valois council began talks for the marriage of Henry of Navarre to Princess Margaret, sister of Charles IX, to bind the two kingdoms closer in friendship. After prolonged deliberations, finally in early 1572 the treaty was signed and on August 18 the wedding was held at Notre Dame in Paris. The marriage and elaborate celebrations were attended by many militant Catholic and Huguenot nobles, who increasingly began to threaten the peace. Several days after attending the ceremony, Admiral Gaspard Coligny was wounded in an attempted assassination plot by members of the Guise faction. The heretics responded by demanding revenge against Charles IX and his court. As the belligerence escalated, Catherine de Medici encouraged her son to arrest the leaders of the anti-papist alliance to thwart the threatening violence. However, rioting quickly resulted when a Paris mob attacked and killed several thousand Protestants, including Admiral Gaspard of Chatillon in the Saint Bartholomew's Day Massacre. The violence spread to numerous towns over the next two weeks, resulting in the murder of over two thousand additional Huguenots. The Valois crown's campaign of promoting toleration and restraint was abandoned and the hostile policies of the Guise family adopted. The non–Catholics gave up any prospects of achieving religious peace through negotiations, returning to defend their fortresses and towns in the south and west.

In the aftermath of the Saint Bartholomew's Day Massacre, the Valois kingdom again erupted into religious civil war. After the withdrawal of the Huguenot magnates from Paris, Charles IX sent his armies to subdue their towns and reimpose his rule. The king's troops besieged Rouen, which was skillfully defended by Count Gabriel of Montgomery, who energetically repelled the assaults of the royalists. While the attack against Rouen faltered, Duke Henry of Anjou advanced against the large fortress at La Rochelle. He laid siege against the city and began an intense artillery bombardment. After weakening the defenses, the loyalists attempted to storm the fortification eight times but the garrison and population withstood their onslaught. Finally, in July 1573 he was forced to abandon his campaign when the king's government failed to raise enough money to support his army, retreating with the Huguenots still in control of their southern and western strongholds. By the summer both religious factions had grown war weary with many of the less militant Catholic nobles renouncing the regime's policy of aggression. With its coffers depleted and support weakening, Charles IX's government opened talks for a truce with the rebels. The Treaty of Boulogne was quickly signed to end the Fourth Religious War, however, with no permanent resolution to the ongoing religious crisis.

By 1574 the health of Charles IX began to rapidly deteriorate. He had always been prone to serious illnesses and these reoccurring attacks were made worse by his tuberculosis, which weakened his resistance and strength. On May 30, 1574, the king died outside Paris in the chateau of Vincennes at age twenty-four after a reign of fourteen years. Charles IX died without a direct male heir and was succeeded to the Valois throne by his brother, Henry III.

Sources

Knecht. *The Valois: Kings of France, 1328–1589.*   Potter. *A History of France 1460–1560.*

Henry III, 1551–1574–1589

In May 1574 Charles IX died without a direct heir and the Valois crown was inherited by his brother, Henry III, who reigned as the tenth French king of the Renaissance. Henry was the fourth of the five sons of Henry II and Catherine de Medici and was born on September 19, 1551, at the Fontainebleau Chateau. At his birth he was named duke of Angouleme and at age nine was ceded the duchy of Anjou. Under the guidance of his mother, renowned scholars were chosen as tutors for his education. Unlike his two older brothers, Henry was a gifted and serious student, excelling in his studies of reading, writing, science, religion, history and languages to include Latin and Italian. He developed a special interest in literature, poetry, dancing and music, becoming a prince of culture and refinement. While his academic education continued, he received instruction from distinguished soldiers in the battle skills of a feudal knight and was proficient in fencing, archery and jousting. With his brothers, Henry was an energetic hunter, and participated in numerous field sports. As a child he was frequently ill and never acquired a robust health. As he grew into adulthood, contemporaries described him as unusually tall and possessing a graceful and easy manner with an attraction to wearing fine clothes and jewelry.

Henry of Anjou was a Renaissance prince of wide ranging interest from court dandy to skilled soldier. He invited scholars to his household to discuss issues of theology and humanism and continued his mother's patronage of Renaissance artists, poets, singers and musicians. The duke was the most intellectual of the late Valois kings and was compared by contemporaries to his grandfather, Francis I. Henry was a devout Catholic and dedicated to the defense of its doctrines and rituals. During the French Religious Wars, he led his brother's army at the Catholic victories at Jarnac and Moncontour, acquiring a reputation for his bravery and military talents. The duke commanded the royal siege against the Huguenot enclave at La Rochelle in 1573, which added to his renown among the European courts. During the investment at La Rochelle, Henry received the reports of his election to the crown of Poland.

In 1572 the king of Poland, Sigismund II Augustus, died without a direct heir, ending the Jagiellon dynasty. Henry of Anjou and three princes of Europe began to contend for their election to the throne. The primary challenger to the Anjou duke's candidacy was the son of Emperor Maximilian II, Archduke Ernest, who commanded the support of the high nobles. However, when the Polish Diet assembled in May 1573 Henry was chosen by a wide majority, as the minor magnates rallied to his election. His selection was not unconditional and after meeting with a Polish delegation in Paris, he agreed to govern under constitutional restrictions and respect religious toleration. In late September Henry traveled to Krakow, making a favorable impression on the Polish court with his gallantry and charm. As the new monarch began to consolidate his regime, on May 30, 1574, his brother, Charles IX, died and as the recognized dauphin, Henry III inherited the Valois monarchy. In June he left Krakow to return to France, advancing through Austria to Venice, where Doge Alvise Mocenigo lavishly entertained him.

In September Henry III crossed the Italian border into France to begin his reign. On February 13, 1575, at the cathedral of Rheims, he was enthroned as king and assumed full control of the government from his mother, who had acted as regent after the death of Charles IX. He intended to rule both France and Poland but was soon forced to abandon the Krakow crown.

Following his coronation Henry III was married to Louise of Vaudemont-Lorraine in Rheims Cathedral. The king and his new wife were initially devoted to each other, developing a close and supportive bond, but their failure to produce a heir slowly created an increasingly strained relationship. Louise began to suffer from periods of depression, withdrawing from court. However, Henry III continued to enjoy a lavish and flamboyant lifestyle of frequent hunting parties, elegant balls and festivals, which the queen opposed. He had many court favorites and spent freely to entertain his friends and courtiers, while Louise was dedicated to the Catholic Church, preferring a moral life of piety and devotion to religious doctrine. Their marriage did not result in the birth of any children, creating a future succession crisis for the French kingdom.

During Henry III's absence at the Krakow court, violence had erupted in France between the two rival religious factions, threatening to plunge the realm into war. As the king established his governing council, he came under the influence of the militant Guise party, which was led by Henry, son of the assassinated Duke Francis II. Henry was born on December 31, 1550, and was the eldest son and heir of Duke Francis II and Anna d'Este of Ferrara. After the murder of his father, Henry inherited his ducal throne and by 1570 through the force of his charismatic personality became the recognized leader of the Catholics. He had earlier fought against the encroachments of the Ottoman Empire in royal Hungary and had participated in the battles of Jarnac and Moncontour against the French Huguenots. Under the exhortations of Duke Henry, the Valois regime initiated an aggressive policy for the subjugation of the Protestants by force of arms by sending four armies into southern France to assert the crown's supremacy and authority of the Catholic Church. However, the royalists lacked the military might and finances to impose the Valois's will and the Huguenots thwarted their campaign, as the conflict developed into a stalemate.

To force religious concessions from the Valois regime, the heretics forged a military partnership with Count John Casimir of Pfalz-Lautern. He was a militant Calvinist who had energetically supported the Protestant Reformation in Germany. In January 1575 Count Casimir entered northern France with four thousand soldiers, joining with the Huguenot army to pillage through Burgundy with impunity. After the failure of Henry III to launch a counterattack against Casimir and the French Protestants, the king's brother, Duke Francis of Anjou, abandoned the royalists and negotiated an alliance with the Huguenots. The duke had ambitions to seize the crown and demanded freedom of worship and an end to the war. The Valois crown lacked the troop strength and money to resist the new coalition by force of arms and Queen Catherine was sent to negotiate a settlement. Confronted by the overwhelming military might of the allies, she was forced to sign the Treaty of Beaulieu on May 6, 1576, which granted most of the heretics' demands. Under the agreement, the Protestants gained the freedom to worship throughout the realm except in Paris, the Saint Bartholomew's Day Massacre was acknowledged as a crime, seized Huguenot lands were to be returned and the Estates-General summoned to resolve the ecclesiastic conflict. The treaty was widely popular with the Protestants but was strongly opposed by the Catholics.

The militant papists countered the sweeping Treaty of Beaulieu concessions by beginning negotiations for a Catholic League under the leadership of Duke Henry of Guise. Emissaries were sent to Rome to gain Pope Gregory XIII's approval and financial aid, while an initiative was begun in France to recruit moderate Catholics to their cause. Henry of Guise and the league attracted many Catholic sympathizers to their coalition as their campaign in defense of their faith became increasingly more aggressive and hostile. In an attempt to thwart the growing power of the Leaguers, Henry III formed a counter faction in December 1576, establishing a separate military force in each province under the command of the local royal governor to enforce his sovereignty. He supported the Treaty of Beaulieu by ordering the religion and property of the Protestants to be respected and any Catholic who failed to obey his authority was branded a traitor. However, his policy failed to attract widespread backing and Henry III was compelled to recognize the Catholic League.

In compliance with the provisions of the Treaty of Beaulieu, in December 1576 Henry III summoned the Estates-General to Blois to resolve the religious dispute. However, when the nobles and clergy met, they came under the domination of the Guise faction. The Estates voted to prohibit all policies of religious toleration and authorized full suppression of the Reformation movement but failed to grant the king the funds necessary to enforce its petition. During the winter months, Henry III prepared for the Sixth Religious War, attempting to raise money and a new army. He was able to muster a small military force and in April launched an attack against the Protestant towns. The royalists captured and brutally sacked several strongholds but due to the lack of money their campaign steadily lost momentum. By September Henry III's coffers were depleted and truce talks were initiated with the rebels. After brief negotiations the Peace of Bergerac was signed, which compelled the heretics to accept some restrictions on the concessions granted by the Beaulieu Treaty. After the restoration of peace in his kingdom, Henry III reorganized his government and appointed Lord Louis Potier of Gesvres secretary of his council. Louis was the second son of Jacques Potier, Lord of Blancmesnil, and Frances Cueillette, daughter of Lord John Cueillette of Freschines and Gesvres, and was born about 1545. Through the lineage of both parents, he was directly related to families with a long history of service to the kings of France as knights, Parliamentarians, lords and royal counselors. He joined the ruling council of Charles IX and in 1567 was appointed as his secretary. After the death of the king, Louis remained at court and served in the regime of Henry III.

Despite a brief renewal of hostilities in 1579, which was resolved by the personal intervention of Catherine de Medici, the Bergerac Treaty resulted in nearly eight years of only isolated skirmishes between the belligerents. With the uneasy peace established, Henry III renewed his policy of religious toleration and restraint, while his brother, Francis of Anjou, became involved in the quest for a separate realm in Flanders. In July he marched his private army to Mons, offering his support to the Dutch Protestants in their ongoing conflict against Philip II of Spain. The Valois government became increasingly alarmed that the dauphin would propel France into war with Philip II. However, after seizing the city of Cambrai Duke Francis of Anjou was repeatedly defeated on the battlefield by the local viceroy and compelled to retreat to France, abandoning his campaign for a personal kingdom. His military incursions created a temporary strain in relations with the Spanish court, but Philip II continued to defend the French Catholics in their struggle against the heretics.

After nearly ten years of childless marriage to Queen Louise, by 1584 it was unlikely that the king would produce a direct successor. As the dauphin, Francis of Anjou was increasingly recognized as heir apparent by the ultra–Catholic party. However, in June he died from consumption, resulting in a succession crisis for the French kingdom. Under the recognized Salic Law, the leader of the Protestants, King Henry of Navarre, became the next in line to the throne. Henry was born on December 13, 1553, in the southwestern city of Pau and was the son of Antoine of Bourbon and Queen Joan III. His father was directly related to the ruling French dynasty and his mother was the daughter and heiress of the king of Navarre. Queen Joan III was a zealous supporter of the Calvinist religion and raised her son as a Protestant. In 1561 the queen took her son to live at the French court where his education was continued in the royal schools with the children of the king's family, including the future Henry III and Duke Henry of Guise.

The prospect of a Huguenot as king of France provoked Duke Henry of Guise and his two brothers, Cardinal Louis of Lorraine and Duke Charles of Mayenne, to form a second Catholic League at Nancy in September 1584 to prevent the heretic from assuming the monarchy, which ignited the War of the Three Henrys. To further their quest for the exclusion of Henry of Navarre, in December the league signed the Treaty of Joinville with Philip II. The Spanish agreed to financially support the war of the league, while the Guise faction pledged to defend the Catholic faith and eliminate all Huguenots from France.

Under the leadership of Duke Henry, the ultra–Catholics mounted an offensive against the isolated Protestant towns and enclaves in the north, capturing numerous fortresses. While the league's campaign gained momentum, many papists rallied to its cause and much of the region north of the Loire came under its control. As the popularity and power of the ultra–Catholics grew, the continued reign of Henry III became increasingly threatened. To avoid war with the duke and preserve his monarchy, the king sent his mother in April 1585 to negotiate a settlement with the league. After three months of talks, the Treaty of Nemours was ratified, which resulted in an end to the crown's policy of religious tolerance, banishment of the Reformation Church and repudiation of Henry of Navarre's blood right to France. After the signing of the Nemours Treaty, the Protestants were forced to again take up arms to protect their religion and lands.

As the prospects for war grew, Henry III raised taxes and received a subsidy from Pope Sixtus V, while the Huguenots negotiated a money grant from Queen Elizabeth I of England and secured German troops from Count John Casimir of Pfalz-Lautern. In April 1586 the king sent three armies south to attack the heretic towns. However, his offensive was limited by the lack of funds and only a few strongholds were seized. His unsuccessful campaign caused widespread dissent among the Catholics, who accused him of not aggressively pursuing the war but favoring a policy of appeasement. Many papist towns willingly gave their allegiance to the league, as Henry of Guise's popularity and power increased, posing a danger to the monarchy of Henry III. In early July 1587 the monarch met with the Guise duke at Meaux to resolve their escalating dispute, but no resolution resulted as the Valois regime's control over the kingdom continued to wane.

With his rule under threat from the Guise faction and Huguenot armies of Henry of Navarre, in August 1587 the king assumed personal command of his military forces. He advanced into the Loire Valley in an attempt to intercept the German mercenaries of Count Casimir, who had again invaded France. However, after ravaging the eastern lordships, the count began to withdraw to Germany. As he retreated his army was defeated by Henry of Guise in two battles, while the royalists under the leadership of the monarch's favorite, Admiral Duke Anne of Joyeuse, were routed by Navarre at Coutras. The duke was a close friend of Henry III, receiving many titles, honors and privileges for his service to the crown. He had fought in the Religious Wars, commanding troops in the attacks against Languedoc and Auvergne and later at the siege of Fere-en-Tardenois.

The lack of victory by Henry III and the successes of the Guise faction further eroded the approval and popularity of the royal regime. As the league gained support among the more moderate Catholics, the king provoked increased disfavor from the nobles by appointing his courtier, Duke John-Louis Epernon, as the new governor of Normandy and admiral of France, while continuing to entertain lavishly with nightly parties, balls and masquerades.

Duke Henry had been banned by the Valois court from entering Paris, but on May 12, 1588, he defied the order and rode into the city to meet with the city council. During the night the Valois regime sent troops into the capital to enforce the ban. The local population responded by rioting and attacking the royalists, in the Day of the Barricades. Fearing for his safety, the king fled from Paris, traveling to Chartres. The loyalists' supporters on the council were replaced by pro–Leaguers, ensuring the Guise faction's full control of the city. After the Day of the Barricades most of northern France pledged its allegiance to Duke Henry as the continued rule of the Valois dynasty became increasingly threatened.

With the north of France and Paris under the control of the Guise faction, Catherine de Medici intervened to persuade the king to negotiate a reconciliation. Under the ensuing Edict of Union, Henry III agreed to dismiss his favorites from his government, grant the Guise family governorships, acknowledge Charles, cardinal of Bourbon, as successor and reaffirm the Treaty of Nemours. Charles was born on September 22, 1523, at Ferte-Sous-Jouare and was the fifth child of Duke Charles IV of Vendome and Frances of Alencon, Duchess of Beaumont. As a younger son, he was chosen for a career in the Catholic Church and rose rapidly through the ecclesiastic government. Charles was appointed as prelate to the bishopric of Nevers in 1540 and eight years later was elected a cardinal by the Holy See. As a cardinal, he attended several conclaves in Rome and served as a church official at the Colloquy of Poissy in July 1561. Through his father's lineage, he was a direct descendent of Louis IX and with Henry III childless the French monarchy passed to him by birthright. Under the terms of the Treaty of Joinville, Charles of Bourbon was recognized as heir apparent by the Catholic League and Philip II of Spain.

The concessions granted in the Edict of Union did little to improve relations with the ultra-Catholic alliance or limit the growing popularity of Duke Henry. To reimpose his usurped authority, Henry III issued a summons for the Estates-General to meet in Blois. In December 1588 the nobles and clerics assembled at Blois to resolve the dissent between the Valois regime and Duke Henry. However, the Estates-General was quickly dominated by supporters of the league and the royal council led by Louis Potier of Gesvres failed to reassert Henry III's sovereignty. As the fear of a Guise led coup escalated, the king arranged the assassination of the duke. On December 23 he was murdered by Henry III's personal bodyguards in the chateau of Blois. The following day Cardinal Louis of Lorraine was killed and surviving leaders of the league arrested, including the cardinal of Bourbon.

After the murders of Duke Henry and his brother, the league issued a summons for all Catholics to take up arms to avenge the killings, as rioting against the Valois regime erupted in Paris. With the papists steadily expanding the territory under their control and with his sovereignty threatened, Henry III was forced to negotiate an alliance with Henry of Navarre and the Huguenots. The crown's secretary of state, Lord Louis Potier, was appointed to lead the royalist envoys and through his exhortations the two kings were brought together. On April 26 the former rivals met and signed an agreement to unite their armies and jointly confront the Catholics. During the summer the combined forces of the new allies drove the Leaguers back from their strongholds and marched against Paris. The capital was placed under siege, while anti–Valois sentiment raged throughout the city and the ultra–Catholics called for the death of the monarch. On August 2, 1589, a fanatical Dominican priest, Jacques Clement, traveled to the royal court at Saint Cloud, claiming to have messages for the king from friends in Paris. The priest had come under the influence of the Catholic League and after approaching Henry III, drew a knife from his cloak mortally stabbing him. Before his death he acknowledged his cousin, Henry of Navarre, as his successor to the crown of France. Henry III died at age thirty-eight after a reign of fifteen years. He was buried at the historic site of interment at the Basilica of Saint Denis with his father, brothers and prior kings of the French Renaissance era.

Sources

Knecht. *The Valois: Kings of France, 1328–1589.*   Potter. *A History of France, 1460–1560.*   Russell, Lord of Liverpool. *Henry of Navarre.*

General Sources for France

Ault. *Europe in the Middle Ages.*   Blum; Cameron; Barnes. *The Emergence of the European World.*   Briggs. *Early Modern France.*   Cameron. *From Valois to Bourbon.*   Castries. *The Lives of the Kings and Queens of France.*   Ferguson. *A Survey of European Civilization.*   Knecht. *The Rise and Fall of Renaissance France, 1483–1610.*   Law. *Fleur de Lys: The Kings and Queens of France.*   Potter. *Kings of the Seine.*   Tilley. *Medieval France.*

PART IV

Renaissance Monarchs of Spain

John II	1405–1406–1454
Henry IV	1425–1454–1474
Isabella	1451–1474–1504
Joanna	1479–1504–1555
Charles I (V of Holy Roman Empire)	1500–1516–1556–1558*
Philip II	1527–1556–1598

Four dates indicate birth, succession, abdication and death.

Genealogical Table

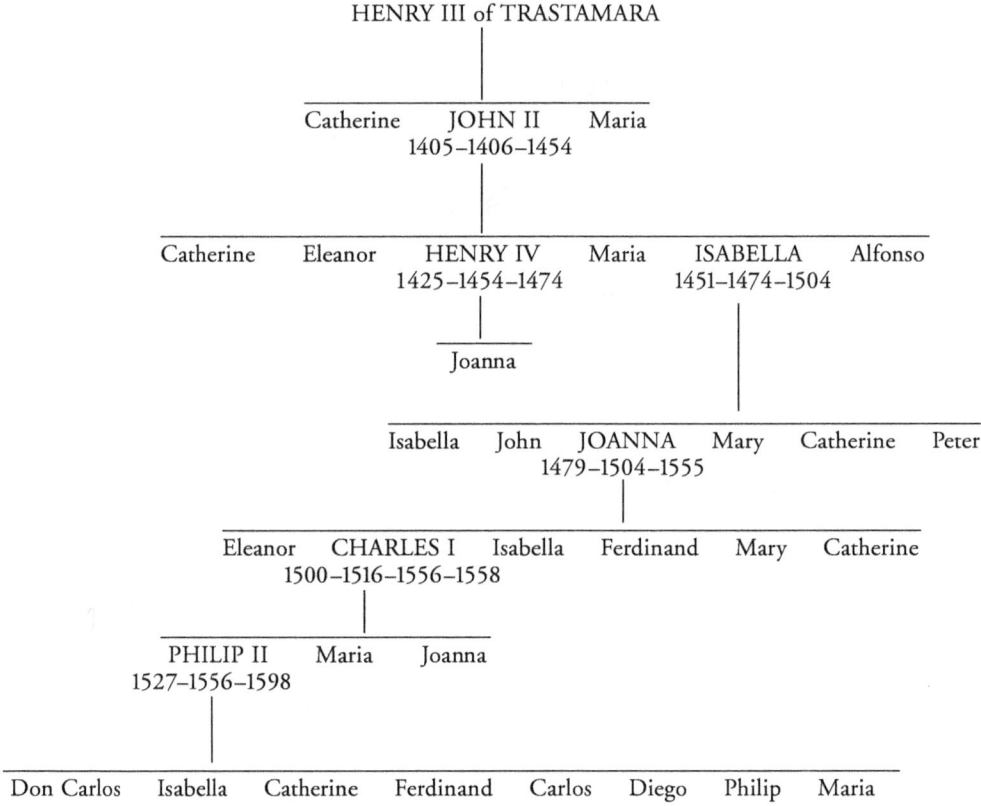

Kings and queens of Spain are in ALL CAPITALS

Overview

In 711 the Muslim Moors from North Africa crossed the Mediterranean Sea and by military might subjugated the fragmented kingdoms of Spain. Slowly the northern Spanish monarchs began to unite and reclaim their territories from the foreign invaders. By the fifteenth century, Castile and Aragon had become the dominant Christian realms and had firmly established their independent rule. During the Renaissance era the kings and queens of Spain completed the ongoing reconquest of their lands from the North African Moors, integrated their tattered Iberian Peninsula into an unified kingdom and created the preeminent European power which ruled half the known world. The first Renaissance king was John II, who assumed the Castilian crown in 1406, advancing his sovereignty into the last bastion of Moorish authority in Granada while defending his demesne against the encroachments of the neighboring kingdom of Aragon. During the kingship of John II, the Renaissance movement began to first appear in Castile under the patronage of his government. He was succeeded in 1454 by his son, Henry IV, whose reign was dominated by the struggle against the attempted usurpation of his throne by King John II of Aragon, rebellion of his recalcitrant nobles in pursuit of their usurped feudal privileges and the succession crisis with his half-sister, Isabella.

The third Renaissance sovereign was Isabella of Castile, who inherited the reins of power in 1474, ruling for thirty years. The queen's reign was occupied with the final defeat of the Moorish invaders, discovery of the New World by Christopher Columbus under her patronage and unification of Spain with her marriage to Ferdinand II of Aragon. Isabella was followed to the throne by her daughter, Joanna, who expanded Spanish influence into northern Europe through her marriage to Archduke Philip of Habsburg. While recognized as queen, in 1506 the Cortes declared her unfit to govern due to insanity and her crown was assumed by her father, Ferdinand II of Aragon, and after his death by her son. To ensure their continued rule, Joanna was imprisoned for the remainder of her life, dying alone and forgotten after fifty-five years of confinement.

The fifth monarch of the Renaissance epoch was Charles I, whose monarchy was dominated by the expansion of Spanish authority into Germany and Italy and the ensuing wars with France. The king sponsored the renewal of exploration into the Americas, resulting in the discoveries and conquests of Mexico and much of South America. As the recognized secular leader of the Catholic Church of Rome and a devout Christian, Charles I defended Spain and its overseas territories against the attacks of the Muslim sea raiders. He was succeeded to the throne by his son, Philip II, whose monarchy of forty-two years produced a Spanish golden age. He ended his father's wars against France and defended his sovereignty and Catholic faith against the encroachments of the Dutch Protestants. During his kingship, he was an enthusiastic patron of the Renaissance, inviting renowned artists, authors, artisans and architects to his court. At the end of his reign, Philip II ruled the Netherlands, Portugal, half of Italy and Spain with its vast overseas colonies and was acknowledged as the dominant power in Europe.

John II, 1405–1406–1454

When the fourth Trastamaran ruler of Castile, Henry III, died in December 1406 his throne was assumed by his son and heir, John II, who reigned as the first Renaissance king of Spain. Prince John was born at Toro in the province of Zamora on March 6, 1405 and was the only son of Henry III and Catherine, daughter of the English duke, John Gault of Lancaster. Through his father's lineage, he was the great-great-grandson of the founder of the Trastamaran dynasty, Henry I, and by his mother he was directly related to the reigning Lancastrian family of England. At birth he was acknowledged as successor designate to his father's kingdom and invested with the title of prince of Asturias. When Henry III died on December 25, 1406 the twenty-two-month-old prince inherited the crown of Castile unchallenged. Prior to his death, Henry III appointed his brother, Ferdinand, and Queen Catherine as regents to govern jointly in the name of the minor sovereign. In January 1407 the Castilian Cortes met in Segovia to officially recognize John II as monarch and authorize the regency of the queen and Ferdinand. However, dissent soon erupted between them, when Catherine came increasingly under the influence of a faction of nobles, who were attempting to regain their usurped feudal powers. As the realm became threatened with civil war, in April the regents agreed to partition Castilian sovereignty with Catherine retaining the north, while Ferdinand assumed authority over the regions of Toledo, Murcia and Andalusia.

As the infant-king's mother maintained his rule over the north, Ferdinand renewed the ongoing Catholic campaign of reconquest against the Moors by launching an attack against the kingdom of Granada. After several inconclusive border clashes, during the late summer of 1407 he captured the fortress of Zahara. As the Castilians continued to advance south into Granada, the Moorish king, Muhammad VII, counter attacked to limit further gains by the Christians. Ferdinand's offensive was increasingly hampered by the lack of money, troops and supplies from the government. As he remained in Granada his requests for military aid were repeatedly ignored by his co-regent, who was advised by her courtiers not to support his initiative to weaken his prestige and authority over Castilian affairs. As the dissent between the two regents escalated, the sovereign's uncle negotiated the backing of the royal council, Cortes and high nobles to compel the queen to dismiss her advisors and withdraw from court. Through his forceful intervention, civil war was averted and the powers of the magnates weakened.

While Ferdinand was taking control of the regime, the king of Granada, Muhammad VII, died and his brother, Yusuf III, assumed the Moorish monarchy, quickly agreeing to a two-year truce with the Castilians. During the ensuing period of peace, Ferdinand consolidated his rule over the recalcitrant nobles to govern uncontested in the name of the king. With unrestricted autonomy he began to reform the Castilian administration, usurping the powers of the royal council. The governments of the large cities were restructured, limiting their authority and reducing local abuses and corruption. With his reign secure, the queen's exiled advisors were permitted to return to court and the kingdom was again divided between the two co-regents. Nevertheless, all decrees still had to be approved by Ferdinand. His centralization policy expanded the supremacy of John II's sovereignty and enhanced his prestige and standing among the magnates and towns.

With his power over Castile secure, the regent mounted a formidable campaign to expand the demesne of John II after the truce expired with Granada in 1410 and laid siege against Yusuf III's great fortress at Antequera. With his stronghold under attack, Yusuf III sent a large relief army to break the investment but his troops were defeated and forced to withdraw. The assaults against Antequera were intensified and following an attempt to storm the defenses, the garrison commander surrendered on September 10 after a five-month siege. With his lands occupied by the Castilians, the Moorish king was compelled to negotiate a truce and under the ensuing treaty agreed to give homage and pay an annual subsidy to the Trastamaran monarchy. The victory at Antequera increased the domain and wealth of John II, enhancing his prestige among the nobles.

Under the terms of the reconciliation negotiated between Catherine and her co-regent in 1407, the Castilian kingdom was divided with the queen gaining supremacy over the northern lordships and custody for her son, while Ferdinand governed the southern provinces. Under their agreement the queen provided for the protection and care of John II and he resided at her court in Valladolid. During the early years of John II's reign, his kingdom remained at peace under the skillful rule of his uncle. In late June 1412 the political stability of the realm became threatened when Ferdinand was elected as the new king of Aragon by the Conference of Caspe. However, after taking the Aragonese throne, he refused to relinquish his co-regency and continued to effectively control all of Castile.

When Queen Catherine assumed nominal control of the northern provinces, the king remained in her household at the castle of Valladolid. Under the direction of his mother, respected tutors from the church and nobility were appointed for John II's education in reading, writing, religion, Latin and literature. He was a serious and dedicated student, developing a special interest in the classics and poetry. John II was introduced to military training and especially enjoyed hunting and martial tournaments. As part of his education, he was instructed in the social graces, mastering the skills of singing, dancing and court etiquette.

While Ferdinand held near absolute power over Castile, the nobility remained loyal and submissive to the regime and the Moors maintained peace along the border. In 1416 John II's uncle died and was succeeded as king of Aragon by his son, Alfonso V, while Catherine became the sole regent for Castile until her death two years later. Following the queen's death, the Castilian Cortes officially ended the minority of John II, recognizing him as reigning king. However, he was ill prepared and had little aptitude or desire to rule. Assuming the reins of government, John II was increasingly challenged for power by the local lords and especially his Aragonese cousins, King Alfonso V, Prince John and Prince Henry. The Aragonese princes had been granted extensive and rich Castilian lands and honors by their father, making them formidable magnates. Henry married Catherine, sister of the Castilian sovereign, and received the march of Villena as the dowry, while John married Blanche, daughter of King Charles III of Navarre and heiress to his throne. Prince John was the second son of Ferdinand of Aragon and Eleanor of Albuquerque and was born at Medina del Campo, Castile on June 29, 1398. After his brother, Alfonso V, inherited the crown of Aragon, he was appointed lieutenant general, ruling as regent during the king's frequent absences in Italy. Through his wife, John was recognized as heir to the monarchy of Navarre, developing a large following of support in the kingdom.

With a strong base of Castilian support, the Aragonese princes attempted to gain supremacy over their cousin and reduce him to their figurehead ruler. Lacking the skills of kingship, the fourteen-year-old king increasingly depended on the advice and protection of his close friend and confidant, Alvaro de Luna, appointing him constable for his kingdom. De Luna was born around 1389 in Cuenca Province and was the son of Alvaro Martinez de Luna, a prominent Castilian courtier during the reign of Henry III, and Mary Fernandez de Jarana. Through the influence of his uncle, Archbishop Peter de Luna of Toledo, he became a page at the royal court in 1410 and during the final two years of Queen Catherine's regency gained control over the young monarch. Alvaro de Luna was well educated and a skilled and unscrupulous politician.

Soon after taking control of the government, Alvaro de Luna finalized the marriage agreement of John II to his cousin, Mary of Aragon. She was the daughter of Ferdinand of Aragon and Eleanor of Albuquerque and was born in 1396. The marital treaty was negotiated to closely bind the Castilian branch of the Trastamaran dynasty to its Aragonese cousins. The relationship between the Castilian king and his queen was frequently tense, as she continually attempted to thwart his initiatives against her brothers and intrigued in court policy. The marriage resulted in four children, including the future King Henry IV, who was born in 1425.

In July 1420 Prince Henry of Aragon attempted to seize power in Castile by force of arms. With the backing of a contingent of soldiers, he broke into the royal palace at Tordesillas, taking custody of John II and holding him as his prisoner. With the king's authority over the kingdom challenged, Alvaro de Luna began to intrigue to arrange his release. Through his initiatives, in November John II managed to escape from Tordesillas and reassumed the monarchy. Under the influence of de Luna, the king ordered the arrest of Henry on charges of treason. His estates were forfeited to the Trastamaran crown and granted by Alvaro to his supporters and friends to closely bind their loyalty to the regime. De Luna was personally rewarded by the throne for his services with his official appointment as constable and commander of all military forces.

As the Castilian king continued to imprison Henry, his brothers, Alfonso V, and the newly anointed monarch of Navarre, John, demanded his release and the dismissal of de Luna, threatening to invade his kingdom. In September 1527 confronted with the united military might of his cousins, John II was forced to remove the constable from his offices and free Henry. Without de Luna's political skills and prestige protecting the king, John of Navarre soon usurped power from his cousin and attempted to rule with his Aragonese relatives and friends. However, he was distrusted by the Castilian council and court, while the nobility refused to accept the presence of the Aragonese and loss of their influence in the ruling administration. Unable to govern, John of Navarre was compelled to permit the recall of Alvaro de Luna to court. After the restoration of the constable, John II was quickly again under his control and the Navarre king forced to return to his realm.

In the aftermath of his failed intervention against Castile, King John of Navarre remained determined to overthrow de Luna and appealed to his brother, Alfonso V, for military aid to crush him. As hostilities between Castile and the Aragonese princes intensified, in 1430 both rivals began to prepare for war. John II's call to arms was fully supported by his nobles and Cortes but Alfonso V was confronted with dissent from his magnates and towns over the increase in taxes to finance the army. Without the backing of his subjects, he was forced to negotiate a five-year truce, leaving de Luna fully in power over Castilian affairs of state.

Following the truce negotiated by Ferdinand with Granada in 1410, the two kingdoms had remained at peace. However, in 1429 the Moorish king, Muhammad IX, refused to pay the agreed annual tribute and became aligned with Aragon against Castile. To enforce the terms of the treaty, the Trastamaran crown formed an alliance with Yusuf IV, grandson of King Muhammad VI, pledging to support his usurpation of the regime for his pledge of vassalage. In the spring of 1431, Castilian troops began to raid the borderlands, while preparations for a major offensive were begun. In June the formidable Spanish army, with the king and his constable in command, marched into the Moorish kingdom and on July 1 defeated Muhammad IX at the battle of La Higueruela near the capital city of Granada. After their victory John II and de Luna returned to Castile and appointed their frontier captains to continue the campaign. Under the renewed attacks of the Castilians and their Muslim allies, the western Granadian lordships were occupied and in January Yusuf IV entered the capital to establish a new government. However, he was unpopular with the local population and was assassinated in March 1432. Muhammad IX regained the Moorish throne and continued the war until a peace treaty was signed seven years later.

During the reign of John II, the Renaissance movement began to first appear in Castile. The king was an enthusiastic sponsor of classical scholarship and literature, while inviting distinguished humanists to his kingdom. He was a renowned patron of poets and authors and his court became an important literary center for the advancement of humanism in Spain. He supported the poet John Alfonso de Baena and ordered the writing of his poem *Cancionero de Baena*. Alfonso de Villasandino became the monarchy's court poet, writing in the lyric style. The king appointed John de Mena as his personal secretary for Latin letters and he became the first humanist poet of Castilian literature.

In the aftermath of the truce negotiated between Castile and Aragon in 1430, Alvaro de Luna's rule over the kingdom was unchallenged. John II remained content to allow the constable to determine his court policy, while pursuing his personal interest in poetry and hunting. At first the Castilian nobles and towns did not demand a voice in his administration but as his authority became supreme they turned slowly more bellicose. The once aggressive Aragonese princes were occupied with the conquest of Naples and posed no immediate threat to de Luna's dominance. For nearly eight years he held the reins of power, keeping the Cortes and magnates in check and maintaining peace over the realm. However, in 1438 Alfonso V and his brothers returned from Italy and began to intrigue with the Castilian nobility against de Luna. As the constable continued to acquire large estates for himself and appoint his supporters and relatives to high offices in the government, the Castilian lords united to press the king to dismiss him and govern alone. As their hostility grew, in October 1439 Alvaro de Luna was exiled from the council for six months.

During the banishment of de Luna, John of Navarre returned to Castile and attempted to assume the constable's role as chief minister to the king. However, John II disliked and mistrusted his cousin and took every opportunity to avoid contact with him. To expand his influence and prestige over the Castilian regime, in 1440 John of Navarre arranged the marriage of his daughter, Blanche, to the monarch's heir, Prince Henry of Asturias. However, when Alvaro returned to the royal council following his expulsion, the power struggle between the two court parties intensified. The princes of Aragon became allied with a faction of rebel Castilian lords and issued a proclamation charging de Luna with usurping the powers of the Trastamaran crown and governing as dictator. With the threat of rebellion from the dissident nobles and towns escalating, John II was again forced to exile his constable.

In the absence of de Luna, the Aragonese princes began to increasingly challenge the Castilian crown by force of arms. King John of Navarre ordered his brother, Prince Henry, to assemble his private militia in Toledo and seize the constable at his Escalena Castle. As Henry laid siege against Alvero's defenses, the king negotiated the surrender of John of Navarre's fortified city of Medina del Campo to draw his cousins away from their siege at Escalena. While John II took possession of the strategic fortress, the Aragonese princes abandoned the attack against Escalena and advanced to recover Medina del Campo. In June 1441, they launched an assault against the citadel, storming the walls and defeating the royalists. During the battle, John II was taken prisoner and his kingdom usurped by his two cousins.

John of Navarre and Henry took control of the Castilian monarchy and established a new ruling administration, appointing many of their Aragonese allies and friends to prominent offices while the king remained imprisoned. The kingdom was now beset with a dysfunctional regime, resulting in misrule, factionalism, internal revolt and impoverishment. After three years of suffering the abuses of power by the Aragonese, Prince Henry of Asturias became allied with his former tutor, Bishop Lope Barrientos of Segovia, and the exiled de Luna to challenge the government. To gain John II's release from the usurpers, the bishop met with him at Tordesillas Castle and formulated a plot of escape. Acting under their plan, on July 15, 1444, the king arranged to go hunting and as his party neared the village of Majador they were intercepted by a contingent of loyalist troops, who freed him. While he was securing his rescue, Prince Henry and de Luna assembled their personal armies and marched to join the royalists for the expected battle against their rivals. However, when confronted by the superior military might of the king, the Aragonese princes abandoned Castile and returned north to muster additional soldiers to regain their lost power.

After the exile of the two Aragonese princes, John II mounted an attack against their Castilian fortifications along the Douro River in the northern provinces. In August 1444 the royalists laid siege and soon occupied the great stronghold at Penafiel. While the monarch continued his Douro River campaign, John of Navarre began preparations to invade his cousin's realm, uniting his army with the private militia of his brother, Prince Henry of Aragon, and dissident Castilian magnates. In February 1445 the king appointed Alvaro de Luna as commander of his army and began to muster his troops at El Espinai to defend his kingdom. When his Aragonese cousins advanced into Castile, John II broke camp and moved to engage them. After several days of hard marching, de Luna intercepted the Aragonese princes near the town of Olmedo. However, John of Navarre refused to fight and withdrew to the protection of the fortified town, while attempting to negotiate a reconciliation. The monarch refused any compromise and after several small inconclusive skirmishes, on May 19 the dissidents finally opened the town's gates to challenge the loyalists. De Luna immediately formed his cavalry and foot soldiers into battle array with their lances, swords and shields gleaming in the late afternoon sun and personally led the charge against the invaders. During the melee he suffered a severe wound to his thigh from a lance but continued with the fight. As the battle remained inconclusive, the royal infantry entered the onslaught and the archers and spearmen decimated the ranks of the rogue forces. The Aragonese army and their allies abandoned the conflict, while John of Navarre and his injured brother fled in disarray to the safety of Aragon. The complete triumph at Olmedo propelled Alvaro back to supremacy over the throne's government to rule without opposition. The rich estates of Prince Henry were forfeited to the crown and the constable was rewarded with the lordship of Santiago.

While Alvaro de Luna governed the kingdom unopposed, the king's heir, Prince Henry of Asturias, came increasingly under the dominance of the ambitious and politically astute John Pacheco, Marquess of Villena. With the support and encouragement of Pacheco, the Asturias prince began to energetically confront the constable for control over the king. His political faction forged coalitions with dissident nobles and challenged the power of de Luna. Despite their threats of armed rebellion and an alliance with Aragon, Alvaro skillfully thwarted their hostilities. However, the rebels found a new ally in 1447 when the constable arranged the marriage of John II to Isabella of Portugal. She was born in 1428 and was the daughter of Prince John, brother of the Portuguese king, Alfonso V. The wedding ceremony was held on July 22 and resulted in two children, the future Queen Isabella and Prince Alfonso. The king and Isabella of Portugal quickly developed a stormy relationship as she schemed to reduce the authority of de Luna and direct court policies. She was young, beautiful, ambitious and strong willed and exerted a strong influence over her husband. The queen resented the constant interference of de Luna in the affairs of the royal household and his supremacy over the king, allying with Prince Henry to oppose the constable. She relentlessly demanded the dismissal of Alvaro but John II remained loyal to his close friend. Finally, in 1453 she convinced the king to force the constable to retire to his estates. Nevertheless, de Luna refused to leave his offices and his arrest was ordered by the Trastamaran crown. He was tried by a court of nobles and declared guilty of seizing the throne and ruling as an usurper. Alvaro de Luna was beheaded on June 2, 1453, in the Valladolid main square. John II soon became distressed and distraught over his involvement in the execution of his lifelong confidant, growing increasingly frail and weak. The king died at Valladolid on July 20, 1454, at the age of forty-nine after a troubled reign of forty-eight years, leaving his kingdom impoverished, the government in shambles and the sovereignty of the Castilian monarchy powerless.

Sources

Miller. *Henry IV of Castile.*   O'Callaghan. *A History of Medieval Spain.*   Phillips. *Enrique IV and the Crisis of Fifteenth Century Castile.*

Henry IV, 1425–1454–1474

In the immediate aftermath of the death of John II, the Castilian crown was inherited by his heir, Henry IV, who ruled as the second king of the Spanish Renaissance era. Henry was born on Friday, January 5, 1425, in Valladolid and was the only son of John II's first marriage to Mary of Aragon. In April he was invested with the title of prince of Asturias in recognition of his blood right as successor to the Trastamaran monarchy. The young prince spent most of his early life away from the royal court in the town of Segovia under the care and protection of the Lord of Baena. The local bishop, Lope Barrientos, was appointed as tutor for his education and Henry received instruction in reading, writing, religion, mathematics, government and literature. He developed a fondness for music, learning to play the lute and as was typical for a Renaissance prince collected rare and exotic animals. A veteran knight from Sevilla, Peter Manuel, was later appointed to provide his military education and he received training in fencing, horsemanship and hunting. As he grew older, he frequently traveled with the royal court to master the skills of kingship, as his father enforced the sovereignty and laws of his Trastamaran throne. In Segovia a small council was created for the Asturias prince and he soon came under the influence of John Pacheco, who became his close friend and confidant. During his childhood he suffered a severely broken nose, which permanently disfigured his face. As the prince grew into adulthood, he was described by contemporaries as unusually tall at over six feet, with blue eyes and blondish hair and beard and a well formed body. He was uncomfortable in large crowds, preferring small informal gatherings.

In 1436 John II began talks with the kingdom of Navarre for the marriage of Henry to his cousin, Princess Blanche, daughter of King John. The Navarre king and his two brothers, Alfonso V and Prince Henry, had inherited large Castilian estates in 1416 after the death of their father, Ferdinand of Aragon. With a formidable base of local support, the Aragonese princes began to aggressively challenge the throne of Castile through diplomacy and military might. John of Navarre strongly favored the marital union to further his quest for power in Castile. While the deliberations continued, John Pacheco convinced Henry to demand an independent court and control of Segovia to secure his approval for the marriage. To gain his backing, the king was forced to agree to his son's terms. In September 1440 the two royal families met in Valladolid for the wedding. However, the pre-marital festivals and military tournaments soon became marred by the deaths of several prominent guests and the elaborate celebrations were cancelled. The wedding ceremony was held on September 15 in the palace instead of the local cathedral with Blanche dressed in a white bridal gown and wearing the

Navarrese crown jewels. The service was followed by a small private banquet in the queen's rooms. While the wedding had turned into a fiasco, the biggest disappointment occurred when Henry failed to consummate the marriage.

With his plans for the peaceful usurpation of Castile shattered by the failed marriage, John of Navarre ordered his brother, Henry of Aragon, to renew their ongoing campaign against the throne by force of arms. Henry mustered his private militia in Toledo, advancing against the regime's constable, Alvaro de Luna, at his fortress of Escalena. With his confidant and close advisor under siege, the monarch traveled with a small contingent of troops to John of Navarre's city of Medina del Campo and bribed the local council to renounce their overlord and acknowledge his sovereignty. After the loss of their strategic castle, the Aragonese princes were compelled to abandon the siege against de Luna and unite their forces to regain the city. In early June 1441, the rebel army of over two thousand men-under-arms was assembled and marched against the king. When they arrived at Medina del Campo, an assault was ordered against the stronghold and in the ensuing battle the walls were breached and the royalists defeated. During the melee John II was taken prisoner by his cousins' soldiers. With control of the king, the princes seized the crown and ruled Castile, establishing their independent council. John II was imprisoned at the castle of Tordesillas and held under close guard.

In the aftermath of his father's dethronement, Henry of Asturias withdrew to his city of Segovia and initially supported his cousin's new regime. However, after three years of misrule, impoverishment and internal rebellion, the Castilian prince's former tutor, Bishop Lope Barrientos of Segovia, convinced him to renounce the Aragonese government and unite with the king and de Luna against the usurpers. In the late spring Henry rode to the castle of Tordesillas, meeting with his imprisoned father and pledging his loyalty. Under the influence of Barrientos, a plot was formed to secure John II's freedom and regain control over the kingdom. On July 15 the king, under custody of the Count of Castro, was permitted to pursue his favorite sport of hunting. However, when the royal party approached the village of Majador, they were intercepted by the crown's troops and John II freed. While he was escaping from his captors, Henry and de Luna mustered their private armies and advanced to join the royalists at Duenas in preparation for battle against the Aragonese and their local allies. Nevertheless, when confronted by the superior military might of the loyalists, the rebels abandoned Castile and returned to their lands to raise additional soldiers to recover the throne.

While the princes recruited a new army in Aragon and Navarre, Alvaro de Luna assumed command of the royalists and in February 1445 began to assemble his troops at El Espinai in central Castile. Later in the month Henry left Segovia with his personal militia and Moorish bodyguards to join his father at El Espinai. When the rebels crossed the border into Castile from the east, de Luna immediately assembled the army to pursue his enemy. After several days the Castilians encountered the princes near the town of Olmedo. However, John of Navarre refused to fight and attempted to negotiate a resolution to his disputes while his forces were steadily reinforced with Castilian dissidents. The fruitless talks went on for several days until finally on May 19 Henry of Asturias with his household cavalry rode close to the defensive walls to challenge his uncles. The rogues responded by sending a contingent of knights to engage him. Outnumbered he was compelled to ride hard for the safety of the Castilian camp. De Luna quickly ordered the army to arms and deployed into battle formation. With the constable commanding the center and Henry on his right with over four hundred men-at-arms, the king gave the command to advance toward Olmedo.

When the loyalists reached the city, the Aragonese and their Castilian allies initially refused to fight but after several hours of delay they opened the gates and rode out in full battle array with pennants flying. John of Navarre with one thousand cavalry commanded the center, while his brother led one thousand five hundred men-at-arms on the left flank. When his cousins approached his lines, John II ordered his trumpeters to sound the charge across the fields of poppy and wheat. The two armies met in a violent clash of arms with de Luna personally leading the assault. After the initial encounter, the two military forces turned and charged again into each other with lances, battle axes and swords. However, the invaders lacked infantry and when the royal spearmen and archers reached the melee they decimated their ranks. The rebels began to abandon the battlefield with the royalists in close pursuit. John of Navarre and his wounded brother fled from Olmedo in disarray. The military might of the Aragonese princes and dissident Castilian nobles was shattered by their decisive defeat, while John II regained supremacy over his kingdom.

Following the battle, the royal army marched north to seize the castles and towns of the vanquished princes and magnates, while Henry returned to Segovia and his private life away from court politics and courtiers. He was rewarded by his father for his participation in the Olmedo victory with the taxes from five towns and with the income from his royal titles and honors became a wealthy prince. Segovia was his favorite residence and he spent his wealth to rebuild and embellish the city. He made improvements to the cathedral, building a new cloister and buying a grand organ. The local castle was redecorated in the Moorish style with a magnificent throne room constructed. Henry greatly enjoyed music, playing the lute well and spending freely for a private choir. He began to collect exotic animals, building a preserve to house his wild lions, bears, boars and bulls. The prince was occasionally recalled to court but after fulfilling his obligations as heir always returned to his beloved Segovia and its surrounding forest of pines.

Remaining in Segovia with his small court of favorites, Henry came increasingly under the influence of John Pacheco. To enhance his personal wealth and esteem, Pacheco encouraged the prince to actively challenge de Luna for authority over his father. Under John Pacheco's prodding, Henry organized an aggressive political campaign to confront the constable. He formed close associations with former Castilian dissidents and began negotiations for an alliance with Aragon. As his rebellion gained strength, the rival court factions began to prepare for civil war. However, in May 1446 the two belligerents peacefully settled their differences by signing the Treaty of Astudillo. Under the agreement Henry and his father pledged to share responsibility for the administration of the government and towns. Despite their apparent reconciliation, neither party honored the resolution, as the Asturias prince and his allies continued to pursue additional power. While maintaining his governmental offices, the constable opened talks for the marriage of the widowed king to a Portuguese princess for an ally to thwart the opposition of a resurgent John of Navarre and Henry of Asturias's expanding coalition.

In April 1446 the marriage contract with Portugal was signed by the Castilians and in July of the following year the wedding ceremony between John II and Isabella was held south of Valladolid at the town of Madrigal de las Atlas Torres. The new queen was beautiful, ambitious, and possessive, quickly exerting a strong influence over her husband. Despite de Luna's attempt to gain an ally against Prince Henry, the queen resented his constant presence and overbearing control of the king. To assert her independence, Isabella became allied with Henry and Pacheco to confront the constable.

While the faction in opposition to the royal regime continued its intrigues, in 1449 Toledo revolted against the rule of John II and declared its independence. Henry agreed to support the uprising for his recognition as co-governor. However, when a plot was discovered in the city to assassinate him, he entered Toledo with a strong contingent of troops to overthrow the government and assume full control. By his decisive actions and show of military might, the Asturias prince was now acknowledged as a powerful rival to de Luna and his administration.

As Henry's political faction was expanding its power and weakening the rule of de Luna, Queen Isabella continued to press her husband to dismiss the constable from his council offices. The Castilian prince remained away from court at his favorite city of Segovia and after twelve years of childless marriage with Blanch of Navarre began negotiations with his cousin, Alfonso V of Portugal, for his marriage to the king's sister, Joanna. The Portuguese favored the continuation of their alliance with Castile and the preliminary agreement was quickly signed. The prince immediately petitioned the church for a divorce and after a hearing in July 1453 the archbishop of Toledo granted an annulment on grounds that the marriage was never consummated. However, the marital union with Joanna was delayed by the rapidly unfolding events at the royal court in Valladolid.

Alvaro de Luna had come under increasing attacks from Queen Isabella and Henry's hostile faction, demanding his dismissal from the government. Finally, in 1453 John II demanded his retirement from the council. However, de Luna refused to leave his offices and his arrest on charges of sedition was ordered by the monarch. After a brief trial by a court of nobles, he was declared guilty and executed on June 2, 1453.

Following the overthrow of the constable, Henry withdrew to his estates, while retaining his powerful coalition in opposition to his father. In late 1453 the king's health began to steadily decline. By June it was clear to the court that he was dying and his son was summoned from Segovia to assume control of the regime. On July 22, 1454, John II died and Henry was recognized as king, quickly overcoming the challenge from Queen Isabella to place her infant son, Alfonso, on the Castilian throne. On July 23, 1454, Henry IV mounted his horse at Valladolid Palace and rode at the head of a brilliant coronation procession, followed by his courtiers and soldiers through crowded streets decorated with tapestries and placards. He was invested with the crown of Castile in the traditional Trastamaran enthronement ceremony.

After assuming control of the monarchy, Henry IV began to establish his ruling administration, retaining many of his father's court officials and advisors. He had received little prior training in preparation for his assumption of the throne and lacking close family support was forced to seek advice from his favorites. As a close friend of the Castilian king, John Pacheco of Villena took a prominent role in the new council and was appointed to the position of steward. To secure his sovereignty, Henry IV initiated a policy of reconciliation, inclusion and patronage with the magnates. He issued grants of titles, lands, money and royal offices to gain their loyalty. New lords were ennobled to dilute the power of the aristocratic grandees, while previously exiled nobles were pardoned and their forfeited estates returned. To enhance the efficiency and quality of his government, he began the practice of including university trained officials in his regime, who owed their allegiance to only him. To strengthen his authority, he extended the practice of sending royal agents into the provinces to ensure compliance with his rule. The Castilian crown's interest was protected by appointing retainers to serve on town councils. The reforms directed by Henry IV weakened the strength of the nobility and cities and expanded the might of his kingship.

During his early reign, the Castilian king began new initiatives to improve the kingdom's economy. Commercial activities with the Low Countries had been a major source of wool and raw materials trade for Castile and he encouraged its expansion. Diplomatic contacts were made with England to repair damaged relations resulting from Castile's support of France during the Hundred Years' War and new treaties of commerce were signed. Henry IV's council opened negotiations with Aragon to establish a new relationship of détente. In October the two realms agreed to the Treaty of Perpetual Peace and Friendship at Agreda on their common border. Under the settlement, John of Navarre, serving as his brother's lieutenant general, pledged to renounce all family claims to Castilian possessions for the annual payment of a large subsidy. To stabilize the monetary system, attempts were made to improve the minting of coins to ensure their quality and reduce the inflationary practice of debasing. The system of weights and measurements was standardized and royal agents sent to ensure compliance. To improve the collection of the sales tax, new decrees were issued to indicate which products were subject to the levy, while making sure fraud was reduced and the clergy and nobles paid their fee. While many of the reform measures were only partially successful and had limited effect, most were continued by following monarchies.

The kingdom of Granada stretched across the southern border of Castile and was the last bastion of Islamic power remaining in Spain. Attempts had been made by prior regimes to conquer the region but its mountainous terrain had limited success. To expand the territory under his rule, in March 1455 the Castilian king mounted a small scale military campaign against his Moorish neighbor. Prior to traveling to Granada to assume command of the army, he appointed the archbishop of Toledo, Alfonso Carrillo, and the Count of Haro as regents during his absence, investing them with full authority to govern in his name. Carrillo was born in 1410 and was the son of Lope Vazquez de Acuna and Teresa Carrillo. Through his father's lineage, he was a direct descendent of a Portuguese noble family. Alfonso was educated by his uncle, Cardinal Alfonso Carrillo of Albornoz, and chosen for a career in the church. After serving in various church offices, he was appointed bishop of Siguenza in 1436 and archbishop of Toledo ten years later. He participated in the battle of Olmedo with his personal ecclesiastic militia supporting the monarchy of John II. As a skilled soldier and diplomat, he was appointed to the court of John II, becoming an influential and powerful royal advisor.

As Henry IV marched toward southern Castile, the royal army was united at Cordoba with the private militias of the Spanish lords and infantry supplied by the towns advancing east unopposed into the Moorish domain. The monarch refused to fight a major battle and launched only small rapid sorties against the Muslims' exposed positions, while avoiding prolonged sieges. To strengthen his initiative against the Moorish king, he negotiated alliances with dissident Grenadian magnates and encouraged his new allies to revolt against their overlord. Under his relentless attacks, Henry IV's invasion continued to make significant gains, securing his border with the Islamic realm and winning sovereignty over the fortresses at Gibraltar and Archidona. By seizing the offensive, his policy of limited engagement weakened the wealth, esteem and power of the Moors, while increasing the demesne under Castilian control. However, despite his successes his nobles disapproved of his strategy of restricted warfare, preferring a large scale attack to acquire personal wealth, lands and martial glory, while the clergy opposed peaceful relations with the non–Christians.

While the Spanish were expanding Christian control into Muslim Granada, the Holy See of Rome was attempting to rally all of Europe for a holy war against the Ottoman Turks, who had recently seized Constantinople. The Castilian crown sent envoys to Rome, convincing Pope Calixtus III to recognize Henry IV's campaign against Granada as a papal crusade. The king was granted the authority to issue church sponsored indulgences and retain the income from the sales. The government utilized the fees from the papal bulls to fund the Islamic war and created the realm's first permanent army of twenty thousand infantrymen and a force of three thousand cavalry.

As the campaign continued against the Moors, in May 1455 Henry IV appointed Peter Giron, brother of Pacheco, to command the army and returned to Cordoba to meet his new wife, Joanna of Portugal. The final marital contract was signed and the private ceremony was performed on May 23 in the local palace. A public mass was held in the cathedral and was followed by a grand banquet with the royal court. After the wedding Henry IV and Joanna traveled to Sevilla, where a series of festivals, banquets and military tournaments was staged to honor the new queen. She was described as beautiful, self-confident, cultivated and fastidious with a fondness for lavish entertainments and parties. The king and his queen were a complete mismatch and their relationship quickly became stormy, ending in divorce in 1468. The marriage resulted in one daughter, Princess Joanna of Castile; albeit with the queen's numerous adulterous affairs there was widespread doubt that Henry IV was the father.

The ongoing peace between Castile and Aragon became threatened in 1458 with the death of King Alfonso V and the succession to the throne of his more militant brother, John II of Navarre. Initially he pledged to respect the Treaty of Perpetual Peace and a period of superficial conciliation followed. To bind the two kingdoms in friendship, Henry IV negotiated the marriage of his half-sister, Isabella, to Ferdinand, son of the king of Aragon. The Castilian grandees considered the union of the two monarchies as a threat to their feudal rights, forming a league to seize control of the council and force the king to appoint his half-brother, Alfonso, as heir designate. Confronted by the challenge of the rebels, the sovereign ordered John Pacheco of Villena to mount a punitive attack. As the revolt turned more bellicose, the archbishop of Toledo, Alfonso Carrillo, joined the insurgents and influenced many of the high nobles to join him. In April 1460 John II of Aragon agreed to support the rogue alliance.

As the hostilities between Castile and Aragon grew, Henry IV began preparations for war against Aragon, negotiating an alliance with Prince Charles of Navarre, the son of John II from his first marriage. The prince was popular in his Navarre kingdom and commanded a large powerbase in the Aragonese province of Catalonia. Before invading Aragon, the king needed to first come to terms with the rebel Castilian league and sent Pacheco to mediate a reconciliation. After talks with the leaders of the insurgency, an agreement was signed with the nobles pledging troops for the conflict and the crown promising to guarantee their feudal privileges, appoint Alfonso as heir and enlarge the council with new grandee members. In January 1461 war erupted in Navarre between Charles and Aragon and when the prince was captured by his father, the Castilians dispatched an army to attack the kingdom. The formidable cavalry force defeated the local Aragonese soldiers and freed Prince Charles. In March Henry IV moved his court to the Aragonese frontier to personally direct the campaign and by early summer his troops had seized many of John II's border towns, despite the death of his ally, Charles of Navarre. With part of his demesne under occupation and his province of Catalonia in revolt in support of the invaders, John II was compelled to open peace talks. On August 26 the two belligerents ratified a treaty, agreeing to appoint a commission to reconcile the terms. By his successful intervention into Aragon, Henry IV won esteem and respect for his rule from the grandees and expanded his power.

In late February 1462 Queen Joanna gave birth to a daughter, Joanna of Castile; to secure the succession of Henry IV's monarchy. On May 9 she was acknowledged as heir apparent by the Cortes and given the title of Princess of Asturias. With the authority of his government enhanced by his successes in Aragon, the king assembled the grandees and high nobles at court to pledge their allegiance and swear to support Joanna as their future queen. With the investiture of the princess as heir, the recent appointment of Prince Alfonso as successor was rescinded and the power of the nobility weakened.

While the court of Castile was celebrating the birth of the new heir, in the Aragonese province of Catalonia civil war had again erupted. In the aftermath of the death of the popular Prince Charles of Navarre, King John II appointed his nine-year-old son, Ferdinand, as his Catalonian lieutenant general with his mother serving as regent. However, the local lords and towns refused to accept their rule and rose in revolt. In August 1462 the rebels offered the Aragonese crown to Henry IV. He quickly accepted the monarchy and while his spies and agents attempted to incite dissent among the Aragonese population, a large contingent of troops was dispatched to buttress the conspirators' defenses against John II's siege at Barcelona. Late in 1462 a formidable Castilian army was mustered for an invasion of John II's kingdom.

With the threat of a Castilian attack imminent, John II began negotiations with Louis XI of Valois, promising to cede him the northern lordships of Roussillon and Cerdagne for French military aid. To further entice the Valois regime into the treaty, the kingdom of Navarre was without a ruler following the death of Prince Charles and it was pledged to the French nobleman Gaston de Foix, husband of the heir designate, Eleanor. The offer was accepted by Louis XI and his army was sent to invade Catalonia. As the French campaign gained momentum, Henry IV agreed to personally negotiate with the French king and resolve the differences between Castile and Aragon. In April 1463 the two kings met on their common frontier and after long deliberations Henry IV pledged to withdraw his forces from Aragon and renounce his claim to the throne, while receiving the Navarre border town of Estella and surrounding region as compensation.

In the aftermath of the peace treaty with John II of Aragon, Henry IV renewed his policy of patronage and reconciliation with the grandees to solidify their allegiance. New grants of honors, titles and lands were bestowed on the magnates and new high nobles created. To secure his borders, he negotiated a peace treaty with Granada and signed an agreement of friendship with his cousin, Alfonso V of Portugal, gaining a formidable ally for support against rebellious magnates and an aggressive king of Aragon.

During the recent invasion of Aragon, the regime's principle advisors, John Pacheco and Alfonso Carrillo, had initiated secret independent negotiations with the French and had pledged to promote Castile's withdrawal from the war, fearing a reduction in their power over the monarchy. Their plot to increase their authority over the government was discovered and they were exiled from court. The king came under the influence of his new confidants, Beltran de la Cueva and the Mendoza family led by Peter Gonzalez. Beltran de la Cueva was born in 1443 at Ubeda and was the second son of Diego Fernandez de la Cueva and Maior Alfonso de Mercado. He became a ward of Henry IV in 1454 and was raised and educated in the royal court. As a favorite of the king, he quickly rose to high offices in the administration and was rewarded for his skills and loyalty with grants of lands, money and titles, including the grand mastership of the Military Order of Santiago. The second of the king's confidants was Peter Gonzalez, who was born on May 3, 1428, at Guadalajara in the province of New Castile and was the fourth son of Inigo Lopez, marques of Santillana. He was a direct descendent from a family with a long history of faithful and heroic service to the throne of Castile. As a younger son, Peter was chosen for a career in the church, rising rapidly to high ecclesiastic posts and in 1452 was appointed bishop of Calahorra by King John II. Under his responsibilities as bishop, he assumed secular command of the local militia and civil government in addition to his religious duties. Serving as leader of the Calahorra levies, Gonzalez led his troops in support of the crown against the dissident lords.

After their forced banishment, Pacheco and Carrillo forged a coalition with other insurgent nobles to regain their council offices. They planned to take control over the sovereign's half-sister, Isabella, and half-brother, Alfonso, and use them as the figureheads of their revolt. As their rebellion gained new supporters, in September 1464 John Pacheco, lord of Villena, and the leaders of the league offered to negotiate a settlement with the Castilian king. However, as Henry IV approached the small town of Villacastin for the talks, a defector from the magnates' faction warned him of the rebel plot to take him prisoner. With the monarchy threatened, the local militia rallied to the king's defense and the conspiracy was thwarted. After their scheme was neutralized, the dissidents issued a proclamation, charging Henry IV with showing favoritism to non–Christians, allowing Beltran de la Cueva to seize royal power and invading Catalonia illegally. To defend his reign against the challenge of Pacheco and Archbishop Carrillo, the king assembled his counselors in Valladolid and despite the protest of Beltran and Peter Gonzalez of Mendoza, who advised an attack against the anti-royalists, ordered new negotiations with the renegade alliance.

The first meeting between the two belligerent factions occurred on October 25, 1464, on an open plain to avoid the possibility of assassination. After brief negotiations a treaty was signed with Henry IV agreeing to disinherit his daughter, appoint Alfonso as heir, and exile Cueva from court for six months, while the rebels promised to respect the peace. To compensate his friend and favorite for his absence from the council, the king granted Beltran the duchy of Albuquerque. The rivals met for a second time on November 20, where a commission was authorized to modify the structure of the ruling council to increase the powers of the nobility in the government. The committee members assembled at Medina del Campo in January 1465 and under the strong leadership of Pacheco and Archbishop Carrillo published a declaration known as the Sentence of Medina del Campo. Under the sentence, Muslims and Jews were to be removed from the administration, an ecclesiastic inquisition created to judge all suspected heretics and no tax levies were permitted without permission from the Cortes. The central provision of the proclamation established a permanent council of high grandees and prelates, whose consent was required for the arrest order of any magnate by the king. With the degradation of his authority to rule independently, Henry IV declared war on the dissident league in defense of his sovereignty and ordered Beltran to muster the army at Segovia. In February the king issued a decree, voiding the sentence. In defiance of the regime, on June 5 the rebel alliance held a mock dethronement ceremony at Avila, no longer recognizing the kingship of Henry IV and crowning Alfonso as the new monarch of Castile.

In the aftermath of the ceremonial dethronement at Avila, Castile was quickly divided into two hostile factions. The rebel league was led by John Pacheco and Archbishop Alfonso Carrillo, while Beltran and the Mendoza family under the leadership of Peter Gonzalez supported the defense of the crown. Henry IV was strongly opposed to war but the attempted usurpation of his power forced him to issue a summons for the kingdom to rally to him with soldiers, money and arms. As he recruited his army, the first clash between the belligerents occurred when Pacheco launched an attack against the fortified city of Simancas. The city commanded a strategic location and the regime encouraged the garrison to resist all assaults. As the loyalists continued to repulse the dissidents' sorties, they were compelled to begin siege operations against Simancas, while the defenders at Jaen in the south thwarted the investment against their town by Peter Giron. The heroic opposition of the two garrisons permitted the throne the time it needed to prepare for war.

In early 1466 the town of Valladolid rose in revolt against the anti-royalists and swore loyalty to the monarchy. The war effort of Henry IV was given further impetus when Pope Paul II recognized him as the legal ruler and sent Leonardo of Bologna as his personal legate to encourage the rebels to reconcile. As support for their league faltered, Carrillo and Pacheco attempted to regain their momentum by marching their forces from Avila and attacking several government held strongholds. When they gained control over Olmedo, the king's army, with the militias of the Mendoza family, Cueva and other powerful magnates, was mustered at Cuellar and on August 18, with pennants flying in the breeze, advanced toward Olmedo. After two days of marching the loyalists were confronted by the waiting Leaguers led by Archbishop Carrillo. The crown's troops were moved into battle formation with Peter Gonzalez commanding the left flank and Beltran on the right. In the mid-afternoon, as the heat intensified, the two forces charged into each other's ranks with lances, swords and battle axes. At first the kingdom's cavalry was driven back and when his knights fled the onslaught, Henry IV withdrew toward Medina del Campo with his personal Moorish guards, leaving Gonzalez and Beltran to direct the fight. Under their command the throne's levies rallied to take charge of the battlefield, holding Carrillo in check. The melee lasted until after dark with the archbishop finally withdrawing with the remnants of the league to the safety of Olmedo. After hours of hard and bloody fighting in the hot August sun, the battle ended in a stalemate with the dissidents still holding Olmedo and the loyalists traveling to Medina del Campo to join the king.

The second battle at Olmedo had ended in an impasse but the royal army had deprived the league of the decisive victory it needed to sustain the rebellion. Castilian magnates and cities increasingly returned their allegiance to the crown and in the late spring of 1468 Sevilla and Toledo opened their gates to the king and pledged their loyalty. When the bishopric of Siguenza became vacant, Henry IV appointed Peter Gonzalez as the successor as reward for his support.

As their uprising continued to lose momentum, in July 1468 Prince Alfonso suddenly died and after the loss of their recognized king, the rebels' cause lost support among the lords, cities and prelates. With the league's revolt in disarray, John Pacheco supported a reconciliation with the throne but demanded Henry IV appoint Isabella as his legal successor and renounce the inheritance rights of his daughter, Joanna. Many of the dissident magnates had become exhausted by the costly war and willingly accepted the reunion with the monarchy. To settle the civil war, in September the king and his council agreed to meet with the Leaguers near Avila on the open plain of Toros de Guisando. Under the treaty signed between the rebel faction and the regime, Isabella was named hereditary princess with immediate possession of the lordship of Asturias and six cities, while Henry IV was acknowledged as ruling monarch with the right to approve the future marriage of his half-sister. To gain fealty of the rogue faction, the crown initiated programs of royal patronage, granting pardons, government offices, money, lands and castles. The administration's allies were rewarded for their continued loyalty with the Mendoza family and the Duke of Albuquerque receiving control of additional towns and estates.

Despite accepting the terms of the Toros de Guisando Treaty, in October 1469 Princess Isabella was married to Ferdinand of Aragon without the approval of her half-brother. Henry IV remained resolved to be succeeded by his daughter and with his sovereignty widely accepted, renounced the Toros de Guisando agreement. In October 1470 Joanna was again proclaimed heir and to provide for the future of the Castilian monarchy was betrothed to the brother of the French king, Duke Charles of Berry. With the promise of marriage to a powerful European dynasty, Joanna's quest for acceptance as successor received broad support. However, Charles died shortly after and despite several new negotiations for a marital contract, no suitable husband was found. While Joanna's prospects for assuming the throne became diminished, Isabella was already married to a formidable and politically skilled nobleman who was heir to the crown of Aragon. Isabella's recognition as successor gained momentum when she gave birth to a daughter, Isabella, increasingly gaining the backing of the grandees, lords, towns and church.

John Pacheco's return to the favor of the king was widely opposed by many of the crown's strongest defenders, who feared the loss of their power and influence at court. In the south the duke of Medina Sidonia, Henry of Guzman, led the city of Sevilla in revolt in opposition to Pacheco of Villena. The throne's prestige and acceptance deteriorated further, when Pope Paul II died on July 26, 1471, and the new pontiff, Sixtus IV, reversed papal policy to support Isabella's political faction. As Pacheco continued to demand more authority, council offices and land, many noblemen, including Peter Gonzalez and his Mendoza family, deserted to the rebel alliance resulting in the additional decline of Henry IV's sovereignty and power.

In late December 1473 Henry IV agreed to meet with Isabella and Ferdinand at the fortress in Segovia to resolve the terms of the succession. After several days of unsuccessful talks, the king was suddenly stricken with a severe abdominal pain following dinner and was serious ill for several days. After partially recovering his health, in March he traveled from Segovia to establish his court at Madrid. However, his illness soon returned and he grew increasingly frail. The king renewed his campaign to secure the crown for Princess Joanna but his declining health limited his initiative. By December Henry IV was too weak to return to Segovia for the Christmas holidays, dying at Madrid in the local castle on December 12, 1474, at the age of nearly fifty after a reign of twenty years.

Sources

Miller. *Henry IV of Castile.*   O'Callaghan. *A History of Medieval Spain.*   Phillips. *Enrique IV and the Crisis of Fifteenth Century Castile.*

Isabella, 1451–1474–1504

When Henry IV died in December 1474 the Castilian throne was assumed by his half-sister, Isabella, who reigned as the third sovereign of the Spanish Renaissance era. Princess Isabella was born in the town of Madrigal de la Atlas Torres on April 22, 1451, and was the daughter of John II and Queen Isabella of Portugal. She was the first child of the king's second marriage and next in the line-of-succession to her half-brother, Henry. She was raised in her mother's household but after the death of her father and the accession to the monarchy by Henry IV, the infant princess was moved from the royal court with the dowager queen and her brother, Alfonso, to the palace in Arevalo. Although John II had provided funds for their upkeep, the new king ignored the wishes of his father and the queen and her children suffered from shortages of money and household staff. In Arevalo Isabella began her education under the direction of her mother, who appointed local tutors and nuns for her limited studies in writing, reading, mathematics, grammar, music and embroidery. The Castilian princess was encouraged to participate in physical activities and enjoyed falconry, horseback riding, games and hunting. The dowager queen was a devout Catholic and instilled her children with the same piety. Princess Isabella remained away from court and uninvolved in crown politics, while Henry IV struggled to maintain his rule against rebellious noble factions. However, as the second issue of John II, she attracted the loyalty of many grandees and towns, who favored her inheritance rights to the Castilian throne.

Isabella and her brother spent most of their early childhood in Arevalo but in late 1461 they were moved to the royal court in Madrid to await the birth of Henry IV's first child. They became a part of Queen Joanna's household, where their education was renewed. In the unfamiliar and strange courtly environment, Isabella came under the influence of Archbishop Alfonso Carrillo of Toledo, who assumed the position of surrogate protector. In February 1462 the king's wife gave birth to a daughter, Princess Joanna of Castile. When her niece was recognized as her father's heiress, the princess was reduced to a minor role at court. During Joanna's baptism ceremony in the palace chapel, Isabella served as one of her godparents. On May 9 Henry IV summoned the Cortes to swear its loyalty to Joanna with Alfonso and his sister acknowledging their niece's legitimacy as successor.

Despite his apparent reconciliation with the nobility in 1462, many powerful magnates and grandees still favored the inheritance rights of Alfonso and Isabella and Henry IV opened negotiations to subdue their mounting rebellion. While Isabella and Alfonso remained under the guardianship of the king, a rebel faction began to form to promote their bloodrights. The league was quickly joined by many high nobles and cities and by summer of 1464 civil war against the throne threatened. To discredit the succession of Princess Joanna, the dissidents issued a proclamation asserting the illegitimacy of her birth. As the strength of their uprising grew, Henry IV agreed to meet with Archbishop Carrillo and Lord John Pacheco to resolve their dispute. After brief negotiations the court pledged to disherit the king's daughter and name Prince Alfonso as heir, provided he was married to Joanna of Castile. When the belligerents met for the second time, a commission was appointed to modify the structure of the royal council and published the Sentence of Medina del Campo, usurping the powers of the monarchy.

Henry IV responded to the threat of rebellion against his rule, by revoking the birthrights of his half-brother and half-sister and declaring war against the dissidents. As backing for the king steadily increased, the rogue league marched its army to seize several towns in an attempt to regain its momentum. The royal council countered the losses by attacking the anti-royalists at Olmedo. The ensuing battle resulted in a stalemate but denied the rebels the decisive victory they needed to sustain their uprising. As the monarchy continued to expand its authority over the nobles and cities, Princess Isabella remained at Segovia under the wardship of her half-brother, adopting a political policy of neutrality. However, in July 1468 Prince Alfonso died and with the loss of its acknowledged symbol of sovereignty, the insurgents' cause lost support among the lords, including its major defender, John Pacheco, who returned his allegiance to the crown. As the throne regained its control, the leaguers were forced to begin reconciliation talks.

In September Henry IV and his council met the rebels a few miles from the walled city of Avila on the plains of Toros de Guisando. The king arrived for the meeting with his chief advisor, John Pacheco, and one thousand men-at-arms, while Isabella appeared on a richly decorated mule with Archbishop Carrillo and over two hundred armed troops. Under the terms of the ensuing treaty, Isabella was appointed hereditary princess, while Henry IV was recognized as ruling monarch with the right to approve the future marriage of his half-sister. In the aftermath of the reconciliation, the Cortes was summoned to formally acknowledge Isabella as heir designate.

Following the Toros de Guisando agreement, many additional dissident lords abandoned the conspiracy movement and returned to the regime. Pacheco had quickly resumed his former office as chief advisor to the monarchy and to protect his extensive holdings in the north against an aggressive King John II of Aragon, influenced Henry IV to approve the marriage of Isabella to Alfonso V of Portugal with their future son acknowledged as heir to Castile.

However, she refused to accept the marital treaty, prompting her half-brother to deny her possession of her inherited towns and castles to force her approval of the wedding to the Portuguese king. Without a designated source of income, she was unable to establish her private household and was compelled to remain at the royal court in Ocana. The Castilian council increasingly regarded the terms of the Toros de Guisando Treaty and Isabella's rejection of the Portuguese marriage as attacks against its independent sovereignty. As her opposition to the crown mounted, the hereditary princess regretted her compromises at Toros de Guisando and forced marriage proposal to Alfonso V, as she again came under the influence of the archbishop of Toledo, Alfonso Carrillo. The archbishop strongly promoted her marital union with Prince Ferdinand of Aragon to protect Isabella's inheritance rights to the Castilian throne. Ferdinand was born on March 10, 1452, in Sos del Rey Catolico in the province of Saragossa and was the second son of John II and his second wife, Queen Joanna Enriquez. In recognition of his place in the line of succession, Ferdinand was named king of Naples and when his older brother died in 1461 was acknowledged as heir to Aragon. He became closely associated with his father's regime and army, learning the skills of government and war. He was a formidable soldier and became renowned for his jousting and martial triumphs.

Despite the opposition of the monarchy, secret negotiations for the marriage of Isabella and Ferdinand were continued between her allies and King John II of Aragon. While the Castilian princess refused to openly challenge her half-brother's rule, resistance to the Portuguese union grew among the grandees and towns. The rebel faction opposed the marriage to the much older Alfonso V, fearing that after his death his successors would attempt to seize the Castilian crown. Finally, in February 1469 with the support for her assumption of power escalating, she agreed to the Aragonese marriage.

In the aftermath of the princess's approval for the marital union with Aragon, Archbishop Carrillo sent envoys to the court of John II in Saragossa to finalize the contract. While the negotiations continued in Aragon, Isabella made arrangements for her escape from Ocana and in July 1469 with Henry IV campaigning against several rebellious cities in the south, she secretly traveled to Madrigal to join her mother. The king was soon informed of her flight and threatened the Madrigal officials with harsh penalties if they continued to support her marriage to the Aragonese prince. Fearing harm to her allies, she moved with her small court to the nearby town of Coca. With the princess in danger, Carrillo marched his personal militia north to provide security and presenting a magnificent ruby, pearl necklace and large sum of gold coins to her as gifts from Prince Ferdinand. In defiance of her half-brother's spies, she publicly wore the necklace, signaling her independence from his crown. To give greater protection to Isabella, in August she rode out of Coca to the safety of the great fortress at Avila. However, the city was beset with an epidemic and Carrillo was forced to change the route, traveling to Valladolid. On August 30, 1469 Isabella was welcomed to the city by crowds of cheering nobles and commoners.

When informed of his half-sister's defiance, Henry IV ordered the royal army to advance north to capture Isabella. As the loyalists moved toward Valladolid, Archbishop Carrillo sent his agents to Aragon with instructions to bring Ferdinand to the princess's court. However, when they reached Saragossa in late September, neither John II nor his son was in the capital. Both kings were in Catalonia, defending their realm against an invasion from France. To protect Aragon's friendship and alliance with the Castilian rebel faction, Ferdinand soon began the journey to Valladolid dressed as a peasant to avoid recognition and seizure by the royalists. On October 14 the prince arrived in Valladolid with an escort led by Archbishop Carrillo to his first meeting with Isabella. The civil wedding ceremony was held four days later with

Archbishop Carrillo reading a papal bull permitting Isabella and Ferdinand, as second cousins, to marry within the forbidden degree of consanguinity. After agreeing to govern as equal rulers, they were married in the late afternoon in the Vivero Palace by Archbishop Carrillo. The religious service was held the next day in front of Carrillo and two thousand guests and was followed by celebrations of dancing, jousting, singing and feasting. However, there was little of the rich pageantry and elaborate parties associated with royal weddings due to the lack of money.

Soon after the wedding ceremony, Isabella and Ferdinand sent their envoys to Henry IV with letters swearing their allegiance and pledging to respect the peace but there was no response. In early November, the king voided the princess's rights and income to the town of Arevalo and seized several castles, leaving the rebels with little money. Later in the month, the regime claimed that the papal bull read by Carrillo at the marital ceremony was forged and the marriage illegal. Many of Isabella's remaining allies now deserted to the crown.

As the princess and Ferdinand struggled to maintain their small court, Henry IV returned to Old Castile, threatening Valladolid and the region with his close presence. Many of their local followers turned hostile and Isabella and Ferdinand were forced to move north to Duenas in March 1470. They were compelled to spend the summer in fear of attack, poverty and diminishing popular support.

On October 2, 1470, the king's half-sister gave birth to her first child, Isabella, who became the recognized successor to the Trastamaran throne by bloodright. However, her birth was greeted with little enthusiasm throughout the kingdom. Isabella's claim to the Castilian crown would have been greatly enhanced if she had delivered a son. The princess's right to the monarchy suffered a further setback, when Henry IV formally disinherited his half-sister and named his daughter, Joanna, as heir. Nevertheless, the appropriation of Isabella's inheritance was widely opposed by the grandees and towns.

In reaction to the monarch's disinheritance decree, whole towns in the north revolted, while in Sevilla the duke of Medina Sidonia led the city in support of Isabella. The crown's backing continued to falter, as the Castilian economy suffered from bad weather, resulting in crop failures and famine, repeated debasing of the coins and widespread brigandage. In early 1471 the king's principal ally, the Mendoza family, abandoned the monarchy and joined with the rebel faction. Continually short of money, Isabella initiated an aggressive campaign to acquire possession of her Aragonese dowry, writing to John II for his personal intervention. Through his involvement, she gained control over her properties and incomes from Naples and Aragon. Support for the throne deteriorated significantly when Henry IV's friend and ally, Pope Paul II, died in July 1471 and was succeeded by the hostile Sixtus IV, who reversed papal policy to promote the rights of Isabella. The anti-royalists' cause was further aided when the new pope issued the papal bull, sanctioning the marriage between Isabella and Ferdinand, as their quest for the realm gained widespread favor.

As the prospects of gaining the crown for Isabella brightened, in June 1472 Cardinal Rodrigo Borgia, serving as Sixtus IV's personal legate, arrived in Valencia with papal instructions to offer assistance in resolving the differences between Castile and Aragon. He also carried the papal bull legalizing Ferdinand and Isabella's marriage. He first met with the Aragonese prince and affirmed the Holy See's commitment to Isabella and Ferdinand's succession to the throne. After leaving Valencia, the ecclesiastic party traveled to Madrid for negotiations with Henry IV. The king was anxious to restore his former friendly relations with the papacy and attempted to win the cardinal's backing but any gains were transitory. He finished his journey with a private meeting with Isabella and Ferdinand at Carrillo's palace in Alcala. Cardinal Borgia left Castile without visiting the queen or Princess Joanna. The papal endorsement brought esteem and repute to the princess and prince, enhancing their campaign to claim the Castilian monarchy.

By the summer of 1473 many towns and prominent nobles had changed their allegiance, pledging their loyalty to Isabella and Ferdinand. In June the captain of Henry IV's favorite city of Segovia, Andres de Cabrera, joined the rebel alliance. As the crown continued to lose power, Pacheco deserted the king and became allied with Isabella's faction to protect his royal offices and estates. Without the political advice of Pacheco, by the winter most of the towns in the south and many in the north now supported the Castilian princess's right to the throne. Finally after Christmas celebrations, Henry IV agreed to meet in Segovia with his half-sister and arrangements were quickly made by the Cabrera family.

Beginning on December 28, 1473, Isabella met privately with her half-brother over the next three days. She attempted to resolve the future succession and her inheritance rights but the king refused to make any commitment. On New Year's Day they were joined by Ferdinand, who met Henry IV for the first time. They spent their time together cordially riding through the streets of Segovia, renewing their talks and attending banquets, dances and parties at night. On Sunday January 9, 1474, Cabrera invited Henry IV, the Aragonese prince and Isabella to a banquet at the residence of the local bishop. After dinner they moved to an adjacent room for the musical entertainment but soon Henry IV became serious ill with a sharp abdominal pain. Isabella and Ferdinand remained close to the sovereign and after several days he began to slowly recover his health. However, there was now widespread suspicion they had poisoned him. The trust that had been established between the two factions was shattered and in the coming days the king avoided all discussions about the succession rights of Isabella. In March Henry IV left Segovia and established his court at Madrid, while the princess assumed control over the town.

From Madrid Henry IV renewed his initiative to secure the monarchy for his daughter, Joanna but was limited by his rapidly declining health. By the approaching holiday season, he was too ill to spend Christmas in his beloved Segovia and died on December 12. Messengers were sent immediately to Segovia with the news of Henry IV's death and on the next day Isabella was hurriedly crowned queen of Castile without Ferdinand. She was advised by her council to act quickly to deter Princess Joanna's political faction from issuing a counter claim for the throne.

Ferdinand had earlier traveled to Aragon to aid his father in defending Catalonia against an invasion from France and after receiving the reports of Henry IV's death quickly returned to Segovia. On January 2 he entered the city to an elaborate reception planned by the queen with cheering crowds, placards of welcome, dancing and music. He was first met by Cardinal Gonzalez, Archbishop Carrillo and many high grandees and prelates and escorted to a church service of thanksgiving in the cathedral. He was finally reunited with Isabella in the palace. Despite their public display of affection, Ferdinand soon began to resent his secondary role as only king consort. He demanded a commission be summoned to determine his legal rights of sovereignty. During the hearing, the queen's position was presented by the cardinal, who stressed the advantages under Castilian law that permitted the eldest daughter to be recognized as heir in the absence of a male issue, which prevented the kingdom from falling under the domination of a foreign prince. The king finally accepted the Castilian concept of female inheritance and withdrew his objections. Isabella was empowered with the right to rule the realm in all affairs of state but Ferdinand was acknowledged as chief military commander and given responsibility for waging war. In spite of her unlimited power, over the next months she ceded Ferdinand the authority to govern as co-sovereign.

Once Isabella was affirmed as queen by the high grandees and prelates, the Cortes met in Segovia to pledge its loyalty to her. However, Princess Joanna still retained a significant base of support among the nobles and towns and in late May claimed the Castilian throne as Henry IV's legitimate heir. To strengthen her inheritance rights, the princess's allies negotiated her marriage to her uncle, Alfonso V of Portugal. Once the marital contract was signed, in May 1475 he led his army into Castile, meeting Joanna and her Castilian sympathizers at Placencia where they were proclaimed co-sovereigns. After a delay to celebrate their betrothal, Alfonso V marched north to capture the fortress at Zamora to ignite the Castilian War of Succession.

As the invaders advanced unopposed into Castile, Isabella rode from town to town recruiting an army, while Ferdinand traveled to the northern provinces, rallying the local troops to the queen's cause. By early July a large military force of mostly militiamen was mustered in Valladolid under the personal command of the king. He organized and trained the royal army and began plans for the campaign against Joanna. To provide revenue for the war, he convinced the church to grant a large loan and was able to now purchase the necessary arms and supplies for the coming attack. With his preparations made, he marched his soldiers west to besiege Zamora, while the loyalists' light cavalry launched destructive raids into Portugal, destroying farms and villages and interrupting Alfonso V's lines of communications. As the war dragged on, many of Joanna's Castilian allies deserted her cause unhappy with fighting for a foreign king.

In late February the Portuguese king advanced his forces to relieve the siege against Zamora Castle. As they made camp before the castle's walls, Ferdinand mounted a surprise attack, driving Joanna's army from Zamora. As the Portuguese withdrew, they were closely pursued by the royalists, who intercepted them near the town of Toro on March 1, 1476. Commanding the center line, the Castilian king maneuvered his soldiers into battle formation and charged into the ranks of Alfonso V's troops. After nearly three hours of hard and bloody fighting, the Castilians forced their enemy from the field as the retreat turned into a rout.

In the aftermath of the defeat of Joanna's army at Toro, Isabella and Ferdinand introduced a wide ranging array of reforms to consolidate their rule. The royal council was restored as the central governing institution for the kingdom and the queen appointed not only high grandees and prelates to serve but also lesser nobles and townsmen. She summoned the Cortes to meet in Madrigal in April 1476 and passed laws to standardize the money system and established regulations for all monetary transactions. The judicial structure was reorganized and a national police force formed to keep the peace and end brigandage. To expand commerce, new roads and bridges were built and existing ones improved, while the merchants were encouraged to advance the highly profitable wool trade with western Europe. To ensure compliance with royal laws, crown agents were sent to live in designated cities and participate in the local councils. While the co-sovereigns gained the support of the towns through their revamping measures, they also issued decrees to weaken the power and privileges of the nobles. Statutes were promulgated forbidding the construction of new castles, while many existing ones were demolished. Private wars were outlawed and the magnates' impunity from the law eliminated. To weaken them financially, the grandees were made to pay a large subsidiary directly to the treasury. When the master of the wealthy Military Order of Santiago died, Isabella denied its appointment to the nobility and chose her husband as the new commandeer, keeping the income for her royal coffers. Through negotiations with Pope Sixtus IV, the regime regained control over Spanish ecclesiastic appointments and qualified clerics were named to the high church offices, who owed their loyalty to the throne. Under the direction of the queen, the church began a broad based initiative to restructure the monastic orders and enforce religious discipline and laws.

While the majority of the grandees and towns had declared their allegiance to the crown, isolated areas of sympathy still remained for Joanna, especially on the border with Portugal in the province of Estremadura. In April 1477 the queen traveled to the west with her court to impose her sovereignty over the defiant city of Trujillo but was refused entry by the mayor. To enforce her authority, she summoned loyal troops from Andalusia and under threat of attack the fortress surrendered. She continued her journey through the rebel lordships forcibly asserting her rule by the power of her presence. While the queen reclaimed southwestern Estremadura for her throne, Ferdinand rode to the northern region with his army and launched assaults against four rogue castles, seizing them by force of arms for the queen. By the end of the year, the province had pledged its loyalty to the regime.

After imposing her rule over the western lordships, Isabella traveled to Sevilla to enforce her law and justice over the mutinous and ungovernable province. She established her court in the local castle and relentlessly prosecuted the civil and criminal cases, while the royal police aggressively pursued the brigands. During her long stay in the city, Isabella gave birth to a son, John, who was recognized as heir to the thrones of Castile and Aragon. The queen's assertive and determined intervention in Sevilla ended years of unrestrained civil disorder and restored her power over the region.

Following the decisive victory at Toro and Isabella and Ferdinand's aggressive campaign of subjugation, many defiant Castilian lords and towns now gave their allegiance to the throne. The city of Madrid, which had long supported Joanna's cause, pledged its loyalty to the queen. As his challenge for the monarchy continued to crumble, in September 1479 after failing to gain French military and financial aid, Alfonso V signed the Peace of Trujillo, renouncing his claims to the realm and annulling his marriage to his niece, while Joanna agreed to retire to a convent in Portugal. After four years of warfare, Isabella was finally the undisputed queen of an united kingdom. John II had died earlier in the year and Ferdinand II had succeeded him to the throne, to rule with Isabella as co-sovereigns of Castile and Aragon.

While Isabella and Ferdinand II were distracted with the Castilian War of Succession, the Granadian king of the last remaining Muslim realm, Mulay Hassan, defiantly refused to pay the agreed annual tribute to the Christians. He had aspirations of reconquering Christian Spain for the Moors and in late December 1481 without warning attacked the Andalusian town of Zahara, killing or enslaving the entire population. The king and queen responded to the breach in the ongoing peace by ordering the marquis of Cadiz, Rodrigo de Leon, to seize the Muslim town of Alhama. On February 28 the marquis overran the fortress and claimed the town for the crown. While he occupied the region, Ferdinand II recruited an army in the north to reinforce the Granadian campaign, while Isabella raised money, arms and supplies for the war effort. After the conquest of Alhama, the conflict developed into a series of sieges as the Christians slowly and relentlessly captured town after town. As the Spanish gained more victories, mercenary soldiers from all of Europe began to swell their ranks, as the offensive became a religious crusade against the Muslims. While the king besieged the Moorish strongholds, a separate force of cavalry was sent to destroy the local farms, crops and orchards. To prevent Mulay Hassan from receiving military aid and supplies from North Africa, Ferdinand II ordered his Aragonese fleet to patrol the south Mediterranean Sea and intercept all Moorish ships.

The Spanish ongoing conquest of Granada was further facilitated by the outbreak of civil war between the supporters of Mulay Hassan and his two sons, Muhammad XII and Yusuf.

Muhammad XII proclaimed himself king and to advance his cause for the throne in 1487 negotiated an alliance with the Christians, agreeing to hold Granada as a tributary kingdom for Isabella and Ferdinand II. With military aid from the Spanish, he and his allies mounted an attack against his uncle, King Muhammad XIII, who had succeeded his brother, Mulay Hassan, to the Moorish throne. While the two Muslim factions fought each other, Isabella and Ferdinand II organized a combined land and sea assault against Granada's second most important city of Malaga. Located on the Mediterranean coast, the fortress port was under the rule of the Moorish king and was defended by a reinforced garrison and large contingent of mercenaries from North Africa. In May 1487 the Spanish laid siege against Malaga and pounded the defensive walls with cannon fire for three months. Finally, in August with food supplies exhausted, the Moors agreed to conditionally surrender. However, Ferdinand II refused to offer any terms and the city was forced to unconditionally submit. The entire population was enslaved with one-third exchanged for Christian captives in North Africa, while the remainder was the property of the co-sovereigns.

Ferdinand II's severe decree against the Malagan population served as a threat to further Moorish resistance and Muhammad XII pledged to renounce control of his occupied Granadian territory in exchange for sovereignty over the four towns still under the rule of his uncle. The king and queen accepted the proposal and in the spring of 1489 began siege operations against Muhammad XIII's capital of Baza. The Moors defiantly refused to surrender and put up a fierce resistance for five months. However, after an offer of generous terms from the Spanish, the garrison commander agreed to submit. Following the fall of his capital the Moorish King abandoned his three remaining fortresses to Isabella and Ferdinand II. After gaining supremacy over the four cities, the king and queen demanded the submission of the capital city of Granada from Muhammad XII. However, he refused to honor his prior commitment and prepared to fight for the remainder of the Moorish kingdom of Granada.

Muhammad XII's small domain was centered in the capital of Granada and Isabella and Ferdinand II directed their offensive against the city. A formidable army of over fifty thousand was mustered and in the spring of 1491 Granada was besieged. The Moors offered little resistance and in October negotiations for surrender were initiated. After two months of deliberations, the Moorish king agreed to accept the generous conditions proposed by the co-sovereigns. Under the resulting treaty, in return for their submission the Moors were permitted to retain their laws, religion and property, while Muhammad XII was granted a new kingdom under Castilian sovereignty. On January 2, 1492, the Moorish king rode out of the city and four days later Isabella and Ferdinand II made their triumphant entry into Granada in a magnificent procession of splendidly armored knights and infantry followed by lavishly robed clerics. In the throne room of the Alhambra Palace, the queen and king officially took possession of the last Moorish kingdom to end nearly eight hundred years of Muslim rule in Spain.

While the Spanish were at war against Granada, in 1486 Queen Isabella was first introduced to Christopher Columbus through the intervention of the Duke of Medinaceli, Luis de la Cerda. Columbus was born in the second half of 1451 in the northern Italian city-state of Genoa and was the eldest son of a local wool weaver, Domenico Columbus. He spent his childhood working for his father, receiving only a limited formal education. At the age of eleven he became a cabin boy, sailing the Italian coastline on commercial vessels. In 1473 Columbus was employed as a merchant sailor, delivering cargo to ports along the Mediterranean coast for various business firms. Three years later he joined his brother, Bartolomeo, in Lisbon and worked as a mapmaker. In Lisbon he was exposed to the latest in navigation and sea exploration to Asia. In 1482 Columbus left Portugal and began trading along the west coast of Africa. He later traveled to southern Castile, gaining the favor of several influential royal courtiers, who were interested in discovering new sea routes to China and Japan. Through their intervention, Columbus was granted an interview with the Spanish court.

During his discussions with the queen, Columbus explained his radical plan to sail to China and Japan by a direct western course, instead of the traditional eastern route. Isabella realized the advantages of trade and an alliance of friendship with the Great Khan but with the struggle against the Moors still unresolved, no financial commitment was made. Nevertheless, the Genoese sailor refused to abandon the expedition and remained at court to constantly press for further interviews. His venture attracted the patronage of several influential courtiers and in early 1492 after threatening to leave for France, he was granted an audience. After a hour's meeting with Isabella and Ferdinand II, the naval expedition was approved. Under the contract, Columbus agreed to sail for Spain and was appointed admiral of the ocean and royal viceroy for new lands discovered, while the crown pledged to provide the funds for the ships, crews and supplies.

In the spring of 1492 Christopher Columbus traveled to the southern port town of Palos on the Atlantic coast and began to assemble his small fleet of three caravels. Under orders from the royal crown, Palos provided the *Pinta* and *Nina,* while chartering the flagship, *Santa Maria,* for the voyage. An experienced local sea captain, Martin Alfonso Pinzon, was appointed co-leader of the expedition and after three months the preparations were completed. On August 3 Columbus sailed in a westward direction toward the Orient with ninety sailors. After seventy days at sea he landed on the Bahaman island of San Salvador, believing it was part of the Asian coastline. On the first voyage he discovered many islands, including Cuba and Hispaniola. In April 1493 Columbus returned to Spain and received a hero's welcome by the royal court at Barcelona. Three more expeditions followed with many additional discoveries. Christopher Columbus's four journeys of exploration opened a new world that became a vast overseas empire, making Spain the wealthiest and most powerful kingdom in Europe.

Under the influence of Isabella and Ferdinand II, the early Renaissance movement blossomed in Spain. The queen was an avid collector of Flemish artists and favored the paintings of Jan van Eyck and Rogier van der Weyden. She sponsored the works of local painters, who developed a new Spanish-Flemish style of art. Isabella amassed a large personal library on a wide range of subjects. When the printing press was introduced into Castile, the co-monarchs were active patrons of its development, granting special tax exemptions and subsidies to promote its expansion. The regime promoted the growth of education and learning, encouraging scholars and humanists from Europe to settle in Spain, while new universities were founded and existing ones enlarged. Literature and poetry flourished under the reign of Isabella with a revival of religious poetry, while court poets wrote in the lyric style. Isabella and Ferdinand II traveled frequently between their many palaces from the Moorish styled Alhambra in Granada to the turreted Segovia Castle. As the queen and king rode across their realm, they asserted their rule through the power and grandeur of their presence and court.

During the final years of the war against Granada, a wave of anti–Semitism swept through Aragon and Castile encouraged by fanatical Catholic priests and the Spanish Inquisition. Anti-Jewish riots erupted in the large cities and the Inquisition prosecuted hundreds of converted Jews as heretics. Isabella and Ferdinand II resisted the petitions from the church to banish the non–Christians to retain the valuable contribution they made to the Spanish economy. However, on March 31, 1492, under increased pressure from the prelates, they signed the Edict of Expulsion, demanding all Jews who refused baptism leave their realm within three months.

The queen and king agreed to issue the decree to promote Spanish unity through the single Christian religion. The non–Christians were ordered to sell their property and depart from the kingdom without taking any gold, silver or jewelry. The money from the sales of their farms, houses, physical property and animals was converted into letters of exchange, which were redeemable by Genoese bankers. Despite efforts from the crown to protect the Jews against abuse, property values fell sharply with the mass selling and they suffered huge financial losses. As many as one hundred fifty thousand were expelled from the land where their ancestors had lived and had prospered for generations. Many families migrated to Portugal, while smaller groups sailed to Italy, Greece and Turkey. Only a small minority chose to remain in Spain and convert to Christianity.

Through the marriage of Isabella and Ferdinand II, Spain became an united and prosperous kingdom and for the first time a European power. To promote and protect the interest of their government, the co-monarchs entered into a series of marriage alliances with the major European courts. In 1490 the eldest daughter, Isabella, was married to Prince Alfonso, heir to the crown of Portugal. The marital union united the two Iberian realms in friendship and lessened the chances of future war. Princess Isabella became a part of the Portuguese court but a few months after the wedding ceremony, Alfonso was killed in a riding accident. The princess returned to the Spanish court, where she implored her parents for permission to join a nunnery. However, four years later to enhance the security of Spain, she reluctantly agreed to marry Alfonso's uncle, Emanuel I, who had succeeded to the Portuguese throne.

To bind the Spanish regime to a central European power and further their policy of containing the aggression of France, in 1496 the co-monarchs negotiated the marriage of their second daughter, Joanna, to Archduke Philip of Burgundy, son of the Holy Roman Emperor, Maximilian I, while the successor to the Trastamaran monarchy, John, was betrothed to Archduchess Margaret of Austria. Following the marriage between Joanna and Philip in Flanders, on April 3, 1497, Prince John was married to Margaret in a service of great pomp and spirituality at the palace of El Cordon. However, six months after the wedding the Spanish heir became seriously ill with a high fever. By the time the king reached his bedside, he was dead.

The death of John had grave ramifications for the future of Spain. Without a male heir, the Trastamaran throne fell to the eldest daughter, Isabella of Portugal, and her husband's family. If the kingdoms of Aragon and Castile were to remain united, it was essential that she produce a son. On August 23, 1498, Isabella died giving birth to a male successor, Miguel, who inherited the crowns of Castile, Aragon and Portugal to unite the Iberian Peninsula under one ruling dynasty. However, he was frail and sickly, dying in less than two years.

In the aftermath of their grandson's death, the queen and king immediately sent to Flanders for their second daughter, Joanna, who was the new successor designate. She had lived in the Flemish court for four years with her husband, Philip of Burgundy, and in February 1500 had given birth to a son, Charles, who was recognized as second in line to the Spanish crown. Joanna and Philip met the royal court in Toledo, where she was reunited with her parents. However, she immediately exhibited signs of mental instability inherited from her Portuguese grandmother and was tormented by attacks of anxiety and jealousy over Philip, refusing to leave his presence. When the archduke returned to Flanders, Joanna soon followed him north leaving her newly born second son, Ferdinand, to be raised by the Spanish royal household.

Through the marriage alliances with the Holy Roman Empire, the Spanish regime became aligned with Maximilian I and his ongoing struggle against France. In 1494 the French king, Charles VIII, invaded the kingdom of Naples with military aid from Duke Ludovico Sforza of Milan. While the Valois army advanced into Naples, Ferdinand II sent Spanish troops to buttress the defenses of his nephew, Alfonso II, against the French. Despite the assistance of the Spanish, by February 1495 Charles VIII had seized control of the Neapolitan realm. However, with the dissolution of Italian security, a Holy League was formed by Pope Alexander VI with Venice, Milan, Mantua, Spain and Maximilian I to force the French out of Naples. In support of the league, Ferdinand II dispatched a second army to Naples under the command of Gonzalo de Cordoba, who attacked and drove the French out of southern Italy.

In 1498 a peace treaty was signed between France and the Holy League but war soon erupted again when Louis XII assumed the Valois monarchy after the death of Charles VIII. He negotiated a treaty of alliance with Ferdinand II and Isabella for the joint conquest of Naples. After the invasion and seizure of the Neapolitan kingdom, dissent broke out between the two allies and Cordoba was ordered to attack the Valois troops. With superior military skills he outmaneuvered the French and forced them out of southern Italy. In September 1504 Louis XII and the Spanish signed the Treaty of Blois with the French agreeing to relinquish all claims to Naples. As the result of Ferdinand II's intervention into Naples, all of southern Italy remained under the rule of the Spanish for the next two hundred years.

The death of her two oldest children, worsening insanity of Joanna and the absence of her two youngest daughters in foreign courts caused great mental anguish to Isabella and her once robust health deteriorated. She increasingly withdrew from court and was confined to her apartments, while the king assumed control of the government. In July 1504 the queen became seriously ill with a high fever. She struggled with her illness during the summer but only became increasingly weak and frail. Isabella died on November 26, 1504, at the age of fifth-three after a reign of thirty years. Before her death she appointed Ferdinand II as regent for Castile until her grandson, Charles, reached the age of majority.

Sources

Fernandez-Armesto. *Ferdinand and Isabella.*   McKendick. *Ferdinand and Isabella.*   Prescott. *History of the Reign of Ferdinand and Isabella.*   Rubin. *Isabella of Castile.*

Joanna, 1479–1504–1555

After the death of Queen Isabella in November 1504 her kingdom of Castile was inherited by her eldest surviving daughter, Joanna, who ruled as the fourth sovereign of the Spanish Renaissance period. Joanna was the third issue of Isabella of Castile and King Ferdinand II of Aragon and was born on November 6, 1479, in the capital city of Toledo. The princess spent her first years in the royal household under the care and guidance of a crown appointed nurse and governess. As the third child she was not expected to assume the Trastamaran throne and was educated to enter a royal marriage with a foreign prince to expand Spain's influence, power and security in European affairs. Renowned humanist scholars and priests were chosen by the king and queen as her tutors. She was an intelligent student, excelling in her studies of reading, writing, foreign languages of Latin and French, religion and the social graces of music, dancing and court etiquette. The princess became a skilled musician, mastering the clavichord and monochord. Unlike her elder sister and brother, Joanna received only limited training in ceremonial functions and traveled with the royal court infrequently. As the princess grew older, she received a small personal household led by a governor to serve her needs.

While Joanna continued her education at the royal court, Queen Isabella and King Ferdinand II entered into a series of marital alliances to contain the aggression of France and expand their influence and prestige with the European powers. In 1496 they negotiated the union of the sixteen-year-old Joanna to Archduke Philip, son and heir of the Habsburg emperor, Maximilian I. To further strengthen their security, the only son of the Spanish king and queen, John, was engaged to Margaret of Austria, daughter of the emperor, while their youngest daughter, Catherine, was betrothed to the English successor, Arthur. Following her proxy wedding, on August 22, 1496, Joanna boarded a ship in the northern harbor of Laredo and was escorted to Flanders by a large fleet. The princess landed in the Netherlands in early September at the port of Middleburg. At the time of her arrival, Archduke Philip was in Germany, attending the imperial diet and Joanna was compelled to travel to Lierre north of Brussels before finally meeting him for the first time. At first sight she fell in love with her handsome and charming husband and never lost her strong affection for him. The formal wedding was held on October 20, 1496, and was followed by days of receptions, festivals, entertainment and tournaments by the Flemish towns in celebration of their new archduchess.

Philip was eighteen years old at the time of his marriage to Joanna and had little interest in personally ruling the Netherlands, leaving the administration of his lands to his Burgundian council. The archduke's advisors favored a friendly relationship with France to safeguard their borders and strongly opposed the marital alliance with Spain. To undermine the influence of the archduchess, they replaced her Spanish household staff with Flemish courtiers, who won her to their cause. When she first arrived in Flanders, her court included over one hundred Spanish attendants, but in less than a year only sixteen of the original members remained. To subordinate Joanna and her retainers further to Philip's authority, she was made totally dependent on him financially and new orders were issued to continue the Burgundianization of her staff. Isolated and under the control of her Flemish counselors, she quickly adapted to her new role and life and traveled frequently with Philip throughout their realm, where they were greeted by large cheering and enthusiastic crowds. In Spain Joanna had been educated by her parents to advance their kingdom but she was now totally devoted to her husband and supported his pro–French policy, ignoring the co-monarchs' repeated requests to promote their interest.

While Joanna remained in Flanders, in late 1496 her elder sister, Isabella of Portugal, became the new successor to the Spanish realm when her brother, Prince John, unexpectedly died. However, two years later Isabella died in childbirth and her newly born son, Miguel, was recognized as heir designate. The Burgundian archduchess was now second in line to the crown to the sickly and frail prince and Queen Isabella sent a special envoy to the Flemish court to collect information about her loyalty to Spain. The queen was informed of Joanna's continued piety, and her lack of desire in promoting Spanish interest was blamed on Philip and his courtiers. Nevertheless, the archduchess's standing with her parents was greatly enhanced on February 24, 1500, when she gave birth in Ghent to a healthy son, Charles. The birth of Charles became more significant to the Spanish court when Miguel died in July and Joanna and her lineage were acknowledged as successors to the Trastamaran kingdom. The co-sovereigns immediately summoned Joanna and Philip to Spain for their formal confirmations as heirs to the throne by the legislative assemblies of Castile and Aragon. Philip began to title himself prince of Spain and sought French support for his claim to the regime

Isabella and Ferdinand II urged their daughter and son-in-law to quickly sail to Spain for their confirmations as successors by the Castilian and Aragonese legislatures, but the Flemish council attempted to impede the journey, fearing its loss of influence and control over the archduke. Despite the advisors' repeated attempts to delay the departure, the voyage was postponed by Joanna's third pregnancy. In February 1501 she gave birth to a second daughter, Isabella, and preparations to leave the Netherlands were soon renewed.

After traveling through France, in early 1502 Joanna and Philip crossed the border into Spain and were met by an escort sent to transport them to the queen and king in Toledo. As they rode through the Basque region into Castile, the local nobles and towns entertained their future rulers with bullfights, lavish displays and banquets to gain their favor. Finally after the long journey, on May 7 they met Isabella and Ferdinand II in Toledo and were greeted by an opulent reception and religious services of thanksgiving. While waiting for the Cortes to assemble, Joanna remained with her mother, while Philip traveled to Aranjuez with his father-in-law for hunting, hawking and jousting tournaments. In Aranjuez Ferdinand II pressed the archduke to abandon his alliance with France and join the Spanish-Habsburg coalition against Louis XII but he remained loyal to the Valois regime. On May 22 the Castilian legislature assembled in Toledo and confirmed Joanna as successor and Philip as prince consort. After the meeting of the Cortes, relations between the Flemish and Spanish deteriorated after Philip was not recognized as king presumptive and he increasingly resented Ferdinand II's continued attempts to turn him against Louis XII.

In July the Spanish king departed for Saragossa to summon the Aragonese Cortes to acknowledge his daughter as heiress. In Toledo hostilities between the Spanish and Philip's supporters intensified, when several of his courtiers were attacked by a mob. In late August the Habsburg archduke and Joanna left the queen in Toledo and traveled to Aragon to await the convening of the local assembly. After a delay of nearly two months, the Aragonese nobles and towns acknowledged their future rulers at Saragossa. However, relations continued to deteriorate and Philip began to make preparations to return to Flanders, despite the pleadings of the king and queen to make Spain his permanent home. He refused to change his plans but with Joanna's advanced pregnancy, agreed to leave her with her parents until after giving birth. When Philip met his wife in Madrid to tell her of their temporary separation, she was enraged at her abandonment, arguing violently with him. When the archduke left later in the year for Flanders, she became increasingly overcome with grief and sorrow, withdrawing to her apartments in solitude.

Following the birth in February 1503 of a second son, Ferdinand of Habsburg, Joanna recovered from her depression and looked forward to the reunion with Philip. However, her despair and despondency soon returned when the journey to the Netherlands was delayed by war between Spain and France over the conquest of Naples. Unable to leave for the Low Countries, her melancholy intensified and she was only consoled by the queen's promise to send her to Philip by sea. In June her mother took her to Segovia in preparation for the departure. However, to ensure their daughter inherited the Spanish throne and not her husband, it was essential the heiress remain in her homeland to defend her bloodrights and Isabella and Ferdinand II refused to permit her to leave. Everyday she remained in Segovia her mental state deteriorated and she now ate and slept little. As Philip traveled through France, she worried about his faithfulness and continued love, growing increasingly jealous over imaginary lovers. The longer she remained away from Philip, the more she doubted his love and fidelity, becoming more depressed. Joanna began to quarrel violently with her mother and finally was ordered to move to separate apartments in the castle at Medina del Campo by court physicians in the hope of improving her mental and physical health.

While Joanna remained isolated at Medina del Campo, in November 1503 she received a letter from Philip asking her to hurry to Flanders. She was elated by his message and gave orders for her baggage to be immediately packed. When informed of her daughter's plans, the queen directed that she be prevented from leaving by any means. When Joanna saw her passage to freedom barred, she was infuriated, becoming uncontrollable with rage. She left her apartments and took refuge in the courtyard, refusing to leave and spending the cold night in the open air. She would not speak to anyone until her mother arrived from Segovia. A violent argument quickly erupted between the two and Joanna was only consoled by the queen's promise to send her to the Netherlands. Despite her assurances, the queen continued to delay her daughter's departure and Joanna's mental state declined into despair. She had to endure three months of additional separation from her beloved Philip until a special Flemish emissary arrived to escort her to the Low Countries and the Spanish co-sovereigns were compelled to permit her to leave. In late May 1504 she sailed from Laredo to her husband's ducal realm.

When the Spanish fleet arrived at the Flemish port of Blankenberghe, Joanna was met by Philip and his Burgundian court. She was escorted to Brussels in a grand procession of receptions and banquets by the nobles and towns. It seemed to her that nothing had changed in their relationship and Philip still loved only her. However, her joy was soon shattered when she discovered her husband had taken a beautiful Flemish noblewoman as his mistress. The archduchess vented her rage on her rival, threatening her life with a pair of scissors. After learning of his wife's outburst, Philip confronted her and a violent argument erupted. As they remained estranged, she attempted to regain his love by turning to the passion charms and potions of her Moorish attendants. However, the archduke rejected her advances and a new series of quarrels developed. When she became violent, Philip ordered her confined to her rooms. She was now sure he had a new mistress, growing more jealous and refusing to eat or sleep. As the archduchess's health declined, Philip yielded to her and became reconciled. However, their reunion was brief when Joanna again accused him of infidelity, becoming increasingly resentful of anything, which would take her beloved husband away from her.

While the archduchess remained in the Burgundian court, becoming ever doubtful of Philip's continued love and fidelity, in Spain on November 26, 1504, Isabella died and Joanna was acclaimed successor. In compliance with the decree signed by the queen, Ferdinand II temporarily assumed sovereignty for Castile and dispatched officials to his daughter and son-in-law in Flanders to proclaim their assumption of power. In Brussels Joanna and Philip I declared themselves queen and king of Castile and sent an envoy to Ferdinand II to announce their preparations for departure to Spain.

Isabella and Ferdinand II had ruled Castile and Aragon jointly, uniting the two separate kingdoms into Spain. With the queen's death, a faction of self-serving Castilian magnates and towns quickly formed a coalition to promote the assumption of the throne by Joanna but Ferdinand II exploited his daughter's deteriorated mental state to claim power under the provisions of his wife's will, which allowed him to rule if she was declared incompetent. He summoned the Castilian Cortes and was recognized as regent after the archduchess was proclaimed unfit to govern.

While the king had secured the approval of the local legislature for his assumption of the Castilian crown, he was still vulnerable to Joanna's opposition faction of grandees and towns and to further strengthen his authority attempts were made to encourage his daughter's renunciation of her realm. He sent the archduchess's former personal advisor and chaplain to Flanders to convince her of the need to transfer Castile to her father. In Brussels under the influence of her trusted confessor, she was quickly won to the king's cause, signing a decree giving Ferdinand II full sovereignty. However, the document was intercepted by Philip I, who persuaded his wife to disavow the letter and rule jointly with him. Joanna could not resist her husband and notified her father of her intention to govern Castile with Philip I. When the Castilian nobles and towns were informed of her decision to personally assume the throne, they rallied to her and the archduke, while Ferdinand II's quest to reign seemed lost. However, Spanish spies in the Brussels court soon informed the archduchess that Philip I had forged an alliance with France and Austria to seize Castile and had been largely responsible for the widespread rumor that she was insane. Enraged by her husband's actions, she attempted to exert her independence against Philip I but her orders were ignored and he had her placed under close confinement to prevent her from secretly giving power for Castile to Ferdinand II.

As Philip I continued to remain in the Netherlands, his support from the Spanish grandees and towns started to wane and the Aragonese king began to regain dominance. To secure authority over Castile, he was compelled to negotiate a treaty with his father-in-law, agreeing to rule the kingdom jointly with him and his wife. Once the Treaty of Salamanca was signed, preparations for the journey to Spain were intensified and on January 8, 1506, Joanna and Philip I sailed from Flanders.

The Burgundian fleet made a quiet voyage south through the English Channel into the Atlantic Ocean, when it was struck by a violent winter storm. Many of the vessels were widely scattered and the archduke and archduchess struggled into the English port of Weymouth with a broken main mast. While their ship was under repair, the royal couple was richly entertained by Henry VII and his court. At Windsor Castle Philip I and the Tudor king agreed to unite against Ferdinand II and France, while Joanna visited with her sister, Catherine. After over two months in England, the fleet was refitted and reprovisioned and in March sailed for Spain, landing at the small port of Corunna in the northern province of Galicia.

After landing on Spanish soil at Corunna, the co-sovereigns were given a formal reception by the local nobles and town officials. However, when asked to take the oath of office, Joanna refused, insisting on first conferring with her father. Philip I realized that if she was permitted to meet with the Aragonese king his chances of succeeding to the Castilian kingship would be impaired and imposed a close watch on his wife to prevent her from transferring power to her father. While she remained under confinement, Philip I sent envoys to his supporters, announcing the arrival of their new queen and king. As the news of their coming spread, the grandees rallied to them, pledging their fealty. The magnates began to assemble in Galicia with their armed retainers ready to defend the crown of Philip I and Joanna. As his strength grew, the king wrote to Ferdinand II disavowing the terms of the Salamanca Treaty to reign alone.

The co-monarchs remained at Corunna for over a month but when Ferdinand II assembled his military forces and began to seize the Galician border fortresses, they were compelled to flee to Castile. In their realm, the local nobles continued to rally to their banner, pledging their loyalty. However, the self-serving grandees became disgruntled at the continued absence of the queen from court and resented the arrogance of the Flemish, increasingly favoring the rule of only Joanna. With his support beginning to deteriorate, Philip I was forced to seek a negotiated settlement with his father-in-law. Confronted by the formidable army of Castilian magnates and hired German mercenaries, Ferdinand II quickly accepted the offer and on June 20 the two kings met at Villafafila in friendship to resolve the succession crisis, while Joanna remained imprisoned. To promote his future recovery of the Castilian crown, it was in Ferdinand II's political interest for his daughter to never reign and he willingly agreed to his son-in-law's demands. Under their resulting treaty, Ferdinand II pledged to surrender Castilian power to only Philip I and exclude Joanna from the throne due to her unstable mental state, while receiving control of the local military orders and half the income from the New World discoveries. The document was signed on June 27 at Villafafila. Despite approving the agreement, as Ferdinand II withdrew to Aragon, he issued a proclamation to the nobles and towns of Castile, repudiating the treaty and claiming it was signed under duress.

While the Castilian king was meeting with his father-in-law, Joanna was sent to the city of Benavente and kept under heavy guard. When informed of the Treaty of Villafafila, she became enraged that the conference had occurred without her approval or presence. When Philip I met with her, a frenzied quarrel erupted, as Joanna attempted to exert her authority as queen, declaring her sole sovereignty. With his quest for the monarchy in jeopardy, Philip I became determined to eliminate the threat of his wife to his assumption of the throne and summoned the Cortes to Valladolid to formally acknowledge him as the only ruler. The grand entry into the city was held on July 10 but when the legislature convened Joanna's faction refused to abandon her, swearing allegiance to both monarchs. The nobility was now divided in its loyalty and the king's control over the regime began to wane. The kingdom was beset with plague and poor harvests and there was little revenue for Philip I to defend his realm.

As the threat of civil war grew, the Castilian king attempted to gain possession of the strategic fortresses and in September traveled with the queen to Burgos. In the fortified city, Philip I became ill with a fever and broke out in a rash. When informed of his illness, Joanna rushed to his bedside, forgetting their animosity and taking charge of his care. She remained with him throughout his sickness never leaving her beloved husband until his death on September 25, 1506.

As the death of Philip I became imminent, a council of grandees representing the factions loyal to the dying king and Joanna was summoned by the archbishop of Toledo, Ximenes de Cisneros, to preserve the peace. Cisneros was a Franciscan friar who had been chosen by Isabella as her confessor in 1492. His strict piety quickly won the favor of the queen and he exerted significant influence over her. In 1495 the friar was appointed to the vacant archbishopric of Toledo and given the position of chancellor for the Castilian government. As the archbishop of Toledo, he promoted the reform of the Spanish clerics and enthusiastically backed the trials of the Inquisition. When the queen died, Cisneros supported the rule of Ferdinand II to prevent the resurgence of the grandees' power and fragmentation of Spain. Following the Treaty of Villafafia and the departure of the king of Aragon, he became allied with Philip I.

The nobles' council met on September 24, electing Cisneros regent for Castile. On the next day he went to the Burgos Castle and assumed control of the government. There was little opposition to his usurpation of power and the queen was once again sequestered and isolated from the outside world. Joanna was still recognized as sovereign and the archbishop was forced to govern through her. However, in defiance of her exclusion from the monarchy, she thwarted every petition he brought to her and the kingdom was thrown into chaos with a dysfunctional administration. With no legal authority to rule, the archbishop's decrees were ignored and private wars between the grandees erupted; brigandage was widespread and famine grew worse. Joanna spent the autumn in Burgos but when plague broke out her household was moved to the castle at Torquemada. The queen had shown little interest in personally ruling her kingdom, but as the shock of her husband's death subsided she began to take control of her realm. In December she revoked all the decrees of Philip I and purged her council of his Flemish nobles. The suspected supporters of her father were banned from court and replaced by grandees faithful to her. With a loyal administration, Joanna announced her decision to personally convey her husband's remains to Granada for burial, according to his wishes. However, the magnates and their private militias commanded by Cisneros surrounded the city and prohibited her from leaving. While Joanna remained under confinement, plague broke out and she was transferred to the nearby town of Hornillos. Fearing imprisonment in the local castle, she refused to enter Hornillos and established her private residence in a local farmhouse. Determined to assert her authority, she summoned her mother's former counselors to the farm and empowered them to assume the reins of government. When they attempted to take power, a clash quickly erupted with Cisneros's faction. As she struggled to rule the chaotic kingdom, the archbishop wrote to Ferdinand II in Naples to encourage him to return to Castile and assume the crown. Without a functioning regime the kingdom fell into despair and anarchy, while support for the Aragonese king among the Castilian towns and nobles steadily grew. On June 4, 1507, he sailed from Italy and landed in his lordship of Valencia.

After landing in Aragon, Ferdinand II sent a message to his daughter asking her to join him in the Castilian city of Tortoles. She gladly agreed to meet the king and ordered an appropriate reception for him. On August 28 he arrived in the city and they met in the local palace with each expressing their devotion and love. The queen and her father attended a mass of thanksgiving and following the services held private talks for two hours. In the aftermath of their discussions, Ferdinand II announced his appointment as regent for Castile by Joanna.

Assuming the reins of power, the king assembled the royal army to enforce the rule of his daughter against the rogue grandees. While the queen took up residence in Arcos, he advanced against the rebellious city of Burgos, quickly seizing the castle. As the war was continued against the rebels, Ferdinand II met with Joanna several times a week, seeking her approval for his policies. As he imposed the crown's authority over the nobles and consolidated his personal control, the queen remained with her small court at Arcos, content that he was governing in her name. Philip I's coffin was moved to the local church and she ensured mass was read daily for the redemption of his soul.

After nine months of campaigning, most of the kingdom was subdued and Ferdinand II was ready to march against the remaining rogue strongholds in Andalusia. To maintain his position as unrestricted ruler, he could not leave the queen unprotected from access by the rebellious grandees, who would unduly influence her against him. He attempted to move her to the castle at Valladolid for greater security but she strongly protested. Unable to relocate the queen to the stronghold, the king was forced to surround Arcos with his troops to ensure his interests. Confined by her father's soldiers, she again became beset with despair and melancholia. Joanna would not eat or sleep and refused to change her clothes. By December she had become seriously ill. If the queen died, all Ferdinand II's schemes to rule Castile would be destroyed with the inheritance of the throne by her eldest son, Charles. To protect his continued reign as regent, on February 15, 1509, the king ordered his daughter taken to Tordesillas, where she would be completely isolated and forgotten.

After signing the Treaty of Villafafila, Ferdinand II had returned to Aragon and had sailed to Naples to expand his influence and presence in Italian affairs. With his assumption of the regency in Castile, he now had the money and military might to more aggressively pursue his quest for power and lands in Italy. He had earlier joined the League of Cambrai with Pope Julius II, Emperor Maximilian I and Louis XII of France to force the doge of Venice, Leonardo Loredan, from his mainland territories. In May 1509 the French army decisively defeated the Venetians at the battle of Agnadello. The doge was compelled to abandon eastern Lombardy and come to terms with the league. For his support in the defeat of Venice, under the ensuing Treaty of Blois, Ferdinand II was recognized as regent for Castile by the European courts until Joanna's eldest son, Charles, reached the age of majority.

In the aftermath of the War of the Cambrian League, France became the dominant military power in northern Italy. Fearing the future expansion of Louis XII into papal territory, Julius II negotiated a treaty of alliance with Venice and separated the Spanish king from his French ally by offering to formally invest him with the crown of Naples. Through diplomacy and with little financial expenditure, in less than two years Ferdinand II had ensured his continued Castilian rule and had legalized Naples as a Spanish possession.

As the French continued to maintain their control over Lombardy, in 1511 Ferdinand II joined a new Holy League forged by the papacy to force them out of Italy. With Louis XII distracted defending his Italian lands, the Spanish invaded his southern vassal-kingdom of Navarre to secure their borders against French invasion. Navarre was lightly defended and by 1512 Ferdinand II's army had occupied the region, expanding the territory under Spanish dominion.

While the king aggressively pursued Spanish foreign policy, Joanna remained at Tordesillas under military guard, totally isolated from the outside world. For security she was confined to a small dark room in the castle and provided a small staff, which was completely loyal to her father. The coffin of Philip I was transferred to the nearby Convent of Santa Clara and the queen could view the nunnery from her captivity. Totally abandoned by her father, the nobility and surrounded by despair, she became increasingly depressed and melancholy. In passive protest of her conditions, Joanna refused to eat, sleep or bathe and over the passing months became increasingly weak and frail. In November 1510 Ferdinand II brought the leaders of the grandee factions to the castle to persuade them that his daughter was mentally unfit to rule. After talking to her the nobles were convinced she was insane and unable to assume the reins of power, pledging their allegiance to the king.

Ferdinand II reigned over Castile and Aragon asserting his authority with little opposition, while pursuing an aggressive foreign policy in Europe to advance Spain as the preeminent power until his death on January 23, 1516. Following the death of her father, Joanna was widely acknowledged as queen of united Spain. However, she was considered unfit to hold the reins of power and her eldest son, Charles, was recognized as her legal guardian and king. To rule during his absence in Flanders, before his death Ferdinand II had named Cisneros to govern Castile and his illegitimate son, Alfonso, archbishop of Saragossa, to govern in Aragon. However, the chief justice of the realm nullified the appointment of Alfonso and the Toledo archbishop continued to administer unified Spain in Charles's name.

Assuming the reins of government, the regent-archbishop reorganized Joanna's household and appointed a new staff, which initiated a series of reforms to improve their prisoner's living conditions. The queen regularly attended mass, visited the gravesite of Philip I at Santa Clara Convent and received guests. The symptoms of her depression lessened and she willingly ate and slept, as her physical health improved.

Soon after receiving the news of his grandfather's death, Charles confirmed Cisneros's appointment as regent for Spain to maintain peace over his new realm against the rebellion of the recalcitrant nobles. With control of the government, the archbishop assembled the high grandees to proclaim Charles as the rightful king. However, it was in the magnates' self-serving interest to promote a weak sovereignty to regain their usurped power and they continued to support Joanna as the lawful heiress to the crown. To enforce his decree, Cisneros threatened to launch the royal army against the grandees and they were forced to comply. With full autocratic powers, the regent-archbishop sent great sums of money to Flanders to encourage the king's quick departure and to fund his preparations for the voyage to Spain. To acquire the large sums needed, he increased the taxes, sold royal offices and confiscated properties. As the Toledo archbishop demanded more taxes and his rule became more dictatorial, widespread dissent among the lords and towns spread throughout the kingdom. As the threat of civil war grew, Charles sent envoys to Spain to act as his personal regents but Cisneros ignored their decrees and continued to govern independently.

Ximenes de Cisneros of Toledo ruled Spain until his death on November 8, 1517. Prior to the archbishop's death, Charles had arrived in Spain but had delayed meeting the archbishop to first visit his mother at Tordesillas to obtain her approval for his assumption of the monarchy. On November 4 with his older sister, Eleanor, he entered the palace and was welcomed with expressions of great joy and love by the queen. They met in a plainly furnished room with Joanna attired in a simple gray wool dress, while her son was dressed in rich and elegant clothes. During their discussions Joanna agreed to confirm her son as Spanish ruler.

After acquiring his mother's approval to assume the throne, the Castilian Cortes was summoned to Valladolid to proclaim Charles as king. However, before the legislative body gathered, he appointed many of his Flemish courtiers to the principal offices in his government and sold others to the highest bidder. The Spanish grandees and towns resented being ruled by foreigners and when the Cortes met on January 4, 1518, the delegates refused to formally acknowledge Charles as sovereign. To gain their approval, he was compelled to pledge to govern only with Spanish advisors and voluntarily resign the kingship should his mother recover her health. On February 7 Charles I was affirmed as king of Spain.

Under the administration of the regent-archbishop's governor, Joanna's mental and physical health had steadily improved and now she posed a threat to the kingship of her son. To protect his continued rule, the king replaced Cisneros's appointees with a new staff that was loyal only to him. The Marquis of Denia was chosen as the queen's guardian and commanded to permit no one to visit her without the king's permission. Imprisoned in the Tordesillas Castle and placed under close guard, the queen's mental state quickly deteriorated, as her despair and depression returned. With Joanna again safely secluded from the outside world, in March Charles I traveled to Aragon for his formal confirmation as sovereign by the local Cortes. After his proclamation as king on July 29 at Saragossa, all of Spain was once again governed by a single ruler.

In the aftermath of his confirmation as king, Charles I and his Flemish counselors initiated a governmental policy to systematically plunder the riches of Spain. As tons of gold and silver, jewelry and other items of value were sent to the Netherlands, discontent steadily grew among the towns, as the administration continued to mandate more money. In early 1519 Emperor Maximilian I died and Charles I became the leading candidate as successor to the Holy Roman crown. To buy the votes of the seven imperial electors, greater demands for taxes were placed on the towns. On June 28, 1519, in Frankfurt, Charles I's envoys outmaneuvered his two opponents to claim the emperorship. The king now had little time for Spanish affairs and devoted his attention toward ruling the empire. As dissent spread among the population, Charles I summoned the Cortes to the distant town of Corunna and with the liberal use of bribes forced the delegates to vote an additional subsidy. With the funds from the Cortes, he made preparations to travel to Aachen for his coronation and May 20, 1520, boarded a ship for the journey to Flanders with his kingdom on the verge of open rebellion.

Before leaving Spain the king appointed Cardinal Adrian Boeyens, bishop of Tortose, as his regent. The vast riches sent to the Netherlands and the selection of the Flemish born bishop as governor were greatly resented by the nobles and towns, who grew increasingly displeased with their foreign rulers. Revolt began to erupt in several isolated towns but quickly spread to the principal cities. The populations of Madrid, Toledo and Segovia took up arms in open rebellion, overthrowing the throne's officials and seizing the local government. As the uprising intensified, on June 20 the cities formed the Holy League of Corporations at Avila and proclaimed the end of the regency and their assumption of power in the name of Queen Joanna to ignite the War of the Comuneros.

With the king's monarchy in jeopardy, his Spanish council appealed directly to the queen for her approval of her son's right to rule. To secure Charles I's kingship, she agreed to ratify a decree in his favor but before signing, the city of Medina del Campo was brutally sacked by the royalists and now all of Spain was in revolt. To prevent the loyalists from gaining the endorsement of the queen, the rebel army advanced to Tordesillas and occupied the town. As the troops marched into the city, Joanna summoned their leaders for an audience. She met with the dissident commander of the Comuneros, John Padilla, who related her kingdom's despair and the taking of arms in protest. Lied to by her captors since her imprisonment sixteen years earlier, she was bewildered and agreed to confer with the heads of the league. On September 24 the queen met with the Junta and asked them to form a council of four members to advise her.

After the Holy League began to assert its power, Charles I replaced Bishop Adrian with two Spanish grandees in an attempt to reclaim his kingdom. The nobility had been largely excluded from the Comuneros's government and had had many of its privileges withdrawn. With the appointment of the two grandees to lead the royal administration, the magnates and knights rallied to Charles I's defense. While the royalists were raising money in Genoa and Portugal and assembling their troops, the loyal servants of the king in his mother's household began to spread suspicion and doubt about the motives of the rebels and Joanna wavered in her support, refusing to sign any league documents. Without written authorization to rule from the queen, the rebellion began to lose its popularity with the population.

When Joanna refused to sign any documents, the Comuneros withheld her food and denied her permission to leave the town. As the queen continued to be imprisoned, rumors spread through the realm that she was being held in confinement against her will and support for the league declined further among the population, who still defended her right of inheritance to the throne. Dissention soon broke out in the rebel army and John Padilla withdrew his forces to Toledo while Peter Giron assumed command of the remaining troops. Lacking adequate military strength, Giron abandoned Tordesillas and on December 4, 1520, the royalists stormed the town to free the queen. However, the grandees remained loyal to the king and Joanna was again held captive with the marquis of Denia ordered to keep her in seclusion.

Assuming his former role as guardian, Denia reestablished his prior harsh treatment of the queen. The palace was cut off from the outside world and Joanna was restricted to a few small rooms. In protest she returned to her passive opposition, refusing to eat, sleep or change her clothes. However, the Marquis ignored her resistance and increased his severe treatment totally isolating her in an inner room and dismissing her confessor. Without her trusted priest, she refused to attend mass and grew increasingly despondent. To ensure his continued kingship in Spain, Charles I had his mother imprisoned for the remainder of her life at Tordesillas. In her degrading environment, the queen's physical and mental health deteriorated steadily through the next thirty-five years. In her final years Joanna's physical state rapidly declined and she was confined to her bed. Queen Joanna died on April 12, 1555, at age seventy-five, isolated and forgotten. She had been held captive for fifty years to ensure the Spanish rule of her husband, father and son. Joanna was interred in the Royal Chapel in Granada, alongside her beloved Philip I and parents.

Sources

Aram. *Juana the Mad.* Prawdin. *The Mad Queen of Spain.*

Charles I, 1500–1516–1558

Charles I assumed the crown in 1516 to rule as the fifth sovereign of the Spanish Renaissance epoch when his grandfather, Ferdinand II, died and his mother, Queen Joanna, was declared incapable of governing due to mental instability. Charles was born in Flanders in the city of Ghent on February 24, 1500, and was the second child of Philip, Duke of Burgundy, and Joanna of Spain. After the death of Queen Isabella of Castile in 1504, her daughter, Joanna, and the Burgundian duke traveled to Spain to impose her rights as heiress to the throne, leaving the four-year-old Archduke Charles in the Brussels court with his two sisters, Eleanor and Isabella. Two years later Philip I died in Spain and his son inherited his duchy of Burgundy. To govern the strategic Flemish region, Charles's aunt, Margaret of Austria, was appointed regent and assumed the guardianship of the young duke. Under the guidance of his well educated and politically astute aunt, renowned scholars were chosen as his tutors for his studies in reading, writing, government, history, religion and the languages of French, Italian and German. His principal teacher was the learned theologian Adrian of Utrecht, who instilled in Charles a deep sense of religious piety, loyalty to the papacy and obedience to the teachings of the Catholic Church. The duke took his studies seriously but was not a gifted student, preferring hunting and field sports. He became a skilled equestrian and enthusiastically participated in military games with the sons of the Flemish nobility. Like his mother, he learned to play the clavichord and always enjoyed listening to music.

Under the direction of Margaret, the duke was exposed to the government of the duchy by attending meetings of the council and conferring with foreign ambassadors and Flemish city officials. In 1513 he made his first visit to a foreign court crossing the North Sea to England and was royally entertained by Henry VIII. Following his contacts with the Tudor regime, he became more involved in European politics and began to assert his independence from Margaret. In early January 1515 Charles reached the age of majority and in a grand and extravagant ceremony in Brussels attended by representatives from the European courts assumed the ducal throne. The coronation was followed by a magnificent procession through Flanders, where he received the homage of the towns.

While the Burgundian duke continued to gain experience in ruling his demesne, in 1516 his maternal grandfather, Ferdinand II, died. The Spanish throne was inherited by the duke's mother, Joanna, but she was declared unfit to govern and the Cortes recognized Charles as her guardian and successor. In his new kingdom civil war threatened to erupt as the magnates and towns attempted to regain their lost feudal privileges against the dictatorial administration of the appointed regent, Archbishop Ximenes de Cisneros. Despite repeated pleas from Cisneros to hurry to Spain to enforce his inheritance rights, the king was in danger of attack from France and was compelled to remain in Flanders until the summer of 1517, when a peace treaty was signed. Preparations were now hurriedly arranged and on September 8 he sailed to his kingdom from the Flemish port of Flushing with a fleet of forty ships.

After a stormy voyage of ten days, Charles and his courtiers landed on the shore of Asturias, but before establishing his government he traveled to Tordesillas to visit Queen Joanna. He spent several days in the city and received his mother's approval to govern in her name. After gaining the queen's consent to supersede her, the Castilian Cortes was summoned to Valladolid where the delegates proclaimed Charles I as king. After formalizing his power over Castile, in January 1518 the Cortes of Aragon met at Saragossa and after gaining concessions from Charles I confirmed his inheritance. To secure the legislature's endorsement, he was forced to agree to dismiss his Flemish advisors, learn to speak Spanish, resign his reign should his mother regain her health and reside in the realm. With his acceptances by both legislative bodies, all of Spain was again united under the rule of a single monarch, Charles I. However, he had arrived in Spain largely ignorant of local affairs and not speaking the language. He had surrounded himself with only Flemish counselors who had alienated the nobles and towns with their arrogance and self-serving policies and his attempts to solidify his regime were increasingly opposed by the hostile population.

Despite his pledges to the Cortes, after gaining authority to govern, Charles I ignored his promises and his Burgundian friends continued to hold the major offices in his regime. The Spanish king was too young and inexperienced to assert his independence and the Flemish nobles led by William of Croy exploited their positions in the administration to renew their plundering of Spanish wealth. Croy enriched himself with his appointments as head of the royal treasury and admiral of the kingdom. He had his nephew, William of Croy, named to the archbishopric of Toledo and shared in its large revenue. As the government demanded more taxes, the magnates and towns grew increasingly hostile.

During the reign of Isabella and Ferdinand II, Spain had initiated the exploration of the western sea routes to Asia. After Charles I was confirmed as sovereign, his government renewed the quest for new discoveries. In March 1518 he agreed to sponsor the voyage of Ferdinand Magellan to the rich Spice Islands in the Orient. After a year's preparation, in August 1519 Magellan's fleet of five vessels sailed from Seville, crossing the Atlantic Ocean and rounding the tip of South America into the Pacific Ocean. Navigating the vast Pacific with only crude instruments and inaccurate maps, he claimed the islands of Guam, the Marianas and Philippines for Charles I. In the Philippines Magellan became involved in a local tribal war and was killed on April 27, 1521. John Sebastian del Cano assumed command of the expedition and after leaving the Philippines signed numerous trade agreements with the sultans of the Spice Islands. He continued the journey to the west and struggled to Spain with the remnants of the crew aboard the only remaining ship, *Victoria*. Del Cano arrived in Seville in September 1522 with a cargo of cloves, ginger, sandalwood and cinnamon to complete the first circumnavigation of the Earth. The voyage of Magellan resulted in new trade with Asia after Charles I sent German ships and merchants to develop the spice markets.

Following the four voyages of Christopher Columbus, Spanish explorers and settlers began to arrive in the New World. During Columbus's second voyage, the first permanent colony was established in 1493 on the island of Hispaniola at Isabella. The island became the center of the crown's overseas government and from the capital of San Domingo the royal governor attempted to impose the regime's rule over the recalcitrant colonists, who continued to unleash merciless assaults against the native Indian population, enslaving them while plundering and seizing their lands. As more Spanish conquistadors came to the Americas, new territories were explored and conquered in the name of the king. In 1502 the Spanish conquistador Vasco Nunez de Balboa began the investigation of South America by exploring and conquering the region near the Atrate River in present day northwestern Columbia. When the newly discovered mainland of Central America was settled, Spanish adventurers began to attack southern Mexico. In 1518 the viceroy of Cuba appointed Hernando Cortes to lead an expedition to explore and secure Mexico for the Spanish throne.

Hernando Cortes was born in 1485 in the Spanish town of Medellin and was the son of the minor nobleman, Martin Cortes de Monroy. At the age of fourteen he studied law at the University of Salamanca but after two years returned to Medellin. After spending two troubled and restless years in the small provincial town, Hernando sailed to Hispaniola in search of adventure and gold. In San Domingo he used his knowledge of law to secure employment as a notary, becoming associated with the island's governor. As Cortes continued to gain the favor of the government, in 1511 he was appointed a captain in the local army and participated in the conquest of Cuba. Following the occupation of the island, he was named as secretary to the newly appointed Cuban viceroy, Diego Velasquez. Through his considerable energy and administrative skills, Cortes later became the mayor of Havana.

In the aftermath of the discovery of silver and gold in Mexico, in 1518 Hernando Cortes was chosen by Diego Velasquez to command the campaign to conquer the Aztec Empire. Sailing from Cuba, he landed in Vera Cruz in March 1519, soon advancing with six hundred soldiers against the Aztec capital at Tenochtitlan. To subjugate the vast Aztec Empire, Cortes secured the military aid of the local tribes, including the Tlaxcaltec and Nahuas, through bribery, threats and diplomacy. By August 1521 with the help of his native allies and reinforcements from Cuba, he had defeated the Aztecs and had subdued Mexico for Charles I. Following the destruction of the Aztec Empire, Cortes began the exploitation of its land, sending tons of gold and silver to the government of the king. In the years after Cortes's expedition, Francisco Pizarro, Francisco Coronado, Hernando de Soto and other conquistadors created a vast and rich empire for Spain that stretched from southern North America through all of Central and South America.

In 1519 Charles I's paternal grandfather, Emperor Maximilian I, died and the king inherited his Austrian lands. With encouragement from William, Lord of Chievres, he initiated a political campaign to gain the emperorship of the Holy Roman Empire. To finance his quest for the imperial crown, increased demands for revenue were placed on the Spanish towns. In June 1519 Charles I was chosen Holy Roman emperor by the seven electors at the cathedral of Saint Bartholomew in Frankfurt and now had little time for his Spanish government, devoting his attention toward ruling the empire. As the king continued to spend Spanish wealth in Europe and requested additional taxes, revolts in protest began to erupt in Toledo, Valladolid, Avila and Segovia. To secure the funds for the journey to Germany for his imperial coronation, Charles I was forced to convene the Cortes in the remote town of Corunna. The hostile delegates finally approved the money after the liberal use of bribes, promises and intimidation. With the subsidy from the Cortes, preparations for travel to Aachen were finalized and in May 1520 the monarch and his inner council sailed for Flanders, leaving his kingdom on the threshold of civil war.

Before departing for Germany, Charles I formed a regency government of his Flemish courtiers and appointed Adrian of Utrecht as his regent. Adrian was born in the Flemish city of Utrecht on March 2, 1459. At an early age his father died and his mother struggled to provide him with an education. He first studied under the Brethren of the Common Life and later at the University of Louvain, graduating with a doctorate degree in theology. He became a renowned teacher at Louvain and was appointed by Emperor Maximilian I in 1507 as tutor for his grandson, Charles. In 1515 Adrian was sent on a diplomatic mission to Spain by Archduke Charles and was later named a cardinal by Pope Leo X.

After leaving Spain the king sailed first to England to gain the support of Henry VIII against an increasingly hostile France. Following inconclusive negotiations, he traveled to the Netherlands and finally to Aachen for his coronation ceremony on October 22, 1520. While the emperor remained in Germany consolidating his imperial power, Adrian attempted to enforce his rule over the Spanish grandees and population. However, he was met by increased resistance by the towns, who resented being governed by a foreigner and the continued exploitation of their realm. As the threat of revolt spread throughout Castile, the representatives from the rebelling towns met in Avila, forming the Holy League of Corporations on July 29. The junta proclaimed the end of Adrian's regency and its assumption of the government in the name of Queen Joanna to begin the Revolt of the Comuneros. To give legality to its regime, the league mustered its army to rescue Joanna from her imprisonment by the royalists, advancing against the king's troops at Tordesillas. After occupying the lightly defended town, the leaders of the Comuneros were summoned to an audience with the queen. Conferring with Joanna, the rebels petitioned her to sign a decree recognizing their administration but she demanded more time.

As the queen continued to delay endorsing the Comuneros Revolt, Charles I reorganized his regency government replacing Adrian with two Spanish grandees in an attempt to reclaim the loyalty of the nobility. The uprising had been initiated by the towns and the magnates had been largely excluded from the ruling junta. There had been isolated attacks against the lands of the lords and many of their privileges had been voided by the insurgent council. To regain their lost rights, the grandees supported the new royal regime led by two prominent nobles, the constable of Castile, Inigo Velasco, and Admiral Fadrique Enriques. While the rebel army was beset with internal dissention, the constable assumed command of the royal troops and private militias of the lords and advanced against the dissidents. The city of Burgos was reoccupied by the loyalists in September and Tordesillas reconquered in December. As Velasco continued to gain new recruits, on April 23, 1521, his forces defeated the rogues at the decisive battle of Villalar. The three leaders of the junta's army were captured and executed on the following day to break the military power of the Comuneros and end the armed resistance against Charles I.

During the Revolt of the Comuneros, Charles I had remained in Germany and the Netherlands, enforcing his sovereignty over his Habsburg demesne and the Holy Roman Empire while defending his lands against the encroachments of France. Following an inconclusive war against Francis I, a peace treaty was signed and after an absence of nearly two years preparations for Charles I's return to Spain were made during the spring of 1522. He appointed a regency administration to rule in Flanders and in May sailed to his Iberian kingdom. Charles I took control of his Spanish council and fully asserted his personal authority. The rebellion of the towns had been crushed by the grandees and after assuming the reins of power, the king was careful to retain their friendship, confirming their privileges and including them in his regime. To gain the support and loyalty of the minor lords, he offered them positions in his government and they served in his army, court and administration.

The Holy League of the Corporations had been formed by the Spanish towns in protest of their king's rule. To prevent a new rebellion, Charles I began an aggressive restructuring of his kingdom. He granted a general amnesty to the rebels and confirmed the privileges of the towns. He agreed to summon the Cortes on a regular basis and the legislature was given a larger role in the administration and collection of taxes. Many causes of the Comuneros were mitigated and numerous reform proposals from the junta enacted into law. Existing universities were expanded and new schools established by the crown to create a source of trained bureaucrats for the government. To retain the loyalty of the nobles and towns, he appointed only Spanish officials to his council, while becoming more closely associated with his subjects by learning their language, customs and culture. In 1526 Charles I was married to Princess

Isabella of Portugal, daughter of King Manuel I. Despite being an arranged marital union for political purposes, the king and Isabella developed a close loving and supportive relationship. During Charles I's many prolonged absences from Spain, she was appointed regent, ruling with an advisory council in the name of her husband. The marriage resulted in the birth of three children, including the future King Philip II, who was born in 1527. The union with Spain's Iberian neighbor and historic ally was widely acclaimed throughout the realm. Through the policies of the crown, the local silk and wool industries expanded through increased demand from the Spanish colonies in the New World. By means of the expeditions of Hernando Cortes, Ferdinand Magellan and many other conquistadors, vast quantities of silver and gold were flowing into the treasury. During the reign of Charles I, the economy entered a long period of sustained growth, making Spain the richest kingdom in Europe and creating a golden age. When he departed for Italy in July 1529 after spending seven years in Spain, his monarchy was at peace and growing increasingly prosperous while his regime was popular and respected by the nobles, towns and population.

While Charles I remained in Spain, his imperial armies had fought three inconclusive wars against the Valois kingdom of Francis I. In July 1529 through the personal intervention of his aunt, Margaret of Austria, and the king of France's mother, Louise of Savoy, a peace treaty was signed at Cambrai. After an absence of seven years, the Spanish king's presence was urgently needed in Germany to contend the mounting Turkish menace in Hungary, the escalating threat of German Protestantism and the uncertainty of relations with France. In July 1529 he sailed to Italy to revive his shattered alliance with the papacy before traveling to Germany. Before leavening Barcelona, he appointed Queen Isabella as regent to rule in his name. Francisco de los Cobos was chosen as her chief counselor and with his skilled advice the nobles and towns remained loyal to the regime.

In April 1533 Charles I returned to Spain after repulsing the Turkish invasion against Vienna by Sultan Suleiman I and confronting the Protestant Reformation in Germany. After assuming the reins of power from the queen, he met with the legislatures of Aragon and Castile to reconfirm their loyalty. During his absence in the Holy Roman Empire, the fleet of the Muslim pirates led by Barbarossa Hayreddin Pasha had repeatedly attacked Spanish shipping and coastal towns to pose a threat to the security of the realm. Barbarossa was a pirate-vassal of the Ottoman Empire and supported its war of expansion by raiding Christian ports and commerce in the Mediterranean Sea. He commanded a large fleet and continually overwhelmed the navies of Venice, Papacy and Holy Roman Empire. In 1532 he defeated the Genoese fleet of Andrea Doria near Preveza and two years later was recognized for his naval skills and leadership by Suleiman I with his appointment to admiral of the Ottoman navy.

To challenge the growing threat of Barbarossa and as secular head of the Catholic Church, the Spanish king became determined to mount a naval expedition against the Muslim raiders. However, he lacked the military strength to confront the powerful pirate fleet alone and negotiated a coalition with Portugal and Genoa for a joint seaborne campaign. In June 1535 the Spanish ships began to assemble in Barcelona and were soon joined by the vessels of the allies. An invasion army of over thirty thousand Spanish, German, Italian and papal troops was mustered on the island of Sardinia and boarded the ships for the attack against the capital of the Moors at Tunis with Charles I in personal command. The harbor was guarded by the fortress of La Goletta and an assault was ordered against the garrison. Despite several sorties, the stronghold was too strong to be captured by storm and was placed under siege. After nearly a month, the allies' artillery finally breached the walls and the Spanish soldiers surged through the openings to quickly overwhelm the defenders.

Following the occupation of the fortress, Charles I ordered the army to attack the city of Tunis and capture Barbarossa. The king personally commanded the assault, encouraging his troops forward with his presence and bravery. As the allies advanced closer to the city, thousands of Christian slaves revolted and aided in the defeat of the Moors. During the battle Barbarossa escaped from the melee, but his fleet of over one hundred ships was seized. The defeat of the powerful ally of Suleiman I was a great political victory for Charles I, resulting in greater respect and influence with the European kingdoms.

After his triumph at Tunis, Charles I traveled to his domain in southern Italy. Isabella again assumed the regency and Francisco des los Cobos served as her principal advisor. The system of government previously established by the king continued to maintain control over the nobles and towns under the capable administration of the queen. In Italy Charles I soon became involved in a new war with France after the appointment of his son, Philip, as the successor to the vacant ducal throne of Milan. He was finally able to return to Spain in the summer of 1538 after signing a truce agreement with Francis I at Nice. During his absence, his Spanish realm had remained at peace and he quickly reasserted his power over the legislatures and grandees. In May 1539 his beloved Isabella died and the grief stricken king retired to a monastery near Toledo for three weeks of prayer and solitude.

Spain had become the center of his vast empire and Charles I preferred to remain in his adopted home. However, in late 1539 a serious revolt erupted in the Netherlands and he was forced to personally intervene to enforce his rule. Before leaving Spain, he appointed his son, Philip, as regent and Francisco de los Cobos was chosen as his chief advisor and secretary of the ruling council. Arriving in Flanders overland through France, Charles I quickly suppressed the rebellion and after meeting with the Imperial Diet at Regensburg was able to return to Spain. However, before leaving Germany he initiated preparations for a campaign to subjugate the revival of Moorish raiding attacks in the Mediterranean.

Following his victory against Barbarossa at Tunis, Charles I had planned an invasion against the Moorish stronghold at Algiers for the next year. However, he was compelled to return to Italy and the expedition was cancelled. As the secular head of the Catholic Church and a devout Christian, Charles I remained determined to mount a holy crusade against the western advance of the Muslims into the Balkans and the campaign against Algiers was the first attack of his grand strategy to recapture the region and march against Constantinople. As he slowly traveled through Germany and Italy, instructions for his fleet and army to assemble were issued and in late October 1540 the offensive was launched, despite the stormy weather.

The royal fleet assembled along the coastline of North Africa and on October 21 arrived at Algiers with Charles I personally leading the campaign. In spite of rough seas, the troops and supplies were landed and a base camp established. On October 24 the army advanced against the city, making significant progress during the first day of fighting. However, during the night the provisions and munitions of the army were destroyed and the fleet dispersed by a violent storm. When the governor of Algiers, Hassan Aga, counterattacked the encroachment quickly lost its momentum and the king was compelled to order a withdrawal.

In the aftermath of Charles I's failure at Algiers, in early December 1540 he returned to Spain, assuming the reins of power from Philip. From his Iberian kingdom, he ruled his vast empire for the next two years. In 1541 Charles I's détente with France collapsed and in the following year war erupted again between the two realms. To fund the conflict, the king summoned the Cortes to approve a large subsidy. However, the legislature resented paying for his foreign wars, only reluctantly granting the money. While negotiating with the Cortes, he initiated talks with the English crown for an alliance against Francis I, signing an agreement in

February 1543. As the war spread in the Netherlands, the king made preparations to return to northern Europe and appointed Philip as his regent. Before leaving, he summoned the legislature to confirm his son as regent and heir. A three member inner council was named to advise him and the sixteen-year-old prince assumed authority for the government. In the spring Charles I departed for Flanders not knowing that he would not return to his beloved Spain for the next thirteen years.

Charles I spent his last reigning years in the Netherlands and the Holy Roman Empire, renewing his ongoing war with France and struggling to find a resolution to his religious differences with the Protestant princes to end their schism from the Catholic Church. In Spain the opposition of the towns had been eliminated by the suppression of the Comuneros Revolt and the power of the nobles greatly limited by their inclusion in the government and reduction in their wealth and privileges. While Philip maintained control over the realm, Spanish troops and money continued to fight and fund the wars and political initiatives of the king.

By 1555 Charles I had grown physically and mentally exhausted from his many years of ruling half the known world. In recent years he had become increasingly frail and suffered from gout, which caused him great pain and severely limited his mobility. In October he abdicated his Burgundian ducal throne and appointed Philip as his successor in a solemn ceremony in the great hall in Brussels attended by the ministers and provincial governors of the Netherlands along with the great imperial lords. On January 16, 1556, he ceded power for Spain and its overseas colonies to his son in a private ceremony in his apartments. Responsibility for governing the Holy Roman Empire had earlier been transferred to his brother, Ferdinand, and now free of all obligations, the king sailed from Zeeland to Spain in September. After landing in his beloved kingdom, he had a small villa built near the San Jeronimo of Yuste Monastery in central Castile. On February 5, 1557, Charles I and his small court moved into the new residence. The interior of the villa was richly decorated with tapestries, furniture and paintings from the Netherlands, along with exquisite clocks and intricate scientific instruments. He had a small library and spent hours reading history, literature and religious books. His household included his private confessor and the king discussed his salvation and religion with him for many hours. He had occasional guests and enjoyed a quiet life during his final years. In the summer of 1558 he became seriously ill with a fever, growing increasingly weak. On September 21 Charles I died at age fifty-eight after a reign as monarch of Spain for forty-two years.

Sources

Brandi. *The Emperor Charles V.* Grant. *Charles V.* Mulgan. *The Renaissance Monarchies, 1469–1558.* Rady. *The Emperor Charles V.*

Philip II, 1527–1556–1598

When the aging Charles I abdicated the throne on January 16, 1556, his son, Philip II, assumed the reins of power to rule as the sixth monarch of the Spanish Renaissance. Philip was the first child of Charles I and Queen Isabella of Portugal and was born at Valladolid in the province of Old Castile on May 21, 1527. Shortly after his birth, he was baptized by the archbishop of Toledo in the church of Saint Paul and given the name of Philip after his paternal grandfather, King Philip I. In the following year the representatives of the Cortes were summoned to the Saint Jeronimo Monastery in Madrid to acknowledge the infant prince as heir to the crown. During his first years he was raised in his mother's court under the care of an appointed nurse and governor. After the king's return to Spain from northern Europe in 1533, he appointed renowned scholars for his son's education in reading, writing, history, mathematics, religion and the languages of Latin, Greek and French. His humanist education included instruction in the social graces of music, dancing and court etiquette. Like his father, the prince was a serious but not gifted student. He took a special interest in music, learning to play the viol and lute. As Philip grew older, experienced soldiers were chosen for his military training and he became skilled in fencing, jousting and equestrianship. He was an enthusiastic hunter, spending many hours in the forest pursuing small game, deer and bear. Under orders from his father, Philip was given his own household with administrative and personal staffs headed by his governor. He was provided a private library and became an avid book collector, mainly of religious and classical literature.

In May 1539 Queen Isabella died and Philip became more closely associated with his father, who was always held in the greatest esteem and respect. Shortly after the death of the queen, revolt erupted in the Low Countries and the king was forced to personally intervene, appointing his son as the nominal regent for Spain. He created an inner council led by Francisco de los Cobos, Cardinal John Tavera of Toledo and the Duke of Alba, Francisco Alvarez de Toledo, to advise the prince. Under the capable guidance of his counselors, the twelve-year-old Philip gained his first experiences in ruling the realm, while continuing his education. During Charles I's absence, Spain suffered from widespread famine and discontent, but under the administration of Philip's council the kingdom remained peaceful.

Following his failed attempt to conquer the Moorish pirates at Algiers, in December 1540 Charles I returned to Spain and assumed the reins of power from his son. To better prepare Philip for his future assumption of the throne, the monarch associated him more closely with the royal regime and court. The prince now traveled with his father, mastering the skills of kingship, as the council asserted its power throughout the kingdom. During the summer of 1542 after first visiting Navarre, Philip rode with Charles I to the city of Monzon to receive recognition as heir from the legislatures of Aragon, Catalonia and Valencia.

In 1542 Philip was fifteen years old and his father began negotiations for his marriage to his cousin, Princess Maria of Portugal, daughter of King John III. The Portuguese kingdom was the historic ally and friend of Spain and the choice of Maria as the prince's wife was widely popular with the nobles and towns. The marital agreement was signed in late 1542 and the wedding ceremony held on November 12, 1543, at Salamanca. However, the marriage lasted less than two years when Maria died at Valladolid shortly after giving birth to a son, Don Carlos.

As war began to spread in northern Europe, in May 1543 Charles I was compelled to return to Flanders to personally lead the fight against France, appointing Philip as regent. Before leaving Spain, the king named Cardinal Tavera, Francisco de la Cobos and the Duke of Alba as Philip's principal advisors. The prince assumed his responsibilities with enthusiasm and dedication while continuing his education. He remained in close contact with his counselors, conferring with them on a regular basis. Cobos held the office of Spanish secretary of state and Philip grew to depend on his wise counsel for local affairs. Major decisions were still made by the sovereign but routine matters were handled by the regent. He began to hold audiences and meetings with foreign ambassadors, grandees and city officials. He made his decisions after discussing the available options with his chief advisors and committees, always encouraging free expression of opinions. In his correspondences with the king, Philip routinely stressed the plight of the Spanish people and their strong opposition to the European war. In 1544 the regent summoned the legislatures of Castile and Aragon to enact new subsidies to help fund Charles I's wars against France and the Ottoman Empire. After securing a small grant from Aragon, the royal prince attempted to personally negotiate with the Cortes of Castile for its approval of funds but the delegates refused to authorize any money. Unable to raise local taxes, Philip diverted shipments of newly arrived American silver and gold from other governmental expenditures to supplement his father's repeated requests for financial support.

In 1546 Prince Philip was compelled to assume independent control of the Spanish regime following the death of Cardinal Tavera and withdrawal of Cobos from court due to serious illness. Acting without the advice of his former counselors, he issued instructions for the legislatures of Castile and Aragon to meet and personally negotiated with the representatives to raise new money for the king. As the prince continued to enforce his power, rebellion led by the conquistador Gonzalo Pizarro erupted in Peru over the crown's implementation of new laws giving rights to the Indians. When the uprising threatened to overthrow the throne's Peruvian administration, Philip sent Peter de la Gasca as his envoy to restore order. Empowered with absolute authority, he mustered a local army and defeated the rebels at the battle of Sacsayhuaman to quickly reimpose the royal government. The Peruvian insurrection was Philip's first experience confronting armed revolt and his decisive orders reestablished the monarchy's rule and increased his respect and esteem with his father.

As Philip continued to master the skills of kingship in Spain, Charles I summoned him to the Low Countries to broaden his personal experiences in European affairs. As heir to half the known world, it was necessary to prepare him for his future assumption of power in the multi-national and diverse empire. The king made preparations for his son's extended absence from Spain by sending his nephew, Archduke Maximilian of Austria, to assume the regency. After the arrival of his cousin, in October 1548 Philip sailed to Italy and traveled overland to the Netherlands. The journey lasted six months and at each city the prince was lavishly entertained by the local rulers with banquets, dancing, hunting parties and military tournaments. The royal prince made his formal entry into Brussels on April 1, 1549, in a magnificent procession and was greeted by his father in the royal palace.

Philip remained in Brussels with the king for the next three months, beginning the task of learning the local politics and meeting his future subjects. He spent several hours daily with his father, mastering the skills of ruling the recalcitrant Netherlanders. In July the prince and Charles I made an extended tour of the duchy's provinces, conferring with the Flemish magnates and city burghers. At each town, Philip was entertained with magnificent banquets, dancing and hunting parties and military tournaments. He made a favorable impression on the nobles and provincial governors, enthusiastically participating in the jousting and festivals. As he traveled through the duchy, he was greatly impressed with the architecture, art and music, sending paintings by Rogier van der Weyden, including *Descent from the Cross,* to Spain, while adding local musicians to his household. In late October Charles I and the Spanish prince returned to Brussels after visiting each of the seventeen provinces, where Philip was formally acknowledged as heir by the regional governments.

The Spanish prince spent the winter months in Brussels at the ducal court, continuing his education for his future assumption of the Burgundian throne, while enjoying hunting and dancing parties, festivals and military tournaments. In late May 1550 Charles I and his son began the journey to Augsburg to attend the Imperial Diet. Traveling through Germany, they visited the large local cities; where Philip was greatly impressed by their splendor, size and wealth. In July they arrived in the imperial free city of Augsburg. Philip frequently attended the Diet, conferring with the Protestant and Catholic princes who were contending for religious supremacy in the Holy Roman Empire. He remained in southern Germany for the next year, extending his knowledge of his father's extensive and diverse empire. In Augsburg he met the Venetian painter Titian, giving him a large commission for a series of mythological paintings. While in northern Europe, Philip met his uncle, Ferdinand of Austria, and was later joined by his cousin, Maximilian, who had left Spain to reunite with the two branches of the Habsburg family. With his advancing age and frail health, Charles I was anxious to bequeath his entire empire to his son but Ferdinand refused to agree. A compromise settlement was later arranged with Ferdinand inheriting the imperial crown and Philip assuming the Netherlands, Naples, Milan and Spain with its overseas territories.

Philip had been absent from Spain for nearly three years and in May 1551 preparations for his return were begun. He departed from Augsburg with a small escort on May 25, traveling to Austria and south into Italy. In early June he arrived in Trent and attended sessions of the Ecclesiastic Council, which was summoned by the papacy to resolve the religious differences between the Catholics and Protestants. In July Philip sailed from Genoa to Barcelona, assuming control of the kingdom from his sister, Maria.

After establishing his government in Valladolid, Prince Philip traveled to Tordesillas to visit his aging grandmother, Queen Joanna, who had grown increasingly mentally incompetent under her continued confinement. The regent-prince spent the remainder of the year ruling Spain alone, while the fragile peace in northern Europe was shattered by the newly formed league between the Protestant princes and France. Under attack on two fronts from the anti–Habsburg league, Charles I was hard pressed to retain his authority in Germany. In Spain Philip supported his father's war by recruiting volunteer soldiers and raising money from the church and legislatures. While the king struggled against the pro–Protestant alliance, the Spanish prince remained in Madrid to reorganize and consolidate his government. In June 1552 he traveled north to Aragon to impose his personal rule by the power of his presence. He met frequently with the Aragonese Cortes, addressing its petitions and resolving local affairs.

In 1553 the military situation in northern Europe stabilized after the Protestants agreed to a truce with Charles I and the Habsburg army counterattacked to contain the French advances. While the war continued against France, in July 1553 Edward VI of England died and the Tudor throne was inherited by his Catholic half-sister, Mary I. The succession of the Catholic queen created an opportunity for an Anglo-Habsburg alliance against France through the marriage of Philip to Mary I. Negotiations for the marital agreement were initiated by Charles I and lasted until April 1554, when the English Parliament ratified the treaty. Under the ensuing marriage accord, the Spanish prince pledged to exclude foreigners from all crown offices, promote peace between England and France, respect the rights and privileges of his English subjects and relinquish the throne if Mary I died. Under the succession terms of the settlement, if a son resulted from the union, he inherited the Netherlands and England, while Spain, the overseas colonies and Italy passed to Philip's heir, Don Carlos. Following the approval of the marriage contract, Philip began arrangements at Valladolid to travel to England, appointing his youngest sister, Joanna, as regent. After prolonged preparations, in July he sailed from Spain on board his flagship, *Holy Ghost,* with an escort of two hundred vessels, landing at Southampton seven days later.

After a delay at Southampton for several days due to stormy weather, Philip traveled to Winchester, meeting Mary I for the first time on July 23, 1554. Prior to the wedding, he received a special gift from Charles I, who announced his formal investiture as king of Naples. The marriage ceremony of great pomp and spirituality was performed by the local bishop in Winchester Cathedral, where the Spanish prince wore a rich white coat decorated with multi-pearls. Following the marital service, Philip and Mary I began a slow journey to London, where they were welcomed with large cheering crowds and lavish decorations. As king consort, he attempted to make a good impression on the English, endeavoring to adapt to their customs and culture. Supporters of the queen were appointed to his household and the prince tried to learn to speak English. In his personal relationship with the queen, he had agreed to the marriage out of a sense of duty to his father but always treated his wife with kindness and generosity. Philip was careful not to interfere in English politics but devoted himself to governing Spain, Milan and Naples. However, he encouraged Mary I to end the religious schism in England and reconcile her realm with the Catholic Church. In late November Mary I and Philip attended a session of Parliament, presiding over the approval of the law returning England to the Holy See of Rome.

After spending over a year in England, Philip was summoned to Brussels by his father to discuss the distribution of his Habsburg Empire, but the queen's announcement of her pregnancy forced him to delay the journey. However, as the expected birth date passed without any signs of labor, she finally accepted that it was a false pregnancy. The prince was now able to prepare for his voyage to Flanders and in September 1555 sailed from Dover.

Due to his advancing age and deteriorating frail health, Charles I had decided to abdicate from the thrones of the Netherlands and Spain and Philip's presence in Brussels was required for the transfer of power. In late October 1555 the lords and provincial governors of Flanders, Habsburg family and neighboring princes assembled in the great hall of Brussels to witness the king's investiture of his son as the new duke of Burgundy. The ceding of Spain and the overseas colonies was made on January 16, 1556, in a private ceremony in Charles I's apartments. In Spain Philip II's succession to the crown was announced at Valladolid on March 28. He now ruled the most extensive empire in Europe, comprising the Burgundian duchy, Milan, Naples and Spain with its vast overseas settlements.

As the ruler of the Netherlands, Spain and half of Italy, Philip II inherited his father's ongoing conflict with France. Surrounded and threatened on three sides by the Habsburgs, the French king, Henry II, had negotiated a military alliance with the anti–Spanish pope, Paul IV. As papal troops continued to harass his Italian lands, the Spanish king ordered his local viceroy, Duke Francisco Alvarez of Alba, to attack the Ecclesiastic States. The localized war quickly expanded when the French armies advanced into Flanders and northern Italy. As the war dragged on inconclusively, in March 1557 Philip II returned to England to raise troops and money. However, his requests were repeatedly denied by Parliament until June when the English dissident, Sir Thomas Stafford, attempted to raise a rebellion in the north with the encouragement and subsidies from Henry II. The French involvement in the insurrection created widespread public resentment against the papal–Franco coalition and on June 7 Queen Mary I declared war against Henry II.

After securing an agreement for military aid and troops from the English, on July 6, 1557 the Spanish king returned to Brussels to personally direct the war effort against France. In late July Henry II's forces invaded the Flemish borderlands, as Philip II quickly assembled his army of Spanish, English, Netherlander and German soldiers and ordered his commander, Emmanuel Philibert of Savoy, to counterattack by besieging the Saint Quentin fortress. When Henry II attempted to relieve the investment, his army under the command of Anne de Montmorency was destroyed on August 10 by Savoy with many thousands killed and captured.

Three days after the battle, the king arrived at Saint Quentin, assuming control of the siege. Later in the month, he personally led the final assault against the stronghold, gaining his first experiences in combat. Following the occupation of the city, Philip II returned to Brussels to renew his quest for money and troops to continue the fight against the French, while writing to his sister, Joanna, encouraging her to press the Cortes for additional financial subsidies. As the conflict remained at an impasse, in October 1558 with both realms growing increasingly war weary and facing bankruptcy, peace negotiations were begun.

While the treaty discussions with the French continued, on November 17, 1558, Queen Mary I died, resulting in the dissolution of the Anglo-Spanish détente and loss of Philip II's influence in English affairs. As the king remained in Brussels, ruling Spain, Italy and the Netherlands, in April a peace agreement with the French regime was signed at Cateau-Cambresis. Under the terms of the settlement, Spain's Italian possessions were confirmed, the French retained the recently seized English enclave at Calais and friendship between the two kingdoms was sealed with the marriage of Philip II to Elizabeth of Valois, eldest daughter of Henry II. The wedding ceremony was held by proxy on June 22 in the Paris Notre Dame Cathedral with the duke of Alba representing the king. With peace finally restored to Europe, Philip II began plans to travel to Spain. Despite the sudden death of the French king from a wound suffered in a jousting tournament and rising threat of the Protestant movement in the Netherlands, Philip II continued his preparations to return home. To rule the Low Countries, he established a regency government, appointing his half-sister, Margaret of Parma, as regent. She was advised by the councils of finance, privy and state but Anthony Perrenot, cardinal of Granvelle, quickly imposed his dominance over the other counselors. On August 25 after a stay of over five years in northern Europe, Philip II boarded his vessel and with an escort fleet of ninety ships sailed for Spain, arriving in early September.

After landing at Laredo, Philip II rode to Valladolid and assumed control of Spain from Princess Joanna. From the royal palace, he began the daily routine of ruling his vast empire. Charles I's wars in northern Europe had depleted the Spanish treasury and the king summoned the Cortes to Toledo to raise the revenue necessary to govern his kingdom. Despite the inflows of silver and gold from the American colonies, the shortage of money remained a constant problem for the regime. During Philip II's absence in Brussels, several factions of Lutherans had been discovered in Spain. He had witnessed the turmoil caused in Germany by the Protestant Reformation and was determined to eliminate all heretics from his lands. He actively supported the intervention of the Inquisition against the anti-papists and personally presided over a judicial session where unrepentant Lutherans were condemned to death and penances imposed on those who recanted. To contain the growth of the non–Catholics, new censorship laws were enacted and a list of forbidden books published. Jews, who had previously converted to Christianity, came under closer scrutiny for possible heretic sentiments. The throne's energetic backing of the Inquisition greatly limited the success of the Protestant movement and allegiance to the Church of Rome remained dominant in Spain.

Philip II had traveled extensively through western Europe, becoming exposed to the art, architecture and music of the Renaissance. After returning to Spain he became Europe's leading patron of artists, purchasing paintings by Titian, Antonis Mor and Hieronymus Bosch. The king's many artistic works decorated his palaces, including Madrid, the Escorial and El Pardo. He also favored Spanish painters, bringing Alonso Sanchez Coello and Pantoja de Cruz to his court. Music played a major role in the Spanish court and the king attended and promoted musical performances. He sponsored many Flemish composers, encouraging Philip Rogier and others to settle in Spain. While he was an enthusiastic collector of art, the major cultural project of his reign was the construction of the monastery of San Lorenzo near the small village of El Escorial. The massive structure served as a monastery for the Jeronimite friars, grand palace and mausoleum for the burial of the royal family. He took an active interest in its design, building and decoration, personally making modifications to the plans. One of the central features of the Escorial was the library with its massive collection of books and rare manuscripts. The king had faith in the healing power of religious relics and housed over seven thousand in the San Lorenzo structure. The monarch's patronage was not limited to only the arts but also included the sciences and medicine.

During Philip II's stay in England and Flanders, the Ottoman Turks continued their advance into Hungary, while their allies in the western Mediterranean renewed their attacks against Spanish commerce and coastal towns. In 1559 the king authorized an expedition against the Muslim stronghold of Tripoli. However, the campaign ended in disaster, when the Ottoman fleet commanded by Turgut Reis defeated the naval forces of Philip II at the battle of Djerba. The Muslim presence in North Africa remained a threat to Spain's security and in 1562 the crown mounted a second sea-borne attack against Tripoli, but the initiative was thwarted by a violent storm with the loss of twenty-five galleys. Without adequate military forces, the Spanish government struggled to protect its Mediterranean possessions and the Ottoman invasions against Oran and Malta were repulsed only with great difficulty.

While Philip II remained engaged against the Ottoman advance into North Africa, Elizabeth of Valois arrived in Spain to finalize the marriage terms under the Treaty of Cateau-Cambresis. In January 1560 the wedding ceremony between the Spanish king and Elizabeth was formalized at Toledo and was followed by a lavish banquet and ball. The celebrations continued into the next day with jousting, bullfights and hunting parties. Elizabeth was young, beautiful and intelligent and their marital union was widely popular in Spain, where it was perceived as a deterrent to future war with France. Despite his marriage, the king renewed his many amorous affairs with the ladies of his court. However, over time he became increasingly devoted to the queen and ended his adulterous relationships. After suffering a miscarriage, she gave birth to a healthy daughter, Princess Isabella, in 1556 and in the following year a second daughter, Princess Catherine, was born. The pregnancies had been difficult for the queen and in the summer of 1568 she died from complications following the birth of a third daughter, who also did not survive.

In 1562 religious conflict erupted in France between the Catholic and Huguenot factions, which threatened to spill over into the Low Countries. With its large cloth markets and merchant fleets, the maintenance of peace with Flanders was vital to the economic interest of the Spanish and the king encouraged his half-sister, Margaret, to keep the advancement of Protestantism in check. Acting on the advice of Cardinal Granvelle, she ruled with a firm hand against the Flemish nobles and towns. As the magnates became increasingly excluded from the government, they wrote to Philip protesting the influence of Granvelle and asking for his dismissal from court.

As the danger of rebellion escalated in the Low Countries, in 1563 Philip II was occupied with sessions of the Castilian and Aragonese legislatures, addressing their concerns and needs, while raising money for his impoverished coffers. Between negotiations with the Cortes representatives, he traveled to many of the principal cities, enforcing his rule through the power of his presence and grandeur of his throne. As Philip II continued to advise Margaret of Parma in Flanders, she finally yielded to the unrelenting pressure of the nobles and asked the king to dismiss Granvelle. While at Monzon attending the Aragon Cortes, he ordered the cardinal to leave the duchy temporarily to restore order. The monarch remained in northern Spain, continuing his meetings with the Cortes until April 1564, when he returned to Madrid.

While Philip II attended to the routine affairs of state from his newly proclaimed seat of government at Madrid, his regime was again compelled to intervene against the rising unrest in the Low Countries. Despite the departure of his trusted advisor, Cardinal Granvelle, the local nobles and burghers demanded increased religious freedom, greater participation in the ruling council and less restrictive heresy laws. In February 1565 they sent Count Lamoral of Egmont to Madrid to personally appeal to the king for reforms. After conferring with Egmont and meeting his counselors, Philip II agreed to limited concessions, approving modifications to his Flemish administration and consenting to reconsider the anti-papists statutes. In early April the count departed for the Netherlands, believing meaningful compromises had been granted. However, in May the execution of six convicted Lutherans was approved by the Spanish council and the Flemish lords protested at the lack of tolerance, threatening civil disobedience.

In 1565 to limit the spread of Lutherism into the Netherlands, the Spanish regime sent Queen Elizabeth with Francisco Alvarez of Alba to meet her mother, Catherine of France, at Bayonne to gain her support in actively confronting the heretics. Under instructions from the government, Alba attempted to convince the French administration to adopt a more aggressive strategy against the Huguenots but Catherine refused to modify her policy, fearing widespread religious rebellion. Her rejection of Alba's proposal compelled the Spanish council to focus its military and financial support on Duke Henry of Guise and his anti–Huguenot league.

Philip II was totally committed to the Catholic Church and when the Council of Trent's religious reforms were proclaimed by the papacy, Spain was the first European kingdom to accept them. As a devout Catholic, he rejected any compromise with the Flemish Protestants and in late August 1565 his government announced its refusal to grant them any religious concessions. When reports of the new policy reached Brussels, William of Orange and Egmont withdrew from the ruling council in opposition. Rumors spread through the provinces that the Inquisition was being introduced into the Low Countries and the king would arrive at the head of a large army to force its acceptance. In April 1566 Count Egmont and Orange issued an ultimatum to Margaret of Parma, threatening to resign from the government unless they were given larger roles in the regime and religious toleration was granted. Lacking adequate military forces to assert the royal will, she was compelled to submit. To defend their acts of defiance, two Flemish noblemen were sent to Spain by the rebel faction to meet with the king. In June the envoys conferred with Philip II at Segovia, expressing the need for toleration and inclusion in the administration. After discussing his options with the council and selected ministers, he announced his decision to travel to Brussels to personally resolve the discord, while rejecting the demands of the Netherlanders. In July he received news from Margaret, reporting that the Flemish magnates were raising money and recruiting troops for rebellion. She urged her half-brother to take firm action or make meaningful concessions.

As the danger of armed insurrection escalated in the Low Countries, the Spanish king authorized Margaret to hire German mercenaries to defend his sovereignty. In September 1566 he received letters from the regent, reporting widespread anti–Catholic rioting and pillaging of local churches. As the uprising spread, the Spanish government began preparations to send an army under the command of Duke Francesco Alvarez of Alba to enforce the peace. In April 1567 he sailed from Cartagena on the eastern Spanish coast to Italy, marching his troops north to Flanders. After an overland journey of four months, the sixty-year-old captain-general entered Brussels with ten thousand Spanish soldiers and full military power to restore order. He began the campaign against the insurrection by arresting the recognized heads of the revolt, Count Egmont and Count Philip Hornes of Montmorency. Under the ruthless and relentless attacks of the Spanish, the crown's rule was imposed by the sword and by the end of the year most of the rebel leaders were either imprisoned or fled abroad.

While the Madrid court awaited new reports on the progress of Alba's offensive in Flanders, in December 1567 the king's son and heir, Don Carlos, began to plot his escape from Spain to the Netherlands. Don Carlos was born in Valladolid on July 8, 1545, and was the only issue of Philip II's first marriage to Maria of Portugal. At an early age he began to show signs of mental instability, which were exacerbated in 1562 from head injuries suffered from a fall. His behavior became more unpredictable and aggressive and his father seriously questioned his son's ability to rule. When Alba was named to command the Flemish campaign, the Spanish prince was enraged, believing as the recognized successor, it was his right to lead the army. He secretly communicated with the conspirators in the Low Countries and in January the king ordered his arrest to prevent him from becoming the figurehead ruler of the revolt. Don Carlos was imprisoned in the castle of Madrid under close guard and denied any visitors. Kept under confinement, his physical and mental health deteriorated rapidly and on July 24, 1568, he died.

Following the death of Don Carlos, the Spanish king's only remaining children were the two infant daughters of Elizabeth of Valois. The queen had died in 1568 and now without a male heir, Philip II was pressed by his counselors to marry again in the hope of producing a son to avoid a succession crisis. Marguerite of Valois was proposed as a possible spouse but the king chose Anna of Austria, daughter of Emperor Maximilian II, as his fourth wife. After the marital negotiations with the emperor were concluded, in September 1570 Anna sailed from the Low Countries to Spain and was welcomed by a magnificent reception in Segovia, where she met Philip II. The formal wedding ceremony was held on November 14 in the presence of the high churchmen and grandees. Despite being an arranged marriage for political reasons, Philip II and Anna developed a deep affection and they became totally devoted to each other. She shared a similar interest with her husband in music, art and plays and with her quiet personality brought tranquility to the royal household. In their over nine years of marriage, Anna gave birth to five children, however, only Prince Philip born in April 1578 survived into adulthood. When his wife died from influenza in October 1580, Philip II was grief-stricken and greatly lamented her loss.

The Duke of Alba's aggressive campaign of subjugation against the Flemish rebels had reimposed the Spanish throne's authority and had captured many of its leaders. However, Prince William of Orange managed to escape to Germany, assuming the role of defender of the Netherlands. He developed close friendships with the German Protestant princes and recruited troops from their lands. To confront the Spanish presence in his homeland, he mounted several raids against Alba's occupation forces but his attacks were repulsed. Emboldened by the incursions of Orange, the Netherlanders strengthened their opposition, compelling the Spanish government to order the execution of Egmont and Hornes for treason to break their resistance. However, the deaths of the two counts only served to intensify the rebellion and Alba was forced to initiate a harsher policy of suppression, executing hundreds of dissidents.

Spain had remained at peace internally since the defeat of the Comuneros Revolt in 1521. However, the tranquility was broken when the Moriscos in the southern province of Granada rebelled against the implementation of new anti–Moorish laws. As the uprising gained strength and arms and volunteers arrived from North Africa, the king's half-brother, Don John, was appointed to command the royal army's campaign of subjugation against the dissidents. Under his relentless and brutal attacks, in November of the following year the rebel leaders agreed to terms. Many thousands of Moriscos were killed during the war and thousands more forcibly expelled to other regions of the kingdom. With most of the crown's military forces in the Netherlands, the revolt in Grenada was a serious threat to the regime's security, but Don John's savage repression policy succeeded in reasserting the rule of the king.

While Philip II was still in Andalusia directing the campaign against the Morisco rebels, Pope Pius V sent him an urgent appeal for military aid for the defense of the Venetian occupied island of Cyprus against invasion by the Turks. After conferring with his council, the king agreed to dispatch military forces to support the Republic of Venice at Cyprus. With Cardinal Granvelle representing the Spanish throne in Rome, a treaty of alliance was signed, binding the Republic of Saint Mark, Spain and the Holy See to the protection of Cyprus. Each realm pledged to provide two hundred warships and fifty thousand troops and to recognize Don John as supreme commander. On June 6, 1471, Philip II received the news of the Holy League's ratification and in the afternoon Don John departed to assemble his navy.

Don John traveled to Sicily by way of Genoa and Naples, arriving at the port of Messina in late August. He took command of the allied fleet of over two hundred fifty vessels and sailed on September 15 to the east. Approaching the western coast of Greece, the Christian navy met the Ottomans in the Gulf of Lepanto on the morning of October 7, deploying into three divisions to attack the Muslims. Under the skilled leadership of Don John, the Holy League won a decisive sea battle, destroying all of Sultan Selim II's fleet except forty ships, while suffering the loss of only ten galleys. The league's triumph at Lepanto severely weakened the naval power of Selim II, securing Spain from a direct Muslim invasion while freeing Philip II to direct his resources and money toward defending his north European possessions.

While Spain and its allies were gaining success in the Mediterranean, in the Low Country the Duke of Alba continued to struggle against the resistance of the local rebels. In April 1572 the Spanish crown's campaign suffered a serious setback when the Flemish privateer William de la Marck and his Sea Beggars seized the town of Brille. Emboldened by the Sea Beggars' victory, Mons opened its gates to Louis of Nassau, younger brother of William of Orange. Soon the principal cities in Zeeland, Holland and Guelderland declared their allegiance to the prince of Orange's faction.

To confront the gains of the dissidents, Alba began a reign of Spanish terror, using the army to indiscriminately suppress the Flemish. Under his aggressive attacks, Mons was recaptured in September and after the surrender of Harlem and Malines his soldiers mercilessly sacked the towns. The duke's subjugation campaign was so ruthless that the Catholic burghers complained directly to the king for relief. However, despite the relentless and brutal assaults of Francesco Alvarez, the Netherlanders continued to resist. By 1573 it was clear to Philip II that the duke's policy had failed and the royal government appointed Don Luis de Requesens as his successor.

Assuming the reins of power, de Requesens abandoned Alba's policy of terror and implemented a strategy of moderation with the limited use of force. In April 1574 the Spanish army was ordered by de Requesens to attack the Dutch forces led by Louis of Nassau. In the resulting battle of Mookerheyde, the rebels were decisively defeated and Louis was killed. Following the defeat, with his troop strength depleted from the losses at Mookerheyde and his coffers exhausted, William of Orange was compelled to negotiate a truce through the mediation of Emperor Maximilian II. The royal governor pledged to withdraw his Spanish soldiers but only if Catholicism was acknowledged as the sole religion. Under his reconciliation campaign, the Spanish reversed many of the gains of the Dutch rebels, but in March 1576 Don Luis died in Brussels. Without the strong hand of the governor-general, the unpaid troops in Antwerp rioted on November 4, 1576, sacking the city and murdering over eight thousand citizens in the Spanish Fury. The news of the attack quickly spread through the Netherlands, uniting the seventeen provinces in common cause against the Spanish occupation. In November the States General met in Ghent, adopting the Pacification of Ghent. Under the ensuing agreement, the provinces pledged to collaborate in the expulsion of the foreigners from the Low Countries.

Following the death of de Requesens, the Spanish king appointed his half-brother, Don John, as successor to the governorship of the Low Countries. Don John was instructed to travel to Brussels as quickly as possible but he continually delayed his departure, not arriving until late in November 1576 at the height of the Spanish Fury. To quell the rebellion, he agreed to a policy of appeasement, evacuating the Spanish infantry, releasing his prisoners and reinstating the privileges and exemptions of the towns. His concessions resulted in a brief period of peace, but William of Orange refused to accept the reconciliation, intriguing against the governor's administration. Under his leadership the nobles and towns renewed their uprising, electing Archduke Matthias of Austria as governor-general and Orange as his deputy of an independent realm. Philip II responded by ordering the Spanish army back to the Netherlands and appointing his nephew, Alexander Farnese, Prince of Parma, to assist Don John. Never liking his role as peacemaker, the Spanish governor quickly assembled his forces and marched against the dissidents, defeating Prince William on January 31, 1578, at the battle of Gembloux. After his victory the predominately Catholic southern provinces agreed to open peace negotiations. Despite his success in the south, Don John did not live to continue his campaign, dying on October 1, 1578, of typhoid. Before his death he named Alexander Farnese as his successor and the king confirmed his choice.

Prince Alexander Farnese was the son of Margaret of Parma and was familiar with Flemish political affairs, customs and culture after spending time in the Netherlands during his mother's regency. He was an experienced soldier and diplomat, utilizing his skills to exploit the racial and religious differences between the southern and northern regions. He negotiated the Union of Arras with the provinces of Artois and Hainault, securing their allegiance to the Spanish crown. William of Orange replied by forging the Union of Utrecht, uniting the seven northern provinces against Philip II's rule. With most of the Low Countries still in revolt against Spanish sovereignty, Farnese marched his troops against Orange, winning several battles. After the military defeats, Prince William was in danger of losing control of the north and was compelled to seek French support to avoid defeat.

While the Spanish throne continued to seek solutions to the Flemish rebellion, in December 1577 Philip II met his nephew, King Sebastian I of Portugal, at Guadalupe in Castile to discuss a joint attack against North Africa. The Spanish king had little confidence in the success of the campaign but promised a contingent of his soldiers. In June 1578 Sebastian I sailed from Lisbon with an army of seventeen thousand men-under-arms to Morocco. Marching into the interior, he encountered the Moors near the town of Ksar el Kebir. During the ensuing battle, the Portuguese were routed and their king killed. Sebastian I had no direct heir and his crown was assumed by his great uncle, Henry I. The new Portuguese king was over sixty six years old and a former cardinal. Without any successors, the future inheritance of the Portuguese monarchy became a matter of great concern to the European courts.

Through his mother, Philip II was directly related to the reigning Portuguese dynasty and a strong claimant to the kingdom. In January 1580 Henry I died after acknowledging

Philip II as his heir. Despite the Spanish king's legal right to the throne, Don Antonio of Beja, illegitimate nephew of Henry I, refused to accept his succession and formed a faction of supporters in opposition. Determined to assert his inheritance, in August Philip II sent the Duke of Alba with a veteran army of fifteen thousand to enforce his rule. The Portuguese militia of Don Antonio was quickly outmaneuvered and overwhelmed by the skilled Alba and Lisbon was captured. In the aftermath of his defeat, Don Antonio fled to the Azores and unsuccessfully attempted to claim Portuguese sovereignty. On April 16, 1581, Philip II officially assumed the crown at Tormar in the presence of the local legislature. He remained in Lisbon until early 1583, establishing his government, imposing his power and integrating the new realm into his empire.

Through diplomacy and military might, Alexander Farnese had regained the loyalty of the Catholic southern provinces of the Low Countries and had weakened the resistance of William of Orange's Union of Utrecht. As the recognized leader of the pro-independence faction, Orange remained determined to end Spanish domination and negotiated an alliance with Francis of Anjou, brother of King Henry III of France. Under the Treaty of Plessis des Tours, Francis was recognized as duke for the northern region, while pledging to respect the privileges of the towns, appoint only Netherlanders to his government and intervene militarily with his private French troops. His rule was acknowledged by numerous nobles and burghers but his authority was undermined by the presence of William of Orange and several Calvinist provinces rejected the Catholic duke's assumption of the ducal throne because of religious differences. With only limited support from the Dutch, when he advanced the army against Parma, his forces were repeatedly defeated on the battlefield. In January 1583 the duke attempted to seize power in Antwerp but his French soldiers were repulsed by the Netherlanders. Anjou was finally compelled to abandon his quest for sovereignty, returning to France in July 1583.

Under the skilled leadership of the prince of Parma, the Spanish continued to recover territories previously lost to William of Orange's northern union, now called the United Provinces. Parma's campaign to reimpose Philip II's sovereignty was aided by the assassination of the charismatic and popular Prince William of Orange in July 1584. With over sixty thousand men-under-arms and sufficient money, the prince regained Ypres, Bruges and Ghent and in August 1585 Antwerp surrendered. The only remaining opposition to the Spanish came from Holland and Zeeland. The Dutch were hard pressed to contain the advance of the Spanish and turned to England for military aid. The Protestant Tudor court had secretly abetted the rebels' cause, sending money to buttress their resistance to Catholic Spain. In August 1585 Elizabeth I signed the Treaty of Nonsuch, agreeing to intervene militarily. In December Lord Robert Dudley arrived with eight thousand troops. Despite the English pledge to support the Dutch, the queen refused to supply needed arms and money to Dudley. Without the full backing of the Tudor government and confronting a seasoned army, Lord Robert's initiative achieved little success. Relations between Spain and England became increasingly strained as Elizabeth I continued to intervene in the Netherlands and France in defense of the Protestants.

In June 1584 Henry III's brother and heir, Duke Francis, died and under the recognized Salic Law the Protestant king of Navarre, Henry Bourbon, was the new successor designate. The accession to power of a heretic was unacceptable to Spain and the government increased its financial payments to the French Catholic League. With the threat of religious war again growing in France, Elizabeth I supported the Huguenot resistance with a large financial subsidy in defiance of Spanish interest. Hostilities between the two rivals were further exacerbated by

Philip II's involvement in the plots to assassinate Elizabeth I and place Mary I of Scotland on the throne, along with the increasing attacks of the English privateers in the Americas against Spanish settlements and silver shipments. In 1585 the Spanish regime lacked the naval power to defend its interest and the king issued orders for the construction of the Great Armada for the invasion of England.

The Spanish king ruled his empire from Madrid and the Escorial but acute attacks of gout forced him to rely more heavily on his council advisors and government ministers. He attempted to find peaceful solutions to the threatening war with the Tudors but as Elizabeth I continued to send her sea raiders to American waters and supported the Dutch revolt, his regime appointed Alvaro de Bazan, Marques of Santa Cruz, to command the invasion against England. In the spring of 1587 Santa Cruz was ordered to prepare to sail with two hundred vessels and escort the seventeen thousand soldiers of Parma from Flanders across the channel to Kent. After landing in England, Farnese was to occupy Kent and take London by storm. Santa Cruz began to assemble the flotilla in Lisbon but in early 1588 he became seriously ill, dying on February 9. Philip II quickly named Alonzo Perez Guzman, Duke of Medina Sidonia, to replace Bazan. Under his directions, preparations were intensified and by the summer the fleet was ready to put to sea.

On July 22, 1588, Medina Sidonia sailed from Lisbon onboard his flagship, *San Martin,* with over one hundred thirty vessels north toward England. Seven days later the great fleet approached the coast of Cornwall. When the armada was sighted by the English, Lord Charles Howard left Plymouth with Sir Francis Drake and Captain John Hawkins to harass the Spanish. Under attack Guzman maneuvered his ships into a crescent shaped formation that the English were unable to penetrate. On August 6 he anchored in the English Channel off the coast of Calais to await Parma and his army. However, Farnese lacked the small boats necessary to ferry his troops from the shore to the larger galleons and needed additional time. While the Spanish vessels remained anchored, during the night Howard launched eight fireships packed with explosives into Guzman's position. The duke's ships were compelled to cut their cables and sail into the channel. As the Great Armada was reforming into the defensive crescent formation, it was attacked by the English near Gravelines. Utilizing their superior firepower, seamanship and maneuverability, Howard's fleet sank five galleons and heavily damaged many others. With his flotilla in disarray, Medina Sidonia was forced to abandon the rendezvous with the Duke of Parma and sail up the channel toward Scotland.

Traveling into the North Sea with many of his ships damaged and water and food supplies nearly exhausted, Guzman was compelled to cancel the invasion of England and return to Spain. As he sailed into the Atlantic Ocean, his fleet encountered large powerful summer storms off the coasts of western Scotland and Ireland which forced many of his vessels onto the shore. As the remnants of the Great Armada struggled southwestward to home, a few ships began to arrive on September 13. Philip II was working at his desk in the Escorial, when the reports of the severity of the defeat reached him. He accepted the loss of the armada as God's will and ordered prayers in the churches and money to alleviate the suffering of the survivors.

Following the destruction of the Great Armada, Philip II's health deteriorated further, as he suffered from depression and the increasing effects of gout, which left him immobile for large periods of time. However, by April 1589 his health improved and he was well enough to travel to Ananjvez in April to enjoy the warm spring weather. In northern Europe he continued to rule over the southern Flemish region, but the United Provinces remained in rebellion. In France his interests were undermined by Henry III's alliance with the Protestant king of Navarre, Henry of Bourbon. In the summer of 1589 they advanced against the Catholic League, but near Paris the French monarch was assassinated and his ally, Henry, acknowledged as ruler under the prevailing Salic Law. The assumption to the French throne by a heretic was contrary to Spanish policy, causing Philip II to increase his military and financial support to the Catholic League. He ordered Parma to aid the papists by raising the Huguenots' siege against Paris and Rouen. Following the relief of the two cites, in January 1593 the Spanish king sent his envoys to Paris to promote the acceptance of either Archduke Ernest of Austria or the fourth duke of Guise, Charles of Lorraine, as the new French king with his daughter, Catherine, as his queen. However, the Spanish intervention in France was weakened when Henry IV abandoned his Protestant religion and recognized Catholicism. Many of the moderate Catholic League's nobles and towns accepted his government and Henry IV steadily consolidated his power, gaining control of Paris in 1594.

The health of the sixty-six-year-old Philip II had continued to decline from the stresses of ruling his vast and diverse empire and the effects of gout. In 1593 his son, Prince Philip, became more closely associated with the regime, assuming a larger role in the administration of the government. While continuing his education, he represented his father in the council and at audiences. As the monarch began the transfer of power to his heir, in France the Spanish army captured Cambrai, Amiens and Calais to solidify the crown's authority in the northwestern region.

After Henry IV renounced his Protestantism, Pope Clement VIII accepted him into the Catholic Church and initiated a political campaign to resolve the Franco-Spanish war. With his realm impoverished and nearing bankruptcy, Philip II appointed his nephew, Archduke Albert of Austria, to represent him at the secret talks with the French at Vervins and on May 6, 1598, a peace treaty was signed. Under the agreement, the Spanish surrendered all their French conquests with the exception of Cambrai, while Henry IV returned the county of Charolais to the Netherlands. Four days later Philip II ratified the decree and transferred sovereignty for the Spanish Netherlands to Archduke Albert, who was to marry his daughter, Isabella. However, the United Provinces remained in rebellion.

The Spanish king had spent his last years attempting to find peace in the Netherlands and supporting the Catholic cause in France, while educating his son to succeed him. After the signing of the Vervins Treaty, he suffered a severe attack of gout and had to be carried by litter from Madrid to his beloved Escorial. In the following months his health rapidly deteriorated and his legs became painfully ulcerated from the gout. Philip II died early in the morning of September 13, 1598, surrounded by hundreds of religious relics in the presence of the archbishop of Toledo, Garcia de Loaysa, and priests from the Escorial after a reign of forty-two years at the age of seventy-one. He was buried in the Escorial mausoleum next to Queen Anna.

Sources

Grierson. *King of Two Worlds.*   Grierson. *The Fatal Inheritance: Philip II and the Spanish Netherlands.*   Kamen. *Philip of Spain.*   Mattingly. *The Armada.*   Parker. *Philip II.*   Petrie. *Philip II of Spain.*

General Sources for Spain

Blum; Cameron; Barnes. *The Emergence of the European World.*   Carr. *Spain: A History.*   Davies. *The Golden Century of Spain, 1501–1621.*   Elliot. *Imperial Spain, 1469–1716.*   Highfield. *Spain in the Fifteenth Century.*   Livermore. *A History of Spain.*

Part V

Renaissance Emperors of the Holy Roman Empire

Sigismund	1368–1410–1437
Albert II	1397–1437–1439
Frederick III	1415–1440–1493
Maximilian I	1459–1493–1519
Charles V (I of Spain)	1500–1519–1558
Ferdinand I	1503–1558–1564
Maximilian II	1527–1564–1576
Rudolf II	1552–1576–1612

Genealogical Tables

CHARLES IV OF LUXEMBOURG

Margaret	Catherine	WENCESLAS	Elizabeth	Anne	SIGISMUND	John	Charles	Margaret
					1368–1410–1437			

Catherine — Henry

(Daughter Elizabeth married ALBERT II of Habsburg)
1397–1437–1439

Anna Elizabeth Ladislaus

HOUSE OF HABSBURG

FREDERICK III
1415–1440–1493

Christopher MAXIMILIAN I Helena Cunegunde John
1459–1493–1519

Philip Francis Margaret Francis

Elenora CHARLES V Elizabeth FERDINAND I Mary Catherine
1500–1519–1558   1503–1558–1564

SPANISH HABSBURGS

Philip II Maria Joanna   AUSTRIAN HABSBURGS
(King of Spain)

Elizabeth MAXIMILIAN II Anna Ferdinand Maria Magdelena Catherine Elenora
1527–1564–1576

Margaret Johann Barbara Charles Ursula Helen Joanna

Anna Ferdinand RUDOLF II Ernest Elizabeth Maria Matthias Maximilian
1552–1576–1612

Albert Wenceslas Frederick Maria Charles Margaret Elenora

Emperors of the Holy Roman Empire are in ALL CAPITALS

Overview

The Holy Roman Empire was a political and military organization established as a central government for western Europe to replace the authority of the fallen Roman Empire. The new empire was created on December 25, 800, when Pope Leo III anointed Charlemagne in Rome with the imperial crown and recognized him as the secular head of the church. However, by the late Middle Ages the Holy Roman Empire had evolved into a loose confederation of mainly German princedoms, which actively contended for supremacy against the sovereignty of the emperor. The eight Renaissance emperors struggled to regain lost power and privileges from the imperial princes, resisted the encroachments of the Turkish Muslims in the Balkans and defended the Catholic Church against the advancement of Protestantism in Germany and Bohemia. The first Renaissance sovereign was Sigismund, who assumed the imperial title in 1410 and was occupied for much of his reign with the suppression of the heretic Hussite religious movement in Bohemia. He was succeeded by his son-in-law, Albert II of Austria, who began over three hundred years of uninterrupted rule by the Habsburg dynasty. Taking the reins of power, he initiated a series of reform measures in an attempt to regain the previously usurped rights of the imperial throne, while solidifying the Habsburgs' presence in Hungary and Bohemia.

Albert II died childless in 1439 and in the ensuing election for emperor his cousin, Frederick III of Habsburg, assumed the crown. The third Renaissance sovereign's regime was beset with ineptness, creating a loss of imperial prestige and power, as the secular and ecclesiastic princes increasingly asserted their autonomous rule. Following his death in 1493, he was succeeded by his son, Maximilian I, who reestablished a measure of the empire's lost authority while extending Habsburg hereditary lands into the Netherlands and Spain. Maximilian I was followed to the throne in 1519 by his grandson, Charles V. Under his emperorship the empire expanded its control into northern Italy in a direct confrontation with France, while defending its eastern demesne against the invasions of the Ottoman Empire. As temporal head of the Catholic Church, he championed the cause of the papacy against the rise of Protestantism in Germany. The policies of Charles V were continued by his brother and successor, Ferdinand I. During his brief reign, he energetically pursued reconciliation with the German Lutherans through tolerance, inclusion and compromise.

The seventh Renaissance emperor was Maximilian II, who claimed the empire in 1564 after the death of his father, Ferdinand I. He renewed the prior administration's quest for religious peace in Germany through negotiations and toleration, while waging war in Hungary against the Ottoman Turks in defense of Habsburg territorial rights. He was followed to the imperial throne by his son, Rudolf II, who was beset with increasing periods of debilitating depression and paranoia. While he was a great patron of the arts, education and the sciences during the Renaissance era, his insanity resulted in a reign that was inept and incompetent, producing a significant deterioration in imperial authority and prestige.

Sigismund, 1368–1410–1437

Following the death of the Holy Roman emperor, Rupert III, in 1410 Sigismund of Luxembourg was elected as his successor, overcoming the opposition of his half-brother, Wenceslaus, and cousin, Jobst of Moravia, to rule as the first Renaissance emperor. Sigismund was the second son of Emperor Charles IV and his fourth wife, Elizabeth of Pomerania, and was born on February 15, 1368, in Nuremberg. The House of Luxembourg had acquired power, wealth and vast territorial holdings, becoming the preeminent dynasty in central Europe with the election in 1308 to the imperial throne of Sigismund's great-grandfather, Henry VII. The family directly controlled the crownlands of Bohemia, Brandenburg and Germany. The Luxembourg prince spent his early years in the Prague court of his father, where he was exposed to the latest in Renaissance art, literature, music, architecture and science. Renowned scholars provided his academic education and he studied languages, religion, reading, writing and government. During his reign as emperor, he became an enthusiastic patron of learning.

In 1373 the Margravate of Brandenburg was ceded to the imperial crown and Emperor Charles IV transferred the fiefdom to Sigismund. He acquired additional lands when his father negotiated his marriage to Mary, daughter of King Louis I of Hungary and Poland. The eleven-year-old Luxembourg prince was sent to the Magyar court to learn the local language, customs and traditions and continue his education. In 1382 Louis I acknowledged Mary and Sigismund as his heirs to both Hungary and Poland. However, when he died in September the Polish nobles and church refused to accept their new rulers, electing Louis I's younger daughter, Hedwig, as their queen. Thwarted in his pursuit of the Polish regime, the Luxembourg lord redirected his initiatives toward securing the Magyar throne.

Soon after the death of her father, Mary was recognized and crowned by the Hungarian church and nobility as queen. However, she was young, highly impressionable and easily dominated by her mother, Elizabeth, who secured control of the royal council and refused to permit her daughter's pre-arranged marriage to Sigismund. Elizabeth replaced the officials in the government with her favorites, attempting to seize total authority over the kingdom. The Magyar lords revolted at the loss of their influence and power, negotiating an alliance with the ruling family's closest male heir, Charles of Naples. Buttressed by the martial might of the rebel Hungarian barons, Charles, supported by his personal small army, landed on the Dalmatian coast to personally contend for the kingship by force of arms. Confronted by the military of the Neapolitan troops and rogue warlords, Elizabeth was soon compelled to admit defeat and acknowledge Charles II as king. With the new ruler's assumption of the throne, Sigismund's quest for the Hungarian realm now appeared hopeless. However, despite the initial success of the renegade faction, the dowager queen refused to accept the loss of Hungary, petitioning Sigismund for his intervention. To enhance his prestige and approval among the magnates, he quickly was married to Mary and began deliberations with the Magyar nobles and church for their backing, promising them a role in his administration.

In October 1385 Sigismund was married to Mary, the daughter of Louis I of Hungary, in a negotiated political union to gain the monarchy of Hungary for the Luxembourg dynasty. The marriage quickly became unhappy with each living in separate households due to their mutual incompatibility and his many infidelities. The queen died in 1395 in a riding accident without producing any children.

Following his marriage to Queen Mary, with the prestige and power of the ruling dynasty supporting him, a political faction began to form around the Luxembourg prince. To raise troops and money for the pursuit of his wife's throne, he traveled to Germany to mortgage Brandenburg to his cousin, Jobst of Moravia. However, while he was in Germany settling the terms for the funds, Elizabeth seized the rising tide of acceptance for Sigismund's cause to arrange the assassination of the newly invested Charles II. The king had developed a formidable power base among the southern Croatians and warlords and under the leadership of the Hovathy family their alliance rose in revolt, seizing the dowager queen and Mary. Sigismund was compelled to abandon his negotiations with Jobst and return to command the campaign against the rebels. Fearing the loss of their influence and power in the government, the high Magyar barons rallied to Sigismund, offering him the crown and on March 31, 1387, he was anointed as monarch. With the military might of the preeminent Hungarian families united around him, Sigismund advanced the royal army south to contend the rebellion and rescue his wife and Elizabeth. The rogue castle at Novigrad was besieged, provoking the Croatians to murder the dowager queen and threaten the life of Mary in retaliation. To secure the freedom of the queen, Sigismund enlisted the diplomatic aid of the Venetians, who acted as intermediaries to arrange her release. In June the insurgents agreed to acknowledge the sovereignty of Sigismund, resulting in an uneasy peace.

Despite the suppression of the southern lords, the Hovathy coalition again revolted against the crown with financial and military support from the monarch of Bosnia, who was plotting to expand his presence into Hungary. Attempting to embolden their campaign with the prestige of a royal house, the rogues offered the Hungarian throne to Ladislaus of Naples, son of Charles II. However, the Neapolitan king was beset with an internal power struggle against Louis II of Anjou and the antipope, John XXIII, and was compelled to remain in Italy. Nevertheless, the Hovathy faction continued to gain momentum and to counter the growing threat to his sovereignty Sigismund forged a counter alliance with the preeminent and powerful Magyar magnate, Miklos Garay. Under the influence of the Garay family, the northern warlords rallied to Sigismund's cause and a large military force was mustered against the dissidents. With the military strength of the formidable barons supporting him, the king marched his troops against the rebels, launching his offensive into the southern provinces. In spite of the loss of the stature of Ladislaus as a figurehead ruler and the persistent attacks of the royalists, the Hovathy insurgents were not overwhelmed and forced to submit until 1395.

With a shaky peace again restored to his southern provinces, the king was free to direct his military and political policies against the growing Turkish menace. Early in the fourteenth century, the Ottoman Empire had begun to expand into the southern Balkans. In June 1389 the Turks defeated the alliance of Albanians, Serbs and Bosnians at the decisive battle of Kosovo and by 1393 their domain stretched through Bulgaria and Serbia, directly threatening Hungary. As the Ottomans marched closer to the Magyar border, Sigismund led several attacks against their advance guard. However, he soon realized that his military was too weak from years of internal warfare to successfully resist the Turks and began to plan for a multi-national army to confront the Muslims. In 1395 the Hungarian monarch prepared for the defense of his realm by dispatching emissaries to the kingdoms of Europe to appeal for a crusade against the Turks. To further the call for the holy war, Pope Boniface IX was persuaded by the Magyar ambassadors to proclaim a papal crusade against the Ottomans' invasion.

The papal summons for the knights of Europe to unite to protect Christendom was met with widespread success and large contingents of warlords from France, England, Burgundy and Germany began to muster for the war in the east. By the late summer of 1396 a formidable army of over fifty thousand men-under-arms had assembled in Buda around Sigismund as leader. The crusaders began the campaign by advancing south against the Turks, seizing their fortress at Widdin. After garrisoning the stronghold, the international army of Poles, Germans, Hungarians, Italians, English, Burgundians and French continued into Bulgaria and in the second week of September began siege operations against Nicopolis. Sigismund's crusade was further augmented by the arrival of a force of Knights Hospitallers and Venetians, as the sorties against the citadel were intensified. To counter the growing threat of the Christian allies, the Turkish sultan, Bayazid I, was compelled to abandon his planned siege against Constantinople and march north with a powerful military force, first encountering the Hungarian king's outposts on September 24. The following day the crusaders formed into battle formation with little order or discipline with the Burgundian and French men-at-arms in the front rank. The first squadron of cavalry under Count John of Nevers, son of the duke of Burgundy, charged wildly into the fortified Turkish position and was repulsed with heavy causalities as the elite Janissaries held their line. The failed assault resulted in confusion among the massed waiting troops, turning into a rout with many thousands killed. As the Turks counter attacked, Sigismund barely avoided capture with his crusade in shambles. The unprotected northern lands of the Balkans were open to attack but avoided disaster when the Mongols invaded eastern Turkey in 1402 and the Turks' became distracted with a succession crisis after the death of the sultan.

Following the failed Nicopolis Crusade, Magyar support for Sigismund's rule rapidly declined, forcing him to remain in the realm to bolster his damaged esteem and authority. To regain the goodwill of his barons and church, in 1397 he summoned the Diet to meet at Temesvar to discuss their demands for reform. To secure the allegiance of the prelates and lords, the king confirmed their traditional privileges, while agreeing to dismiss his Czech and German advisors, who had grown increasingly unpopular. He further promised to replace his foreign counselors with Hungarian magnates. The crown's conciliation initiative temporarily pacified the Magyars and Sigismund's sovereignty was accepted by the clerics and barons.

With his monarchy secured by his concessions at Temesvar, the king was free to intervene in Bohemian political affairs to expand his kingship, lands and prestige. His half-brother, Emperor Wenceslaus, had alienated the local clerics and lords with his misgovernment of favoritism and oppression, forcing the Czechs to revolt in defense of their rights. While the emperor was involved with reimposing his power over Bohemia by force of arms, he became increasingly estranged from the Holy Roman Empire's ruling Diet when his policies in Italy weakened the imperial crown's authority, his repeated attempts to end the church's Great Schism failed and his initiatives in Germany were unable to bring peace. In 1400 the imperial princes voted to depose Wenceslaus, appointing Rupert III of the Palatinate as his successor. With his half-brother also threatened with the loss of his Czech monarchy, Sigismund advanced into the kingdom with an army of Hungarian troops to secure the throne for him. He was rewarded for his intervention by the Bohemian king with his appointment as royal governor, effectively becoming ruler of the realm.

While Sigismund was expanding his sovereignty over Bohemia, his rule grew increasingly unpopular in Hungary. He failed to implement the reforms promised at Tremesvar and his foreign favorites continued to administer his government. The military expenditures against Turkey and Bohemia had forced a crushing tax burden on the Magyar realm, further alienating the nobles and church. When the king returned to Hungary in the spring of 1401 from Bohemia, he was imprisoned by the magnates under the leadership of the prelate of Esztegom and held for five months before negotiating his release. However, the Magyars remained unpacified and in the following year a large militant faction again offered the throne to Ladislaus of Naples. Ladislaus had successfully defended his reign against the attempted usurpations of Louis II of Anjou and the anti pope, John XXIIII, and in July 1403 landed on the Dalmatia coast to contend for the Hungarian monarchy with the support of the local rebel army. Sigismund rallied a formidable counteralliance, defeating Ladislaus at the battle of Raab and by early 1404 eliminating the last pockets of resistance. To impose his kingship, the insurgents were pardoned to prevent a cause for future revolt and the regime's allies were rewarded with grants of titles and lands.

Following the death of Queen Mary in 1395 Sigismund had not remarried. However, in 1408 to further his quest for political stability in Hungary through a military alliance with the prominent Cilli faction, he negotiated his marriage to Barbara, daughter of the Cilli count, Herman II. The Cilli family was directly related to the rulers of Bosnia, Serbia and Croatia, bringing influence and esteem to Sigismund's reign. Barbara took an active role in Hungarian politics and was instrumental in the formation of the Order of the Dragon, using the prestige of her dynasty to promote the new brotherhood. The marital union resulted in the birth of one child, Elizabeth, who was later married to the future Emperor Albert II.

After regaining authority over his realm, Sigismund began a series of reforms to consolidate his rule and unite the nobility to his overlordship. He energetically sponsored the growth and economic development of the towns while promoting improvements to the legal and criminal systems. New rights were propagated to the peasants, allowing more freedom of movement and independence. A royal league, the Order of the Dragon, was organized to formally bind the leading magnates to the crown. The grants of castles and lands were expanded, creating a class of great barons who owed their allegiance to only Sigismund. To protect his southern borders against a renewal of the Turkish onslaught, a large construction program of new strongholds was initiated along the frontier and diplomatic attempts made to unite the Balkan monarchies into an unified front. While involved in his reform initiatives, as governor of Bohemia, Sigismund became increasingly involved in German and Czech affairs, resulting in his election as emperor of the Holy Roman Empire in 1410.

In the aftermath of the death of Emperor Rupert III in May 1410, Sigismund forged an alliance of temporal and ecclesiastic princes to contend for the imperial crown. He was challenged for the emperorship by his half-brother, Wenceslaus, and cousin, Margrave Jobst of Moravia, who each formed counterfactions. However, the Hungarian king politically outmaneuvered his opposition and on September 1 was elected emperor. Despite Sigismund's election to the throne, Jobst refused to accept the vote of the princes and in October was proclaimed sovereign in Frankfurt by his supporters. With his emperorship opposed, Sigismund began to prepare for war against his cousin when in early 1411 Jobst unexpectedly died. The Magyar ruler was able to reconcile the dissenting nobles and prelates to his cause with promises of imperial patronage and in July was confirmed as emperor and king of the Romans, solidifying his assumption of power.

At the time of Sigismund's succession to the Holy Roman crown, the political stability of the empire had steadily deteriorated into a loose confederation under the inept reigns of the two prior emperors. The unity and supremacy of the central governing institution was threatened by an ongoing power struggle between the imperial fiefs, free cities and sovereign, which was intensified by the lack of revenue and rebellion in the Italian states. To reassert the throne's control, in 1411 the emperor advanced his army across the Alps into northern Italy to contend with the Venetians, who had illegally seized territories along the Adriatic coast. However, he lacked adequate military might to force a decisive victory and the campaign dragged on inconclusively for two years before a truce was arranged. Despite the failure to fully impose his will, the war reestablished peace in the region and Sigismund was able to claim a measure of success. After the conflict with Venice was resolved, he attempted to restore imperial rights over the duchy of Milan, which had openly defied the Holy Roman Empire under Filippo Maria Visconti. As Sigismund marched against the duke, the Italians withdrew to the safety of the fortified city of Milan. Visconti held a secure position behind the walls of the fortress and Sigismund's troops made little gain. The imperial attacks ended in defeat with the army compelled to abandon the siege and retreat to Germany. He returned to the imperial court after over three years with Italy still in revolt and the Holy Roman Empire's authority ignored.

While in northern Italy, Sigismund arranged to meet with the schismatic pope, John XXIII, seizing the opportunity to restore the preeminence of the Holy Roman Empire by resolving the ongoing Great Schism in the church through diplomacy. John XXIII was born in 1370 on the island of Procida and was a descendent of the impoverished noble Neapolitan Cossa family. After joining the army and taking part in the Angevin-Neopolitan War against King Ladislaus, he studied law at Bologna University, receiving his doctor's degree. Following the completion of his studies, Cossa was appointed to an office in the Papal Curia. He was recognized for his administrative abilities and energy in February 1402 when Pope Boniface IX named him cardinal for Saint Eustachius and legate for Romandiola. Cossa took control of the papal territory in Bologna in the following year and gained renown for his skills as a statesman and military commander. Cardinal Baldassare Cossa played a dominate role in the Council of Pisa and orchestrated the election of Pope Alexander V, following the dethronements of Gregory XII of Rome and Benedict XIII of Avignon. When Alexander V died in 1410, Cossa was elected as his successor.

The unity of the Holy See had been split into three papal factions, each supporting a separate pontiff. John XXIII had been forced to abandon Rome following the invasion of his papal lands by the king of Naples and petitioned the emperor for his restoration as the head of the church. As the titular secular leader of Christendom and with John XXIII under his protection, Sigismund issued a demand for the two remaining popes to attend the Council of Constance to settle the ongoing conflict and enact new reforms.

The first session of the Council of Constance was opened on Christmas Day 1414 with a ceremony of great pomp and pageantry with Sigismund enthusiastically participating in the services. He took the leading role in the deliberations, arguing that no resolution to the Great Schism was possible without the resignations of all three popes. When his requests for the renunciation of the papal throne were rejected by the pontiffs, Sigismund traveled throughout the European courts during the following year to secure international support for the synod. He met with Ferdinand I of Aragon, convincing him to sanction the abdication of the pontiffs. From Spain he visited the realms of England, Burgundy and France to gain their endorsement. The emperor returned to Constance in early 1417 with the major European monarchies backing his plan for the expulsion of the church rulers. As his quest to unify the church gained momentum, he renewed his initiatives for ecclesiastic reforms and an end to the schism. Under the diplomatic leadership of Sigismund, finally on November 11 after the resignations of John XXIII and Gregory XII and the council's repudiation of Benedict XIII a new pope, Martin V, was proclaimed after forty years of disunity. However, the emperor's successful role as arbitrator of the divided church at Constance soon led to his greatest failure in confronting the opposition of the Hussite Revolt.

Beginning in the late fourteenth century there had been an ongoing movement in many parts of Europe, demanding ecclesiastic reforms in the Holy See. In Bohemia Jan Hus assumed the leadership of the local revisionists, attacking the wealth and extravagances of the prelates, vices of the monks and lack of social justice. However, his condemnation of the papal practice of selling crusader indulgences finally aroused the wrath of the church and he was summoned by the Council of Constance to answer charges of heresy. Traveling on a safe conduct issued by Sigismund, in 1414 Hus rode to the conclave to defend his doctrines. Nevertheless, despite the imperial safeguard, he was arrested on his arrival and on July 6, 1415, burned at the stake as a heretic. The execution of Hus, who had been highly popular and respected in the Czech demesne, resulted in the armed rebellion of the Hussites and their denunciation of the emperor.

Following the revolt of the Hussites, the empire was distracted with internal dissension and unable to directly intervene against the heretic movement until the death of the king of Bohemia, Wenceslaus, in 1419. The imperial electors appointed Sigismund as the successor to the Czech crown but the local nobles and towns refused to accept him as their ruler because of his involvement in the murder of Hus. The emperor was determined to claim the throne and began to prepare for war. To further his cause for the kingship, he secured the support of Pope Martin V, who agreed to promulgate a crusade against the Hussites. By May 1420 a large army of multi-national crusaders was assembled and the emperor advanced his troops into the rogue kingdom. The radicals driven by religious and nationalist zeal rallied around Jan Ziska, who molded his soldiers into a disciplined and aggressive military force. Over the next year the imperialists were repeatedly defeated and finally driven back into Germany. A second holy expedition was launched two years later but it was easily vanquished by the skilled Ziska. In the following year a third crusade was mounted only to be routed at Kuttenberg. After four years of warfare, Sigismund was compelled to abandon his campaign against Bohemia, having accomplished little in his quest for the monarchy.

While the emperor was attempting to impose his authority over Bohemia, he was also involved with the administration of his government in Hungary. In the southern Magyar provinces the construction of the defensive barrier against Turkish incursions was expanded, establishing a double line of strongholds stretching from the Adriatic coast to the Danube with the great fortress at Belgrade anchoring the whole system. A mobile reactionary strike force was created and augmented with light cavalry for rapid response to any Turkish raid. The crown's diplomatic initiatives succeeded in binding the border Magyar barons with the Serbian and Bosnian kingdoms, providing a unified front against the Ottoman Empire's advance north. Despite the king's successes in protecting his southern frontier, the Dalmatia region was lost to Venetian conquest, while northern territories of his realm were seized by the attacks of Poland. While he continued to defend his lands against foreign encroachments, to buttress his local support, Sigismund sponsored the growth of the merchant class and development of the towns into market centers. To stimulate trade, attempts were made to standardize the weights and measurements and establish a uniform coinage system. Under the protection of the great Magyar magnates and the church, the monarch's rule remained popular and peaceful.

Sigismund spent little time in Hungary, remaining in Germany dealing with reforms to strengthen his autonomy against the repeated encroachments of the electors and making improvements to the military. However, German political factionalism and resistance to change from the native princes seriously limited his initiatives. Nevertheless, attempts were made to restore the central power of the throne by advocating a yearly diet, professional army and local imperial superior courts.

After the crushing defeats of the imperial crown against the Czech Hussites, where its troops had been repeatedly outfought and outmaneuvered, attempts were made to restructure the failing military system. Under the emperor's sponsorship, at the 1427 Diet at Frankfurt a professional army was created, tax measures enacted to provide the necessary funds to renew the Hussite Crusade and a war council formed to coordinate all activities. Sigismund also renewed his initiatives to regain imperial powers that had been lost to the local princes by refashioning the constitution in favor of the central ruling authority.

To impose his Bohemian kingship, in May 1427 Sigismund launched a fourth crusade against the heretics. Emboldened by their earlier successes against the imperial armies, the Hussites, under the leadership of Prokop Veliky, had marched into German and Hungarian lands, occupying numerous border towns. Using the encroachments against the Holy Roman Empire as a call to arms, the emperor mustered a large military force, launching an offensive by besieging the fortress of Mies. However, the Czechs counterattacked the Germans at Tachov, compelling the imperial troops to withdraw in a humiliating defeat. Despite the failure, the emperor was determined to assert his control over Bohemia and in March 1431 summoned the Diet to Nuremberg to plan a fifth holy expedition. The legislative assembly authorized a three pronged campaign against the rebels and in the summer the great armies were assembled. Duke Albert V of Austria commanded the initial assault against the Moravian region, while a second military force advanced to recapture the German territories previously seized by Prokop. The first two initiatives achieved some successes but when the crusaders of the margrave of Brandenburg were decisively routed, the emperor was compelled to end his quest for the Czech crown by force of arms and return to negotiations.

Following the failed fifth crusade against the Czech kingdom, the emperor began talks with the Holy See and German princes to gain their support for a new attempt to settle the Hussite War through negotiations at an imperial diet. While the arrangements for the council were being made, he traveled to the Italian city-state of Siena for his coronation as emperor of the Holy Roman Empire by Pope Eugene IV. Before his investiture Sigismund opened negotiations with the pontiff for the Holy See's recognition and approval of the new imperial assembly. In May 1433 Sigismund was anointed with the imperial crown in a ceremony of great grandeur with a rich mixture of pomp and spirituality. Following the emperor's formal enthronement, the pope gave his endorsement for the Diet, adding the power and prestige of the papacy to the initiative to peaceably end the Hussite War.

Under the sponsorship of the Holy See, a General Council was summoned to Basel with emissaries from Bohemia led by Prokop and Bishop Nichols of Pelhrimov invited to discuss terms for a resolution of the ongoing Hussite Revolt. There was little progress at the initial Diet and a second meeting was convened at Prague in November 1433. The deliberations again resulted in little success. After two failed attempts to find reconciliation through negotiations, Sigismund abandoned the diplomatic initiative and began plans to invade Bohemia. In May 1434 he advanced his army into the Czech kingdom, encountering the Hussites commanded by Prokop at Lipany on May 30. The heretics held a strong defensive position, challenging the Bohemian League of Catholics and local magnates to mount an assault. The Leaguers attempted to avoid war, offering to negotiate a settlement but after three days of fruitless talks they began to withdraw. However, as the imperial army feinted its retreat, the reformers abandoned their fortified defenses, launching an attack against the Catholics. At the approach of the rebels, the emperor's troops turned and charged into the unsuspecting heretics, inflicting heavy losses. The battle quickly turned into a rout with the devastating sortie of the imperial cavalry. The military power of the Hussites army was broken at Lipany and with the death of its commander, Prokop, ceased to be an effective fighting force, opening the path to serious negotiations.

In the aftermath of the decisive defeat at Lipany, the Czech rebels returned to the Prague Diet and following long deliberations a compromise was finally accepted by the Bohemians and imperialists. Under the Compact of Basel, the church promised to enforce stricter discipline on the clergy and gave the Hussites freedom of religion, while the Czechs pledged homage to the emperor. The compact was ratified in early July 1436 and Sigismund finally entered Prague as the acknowledged sovereign.

While Sigismund had been formally crowned as the Czech king, his involvement in the death of Jan Hus and his years of war against the reformers had caused a lasting resentment. He remained in Bohemia attempting to gain respect and acceptance as ruling monarch but with little success. In 1437 his health began to quickly deteriorate from gout and exhaustion from his many years of combating dissension from the imperial princes and Hussites. The last Luxembourg emperor died without a direct heir on December 9, 1437, at age sixty-nine after a reign of twenty seven years. He was succeeded to the imperial throne by his son-in-law, Albert II of Habsburg.

Sources

Heer. *The Holy Roman Empire.*   Main. *The Emperor Sigismund.*

Albert II, 1397–1437–1439

The election of Duke Albert V of Austria to the throne of the Holy Roman Empire in 1437 marked the beginning of over three hundred years of uninterrupted rule by the House of Habsburg and the assumption of power by the second Renaissance emperor. Albert was born in Vienna on August 16, 1397, and was the only son of Albert IV, duke of Austria, and Jean of Bavaria. As the only male issue, Prince Albert was recognized as the Austrian heir designate at birth and through the prior diplomatic initiatives of his father inherited a succession claim to the kingdoms of Hungary and Bohemia. In 1404 the duke died on a punitive campaign against Moravian raiders who had pillaged his lands and was succeeded by his seven-year-old son, Albert V. A regency council was created to rule in the name of the minor duke. During the minority years of his reign, the duchy was governed by members of the Habsburg family, who acted as guardians for the young lord. Renowned clerical tutors were provided for his education and he was taught reading, writing, languages and religion. The Habsburg prince was a gifted and serious student, excelling in his studies, acquiring a well rounded education. However, the focus of his training was the development of his military skills, where he received instruction in the martial arms and tactics for his future role as captain-general of the army. Albert V was a natural and dynamic leader, growing into a tall powerfully built warrior, becoming proficient in equestrianship and weapons.

During the guardianship years of Albert V, the Austrian government was administered by his relatives from the Habsburg Leopoldine branch. Under the rule of the cadet arm, the duchy was mismanaged with a policy of oppression and brutality directed at the suppression of the magnates. In 1411 the Austrian nobles rebelled, overthrowing the regents and announcing an end to the minority of Albert V, allowing him to assume the ducal throne at age fourteen. Taking control of the realm, he appointed talented and loyal advisors from the nobility and church to his council and initiated new reform measures directed at reconciliation, inclusion and reform, bringing peace and prosperity to his demesne.

With his rule in Austria secure, in 1420 Albert V began to intervene diplomatically and militarily to expand the lands under his authority. To gain favor with the Holy Roman Empire, he formed an alliance with Emperor Sigismund, assuming command of the imperial army and providing ducal troops for the wars against the Hussites in Bohemia. He also actively supported the imperial initiatives against the Ottoman Empire's encroachments into Hungary and the Balkans by personally leading his Austrian contingent into battle, gaining recognition for his combat skills and bravery. During the campaigns of the empire, Albert V repeatedly displayed his leadership and energy, winning widespread acclaim throughout the European courts as a renowned military captain.

While Albert V was occupied with his army in Bohemia defending the succession rights of the emperor, his Austrian lands were ravaged by the Hussites. Following the Czech attack, the local Jews were suspected of collaboration with the religious radicals. The Jews had been subjected to persecution during the early reign of the duke and after the 1420 pillaging assault they were ordered imprisoned and forced to convert to Christianity. The non–Christians, who refused to accept the new religion, were exiled, while the wealthy Jews remained under arrest. In March 1421 Albert V sentenced over two hundred heretic men and women to death by burning. He issued a ban against all Jews in his duchy, while demolishing their synagogues and seizing their properties.

Through his alliance with the imperial crown, Albert V had developed a close personal friendship with Sigismund and his formidable military aid had proven invaluable at a time when the emperor had been forced to confront internal disorder among his princes and the Bohemian heretics. As the result of his relationship with Sigismund, in 1422 the Austrian duke negotiated his marriage to Elizabeth, the only issue of the emperor and his second wife, Barbara of Cilli. The marital union secured the neighboring margravate of Moravia for Albert V as the dowry, while greatly enhancing his succession rights to the Holy Roman throne. As a direct descendant of the Cilli family, Elizabeth was related to the Hungarian, Croatian and Serbian ruling houses, which brought the Austrian prince hereditary claims to several Balkan kingdoms. After he later became king of Hungary, in 1438 Albert V utilized his wife's ancestral affiliations to form a local political faction to increase his stature, presence and esteem among the Magyar warlords and appointed his wife as regent for the realm during his absences. The marriage resulted in the birth of two daughters, Anne and Elizabeth, who were married to the rulers of Saxony and Poland respectively to enhance the political influence and prestige of the duke. His only son, Ladislas, was later recognized as king of Bohemia and Hungary by Emperor Frederick III but died in 1457 before reaching the acknowledged age of majority.

As a member of the Holy Roman court, Albert V began to participate in the government of the Empire, becoming a member of the inner ruling council and advisor to the emperor. When the imperial electors recognized Sigismund as Czech king, the Habsburg prince energetically supported his father-in-law's pursuit of the Bohemian throne, serving in his crusades against the local heretic Hussites. The Austrian duke had a hereditary right to the Czech kingdom and his position within the imperial family gave him a strong claim to succeed the emperor. By 1429 Sigismund had launched four unsuccessful holy wars against the Bohemian radicals, who were driven by nationalist energy and religious zeal in the defense of their realm against foreign invasions. Determined to impose its authority over the Czechs, in March 1431 the imperial council summoned the empire's ecclesiastic and secular princes to the Diet at Nuremberg to authorize a fifth crusade. Under pressure from Sigismund and Albert V, the National Council sanctioned a new holy war and approved the creation of three armies. The Habsburg warlord was appointed to command the initiative against the rogues of Moravia, while a separate military force attacked directly into Bohemia and the third advanced to recapture the German territories previously occupied by the rebels. In the summer the multinational levies were mobilized, beginning their separate campaigns. As the imperialists mounted their invasions, the commander of the Hussites, Prokop Veliky, mustered his troops in defense of the Bohemian kingdom. The duke's offensive initially succeeded in overwhelming the Moravians' resistance; however, when Prokop defeated the imperial forces led by the elector of Brandenburg, Frederick I, on August 14 at the battle of Domazlice, he was compelled to abandon his gain. Prokop was born around 1380 and was from a prominent Prague family. Despite serving as an officiating priest, at the outbreak of the Hussite War, he joined the Protestant army, rising to positions of prominence. Following the death of Jan Ziska in 1424, Prokop assumed command of the heretic army, gaining significant victories over the Catholics. He led the Czechs during their frequent encroachments into Hungary and Germany and in 1429 harried the region around Nuremberg with a large military force.

After the defeat of the fifth crusade, Sigismund began negotiations for an imperial diet to resolve the Hussite War through diplomacy, inviting the Bohemian rebel faction led by Prokop and Bishop Nichols of Pelhhmov to participate. Albert V actively supported his father-in-law's political initiatives and was instrumental in the summoning of the Basel and Prague Diets in 1433. However, the assemblies failed to bring peace and the emperor once again mustered the imperial army to compel a resolution through force of arms. The duke of Austria provided troops for the new invasion against Bohemia, participating in the battle at Lipany, where the heretic rogues were decisively defeated and their commander, Prokop, killed. As the result of their crushing subjugation at Lipany, in 1436 the Hussites agreed to terms and Sigismund was finally accepted as Bohemian king. The emperor appointed Albert V as his successor to the Czech crown in recognition of his continued loyalty and administrative and military skills.

After the triumph in Bohemia, the health of Sigismund steadily deteriorated and in December 1437 he died without a direct male heir, resulting in the extinction of the House of Luxembourg. Before his death, he persuaded the imperial princes to name Albert V as his successor to the throne of the Holy Roman Empire. While negotiating with the electors, he summoned the magnates and prelates from Bohemia and Hungary, petitioning them to recognize his son-in-law as his heir. Following the death of Sigismund, in January 1438 the Austrian duke was anointed king of Hungary and in March formally elected emperor at the Frankfurt Diet.

The sovereignty of Albert II had been recognized by the Czech Catholics but the Hussites revolted at his election, compelling him to invade the kingdom of Bohemia to enforce his rule. As the emperor prepared to attack, the heretics led by Bedrich of Straznice strengthened their defenses against the king by forming an alliance with Ladislaus III of Poland, who was threatened by the growing power of the unified Holy Roman Empire, Hungary and Austria. Ladislaus III was the second Polish ruler of the Jagiellon dynasty and ascended to the throne at age ten under the regency of Cardinal Olesnicki. In 1438 he reached the age of majority and assumed full control of the realm. The Polish monarch began his independent reign by pledging to defend Czech rights in their war against the imperialists. The Hussites agreed to accept the brother of the Polish king, Prince Casimir, as their new overlord to bind the two kingdoms in friendship. In support of the Hussite war against Albert II, the Polish forces advanced into Moravia, while Casimir marched against the royalists with a second army into Austrian held Bohemia. Despite the initial successes of the two Polish offensives, by the summer of 1438 the emperor had driven the rebel Bohemians and their allies from Prague and was crowned king but the Hussites continued to challenge his power.

Due to the diplomatic initiatives of Emperor Sigismund in Hungary, Albert II had been acknowledged as king by the realm's great barons and prelates; however, the minor magnates favored a government dominated by a national diet and weak monarchy. Before accepting Albert II as their overlord, they succeeded in negotiating a series of restrictions on his power to rule. Under the ensuing agreement, Albert II pledged to reside in Hungary, not sell or grant royal lands or titles without the consent of the assembly, discuss the marriages of his children with the Diet and limit the rights of the barons.

While Albert II was imposing his rule over the Hussites and negotiating a settlement with the Hungarian barons and minor nobles, he began to initiate measures to refashion the cumbersome and restrictive imperial constitution and legal code of the Holy Roman Empire. Sigismund had earlier introduced the reforms late in his reign but lacked the energy and resources to have them implemented. The authority of the emperor had been seriously eroded by the constant encroachments of the ecclesiastic and temporal princes and Albert II was determined to regain the usurped rights.

As the emperor was enacting policies to recover the lost imperial powers, he intervened in the ongoing power struggle between the papacy and Council of Basel. The Holy See was once again beset with internal disputes, when the prelates attending the Council at Basel attempted to reduce the pope to a figurehead and eliminate all papal revenues. Albert II supported the church in its conflict against the council and at the request of Pope Eugene IV withdrew his emissaries from the assembly, while endorsing the Holy See of Rome's new conclave at Florence. The imperial initiative won the favor of the Pope, binding the two realms closer in friendship and securing an ally for Albert II's pursuit of constitutional changes in the Empire. Eugene was born in 1383 and was from the wealthy Venetian Condulmaro merchant family. After inheriting a large sum of money during his youth, he gave it to the poor and sick, entering the Order of Saint Augustine in the monastery of Saint George. In 1407 his uncle, Pope Gregory XII, appointed him archbishop of Siena, but he was soon forced to resign when the local population objected to his foreign nationality. In the following year he was named a cardinal and sent to San Clemente by his uncle. During the reign of Pope Martin V, the cardinal served as his legate for Ancona and later took command of the papal campaign to subdue the rebellion of Bologna against the Holy See. Following the death of Martin V, Cardinal Condulmaro was elected as his successor, taking the name of Eugene IV. After assuming the papal throne, he soon became involved in an ecclesiastic conflict with the newly convened Council of Basel.

In early 1439 the Turks renewed their war of conquest against the Balkans, advancing across the border of Hungary. In response to the attack, Albert II assembled an army in Buda, marching south to defend his kingdom. However, he was soon struck with dysentery and forced to abandon his campaign, retreating to Buda. The emperor attempted to return to Vienna on a litter but his illness grew worse. Albert II died in Hungary at Neszmely on October 27, 1439, at age forty-two after a reign of only two years and was succeeded to the imperial crown by his Habsburg cousin, Frederick III.

Sources

Bryce. *The Holy Roman Empire.* Crankshaw. *The Habsburgs.* Heer. *The Holy Roman Empire.* Wheatcroft. *The Habsburgs.*

Frederick III, 1415–1440–1493

In October 1439 while defending Hungary against invasion by the Ottoman Empire, Albert II died and was succeeded to the Holy Roman throne by his cousin, Frederick III of the Habsburg Leopoldine family, who reigned as the third Renaissance emperor. Frederick was born on September 21, 1415, in Innsbruck, Austria, and was the eldest son of Duke Ernest the Iron and Cymburgis of Masovia. He spent his childhood in the ducal court, where tutors were appointed for his education. The young lord was a gifted and serious student, excelling in his studies of reading, writing, languages and religion, developing a lifelong devotion to learning. He later had an interest in astrology, botany and astronomy and was an enthusiastic collector of rare stones. Physically Frederick was described by contemporaries as tall with a large body frame, blondish hair and a long face. After assuming the emperorship, he was characterized as presenting a regal bearing with a mild manner but exhibiting little leadership and totally lacking the skills of a warrior. With age Frederick grew increasingly obese and lethargic, becoming disinterested and withdrawn from the affairs of his empire.

In 1424 Ernest died and his Austrian lands of Styria and Carinthia were inherited by the nine-year-old Frederick V and his brother, Albert VI. A regency government was appointed to rule the ducal demesne for the minor brothers with their uncle, Count Frederick IV of Tyrol, elected as guardian. Frederick V and Albert VI remained under the protection of the Tyrol count until 1435, when they assumed their autonomous co-suzerainty of Upper Austria. Shortly after taking control of his inheritance, Frederick V made the long, dangerous voyage to Jerusalem as a pilgrim in a visible display of his Christian piety and devotion to the church, while his brother solely administered their fiefs. However, after his return from the Holy Land, Albert VI refused to relinquish his possession of the realm or share the revenues from Styria and Carinthia, forcing Frederick V to actively contend for his birthright by force of arms and diplomacy. The struggle between the two dukes was intensified after the death of Count Frederick IV in 1439. Before he died, the Tyrol count had designated Frederick V as regent for his countship and ward for his minor heir, Sigismund. With jurisdiction over the young successor, the duke governed Tyrol independently but Albert VI began to plot against his brother's new authority. The ongoing conflict between the two Habsburg princes lasted until the death of Albert VI in 1463.

As Frederick V was pursuing his inheritance to Upper Austria, his initiatives were repeatedly thwarted by his brother. Albert VI was a natural leader and skilled soldier and diplomat, who utilized his talents to retain control over the majority of the duchy. However, in 1439 the future outlook of the elder duke changed dramatically with the sudden death of Emperor Albert II and his assumption of the leadership of the Habsburg dynasty.

At the time of Albert II's death, the Holy Roman Empire was beset with disunity and internal dissension, as the ecclesiastic and secular princes contended for imperial power against the emperor. As the authority and military might of the empire ebbed, the central European lands were increasingly threatened from the south by the relentless advance of the Ottomans, while to the east the resurgent Polish and Hungarian armies pushed their borders into German territories with impunity. The Holy Roman Empire had previously been shaken by the zeal of the religious revolts of the Hussites in Bohemia. In need of a dynamic, forceful ruler, the electors returned to the Habsburg lineage, which had in prior periods of crisis provided strong and energetic leadership. As the eldest member of the Habsburgs and with his father's reputation as the defender of Christendom against the onslaught of the Turks in the Balkans, Frederick III was elected emperor on February 2, 1440, at Frankfurt in the Cathedral of Saint Bartholomew by the seven electors and officially crowned on June 17, 1442, in Aachen.

The Habsburg dynasty had its origins in northern Switzerland, beginning in the early eleventh century. Through force of arms, imperial grants and marriages, succeeding generations had extended the territories under their control to the eastern cantons. However, the Swiss grew increasingly hostile to their rule and in 1273 during the reign of Rudolf I they revolted, forming the anti–Habsburg league known as the Swiss Confederation. Through the next two centuries the Habsburgs were slowly driven out of the cantons into Austria. After Frederick III assumed the imperial crown, civil war erupted among the Swiss Cantons. Seeking to regain his family's lost influence and lands in Switzerland, in 1443 he forged a coalition with the city of Zurich, agreeing to support its fight against the Swiss Confederation.

The canton of Zurich under its energetic mayor, Rudolf Stussi, had steadily extended the domain under its power. Stussi was first appointed to a minor city office in 1414 and through his administrative skills by 1430 rose to the position of mayor. Three years later he served as Zurich's representative to the imperial coronation of Emperor Sigismund in Rome. Under his aggressive leadership, he initiated policies to expand the city's influence and territory under its rule. In 1436 the count of Toggenburg, Frederick VII, died without a direct heir and his demesne was claimed by the Zurich mayor. However, the remaining cantons of the Old Swiss Confederation opposed the expansion of Zurich by making a counter-claim. When the area was occupied by Stussi, the Confederation members responded by declaring war. Confronted by the overwhelming military might of the league, Stussi used his influence at the imperial court to negotiate an alliance with Frederick III to enforce his rights to Toggenburg.

Emboldened by their military coalition with Frederick III, the Canton of Zurich began to recruit soldiers, raise money and stockpile military arms and supplies for the coming conflict. As the city continued to defy the cantons and strengthen its defenses, in July 1443 the Old Swiss Confederation mounted an invasion into the rebel region, advancing against Zurich. To protect the city Rudolf Stussi established his protective perimeter along the Sihl River. However, on July 22 he was attacked and outmaneuvered by over twenty thousand confederation troops at Saint Jacob's Bridge and driven back in defeat. When the remnants of the rogue army retreated to Zurich, the stronghold was placed under siege, as appeals for military intervention were hastily sent to the emperor.

When Frederick III received the reports of the confederation's victory, he lacked the military and financial might to personally respond. He was forced to send urgent appeals for aid to the European courts. Charles VII of France, who was seeking to regain his lost presence in the western Swiss Basel region, agreed to launch an offensive in support of the Canton of Zurich. In the following summer under the command of the dauphin, Louis, the French force of over ten thousand men-under-arms marched into the Swiss cantons. However, after besieging Basel and defeating a Swiss relief army at Saint Jacob, Louis was wounded and forced to withdraw from the war. The abandonment of the French initiative was a serious setback to Frederick III's campaign to confront the confederation and regain his lost power and authority over Switzerland.

As the Basel army was defending western Switzerland, the confederation renewed the war into the Zurich canton. The local population continued to resist their onslaught and by 1445 both rivals became exhausted, resulting in the beginning of peace negotiations. After prolonged deliberations, in 1446 the Peace of Constance was signed. Under the treaty Zurich was re-admitted to the confederation with some minor territorial gains, while pledging to dissolve its alliance with the Habsburgs. The agreement created a loss of prestige for the emperor and forced him to abandon his family's historic presence in Switzerland and turn to eastern Europe for future aggrandizement.

While Frederick III was attempting to reestablish his overlordship against Switzerland, in 1445 he began to negotiate with Pope Eugene IV for papal support against the renegade factions of his Holy Roman princes. The pope had been confronting the dissident bishops of the Council of Basel and their alliance of imperial rulers for control of the German church and in July 1439 had been deposed by the prelates. In need of an ally to confront the increasingly hostile rebel churchmen and nobles, he negotiated an agreement with the emperor. Under their accord, Frederick III pledged to defend Eugene IV in his dispute against the rogues, while the Holy See granted the Holy Roman crown the right to nominate six major bishoprics, authority to appoint one hundred benefices and a large sum of money for use in its quest for supremacy against the rebelling imperial fiefs. To promote peace between the papacy and German princes, the emperor summoned the Diet to Frankfurt in September 1446, where under his direction a reconciliation was reached between the two parties. Under the resolution, the See of Rome's prerogatives were defined and accepted in Germany, while the bishops and princes pledged to submit to the church. The ecclesiastic and secular lords won the right to call a new religious council, while the German church reform measures previously adopted by the Basel Council were approved by the pontiff and the deposed archbishops reinstated. A formal treaty known as the Concordat of Vienna was signed by Frederick III and the new pope, Nicholas V, in February 1448. The settlement solidified the church's power over German ecclesiastic affairs and enhanced the emperor's rule over his recalcitrant lords.

Under the provisions of the Vienna Concordat, Pope Nicholas V had pledged to consecrate Frederick III as emperor in Rome. The Habsburg emperor was fully aware of the symbolic importance attached to the coronation regalia and ceremony as a means of enhancing his prestige and power and an elaborate and grandiose enthronement celebration was planned. As he entered Italy, the imperial court was welcomed by each city with increasingly splendid receptions. Traveling south the Habsburg entourage visited Florence and Frederick III met with the city's ruler, Cosimo de Medici, discussing Italian politics and viewing the Renaissance art of Donatello, Filippo Brunelleschi, Filippo Lippi and Fra Angelico. When the emperor arrived in Rome, he was personally met by Nicholas V and escorted into the church of Saint Peter. On March 19, 1452, Frederick III was married to Eleanor of Portugal and crowned Holy Roman emperor by the pope. The papal investiture was a great promotional success, which served to rebuild the shattered structure of imperious authority in German political affairs in the person of the emperor. However, all the gains were soon transitory under the inept and unenergetic rule of Frederick III.

In March 1452 as part of Frederick III's coronation ceremony in Rome, he was married to Eleanor, daughter of the king of Portugal. Despite being an arranged political union, the emperor became totally devoted to his wife, refusing to remarry after her death in 1467. Under Eleanor's influence, the emperor's court at Wiener Neustadt and ducal capital at Graz became centers of art, cultivation and learning, rivaling any in eastern Europe. The marriage of Frederick III and Eleanor resulted in five children with only two surviving to maturity.

After the death of Emperor Albert II in 1439 his minor son, Ladislaus, was recognized as the successor to the thrones of Hungary, Bohemia and Lower Austria. As the senior member of the Habsburg family, Frederick III was appointed as guardian for the infant heir. With control over the minor Ladislaus, the emperor acted as regent-ruler for his two kingdoms and duchy. In Hungary his regency for Ladislaus was acknowledged by the northern barons, while the southern region rebelled, electing Ladislaus III of Poland as their overlord. As the tension between the two rival parties intensified, a brief civil war erupted, ending in a stalemate with the Habsburg faction still holding Upper Hungary. However, power over the north was seized by the dominant local warlords, who governed the area largely ignoring the authority of Frederick III. The emperor was still recognized as king but lacked the force of personality and military might to enforce his rights.

As the acknowledged guardian for Ladislaus, Frederick III also assumed authority for the crown of Bohemia as regent-king. However, the Czech magnates refused to recognize his sovereignty. In the absence of a central governing institution, the Catholic and Hussite factions began to confront each other for control of the kingdom. The Hussites were united under George of Podebrady, while the Catholic Party rallied to Ulrich von Rosenberg. The lord of Podebrady was from a prominent Bohemian noble family, taking up arms against the Catholics at a young age and participating in the battle of Lipany against the imperialists of Emperor Sigismund. He later commanded the Hussite army against Albert II and was chosen as head of the heretic religious alliance for his military and leadership skills. As the hostilities between the pro-papists and reformers grew, attempts were made to find a peaceful reconciliation, but in 1448 war erupted. As the conflict escalated, Frederick III was confined to his lands in Austria, lacking the military might and force of personality to intervene to enforce his acceptance as ruler. By 1451 Rosenberg was defeated and the emperor endorsed George of Podebrady as his governor for Bohemia to gain some limited measure of influence in local affairs and acceptance as king.

While Frederick III struggled to enforce his supremacy over Hungary and Bohemia, he initially secured his recognition as regent for the Lower Austrian region. However, his administration was ineffective and unpopular among the nobles, and support for the independent rule of Ladislaus grew. After his return from the Rome coronation, the dissident faction rose up in revolt, forming the Mailberg League with Hungary and Bohemia to challenge the power of Frederick III. The allies launched an attack against the emperor, besieging his castle near Vienna and forcing him to release his ward. Ladislaus was acknowledged as the ruler of Lower Austria, Bohemia and Hungary under three local regency governments and Frederick III was left to contend with his brother, Albert VI, for power in only Upper Austria. As he continued to oppose Albert VI's encroachments into Habsburg Austria, his nominal and incompetent emperorship of the Holy Roman Empire was largely ignored by the secular and ecclesiastic princes, who continued to usurp imperial power and govern their fiefs with little regard to the emperor. However, the unexpected death of Ladislaus in 1457 presented the emperor new opportunities for the aggrandizement of the defiant kingdoms.

Frederick III became the senior member of the Habsburg dynasty with the death of Ladislaus, becoming the rightful heir to the duchy of Lower Austria and the realms of Hungary and Bohemia. In defiance of his succession rights to the kingdoms, local political factions challenged his power, while in Austria Albert VI launched his army against his brother's ducal inheritance. In Hungary the formidable Hunyadi party forged a series of coalitions with the preeminent noble families and in January 1458 the Magyar Diet elected Matthias Corvinus as king, ignoring the Habsburg birthright of Frederick III. Under the tutelage of his father, John Hunyadi, Matthias had received a scholar's education, excelling in his studies. At a young age, he began to participate in the military campaigns of his family's alliances, quickly exhibiting his natural leadership and martial skills. During an attack against the Ottoman Empire, he was knighted for bravery during the siege at Belgrade. At the same time as Hungary was choosing a new monarch, in Bohemia the magnates summoned their Diet to appoint George of Podebrady as the successor to Ladislaus. The political encroachments of the national Parliaments usurped Frederick III's claims to the Czech and Magyar monarchies, while his control over Lower Austria was increasingly confronted by his brother.

While Frederick III contended for authority in Austria, his powers as Holy Roman emperor continued to be usurped by the imperial ecclesiastic and secular princes. He lost additional prestige, when his repeated calls for a crusade against the Ottoman Empire's seizure of Constantinople in May 1453 were ignored by the great European courts and imperial princedoms. The emperorship provided no income to recruit an army to enforce his inheritance rights to Hungary and Bohemia, while his imperial crown lost relevance due to his inability to personally intervene in German affairs. Due to his lack of resources and military might, he was confined to his government in Austria, participating little in the diets of the Holy Roman Empire. As the result of Frederick III's impotency, his rule became increasingly irrelevant in European affairs, lacking the revenue and force of arms to respond to any challenge or crisis.

Following the death of Ladislaus, after years of contending for control of hereditary Austria Frederick III and Albert VI agreed to partition the duchy with the emperor ruling the lower fiefdoms and his brother the upper area. However, the settlement was soon broken, when Albert VI began to occupy the Vienna region by force of arms. He formed an alliance with George of Podebrady and their united armies invaded Lower Austria, forcing Frederick III and his family to retreat to the safety of Vienna Castle. Despite the allies' successes, in 1463 Albert VI unexpectedly died and with reinforcements from his loyal vassals in Styria the emperor broke the siege, driving the Czech and rebel Austrian troops from his lands. Without the leadership and military skills of Albert VI, the emperor was able to reassert his authority into Upper Austria and consolidate the two duchies. Nevertheless, the Bohemians continued to ravage his border territories with impunity. With his preoccupation with local events and weak financial and military position, Frederick III became increasingly withdrawn from imperial affairs, prompting the electors to plot his dethronement. He was able to maintain the crown only when the princes and prelates failed to unite around a common successor.

As the emperor was defending his Austrian duchy, he began to plot with dissident Hungarian warlords who were contesting the election of Matthias as monarch. In 1459 a small rebel faction recognized Frederick III as their sovereign. However, lacking the finances and military might to enforce his rule, he began to negotiate a resolution to his sovereignty claims with the royal Magyar court. In 1463 a compromise was reached with the emperor acknowledging Matthias as king, while retaining numerous western border counties and adopting him as his son with the right of inheritance to the Magyar crown if he died without an heir. Nevertheless, Frederick III could only maintain peace with the energetic and ambitious Matthias by granting numerous political and territorial concessions. In 1467 Frederick III used his influence with the Hungarians to forge an alliance against George of Podebrady to end the Czech pillaging attacks into his ducal demesne.

With his Austrian lands now secure, the emperor began negotiations for the marriage of his heir, Maximilian, to bind the Habsburg dynasty to an alliance that would expand his territorial holdings, power and wealth. He became increasingly drawn to Princess Mary, daughter of Duke Charles of Burgundy, who controlled vast territories in the Netherlands and along the Rhine River. In 1473 he met with the duke at Trier to arrange the marital treaty, but no settlement could be reached and the deliberations ended on unfriendly terms with the emperor secretly departing in haste. An agreement was only realized two years later after Charles suffered a serious defeat in Switzerland and his siege against the imperial city of Neuss was thwarted by the threat of the intervention of Frederick III's army. In need of an ally and friend to guarantee the peace on his eastern border, the Burgundian duke consented to the union of Mary to the emperor's son. However, before the ceremony could be performed, Charles was killed in the battle of Nancy and the marriage to Mary became jeopardized with her seizure by the burghers of Ghent.

With his plans for Habsburg aggrandizement jeopardized, Frederick III ordered his son to Ghent to begin negotiations with the rebel leaders. In August 1477 he arrived in the city, winning the support of the local burghers through the force of his personality and was quickly married to Mary. Through the marriage, the Habsburg family gained possession of the Netherlands, Burgundy and numerous lordships and cities along the Rhine River. The new acquisitions marked the beginning of the ascension of the dynasty as the dominant political power in central European affairs for the next four hundred years and was the most significant achievement of the long reign of the emperor.

By 1480 Matthias Corvinus of Hungary had seized control of the southern Bohemian region and had secured his borders against the Ottoman threat. To expand his demesne to the west, he directed his powerful professional army, united with the troops of the archbishop of Salzburg, against his former ally, Frederick III, and his Austrian homeland. The Magyars slowly drove the emperor from his lands and in June 1485 after a long siege gained possession of Vienna. Matthias continued his military campaign westward, conquering most of Lower Austria and forcing Frederick III to reestablish his capital in Linz. The Hungarian victories greatly reduced the territorial holdings and wealth of the emperor, severely limiting his power, as Maximilian increasingly began to assume authority for Habsburg and Holy Roman affairs. The lost fiefs were regained only after the death of Matthias in 1489 as a resurgent Austrian military under the command of Maximilian reoccupied the eastern lands.

As Frederick III grew increasingly lethargic and removed from the affairs of state, in 1486 Maximilian was elected German king and acknowledged as successor designate by the Imperial Diet. The emperor remained isolated at his Linz court, living the remainder of his life in virtual exile. He returned to his studies of astrology and alchemy while tending his gardens. Frederick III died on August 19, 1493, at age seventy-eight after a reign of over fifty-three years.

Sources

Bryce. *The Holy Roman Empire.* Crankshaw. *The Habsburgs.* McGuigan. *The Habsburgs.* Wheatcroft. *The Habsburgs.*

Maximilian I, 1459–1493–1519

At the end of the long reign of Frederick III in 1493 his only surviving son and heir, Maximilian, was elected by the imperial princes as successor to the Holy Roman Empire, assuming power as the fourth Renaissance emperor. His ascension to the throne marked the continuation of the Habsburg lineage that ruled central Europe for the next four hundred years. Maximilian was the second of the three sons of Frederick III and Eleanor of Portugal and was born on May 22, 1459, at Neustadt near Vienna. He was named after the patron saint of his father. The bishop of Wiener Neustadt was appointed as his private tutor and the young lord received instruction in reading, writing, languages to include German, Latin, French, Italian and Flemish, history, mathematics and religion. He was a gifted and dedicated student, excelling in his studies, which were pursued all his life. While receiving a well rounded humanist education, he was also trained in various crafts, including carpentry, blacksmithing and farming. At his father's court he was exposed to the arts, learning to paint and play various string instruments, becoming an accomplished musician. However, the focus of his training was centered on his preparation for kingship. Unlike his father, the Habsburg prince was a natural leader and skilled soldier. He became renowned throughout the courts of Europe for his many acts of chivalry and his battle prowess as a knight.

Maximilian spent his early life in the turbulent court of his father, who was engaged in a civil war against his brother, Albert VI, for possession of Austria. By 1463 Frederick III had been defeated and forced to retreat to the security of his castle in Vienna. The fortress was placed under siege and during the lengthy investment by his uncle, the young Habsburg prince was subjected to privation and near starvation. However, with Albert VI's unexpected death Frederick III reasserted his authority, gaining control over a united Austria. During the conflict against his uncle, Maximilian became exposed to warfare, developing an interest in weapons, armor and the battle skills of a soldier.

While Frederick III continued his ineffective and weak reign as emperor, Maximilian remained with the Habsburg household, resuming his education and military training. In 1467 his mother died and he became closely associated with his father, who exposed him to the administration of the government and affairs of state to prepare him for his future assumption of power. In 1468 the emperor began to make plans for the marriage of his son to Mary, daughter and heiress of Charles of Burgundy, sending his envoys to the duke's court to begin negotiations. Despite the offer of a kingship from Frederick III, which had been demanded by Charles, the discussions ended without an agreement. After the initial failure, the deliberations were later renewed, while Maximilian increasingly assumed control of his father's duchy and army. After prolonged talks, in 1476 a marital treaty was finally ratified with the Burgundian duke. However, the settlement was thrown into jeopardy with the unexpected death of Duke Charles in the battle of Nancy and the imprisonment of Mary by the burghers from the city of Ghent.

While Mary remained a prisoner in Ghent, Frederick III and his son were compelled to stay in Austria beset with the danger of invasion from Matthias of Hungary and the lack of money to fund Maximilian's intervention in the Netherlands. Finally in August 1477 the Habsburg prince made his entrance into Ghent to begin negotiations for his marriage to Mary. Through the force of his personality, he won the favor of many of the burghers but no marital agreement was signed. However, in need of a strong ally after Louis XI began to annex the Flemish borderlands by force of arms, the cities and nobles accepted Maximilian as the new duke. With the support of the local lordships, on August 19 he was married to Mary. The union with the House of Burgundy brought to the Habsburg dynasty territorial acquisitions in the Netherlands, Burgundy and numerous cities and countships along the Rhine River.

Despite being an arranged marriage for political reasons, Maximilian and Mary were well suited to each other, quickly developing a supportive and loving relationship. She was described as a princess of beauty, grace and intelligence, becoming totally devoted to her husband. The duchess was a zealous sportswoman, excelling in equestrianship and hunting with falcons and hounds. The future succession of the Habsburg dynasty was secured in 1478 with the birth of a son, Philip, and was followed two years later with the birth of a daughter, Margaret. However, their happy marriage was short-lived with the sudden death of Mary in a riding accident in 1482.

Following the wedding ceremony, Maximilian assumed control of the Burgundian government and army. After receiving homage from the nobles and city burghers, he began to mobilize and train troops for the defense of his borders and recovery of the French seized lordships. In 1478 he renewed the war against Louis XI by marching his militia south to recapture the city of Cambrai. In the following year the French countered the loss of the city by sending an army into Flanders, which was met by Maximilian at Guinegate. In the resulting encounter, when the attack of the Flemish cavalry was driven back, the Habsburg prince personally turned the tide of battle with his spirited leadership of the pikemen. The victory was followed by a papal negotiated truce, which lasted until April 1481. Maximilian utilized the period of peace to solidify his political power over the burghers and strengthen his military forces. However, the death of Mary in a riding accident seriously jeopardized his continued rule in the Netherlands.

Under the terms of the marital treaty signed by Maximilian in 1477 with the burghers of Ghent, he had pledged to relinquish control of the Burgundian government at the death of Mary and now his only claim to continued power was as regent for his young son, Philip. However, the Flemish refused to accept an alien prince, rebelling against his administration and ignoring his authority by beginning independent peace talks with Louis XI. After the burghers negotiated the Treaty of Arras in March 1483, to retain his rule Maximilian was forced to agree to the settlement and approve the marriage of his daughter, Margaret, to the Dauphin Charles of France with a dowry of Artois and Franche-Comte, while compelling his son, Prince Philip, to give fealty to the French crown for Flanders.

After the signing of the Arras Treaty, many of the provinces in the Netherlands in defiance of the agreement refused to acknowledge Maximilian as duke, compelling him to assert his authority by force of arms. He began his quest for supremacy by raising an army from his loyal fiefdoms and in July 1485 subdued the rebelling Bruges and Ghent regions, entering the cities in triumph. The Habsburg lord was formally proclaimed regent for Philip, again assuming full control of the government. To win the loyalty of the burghers, he initiated a policy of toleration, inclusion and leniency, gaining the support of additional towns and nobles.

While Maximilian was enforcing his authority over the Burgundian lands, Frederick III was beset with the seizure of his Lower Austrian demesne by Matthias of Hungary. The loss of the duchy and the occupation of Vienna further eroded the already deteriorated stature and support for the emperor among the electors of the Holy Roman Empire, who increasingly began to favor Maximilian as the next sovereign. The princes of the Empire regarded Frederick III's rule as weak and ineffective and as the most powerful German prince and lord of the Netherlands, the Habsburg duke began to plot against his father for the emperorship. In early 1486 the Holy Roman Diet elected Maximilian as German king and emperor apparent. On April 9 he was formally anointed at the church of Charlemagne in Aachen with the crown of Germany.

Following his coronation as king, Maximilian returned to the Netherlands where his rule as regent soon became increasingly unpopular among the Flemish provinces, when his economic policies caused the loss of their highly profitable cloth trade with England. As the cities began to prepare for rebellion, the French declared war against the duke in defense of the burghers. To regain the loyalty of Bruges, the duke traveled to the city to begin negotiations for a reconciliation but was seized and held captive by the local merchants. With support for the uprising mounting, the governing council of Ghent joined the civil war, forming an alliance with Bruges.

While Maximilian remained imprisoned and the troops of Bruges and Ghent ravaged his supporters in the province of Brabant, he sent messengers to his father, appealing for military aid. Frederick III responded by raising an army of over twenty thousand German men-under-arms, marching toward Liege in May 1488 to the relief of his son. At the approach of the powerful imperial force, the rebels agreed to negotiate a settlement with the duke. Under the terms of the ensuing treaty, to gain his freedom Maximilian pledged to renounce his regency for Flanders, honor peace with France and withdraw the imperial soldiers to Germany. After ratifying the accord, he was released and joined the Holy Roman army, However, the emperor refused to accept the conditions of the agreement, advancing his army against Ghent to enforce his son's rights to the ducal crown. The city was besieged but the defenders defiantly resisted the German attacks and with his coffers exhausted Frederick III was compelled to withdraw in October in defeat.

After the victory of the Flemish rogues and his overthrow, Maximilian appointed Duke Albert III of Saxony as his governor for the Netherlands, returning to Germany to personally assume his duties as king. Albert III was the ruler of Meissen and a prominent member of the imperial court, participating in the campaigns against Charles of Burgundy and leading an expedition against Matthias of Hungary. In 1488 he advanced with the emperor's army to negotiate the release of Maximilian from his imprisonment in Bruges. While Maximilian administered the German government, Albert III rallied the loyal provinces and aggressively attacked the dissident cities to regain control over Brabant and pursue the war into Flanders. Suffering from the relentless ravaging of their lands by the duke, in July 1489 the rebelling countships agreed to discuss reconciliation. Under the resulting Treaty of Frankfurt, the Netherlanders pledged to honor the peace, submit and acknowledge Maximilian as regent for his son.

Acting under the terms of the Treaty of Frankfurt, Maximilian reasserted his authority over the Netherlands. After securing the fealty of the Burgundian fiefdoms, to protect his lands against future aggression from France, he began negotiations for his marriage to Anne, the successor to the duchy of Brittany. The Bretons were aggressively resisting the expansionist policies of the new French king, Charles VIII, and in need of a powerful ally. The acquisition of Brittany would enhance Maximilian's territorial holdings and wealth, while providing a second front for military operations against France if the Netherlands was attacked by Charles VIII. On March 31, 1490, the marriage treaty was signed and the ceremony performed by proxy later in the year. However, Maximilian delayed his formal entrance into Brittany to receive his homage from the local lords by remaining in the east, renewing the war against Hungary for control of Lower Austria.

In April 1490 King Matthias of Hungary died without a direct heir, creating a succession crisis in his lands. To exploit the lack of a recognized central ruling authority, Maximilian began to raise an army for the recovery of the Lower Austrian Duchy. His summons to arms was met with great enthusiasm and at the end of June he began his campaign of reconquest. At the approach of the Austrian troops, the Magyars offered only token resistance, resulting in the recapture of Vienna and subjugation of the duchy by August. With all of Austria under Habsburg power, Maximilian continued the offensive into Hungary. However, after initially encountering limited opposition, when he advanced against Buda, the garrison stubbornly resisted his attacks. While the Holy Roman king became delayed by the siege against the city, Vladislav II of Bohemia, who had been elected to the throne of Hungary, began to threaten an invasion against Vienna from his Czech lands. Vladislav II was born in Cracow and was a member of the Polish ruling Jagiellon dynasty. After the death of King George of Podebrady in 1471, the Bohemian crown was vacant and the Czech nobles chose Vladislav II as his successor. With the Czech army assembling for war on his border, the Habsburg prince was compelled to abandon the Buda investment and his recent conquests to defend his capital. By July 1491 he was exhausted from the conflict and forced to open peace negotiations with the Magyar court. In the ensuing Treaty of Pressburg ratified in November 1491, Vladislav II was acknowledged as the new monarch of Hungary, while Maximilian retained all of Austria and the inheritance right to the Magyar crown if there was no direct Jagiellon successor.

While Maximilian was pursuing the conquest of Lower Austria and Hungary, Anne of Brittany was beset with the renewal of hostilities by Charles VIII. By May 1491 the Breton army was defeated and much of the duchy occupied with French troops. With Maximilian's extended absence in the east and Anne under siege in her capital of Rennes, she was forced to negotiate peace terms from a position of weakness with the French court. After prolonged talks, a treaty was signed in November 1491 with the central provision providing for the marriage of the duchess to Charles VIII. On December 6 in the Loire Valley chateau of Langeais the formal ceremony was held effectively ending the independence of the Brittany duchy.

Under the 1483 Treaty of Arras, peace between France and Burgundy was guaranteed by the pledged marriage of Charles VIII and Margaret, the young daughter of Maximilian. By agreeing to marry Anne, the French king was compelled to repudiate the Habsburg princess and her father demanded the return of the dowry of Franche-Comte and Artois. However, Charles VIII ignored all requests, compelling Maximilian to take the fiefdoms by force of arms. To advance his claim, he invaded the Franche-Comte, conquering much of the region. The French finally agreed to open talks and on May 23, 1493, the Peace of Senlis was signed. Under the terms of the treaty, Maximilian regained Franche-Comte, Artois and some minor Flemish cities but the long delays in Lower Austria and Hungary had cost him the opportunity to acquire the major prize of Brittany, which was lost to France.

Under the provisions of the Peace of Senlis, the French seized Burgundian countships were occupied by Maximilian's troops and his government reestablished. While he ruled as German king and duke of the Burgundian lands, in August 1493 Emperor Frederick III died after a reign of over fifty years. After the death of his father, Maximilian imposed his rule over the Habsburg crownlands in Upper and Lower Austria and with his 1490 purchase of the Tyrol region, the entire duchy was unified under his authority. As the emperor elect, he also claimed the throne of the Holy Roman Empire to unite with his eastern fiefs, creating an empire stretching from the Atlantic Ocean to the Danube River.

As Maximilian I assumed control of the Holy Roman and Austrian realms, changes in the political status quo of Italy soon involved him in the power struggle between Milan and France. Ludovico Sforza had seized the Milanese ducal administration to unlawfully rule as regent for his nephew, Gian Galeazzo. Ludovico was born on July 27, 1452, in Lombardy at Vigevano and was the fourth son of the Milanese duke, Francesco I, and Bianca Maria Visconti. At the direction of his mother, he received a broad based humanist education under renowned tutors, studying the classics, religion, government, warfare, the arts and letters. When his eldest brother, Galeazzo Maria, who had succeeded Francesco I to the ducal throne, was assassinated in 1476, Ludovico became the leader of a militant faction usurping the new regency government of his minor nephew. In 1491 he married Beatrice d'Este, daughter of Duke Ercole I of Ferrara, and under her influence the Milanese court became a center of Renaissance artists, poets, and philosophers. Under the patronage of the duke, Leonard de Vinci received the commission to paint the *Last Supper* in the Santa Maria Della Grazie Church. To give legality to his usurped regime, Ludovico sent his envoys to the imperial court, proposing the marriage of his niece, Bianco Maria, to the emperor and a substantial cash dowry for his formal investiture as duke. In need of money for his planned crusade against the Turks in the Balkans in defense of his Hungarian territories, the offer was accepted by Maximilian I. The wedding ceremony was held in Tyrol on March 9, 1494.

While the emperor remained in Germany negotiating the restructuring of the empire's governmental and judicial systems with the imperial princes, in Italy the king of Naples died and with the earlier death of Lorenzo de Medici in 1492 the shaky political stability of the region was thrust into disarray. Seeking to exploit the growing turmoil and uncertainty, Charles VIII of France began to assemble an army for the invasion of Naples in support of his hereditary claim to the realm. In the summer of 1494 he marched his formidable military across the Alps, overcoming all Neapolitan resistance and establishing his regime in February 1495 in Naples. However, the Italian rulers began to fear the presence of the new foreign power and under the leadership of Duke Ludovico and Pope Alexander VI a league was hastily formed with Ferdinand II of Spain and the doge of Venice. Acting under the influence of the Milanese duke, Maximilian I joined the growing faction to expand Habsburg territory and presence in Italy. The treaty was ratified by the marriage of his son, Duke Philip of Burgundy, to Joanna of Spain, daughter of Ferdinand II and Queen Isabella.

After agreeing to join the anti–French league, Maximilian I began to prepare for the imperial army's intervention in Italy in support of Duke Ludovico. However, the emperor lacked the money to launch his campaign and was compelled to summon the Imperial Diet to grant new taxes to fund the war. When the electors, princes and imperial free cities assembled in Worms, they refused to provide any revenue unless the emperor first pledged to reform the Empire's government. He was able to thwart their attempts to severely curtail his power but was forced to accept the establishment of a central imperial court, abolishment of all private wars and summoning of the diet annually in return for the creation of a universal tax, for the funding of the Italian war. Nevertheless, despite the approval of the funds, during the prolonged negotiations Charles VIII was compelled to abandon Naples by the mounting military might of the league, as Maximilian I remained in Germany mired in deliberations with the empire's princes.

After returning to France from his failed Naples war, in the autumn of 1496 Charles VIII began preparations for a new Italian invasion, forging an alliance with Florence and recruiting Swiss mercenaries. In response to the mounting French threat, a new holy league was formed by the pope with Venice, Ludovico of Milan and the Holy Roman Empire. To fund his military campaign Maximilian I was compelled to summon the Imperial Diet. However, when the assembly met the princes again refused to grant any new taxes and the emperor was forced to borrow the needed money from the Augsburg bankers to participate in the war.

By the summer of 1497 Maximilian I had assembled a small army, crossing into northern Italy to join the league in Genoa. However, dissension soon erupted between the allies and the emperor decided to invade the Republic of Florence without the support of the coalition. To undermine the resolve of the Florentines, he advanced his German forces against the republic's seaport at Livorno. The city was besieged but lacking adequate troops and with the arrival of reinforcements from France, Maximilian I was compelled to abandon the attack. Disappointed at the absence of an unified war effort, the emperor withdrew from the holy league, returning to Austria. His unsuccessful campaign left the French king's political influence in Italian affairs more powerful than ever.

As Maximilian I was attempting to thwart French aggrandizement in Italy, the Swiss cantons revolted at their nominal allegiance to the Holy Roman Empire, refusing to honor its rule. After returning to Austria, the emperor demanded the Swiss comply with the reform measures of the Diet of Worms by paying the universal tax and contributing soldiers to the imperial army. The cantons defiantly responded to the challenge against their new independence by launching plundering raids against the German border region. As the conflict escalated, in early 1499 Maximilian I issued a summons for his military forces to muster. However, his army was largely comprised of undisciplined private levies from the Empire's princes and his attacks against the Cantons were repeatedly defeated. To force the subjugation of the dissidents, in the early summer a new offensive was launched into Switzerland, advancing toward Dornach Castle. At the approach of the Germans, the Cantons rallied their town militias and mounted a counterattack, decisively crushing Maximilian I's troops. Following the Dornach defeat, the emperor was compelled to open peace negotiations, resulting in the Treaty of Basel. Signed on September 22, 1499 the agreement granted Switzerland freedom from the jurisdiction of the Empire and virtual autonomy.

Following the loss of imperial power in the Swiss Cantons, Maximilian I returned to Germany and the government of the Holy Roman Empire. In order to prevent the reccurrence of the military setbacks that occurred in Italy and Switzerland and provide a permanent source of unrestricted taxes to pursue his foreign policy, in 1500 he summoned the princes to the Diet of Augsburg. He proposed the creation of a permanent military force and the funds necessary for its maintenance. However, his initiative was received with widespread animosity and he was forced to accept the mobilization of an army for only six years and establishment of a new Regency Council, which usurped imperial power by assuming control of all foreign affairs.

Maximilian I soon found the restrictions on his rule from the Regency Council intolerable and began to plot against the leaders of the Diet. When he attempted to raise an independent army and threatened civil war, the empire was thrown into widespread political disunity. The growing dispute erupted into open conflict during the succession crisis in Bavaria-Landshut, when Maximilian I supported Albert IV in his quest for the vacant ducal title in opposition to Philip, imperial elector of the Palatinate. The emperor marched his forces against Philip and after several inconclusive encounters decisively overwhelmed the Palatinates near Regensburg, where he distinguished himself with his leadership and personal bravery. The Regensburg triumph was followed by the capture of the Tyrolean city of Kufstein, compelling the elector to acknowledge defeat. The seizure of Kufstein resulted in a truce with peace negotiations soon following. In August 1505 Maximilian I dictated the terms of a settlement at the Diet of Cologne, securing Bavaria-Landshut for Albert IV and personally was ceded numerous lordships from Philip. The victorious campaign greatly enhanced the emperor's power and prestige, allowing him to again reassert his authority over the empire's princes to govern independent of the Regency Council.

Throughout his reign Maximilian I was a patron and friend of the arts, letters, learning and the sciences, while encouraging eminent scholars to reside at his court. He actively sponsored the artworks of Hans Holbein and Albrecht Durer, along with the leading sculptors and was responsible for first introducing the Renaissance movement into Germany. Under Maximilian I's direction, Vienna became the center of music in Europe. In 1498 he reorganized the imperial orchestra, summoning the most renowned musicians to his court, while ordering the formation of a new choir that became the Vienna Boys' Choir. The emperor also fostered the development of education, encouraging the establishment and expansion of German universities. He took a special interest in the advancement of the imperial army, personally making improvements in the artillery and was responsible for the creation of the *Landsknechts*, companies of professional pikemen, who became feared on the battlefields of Europe.

After the Diet of Cologne, Maximilian I's rule over the Holy Roman Empire was unchallenged, allowing him to begin preparations for the expansion of his demesne into northern Italy and his long delayed coronation as emperor by Pope Julius II. However, his quest for Italian aggrandizement was thwarted by the imperial princes' refusal to grant the necessary money and the campaign was delayed. To formally receive the title of emperor, Maximilian I was compelled to break with the prior traditions of a Roman investiture and on February 4, 1508, was crowned as the imperial sovereign in the cathedral of Trent.

Despite the set back to his plans for Italian aggrandizement, Maximilian I remained resolved to acquire additional territories in Lombardy. In March 1508 after securing funds from the diet for the campaign, he declared war against the Venetian doge, Leonardo Loredan, for his recent occupation of Milanese territory, where his wife held hereditary claims, sending the imperial army into northeastern Italy. After some initial successes by the imperialists in Veneto, the Venetians rallied their troops and steadily recaptured the lost towns, continuing their advance into the demesne of the Habsburgs. By June Maximilian I was forced to negotiate a three year truce with the doge retaining control over the seized Habsburg lands.

The failed initiative into Italy served to strengthen Maximilian I's resolve to defeat the Venetians. He put aside his differences with Louis XII of France and opened talks for a military alliance for the partition of Venice. The deliberations were later expanded to include the Holy See and Naples, resulting in the Treaty of Cambrai, which was ratified on December 10, 1508. While the emperor summoned the Diet to grant the funds for the invasion of Italy, the war was begun in May 1509 with the French victory at Agnadello and was followed by Pope Julian II's occupation of Romagna. After his successful negotiations with the imperial princes, in the summer Maximilian I personally opened his campaign, advancing virtually unopposed to recover his lands lost in the prior year and marching into the doge's Veneto domain, capturing the principal cities of Verona and Padua. However, the papacy and Naples soon achieved their war goals and withdrew from the league, allowing the Venetians to consolidate their forces against the imperialists. Limited by the lack of troop strength and money, the emperor was unable to repel the doge's attacks, quickly losing his recent Venetian conquests. With his offensive crushed, in October Maximilian I withdrew across the Alps with the bulk of his army, leaving his German allies to defend his remaining Italian towns.

Following the collapse of the Cambrai Treaty, in March 1511 Pope Julius II began to increasingly fear the presence in Italy of the French and imperialists. In October he formed a holy league with Naples and his former foe, Venice, to force the foreigners out of Italy. Lacking the necessary financial resources and military might to contend the new league alone, the emperor was compelled to forge a counterfaction with Louis XII. However, when the French king initiated the war against the papacy in 1512, Maximilian I exhibited little enthusiasm for the conflict, remaining in the empire and negotiating a separate truce with Venice. After the defeat of the French army at Ravenna, he totally abandoned Louis XII, joining the pope's coalition and declaring war against France. Nevertheless, the death of Julius II in January 1513 and the election to the Holy See of Leo X, who demonstrated little interest in the anti-foreigner war, resulted in the disbandment of the league, forcing the emperor to seek new allies for his anti–French campaign. Leo X was born in Florence on December 1, 1475, and was the second son of Lorenzo de Medici and Clarissa Orsini. At an early age his father chose him for an ecclesiastic career and in 1489 he was appointed cardinal for Santa Maria in Domnica. Under the direction of Lorenzo, his son received an extensive humanist education under renowned scholars. In March 1492 Cardinal Giovanni was admitted to the Sacred College and departed for Rome. However, when his father died, he returned to Florence and remained until the overthrow of his family by the Dominican friar, Savonarola. Without a supportive power base in Italy, he was forced to spend the next several years in the courts of Europe before finally returning to Rome in 1500. When Pope Julius II was elected to the papacy, Giovanni de Medici found favor with him and was appointed papal legate for Bologna. In 1512 he was given command of an army and sent to reimpose papal rule over Florence. After the surrender of the city, the cardinal assumed power in the name of the Holy See. Following the death of Julius II in early 1513, Giovanni was chosen as Julius's successor, taking the name of Leo X. As pontiff, Leo X was a great patron of the Renaissance, sponsoring renowned musicians, scholars, writers, poets and artists, including Raphael and Michelangelo.

Soon after the breakup of the Cambrai League, Maximilian I began talks with Henry VIII of England and Ferdinand II of Spain for a new military coalition in support of the Swiss Cantons' ongoing war against Louis XII. On April 5, 1513, a treaty was signed with the allies agreeing to a joint invasion of France. While the emperor marched his small army south to join the conflict, in June the Tudor king launched his campaign from Calais with the Habsburg troops soon participating in the English siege against the fortress of Therouanne. Louis XII responded to the encroachment against his demesne by sending a large force of cavalry to relieve the investment. As the French approached Therouanne, Maximilian I personally commanded the allies' attack at the Battle of the Spurs on August 16, overwhelming Louis XII's soldiers and compelling the surrender of the stronghold. After razing the citadel, the allies advanced against the bishopric of Tournai, which was soon captured after only token resistance. Following the seizure of the two cities, the war was suspended until the spring with the three sovereigns pledging to renew their offensive under the Treaty of Lille, which was signed on October 13. However, the accord was short-lived when Ferdinand II and the emperor negotiated separate peace agreements with Louis XII early in 1514.

After the end of the war against France, Maximilian I returned to the empire and the administration of his lands, where he continued to introduce reform measures to improve his government. However, the newly negotiated political stability with France was shattered on January 1, 1515, with the death of Louis XII and the assumption of the crown by the energetic and militant Francis I. The Valois king inherited a blood claim to the duchy of Milan and with his rule over France secure, soon began plans for an Italian campaign to assert his hereditary rights. To counter the mounting French threat, a papal sponsored coalition was forged between the emperor, Pope Leo X, Ferdinand II and Duke Massimiliano of Milan. While Francis I advanced into Italy capturing Milan in September, Maximilian I remained in Vienna taking no part in the league's war effort, distracted with the prolonged negotiations for peace in eastern Europe with Vladislav II, king of Hungary and Bohemia, and his brother, Sigismund I of Poland. Under the ensuing First Congress of Vienna Treaty, the emperor secured the future expansion of the Habsburg demesne by arranging the marriage of his grandson, Ferdinand, to Princess Anna, daughter of the Hungarian and Bohemian sovereign and the marriage of his granddaughter, Mary, to Louis, brother of Anna. The agreement resulted in the Habsburgs' ascension to power in the two kingdoms in 1526 after the death of Louis.

After the successful conclusion of his deliberations with Vladislav II and Sigmund I, in early 1516 the emperor returned to the conflict against the French in Italy. In February he marched his imperial army, augmented with Swiss mercenaries, against Francis I's ally, Venice, capturing Verona and numerous towns in the Veneto district. However, his campaign soon lost momentum and after garrisoning his recent conquests, Maximilian I withdrew to Innsbruck. Restricted by the lack of financial resources and troop strength to pursue the war, he was compelled to sign the Treaty of Brussels agreeing to a six month truce, which later resulted in a permanent peace in July 1518.

While the final peace negotiations with France and Venice continued, in the summer of 1518 Maximilian I summoned the Imperial Diet to Augsburg to secure the election of his heir and grandson, Charles, as German king. Despite his increasing infirmity, he was eager to command a crusade against the Muslims in the Balkans and pressed the princes, electors and imperial free cities for the money to fund the war, but his requests were rejected by the Diet. Following the failure of the Augsburg Diet, the emperor traveled to Wels in Upper Austria, where his health rapidly deteriorated from the effects of gout and stresses of a turbulent twenty-five-year reign. Maximilian I died on January 12, 1519, at age fifty-nine and was succeeded to the imperial throne and Habsburg hereditary crownlands by his grandson, Charles V.

Sources

Hare. *Maximilian the Dreamer: Holy Roman Emperor, 1459–1519.*   Wandruszka. *The House of Habsburg.*
Watson. *Maximilian I, Holy Roman Emperor.*

Charles V, 1500–1519–1558

Through the political marriages, alliances and wars of his paternal grandfather, Maximilian I, in 1516 Charles of Habsburg became the acknowledged king of Spain and three years later the fifth emperor of the Renaissance epoch. Charles was the second of the six children of Philip, Duke of Burgundy, and Joanna of Spain and was born on February 24, 1500, in the Flemish city of Ghent. He spent little time with his parents, who traveled to Spain in 1504 to assert Joanna's rights of inheritance to the throne of Castile. In 1506 Duke Philip died and as his direct heir and successor, Charles assumed the ducal title of Burgundy at age six. To rule the strategic duchy, Emperor Maximilian I appointed his daughter, Margaret of Austria, as regent and guardian for his young grandson. Remaining in the Netherlands, renowned scholars were appointed as tutors for Charles's academic education and future assumption of power. He was instructed in reading, writing, history, government, religion and languages, becoming fluent in Flemish, French, German, Italian and later Spanish. His principal teacher was the future Pope Adrian VI from whom the duke acquired a deep sense of religious piety. Charles was a serious but not gifted student, preferring hunting and field sports at which he excelled.

As the Habsburg prince continued his education, Margaret ruled the scattered and turbulent domains of her nephew, growing increasingly unpopular with the nobility and city burghers. In 1514 the magnates revolted against her pro–Habsburg policies, favoring the assumption of power by the duke. As the rebels' insurgency movement gained momentum, they forced the regent from office, recognizing the accession to the ducal throne by Charles. On January 5, 1515, in a grand and opulent ceremony in Brussels, he officially took the reins of government from his aunt.

While Charles asserted his Burgundian rule as duke, in Spain his maternal grandfather, King Ferdinand II of Aragon, died in 1516. Through his mother's lineage Charles I was the acknowledged successor to the thrones of Castile and Aragon. In September 1517 he appointed a regency council to govern the Netherlands in his absence and departed to his new realm by ship. Landing in Spain after a stormy ten day voyage, Charles I was exuberantly greeted by his subjects and accepted as sovereign by the local Cortes. However, he quickly alienated the nobles with his repeated demands for money and appointments of his Burgundian favorites as court officials and high ministers in his government. The simmering discontent was exacerbated in 1519 with the death of Emperor Maximilian I and the election of the Spanish king as his successor. In the following year when he began the journey to Germany to assume the Holy Roman crown the Spanish kingdom was on the verge of open rebellion.

After the death of his grandfather, Maximilian I, in January 1519, Charles I began an aggressive political campaign from Spain to win the imperial throne. Through the plotting of Margaret of Austria, generous bribes and intimidation, he outmaneuvered his principal rival, the Valois king of France, Francis I, to secure his election as ruler of the Holy Roman Empire. With his ascension to the emperorship, he controlled the German princedoms along with his inherited lands in the Netherlands, Spain, Italy, and Austria, becoming the most powerful sovereign in Europe. On October 22, 1520, in the cathedral of Charlemagne's capital at Aachen, Charles V was crowned emperor.

During the reign of Maximilian I, numerous attempts had been made by the electors, princes and imperial free cities to reform the government of the Holy Roman Empire. After assuming the Holy Roman crown, Charles V summoned his first Diet to Worms in January 1521, where the temporal and ecclesiastic princes, seeking to weaken imperial power and expand their authority, immediately petitioned him for the establishment of a Regency Council as a new central governing body. As the sovereign of other non-imperial kingdoms, Charles V would be absent from Germany for extended periods and needed to set in place an administration that remained loyal to him and his policies. After extended negotiations, in May a compromise agreement was signed and a new council empowered. A twenty-two member board was approved with Charles V appointing the principal governor and five regents, which was to rule only when he was not in Germany. The settlement satisfied the Estates, giving it part of its demands, while retaining independent control for the emperor.

Through the writings and preaching of Martin Luther, the Catholic Church reform movement, later known as the Protestant Reformation, had gained widespread popularity in Germany. Luther was born in the small German town of Eisleben in the Holy Roman Empire on November 10, 1483, and was the first son of Hans Luther, who was the lessee of a copper mine and member of the local town council. After his basic education, Martin entered Erfurt University in 1501, receiving his degree four years later. He continued his education, first enrolling in law school but soon abandoned his studies to enter an Augustinian friary and was ordained a priest in 1507. In the following year he began to teach theology at Wittenberg University. Luther first became active in religious dissent in 1517 when he protested the papal sale of indulgences to fund the rebuilding of Saint Peter's Basilica in Rome by nailing his Ninety-Five Theses to the castle church door on October 17. As his campaign for reform continued to expand, increasingly threatening the power of the papacy, in June 1520 Pope Leo X excommunicated the outspoken monk. As the newly elected emperor and acknowledged defender of the pope and his church, Charles V was pressed by papal envoys to declare Luther an outlaw. He was easily won to their cause during the Diet of Worms, ordering a vote on the banishment decree. However, the imperial princes were not willing to provoke revolt among Luther's many supporters and demanded his summons to Worms to openly recant his heretic dogma. In April Luther appeared before the assembly, justifying his attacks against the church and refusing to abandon his doctrine. As a devout follower of the Holy See of Rome, Charles V was determined to eradicate heresy and on April 19 read his verdict to the Diet, declaring Luther guilty. Nevertheless, the Edict of Worms only served to inflame the anti-papist faction and the emperor was forced to defend the papacy for the remainder of his reign.

While Charles V continued his deliberations with the Diet of Worms, negotiations were begun for the appointment of his brother, Ferdinand, as the principal governing regent for the Holy Roman Empire. Under the newly created Regency Council, the emperor had to appoint a ruling surrogate during his absences from Germany, turning to his brother as a trusted and loyal deputy. In February 1522 the agreements were finalized and signed in Brussels, naming Ferdinand as the emperor's chief imperial representative. In order to enforce his sovereignty rights over the Diet, Ferdinand was named as the ruler for the Austrian Habsburg crownlands and elevated to archduke.

Following the close of the Diet of Worms on May 25, 1521, the emperor returned to the Netherlands, remaining for the next year. He assumed the local government from his regent and traveled to the provinces to reassert his power. While Charles V administered his vast empire from Brussels, Francis I, who had seized Milan in 1515, became alarmed at imperial opposition in Italy. To keep the emperor occupied and distracted in northern Europe, the French actively encouraged Lord Robert III of Marck to attack the eastern border lordships of the Netherlands to enforce his territorial claims. As the prospects for open confrontation escalated, Cardinal Thomas Wolsey of England with papal support began peace negotiations in Calais with the envoys of Charles V and Francis I, however, with little success. Growing impatient at the lack of progress through diplomacy, the emperor ordered an assault against the French city of Mezieres but was soon checked by the stubborn resistance of the local garrison. Nevertheless, a second imperial army besieged Tournai and forced the surrender of the bishopric in December. After the victory at Tournai, the war soon entered a stalemate with little gain for either rival with the onset of the winter season.

Charles V had been absent from Spain since the autumn of 1520 and began to prepare for his return. To govern the Netherlands in his absence, Margaret of Austria was once again appointed regent and after securing the loyalty of the cities, in May 1522 the imperial fleet departed for Spain. However, en route the emperor visited Henry VIII in England to conclude the ongoing negotiations for an alliance against France. On June 16 the Treaty of Windsor was ratified, which formally committed the two realms in the war against Francis I and authorized a joint invasion for 1524. Following the conclusion of the talks, in early July the voyage was continued south to Spain.

The emperor landed in Spain on July 16, 1522, to a dramatically altered political environment. Soon after his departure for Germany in 1520, the towns had rebelled against the constant demands for new taxes and appointments of alien ministers to the court and administration. When the rebels attacked the estates and privileges of the great noble families, they rallied to the king, who gained their loyalty by appointing two of their prominent members as co-regents for Spain. By April 1521 the military might of the royalists' forces had overwhelmed the insurgency movement to reassert Charles V's power. Following his return to Spain, the emperor assumed personal control of the kingdom and to prevent the reccurrence of the Comuneros Revolt embarked on an aggressive governmental restructuring program.

To retain the loyalty of his subjects, Charles V replaced his Burgundian advisors and courtiers with Spanish officials and became closely associated with their local culture and customs. His marriage in 1526 to Isabella of Portugal was popular with the people, binding her dynasty with Spain. Measures were taken to improve economic growth and with the discovery of gold and silver in the newly conquered American colonies, Spain was propelled into the beginning of a golden age. The policy of inclusion and reconciliation with the magnates and towns along with the expanding economy resulted in a prolonged period of peace and prosperity.

While Charles V remained in Spain, forging the kingdom into the powerhouse of his empire, the conflict in Italy against Francis I was continued. Before departing from the Netherlands, the emperor negotiated a new anti–French league with the papacy, Florence, Mantua and England to confront the aggression of Francis I in Lombardy. Implementing the campaign approved by the emperor, in 1521 the allies advanced their armies against French occupied Milan, forcing the garrison to abandon the city. In the following spring the Valois king sent reinforcements to the duchy in an attempt to recapture the region. However, Francis I's forces were routed by the imperial, Spanish and papal troops led by Prospero Colonna at Bicocca on April 27, 1522, compelling the French to withdraw from Lombardy and permitting the Habsburg emperor to establish his authority over Lombardy.

Following his defeat in Italy, Francis I remained determined to regain the duchy of Milan and launched a new military initiative into Lombardy in the spring of 1523. At the approach of the invading army, the allies abandoned the countryside, withdrawing to the protection of the citadel in Milan and forcing the French into prolonged siege operations. As the investment wore on, in April 1524 exhausted by the harsh winter conditions, constant harassing sorties from the garrison troops and the approach of an imperial relief force, the Valois commander was compelled to abandon his campaign. While the French were besieging Milan, the league mounted a diversionary attack against Ile de France and sent a second army into southern France to impose the allies' authority. However, both offensives resulted in little success as the war reached an impasse.

To force a resolution to his hereditary rights to Italy, in 1524 Francis I again assembled an army and personally marched against Milan. Crossing the Alps into Lombardy, Milan was quickly reoccupied when the imperial forces withdrew to the fortified fortress at Pavia. To secure his control over the duchy, the Valois king was compelled to pursue and besiege Charles V's troops at Pavia. As the investment dragged on through the winter months, on February 25, 1525, with supplies exhausted the imperial cavalry mounted a desperate sortie, completely surprising Francis I. In the ensuing battle the French were decisively defeated and their king taken prisoner. After his capture he was sent to Madrid to better facilitate the negotiations for the terms of his release. Following prolonged deliberations on January 14, 1526, Francis I was compelled to sign the Treaty of Madrid to win his release. Under the central provisions of the agreement, he pledged to honor the peace, renounce all claims to Italy and abandon the duchy of Burgundy. The resolution was a great personal triumph for the emperor, securing the return of his historic Burgundian heartlands and eliminating the Valois threat to Italy, while greatly enhancing the prestige and power of his reign. However, after gaining his freedom, Francis I soon defied the terms of the Madrid Treaty by forging the anti–Habsburg League of Cognac with Venice and Pope Clement VII and began to intrigue into Italian affairs. Clement VII was born Giulio de Medici in Florence on May, 26 1478, and was the posthumous illegitimate son of Giuliano de Medici. In the month before his birth his father was assassinated during the Pazzi conspiracy and Giulio was adopted by his uncle, Lorenzo, and raised in his household. Along with his cousins, Giulio received an extensive humanist education and at a young age was chosen for a career in the church. He entered the priesthood and became prior for Capua. When his cousin was elected Pope Leo X in 1513, Giulio was appointed a cardinal and moved to Rome, playing a major role in the administration of the new pontiff.

During the third Valois-Habsburg War, Charles V was married to Isabella of Portugal, sister of King John III. Despite being an arranged marital union, the emperor and Isabella through the years developed an ever deepening love and caring bond. She was described as a princess of beauty, intelligence and great piety. The empress became an unofficial advisor to her husband, serving as Spanish regent during many of his prolonged absences. The future of the Spanish Habsburg dynasty was secured in 1527 with the birth of the future King Philip II and later two daughters, Isabella and Catherine, whose political marriages with the courts of Europe expanded the family's presence and influence. At the death of Isabella in May

1539, Charles V expressed great sorrow, withdrawing to the solitude of a monastery for three weeks.

After his return to France from his Madrid captivity, for most of the next year Francis I became involved with internal problems, taking little interest in the League of Cognac. With the French distracted, in late 1526 Charles V sent an imperial army, augmented with largely German Lutheran mercenaries under the command of George von Frundsberg, to attack the fiefs of the papacy in Italy. Frundsberg was born on September 24, 1473, at Mindelheim in southern Germany into a family with a long history of distinguished military service. He was a natural leader with a charismatic personality and quickly advanced to positions of high command in the Habsburg army. In 1504 he took part in Emperor Maximilian I's campaign against Elector Philip of the Palatinate, winning recognition for his bravery and martial skills during the siege at Regensburg. Frundsberg assisted the emperor in the creation of the *Landsknechts* and soon assumed command of the professional pikemen forces. He led the German pikemen in Maximilian I's war against Venice in 1509, gaining repute for his heroic defense of Verona. He continued to serve the Habsburg emperors, fighting in their Italian wars against the French, Venetians and papal soldiers. In 1522 George von Frundsberg again answered Charles V's call to arms and crossed the Alps with his *Landsknechts* to play a leading role in the imperial victory at the battle of Bicocca.

After invading the Papal States, the imperial troops, who had not been paid for many months, mutinied, quickly turning into a lawless and uncontrollable mob. The rioters disregarded the commands of Frundsberg and marched south to Rome looking for plunder and on May 5, 1527, launched a merciless assault against the city. The defensive walls were easily breached and the soldiers poured into the streets, beginning the sack of Rome that continued until December. Pope Clement VII became a virtual prisoner in his fortress at Castel Sant' Angelo, withdrawing from the Cognac League and ending his involvement in the conflict against Charles V.

With the departure of the Holy See from the war, Francis I began negotiations with Henry VIII for a new ally, winning his agreement for an anti–Habsburg alliance for the promise to support his quest for a divorce from Catherine of Aragon. With England not a threat to attack France, in August 1527 the Valois king again sent his army into northern Italy, quickly overrunning much of Lombardy but failing to seize Milan. While Charles V's German troops continued to hold the city, his Spanish forces landed in Genoa, advancing to the relief of the capital and encountering the waiting French at Landriano. In the ensuing battle, Francis I's soldiers were overwhelmed and after a second French army in Naples was dealt a similar defeat, he was compelled to withdraw from Italy. After the destruction of his fourth Italian initiative, Francis I began reconciliation talks with Margaret of Austria, aunt of Charles V, with his mother, Louise of Savoy, serving as his envoy. In the resulting Treaty of the Two Ladies, peace was restored between the two realms with the French court again pledging to repudiate its hereditary claims in Italy and recognize Habsburg rights to Flanders, while the emperor abandoned his demand for Burgundy.

Following the return of peace to Italy, as the secular leader of the Catholic Church, Charles V was anxious to personally meet with Pope Clement VII to restore their shattered alliance and receive his formal investiture as emperor by the church. In July 1529 he sailed from Spain finally arriving in Bologna in November for the prearranged talks with the papacy. To gain the goodwill of the Holy See, he agreed to supply imperial troops to Clement VII for his conquest of Florence, while the papacy pledged to support numerous initiatives favored by the Habsburgs and recognize Charles V's rights to Lombardy. The discussions ended amicably, reestablishing a more cordial relationship between both courts. Following their reconciliation, on February 24, 1530, Charles V was anointed in the Bologna Cathedral by Clement VII as emperor of the Holy Roman Empire.

In the aftermath of his Bologna coronation, Charles V traveled north to Austria, meeting his brother, Ferdinand, in Innsbruck. During the emperor's nine-year absence in Spain, significant changes had occurred in Germany where the Protestant cause had firmly taken hold in many princedoms. Lacking the full authority of the emperor, Ferdinand, acting as regent, had been unable to contain the expansion and popularity of the heretic movement. To address the growing religious division between the Catholic Church and the followers of Luther, Charles V summoned the Diet to Augsburg in July 1530.

Before the Augsburg Diet assembled, the emperor issued a three part agenda for debate with the ecclesiastic and secular princes, calling for unification of the German church, launching of a crusade against the Turks in the Balkans and election of Ferdinand as king of the Romans. When the Catholic and Protestant princes met, the growing hostile division between the two religious factions quickly became the central issue. At the emperor's request, the Lutherans presented their religous beliefs in the *Confession of Augsburg*, offering modest compromises. However, when the Catholics responded with the *Confutation*, the differences between the two doctrines were too wide to resolve. Negotiations were continued but when the Diet recessed in September no settlement was found and dissent between the two religious parties intensified with a final attack against Protestant dogma. As the threat of war grew, in early 1531 the Lutheran princes and towns united at Schmalkaldic to form a league for their common defense.

By 1531 the Ottoman Empire had conquered much of Hungary and was advancing against Vienna, threatening the whole of eastern Europe. The approval of a crusade to defend Christendom was now in the common interest of both the Catholic and Protestant factions. Responding to the request of the emperor, in May 1532 the German princes assembled in Nuremberg, agreeing to temporarily put aside their religious differences and unite in a holy war against the Turks, who were commanded by Sultan Suleiman I. In August a great combined military force was mustered, beginning the march to the east. However, by the time the imperialists reached the Hungarian border, Suleiman I had ended his campaign and had withdrawn south due to the approach of the winter season. Charles V had managed to engage the Turks in several brief skirmishes, winning victories, but his grand crusade ended with the Ottoman menace still intact.

Charles V had been absent from Spain for over four years and was now anxious to return home. Following the crusade against Suleiman I, he began the long journey south. Traveling through Italy, he met the pope in Bologna to discuss reconciliation with the German Protestants and the possibility of a campaign against the growing danger of Turkish sponsored pirates in the Mediterranean Sea. Arriving in Spain in late April 1533, the emperor assumed personal control of the government from his wife and soon began to meet with the Parliaments of Castile and Aragon. There were endless welcoming court banquets and hunting parties to attend, while the negotiations continued with the regional assemblies. The Castile Cortes had been held in check by Empress Isabella, but the towns and nobles in the Aragonese legislative body argued over numerous complaints and heavy taxes.

After two years in Spain, the emperor sailed to his southern Italian kingdom, receiving a triumphant welcome and staying for the winter, governing his vast empire, while enjoying numerous banquets, costume balls and hunting parties. While Charles V remained in Naples, the duke of Milan, Francesco II Sforza, died and the emperor's son and heir, Philip, was appointed as his successor. Francis I became alarmed at Habsburg expansion into Lombardy and again renewed his quest for Italian land. The French launched their attack in March 1536 into the northern duchy of Savoy, capturing Turin. Charles V thwarted the Valois campaign by ordering imperial troops to reoccupy the duchy. With the two realms at war, in the summer of the following year, Charles V adopted a new offensive strategy of carrying the fighting directly to the enemy's soil, sending an army to invade the southern French region of Provence. However, the initiative ended in disaster when the local French commander, Duke Anne Montmorency, withdrew into the interior, leaving only a scorched earth behind. Suffering from heat, disease and lack of water and food, in September the shattered imperial force retreated. The conflict dragged on into 1537 with only sporadic skirmishes in Artois, as a stalemate once again developed. After three years of inconclusive war, both kingdoms were exhausted and nearly bankrupt, welcoming a papal sponsored truce, which was signed in June 1538. The new pope, Paul III, had personally intervened brokering the settlement and arranging for both sovereigns to hold personal talks at Aigues-Mortes near Nice. At the meeting Charles V and Francis I expressed their friendship and agreed to continue negotiations for a permanent peace.

Following the Truce of Nice, Charles V returned to Spain, which he considered his home and heartland of his empire. Relations with France continued to be friendly and Europe remained at peace, allowing him to travel throughout his Spanish realm, administering his government and dealing with the local legislatures. However, in late 1539 he was forced to personally intervene in the escalating revolt in Flanders. The journey to the Low Countries was made overland through France, where the emperor was met at the border and accompanied by Francis I, who arranged a grand procession of banquets and parties as they traveled north. The two sovereigns parted with pledges to retain their cordiality and renew negotiations for a permanent peace.

The center of the Flemish insurrection had been in the city of Ghent, which had risen in revolt, overthrowing the imperial government. Arriving in the Netherlands, Charles V was determined to prevent future rebellions by making a harsh example of Ghent. He entered the city in February 1540 with a strong military force, easily suppressing the rebels and after a short trial executing their leaders. The special privileges previously granted to the population were voided and the city was occupied with a permanent garrison. For the remainder of his reign, the Netherlands provinces maintained peace with Charles V.

Following the subjugation of the Flemish rebellion, Charles V summoned the Imperial Diet to Regensburg to make another attempt to end the religious division between the Catholics and Protestants. However, both parties refused any meaningful compromise and the assembly ended without any resolution of the schism. With no possibility of finding reconciliation, the emperor returned to Spain.

By 1541 the détente with France had deteriorated and from Spain Charles V spent the year preparing for the renewal of the war. In the following spring Francis I launched his army into Flanders, while his ally, John, Duke of Cleves, attacked northern Netherlands. After limited successes their campaign was thwarted by the stiff local resistance and the conflict ended the year without any resolution. During the winter Charles V intensified his ongoing negotiations for a coalition with Henry VIII, finally resulting in an agreement in February 1543. However, before the allies mounted their combined initiative, Francis I renewed his incursion in Flanders, seizing several towns and pressing his assault. In the spring the emperor departed for the Netherlands, assuming personal command of the imperial war effort. As the French continued to advance into Flanders, he launched a counterattack against Cleves, defeating

Duke John and forcing his withdrawal from the Valois alliance. With the north protected the Habsburg troops marched against the French, compelling them to abandon their recent conquest. The campaigning season ended with little gain for Francis I and the emperor in control of Cleves.

During the winter months of the new year, Charles V and Henry VIII pledged to mount a double invasion of France to end the stalemate. Under their agreement the English were to break out from Calais, while the imperialists marched west from Metz toward Paris. In May the allies launched their campaign with Henry VIII overrunning Picardy, as the Habsburgs crossed the Marne River. However, Charles V's attack lost its momentum at the month long siege at Saint Dizier and when his soldiers renewed their advance; they were slowed by the summer heat and scorched earth tactics of the French. By September Charles V's finances and troop strength were depleted, compelling him to order a withdrawal. After three years of war both rivals were exhausted and anxious to negotiate a final settlement. Meetings were soon scheduled between Valois and Habsburg envoys, resulting in the Treaty of Crespy. Under the agreement, peace and the status quo were reestablished, Francis I pledged to repudiate his claim to Savoy, while Charles V agreed to the marriage of a member of the Habsburg family to a son of the Valois king with either Milan or Flanders as her dowry and the French promised to aid the Catholic cause against the German Lutherans. The 1542–1544 Valois-Habsburg War was Charles V's last encounter with Francis I, who died two years later.

The Schmalkaldic League had been formed by nine Protestant German princedoms in 1531 in defense of their religious doctrine against the Catholic Holy Roman Empire. In lieu of an armed confrontation against the heretics, Charles V had attempted to negotiate a reconciliation but his numerous efforts had failed. After making peace with France and with the Ottoman Empire temporarily contained in the east, he became resolved to force a settlement of the religious schism through military might. In late 1546 the imperial army with the emperor in personal command was mustered at Regensburg, beginning the campaign of subjugation by first seizing control of southern Germany. After occupying the conquered region, the Habsburg troops turned north to attack the Ernestine Saxon lands of the leader of the Schmalkaldic League, John Frederick I. The elector of Saxony was a personal friend of Martin Luther and a faithful and forceful supporter of the Protestant Reformation. He continually defied the emperor by aggressively introducing the Lutheran religion into new German territories. At the approach of the imperialists, the Saxons began to withdraw to the protection of the fortified city of Magdeburg. However, on April 24, 1547, they were outmaneuvered by Charles V near Muhlberg and completely routed with John Frederick I taken prisoner.

After his military triumph at Muhlberg, the emperor summoned the Imperial Diet to Augsburg to impose a religious settlement with the reformers. However, the princes both Catholic and Protestant feared the loss of their individual authority and rights, thwarting all of his initiatives. He was compelled to accept a compromise, approving the *Interim,* which temporarily re-aligned the Protestant dogma into more traditional Christian beliefs until a papal general council could resolve the issue. Despite the victory at Muhlberg, the disappointed emperor still lacked the political might to force an end to the religious schism.

Charles V remained committed to ending the defection of the Lutherans from the Catholic Church and in 1551, as a result of his ongoing deliberations with the Holy See, a papal council was called to Trent to address the schism. While he was distracted with the council, in Protestant Saxony Duke Maurice, fearing an end to his freedom of worship, began to prepare his army for war against the emperor. Alliances were forged with the militant heretic princes and in January 1552 a treaty was signed with the new French king, Henry II. In the spring the anti–Habsburg league launched its attack in Germany with the French seizing the bishoprics of Metz, Verdun and Toul, while Maurice advanced against Innsbruck, forcing Charles V to abandon the city. After their seizure of parts of Tyrol, lacking the military might for a prolonged war, the anti-papist princes offered to negotiate a settlement. Physically wornout from years of fighting and suffering from gout, Charles V reluctantly accepted the proposal and the result of the talks was the Truce of Passau, which finally ended the religious wars in Germany. Under the agreement, which was later made permanent under the Peace of Augsburg, the Protestant doctrine was formally recognized and the rights of the princes acknowledged by the emperor.

While the German princes had agreed to the Truce of Passau, Charles V remained at war with Henry II. After a failed campaign to expel the Valois garrison from Metz in 1552, the emperor invaded Picardy, quickly seizing the strategic fortress of Therouanne. The French countered by attacking Flanders, occupying parts of the southern lordships. As the conflict dragged on in northern Europe, to gain an ally and a foothold in Italy for future aggrandizement, Henry II supported the rebellion of the city of Siena against Habsburg control by sending money and troops. In 1553 to protect his interest in northern Italy, Charles V negotiated an alliance with Duke Cosimo I of Florence, who laid siege against Siena and forced the French defenders to surrender in the following year. The war continued another two years with only inconclusive skirmishes in Flanders and Italy and with both rivals again exhausted and nearly bankrupt, a truce was arranged in 1556.

Charles V had ruled half the known world for over thirty-six years and was now mentally and physically exhausted from the prolonged stress and the effects of gout. As his health deteriorated, in October 1555 he abdicated the Burgundian throne, appointing his son, Prince Philip, as his successor. Two months later, the emperor ceded Spain with its overseas colonies to his son. The responsibilities of emperor had previously been transferred to his brother, Ferdinand, and freed from the burdens of government, Charles V retired to his beloved Spain, leaving the Netherlands in September 1556. A small villa near the San Jeronimo of Yuste Monastery was built for him and he spent his remaining years preparing his soul for death. Charles V died at age fifty-eight on September 21, 1558, after a reign of forty years.

Sources

Brandi. *The Emperor Charles V.*   Grant. *Charles V.*   Mamatey. *Rise of the Habsburg Empire.*   Mulgan. *The Renaissance Monarchies, 1469–1558.*   Rady. *The Emperor Charles V.*

Ferdinand I, 1503–1558–1564

Ferdinand of Habsburg officially ascended to the throne of the Holy Roman Empire in 1558 after the death of his brother, Charles V, reigning for less than five years as the sixth Renaissance emperor. He was the second son of Duke Philip of Burgundy and Queen Joanna of Spain and was born on March 10, 1503, at Alcala de Henares near Madrid, Spain. In 1506 his father unexpectedly died and with the resulting insanity of the queen, the guardianship for the Habsburg prince was assumed by his maternal grandfather, King Ferdinand II of Aragon. He was raised in the Spanish royal household, receiving a well-rounded education in reading, writing, the sciences, literature, and the languages of Spanish, French and later German. Ferdinand was a dedicated student and later as Roman king and emperor enthusiastically encouraged renowned scholars to reside at his court. He was a zealous sponsor of the humanist movement and patron of architecture, supporting the rebuilding of Prague and Vienna. Through the influence of the king of Aragon, he became a devout Catholic and defender of the teachings of the Holy See of Rome. With the inability of Joanna to rule, Ferdinand II began to educate and train his grandson in statesmanship and government for his future accession to the Spanish crown.

As Ferdinand continued his education for his succession, in 1516 his maternal grandfather died. The Habsburg prince had been born and raised as a Spaniard and a local political faction began to rally around him, favoring his recognition as heir. However, his elder brother, Charles, asserted his inheritance rights to the crown and in September 1517 sailed from the Netherlands to Spain to impose his rule. He was readily accepted as king by Ferdinand and the great grandees, who pledged their oaths of fealty in the February 1518 formal ceremony of submission. After securing his acknowledgement as sovereign, Charles sent his brother to the Netherlands to prevent a rival party from again forming in Ferdinand's support. In Brussels he became a part of the court of his aunt, Archduchess Margaret of Austria, who was acting as regent for Charles. While governing the Burgundian lands, Margaret was also a patron of the Renaissance movement, sponsoring and encouraging many poets, artists, composers and musicians in the Low Countries. In the Brussels court Ferdinand continued his education, becoming exposed to the art, literature, and music of the Renaissance.

While Ferdinand remained in the Netherlands, in 1519 Charles V was elected emperor of the Holy Roman Empire, becoming the most powerful ruler in Europe, controlling the German princedoms and his inherited Habsburg demesne. Two years later the emperor departed from Spain to Germany, summoning his brother from Brussels to attend the Imperial Diet at Worms, where Ferdinand was present during the heresy trial of Martin Luther. After declaring Luther an outlaw, Charles V was confronted by the German princes, who were attempting to increase their power through the creation of a Regency Council. After prolonged talks a compromise agreement was approved, establishing a new regency government under the authority of a deputy emperor who was to rule the empire in the emperor's absences. In need of a loyal and capable surrogate, Charles V began negotiations to secure the appointment of his brother as regent. In February 1522 the treaty was finalized and Ferdinand formally acknowledged as the deputy emperor. As part of the settlement, Charles V ceded the Austrian Habsburg crownlands along with the title of archduke to his brother to provide him with the political and military might to enforce his sovereignty rights over the imperial princes and cities, while pledging to support his election as king of the Romans. Following the end of the Worms Diet, Ferdinand traveled to Innsbruck to preside over his court and impose his supremacy in Austria.

After his assumption of power in Austria, Ferdinand reorganized the existing governmental structure, creating a permanent ruling council and office of tax collector. However, he named his Spanish and Burgundian advisors and friends to the positions, creating ill will and resentment among the nobles at their loss of influence at court. As the dissent became more widespread, he agreed to appoint only local magnates to his regime and add a chancery and treasury to his administration to give more authority to the Austrian magnates.

While asserting his ducal rule over Austria, Ferdinand served as his brother's deputy emperor in German affairs, attending the sessions of the Imperial Diet and presiding over the Regency Council. The government soon came under the domination of the Austrian archduke due to the continuous fragmentation of the nobles and imperial free cites into differing political factions who failed to unite to assert their rights. With control over the regency, he utilized the council to advance the policies of the Habsburgs, however, lacking the power and prestige of an anointed sovereign his decrees had little authority, resulting in the deterioration of imperial supremacy. During Ferdinand's over thirty years as regent his administration was seriously challenged by the rise of Protestantism, the Turkish menace in the east and peasants' revolts in 1524 and 1525.

As Ferdinand attempted to maintain peace in the Holy Roman Empire, in southern Germany the peasants and towns rose up against the harsh economic policies of the local ruling princes. As the revolt spread over much of Swabia, Franconia and Thuringia in 1524, the rebels organized into peasant armies, attacking their overlords and demanding religious freedom, reduction in their feudal rents and abolishment of serfdom. The nobles were hard pressed to contain the violence, compelling Ferdinand to order the troops of the Swabian League to suppress the rebellion. Poorly organized and lacking leadership, by late 1525 the rogue forces were completely overwhelmed and the power of the magnates restored. By his decisive response, the archduke had reasserted the authority of the empire and had enhanced the prestige and stature of the emperor.

To expand the Habsburgs' influence and presence into eastern Europe, in 1515 Emperor Maximilian I had negotiated the marriage of his grandchildren, Ferdinand and Mary, to the daughter and son of the ruler of Bohemia and Hungary. The terms of the treaty were finally ratified in 1521 by the archduke's marriage to Princess Anna and the marital union of his sister to King Louis II of Hungary. While Ferdinand remained occupied in Austria and Germany, in August 1526 his childless brother-in-law, Louis II, was killed fighting the Turks at the battle of Mohacs. After the death of the king, the Austrian duke claimed the crowns of Hungary and Bohemia through the inheritance rights of his wife and sister. Seizing on the political fragmentation among the Czech nobles resulting from the absence of a recognized central authority, Ferdinand was quickly elected sovereign after pledging to respect the privileges and religious freedom of the cities. On February 24, 1527, he was anointed monarch, assuming the reins of Bohemian power in Prague. However, he was compelled to contend by force of arms the succession challenge of John Zapolya of Transylvania for the throne of Hungary.

Zapolya had been intriguing in Hungarian political affairs for many years, developing a large base of support. In November 1526 he exploited his widespread popularity by securing his election as king by the Diet. With Ferdinand distracted by Emperor Charles V's war against France and the governing of the Holy Roman Empire and Austria, John I successfully asserted his power over much of Hungary. After gaining control of the realm, he attempted to forge an alliance with the Habsburg Archduke; however, all his initiatives were rejected. In December Ferdinand openly challenged John Zapolya's claim to the throne by having himself anointed Hungarian king.

Ferdinand had aided Emperor Charles V's war against Francis I financially and by sending German troops to Italy. In May 1527 the imperial army sacked Rome, compelling France's ally, Pope Clement VII, to withdraw from their league. With the removal of the papal forces from the conflict, the Austrian archduke was free to transfer his soldiers from Italy and pursue his conquest of Hungary. In the summer he personally led his German army, augmented with seasoned mercenaries, against the militia of John I. The Magyars were easily overwhelmed by the military might of the Habsburgs and Zapolya was forced to flee to Poland. The imperialists marched into Buda unopposed, imposing the authority of Ferdinand as king of Hungary.

While Ferdinand was attempting to further assert his power into the area south of Buda, from his sanctuary in Poland Zapolya forged an alliance with the Ottoman sultan, Suleiman I. The sultan had succeeded to the throne of the Ottoman Empire in 1520 and through the charismatic force of his personality had reenergized the expansionist policies of the Turks into the Balkans, Middle East and North Africa. In 1521 he personally commanded his army into the Balkans, capturing Belgrade, Buda and occupying the duchy of Transylvania. In the following year, Suleiman I defeated the Knights of Saint John, seizing their island of Rhodes. While pursuing the aggrandizement of Christian territory by military might, he was also a patron of culture, sponsoring and encouraging painters, goldsmiths, artisans, jewelers and poets to his Topkapi Palace in Constantinople in a golden age of artistic achievement. The sultan was a renowned poet with many of his verses known throughout the Muslim empire.

As the result of John Zapolya's negotiations with the Ottoman Empire, the Treaty of Constantinople was ratified. John became the vassal of the Turks, while the sultan recognized him as Magyar king and pledged assistance for the reconquest of his usurped realm. In the summer of 1529, the Ottoman army advanced into Hungary, quickly driving the Habsburg troops from Buda and reinstating Zapolya as ruler. After occupying the capital, the Turks continued their offensive, crossing the border to besiege Vienna on September 27 and compelling Ferdinand to flee to Bohemia. However, the Austrian garrison defiantly repulsed the Turkish attacks and Suleiman I was forced to order a retreat. As the Muslims withdrew into western Hungary, they were repeatedly harried by the Habsburg soldiers, enabling the archduke to reimpose his local authority. The year ended in an uneasy truce with Ferdinand acknowledged as sovereign in the newly seized region known as Royal Hungary and John I controlling Buda and the southern lordships as a retainer of the sultan.

With the war in Hungary in a stalemate, in 1530 Ferdinand traveled to Innsbruck to meet his brother, Charles V, who had come to Germany to personally settle the growing religious schism between the Catholics and Protestants. During the emperor's nine-year absence, his surrogate ruler had been unable to check the spread and popularity of the Lutheran movement. As devout supporters of the papacy, the Habsburgs were determined to impose the authority of Pope Clement VII, summoning the Imperial Diet to Augsburg to negotiate a reconciliation with the anti-papists. Ferdinand attended the meetings with his brother, but no compromise resolution was found and the assembly ended with hostilities between the religious factions intensified. The heretic princes and towns later met at Schmalkaldic, forming an alliance against the loss of their freedom to worship and the threat of war with the Catholics. Despite the failure of the Augsburg Diet, Charles V was able to secure the election of Ferdinand as king of the Romans in January 1531.

After solidifying his power over southern Hungary, in the summer of 1532 Suleiman I again marched his army against Austria. With Germany under threat of invasion, the Catholic and Protestant princes put aside their religious differences, agreeing in Nuremberg to unite and launch a holy war against the Turks. Ferdinand energetically supported the crusade and assembled his German and Austrian troops, augmented with contingents from Bohemia, for the coming conflict. In August he joined his soldiers with Charles V's forces and together their great army advanced east. However, by the time they reached eastern Austria, the Ottomans had withdrawn to Buda. As defenders of the Christian faith, the failure of the war to decisively defeat the Muslims was a personal disappointment to the emperor and his brother, while leaving the security of Austria still in peril and the Hungarian succession unresolved.

Following the crusade against the Ottoman Empire, Ferdinand continued to intrigue in Hungary, attempting to gain the support of the nobles to expand his lands and spheres of influence. He ruled the newly occupied Royal Hungary from Vienna, keeping in place the former governmental structure, while adopting a policy of subjugating the local administration to Habsburg control. A loyal viceroy was appointed to administer the region and slowly the power of the Roman king was increased as the former Magyar institutions lost importance and Royal Hungary came increasingly under Austrian supremacy.

While successfully asserting his authority over Royal Hungary, Ferdinand lacked the military might to enforce his rule over the region under John I's control. There were frequent armed encounters between the forces of the two kings but no resolution for the partitioning of the kingdom resulted. Finally in late 1537 negotiations were begun between the envoys of the rival courts for the reunification of the realm. In the ensuing Treaty of Nagyvarad, the archduke was recognized as heir to the childless John I, while pledging to defend Hungary with the imperial army against future Ottoman advances. However, the settlement proved irrelevant with the marriage of Zapolya to Isabella of Poland and the birth of a son, John II, in 1540. Shortly after the birth of the heir, John I died and the infant was crowned king by his sympathizers and acknowledged as successor by the Ottoman Empire. To fill the power vacuum in Buda, the reins of the Magyar regime were assumed by John II's mother, who governed the kingdom as regent with the support of Suleiman I. To enforce the terms of the Nagyvarad accord and gain supremacy over all of Hungary, Ferdinand launched two attacks against the Turkish vassal-state but both incursions ended in failure due to the lack of troops and money. After his unsuccessful invasions, to secure peace along the Hungarian border, in 1544 the Roman king signed a truce with Suleiman I, agreeing to pay a yearly tribute for Royal Hungary.

As Ferdinand attempted to expand his realm into occupied Hungary, in the Holy Roman princedoms the spread of Protestantism continued unfettered. In 1534 the Habsburg duchy of Wurttemberg was seized by Philip of Hesse and the previously deposed Lutheran duke, Ulrich, reinstated as the local ruler. With the Roman king engaged in Hungary and Charles V distracted with his war against France, no attempt to reclaim the lost territory was possible, causing an erosion of prestige for the German crown. Ferdinand remained a strong defender of the Catholic Church but lacked the financial resources and military might to force a resolution, permitting the rapid spread of Lutheranism into northern Germany with the magnates of Brandenburg, Mecklenburg and Saxony abandoning the Holy See. The Habsburg archduke created a Catholic League to reassert the Roman church but his efforts produced only limited success. In 1540 Charles V assembled the Diet at Regensburg to use the power of his office to negotiate a reunion with the anti-papist league. However, both rival religious parties refused to offer any meaningful concessions and the Diet ended in disappointment. While no permanent settlement resulted, a temporary reconciliation treaty was signed in July 1541. Under the agreement, the imperial princes, free cities and emperor pledged to end the religious schism by summoning a general church council and to maintain the peace.

Following the failed Regensburg Diet, hostilities erupted between the emperor and Francis I. Ferdinand again actively supported his brother's war effort by supplying imperial troops and money. With both Habsburg rulers distracted in France, any meaningful attempt to resolve the religious schism in Germany was delayed. However, by 1546 the conflict with France had been settled, permitting Charles V to abandon his reconciliation policy and begin preparations to force a settlement with the Protestants through military might. Answering the call to arms, Ferdinand assembled his imperial forces, joining Charles V at Regensburg. However, when he attempted to recruit levies for the war from Bohemia, the local nobles revolted, delaying the campaign. The archduke was compelled to send his soldiers, augmented with a Spanish contingent from his brother, to subjugate the rebels. With the Czech uprising suppressed, the imperial offensive was mounted and by the following year southern Germany subdued. After the conquest of the south, the Catholics marched against the leader of the

Schmalkaldic League, Elector John Frederick I of Saxony. In April 1547 the Holy Roman army, with Ferdinand commanding the second line of troops, attacked the elector at the town of Muhlberg near the Elbe River. Believing he was protected by the river, John Frederick I ignored the approach of the Habsburgs and continued his retreat toward the fortified city of Magdeburg. However, a little known crossing was found and the emperor launched his assault, catching the elector totally unprepared. In the ensuing battle the Protestants were completely routed and John Frederick I taken prisoner. In June the remaining princes of the Schmalkaldic League surrendered and the authority of the Habsburg family was recognized.

Seeking to exploit his triumph at Muhlberg as a means to force a settlement of the religious schism with the Protestants, Charles V and the Roman king summoned the Imperial Diet to Augsburg. Along with the emperor, Ferdinand was energetically involved in the negotiations with the German princes but no reconciliation was found. After the failure of the anti-papists to offer any significant compromise, in May 1548 Charles V issued the Augsburg Interim, ordering the heretic faction to readopt the established Catholic doctrines and practices. The decree was unpopular throughout the Empire and widely ignored.

While remaining in Germany, in 1550 the fifty-year-old Charles V began discussions with Ferdinand for the partition of his empire after his death. The two brothers spent most of the year discussing a resolution, finally agreeing to the inheritance of Ferdinand to the crown of the Holy Roman Empire with the emperor's son, Philip, succeeding his uncle. However, the settlement later proved impracticable and Ferdinand's son, Maximilian, was recognized as his father's heir to the empire, while Philip was to rule Spain, the Netherlands and Habsburg Italy.

By 1551 the Interim settlement dictated at the Diet of Augsburg was in shambles and despite the summoning of a papal council to Trent to discuss the religious schism, the Protestant princes and the empire were on the verge of war. In defense of his independence and freedom of worship, the new elector of Saxony, Maurice I, formed a league with the militant nobles and negotiated a military alliance with Henry II of France. Maurice I was raised a Lutheran and in 1541 inherited the Albertine lands of the Saxon duchy from his father. While expanding and encouraging the new religion into his demesne, he refused to join the militant Schmalkaldic League, pursuing friendship with Emperor Charles V. During the war against the league, the duke joined his troops with the imperial army, participating in the campaign into southern Germany and victory at Magdeburg over the leader of the Protestant faction, Elector John Frederick I. In order to escape execution for treason, the elector was forced to cede his title and estates to Maurice I. However, when the emperor attempted to reintroduce Catholicism into the Protestant princedoms, Elector Maurice I abandoned the imperialists, joining the anti–Habsburg league. In the spring of 1552 the allies launched their attacks with the French seizing the ecclesiastic fiefs of Verdun, Toul and Metz, while the Saxon elector invaded the Tyrol region of Austria. However, when the emperor transferred Spanish troops from Italy and recruited a mercenary army to confront the league, Maurice I was compelled to open peace talks with the Roman king, resulting in the Truce of Passau, which guaranteed the status quo.

Following the Passau agreement, the emperor adopted a more bellicose policy toward the Lutheran faction, while his brother sponsored a program of conciliation and accommodation. However, after his failure to form an anti–Protestant league and the repulse of his counterattack against Metz, in 1554 Charles V could no longer resist the demands for a permanent resolution and approved the non-aggression policy of Ferdinand. In February 1555 the Imperial Diet met at Augsburg with Ferdinand representing the emperor. Under the

Roman king's leadership, the Protestant and Catholic parties agreed to the Treaty of Augsburg, which formally recognized the reformer doctrine and rights of the princes while establishing peace.

After the religious reconciliation at Augsburg, in September 1556 Charles V returned to Spain and after his death two years later Ferdinand I was officially acknowledged as his successor in Germany. On March 24, 1558, he was crowned in Frankfort as emperor of the Holy Roman Empire. As a devout Catholic and advocate of the Counter-Reformation, Ferdinand I spent much of his short reign backing the efforts of the Papal Council of Trent to end the Protestant schism, earning the title protector of the council. However, frequent disagreements with the papacy over concessions for the Lutherans prevented any meaningful results and the reform movement continued to expand. While supporting the Trent Council, Ferdinand I invited militant Jesuits to establish a presence in his lands to act as a deterrent against the rise of Protestantism. While promoting the reunion of the heretic faction with the Holy See through diplomacy, the emperor renewed his attempts to centralize the government and restructure the monetary system in his vast central European empire. Seeking to protect his exposed demesne in Royal Hungary, he negotiated military alliances with his neighboring kingdoms to contend the Turkish menace.

Despite over one hundred years of uninterrupted rule, the unchallenged inheritance rights of the Habsburg family to the imperial throne had not been firmly established and to ensure the continuance of the dynasty's authority, in November 1562 Ferdinand I had his son and heir, Maximilian, invested as king of the Romans and recognized as successor to the Holy Roman Empire. By 1564 Ferdinand I's health began to seriously deteriorate and on July 25 he died at age sixty-one in Vienna after a reign as emperor of less than five years.

Sources

Crankshaw. *The Habsburgs.* Kann. *A History of the Habsburg Empire, 1526–1918.* Mamatey. *Rise of the Habsburg Empire.* Wheatcroft. *The Habsburgs.*

Maximilian II, 1527–1564–1576

After the death of Ferdinand I in July 1564, his eldest son and heir, Maximilian, was invested with the crown of the Holy Roman Empire by the church in Nuremburg, taking the reins of power as the seventh Renaissance emperor. Maximilian was born on July 31, 1527, in Vienna and was the first son of Ferdinand of Habsburg and Anna of Hungary. To bind his family to the local lordships, his Spanish born and raised father named Maximilian after his paternal grandfather, who was popular among the German and Austrian nobles and population. He was appointed Archduke of Austria soon after his birth and as the first male issue inherited the blood claim to the Habsburg kingdoms of Hungary and Bohemia and the duchy of Austria. The young archduke spent his early years at the royal court in Innsbruck, where a school was established for the education of the monarch's children. To prepare Maximilian for his future assumption of power, Ferdinand carefully chose his son's tutors and he was instructed in reading, writing, religion, science and languages to include Latin, German, French, Italian, Czech and Spanish. He was a gifted and devoted student, excelling in his studies, especially of languages. In 1538 Maximilian began his public life, riding with the German king to Vienna and later Prague to participate in the administration of the Habsburg government by attending court, council sessions and audiences with foreign diplomats and local lords. To expand the training for his succession to the throne, in March 1544 the Habsburg prince was sent to the imperial household of his uncle, Charles V. Traveling with the emperor, he visited the princedoms of the Holy Roman Empire, meeting with the local rulers and their nobles.

Before Maximilian departed to the imperial court, war had again erupted between the Habsburgs and the Valois king, Francis I. After touring the Holy Roman princedoms, the archduke was anxious to join his uncle in confronting the French. While the Habsburgs' ally, Henry VIII of England, mounted an attack against France from Calais, in the spring of 1544 the emperor launched a second offensive from the east. Maximilian advanced with the German army into France, remaining with the imperial headquarters to continue his military education. However, in spite of some early successes, by September the initiative had lost its momentum and the archduke was forced to withdraw with the retreating troops. Despite the failure of the campaign, he gained his first combat experiences, displaying natural leadership and martial skills.

While the invasions of the Habsburgs and English into France had ended in disappointment, the attacks had weakened the resolve of Francis I to renew the war, resulting in the signing of the Peace of Crespy. With his western borders secure, Charles V was free to abandon his policy of peaceful negotiations and confront by force of arms the growing Protestant movement in Germany. In late 1546 he assembled the imperial army at Regensburg, launching his offensive into the southern German princedoms. Maximilian again joined his uncle's campaign and was appointed to command a division of cavalry. During the siege against Ingolstadt in Bavaria, he distinguished himself with his bravery and military skills. By early the next year, the region had submitted and the emperor marched his troops north into Saxony with the Austrian archduke remaining with the military forces. In April Maximilian participated in the battle of Muhlberg, where the army of the Saxon elector, John Frederick I, was decisively defeated. The victory at Muhlberg was followed by the summoning of the imperial diet to Augsburg, where the emperor and his brother negotiated a temporary peace settlement with the reformists. Maximilian attended the Parliament, serving as president, while establishing a following among the German ecclesiastic and secular princes.

During the war against the Protestant princes, the emperor and Ferdinand had begun talks for the marriage of Maximilian to his cousin, Maria of Spain, daughter of Charles V. To provide Maximilian with a royal title for his marriage into the imperial dynasty, Ferdinand appointed his son to the kingship of Bohemia. In 1548 he traveled to Spain for the wedding and to act as regent for his cousin, Philip, who was leaving the kingdom for an extended stay in the Netherlands and Germany. Arriving in the Castilian capital of Valladolid after a journey through northern Italy, the wedding ceremony was held on September 13. He assumed the reins of power from Philip, administering the routine affairs of state. However, his authority to govern was limited by the emperor and all major policy decisions were deferred to him. Nevertheless, his three years of ruling the Spanish regime provided valuable experiences in dealing with local legislatures, finances, and foreign diplomats for his future assumption of the imperial throne. While in Spain he stayed in contact with the courts of the Holy Roman Empire and in particular with the Czech realm. In his heart the Bohemian king remained a German and missed his homeland.

As the result of negotiations between the two branches of the Habsburg dynasty, Maximilian was married to his cousin, Maria of Spain, in September 1548. Unlike her husband, she was a devout Catholic and strongly supported the teachings of the papacy while attempting to influence the religious beliefs of the archduke. Maria was a princess of intelligence, resolve and moderation, becoming active in Maximilian's court and playing a significant role in religious and dynastic issues. Despite being an arranged union, the archduke and Maria became devoted to each other, developing a lifelong loving and supportive relationship. The future of the Austrian Habsburg family was secured in 1552 with the birth of Rudolf and was followed by fourteen additional children. Along with his wife, Maximilian was a patron of culture, sponsoring and encouraging artists, musicians and scholars to his court. He took a special interest in choral music, establishing his own chapel choir with over seventy singers.

In 1550 Charles V and Archduke Ferdinand began discussions for the future division of the Habsburg Empire. The emperor agreed to recognize his brother as heir to the imperial crown but demanded that his son, Philip, be appointed to succeed his uncle. Ferdinand refused to accept the proposal, summoning his son from Spain in October, as negotiations between the two brothers reached an impasse. It was only through the diplomatic intervention of their sister, Mary of Hungary, that a compromise settlement was finally signed. Under the treaty Philip was to follow his uncle to the emperorship with Maximilian acknowledged as next in line. However, the Bohemian king rejected the arrangement, believing the imperial throne was his by birthright, resulting in increased tensions between the two branches of the family.

Following his rupture with the imperial court, Maximilian withdrew to Vienna, assuming the reins of power during his father's many absences, while plotting with both Catholic and Protestant princes to gain their support for his succession to the throne of the Holy Roman Empire. While relations with the emperor remained strained, in 1552 Maximilian was appointed by his father to command the defenses in Royal Hungary and ordered to keep the Turkish encroachments in check. From Austria the Bohemian king continued to maintain his friendships with the German rulers, working with Archduke Ferdinand to bring reconciliation to the religious schism between his uncle and the Lutheran princes through peaceful means. The discord between the two branches of the dynasty was only resolved in 1554 when Charles V negotiated the marriage of his son to Queen Mary I Tudor of England, withdrawing his objections to the ascension of Maximilian to the imperial crown.

The 1547 Diet of Augsburg's approval of the Interim agreement had temporarily imposed a resolution to the ongoing schism between the followers of Luther and the Catholic Church. However, the religious dispute soon began to reemerge, prompting Charles V to abandon his strategy of toleration to promote a settlement by force of arms. Maximilian had cultivated the goodwill and friendship of both Protestants and Catholics in his quest for the imperial crown and to advance his relationships with the princes, openly opposed the bellicose policy of the emperor. To peaceably resolve the religious schism, in 1553 the Habsburg archduke strongly endorsed the creation of the Heidelberg League, gaining the favor of the German lords, while influencing his father to join the faction. When the Heidelberg initiative failed to end the religious strife, the archduke enthusiastically approved Ferdinand's negotiations, leading to the Treaty of Augsburg, which confirmed the freedom of worship and privileges of the anti-papist magnates and towns.

Through his friendships and relentless support for the Protestants, Maximilian had developed a large political base, which gave increasing cause to doubt his Catholic beliefs among members of the Habsburg family. His father pressed him to abandon his circle of reformist friends and meetings with perceived heretic ministers. In 1559 Ferdinand I threatened to disinherit his son for his liberal religious beliefs and appoint his second son, Ferdinand, as successor. However, despite his ongoing backing of the rights of the Lutherans and repeated calls for internal reforms to rid the Holy See of abuses, the archduke continued to practice the dogma of Rome, declaring in February 1562 to never forsake the church.

After the archduke's pledge to remain Catholic, his father became committed to his eldest son's succession to the imperial crown. In early 1562 Ferdinand I, whose health was beginning to fail, initiated a political campaign to secure the election of Maximilian as his designated heir. The Habsburg prince had maintained his strong backing among the Protestant electors, who considered him the champion of their religious interests. His continued defense of the 1555 Treaty of Augsburg as the means to achieve lasting religious peace was popular among the reformist rulers, buttressing his support.

While the Protestants favored the selection of Maximilian to the Holy Roman crown, the Catholic princes found reason to doubt his fidelity to the teachings of Rome. However, with Ferdinand I's enthusiastic support for his son's election and the Habsburg prince's declaration to remain with the traditional church, the Catholic electors withdrew their objections. With the backing of both religious factions, in December 1562 the archduke was elected king of the Germans and acknowledged as imperial successor in Frankfurt at the Cathedral of Saint Bartholomew. In the following year through the negotiations of his father, Maximilian was anointed king of Hungary and with his prior succession to the thrones of Bohemia and Austria continued the Habsburg dynasty's domination of central Europe.

After Maximilian's election as the emperor's designated successor, the health of Ferdinand I began to rapidly deteriorate and his son increasingly became associated with the administration of the Holy Roman Empire and the family's hereditary domains. In July 1564 Ferdinand I died and the German king ascended to the imperial throne unchallenged. After assuming the reins of power, he continued to implement the reform programs previously adopted by his father. The existing governmental structure was largely left intact with the new emperor retaining control over the ruling council. Changes were made to the chancellery to improve the security of court documents and the flow of information between Maximilian II and his foreign ambassadors. However, he primarily directed his policy restructuring measures at the treasury. The record keeping and accountability of the tax collectors were reformed to increase the money inflows to the imperial coffers. He introduced cost saving initiatives into his government, while seeking new sources of revenue. To expand trade and commerce, the coinage was put on a sounder basis. To create a competent bureaucracy, he constantly sought experienced and skilled nobles and clergy for his government from all parts of his extensive empire. The emperor worked relentlessly to advance the realm's fiscal position; however, despite his many improvements, the goal of finding adequate funding for his regime was only partially resolved.

At the time of Maximilian II's succession to the imperial crown and the Habsburg hereditary lands, the Ottoman Empire had seized over two-thirds of Hungary, leaving the emperor controlling only the western lordships. In 1562 to secure peace along the border, Ferdinand I and his son had negotiated a truce with Sultan Suleiman I. After his assumption of power, Maximilian II assured the sultan of his continued peaceful rule, sending envoys to Constantinople to begin talks for a permanent settlement over the divided Hungary. However, while the deliberations continued, war erupted in Hungary when the Turks' vassal, John II Sigismund Zapolya of Transylvania, launched an encroachment into Habsburg lands, besieging several castles. In defense of Royal Hungary, the emperor mobilized his army and counterattacked to seize John II's fortifications along the Tisza River. As the Habsburg troops retained their conquest, Suleiman I sent reinforcements to aid his retainer, as the danger of an expanded confrontation escalated.

In late 1565 the sultan began to prepare his military for an attack against Royal Hungary in defense of John II Sigismund. Maximilian II responded to the mounting threat by summoning his first Imperial Diet to meet in Augsburg. Through the years the Habsburg emperor had cultivated the friendship and support of the princes and they pledged to mobilize a large fighting force. In July 1566 Habsburg and German soldiers began to assemble in Vienna, as Maximilian II labored diligently to find arms, provisions and money for the campaign. In the following month his army marched east with Maximilian II personally in command. Arriving at the Hungarian border, he expected to engage the approaching forces of Suleiman I. While the emperor waited along the frontier for the Muslims, in Constantinople the sultan died and his offensive against Royal Hungary was cancelled and the troops withdrawn.

The prolonged period of inactivity at the border and lack of supplies had seriously deteriorated the morale and discipline of the imperial military forces and in September to gain some advantage from the campaign, Maximilian II advanced his militia against the Turkish held fortress at Esztergom. However, many of his troops refused to fight, deserting his army to return home. With his remaining soldiers, he attempted to besiege the Szekesfelervar Castle in central Hungary, but his sorties failed and the Habsburgs were soon compelled to abandon their attack. In late October the bitterly disappointed emperor was forced to retreat to Vienna with the remnants of his army. With the war at an impasse, a truce was negotiated in 1568 with the Habsburgs retaining their western Hungarian lordships and agreeing to pay a yearly tribute to the new sultan, Selim II. The emperor's failure to defeat the Turks resulted in a loss of personal prestige and stature among his imperial and Habsburg crownland nobles and prelates, weakening their commitment to support his initiatives and policies.

Maximilian II had fully supported the Peace of Augsburg negotiated in 1555 to bring reconciliation between the Lutheran and Catholic princes and prelates. However, since its acceptance several new Protestant splinter religions had evolved, threatening the bipartisanship of the Augsburg agreement. The Calvinists had been particularly successful in winning converts and when the emperor attended the 1565 Diet at Augsburg, he announced his decision to eliminate the movement from his demesne. However, fearing further restrictions on their religious freedoms, the Lutherans refused to back the emperor. While the Parliament ended with the approval of Maximilian II's request for military aid to counter the Turks, he failed to gain the support of the Lutherans against the Calvinists.

Following the adjournment of the Augsburg Diet, the emperor was forced to intercede in the escalating dispute between the elector of Saxony, Augustus, and the previously deposed Saxon elector, John Frederick I, which threatened to further disrupt the already shaky peace between the imperial princedoms. In late 1566 the crisis escalated when John Frederick I negotiated an alliance with the French king, Charles IX, and the Calvinist factions, compelling Maximilian II to order an attack against the dissidents. With the support of the imperial crown, Augustus launched an incursion against his rival, capturing him at the stronghold of Gotha and crushing his uprising. The quick and decisive response to the mounting danger of open revolt helped to repair Maximilian II's damaged reputation and prestige in the aftermath of his failed campaign against the Turks.

While Maximilian II was confronting the rebellion of John Frederick I, his Habsburg cousin, Philip II of Spain, was preparing to assert his rule by force of arms in the Netherlands against the mounting threat of revolt by the Protestants. The Spanish king was determined to purge the anti–Catholics from his lands, sending an occupation army to subdue the insurrection. In September 1566 the dissidents responded by burning Catholic churches and harassing papal followers. As the disruptions escalated, Philip II ordered the arrest of the insurgency leaders and appointed the locally unpopular duke of Alba, Don Fernando Alvarez de Toledo, to command his troops in the Low Countries.

As the tensions grew in the neighboring Netherlands, the emperor grew increasingly alarmed that the conflict would spill over into the Holy Roman Empire. The Lutherans in the Low Countries believed they had been included in the 1555 Peace of Augsburg and looked to the imperial princes for protection. To limit German involvement in the war, Maximilian II initially denied Philip II's request to recruit troops from the empire and offered to mediate the dispute, while urging tolerance and leniency. However, by early 1567 under the influence of Pope Pius V, who demanded the elimination of all heretics, the Spanish king grew more militant. Under mounting pressure from Madrid, the emperor allowed the enlistment of Catholic soldiers from imperial lands but did not prohibit the German Lutheran princes from aiding the Dutch insurgents to maintain peace in the empire. In September Alba arrested two leaders of the rebellion, Counts Egmont and Hornes, while launching an aggressive subjugation of the reformers in the Spanish Netherlands.

When the Spanish initiated additional repressive measures against the reformers, the imperial magnates exhorted the emperor to intercede against his cousin's aggression. In late autumn Alba began to raise troops in Germany, while William of Orange assumed command of the Protestant uprising in the Netherlands and despite a decree banning the recruitment of Lutherans began to enlist soldiers from the Empire. Maximilian II refused to intervene against the Dutch Protestants but when Alba marched into the northwestern German territory of William's brother, Louis of Nassau, the princes intensified their pressure on him to react. However, since the Nassau count was a Calvinist, Maximilian II refused to intervene, which further eroded his support among the Lutherans. The emperor continued to promote a policy of moderation in the Netherlands, while remaining committed to avoiding a direct confrontation between the Empire and the Spanish Netherlands.

As the conflict in the Low Countries continued to escalate and Maximilian II's stature among the Protestants waned, in December 1568 he sent his brother, Archduke Charles, to Madrid to negotiate a moderation in Philip II's policy toward the Netherlands. The emperor pressed his cousin to begin reconciliation talks with William of Orange but the Spanish king remained intransigent. In January 1569 Philip II dispatched a message to the emperor, hardening his position by affirming Spanish sovereignty over the Netherlands under the Church of Rome.

While deliberations were being pursued with Spain, Prince William of Orange began to establish a military presence in southwestern Germany, threatening the already shaky stability of the empire. In defense of his territorial rights, Maximilian II issued a decree outlawing the Orange magnate and declaring his imperial lands forfeited. To regain authority over the militant imperial Protestant faction, in early 1570 the emperor summoned the Diet to Speyer. When the princes met, he attempted to contain the growing danger against unity in the empire by sponsoring imperial decrees for the creation of a permanent army and limitation of foreign recruitment of German troops. However, the princes both Catholic and Lutheran refused to approve any of his reform measures. Having failed to restore his power over the Diet, Maximilian II could do little more than renew his prior policy of urging toleration and peaceful reconciliation, as he became increasingly ignored by the combatants of both parties.

As Maximilian II's policies were rejected by the Protestants, he moved closer to the political and religious orientation of Madrid. He supported a pro–Catholic agenda by advancing the Papal Council of Trent's initiatives, promoting the teachings of the Jesuits and refusing to allow the Bohemian reformers the protection of the Augsburg Peace. The emperor buttressed the Catholic cause in the Spanish Netherlands by refusing to recall German troops fighting for Philip II. However, while his backing of papal interest had shifted in the Catholics' favor, Maximilian II remained committed to a peaceful resolution between the two rival religious parties through negotiation. Nevertheless, lacking the political and financial might to force a reconciliation, he continued to appeal to the two factions for toleration and patience, while taking no offensive action to inflame the already tense situation.

In 1571 the emperor began a diplomatic campaign to secure the imperial throne for his heir, Archduke Rudolf. However, the German Protestant princes regarded the archduke as too pro–Catholic and a zealous supporter of Spanish policies. Maximilian II easily won the backing of the ecclesiastic electors and in 1575 convinced the Lutherans that a Habsburg emperor was in their best interest. On October 9 Rudolf was anointed with the crown of the Holy Roman Empire and recognized as next in line for the emperorship. While Maximilian II was negotiating with the imperial princes for his son's election, he opened talks with the Czech nobles for the appointment of the archduke as successor in Bohemia. At the 1575 Czech Diet, the delegates voted the monarchy to Rudolf and in October the coronation ceremony was held in Prague. With his prior ascension as king of Hungary and his investiture of Bohemia and the Holy Roman Empire, the Habsburg family continued its domination as the preeminent political and military power in central European affairs.

In 1572 the king of Poland, Sigismund II Augustus, died without a direct successor to end the Jagiellon dynasty. The Habsburgs had long standing territorial interest and ambitions in their neighbor to the northeast and Maximilian II began to maneuver to gain the Polish monarchy for his second son, Ernest. Henry Valois of France, Ivan IV of Russia and Stephen Bathory of Hungary also began to openly campaign for their election. The emperor had the support of Philip II and Pope Pius V, who both sent money to influence the decision of the Poles. The Habsburgs' initiative gained the approval of the high magnates but the majority of the nobility favored Henry and in August 1573 he was chosen as the successor to the Polish monarchy. Nevertheless, the throne again became available the next year when the Valois duke departed from Poland to assume the sovereignty of France after the death of his brother, King Charles IX. When a new Diet was held late in the following year, the high nobles elected Maximilian II as king without the approval of the minor lords and knights, who held a separate vote, selecting Stephen of Hungary. To advance his kingship, Maximilian II forged an alliance with Moscow and the city of Danzig, attempting to defend his rights by force of arms. However, when the Danzig army was defeated by Bathory and with his inability to raise troops and financial funds from the empire, Maximilian II was compelled to abandon his quest for the Polish crown and recognize the new ruler.

Maximilian II had long suffered from heart ailments and by 1575 it was increasingly clear that he would live only a short time longer. He suffered from gout and intestinal disorders, which weakened his strength further. In June 1576 he attended the Imperial Diet at Regensburg to personally plead with the magnates for financial aid and troops to confront the attacks of the Turks on the Austrian frontier. However, the Diet refused to discuss taxes and focused solely on religious issues. By September the emperor was confined to his bed as his cardiac seizures became more severe and frequent. On October 12 Maximilian II died at age forty-nine after a reign of twelve years. He was interred along side his father and mother in the Cathedral of Saint Vitus in Prague.

Sources

Fichtner. *Emperor Maximilian II.* Heer. *The Holy Roman Empire.* McGuigan. *The Habsburgs.* Wandruszka. *The House of Habsburg.*

Rudolf II, 1552–1576–1612

In the aftermath of the death of Maximilian II in October 1576, his son and heir, Rudolf II, succeeded unchallenged to the throne of the Holy Roman Empire to rule as the eighth emperor of the Renaissance era. He was born in Vienna on July 18, 1552, and was the second son of Maximilian of Habsburg and Maria of Spain. Soon after his birth he was given the title of Archduke of Austria. As the eldest surviving grandson of the reigning emperor, Ferdinand I, the infant became the recognized future heir to the Habsburg hereditary lands of Austria, Bohemia and Hungary. The archduke spent his first eleven years at the Vienna ducal court, where his education was provided by private tutors. He was a dedicated student, excelling in his studies of reading, writing, religion, sciences and the languages of German, Spanish, Latin and Italian. While Rudolf was a gifted student and received a well-rounded humanist education, unlike his father, he was not a natural leader and lacked the skills of a warrior.

In 1563 under the influence of his Spanish mother and her brother, King Philip II of Spain, Rudolf and his brother, Ernest, were sent to the Madrid court to continue and broaden their education. The two brothers spent their first months with Philip II at the royal castle in Aranjuez, occupied with hunting and practicing their equestrian and fencing skills. In the autumn they traveled to Madrid and later to the new palace at Escorial, where their studies were renewed under Jesuit tutors appointed by the king. Remaining in the conservative household of his pious uncle, the archduke became a zealous follower and supporter of the dogma of the Holy See of Rome and protector of the rights of the pontiff. During the time of his stay in Spain, the kingdom was nearing the summit of a golden age and he was exposed to the latest in Renaissance architecture, art and music. In February 1570 Rudolf and Ernest traveled to the southern province of Andalusia with the Spanish king, visiting the principal cities. The archdukes attended sessions of the Castilian Cortes in Cordoba and later were welcomed by the city of Seville with a magnificent reception. The eight years that Rudolf spent in Spain had a profound influence on his religious and political beliefs and future policies as emperor. Through his close associations with Philip II's court and government, the archduke developed a decidedly Spanish focus and bond, while becoming noticeably more aloof and withdrawn after his return to Austria.

In 1571 the nineteen-year-old Rudolf departed for the Austrian Habsburg court to a dramatically altered political environment. His father was now emperor of the Holy Roman Empire and struggling to retain his authority in Germany over the increasingly militant Lutheran faction, while contending the Turkish menace in Hungary and attempting to avoid imperial involvement in the war in the Netherlands between Spain and the local Protestant lords. Following Rudolf's arrival in Austria, Maximilian II began to associate him more closely with the administration of the Habsburgs' vast central European empire in preparation for his succession of power. During the time his son was in Spain, the emperor had initiated discussions with the Bohemian Diet for Rudolf's assumption of the Czech crown. However, the talks ended in failure when the Protestant nobles demanded guarantees for their religious freedoms. Shortly after the archduke's return from Madrid, Maximilian II began negotiations with the imperial electors to secure the throne of the Holy Roman Empire for the Habsburg archduke. While the Catholic princes quickly offered their support, the reformers considered him a zealous follower of the Holy See and too closely aligned to the Spanish court, initially withholding their approval.

While discussions were renewed with the empire's magnates and Prague court for the recognition of Rudolf as ruler, in 1572 the emperor secured the approval of the Royal Hungarian

Diet for the election of his son as king. After his succession as co–Magyar monarch with his father, under relentless political pressure from Maximilian II, the imperial electors were finally convinced that it was in their best interest to continue the overlordship of the Habsburgs as emperor. Following Rudolf's anointment as German king on October 9, 1575, the emperor summoned the Bohemian nobles to Prague to negotiate the appointment of the Austrian archduke as his heir to the Czech throne. To win the consent of the nobles, he was compelled to accept the *Bohemian Confession*, which guaranteed local religious freedoms and permitted Protestant churches to have their own ecclesiastic administrations. In late October Rudolf was crowned as heir apparent to the Bohemian kingdom. The emperor had labored for over four years to advance his son's claims of sovereignty and by 1576 was physically exhausted, growing increasingly frail with repeated heart seizures. In October 1576 Maximilian II died and was succeeded unchallenged by Rudolf II, who was invested in Frankfurt on November 1 with the imperial emperorship.

Rudolf II inherited a German kingdom that was divided by militant Protestant and Catholic factions and under threat from the Turkish menace in the east. His father's government had promoted a doctrine of tolerance and negotiations to resolve the religious schism in Germany. However, as the new emperor began his reign, he came under mounting pressure from the Spanish court to aggressively pursue the Counter-Reformation and directly confront the non–Catholics. Many of the peaceful initiatives of Maximilian II were reversed and attacks launched against the freedoms and privileges of the German reformers. Nevertheless, the bellicose policies of Rudolf II failed to reconcile the two rival parties, resulting in greater mistrust and unrest. He lacked the force of personality and authority to compel the high magnates to accept a settlement. Imperial diets were now held only infrequently and Rudolf II's influence and power over the princes steadily declined. As the discontent of both Catholic and Protestant princes grew, the emperor increasingly became subject to bouts of melancholy and indifference, withdrawing from the daily administration of the empire, which was assumed by his inept and self-serving ministers.

After his assumption of power, Rudolf II began to increasingly favor the city of Prague, moving his capital there in 1583 and establishing his household in the Hradschin Castle. Bohemia became the focal point of his central European empire. He was a highly cultured and intelligent prince, with a zeal for the advancement of the Renaissance movement into Germany and his hereditary Habsburg crownlands. Under the emperor's direction his Prague court became the center for European scientific studies and the arts. He became the greatest patron of his age, inviting the most renowned humanists, artists, craftsmen and scientists to reside in Prague. The emperor was also a collector of rare gemstones and unusual animals, maintaining a private zoo on his palace grounds.

Rudolf II attracted the eminent Danish astronomer Tyche Brahe to his court, who used telescopes of his own construction to measure the movements of the planets and stars. From his observations he considered Earth to be the center of the universe, while the other planets revolved around the sun, which in turn orbited Earth. When the emperor's cousin, Archduke Ferdinand, outlawed the German mathematician, Johannes Kepler, from his duchy, Rudolf II invited him to Hradschin. Kepler became an assistant and collaborator to Brahe and later used the astronomer's voluminous data to formulate the three basic laws of planetary motion. His calculations also suggested the moon was responsible for Earth's tides. He combined his and Brahe's works into the *Rudolfine Tables*, named after his patron, Rudolf II, which became the basis of modern astronomical study.

The Habsburg emperor became the greatest collector and patron of the arts in the late sixteenth century. He sent his agents throughout Europe to purchase the works of the most celebrated artists including, Durer, Correggio and Brueghel, while sponsoring the best contemporary painters and sculptors. Rudolf II's skilled artisans fashioned magnificent pieces in gold, enamel and glass, while his craftsmen and metal workers produced a wide variety of decorative objects, including clocks, compasses and musical instruments. His art gallery at Hradschin Castle became the largest and most impressive in Europe.

Rudolf II sponsored the popular Renaissance sciences of astrology and alchemy. The emperor had a private laboratory built in the castle, where he performed his own experiments in alchemy. Seeking to change metal into gold, he energetically searched for the philosopher's stone, inviting Europe's esteemed alchemists to his court. The renowned English astrologer John Dee came to Prague and prepared detailed astrological charts for the Habsburg emperor. Rudolf II's pursuit of the occult sciences produced rumors of magical potions and supernatural creatures which spread throughout Europe, giving Prague a reputation for the mystic.

Shortly before his death, Maximilian II had bequeathed Lower Austria to Rudolf II as part of the Habsburg hereditary demesne. During Rudolf II's rule, the Austrian duchy was beset with repeated periods of social disorder as the peasants demanded relief from their harsh agrarian conditions and religious freedoms. Under the influence of the reactionary bishop of Vienna, Melchior Khlesl, the emperor resisted any change to the existing economic structure, while enlisting the Jesuits to defend the dominance of the Catholic Church. The peasant uprisings were severely repressed and the power of the Habsburgs enforced. While Rudolf II was imposing his authority over the eastern region, his nephew, Ferdinand, initiated a crushing campaign of suppression against the Protestants in western Austria. Ferdinand attacked the heretics, burning their churches and forcing them from the duchy while eliminating all freedom of worship.

During much of 1591 border encounters between Royal Hungarian troops and the Ottomans had intensified. To end the escalating threat of war, Rudolf II and the Turkish sultan, Murad III, agreed to renew their existing truce. However, the Muslims soon renewed their attacks and when they were decisively defeated by the Habsburg army at Sziszek, the sultan declared war. The emperor attempted to rally all of Europe in a holy war against the Ottoman Empire, but his appeals met with only limited success. A Christian League was formed but it largely contributed only money and few soldiers to Rudolf II's war effort. However, the elector of Saxony, Christian II, responded to the emperor's request by sending a contingent of troops and established an alliance of friendship with the Habsburgs. Despite the failure to unite Christendom in a crusade, Rudolf II appointed his brother, Matthias, as commander of his army, pursuing the conflict with his Magyar and Austrian forces. By 1595 the archduke had driven the Turks from much of central Hungary and broadened his campaign of conquest by negotiating an alliance with Prince Michael of Wallachia, Sigismund Bathory of Transylvania and the magnates of Moldavia. The Protestant duchies had previously been allied with the Ottomans but with their defection to the Habsburg cause, the sultan was compelled to fight the conflict on two fronts. With their forces united, the Habsburg allies continued to make gains, seizing the strategic fortress at Estergom in September 1595. As Matthias continued to drive the Muslims from Hungary, Rudolf II grew increasingly jealous and resentful of his brother's successes, replacing him as captain-general.

With his military initiative shattered, in the following year the new sultan, Mehmed III, traveled from Constantinople to assume personal command of his troops. He advanced against the fortified city of Eger in September, overrunning the fortress and reoccupying the local region. He continued his offensive, reconquering additional lands and winning a decisive victory at the battle of Mezokereztes before the end of the campaigning season. In 1597 due to the threat of attack against his Turkish eastern territory of Anatolia and increasing poor health, the sultan was compelled to remain in his capital and without his presence on the battlefront the war entered a prolonged period of stalemate. In 1599 Rudolf II attempted to negotiate a truce with the Turks, but Mehmed III refused and the conflict was renewed with neither army able to force a resolution.

While Rudolf II remained in Prague largely isolated from the conduct of the war, in 1598 Matthias was reappointed to command the Hungarian offensive. He renewed the Habsburgs' cause against Mehmed III but was unable to decisively defeat him. After failing to bring an end to the fighting, he was replaced as commander of the military forces by George Basta. After assuming control of the imperial troops, Basta was ordered by the emperor to forcibly annex the lands of his Protestant allies in Wallachia, Transylvania and Moldavia and deprive them of their rights of religious freedom. When the Habsburgs marched into Transylvania, inflicting a devastating attack against the local population, the nobles rebelled, breaking the alliance that had been orchestrated by Matthias. Following the abdication of Prince Sigismund Bathory in 1599, Stephen Bocskai assumed command of the rebel army and in defense of the independence and Protestantism of the duchy forged an alliance with the Ottoman Empire. Under the attacks of Bocskai and his Turkish allies, by 1604 the imperialists had been forced out of northern Hungary and the duchy of Transylvania. Stephen Bocskai was born in Transylvania at the free town of Cluj-Napoca on January 1, 1557, and was the son of Gyorgy Bocskai and Krisztina Sulyok. He was a descendent of a family with a long history of service to the rulers of Transylvania and became an advisor to Prince Sigismund Bathory. Under Stephen's influence, in 1595 the prince abandoned his ties with the Ottoman Empire and negotiated an alliance with Rudolf II. During the deliberations with the imperialists, Bocskai served as a diplomat to the Habsburg court in Prague.

Bocskai was regarded as the defender of the native political and religious rights and in February 1605 the Transylvanian nobles elected him prince. As the rebels and their Turkish allies renewed their offensive, the imperialists became increasingly exhausted from the conflict and agreed to open peace talks with Bocskai. The Protestants had suffered the devastation of their estates and towns for many years and were anxious to find a settlement, signing the Peace of Vienna on June 23, 1606. The accord guaranteed freedom of worship and confirmed the privileges of the nobles, while acknowledging Bocskai as prince of Transylvania. The Hungarian fortress of Tokai and the lordships of Bereg, Szatmar and Ugocsa were ceded to the prince. As part of the resolution, the Habsburgs pledged to begin deliberations with the Ottoman Empire and with Bocskai acting as mediator in November 1606 a treaty was ratified, finally ending the Fifteen Years' War. Under the terms of the agreement, Rudolf II's annual tribute to the Turks for Royal Hungary was eliminated for a one time payment and each realm retained the territory currently under its control. Sultan Ahmed I also pledged to acknowledge the emperor as an equal in diplomatic negotiations, enhancing the prestige of the imperial regime among the European courts.

By 1606 Rudolf II had become increasingly beset with extended periods of depression, rage and paranoia. As he withdrew from the routine administration of his demesne, the chief minister assumed responsibility for the government, but lacking the acknowledged authority of a crowned sovereign his decisions were largely ignored. As the religious tensions escalated in Germany between the Catholics and Lutherans, the count of the Palatinate, Frederick V, formed the Protestant Union to defend the reformers' freedom of worship and privileges, while the traditional church countered with the Catholic League under Duke Maximilian of

Bavaria. With the empire and Habsburg hereditary lands on the brink of civil and religious war, Matthias summoned the members of the royal family to Vienna to force the inept Rudolf II from power. The Habsburg archdukes and cousins appointed Matthias as regent for Austria and head of the house. Acting under his new empowerment, he raised an army and in June 1608 marched against Prague, compelling Rudolf II to relinquish control of Austria and Hungary, while the emperor still retained Bohemia and the Holy Roman Empire.

Following the revolt of his family, Rudolf II attempted to rally support for his restoration to Austria and Hungary from the princes of the Empire, but his appeals were ignored. As his power continued to weaken, the Protestant magnates in Bohemia threatened him with rebellion unless he agreed to affirm their rights of free worship. Abandoned by his nobles, on July 9, 1610, he was compelled to sign the *Rudolfhine Letter of Majesty*, which guaranteed religious freedom for all the Czech population and reconfirmed the *Bohemian Confession,* previously issued by Emperor Maximilian II in 1575.

Embittered by his forced concessions and the rebellion of Matthias, the emperor began to plot to regain his lost crownlands. He forged an alliance with Leopold, bishop of Passau, who invaded Bohemia in 1611 to enforce the sovereignty of Rudolf II. However, the bishop's troops were easily defeated and under pressure from the Bohemian nobles, Rudolf II was compelled to abdicate the Czech throne in favor of his brother.

After the usurpation of his crowns, Rudolf II was forced to retire to his favorite Prague castle, where he spent his few remaining months. Broken by the strains of his humiliating defeats and his persistent attacks of depression, the emperor died on January 20, 1612, at age fifty-nine after a reign of thirty-five years. He had never married and as the oldest surviving member of the family his brother, Matthias, was recognized as heir to the Habsburg lands and five months later succeeded Rudolf II as emperor of the Holy Roman Empire.

Sources

Crankshaw. *The Habsburgs.*   Evans. *Rudolf II and His World.*   Fichtner. *The Habsburg Monarchy, 1490–1848.*

General Sources for the Holy Roman Empire

Ferguson. *A Survey of European Civilization.*   Sugar. *A History of Hungary.*   Zamoyski. *The Polish Way.*

Bibliography

Allman, Christopher. *Henry V.* Berkeley: University of California Press, 1992.
Aram, Bethany. *Juana the Mad.* Baltimore: Johns Hopkins University Press, 2005.
Ashley, Mike. *A Brief History of British Kings and Queens.* New York: Carroll & Graf, 2002.
Ault, Warren O. *Europe in the Middle Ages.* Boston: D. C. Heath, 1937.
Barrell, A. D. M. *Medieval Scotland.* Cambridge: Cambridge University Press, 2000.
Baumgartner, Frederick J. *Louis XII.* New York: St. Martin's Press, 1996.
Bernardy, Francoise de. *Princes of Monaco.* London: Arthur Barker, 1961.
Bevan, Bryan. *Henry IV.* New York: St. Martin's Press, 1994.
_____. *Henry VII.* London: The Rubicon Press, 2000.
Bingham, Caroline. *James V: King of Scots.* London: William Collins Sons, 1971.
_____. *James VI of Scotland.* London: Weidenfeld and Nicolson, 1979.
Blackie, Ruth, Graham Donaldson, and Douglas McKenzie. *James IV: A Renaissance King.* Edinburgh: Canongate Books, 1996.
Blum, Jerome, Rondo Cameron, and Thomas G. Barnes. *The Emergence of the European World.* Boston: Little, Brown, 1966.
Boardman, Stephen. *The Early Stewart Kings.* East Lothian, Scotland: Tuckwell Press, 1997.
Brandi, Karl. *The Emperor Charles V.* London: Jonathan Cape, 1939.
Briggs, Robin. *Early Modern France.* Oxford: Oxford University Press, 1977.
Brown, Michael. *James I.* East Linton, Scotland: Tuckwell Press, 2000.
Bryce, James. *The Holy Roman Empire.* New York: Schocken Books, 1961.
Butler, Mildred Allen. *Twice Queen of France.* New York: Funk & Wagnalls, 1967.
Cameron, Jamie. *James V.* East Linton, Scotland: Tuckwell Press, 1998.
Cameron, Keith. *From Valois to Bourbon.* Exeter: University of Exeter, 1989.
Cannon, John, and Anne Margreaves. *The Kings and Queens of Britain.* Oxford: Oxford University Press, 2001.
Carr, Raymond. *Spain: A History.* Oxford: Oxford University Press, 2000.
Castries, Rene de La Croix. *The Lives of the Kings and Queens of France.* New York: Alfred A. Knopf, 1979.
Champion, Pierre. *Louis XI.* New York: Dodd, Mead, 1929.
Cheetham, Anthony. *The Life and Times of Richard III.* London: Weidenfeld and Nicolson, 1992.
Chidsey, Donald Barr. *Elizabeth I: A Great Life in Brief.* New York: Alfred A. Knopf, 1966.
Chrimes, S. B. *Henry VII.* Berkeley: University of California Press, 1972.
Cleugh, James. *Chant Royal: The Life of King Louis XI of France.* New York: Doubleday, 1970.
Clive, Mary. *This Sun of York.* New York: Alfred A. Knopf, 1974.
Crankshaw, Edward. *The Habsburgs.* New York: Viking Press, 1971.
Davies, R. Trevor. *The Golden Century of Spain, 1501–1621.* New York: St. Martin's Press, 1956.
Denieul-Cormier, Anne. *Wise and Foolish Kings—The First House of Valois.* New York: Doubleday, 1980.
Dockray, Keith. *Edward IV.* Thrupp, Stroud, Gloucestershire: Sutton, 1999.
Donaldson, Gordon. *Scotland: James V—James VII.* Edinburgh: Oliver & Boyd, 1978.
_____. *Scottish Kings.* New York: Barnes & Noble, 1967.
Elliot, John H. *Imperial Spain, 1469–1716.* London: Penguin Books, 1990.
Erickson, Carolly. *Bloody Mary.* New York: Doubleday, 1978.
_____. *The First Elizabeth.* New York: Summit Books, 1983.

Erickson, Carolly. *Great Harry*. New York: Summit Books, 1980.
Evans, R. J. W. *Rudolf II and His World*. New York: Thames and Hudson, 1997.
Ferguson, Wallace K. *A Survey of European Civilization*. Boston: Houghton Mifflin, 1939.
Fernandez-Armesto, Felipe. *Ferdinand and Isabella*. New York: Dorset Press, 1991.
Fichtner, Paula Sutter. *Emperor Maximilian II*. New Haven: Yale University Press, 2001.
_____. *The Habsburg Monarchy, 1490–1848*. New York: Palgrave MacMillian, 2003.
Frazer, Antonia. *King James VI of Scotland*. New York: Alfred A. Knopf, 1975.
_____. *The Lives of the Kings and Queens of England*. New York: Alfred A. Knopf, 1975.
_____. *Mary Queen of Scots*. New York: Greenwich House, 1983.
Grant, Neil. *Charles V*. New York: Franklin Watts, 1970.
Grierson, Edward. *The Fatal Inheritance: Philip II and the Spanish Netherlands*. Garden City, NY: Doubleday, 1969.
_____. *Kings of Two Worlds*. New York: G. P. Putnam's Sons, 1974.
Griffiths, R. A. *The Reign of Henry VI*. Thrupp, Stroud, Gloucestershire: Sutton, 1998.
Hackett, Francis. *Francis the First*. New York: The Literary Guild, 1935.
Hare, Christopher. *Maximilian the Dreamer: Holy Roman Emperor, 1459–1519*. New York: Charles Scribner's Sons, 2009.
Heer, Friedrich. *The Holy Roman Empire*. New York: Frederick A. Praeger, 1968.
Hicks, Michael. *Edward V: The Prince in the Tower*. Stroud, Gloucestershire: Tempus, 2003.
Highfield, Roger. *Spain in the Fifteenth Century*. New York: Harper & Row, 1972.
Hutchison, Harold. *King Henry V*. New York: Dorset Press, 1967.
Kamen, Henry. *Philip of Spain*. New Haven: Yale University Press, 1997.
Kann, Robert A. *A History of the Habsburg Empire, 1526–1918*. Berkeley: University of California Press, 1980.
Kendall, Paul Murray. *Louis XI*. New York: W. W. Norton, 1971.
Knecht, R. J. *French Renaissance Monarchy: Francis I and Henry II*. London: Longman Group Limited, 1984.
_____. *Renaissance Warrior and Patron*. Cambridge: Cambridge University Press, 1994.
_____. *The Rise and Fall of Renaissance France, 1483–1610*. Oxford: Blackwell, 2001.
Knecht, Robert J. *The Valois: Kings of France, 1328–1589*. London: Hambledon and London, 2004.
Lacey, Robert. *The Life and Times of Henry VIII*. New York: Welcome Rain, 1998.
Law, Joy. *Fleur de Lys: The Kings and Queens of France*. New York: McGraw-Hill, 1976.
Livermore, Harold. *A History of Spain*. New York: Farrar, Straus and Cudahy, 1958.
Loach, Jennifer. *Edward VI*. New Haven: Yale University Press, 2002.
Lockyer, Roger. *Henry VII*. New York: Longman Group Limited, 1968.
Lynch, Michael. *Scotland: A New History*. London: Pimlico, 1992.
Macdougall, Norman. *James IV*. East Linton, Scotland: Tuckwell Press, 1997.
Mackie, J. D. *A History of Scotland*. New York: Dorset Press, 1985.
Mackie, R. L., and J. Ross. *Kings and Queens of Scotland*. New Lanark, Scotland: Gedders & Grosset, 2000.
Magnusson, Magnus. *Scotland*. New York: Grove Press, 2000.
Main, Archibald. *The Emperor Sigismund*. London: Simpkin, Marshall, Hamilton, Kent & Co., 1903.
Mamatey, Victor S. *Rise of the Habsburg Empire*. Malabar, FL: Krieger, 1995.
Marshall, Rosalind K. *Elizabeth I*. Owings Mills, MD: Stemmer House, 1992.
Mattingly, Garrett. *The Armada*. Boston: Houghton Mifflin, 1959.
McGuigan, Dorothy Gies. *The Habsburgs*. Garden City, NY: Doubleday, 1966.
McKendick, Melveena. *Ferdinand and Isabella*. New York: American Heritage, 1968.
Miller, Townsend. *Henry IV of Castile*. Philadelphia: J. B. Lippincott, 1972.
Morrison, N. Brysson. *Mary—Queen of Scots*. New York: Vanguard Press, 1960.
Mortimer, Ian. *The Fears of Henry IV*. London: Jonathan Cape, 2007.
Mulgan, Catherine. *The Renaissance Monarchies, 1469–1558*. Cambridge: Cambridge University Press, 1998.
Neillands, Robin. *The Hundred Years' War*. London: Routledge, 1990.
O'Callaghan, Joseph F. *A History of Medieval Spain*. Ithaca: Cornell University Press, 1975.
Oram, Richard. *The Kings & Queens of Scotland*. Stroud, Gloucestershire: Tempus, 2001.
Parker, Geoffrey. *Philip II*. Chicago: Open Court, 1998.
Penman, Michael. *David II*. East Linton, Scotland: Tuckwell Press, 2004.
Petrie, Charles. *Philip II of Spain*. London: Eyre & Spottiswoode, 1963.
Phillips, William D. *Enrique IV and the Crisis of Fifteenth Century Castile*. Cambridge, MA: The Medieval Academy, 1978.
Pickering, Andrew. *Lancastrian to Tudor*. Cambridge: Cambridge University Press, 2000.
Pollard, A. F. *Henry VIII*. New York: Harper Torchbooks, 1966.

Potter, David. *A History of France, 1460–1560*. New York: St. Martin's Press, 1995.
Potter, Philip J. *Gothic Kings of Britain*. Jefferson, NC: McFarland, 2008.
_____. *Kings of the Seine*. Baltimore: PublishAmerica, 2005.
Prawdin, Michael. *The Mad Queen of Spain*. Boston: Houghton Mifflin, 1939.
Prescott, H. F. M. *Mary Tudor*. London: Phoenix, 2003.
Prescott, William Hickling. *History of the Reign of Ferdinand and Isabella*. New York: Heritage Press, 1967.
Putnam, Ruth. *Charles the Bold*. New York: BiblioBazaar, 2007.
Rady, Martyn. *The Emperor Charles V*. London and New York: Longman Group Limited, 1988.
Read, Conyers. *The Tudors*. New York: W. W. Norton, 1964.
Robinson, John Martin. *The Dukes of Norfolk*. Chichester, West Sussex: Phillimore, 1995.
Roll, Winifred. *Mary I*. Englewood Cliffs, NJ: Prentice-Hall, 1980.
Ross, Charles. *Edward IV*. Berkeley: University of California Press, 1974.
_____. *Richard III*. Berkeley: University of California Press, 1981.
Rubin, Nancy. *Isabella of Castile: The First Renaissance Queen*. New York: St. Martin's Press, 1991.
Russell, Lord of Liverpool. *Henry of Navarre*. New York: Praeger, 1970.
Scarisbrick, J. J. *Henry VIII*. London: Eyre & Spottiswoode, 2005.
Seward, Desmond. *The Hundred Years' War*. New York: Atheneum, 1978.
_____. *Prince of the Renaissance: The Life of Francis*. London: Sphere Books, 1974.
_____. *Richard III England's Black Legend*. New York: Franklin Watts, 1984.
Simpson, Helen. *Henry VIII*. London: Peter Davies, 1934.
Skidmore, Charles. *Edward VI*. New York: St. Martin's Press, 2007.
Sugar, Peter F. *A History of Hungary*. Bloomington: Indiana University Press, 1994.
Tilley, Arthur. *Medieval France*. New York: Hafner, 1964.
Tittler, Robert. *The Reign of Mary I*. London and New York: Longman Group Limited, 1991.
Vale, M. G. A. *Charles VII*. Berkeley: University of California Press, 1974.
Vaughn, Richard. *Philip the Bold*. London: Longman Group Limited, 1979.
Wandruszka, Adam. *The House of Habsburg*. Garden City, NY: Doubleday, 1965.
Watson, R. W. Seton. *Maximilian I, Holy Roman Emperor*. London: Butler & Tanner, 1902.
Weir, Alison. *The Princes in the Tower*. New York: Ballantine Books, 1992.
Wernham, R. B. *Before the Armada: The Emergence of the English Nation*. New York: Harcourt, Brace & World, 1966.
Wheatcroft, Andrew. *The Habsburgs*. London: Penguin Books, 1995.
Wilkinson, Burke. *Francis in All His Glory*. New York: Farrar, Straus & Giroux, 1972.
Williams, Neville. *The Life and Times of Elizabeth I*. London: Weidenfeld and Nicolson, 1972.
_____. *The Life and Times of Henry VII*. London: Weidenfeld and Nicolson, 1973.
Wolffe, Bertram. *Henry VI*. New Haven: Yale University Press, 2001.
Zamoyski, Adam. *The Polish Way*. New York: Hippocrene Books, 1994.

Index

Agincourt Battle 6, 21, 171, 177
Albert II (Holy Roman Emperor) 297, 301, 304–309, 311–312
Alexander (Lord of the Isles) 119–120
Alexander VI (Pope) 65, 136, 193–194, 199–200, 202–203, 257–258, 264, 319
Alfonso I (Duke of Ferrara) 204
Alvarez, Don Fernando (Duke of Alba) 100, 220, 227, 281, 284–285, 287–289, 291, 342
Anne of Brittany 61, 191–193, 199, 202, 207, 212, 317–318
Anne of Cleves (Queen of England) 74–75, 87, 95
Anne of Valois (Regent of France) 189–191, 197–198
Archibald (Earl of Angus) 140–143, 147
Archibald (Fourth Earl of Douglas) 12, 52, 114–115, 117–119, 175
Arthur (Prince of Wales) 60–61, 64, 66, 265

Barbarossa Pasha (Moorish Pirate) 278–279
Barnet Battle 35, 40, 44–45, 50–51, 53
Bernard VII (Count of Armagnac) 19, 21–23, 170–171, 174
Boeyens, Adrian (Spanish Regent) 272–274, 276–277, 323
Boleyn, Anne (Queen of England) 71–73, 85–86
Bosworth Battle 6, 57, 59, 136, 195
Brandon, Charles (Duke of Suffolk) 70, 76, 81, 210

Cade, Jack (Leader of Kent Rebellion) 30
Carrillo, Alfonso (Archbishop of Toledo) 249–253, 255–258

Castilian War of Succession 259–260
Catherine of Aragon (Queen of England) 61, 64, 66, 69–73, 85–86, 91, 94, 144, 213, 265, 268, 327
Catherine of Lancaster (Queen of Castile) 240–241
Catherine of Valois (Queen of England) 19, 24–26, 40
Cecil, Robert (Lord Chancellor of England) 104–105, 159
Cecil, William (Lord Chancellor of England (97–99, 102
Charles (Cardinal of Bourbon) 234–235
Charles (Duke of Burgundy) 35, 39–42, 44, 49–50, 52, 185–189, 313, 315, 317
Charles III (Duke of Bourbon) 70, 208, 210–212
Charles V & I (Holy Roman Emperor & King of Spain) 2, 68–72, 74, 76, 82–83, 86–92, 142, 145–146, 203, 207–214, 218–220, 223, 228, 239, 263–265, 270–285, 297, 322–338
Charles VI (King of France) 10, 19, 23–24, 26, 166–175
Charles VII (King of France) 23–29, 31, 117, 120–121, 166, 168, 171–184, 208, 310
Charles VIII (King of France) 59, 61–62, 65, 166, 183, 189–200, 206–207, 263–264, 316–319
Charles IX (King of France) 149, 166, 224–232, 341, 343
Cisneros, Ximenes (Archbishop of Toledo & Spanish Regent) 269, 271–272, 274
Clement VII (Pope) 70–72, 144, 212–213, 217, 326–328, 333–334
Columbus, Christopher (Spanish Explorer) 65, 239, 261–262

Comuneros Revolt 273, 277, 280, 325
Cornwall Rebellion 63, 136
Cortez, Hernando (Spanish Conquistador) 275–276, 278
Cranmer, Thomas (Archbishop of Canterbury) 72–73, 75, 78, 80, 83–84, 92, 94
Crichton, Lord William (Scottish Regent) 123–124
Cromwell, Thomas (Lord Chancellor of England) 74–75, 85, 94

David II (King of Scotland) 15, 110–111
Devereux, Robert (Earl of Essex) 103–104
Don Carlos (Heir to Spanish Crown) 281, 283, 288–290
Don John of Austria (Governor of the Spanish Netherlands) 101, 288
Douglas, James (Earl of Morton) 155–157, 159
Dudley, John (Earl of Warwick) 81–82, 84, 88–89, 95–97
Dudley Lord Robert (Courtier of Elizabeth I) 98–99, 101–103, 291

Edmund (Duke of Somerset) 29–31, 40–41, 50–51
Edward IV (King of England) 6, 33–48, 53–54, 56–60, 62, 65, 127–131, 135–136, 184, 186, 188
Edward V (King of England) 6, 42–48, 53–56, 58
Edward VI (King of England) 6, 74, 77–90, 94–96, 98, 102, 147–148, 150, 217, 283
Elizabeth I (Queen of England) 1, 7, 73, 79–80, 83, 86–88, 94–105, 150–157, 159–160, 228, 233, 291–292

353

Index

Emmanuel Philibert (Duke of Savoy) 93, 97, 220–221, 224, 284
Epiphany Rising 11, 16

Farnese, Alexander (Duke of Parma) 103, 290–293
Ferdinand (King of Aragon) 240–241, 245, 302
Ferdinand I (Holy Roman Emperor) 219, 263, 266, 280, 283, 322, 324, 328–340, 344
Ferdinand II (King of Spain) 41, 45, 61, 64, 66–68, 138, 191–192, 194–195, 200–201, 203–204, 239, 250–251, 253–254, 256–271, 274–275, 297, 319, 323, 331–332
Francis (Duke of Guise) 218–220, 223–226, 231
Francis I (King of France) 1, 68, 71, 74–76, 85, 87, 141, 144, 146, 148, 166, 206–216, 218, 221–223, 230, 278–279, 322, 325–327, 329–330, 333, 335, 338
Francis II (Duke of Brittany) 58–59, 61, 184–188, 190–192, 197–198
Francis II (King of France) 69, 98, 149, 152, 166, 217, 222–225
Francis of Anjou (French Heir and Brother of Henry III) 101, 232, 291
Frederick III (Holy Roman Emperor) 62, 182, 188, 297, 306, 308–318
Frederick V (Count of the Palatinate) 161, 347
French Wars of Religion 226–235

Gardiner, Stephen (Lord Chancellor of England) 89–92
Gaspard of Chatillon (Lord of Coligny) 224–225, 228–229
Glendower, Owain (Prince of Wales) 11–15
Gouffier, William (Lord of Bonnivet) 85, 209–211
Grey, Lady Jane (Queen of England) 83–84, 88–90, 96, 98
Guzman, Alonzo Perez (Duke of Medina Sidonia and Commander of Spanish Armada) 103, 292

Hamilton, James (First Earl of Arran) 138, 140–143
Hamilton, James (Second Earl of Arran) 79, 147–148, 152
Hastings, Sir William (Baron of Hastings) 45–47, 49–50, 53–55

Henry (Duke of Guise) 231–234, 287
Henry II (King of France) 82, 93, 148–149, 151, 166, 211, 214–222, 224, 284–285, 330–331, 336
Henry III (King of France) 100–101, 166, 227–235, 291–293, 343
Henry IV (King of Castile) 186, 239, 242–259
Henry IV (King of England) 1, 6–18, 20, 113, 117, 170
Henry IV (King of France) 103, 166, 228–229, 232–235, 291–293
Henry V (King of England) 1, 6, 13–26, 67, 117, 171–174
Henry VI (King of England) 1, 6, 25–41, 48, 50, 53, 57–58, 65, 1118, 120–121, 126–129, 173, 175, 177–179, 183, 195
Henry VII (King of England) 6, 24, 40–41, 55–67, 73, 80, 135–136, 191–192, 268
Henry VIII (King of England) 1, 6, 65–81, 84–87, 90–91, 94–95, 98–99, 138, 141–144, 146–148, 205, 210–211, 213–215, 274, 276, 322, 325, 327, 329–330, 338
Hepburn, James (Earl of Bothwell) 152–153, 155
Howard, Catherine (Queen of England) 74–75, 87, 95
Howard, John (Duke of Norfolk) 41–42, 52, 54–56, 58
Howard, Thomas (Duke of Norfolk) 69, 73, 75–77, 90, 99–100, 154
Hundred Years' War 1, 6, 9, 19, 67, 117, 166–169, 171, 180, 182–183, 249
Hussite Revolt 297, 302–309

Isabella (Queen of France) 23, 168, 170–171, 173–174
Isabella (Queen of Spain) 2, 41, 45, 61, 64, 191–192, 194–195, 200, 239, 250, 253–267, 269, 274–275, 319

James I (King of Scotland) 109, 111, 115–123, 125, 175, 181
James II (King of Scotland) 109, 122–131, 135
James III (King of Scotland) 34–35, 37, 48, 52, 56, 109, 125, 127–135, 140
James IV (King of Scotland) 1, 63–64, 68, 109, 130, 132–140, 151, 157

James V (King of Scotland) 79, 109, 137, 139–147, 150
James VI & I (King of Scotland & England) 99, 105, 109, 152–162
Joan of Arc 175–177, 183
Joanna (Princess of Asturias) 250, 253–255, 257–260
Joanna (Queen of Spain) 239, 263–274, 277, 283, 323, 331–332
John II (Duke of Burgundy) 170–172, 174, 300
John II (King of Aragon) 241–247, 249–251, 255–257, 260
John II (King of Castile) 239–249, 251, 254
John XXIII (Anti-Pope) 299–300, 302
Julius II (Pope) 67–68, 71, 138, 203–205, 270–271, 320–321

Kennedy, James (Scottish Regent & Bishop of Saint Andrews) 128
Kett, Robert (Rebel Leader) 80–81
Knox, John (Presbyterian Reformer) 150

Lancaster, George (Duke of Clarence) 39–40, 42, 44, 48–51, 60
Lancaster, Richard (Duke of York & Brother of Edward V) 46–47, 54–55
League of Public Weal 185
Leo X (Pope) 68, 208–209, 276, 321–322, 324, 326
Lepanto Battle 289
Lipany Battle 304, 307, 312
Livingston, Alexander (Lord of Callendar) 123–125
Lollardy Rebellion 19
Lords Appellant (English Regency Council) 8–10
Louis I (Prince of Conde) 223–228
Louis XI (King of France) 1, 34–35, 38–40, 42–44, 49–50, 52, 121, 166, 173, 178, 180–190, 196–197, 251, 310, 315–316
Louis XII (King of France) 67–68, 138, 160, 190–207, 264, 266, 270–271, 321–322
Luna, de Alvaro (Constable of Castile) 241–245
Luther, Martin (Protestant Reformer) 324, 328, 330, 332

Macdonald, John (Lord of the Isles) 125–126, 131, 135

Index

Mad Wars 191, 197–198
Magellan, Ferdinand (Spanish Explorer) 275, 278
Margaret of Anjou (Queen of England) 28, 32, 34–38, 40–41, 50
Martin V (Pope) 120, 302–303, 308
Mary (Duchess of Burgundy) 189, 313–316
Mary I (Queen of England) 6, 70, 73, 76, 83–94, 96–98, 150, 219–220, 283–285, 339
Mary I (Queen of Scotland) 76, 79, 82, 98–99, 101–102, 109, 145–157, 217, 222, 292
Mary of Guise (Queen of Scotland) 145, 147–148, 150–151
Matthias Corvinus (King of Hungary) 312–317
Maximilian I (Holy Roman Emperor) 62, 66–68, 189, 191–194, 198, 200–201, 203–205, 263–265, 270, 272, 276, 297, 313–325, 327, 333
Maximilian II (Holy Roman Emperor) 229–230, 282–283, 288–289, 297, 336–346, 348
Medici, de Catherine (Queen of France) 100, 144, 149, 217, 221–226, 229–232, 287
Melville, Andrew (Presbyterian Reformer) 159
Montmorency, Anne (Duke of Montmorency) 213, 217–218, 220, 226–228, 284, 329
Muhammad XII (King of Granada) 260
Muhlberg Battle 330, 336, 338

Nevill, Richard (Earl of Warwick) 31–41 43–44, 49–50
Northampton Battle 34, 36

Olmedo, First Battle 244, 246–247
Olmedo, Second Battle 253, 255

Pacheco, John (Marques of Villena) 244–245, 247–248, 250–255, 257
Parr, Catherine (Queen of England) 76–77, 79, 84, 87, 95
Percy, Henry (Duke of Northumberland) 12–14, 17, 1115
Percy, Henry Hotspur (Heir to Northumberland) 12–13, 115
Philip I (King of Spain & Duke of Burgundy) 62, 263, 265–271, 274, 280, 315–316, 319, 323, 331

Philip II ((Duke of Burgundy) 167–170
Philip II (King of Spain) 2, 90–93, 96–99, 101–104, 157–158, 161, 214, 219–222, 227–228, 232–233, 239, 278–293, 326, 328, 331, 336, 338–339, 341–344
Philip III (Duke of Burgundy) 24–25, 27, 125, 172, 174, 176–178, 184–186
Podebrady, George (Hussite Revolt Commander) 312–313, 317
Pole, de la Reginald (Cardinal & Advisor to Mary I) 91–93, 98
Pole, de la William (Duke of Suffolk) 27–30
Potier, Louis (Lord of Gesvres and Henry III's Council Secretary) 232, 234

Rene I (Duke of Anjou) 28, 183, 189, 192, 198
Richard (Duke of York) 27, 30–37, 48, 178
Richard II (King of England) 6–12, 14–16, 18, 111–113, 168–169
Richard III (King of England) 1, 6, 41, 43, 45–59, 132, 135
Richemont, de Arthur (Constable of France) 28–29, 176–179, 181
Ridolfi Plot 100
Robert II (King of Scotland) 110–112, 122
Robert III (King of Scotland) 109–116, 118
Rudolf II (Holy Roman Emperor) 2, 297, 339, 343–348

Saint Albans First Battle 32–33
Saint Albans Second Battle 34, 37, 39, 53, 128
Saint Ledger, Sir Thomas (Courtier & Brother-in-Law of Edward IV) 41, 55
Schiner, Matthaus (Cardinal & Papal General) 204–205, 208
Scope, Richard (Archbishop of York) 14
Seymour, Edward (Lord Protector) 76–82, 86–88, 95, 97, 148–149
Seymour, Jane (Queen of England) 73, 77–79, 94–95
Seymour, Thomas (Lord High Admiral) 79, 95
Sigismund (Holy Roman Emperor) 22, 170, 297–307, 309, 312
Simnel, Lambert (Pretender to English Crown) 60–62, 64–65
South Hampton Plot 20

Stafford, Henry (Duke of Buckingham) 45–47, 53–55, 58
Stewart, Alexander (Duke of Albany & Brother of James III) 43, 53, 131–132, 140
Stewart, David (Heir to Scottish Crown) 113–116
Stewart, Esme (Earl of Lennox) 156
Stewart, Henry (Lord of Darnley) 99, 152–155
Stewart, James (Earl of Moray) 99, 151–155
Stewart, John (Duke of Albany & Regent of Scotland) 69, 140–142, 147
Stewart, Murdac (Duke of Albany) 109, 117–119, 172
Stewart, Robert (Duke of Albany) 109, 112–113, 122, 172
Suleiman I (Sultan of the Ottoman Empire) 213–214, 278–279, 328, 333–335, 340–341

Talbot, John (Earl of Shrewsbury) 29, 31–32, 179
Tewkesbury Battle 6, 35, 45, 51, 53
Towton Battle 34, 37, 41, 44–45, 48, 53, 57, 184
Tudor, Jasper (Earl of Pembroke) 37, 40–41, 50–51, 57–60
Tyrone's Revolt 104

Verneuil Battle 175

Warbeck, Perkin (Pretender to English Crown) 62–64, 136
Wars of the Roses 1, 6, 32–33, 40, 45, 57, 60–61, 127–128, 184
William (Eighth Earl of Douglas) 124–126, 134–135
William (Prince of Orange) 102, 287–291, 342
William of Croy (Lord of Chievres) 275–276
Wolsey, Thomas (Lord Chancellor of England & Cardinal) 66–69, 71–72, 75, 209, 325
Woodville, Anthony (Earl of Rivers & Guardian for Edward V) 44–45, 53–54
Woodville, Elizabeth (Queen of England) 39, 42–44, 46–47, 49, 53–54, 56, 58, 60
Wyatt, Sir Thomas (Leader of Wyatt's Rebellion) 90, 96

Yolande of Anjou (Advisor to Charles VII) 173–177

Zappyla, John I (King of Hungary) 333–335

www.ingramcontent.com/pod-product-compliance
Lightning Source LLC
Chambersburg PA
CBHW081536300426
44116CB00015B/2653